Global Life Systems

Global Life Systems

Population, Food, and Disease in the Process of Globalization

Robert P. Clark

ROWMAN & LITTLEFIELD PUBLISHERS, INC.
Lanham • Boulder • New York • Oxford

ROWMAN & LITTLEFIELD PUBLISHERS, INC.

Published in the United States of America
by Rowman & Littlefield Publishers, Inc.
4720 Boston Way, Lanham, Maryland 20706
http://www.rowmanlittlefield.com

12 Hid's Copse Road
Cumnor Hill, Oxford OX2 9JJ, England

British Library Cataloguing in Publication Information Available

Library of Congress Cataloging-in-Publication Data

Clark, Robert P., 1940-
    Global life systems : population, food, and disease in the process of globalization /
Robert P. Clark.
        p.   cm.
    Includes bibliographical references and index.
    ISBN 0-7425-0074-8 (cloth : alk. paper) — ISBN 0-7425-0075-6 (pbk. : alk. paper)
    1. Human ecology.   2. Globalization.   3. Population.   4. Food supply.
    5. Diseases and history.   6. Evolution (Biology).   7. Social evolution.   I. Title.

    GF50 .C53   2000
    304.2—dc21
                                                                    00-040300

Printed in the United States of America

⊚™ The paper used in this publication meets the minimum requirements of American
National Standard for Information Sciences—Permanence of
Paper for Printed Library Materials, ANSI/NISO Z39.48-1992.

To Mirentxu

Contents

Acknowledgments

I wish to thank my friend and George Mason University colleague, Michael Emsley, Professor of Biology, for his invaluable assistance in the preparation of this book. Mike read two drafts of an early article-length statement of my central argument. He then read the entire first draft of the book manuscript, and most of a revised draft. At each stage, he provided me with numerous suggestions for improvements. Most importantly, he provided support and encouragement for the overall enterprise. Of course, I alone am responsible for whatever flaws that remain in the final product.

Part I

Global Life Systems

Chapter One

Life Systems and Globalization

On the morning of October 12, 1492, when Christopher Columbus and his crew came ashore on an island in the West Indies, they found people much like themselves—physically, at least, if not culturally.[1] Other European explorers had similar experiences: Almost everywhere they landed there were human beings. According to Clive Gamble, they were not particularly surprised by this, because European folklore had told of a world more or less fully populated.[2] In retrospect, however, they should have been astonished, for we began as a species confined to a very small portion of the Earth, and our expansion to become global has been a long, difficult, and costly journey whose "success" (if it can be called that) has been far from assured.

Humans did not begin as a global species; we had to expand to become one. And we could not have done so without other living organisms becoming global along with us. In this book, I examine the interconnectedness of global systems based on living organisms, or "global life systems." Following the work of Henry Hobhouse,[3] the objects of my analysis are human beings, plants and animals domesticated for food, and pathogenic micröorganisms. Because these life systems are highly interconnected with one another, they have all become, or are becoming, global more or less together. A global perspective helps us understand more clearly how these biological forces mutually reinforce one another and what their globalization[4] has meant for the biosphere.

About one million years ago, our distant ancestors, *Homo erectus*, began to leave East Africa and migrate long distances across the Earth.[5] By about one hundred thousand years ago, the first anatomically modern humans (*Homo sapiens*) appeared. Gradually, but at an accelerating pace, we spread across the planet in a process that yielded global life systems—that is, a number of interconnected life systems living more or less everywhere on Earth.

Terrestrial life systems could not have become global without humans to assist and accompany them;[6] but the dependence is mutual. As long as we lived by hunting and gathering our food, we never could have become global in numbers beyond the Earth's natural (that is, without technology) carrying capacity of four to six million. To grow beyond this limit, humans needed the help of domesticated plants and animals. By living in close proximity with, and eating, these organisms, we came into contact with their parasites; so the globalization of life systems has been, and continues to be, characterized by the coevolution of humans, plants, animals, and diseases. Humans did not dominate and control the other global life systems. Rather, we were, and still are, one component in a package of interdependent life forms that continue to adapt to each other.

In the chapters that follow, I examine the biological dimensions of globalization. A global system requires a global population, so chapter 2 addresses the world's demographic history. Early on, the principal obstacle to globalization was food, so chapter 3 reviews the history of world food supplies. But expansion of the world's human population and food supply involved exposure to harmful microörganisms, so chapter 4 examines the connections between globalization and disease. Four chapters then present case studies of how, in the course of globalization, one set of coevolved life systems invaded the space of another: the arrival of agriculture in Europe; the biological dimensions of the Silk Road; the arrival of Europeans in eastern North America; and the impact of fossil fuels and refrigeration on the globalization of food supplies. Chapters 9, 10 and 11 examine three consequences of globalization: the transformation of the world's food system in the Information Age, the emergence of infectious diseases, and the loss of biodiversity. A concluding chapter addresses the biological implications of our momentous adventure to other worlds.

EVOLUTION AND COEVOLUTION

Globalization could not have occurred without coevolution, so our inquiry begins with two central concepts: how a single species changes over time (evolution), and how systems of species change by means of mutual adaptation (coevolution).[7]

The fit between any living organism and its environment is the result of a long process of adaptation. For a species to become global, its members must adapt to multiple environments across many millennia. According to Jonathan Marks, the process of adaptation takes place

> by the fact that all members of a species do not survive and reproduce with equal efficiency. The consistent ability of organisms with certain attributes to perpetuate themselves more efficiently than other members of the same species lacking those attributes results in the apparent transformation of a species over time. . . . It is the environment . . . that determines which characteristics permit an organism to survive and reproduce disproportionately in nature. . . . The selective action of nature . . . favors simply the survival and propagation of those organisms that are best equipped to function within that particular environment.[8]

The globalization of many species—particularly diseases and domesticated plants and animals—has taken place in accord with the rules of biological evolution: heritable variation, the filtering of these variations via natural selection, and the gradual accumulation of these variations to produce observable differences in species across long spans of time.[9] Species change from generation to generation by mixing together genetic information of parents, and by transmitting new genetic information to their offspring. Individuals with characteristics that make them more successful in the competition for scarce resources leave behind more offspring, and thus their genetic material gradually becomes more prevalent in the population. Observable changes in a species occur through the gradual accumulation of tiny variations over many generations.

So much has been claimed (and disputed) for the theory of evolution by natural selection that it is worth a brief acknowledgment of what evolution is *not*.[10] First, adaptation to the environment is not the only evolutionary force operating. Some changes in an organism occur as random mutations in genetic material. When these changes spread through a population (usually a very small one) without regard for environmental pressures, the process is known as "genetic drift." Other changes may occur in response to adaptations elsewhere in an organism (for example, an increase in body size may necessitate changes in an animal's circulatory system). Finally, some physical attributes of an organism are the product of combinations of genes, and change in these attributes occurs when these genes combine and recombine in novel and unexpected ways.[11]

Evolution is neither intentional nor goal directed. Organisms do not "decide" to change their genetic material or their heritable physical traits to become more competitive; and evolution does not lead toward some final destination but is simply the result of competition, survival, reproduction, and selection of traits over many generations. Moreover, the evolutionary success of one population over another says nothing about the intrinsic worth or moral or esthetic superiority of the former; it simply says that the successful population was able to leave behind more of its genetic material in the next generation. It is still being hotly debated whether adaptations occur gradually via imperceptible changes, or suddenly and abruptly in great leaps, but this controversy involves changes that occurred for the most part long before humans began their global expansion.[12] Finally, there is no requirement that the competition between populations be violent or that their struggle for existence be bloody. Indeed, cooperation and group solidarity may be, for some species, precisely the traits that make their members fitter in a given environmental context.

When we apply the evolution paradigm to globalization, we must extend it in two directions. The first takes evolution into culture and identifies both genes and memes as entities by which information is transmitted. The second introduces new levels of selection, action, and analysis beyond the gene and the organism, to the population and the larger systems of which they are part: the ecosystem and the social system.

Biology and Culture

Some biologists contend that evolution involves not individual organisms such as humans, horses, and wheat, but rather the genes carried within these organisms. For Richard Dawkins, for example, genes are the agents of replication in nature; organisms are simply their vehicles, their "machine[s] for survival."[13] Natural selection works indirectly on genes by granting greater or lesser success to their phenotypic expressions in plants and animals. From this perspective, when we speak of farmers and their crops and livestock coevolving to create the Neolithic Revolution, what Dawkins would claim we really mean is that it was the genes within each respective organism that were being selected and passed on (or not, as the case may have been) to the next generation of organisms. This perspective remains the subject of considerable controversy among biologists; but it is clear that the process of globalization was brought about by individual organisms (organized as coevolved life systems and as cultures), regardless of whether it was their genes that were the ultimate objects of natural selection.

With important exceptions such as skin pigmentation, blood groups, or disease resistance, genetic changes occur too slowly for their impact to show up in humans in the last ten millennia or so, the period during which globalization has occurred. For this reason, social scientists define evolution and coevolution to include cultural adaptations as well. In using evolution to illuminate the globalization of life systems, we are describing intraspecific adaptations at both the biological level, where the carrier of change is the gene, and the cultural level, where the carrier is the meme, idea, or symbol.[14]

Genes and culture constitute two distinct systems of information that interact to shape human phenotype and behavior.[15] These systems are parallel, but they interact extensively throughout our lives, affecting each other as well as their human carriers. There are major differences between the two systems, of course. The codes used to store information have very different properties (DNA, memes); the information is stored and processed in very different, highly specialized structures in the body (cells, the brain); and the information is transmitted via very different media (sexual intercourse, symbolic communication and language). However, the similarities between the two systems are of enormous significance to any understanding of human behavior: both systems store and transmit information that can be divided into recognizable subunits (genes, memes); within all populations, there are sources of variation for both (mutation, recombination, migration; innovation, synthesis, diffusion); and in both systems, there are media of transmission that can convey these units through the population.

John Tyler Bonner, in his book *The Evolution of Culture in Animals*, writes that evolution is a way of explaining change that comes about via the transmission of information from one generation to another.[16] Some information is transmitted genetically. The genome is the agent of transmission, and changes are minute and spread through the population extremely slowly. Other kinds of information are transmitted culturally—that is, by means of one animal teaching another. Here, the agent of transmission is the brain, and changes have the potential to be large and to spread through the population extremely rapidly. Though they are clearly different kinds of information-transmission processes, genes and culture are both ultimately biologically conditioned since both have a biological component or foundation.

"Perhaps the most striking feature of human evolution," writes Jonathan Marks, "is the niche that characterizes the species: symbolic creative thought and its expression in ways of coping with the environment and obtaining the necessities of life through the use of material culture."[17] Adaptation via culture rather than via genetic changes offers humans a number of significant advantages. Culture offers greater flexibility than biology; culture can spread faster and affect more members of a population more directly and more rapidly than can biological change; culture can develop its own history largely independently of the biological history of the individuals that use it; and cultural changes can be transmitted both horizontally across space (within generations) as well as vertically across time (from one generation to the next).

For humans, most adaptation during the past five to ten millennia has occurred via cultural evolution. The central role of coevolution in globalization highlights David Rindos's contention that "cultural traditions that maximize fitness during the evolution of agricultural systems will have an inherent tendency to spread differentially by means of the enhanced reproductive success of individuals within that tradition."[18] Rindos characterizes this paradigm as

> a biological approach to the study of cultural events that accepts the primacy of variability, heritability, and differential fitness in explaining the cultural evolution of organisms (especially *Homo sapiens*). Cultural selectionism accepts that human behavior is determined by the interaction of two inheritance systems—the genetic and the cultural—and generally places its emphasis upon the latter. . . . Although human cultural behaviors may enhance biological survival, the specific differences determining cultural traits have acted largely within the cultural, and not the genetic, inheritance system.[19]

One of the unique properties of human evolution is what Marks calls "the coercive authority of culture."[20] In other species, the behavior of an individual must be in some way in its own best interests, or at least in the best interests of its genes. Culture, however, can make humans take short-term losses in exchange for future gains, or to make sacrifices for the gain of others. Cultures take on their own historical lineages apart from the individual members of a population. Cultural selection differs from natural selection, then, in that cultural adaptations need not directly benefit specific individuals.

The use of evolution to illuminate cultural changes must be approached with caution. In this study of technological creativity, Joel Mokyr asserts that "techniques—in the narrow sense of the word, namely, the knowledge of how to produce a good or service in a specific way—are analogues of species, and that changes in them have an evolutionary character." The idea . . . of how to produce a commodity may be thought of as the genotype, whereas the actual technique . . . may be thought of as the phenotype of the member of a species."[21] Mokyr is careful to use the phrase "may be thought of" instead of "is" to reflect the fact that his approach uses evolution by natural selection as an analogue or metaphor to throw light on the process of cultural adaptation. Similarly, in his history of the development of mechanical refrigeration in the nineteenth century, Mikael Härd makes it clear that his use of the term "evolution" does not suggest any biological parallels, and instead "only alludes to a process of gradual change."[22] Härd sees inventive activity as the accumulation of tiny changes via a gradual process of accretion.

On the other hand, in his study of the evolution of complexity, John Tyler Bonner writes that

> there are close parallels between the organization of cells within a multicellular individual and that of a group of individuals in an animal society. The parallels are no mere analogy, for the same forces of natural selection act at both levels. . . . [T]here is an enormous difference between the mode of inheritance of flexible behavior and of structure. The latter is directly controlled by genes, while the former is passed from one individual to another by nongenetic or behavioral transmission. These are two kinds of inheritance which operate by totally different mechanisms, but dovetail with one another and are both under the direct influence of selection. . . . Both are ultimately controlled by genes, but the connection between flexible behavior and the genome is remote; what is inherited is a capacity to learn and invent and instruct.[23]

No matter which perspective we select—whether we see biological change as simply an analogue of cultural change or as the ultimate shaper of culture—as we proceed with our analysis of globalization via coevolved life systems, it would be wise to keep in mind this admonition of ecological historian William Cronon:

> Efforts to describe ecological history simply in terms of the transfer of individual species between segregated ecosystems . . . are . . . bound to be incomplete. Important as organisms like smallpox, the horse, and the pig were in their direct impact on American ecosystems, their full effect becomes visible only when they are treated as integral elements in a complex system of environmental and cultural relationships. The pig was not merely a pig but a creature bound among other things to the fence, the dandelion, and a very special definition of property. It is these kinds of relationships, the contradictions arising from them, and their changes in time, that will constitute an ecological approach to history.[24]

Genes, Organisms, and Systems

If the concept of evolution must be expanded to encompass both biological entities and culture, the idea of coevolution requires that we expand our definition of the appropriate units of selection, action, and analysis as well. "Ultra-Darwinists" believe that selection works only on genes by indirectly favoring one organism over another.[25] They argue that a theory of how selection might favor one entire collection of organisms (such as a population) over another population raises the evolution paradigm to an unacceptably broad level of abstraction and generalization. Such a theory, they believe, will inevitably lack confirming empirical evidence and even seems implausible, given the incentive of each organism to cheat on the group by being a "free rider" on the properties that give a group superior fitness over another competing group.

The coevolution paradigm, in contrast, asserts that selection does not work in a vacuum. Organisms live in populations; and these live in larger and more inclusive systems; and the whole package confronts the pressures of selection as a unit. Thus, while selection may work at the level of the organism, some organisms are favored over others because of how they fit into, and contribute to, the properties of the larger system. Moreover, organisms are not the passive recipients of selection forces; they are actively shaping their environment to cause the environment to adapt to them as well. As Steven Rose puts it, "organisms evolve to fit their environments, and environments evolve to fit the organisms that inhabit them."[26]

D. H. Jansen defines coevolution as "an evolutionary change in a trait in the individuals of one population in response to a trait of the individuals of a second population, followed by an evolutionary response by the second population to the change in the first."[27] In becoming global, humans, plants, animals, and diseases have coevolved; that is, they have evolved together as a package of interdependent life systems.

For David Rindos, coevolution "is an evolutionary process in which the establishment of a symbiotic relationship between organisms, increasing the fitness of all involved, brings about changes in the traits of the organisms." Rindos maintains that "coevolutionary sequences frequently may be described as cooperation, but they do not depend on any recognition by the organisms of the advantages involved. Most interspecific forms of coevolution began with a situation in which one organism was the prey of the other."[28]

Coevolution is an essential feature of any complex ecological community, because, as John Tyler Bonner explains, a community is a collection of niches that

> reflect different ways animals or plants can maintain a place in the community. This is hardly identical to the kind of division of labor within the body in the form of cells and tissues, but it is a close parallel. If one thinks of niches as slots where organisms can lead a different kind of existence, functioning and behaving in specialized ways, then, if it is not a strict division of labor, it is a division of ways of living. . . . [T]he way one type of organism lives is a necessary requirement for the existence of another type, a kind of interdependence clearly analogous to that of the parts within the body of an individual organism.[29]

For a process as complex as the globalization of a species, coevolution must involve both biological and cultural adaptations.[30] Indeed, William Durham uses the term to describe "the parallel action of cultural selection and genetic selection in the evolution of human phenotypes, especially behaviors."[31] He asserts that "both genes and culture constitute systems of organized information; that both exert profound influence on human phenotypes; and that both are capable of evolutionary transformation through space and time."[32] Ernst Mayr argues that the individual genotype is a well-integrated system whose component parts interact in ways far more complex than that conceived of in classic population genetics, which focuses on the adaptation of single genes. Instead, Mayr urges a holistic view that sees entire organisms as packages of genetic combinations that are subject to selection pressures as a unit.[33] Robert Wesson takes the argument one step further and asserts that the entire ecosystem evolves as a unit, and thus the system is the target of selection pressures: "Adaptation usually depends less on fitness for physical conditions than on interactions with other species."[34] He adds: "The evolution of the symbiotic unit is more complex than that of an individual, and its ability to make difficult adaptations is enlarged."[35]

The coevolution paradigm opens up new windows into the globalization process. For example, seen from this perspective, the domestication of plants for food occurred not by humans imposing their will on the plant world, but through mutual adaptation, or coevolution, of plants biologically and humans culturally. David Rindos explains the evolution of agriculture as the genetic adaptation of plants to humans and the cultural adaptation of humans to plants, with natural and cultural selection filtering the transmission of traits of both from one generation to the next. Even before humans consciously planted and cultivated plants for food, they were affecting the survival of some plant species over others through their unconscious actions: protecting plants from predators, raiding the hoarded seed caches of other animals, such as squirrels, and dispersing seeds through their gut or on their skin.[36] Of the thousands of plants that could conceivably have been grown by humans for food, only a very small number have adapted successfully to human needs. Some, such as maize, grapes, and roses, have adapted so well to humans that today they cannot survive without human actions to fertilize and breed them.

A similar dynamic can be described in the domestication of animals, as Stephen Budiansky does in his work, *The Covenant of the Wild*.[37] Budiansky argues that humans did not tame animals so much as participate in a process of coevolution wherein humans and animals adapted to each other. At one time or another, humans tried to domesticate virtually every large, noncarnivorous mammal on the Earth, a number Jared Diamond puts at 148,[38] but only a very few have ever been domesticated as a food supply. The process of coevolution selected for cows, pigs, and sheep rather than, say, gazelles, zebras, or kangaroos, because the former group adapted to acquire (or already possessed) the characteristics humans needed: neoteny (the retention into adulthood of juvenile traits, such as docility, submissiveness, playfulness, and respect for hierarchy) and an ability to digest plant matter that humans could not (they occupied different niches from that of humans). One important genetic consequence of human–animal systems involved diseases. The coevolution of diseases and humans began as humans started to live in close quarters with animals and with each other, five to ten thousand years ago. The divergent paths taken by human populations in adapting to animal-borne pathogens can be seen clearly in the different genetic endowments of Europeans and Amerindians, which made the latter supremely vulnerable to diseases carried by the former, such as smallpox or measles.[39]

William Durham has identified a number of instances in which genes and culture coevolved to yield significant changes in human phenotypes and behaviors. Two of these were important to the process of globalization: lactose intolerance and sickle-cell anemia.[40]

The advertising slogan, "You never outgrow your need for milk," strikes most North Americans and Europeans as self-evident. Yet only about 30 percent of the world's population possess the ability to digest lactose as adults, and they are found largely in northern Europe, the Middle East, and East Africa.[41] Alfred Crosby claims that the ability to digest milk gave Europeans an advantage in global exploration, since—unlike Asians, Amerindians, and most Africans—they could carry their protein supply with them in the form of cows.[42] By means of comparative analyses of genetic and other data, Durham shows that the ability to digest lactose as adults has evolved within certain populations who (1) have practiced dairying for several millennia, (2) have a taste preference for fresh milk as opposed to processed milk products such as yogurt or cheese, (3) live at latitudes distant from the equator and thus (4) receive relatively less direct sunlight and less UV-B radiation, leading to (5) a potential vitamin D deficiency, which can only be remedied by (6) skin depigmentation and (7) high rates of fresh milk consumption.[43]

The same complex gene–culture interaction can be seen in the case of sickle-cell anemia. Many West Africans and their descendants (and virtually no other population) carry a gene that disposes them to this malady, so-called because the red blood cells are stretched into the shape of a sickle. The forces of natural selection would have gradually worked to delete this gene from the human population were it not for the fact that it also protects the carrier against malaria, thus making it a source of increased fitness in parts of the world where malaria exists.[44] However, Durham demonstrates that malaria has been extensive in West Africa only where slash-and-burn agriculture and yam cultivation have destroyed forest ecosystems. Without extensive tree cover, the land does not drain rain water away so readily, and water collects in pools where mosquitoes breed. As malaria follows the wave of deforestation in the service of agriculture, so does the pattern of sickle-cell anemia. In areas of West Africa that have not undergone such extensive deforestation, mosquitoes do not breed so extensively, malaria does not flourish, and the genetic form that disposes carriers to sickle-cell anemia has not been preserved.[45]

ENERGY FLOWS WITHIN COEVOLVED SYSTEMS

In 1925, Alfred Lotka formulated his law of maximum energy, which has been paraphrased by Vaclav Smil as follows:

> Natural selection will tend to increase the total mass of an organic system, and this will increase the rate of circulation of matter as well as the total energy flux through the system—as long as there is a surplus of available energy. The history of successive civilizations, the largest and most complex organisms in the biosphere, has followed this course. Human dependence on ever higher energy flows can be seen as an inevitable continuation of organismic evolution.[46]

How living systems attain increased efficiency in acquiring and processing energy has been studied by Jeffrey Wicken. "Living systems," he writes,

> are processes rather than things, and their existences are contingent on steady throughputs of matter and energy. More precisely, living systems are processes *composed of* things—of spatial entities that exhibit some intrinsic degree of stability. It is only thus that they solve the evolutionary job of acquiring and processing information.[47]

With this statement, Wicken sets forth the principal tasks to be performed by living organisms: to acquire matter and energy (or low entropy) from sources in the environment, and to dissipate waste and heat (or high entropy) back into sinks in the environment. Indeed, Wicken defines life as the ability of an entity to fulfill these requirements: process energy, dissipate entropy, and thereby resist decay.[48] These tasks confront all living organisms because of the Second Law of Thermodynamics and the inescapable generation of entropy through the metabolic processes that sustain life.

Entropy must be gotten rid of through channels that Ilya Prigogine has labeled "dissipative structures"[49] and that Wicken calls "kinetic pathways"—the ability of an organism to construct and maintain such pathways depends on the capacity of that organism to receive and act on information.[50] This is why Wicken refers to all "natural organizations" (that is, organisms, ecosystems, or society as a whole) as "informed dissipative systems."[51] The interaction of energy and information must be viewed as a whole if we are to understand what makes living organisms different from other physical systems:

> A thermodynamic system is not an entropy-producing black box. It has a material structure, and a finite set of kinetic possibilities within this structure. For a system to accommodate prevailing energy gradients in the production of entropy, it must adopt some kinetic regime—and . . . these involve *organization*. This is the basis of the "dissipative structures" schema, and it is of universal application to all systems that achieve their identities through the irreversible degradation of energy. . . . Thermodynamic systems are wholes, imposing their physical nature on what happens

within them. There is no way to understand a "part" in a thermodynamic system without reference to the system's total activity of energy-processing.[52]

For Wicken, individual organisms do not experience these processes in isolation. Rather, entire ecosystems function as integrated units, importing, processing, and exporting resources and wastes in an endless cycle.[53] The connections between and among parts of the ecosystems—what we are calling here the coevolved life system—provide the kinetic pathways or dissipative structures by which living organisms accomplish their vital tasks. Natural selection works, according to Wicken, to favor those organisms and connections that are "the most effective in channeling energy flows through themselves and, at the same time, in increasing total flow through their ecosystems."[54] Of course, genetic selection continues to favor some individual organism traits over others. "Ecosystem flow patterns," he writes,

cannot develop, however competitively advantageous they might prove to be, except through individual or group strategies for surviving and leaving offspring. Conversely, the competitive success of ecosystemic flow patterns imposes selective conditions on the evolution of individual adaptive strategies. Mutualistic interactions . . . which reduce specific dissipation and increase biomass/throughput ratios at the macroscopic level, are selected by the competitive advantages they accord *individuals* at the mesoscopic level.[55]

In other words, instead of Dawkins's "selfish genes," Wicken sees the "selfish thermodynamic system" as the driving force in evolution.

Coevolution manifests itself in three ways: competition, exploitation, and mutualism.[56] Competition is interaction in which the presence of one species inhibits the population growth of another. If the two species compete for a single resource, such as the same food supply, one or the other will be eliminated. However, if they compete for a range of resources, then it is possible that they will evolve in such a way as to apportion the resources among them. Competing species tend strongly to diverge, which partially explains why the earliest herders chose to domesticate animals such as cattle or sheep, which do not compete with humans for food.

Exploitation is interaction in which the presence of one species A stimulates the growth of a second species B, while the presence of B inhibits the growth of A. Also called antagonistic interactions (interactions in which members of one species feed off members of another), exploitation occurs "because living organisms are concentrated packages of energy and nutrients . . . and because resources are limited."[57] There are three kinds of exploitative interactions, determined by distinctive modes of feeding: parasite-host, grazer-host (such as plant-herbivore), and predator-prey.[58] Parasites live in or on their host in an intimate association that lasts for most of the parasite's life. Virtually all of the parasite's food is derived from its host, and the death of the host usually means the death of the parasite as well, unless or until the parasite has matured to the point where it can leave

the host for another. Many diseases that afflict human populations are examples
of host-parasite interactions. Grazers, in contrast, may interact with many hosts
over a relatively short time. Grazers usually do not cause the death of their host,
but they may cause it some detrimental effects. Interactions of animals and plants,
including human-plant interactions, belong to this category. Predators, on the
other hand, kill their prey, which consequently have a relatively short time in
which to react to the predator. Predators may kill and eat many prey during their
lifetime—unlike parasites, which usually live off of a single host. The human consumption of game animals is an example of a prey-predator relationship.

Mutualism is interaction in which the presence of each species stimulates the
growth of the other. John Thompson describes mutualism as a system of mutual
dependence, wherein one species (the host) provides either food or a safe place
to live for the other species (the visitor).[59] The host derives significant advantages
from the relationship, and the visitor has significant obligations to contribute to
the well-being of the host and thus to the strength of the pairing.

Thompson has identified a number of conditions under which exploitative or
competitive interactions may lead to mutualism.[60] The most likely of such conditions obtains when three species interact such that A and B compete for the same
food supply, but they still evolve as mutualists because A protects B against C.
Mutualists do not even have to belong to the same food chain to experience thermodynamic benefits from their connections.[61] Inasmuch as mutualisms may
evolve from exploitative interactions, the mutualisms may also exhibit relationships that are parasitic, grazing, or predatory. Humans are involved in all three.
Since their transition to agriculture, humans have sought to fashion mutualistic
systems with plants, on which we graze, and other animals, on which we prey. This
latter connection has exposed us to parasites, to which we continue to be linked
(often fatally). Indeed, one way to describe the Neolithic Revolution is as an effort by human beings to transform numerous, exploitative, coevolved systems into
mutualistic ones.

One may wonder how such mutualisms came to be and how they endure, when
it appears superficially as if one party (the visitor) derives all the benefits and the
other (the host) bears all the costs. In fact, hosts derive significant benefits from
the relationship, such as protection from "thieves" or "cheaters" (organisms that
try to use the host's resources without contributing anything to the relationship).
These and other benefits that accrue to the hosts—such as mobility, aid in reproduction, or a more secure food supply—are explored in chapter 3.

Mutualism also has meaning in cultural coevolution as well. Anthropologists
use the term to mean "when two populations exchange goods or services to co-
operatively exploit a range of resources."[62] Mutualism can include a wide variety
of relationships, from intense and direct to subtle and indirect, but in all cases
the relationship results in what Susan Alling Gregg calls a "higher carrying capacity
for the interacting populations," by which she means an increased fitness of both
populations in an evolutionary sense.[63]

Indirect mutualists create conditions leading to increased resources for each other without actually coming into contact, while direct mutualism refers to relationships in which populations actually provide each other with food or services, especially shelter, protection, and transportation. There may be a physiological link between the populations (for example, they provide each other with mates), but there need not be. Ecologists also classify mutualistic relationships into obligate (essential to survival) and facultative (not essential to survival, but without it carrying capacity is reduced). Mutualistic relationships may be asymmetrical—that is, obligate for one population and facultative for the other. If obligate for both, the two populations are truly locked together, since a decline in either population dooms both to extinction.

Mutualism arises when two populations engage in frequent interactions that result in significant fitness gains for both, when exchange proceeds at low cost but yields relatively higher benefits, when alternatives are ineffective or nonexistent, and when the prospects are good for continued long-term interaction. Exchanges are almost always complementary, with each population offering in exchange something it can produce either in excess of its own needs or as a by-product of its own subsistence production. Finally, at least one of the populations must be mobile, since the concept of mutualism requires that populations that do not reside together must still establish contact sufficient to carry on exchange on a regular basis.

Such a wide variety of interactions has yielded many different patterns of coevolution, a number of which have been identified by John Thompson.[64] Coevolutionary alternation is a process wherein a parasite attacks a host, the host mounts an effective defense, and the parasite shifts to a third species (all of this happening over evolutionary time). Successional cycles occur when an ecosystem experiences upsetting change, and one set of coevolved species is transformed into another, then a third, and so forth. Coevolutionary turnover occurs more frequently on islands or in other constricted spaces, where the invasion of one set of coevolved species displaces an indigenous set, which must either leave the space or face extinction. In escape-and-radiation coevolution, a host species evolves characteristics that make it unpalatable to its grazers, which then radiate into a new environment. Their place is taken by a second set of grazers, for which the evolved hosts have now become attractive. Finally, the interaction between mammals and the seeds of trees and fruit has been studied as a highly complex, dynamic process through which the habitat of all the species concerned is constantly on the move (again, over evolutionary time).

COEVOLUTION IN THE HISTORY OF GLOBALIZATION

John Thompson has observed that the complex patterns of coevolution involve so many species interacting in so many ways that we may never hope to understand them completely or capture their complexity in any simple hypothesis.[65]

Nevertheless, the paradigm of coevolution and energy flows enables us to envision sets or "packages" of life forms as systems viewed in a global framework. The following are some overly simplified graphics that attempt to portray some of these systems that have been significant in the history of globalization.[66]

Figure 1.1 illustrates the general pattern of energy flows within a coevolved life system that consists of humans, some other large animals, plants, and micröorganisms. Small-scale examples of energy flows between coevolved species are abundant. Figure 1.2 illustrates the flow of energy within the system known as pastoral nomadism, a lifestyle seen for millennia on the steppes of Eurasia or in East Africa. The sun's energy is captured by grass growing on the steppes, where it is turned into plant matter by the process of photosynthesis. Cattle and horses eat the grass and metabolize the food to produce energy for their own physical processes. Human herders consume the energy primarily via the milk and blood of their livestock. Humans contribute to the system by moving their herds from one grazing land to another, thereby protecting and conserving the precious storehouse of energy in the grasslands.[67] Rats and fleas follow the trail of these moving hosts, living off their energy. Eventually, in the fourteenth century, the microparasites carried in these latter organisms made their way to Europe, and the Black Death was the result.

Figure 1.3 shows how this paradigm can be raised to the level of a global system: the Columbian Exchange.[68] Three human populations were involved in this historic exchange: tens of millions of Africans and Europeans moved from the Old World to the New, while tens of millions (perhaps as many as 100 million) of Amerindians died from contact with European diseases, including smallpox and measles. Europeans, in turn, carried syphilis back to the Old World from the Caribbean. Solar energy was captured by numerous crops that became global, including wheat, rice, maize, and potatoes. Other grazers were carried across the Atlan-

Figure 1.1   Energy Flows within Coevolved Life Systems: The General Pattern

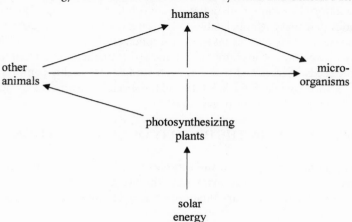

Figure 1.2   Energy Flows in the Pastoral Nomad System

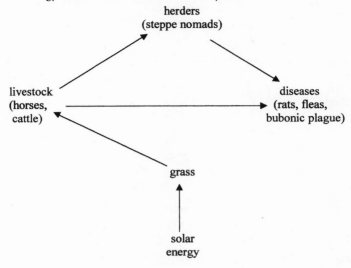

tic by the Europeans, including horses, cattle, pigs, and sheep. Many historians consider the Columbian Exchange the most significant change in life on Earth since the end of the last Ice Age, about twelve thousand years ago.

Figure 1.4 shows the patterns of energy and information flows among three life systems—(European) humans, sheep and dogs—as they coevolved to become

Figure 1.3   Energy Flows in the Columbian Exchange

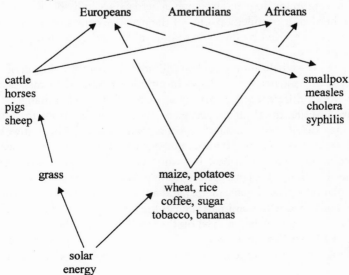

Figure 1.4   Energy Flows in the Sheepherding System

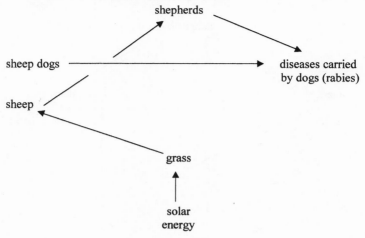

global. None of these three species was native to New Zealand; but, thanks to the steamship and mechanical refrigeration, millions of all three live there today.[69] In the sheepherding system, solar energy enters again via plant photosynthesis and is converted into animal tissue by the grazing sheep. Humans "harvest" the energy via the sheep's meat, milk, and wool. Humans adapted culturally by learning how to train dogs to care for sheep, giving them protection from predators and even assisting the ewes in giving birth. Sheep dogs adapted by becoming the protectors of sheep rather than their predators, and by accepting the discipline and respect for hierarchy that wild dogs do not exhibit. Sheep adapted by living with and raising young dogs and by living in herds, since individualistic wild sheep cannot be herded or rounded up. One of the negative consequences for humans was the diseases carried by dogs, including rabies and distemper, from which measles is evolved.

The history of globalization is replete with instances of the collision of two sets of coevolved life systems, two packages of interdependent life forms, each representing a wholly different way of arranging energy flows and exchanges. One example involved the Amerindian package of life systems that prior to 1600 occupied the area called "New England" by European settlers.[70] This native package included some 60,000 to 70,000 human beings who had divided themselves into at least ten populations, or "tribes," but who frequently were lumped together by Europeans as simply "Indians." These humans had evolved a food system that included plants (squash, beans, maize) and animals that were hunted (deer, turkeys, bear) or fished. Other animals such as the beaver provided fur for clothing, and predators such as wolves preyed on the smaller mammals. All these animals and plants had coevolved in a forest setting that the natives had managed for centuries by means of fire and felling trees so as to control and channel the movement of deer, elk, moose, and other game animals. While this system changed periodically with the seasons, it had reached a level of equilibrium, and the component parts of the package had worked out a kind of symbiosis with one another. Key to this equilibrium was the willingness of the humans in the package to restrain their appetites and to settle for a level of material life that Europeans would describe later as "impoverished."

Into this setting in the seventeenth century came a new set of life systems, introduced by European settlers. After a transition period when they depended on native food supplies, the Europeans brought and reproduced their own preferred food products and draft animals, including horses, oxen, cattle, pigs, and sheep, as well as staple grains such as wheat and rye. Along with these plants and animals came parasites and grazers of varying sizes and forms: dandelions and other weeds, "animal weeds" such as rats and field mice, and microparasites like smallpox and the bubonic plague. The interaction between these two sets of coevolved life systems had a decisive impact on the history of New England, not to mention the connections of the region to the global economy.

These kinds of interactions between sets of life systems have been a central feature of the process of globalization. The cases presented in chapters 5 through 8 illustrate the interconnectedness of biological and cultural forces as one set of coevolved life systems invades another. The biological side involves energy flows and exchanges, and natural selection of genetic material. On the cultural side, we examine sex roles; class, racial, or ethnic relationships; and technologies, religions, and legal and property systems as they affect the transformation of life systems. Above all, we focus on the ways these system interactions affect, and are affected by, the process of globalization.

The history of globalization is the story of the expansion of coevolved life systems, with humans as the principal carriers and the principal (but certainly not the only) beneficiaries. Because of the differences in climate and terrain, different sets of life systems have evolved at different places. John Thompson refers to such diversity as a "geographic mosaic."[71] He has suggested that

the theory of coevolution must be based upon the view that the geographic mosaic of interactions molds the overall pattern and dynamics of adaptation between interacting species. This mosaic, forged by the geographic subdivisions of populations and natural selection acting within local populations, will then be modified by three important aspects of geographic structure: gene flow, genetic drift, and local extinction.[72]

As life systems expanded, they inevitably encountered other systems that had already adapted to local conditions. The expanding, intruding life system thus had to compete with the local, native, or indigenous system for resources. How the interaction between the indigenous and the intruding life systems worked out depended to a great degree on their relative strengths and weaknesses (see Figure 1.5). "Strength" and "weakness" in this context meant thermodynamic

Figure 1.5   Possible Outcomes of the Interaction of Two Coevolved Life Systems

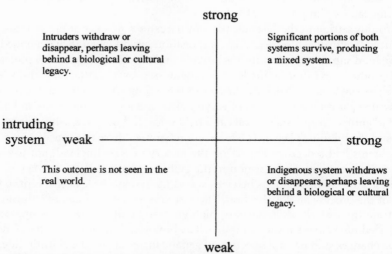

**indigenous
system**

strong

Intruders withdraw or
disappear, perhaps leaving
behind a biological or cultural
legacy.

Significant portions of both
systems survive, producing
a mixed system.

**intruding
system   weak** ─────────────────────┼───────────────── **strong**

This outcome is not seen in the
real world.

Indigenous system withdraws
or disappears, perhaps leaving
behind a biological or cultural
legacy.

weak

Note: The labels "weak" and "strong" refer in this context to the capacity of a given coevolved life system to process energy more efficiently, to provide a relatively greater supply of energy, and/or to increase the storage or mobility of energy (i.e., the system's thermodynamic efficiency). There is no presumption of superiority or inferiority in these labels. Moreover, systems labeled "weak" may possess certain advantages, and systems labeled "strong" may possess certain defects or weaknesses. Thus, the outcome of competition between two systems can never be predicted in advance.

efficiency: their relative capacities to capture energy from the environment; process it efficiently by metabolism; increase the overall supply, storage, and mobility of energy (especially, in the beginning, food); while dissipating entropy efficiently in the process.[73]

Jeffrey Wicken emphasizes the competition for energy in his discussion of succession, the process by which sets of plants and animals enter a habitat and compete with indigenous organisms for space and other resources in it. In the earliest stages of succession, a wide diversity of species stake out their respective claims to solar energy inputs, of which there are enough to support substantial diversity. As the habitat matures, the selective pressures of competition begin to favor "the most effective pathways for energy flow."

Here, competition for energy resources within the economic base establishes a selective premium on mutualistic interactions among species, with higher-order flow patterns becoming units of competition. Now, species diversity declines and specificity of flow increases—and with it, the ascendancy of the system.[74]

When two coevolved life systems came into contact, it was almost always because one system intruded into the habitat of the other. Such a dynamic, when a group of foreign species is thrust into a novel environment, is called a "biological invasion."[75] When the indigenous flora and fauna are innocent of previous contact with alien life systems, they are commonly called "naïve".[76] Unless they occupied nonoverlapping niches, which was unlikely, the two systems competed for scarce resources. Usually, but not always, the intruders enjoyed certain advantages, if only because they had demonstrated a greater capacity for mobility. If the intruding system had its origin in a continent-sized land mass, and the invasion took place on an island (even a very large island like Australia, Madagascar, or New Zealand), the invaders usually possessed certain advantages simply because of this difference. Adaptations brought forward from ancient interactions tended to influence how new interactions were formed. As John Thompson puts it, "A species colonizing a new community, such as a parasite from Europe introduced into North America, is likely to interact with species in the new community in ways that are similar to its interactions with species with which it has evolved."[77] Nonetheless, species transported into a new habitat are, in Thompson's words, "stripped of their old interactions and acquire new ones. . . . If the colonizing species can fit in, survive, and reproduce successfully, it becomes part of its adopted assemblage of species."[78]

Usually, but not always, the indigenous system was at a disadvantage because of its role as recipient in the exchange. Even though the indigenous system had existed for centuries or even millennia, it was not invulnerable. Often, as in the case of the eastern North American Indians, a life system that had endured for thousands of years gave way to intruders in less than three centuries. Nevertheless, the outcome of the competition was usually much more complex than simply one side being the victors and the other the vanquished.

Sometimes the intruding system vanquished the native system and either replaced it or absorbed it to such a degree that the native system virtually vanished. Two of the case studies (the spread of agriculture to Europe, and the impact of Europeans in eastern North America) show that when such a process begins, the intruding system is still relatively weak and vulnerable, and thus dependent on the local system for survival. The intruder system begins to adapt successfully to local conditions, and some local systems begin to adapt successfully to the intruders. Some (perhaps most) of the components of the local system then become vulnerable to the intruder via disease or technology. The intruder system eventually displaces most of the local system either by destroying, absorbing, ejecting, or transforming it. Some parts of the local system will be retained either in a marginalized role (such as museum exhibits) or via mutual adaptation (as in Europeans and the potato). Eventually, a new hybrid system arises in the local habitat, containing elements of both the intruding and the local life systems. The hybrid will always be connected, however, to global systems via bulk-flow technologies and institutions.

On other occasions, the intruders failed to defeat the natives and were forced to withdraw (sometimes after a very long time). Often the reasons for this outcome were not technological but biological. Presumably, intruding systems were superior to native systems in technology, and perhaps in social organization as well. Such an imbalance explains why one system plays the role of "discoverer" and the other the role of "discovered." But in some instances, the local, native biological systems proved to be stronger than intruding systems. Perhaps the force at work was food supply; perhaps it was disease. One such instance involved the expansion and retreat of the Eurasian steppe nomads via the Silk Road and other ancient trade and migration routes.

Even in these instances, however, the process of ebb and flow still contributed to the globalization of life systems. In some cases, the intruding system managed before they withdrew to leave behind part of their life system (bubonic plague in Europe, mestizos in Mesoamerica, the horse in North America, coffee and sugar in the Caribbean) or their cultural legacy (the Spanish language in Mexico, the Catholic Church in the Philippines, the railroad in India).

In the long run, however, the way Europeans and neo-Europeans managed to globalize themselves after 1500 A.D. was by devising global, bulk-flow networks of transport and communication to bring the resources of the world to the industrial and postindustrial cities of North America and Europe. If European life systems could not colonize all the world, they would bring the world to them by technology.

A book that attempts to explain an extremely complex human experience (globalization) by means of some fundamental scientific principles (coevolution) risks being assailed by critics as espousing "biological determinism."[79] This is not my intent. Any process as complex as the global spread of humans, plants, animals, and diseases over the past one hundred thousand years can hardly be reduced to a single, formulaic explanation. But if human inventions like the lateen sail, the steam engine, or the computer have been critical to globalization, so have wheat, the horse, and smallpox. Globalization is, it seems to me, the product of the interaction of systems of living organisms (genes) and the cultural artifacts invented by the members of one keystone species in those systems (memes). A focus on the biological dimensions of globalization is put forward here not to privilege one of the driving forces of change, but simply to recognize that the biosphere places limits on what humans have achieved, and what we may achieve in the future. The biosphere does not determine history, but it certainly does establish the boundaries or limits within which this history has unfolded. Globalization has been achieved at a huge biological price, much of which has been paid by members of species other than our own. It is unrealistic for us to expect that we can continue indefinitely to pass these costs on to other living organisms distant from us in time and space. Eventually the bill will be presented to us for payment in full, and if we are not careful we may find that we have bankrupted ourselves without being fully aware of what we have done.

NOTES

1. I. Bernard Cohen, "What Columbus 'Saw' in 1492," *Scientific American* (December 1992): 100–106; Joseph Judge, "Where Columbus Found the New World," *National Geographic* 170, no. 5 (November 1986): 566–99.

2. Clive Gamble, *Timewalkers: The Prehistory of Global Colonization* (Cambridge: Harvard University Press, 1994).

3. Henry Hobhouse, *Forces of Change: An Unorthodox View of History* (New York: Little, Brown, 1989).

4. "Globalization" is here defined as "the process by which people come to experience the world as a single place." For more on globalization, see the following: Roland Robertson, *Globalization: Social Theory and Global Culture* (London: Sage, 1992), chapters 3, 8; Anthony Kind, "Architecture, Capital and the Globalization of Culture," in *Global Culture: Nationalism, Globalization and Modernity,* ed. Mike Featherstone (London: Sage, 1990); Roland Robertson, "Globalization Theory and Civilizational Analysis," *Comparative Civilizations Review* 17 (1987): 20–30; Eleonore Kofman and Gillian Youngs, eds., *Globalization: Theory and Practice* (London: Pinter, 1996); Malcolm Waters, *Globalization* (London: Routledge, 1995).

5. Gamble, *Timewalkers*, passim; Luigi Luca Cavalli-Sforza and Francesco Cavalli-Sforza, *The Great Human Diasporas: The History of Diversity and Evolution,* trans. Sarah Thorne (Reading, Mass.: Addison Wesley, 1995); Luigi Luca Cavalli-Sforza, Paolo Menozzi, and Alberto Piazza, *The History and Geography of Human Genes* (Princeton, N.J.: Princeton University Press, 1994).

6. Marston Bates, "Man as an Agent in the Spread of Organisms," in *Man's Role in Changing the Face of the Earth,* ed. William Thomas (Chicago: University of Chicago Press, 1956), pp. 788–803.

7. The term "coevolution" was coined by Paul Ehrlich and Peter Raven in their article, "Butterflies and Plants: A Study in Coevolution," *Evolution,* vol. 18 (1964); 586–608. The original meaning referred to interdependent genetic evolution in two species. Edward O. Wilson has referred to the coevolution of genes and culture as the conceptual bridge between the physical and social sciences, in *Consilience: The Unity of Knowledge* (New York: Knopf, 1998), chapter 7.

8. Jonathan Marks, *Human Biodiversity: Genes, Race, and History* (New York: Aldine de Gruyter, 1995), pp. 26–28.

9. Peter Bowler, *Evolution: The History of an Idea,* rev. ed. (Berkeley: University of California Press, 1989); Daniel Dennett, *Darwin's Dangerous Idea: Evolution and the Meanings of Life* (New York: Simon & Schuster, 1995).

10. Michael Denton, *Evolution: A Theory in Crisis* (Bethesda, Md.: Adler and Adler, 1986); Robert Wesson, *Beyond Natural Selection* (Cambridge, Mass.: MIT Press, 1991, 1997).

11. Fritjof Capra, *The Web of Life: A New Scientific Understanding of Living Systems* (New York: Doubleday, 1996), chapter 10.

12. Niles Eldredge, *Reinventing Darwin: The Great Debate at the High Table of Evolutionary Theory* (New York: Wiley, 1995).

13. Richard Dawkins, *The Selfish Gene* (Oxford: Oxford University Press, 1976), p. xx. See also Richard Dawkins, *The Extended Phenotype: The Gene as the Unit of Selection* (Oxford and San Francisco: Freeman, 1982), pp. 239–47.

14. Aaron Lynch, *Thought Contagion: How Belief Spreads through Society* (New York: Basic, 1996); David Rindos, "Darwinian Selection, Symbolic Variation, and the Evolution of Culture," *Current Anthropology* 26, no. 1 (February 1985): 65–77; Dawkins, *The Selfish Gene*; Dennett, *Darwin's Dangerous Idea*, pp. 342–68.

15. William Durham, *Genes, Culture, and Human Diversity* (Stanford, Calif.: Stanford University Press, 1991), pp. 419–26, and Table 8.1.

16. John Tyler Bonner, *The Evolution of Culture in Animals* (Princeton, N.J.: Princeton University Press, 1980).

17. Marks, *Human Biodiversity*, p. 44.

18. David Rindos, *The Origins of Agriculture: An Evolutionary Perspective* (Orlando, Fla.: Academic Press, 1984), pp. 74–75.

19. Rindos, *The Origins of Agriculture*, p. 216.

20. Marks, *Human Biodiversity*, pp. 198–99.

21. Joel Mokyr, *The Lever of Riches: Technological Creativity and Economic Progress* (New York: Oxford University Press, 1990), p. 275. See also George Basalla, *The Evolution of Technology* (New York: Cambridge University Press, 1988), pp. 135–39.

22. Mikael Härd, *Machines Are Frozen Spirit: The Scientification of Refrigeration and Brewing in the 19th Century—A Weberian Interpretation* (Boulder, Colo.: Westview, 1994), p. 53. Note, however, that Dennett, in *Darwin's Dangerous Idea*, argues that Darwin's singular contribution to thinking about change lay in just such an observation: that tiny changes accumulated over very long spans of time would yield changes as large as the emergence of new species.

23. John Tyler Bonner, *The Evolution of Complexity by Means of Natural Selection* (Princeton: Princeton University Press, 1988), p. viii.

24. William Cronon, *Changes in the Land: Indians, Colonists, and the Ecology of New England* (New York: Hill & Wang, 1983), p. 14.

25. Steven Rose, *Lifelines: Biology beyond Determinism* (New York: Oxford University Press, 1998); Eldredge, *Reinventing Darwin*.

26. Rose, *Lifelines*, p. 140.

27. Cited by Rindos, *The Origins of Agriculture*, p. 99.

28. Rindos, *The Origins of Agriculture*, pp. 99–100.

29. Bonner, *The Evolution of Complexity*, p. 100.

30. Marks, *Human Biodiversity*, pp. 187–91.

31. Durham, *Genes, Culture, and Human Diversity*, p. 166, n. 8.

32. Durham, *Genes, Culture, and Human Diversity*.

33. Ernst Mayr, "Driving Forces in Evolution: An Analysis of Natural Selection," in *The Evolutionary Biology of Viruses*, ed. Stephen Morse (New York: Raven, 1994), pp. 33–36.

34. Wesson, *Beyond Natural Selection*, p. 157.

35. Wesson, *Beyond Natural Selection*, p. 162.

36. Rindos, *The Origins of Agriculture*, pp. 99–120; Jared Diamond, *Guns, Germs, and Steel: The Fates of Human Societies* (New York: Norton, 1997), chapter 7. Jared Diamond, "How to Tame a Wild Plant," *Discover* (September 1994), 101–06.

37. Stephen Budiansky, *The Covenant of the Wild: Why Animals Chose Domestication* (New York: William Morrow, 1992), Stephen Budiansky, "In from the Cold," *New York Times Magazine*, December 22, 1991, pp. 18–23.

38. Jared Diamond, "Zebras and the Anna Karenina Principle," *Natural History* (September 1994), 4–10; Jared Diamond, *Guns, Germs, and Steel: The Fates of Human Societies*

(New York: Norton, 1997), chapter 9. The great majority of the preferred candidates for domestication were large mammals that had their origin in Eurasia. For a discussion of the reasons for this, see Edward O. Wilson, *The Diversity of Life* (Cambridge: Harvard University Press, 1992), pp. 120–30.

39. William McNeill, *Plagues and Peoples* (New York: Doubleday, 1989); Alfred Crosby, *The Columbian Exchange: Biological and Cultural Consequences of 1492* (Westport, Conn.: Greenwood, 1972).

40. Durham, *Genes, Culture, and Human Diversity,* chapters 3, 5.

41. Julian Thomas, *Rethinking the Neolithic* (Cambridge: Cambridge University Press, 1991), p. 24; *American Demographics* (January 1995): pp. 47–48; Marks, *Human Biodiversity,* pp. 195–196.

42. Alfred Crosby, *Ecological Imperialism: The Biological Expansion of Europe, 900–1900* (Cambridge: Cambridge University Press, 1986), pp. 26–27.

43. Durham, chapter 5.

44. Henry Hobhouse, *Seeds of Change: Five Plants that Transformed Mankind* (New York: Harper and Row, 1985), chapter 1; Wilson, *The Diversity of Life,* 35 pp. 76–80; Marks, *Human Biodiversity,* pp. 146–147.

45. Durham, chapter 3.

46. Vaclav Smil, *Energy in World History* (Boulder, Colo.: Westview, 1994), p. 1.

47. Jeffrey Wicken, *Evolution, Thermodynamics, and Information: Extending the Darwinian Program* (New York: Oxford University Press, 1987), p. 70 (emphasis in the original). For another approach connecting entropy to evolution, see Daniel Brooks and E. O. Wiley, *Evolution as Entropy: Toward a Unified Theory of Biology,* 2d ed. (Chicago: University of Chicago Press, 1988).

48. Wicken, *Evolution, Thermodynamics, and Information,* chapter 2.

49. Ilya Priogogine and Isabelle Stengers, *Order out of Chaos: Man's New Dialogue with Nature* (New York: Bantam, 1984), chapter 4.

50. Wicken, *Evolution, Thermodynamics, and Information,* chapter 3.

51. Wicken, *Evolution, Thermodynamics, and Information,* p. 60.

52. Wicken, *Evolution, Thermodynamics, and Information,* p. 64 (emphasis in the original).

53. Wicken, *Evolution, Thermodynamics, and Information,* pp. 74, 117.

54. Wicken, *Evolution, Thermodynamics, and Information,* p. 135; see also, p. 145.

55. Wicken, *Evolution, Thermodynamics, and Information,* p. 137 (emphasis in the original).

56. John Thompson, *The Coevolutionary Process* (Chicago: University of Chicago Press, 1994), p. 20; John Maynard Smith, *Evolutionary Genetics* (New York: Oxford University Press, 1989), pp. 292–302.

57. John Thompson, *Interaction and Coevolution* (New York: Wiley, 1982), p. 6.

58. Thompson, *Interaction and Coevolution,* chapter 2.

59. Thompson, *Interaction and Coevolution,* chapter 6.

60. Thompson, *Interaction and Coevolution,* chapters 4, 5.

61. See Wicken, *Evolution, Thermodynamics, and Information,* p. 165, for an example of this.

62. Susan Alling Gregg, *Foragers and Farmers: Population Interaction and Agricultural Expansion in Prehistoric Europe* (Chicago: University of Chicago Press, 1988), pp. 42–48.

63. Gregg, *Foragers and Farmers,* p. xx.

64. Thompson, *The Coevolutionary Process*, chapters 15, 16.

65. Thompson, *The Coevolutionary Process*, pp. 281–87.

66. For examples of the graphic depiction of energy flows in ecosystems, see the following: Vaclav Smil, *Cycles of Life: Civilization and the Biosphere* (New York: Scientific American Library, 1997); A. J. McMichael, *Planetary Overload: Global Environmental Change and the Health of the Human Species* (Cambridge: Cambridge University Press, 1993); K. D. Thomas, "Hierarchical Approaches to the Evolution of Complex Agricultural Systems," in *The Beginnings of Agriculture*, ed. Annie Milles, Diane Williams, and Neville Gardner (Oxford: Symposia for the Association for Environmental Archaeology, no. 8, BAR International Series 496, 1989), pp. 55–73; Sally Morgan, *Ecology and Environment: The Cycles of Life* (New York: Oxford University Press, 1995), chapter 2, Wicken, *Evolution, Thermodynamics, and Information*, pp. 155–56.

67. Claudia Chang and Harold Foster, *Pastoralists at the Periphery: Herders in a Capitalist World* (Tucson: University of Arizona Press, 1994).

68. Crosby, *The Columbian Exchange*; Alfred Crosby, "The Demographic Effect of American Crops in Europe," in Crosby, *Germs, Seeds and Animals: Studies in Ecological History* (Armonk, N.Y.: Sharpe, 1994), pp. 148–66.

69. Andrew Clark, *The Invasion of New Zealand by People, Plants, and Animals: The South Island* (New Brunswick, N.J.: Rutgers University Press, 1949).

70. Cronon, *Changes in the Land*; Carolyn Merchant, *Ecological Revolutions: Nature, Gender, and Science in New England* (Chapel Hill: University of North Carolina Press, 1989).

71. Thompson, *The Coevolutionary Process*, passim., but esp. table 13.1, pp. 221–22.

72. Thompson, *The Coevolutionary Process*, p. 225.

73. Wicken, *Evolution, Thermodynamics, and Information*, pp. 148–51.

74. Wicken, *Evolution, Thermodynamics, and Information*, p. 157.

75. Rob Hengeveld, *Dynamics of Biological Invasions* (London: Chapman and Hall, 1989); Colin Tudge, *The Time before History: 5 Million Years of Human Impact* (New York: Simon & Schuster, 1996), pp. 97–102.

76. Jonathan Kingdon, *Self-Made Man* (New York: Wiley, 1993), p. 87.

77. Thompson, *The Coevolutionary Process*, p. 19.

78. Thompson, *The Coevolutionary Process*, p. 61.

79. Matt Cartmill, "Oppressed by Evolution," *Discover* (March 1998), pp. 78–83.

Chapter Two

Population

A global society requires first and foremost a global population—that is, humans living virtually everywhere that humans can live. We did not begin our presence on Earth living everywhere; the first members of our species were a tiny group, probably no more than a few tens of thousands, living in the Rift Valley of East Africa. To become a global species, we had to expand our number and our reach to global proportions. It may be that, as Carl Sauer wrote years ago, "Built into the biologic nature of man . . . appear to be qualities tending to maximize geographic expansiveness,"[1] but such an accomplishment was not easy or cheap and required more than 100 millennia to complete.

Over the last ten thousand years, the human population has experienced a number of interconnected changes, any one of which by itself would have been significant: an increase in our numbers from four to five million to nearly six billion, and in our population density from an average of 0.04 persons per square kilometer to more than 40, in both instances an increase of three orders of magnitude; a threefold increase in life expectancy, from twenty-five years to seventy-five; and the migration of humans from our origin in East Africa to virtually everywhere. For us to have undergone all these changes more or less together, and compressed within the brief span of only ten millennia, must surely be one of the most dramatic biological events in the history of our planet. Even more remarkable is the fact that the bulk of these changes have not been spread evenly across the last ten thousand years but have been compressed into the last five hundred!

HOMO SAPIENS

Visualize the length of the history of our planet as represented by the 3,900 kilometers (2,400 miles) across North America.[2] The beginning of the Earth, about 4.54 billion years ago, is represented by the Golden Gate Bridge in San Francisco; "today" is at the Washington Monument in Washington, D.C. On this scale, the origin of life as bacteria some 3.7 billion years ago is at the state line between Nevada and Utah. The first life with complex cells, called eukaryotes and about 1.5 billion years ago, is at St. Louis, on the Mississippi River. The dinosaurs appeared 250 million years ago, near the state line between West Virginia and Virginia; and they disappeared about sixty-five million years ago, near the Virginia town of Warrenton, about thirty-five miles from downtown Washington. Our prehuman ancestors, *Australopithicus,* made their appearance about 4 million years ago, near Rosslyn, on the Virginia side of the Potomac River. Our immediate predecessor, *Homo erectus,* dates from 1.5 million years ago, at the Lincoln Memorial, about 1,300 meters (4,000 feet) from the Washington Monument; and *Homo sapiens* appears about 200 millennia ago, only 170 meters (500 feet) from the monument. We have occupied our place on the Earth for only a tiny fraction of the total time the planet has existed; but we have compressed a huge amount of change into that brief moment.

"Like it or not," writes Colin Tudge, "all creatures that aspire to live in a particular way find themselves subject to particular physical laws that must be respected and that largely determine what form they take."[3] Gravity and thermodynamics place inescapable limits on the body size, shape, and lifestyle of any land creature.[4] Moreover, there is only a finite number of ways to fit body parts together, and these all tend to be repeated, with some variation, within genera. Each general pattern for the arrangement of body parts constitutes what Robert Wesson calls an "attractor," or a form that imposes organizational discipline on every organism within the species or genus.[5]

For *Homo sapiens,* our place on the Earth was eventually shaped by the fact that we were a land animal, homeothermic (that is, able to maintain a constant body temperature through our own metabolic processes), of considerable size (relative to most other organisms), with considerable mobility thanks to our bipedalism, and containing a large and complex brain. Not incidentally, similar forces were also at work shaping the other animals in the biosphere: those with which we would compete, those that preyed on us, those on which we preyed, and those we domesticated and with which we coevolved.

On the face of it, it would appear that our large size gave us significant advantages, and indeed it did: greater size usually translates into greater strength and speed, special advantages of predators over prey. But size can be a big disadvantage as well. Large animals need more time to mature, so they cannot leave behind as many offspring. Large, homeothermic animals have slower metabolic rates than do small homeotherms, and so need less food per unit of body weight, but in absolute terms they need much more food to survive. In theory, big carnivores can catch a greater range of prey than can small ones, but in practice it does not pay in energy terms for a carnivore to eat an animal much smaller than itself. Generally speaking, a carnivore converts only about one-tenth of the food it consumes to its own tissue. The remainder is consumed via metabolism to fuel its own physical processes and behavior. So large carnivores are restricted to a much smaller range of ecological niches than are small, large carnivores need a much greater range than do small, and the population of large meat eaters is usually much smaller as a result.

The consequences of size are all a matter of geometry or proportion. The surface of an animal increases in proportion to the square of its linear dimensions, while volume increases in proportion to the cube. All other things being equal, an animal that triples its linear dimensions (length, width, height) increases its surface area nine times and its mass, or volume, twenty-seven times. Also, as linear dimensions increase, the supporting limbs must thicken disproportionately to keep up with the increase in body mass. Big homeotherms need to eat a lot, and that dictates a large mouth and head, which in turn demands a strong, thick neck.

Large homeothermic animals all face similar problems: how to get enough to eat while avoiding being eaten. There are several options available to solve these problems. Some species, like the rhino, adopted a defensive strategy and evolved what Tudge calls the "tanklike" body form. Others, like the camel and the giraffe, opted for a long neck carried more or less erect: the "Eiffel Tower" morph. And there are the primates, which solved the problem by retaining and building on a number of primitive body parts, especially dexterous, five-fingered, upper and lower limbs that enabled them to climb and live in trees. While other mammals became specialists in a given environmental context, the primates succeeded by the opposite strategy: by remaining generalists, with the flexibility they would need to adapt to changing circumstances.[6]

Primates possess few if any features that are not possessed by other mammals; their great flexibility is owed directly to this generality and thus to versatility. Life in the trees gave the earliest primates flexibility of the joints, strength and sensitivity of grip, and binocular vision and hearing developed in three dimensions. After several million years, these animals had evolved what would prove to be the crucial characteristic of *Homo*: the ability to descend to the forest floor, to stand and move about upright on two legs, and to use the hands to manipulate objects.

To say that there is considerable controversy and disagreement among experts about the origins of our species would be a major understatement.[7] Moreover, new fossil discoveries that challenge mainstream paradigms are frequently reported in the daily press.[8] If there is a consensus scenario about human origins, it probably goes something like this:[9] Between five and eight million years ago, a genus known as *Australopithecus* emerged in the newly formed Rift Valley of East Africa, probably in response to changes in climate.[10] As the forests of East Africa declined and gave way to grasslands, our ancient ancestors adapted by becoming bipedal. It was something of a faustian bargain, for what we gained in mobility and in the use of the hands we lost in climbing ability and, perhaps most significantly, in energy efficiency, for bipedal humans are less energy efficient than are quadrupeds such as dogs or horses. So long as our ancestors remained tree dwellers, quadrupedalism continued to be more energy efficient than bipedalism; but once on the ground, chimpanzees and apes lost their advantage—a chimpanzee is about 50 percent less energy efficient than a human when walking on the ground. So when we became terrestrial creatures, locomotor efficiency favored bipedalism, despite its relatively greater energy requirements.[11]

For the next several million years, the australopithecines lived a precarious existence on the grasslands across southern and eastern Africa. Sometime between 1.5 and 2.5 million years ago, their genus evolved into (and gave way to) the genus *Homo*, a diverse and complex set of species, of which only one, *Homo sapiens*, remains today. Between 0.5 and 1.6 million years ago, an early species of *Homo*, *H. erectus*, evolved in Africa and began to migrate to Eurasia. Two diametrically opposed hypotheses have been advanced to explain what happened next, and how *Homo erectus* was replaced by *Homo sapiens*.

Some scholars believe that local populations of *erectus* in Africa, Asia, and Europe evolved separately into *H. sapiens* with a considerable amount of interbreeding, or sharing of genetic material across space and between populations. This paradigm is known as the "multiregional" or "regional continuity" hypothesis. Others believe that *erectus* eventually died out in Europe, Africa, and Asia and was replaced by modern humans, *H. sapiens*, which evolved independently (that is, without interbreeding with *erectus*) in Africa and spread from there to Eurasia, the Americas, and Australia. This paradigm is known by several names, including the "Out of Africa" hypothesis.

On three occasions in 1997, new findings were released that appeared to shift the balance of scholarly support in favor of one or the other of these hypotheses. In mid-1997, researchers at the University of Munich reported that they had isolated a very tiny portion of mitochondrial DNA from the original Neanderthal fossil remains and had compared it with a comparable portion of contemporary human DNA.[12] The results showed that it was virtually certain that Neanderthals did not interbreed with, and thus did not evolve into, *Homo sapiens*. Moreover, the split between Neanderthals and modern humans dates from between 550,000 and 690,000 years ago, long before there were hominids in Europe. Later in the year, at a conference on human evolution at the Cold Spring Harbor Laboratory on Long Island, New York, a number of population geneticists reported their findings, also based on DNA comparisons. They concluded that our species originated in Africa 130,000 to 170,000 years ago, and migrated out of Africa about 137,000 years ago in small groups that in total probably numbered no more than two hundred to five hundred individuals.[13] These findings would appear to settle the debate in favor of the "Out of Africa" paradigm, at least for the time being. Other scientific papers, however, also based on DNA analyses and presented at a meeting of physical anthropologists in St. Louis earlier in the spring suggested that both hypotheses may be too extreme, and that the truth may lie somewhere in between. This analysis suggested that while the earliest ancestors of *Homo sapiens* appear to have left Africa some 200,000 years ago, there was also considerable movement of people back into Africa from Asia and thus a sharing of genetic material over substantial distances and times.[14] No doubt, this debate will continue.

Whichever hypothesis is correct, early humans had to contend with a bioge-ography that was markedly unstable. And the characteristics, both genetic and cultural, we evolved to cope with such instability continue to shape our place in the world today.

Any discussion of early climate changes must begin with temperature, with major consequences for sea level and rainfall.[15] As a result of periodic changes in the Earth, including a certain amount of "wobbling" on its axis ("tilting") and its orientation toward, and its orbit around, the sun, our planet's weather changes in very broad cycles. During each cycle, covering a span of roughly one hundred millennia, the Earth experiences a series of fluctuating cold spells lasting about ninety millennia, followed by about ten thousand years of relative warming. Over the past 3.5 million years, there have been twenty-seven such major climatic cycles. Additional variations have been introduced by changes within the Earth itself, including vulcanism and the shifting of tectonic plates. This latter set of changes has caused the continents to change their positions relative to each other, affect-ing wind and ocean currents.

One of the most significant consequences of such variations in temperature involved the size of the polar ice caps. When temperatures plunged, the glaciers expanded, sea levels dropped, and exposed land masses grew. Land bridges ap-peared where water had been before, and continents and islands previously sepa-rated became joined. Britain and Ireland were once part of the European conti-nent; Indonesia was joined to the Asian mainland; and the Bering land bridge connected North America and Asia. The appearance and disappearance of these land connections can be likened to a series of huge gates opening and closing. When the Earth's temperature was cold, humans and other animals migrated into new lands; when the temperature rose, so did sea levels, and the gates to expan-sion were closed, at least until the next Ice Age.

Flora and fauna instability would have been a second major consequence of climatic changes. Eastern and southern Africa constituted one huge ecosystem of great diversity, ranging from dense forests to open grasslands. The population of large animals, both herbivores and the carnivores that preyed on them, was huge and constantly in flux. The rise and fall of species populations, a function partly of diet and food supply, would have yielded a broad mosaic of fauna and the or-ganisms they ate. Contemporary African game preserves possess animal biomass weighing 12,000 to 18,000 kilograms per square kilometer, an indication of what the primordial savanna might have harbored at the dawn of humankind.[16] Many of these animals actively competed with humans for food; others preyed on hu-mans as well. Only a few herbivores were accessible to humans as a major food source. Over time, these food sources, as well as those derived from plant matter or from aquatic animals, would have been highly unstable, and under the best of circumstances, food was scarce. Food scarcity and instability, in turn, led to two characteristics of the earliest human populations: sparse concentrations and more or less constant movement.

Rick Potts has proposed a view of human origins that is grounded in ecological instability.[17] During periods of great fluctuations in climate, and in plant and animal life, the versatility and flexibility of our species made it possible for us not only to survive but also to compete and flourish. The time when hominids first appeared on the East African savanna, some four to six million years ago, was marked by oscillations of global climate that were on average larger and more frequent than those of any preceding age. Even during the next million years or so, when global climate changes became less frequent, they were still marked by large swings in temperature. The earliest lineages of hominids had to cope with these changes, leading, argues Potts, to "the creative change to human evolution."[18]

Thus, the key features of humans evolved as coping mechanisms of organisms faced with a highly unstable environment. Bipedalism came first, which gave our earliest ancestors the mobility they needed to transcend the limited range and food supply of the other primates. This mobility allowed hominids to range far afield, gathering food (especially meat) and stones (from which to make tools), and to assemble these ingredients at central feeding sites. The use of stone edges to cut meat made *Homo* the first animal to make tools to process food outside their body, leading to important dietary changes that did not require commensurate physical changes (for example, the digestive system).

The introduction of meat into our ancestors' diet was a change of huge significance, principally because of its impact on the size of the body generally, and of the brain in particular. Many of the conditions facing *Homo sapiens* derive from our size. We are large animals, and this seems to give us certain advantages, especially in the predator-prey dynamic. However, as Colin Tudge puts it, "big animals are far more vulnerable than they seem."[19]

Big animals confront three significant problems resulting from their size. First, they are conspicuous and thus easy to find and track. Moreover, their size rewards predators with a huge prize of energy, and thus encourages other species to hunt them. Second, animal populations need to be big if they are to survive over the long term. Populations of any species that number in the hundreds are likely to be wiped out in centuries, if not decades, by physical accidents such as epidemics, or statistical accidents such as a skewed sex ratio. Yet a sizable population of large animals needs enormous space to sustain them, given the inefficiencies inherent in the energy networks in nature.

Finally, large animals pursue the K-strategy of reproduction (to be discussed presently), which means that they produce a few progeny at a time over fairly long intervals, and then invest huge amounts of energy in ensuring their survival. Under certain conditions, this strategy makes genetic sense, but it does have a drawback: when the population of a K-strategy species is reduced, it needs a long time to recover. If the disturbance that reduces their numbers lasts for a fairly long time, it may cause the extinction of the species altogether.

Clearly, humans have been able to resolve this problem of reproduction, since over the past several hundred millennia we have been a hugely successful species (measured by the increase in our numbers). Changes in the size and structure of our brain were the factors that conferred on us our competitive advantage.[20] Despite the complexity of these changes, however, they could actually have resulted from mutations in a very few genes, especially if these mutations affected the regulator genes that control the speed, timing, and sequencing of somatic development.

The human brain differs from the brain of other primates in three crucial ways. First, while our heart, lungs, kidney, and liver are about the size one would expect, our brain is about three times as large as it should be for a primate our size. This extra size is a consequence of an unusually long growth period. The brain of a human grows at about the rate one would expect for a mammal, but it continues to grow for a very long time, mostly after birth. As far as brain size and complexity are concerned, human infants are born "prematurely." If birth were delayed until the brain had matured, the infant's skull would be so large that it would not fit through the mother's birth canal. Expanding the pelvis would have interfered with bipedal locomotion, so the only other evolutionary solution was to defer brain maturation.

Next, the proportions of the human brain are different from those of monkeys and apes. A much greater percentage of the human brain is devoted to the structure called the lateral nuclei, the portion of the thalamus that sends information to the cognitive areas of the neocortex. Finally, the human brain is much more highly specialized. The brains of all mammals are divided into two hemispheres, but while most animals duplicate the functions performed in each hemisphere, in humans each side specializes in a different set of activities. This specialization is especially important for language and speech because these activities require a lot of brain tissue, which would not be available if the brain were not as specialized as it is.

From increased brain size, complexity, and specialization we get the ingredients of culture: technology, language, organization, inventiveness, creative problem solving. But there has been a price to pay for these advantages: energy. The brain is only 2 percent of a human's body weight, but it consumes 20 percent of our energy, about three times the energy required by the brain of a chimpanzee.[21] Moreover, since the brain continues to mature long after birth, for years the human child remains helpless, at the mercy of the environment and dependent on his or her elders for survival. The payoff, however, is critical to our success as a species: social learning, leading to versatility, flexibility, and a capacity for coping with an unstable environment.

In sum, our earliest ancestors had to make their way through a challenging and highly unstable environment. To succeed in this endeavor, they had to evolve mobility and a kind of generalist flexibility rooted in the learned behavior made possible by large, complex brains and culture. The first characteristic enabled them to become long-distance migrants and thus to eventually become a global species (at least in small numbers). The second characteristic, culture, enabled humans to coevolve with plants and animals (via agriculture and animal husbandry). With our food supply thus expanded manyfold, the way was open for *Homo sapiens* to achieve a global population three orders of magnitude greater than when our odyssey began ten thousand years ago.

THE DYNAMICS OF HUMAN POPULATION

Since the preceding section raised the issue of reproductive strategy, it is time to consider this question in detail with regard to the human population.

Living organisms that reproduce sexually (as opposed to those that do so asexually, or by cloning) have to develop an effective reproductive strategy.[22] Small organisms such as insects or mice generally employ an r-strategy: after a short gestation period, they produce huge numbers of offspring at very frequent intervals and invest virtually nothing in their survival. Not surprisingly, most of them die before reaching maturity, but their large numbers make that less of a problem. These organisms mature rapidly and live a brief but explosive life. They have a high growth potential, but they are also vulnerable to population collapse as well, and their populations tend to exhibit wide swings of growth and decline.

Large animals, such as elephants or humans, employ the K-strategy: after a long gestation period, they produce small numbers of offspring (frequently, only one) at very wide intervals, and invest a lot of energy in their survival. Most of them make it through to maturity, at which time they can reproduce themselves. The young of K-strategists mature slowly and live long lives. Their lengthy maturation leaves much time for social learning (or culture), but they are dependent on the older members of their population for a long time as a result.

Jeffrey Wicken has argued that the choice of reproduction strategy is a function of ecological circumstance.[23] For organisms colonizing a new ecosystem, where resources are abundant and competition low, the r-strategy is optimal, as it diverts large amounts of energy into the production of large numbers of offspring that mature quickly, ensuring thereby that they remain fairly small. In saturated ecosystems, where the increased competition puts pressure on species to grow larger, the optimal strategy is the K-strategy, because it encourages species to invest energy carefully in the production of small numbers of slow-maturing progeny. Being a late arrival in the rich and competitive East African ecosystem, *Homo sapiens* evolved the latter strategy for reproduction.

Although this book deals separately with human population and food, in fact the two systems had to expand more or less together, because the process of globalization is fundamentally a transformation of the ways people discovered and exploited energy sources. As we became more proficient at creating energy networks of humans, plants, and animals, and later of industrial energy, we were able to use the increased energy supply to increase our number and to spread ourselves more widely across the Earth.

Calculations of world population for periods further back in time than a millennium or so are exercises in estimation and speculation. Reliable census figures date only from the late eighteenth and early nineteenth centuries, and then only for a small number of countries. Earlier estimates rely on indirect measures such as church registries of births, marriages, and deaths, or tombstone surveys. As we recede further into the past, archeological evidence such as the size of rooms in houses or the number of houses in a village can be translated into a resident population. For populations before the Neolithic, anthropologists extrapolate from contemporary hunter-gatherer societies.

Because they range back to include the pre-*sapiens* period, the data of Michael Kremer (table 2.1) illustrate well the dynamics of world population growth.[24] The picture they paint is of small populations and slow growth rates for a very long time, punctuated by reversals from time to time in the face of disease, war, or upheaval. Nevertheless, the K-strategist species is relentless, and, once endowed with the technologies necessary to defeat most of their microbial enemies, humans began to expand their numbers at steadily increasing rates.

Demographers may disagree about the specifics of timing and causes, but they agree that the human population grew in phases that were demarcated by the availability of energy supplies. One very influential formulation advanced some years ago was that of Edward Deevey, who argued that human population experienced three periods of rapid increase.[25] The first expansion occurred about 100,000 B.C., occasioned by the invention, fabrication, and use of stone tools. During this period, the population was limited by the energy naturally available in biomass. The second wave of growth took place between 8000 B.C. and 4000 B.C., brought about by the invention of agriculture and cities. Following the Neolithic Revolution, the population was constrained by the energy available in plants, animals, moving water, and wind. The third period of growth began in the eighteenth century A.D., made possible by the Industrial Revolution and the liberation of the energy stored in fossil fuel.

Of particular interest is the relative speed with which population increased after the Neolithic Revolution, compared with the slow rate of growth in the first and third expansion cycles. Slow population growth during the first wave of growth is usually attributed to the stress of primitive life: food scarcities, high infant-mortality rate, low life expectancy, and so forth. Slow rates during the third phase are attributed to the lethality of urban life, particularly owing to the crowding diseases of early industrial cities. Once these hazards were overcome by public health measures—better sewage and water treatment technologies, and so forth—growth rates accelerated after World War II to produce the "demographic explosion" of the second half of our century.

Hunter-gatherers are usually given great credit for being able to live within their limitations, especially where their own population growth was concerned. We may not necessarily attribute to these early humans any great moral virtue or even any significant ecological awareness. They may have known the origins of their

Table 2.1   World Population Growth, 1,000,000 BC
to 1990

Year	Population (millions)
−1,000,000	0.125
−300,00	1
−25,000	3.34
−10,00	4
−5000	5
−400	7
−3000	14
−2000	27
−1000	50
−50	100
−200	150
1	170
200	190
400	190
600	200
800	220
1000	265
1100	320
1200	360
1300	360
1400	350
1500	425
1600	545
1700	610
1750	720
1800	900
1850	1200
1900	1625
1950	2516
1990	5333

Source: Michael Kremer, "Population Growth and
Technological Change: One Million B.C. to 1990," *Quarterly
Journal of Economics*, vol. 108, no. 3 (August, 1993), pp. 681-
716, Table 1, p. 683. © 1993 by the President and Fellows
of Harvard College and the Massachusetts Institute of Technology. Reprinted by permission.

limitations, or they may simply have lived "within ecosystems where regulation
of numbers was more a property evolved by the prey than a product of prescient
self-control exercised by the predator."[26] Faced with the burden of living off scarce
resources in a highly competitive environment, humans resorted to numerous
techniques to limit their population: birth spacing by means of lengthy

Table 2.2   Population Dynamics, 10,000 BC to 1990

	10,000 BC	0	1750	1950	1990
Population (millions)	6	252	771	2530	5292
Annual growth (%)	0.008	0.037	0.064	0.596	1.845
Doubling time (years)	8369	1854	1083	116	38
Life expectancy (years)	20	22	27	35	55

Source: Massimo Livi-Bacci, *A Concise History of World Population*, trans. by Carl Ipsen (Cambridge, Massachusetts: Blackwell, 1992), Chapter 1, Table 1.2, p. 31. © 1992 Blackwell Publishers. Reprinted by permission.

breastfeeding, abortion, infanticide, and abandonment of the young or infirm. They also moved constantly in search of new food supplies.

For the greater part of our time on Earth, the human population has been small and growing at an extremely slow rate. The processes of fertility and mortality that have preserved this rough balance are far from understood, although diseases certainly have played a key role. Figure 2.2 shows the survival curve for a group of hunter-gatherers who lived about 15,000 years ago on the Mediterranean coast. Only half the group survived past the age of ten years, and only about one-fifth reached the age of forty years or beyond. Population units probably ranged in size

Table 2.3   Distribution of World Population, 400 BC to 1990 (in millions)

Year	Asia	Europe	Africa	Americas	World
400 BC	95	19	17	8	153
0	170	31	26	12	252
200	158	44	30	11	257
600	134	22	24	16	208
1000	152	30	39	18	253
1200	258	49	48	26	400
1340	238	74	80	32	442
1400	201	52	68	39	375
1500	245	67	87	42	461
1600	338	89	113	13	578
1700	433	95	107	12	680
1750	500	111	104	18	771
1800	631	146	102	24	954
1850	790	209	102	59	1241
1900	903	295	127	165	1634
1950	1393	395	219	330	2530
1990	3113	498	642	724	5292

Source: Massimo Livi-Bacci, *A Concise History of World Population*, trans. by Carl Ipsen (Cambridge, Massachusetts: Blackwell, 1992), Chapter 1, Table 1.3, p. 31. © 1992 Blackwell Publishers. Reprinted by permission.

Figure 2.1   Survival Curve for Hunter-Gatherer Population, c. 15,000 Years before Present

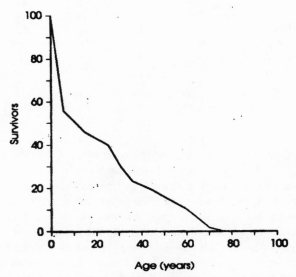

Note: This curve represents the survival profile for a hunter-gatherer population of approximately 15,000 years ago on the Mediterranean coast. The curve shows high child mortality, with only about half of the population surviving past age 10.

Source: Roy Anderson and Robert May, *Infectious Diseases of Humans: Dynamics and Control* (Oxford: Oxford University Press, 1991), Chapter 23, Fig. 23.15, p. 653. © 1991 Oxford University Press. Reprinted by permission.

from about twenty to at most one hundred; and the total world population of *Homo sapiens* remained under five million until the Neolithic Revolution.

Beginning about ten thousand years ago, the nomadic lifestyle of hunter-gatherers began to give way to food production, leading to an increase in both total population and in population density. For the first half of the Neolithic period, from about 8000 B.C. to about 3000 B.C., world population grew some twentyfold, from five million to about one hundred million—one of the fastest rates of population growth ever experienced. Until relatively recently, it was customary to explain such a phenomenal rate of growth by the improved diet of humans caused by the invention of agriculture. We now understand, however, that the impact of agriculture on human populations was much more complex than that.[28]

On the one hand, mortality rates did not decline and life expectancy did not increase. The impact of agriculture on nutrition was mixed, but probably on the whole negative.[29] Agriculture made possible greater reserves, but the human diet probably declined in quality and diversity, and food supplies became more unstable because of reliance on only a few staple items. Mortality rates were kept high or driven even higher by humankind's new experiences with diseases, which afflicted populations of greater density in ways that hunter-gatherer societies had never confronted. In particular, infant-mortality rates rose, and overall life expectancy, if anything, declined. The threat from predators was probably reduced as sedentary communities now found ways to build walls and ditches around themselves. Human predators (bandits and thieves) became much more of a problem, however, since populations had accumulated food surpluses that made plunder worthwhile.

On the other hand, birth rates increased dramatically once agriculture appeared. The chief factor appears to have been the sedentary lifestyle that agriculture makes possible. The cost of childbearing declined, and the relative value of additional children increased, so the interval between births shortened, and fertility rates and family sizes increased. Thus, while death rates were not significantly improved, birth rates rose so high that they alone were able to account for an unprecedented population increase.

For the next five thousand years—that is, from about 3000 B.C. until about 1800 A.D., population grew only fivefold, from 100 million to 500 million, only one-fourth as fast as during the preceding five thousand years. Why the sharp decrease in growth rate? We have little evidence of a reduction in fertility rates, so we should look at the possibility of increased mortality rates. Here we find two possible factors, both related to disease: one, the urbanization we associate with the last five millennia certainly encouraged the emergence and spread of diseases that need a dense host population to survive and flourish; and two, the last five thousand years also witnessed the first large-scale movements of people and commerce across long distances, which spread more exotic disease pools around the world and exposed more people to pathogens that they had never known before. The interaction of urbanization and globalization led frequently to the catastrophic spread of diseases and the decline of population. The best-known cases occurred in Europe in the fourteenth century, when the bubonic plague killed about one-third of the population between 1340 and 1400; and in the Americas, where the arrival of European diseases after 1492 killed as many as 90 percent of the native people.

Since the globalization of the human population was (and still is) essentially the history of human migration and colonization, we need to recognize the special dynamics of population change and structure in areas undergoing colonization.[30] The populations involved in initial migration are heavily weighted toward young adult males; only much later do other age groups and females begin to approach their normal proportions in a population. As a population lengthens the time it occupies a given site, growth rates change from high to low, females achieve something approaching parity in sex ratio, fertility rates rise, and in-migration becomes a minor factor in population growth.

The dynamics of fertility rates are of great interest to us in understanding changes in migrating populations. At the leading edge of the population wave, fertility tends to be somewhat lower than average. Fertility rates rise dramatically just behind the leading edge, through the second and third generations of migrants, with the second generation (the first residents native to a particular site) having the highest rates of all. Fertility rates then decline as one moves behind the leading edge; and the farther one goes away from the frontier, the lower the fertility rates become. At the same time, among sedentary agriculturalists, rates of miscarriages and of infant mortality rise, principally because of the degradation of the environment and the increased chances for the transmission of diseases through the air, direct human contact, or human waste. Finally, as available land and resources are taken, new families and individuals find they must move on to the next fresh territory. The result of all these factors is a decline in the rate of population increase at some distance behind the wave of advancing population.

Since the advent of the Industrial Revolution, around the middle of the eighteenth century, the human population has grown at rates and in quantities without precedent. The explanation for this lies in the demographic transition (see figures 2.2 and 2.3). At the heart of the transition is the fact that the impact of industrialization and modernization is felt first in death rates, which fall, and only somewhat later in birth rates, which begin to decline a generation or more than death rates.

Before industrialization and modernization, a society typically exhibits birth rates in the range of 40 to 50 per 1,000 population, death rates in the range of 30 to 40 per 1,000, and consequent population growth rates between 0 and 10 per

Figure 2.2   Typical Survival Curves for Human Populations in Developed and Developing Countries

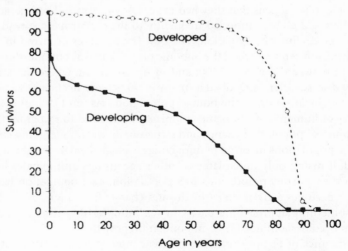

Source: Roy Anderson and Robert May, *Infectious Diseases of Humans: Dynamics and Control* (Oxford: Oxford University Press, 1991), Fig. 1.4, p. 5. Based on data in D.J. Bradley, "Regulation of parasite populations: A general theory of the epidemiology and control of parasitic infections," trans. R. Soc. Trop. Med. Hyg., vol. 66, no. 5 (1972), pp. 697-708.

Figure 2.3   Demographic Transition Model

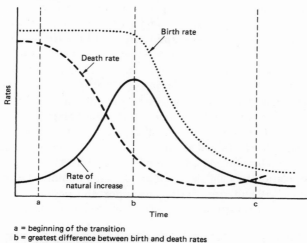

a = beginning of the transition
b = greatest difference between birth and death rates
c = end of the transition

Source: Massimo Livi-Bacci, *A Concise History of World Population*, trans. Carl Ipsen (Cambridge, Massachusetts: Blackwell, 1992), Fig. 4.2, p. 103. © 1992 Blackwell Publishers. Reprinted by permission.

1,000 (1 percent or less). Once industrialization and modernization are under way, death rates decline to perhaps 10 to 20 per 1,000. The reasons behind the decline are easy to see: better food and water, sewage and waste-water treatment, hospitals and health care professionals, medicines and other health care technologies. Above all, the infant mortality rate is brought down, which has the effect of adding to life expectancy. Even though death rates decline, birth rates remain high, apparently because human values and behaviors regarding fertility are much more resistant to change. The result: population growth rates rise to the range of 30 to 40 per 1,000 (3 to 4 percent). Instead of remaining more or less stable or, at most, doubling once every seventy-five to one hundred years, population during this phase doubles every twenty to twenty-five years.

At some point, however, human values and behaviors begin to change.[31] Since more children are being kept alive to adulthood, the value of each additional child begins to decline. Parents understand that they do not need to bring four to six new babies into the world in order to see two reach adulthood, so the fertility rate (the number of children born to each woman during her life) begins to drop to near replacement level of 2.1. As a society's overall level of wealth rises, enormous changes are wrought in the status and role of women. The education level of women rises to approximate parity with that of men; and women enter the salaried work force at levels approaching those of men. Empowered women now envision social roles that are alternatives to that of mother. Thus, birth rates begin to decline to levels that approach death rates, and the population growth rate returns to the preindustrial level: 0 to 10 per 1,000 (or 1 percent or less).

The demographic transition has been under way for about two centuries, with enormous consequences for the size and character of the world's population.[32] Population has been growing at unprecedented rates since the early nineteenth century, reaching 1 billion in 1804, 2 billion in 1927, 3 billion in 1960, 4 billion in 1974, 5 billion in 1987, and 6 billion in 2000. This population "momentum" of about 90 million net additional people each year will continue through the first decade of the next century, but the decline in birth rates (already visible throughout most of the world except Africa)[33] will eventually cause population growth rates to decline as well. The United Nations now expects world population to reach 7 billion in 2011, 8 billion in 2025, 9 billion in 2041, and 10 billion in 2071. They also expect population to stabilize at about 10.7 billion about the year 2200 or shortly thereafter.[34] Whether the Earth can support this population will occupy our attention when we return to this subject near the end of the book.

MIGRATION AND THE GLOBALIZATION OF THE HUMAN POPULATION

To become global, life systems must have moved, or been moved, across great distances, starting with humans. All animals have the potential for migration; indeed, migration as a means of adaptation to environmental stress is a fundamental property of all forms of life.[35] Niles Eldredge writes:

> By far the most common response of species to environmental change is that they move. . . . In the face of environmental change, organisms within each and every species seek familiar living conditions. . . . This is "habitat tracking," the constant search for suitable habitat going on continually, generation after generation, within every species on the face of the earth.[36]

Those animals that choose to migrate do so when they perceive that the suitability of the potential habitat is so superior to that of the current habitat that the difference outweighs the costs of migration. At the most fundamental level, habitat suitability is a function of the food resources the animal needs to survive and to reproduce. The challenge, of course, is to acquire and process the information necessary to be able to assess the differences in suitability of two habitats. The difficulty of accomplishing these tasks mounts proportionately as the distances to be covered increase.

To meet this challenge, hominids had two advantages: a social organization large enough and differentiated enough to be able to send some members to scout ahead to find better food supplies and bring that information back to the main group; and brains large enough to do something productive with that information once it was received. In this way, our earliest ancestors made their way across the East African savanna via routes that must have resembled "calculated wan-

dering." Gradually, almost imperceptibly, they migrated in search of fresh landscapes, fauna, and food supplies. Eventually, moving at the rate of perhaps a kilometer a year, some of the more daring, or more desperate, left Africa and turned
north and east.

For Rick Potts, the ability of human beings to disperse, to migrate over long
distances, and to colonize uninhabited spaces is a product of evolution in highly
unstable environments. "The inclination to colonize new regions," he writes,

> required only an amalgamation of the two basic responses to environmental fluc-
> tuations: to follow vital resources, which requires mobility; and to expand the life
> conditions in which survival is possible, which requires flexibility and ways of
> buffering change. Over the past 1 million years, hominids became masters of both.[37]

According to Potts, the earliest tool makers in East Africa, some 1.8 million years
ago, occupied a home range of about thirty square kilometers, but their travels
traversed distances of perhaps three hundred square kilometers. By between 1
million and seven hundred thousand years ago, hominids traveled over forty kilometers to obtain raw materials, which suggests a territorial range of sixty-six
hundred square kilometers. And as the Ice Age neared its end, during the last fifty
to one hundred millennia, trips of two hundred kilometers and ranges of more
than thirty thousand square kilometers were not uncommon.[38]

Our ancestors were able to conquer distance in part because of their own mobility, and in part because they could impart mobility to other living organisms,
an ability they possessed as a result of their capacity for social organization and
for fabricating technologies out of the materials nature provides. As they moved
themselves, humans also moved many other organisms, some intentionally (livestock moved in herds, grain transported in baskets), and some unthinkingly
(microörganisms).

To be the carriers of globalization, eventually humans had to fashion organizations and technologies of transport and communication, or bulk-flow systems.[39]
Bulk flow requires the technological and organizational capabilities to package
materials; load them into some container; transport that container; and unload,
unpackage, and distribute the materials at destination. Globalization was made
possible by our ability to fashion the bulk-flow technologies necessary to move
matter, energy, and information to virtually every place on the planet. The global spread of human beings and their cultures has occurred in seven episodes, each
characterized by distinctive systems of bulk-flow transport and communication
whose power and efficiency have been steadily increasing (see table 2.4).[40]

Earlier, I noted the competing explanations for how humans came to live more
or less everywhere: the multiregional hypothesis, and the Out of Africa hypothesis. These two hypotheses agree that the first hominid traveler was our distant
ancestor, *Homo erectus.*[41] Fossil evidence suggests that *erectus* left Africa and migrated as far as Southeast Asia by about 1.6 million years ago, but this represents
the limits of their travels. Just why *erectus* would have wanted to migrate is, of

Table 2.4. Seven Episodes of Globalization, Related Bulk Flow Systems, and Changes in World Population

Episode	Approximate Dates	Bulk Flow Systems (typical examples)	World Population (millions)			
			Start	Close	Increase	Per Decade
Out of Africa	100,000+ ybp to 10,000 ybp (8000 BC)	humans	1	5	4	0.0004
The Neolithic Revolution	8000 BC to 3000 BC	animals, plants, pottery, baskets, sledges, canoes	5	14	9	0.18
Ancient Cities and Trade Routes	3000 BC to 1400 AD	draft animals, human porters, wheeled vehicles, sailing ships	14	375	361	0.82
Age of Discovery	1400 to 1800	caravel, trading companies	375	954	579	14.48
Partnership of Steam and Coal	nineteenth century	steamship, railroad, telegraph, telephone	954	1,634	680	68.00
Petroleum and the Internal Combustion Engine	twentieth century	automobile, truck, airplane, radio	1,634	2,530	896	179.20
The Information Age	1960 to 1990	digital information, computers, television	2,530	5,292	2,762	690.50

Sources: Titles and chronologies of episodes from Robert Clark, *The Global Imperative: An Interpretive History of the Spread of Humankind* (Boulder, Colorado: Westview Press, 1997). Population data from Massimo Livi-Bacci, *A Concise History of World Population*, trans. by Carl Ipsen (Cambridge, Massachusetts: Blackwell, 1992), Tables 1.2 and 1.3, p. 31; and Joel Cohen, *How Many People Can the Earth Support?* (New York: Norton, 1995), Appendix 2, pp. 400-401.

course, a matter of speculation. Successful species spread themselves across the landscape as a way of enhancing their intake and processing of energy; and *erectus*, with their large frame and relatively large brain were certainly intensive consumers of food energy. But *erectus* also enjoyed a number of significant advantages that earlier bipeds lacked. The lower back was constructed in such a way as to facilitate running long distances, and they were apparently the first animals to control fire. After 500 or so millennia of living in the grasslands of eastern Africa, *erectus* would have acquired the "mental mapping" ability to navigate across spaces that lack many recognizable landmarks. But they were slowed in their migration because the route from East Africa to Java was probably never a single, unbroken stretch of grassland; and the rain forests, rivers, and mountains that lay in their path would have presented difficult obstacles to overcome.

After *Homo erectus*, the two paradigms diverge. The multiregional hypothesis holds that anatomically modern humans evolved from local *erectus* populations more or less at the same time in many different places in Africa, Asia, and Europe. These locally evolving populations interacted with each other, and exchanged genetic material to yield a single gene pool of *Homo sapiens*. The Out of Africa hypothesis argues that modern humans evolved from *erectus* only in Africa, about six hundred thousand years ago. This *sapiens* population then migrated out of Africa to Europe and Asia, where they displaced the local *erectus* populations to the point where, some thirty thousand years ago, the last *erectus* individuals—the Neanderthals—disappeared, leaving behind virtually nothing of their genetic material. While the debate over human origins will no doubt continue, some of the DNA discoveries in 1997 (mentioned earlier) certainly strengthen the Out of Africa hypothesis.

Long-distance mobility has been one of the key features of our species from its primordial origins. Early humans had no means of mobility other than walking and no bulk-flow systems capable of transporting food energy over any appreciable distance. Nevertheless, humans needed a great deal of food energy to pay for their bipedalism as well as to fund the high energy requirements of their large brains.[42] Hundreds of millennia ago, early humans living in East Africa met this challenge by being scavenging carnivores. Their only mobility requirement was to bring together the carcasses of dead animals and the flint tools they needed to butcher them and prepare the meat for consumption. They solved this problem by the ingenious siting of base camps where they could conveniently assemble all the ingredients they needed to sustain a diet that included meat.[43]

For reasons having to do mostly with the scarcity and unpredictability of the food supply, until relatively recently human populations were sparsely distributed across the landscape.[44] The typical population unit would have numbered between twenty-five and fifty individuals, and the maximum number of such units that could have remained in contact with each other would have been about fifty. The average tribal population, then, would have ranged between two hundred and one thousand individuals, although these people would not have all occupied the same territory. Rather, they would have been widely dispersed across many hundreds of square kilometers. Average densities of foraging populations ranged from one person to perhaps several hundred persons per one hundred square kilometers.[45] The earliest inhabitants of subtropical savanna would have needed on average about two square kilometers to support each person.

These earliest peoples were constantly on the move in search of fresh landscape and food supplies.[46] These migrations took humans out of their African origins across Eurasia and eventually into Australia, the Pacific islands, and the Americas.[47] There were three principal routes of diffusion between Africa and Asia, each with its own ecology[48] To the north lay the path across the great Eurasian steppes, a zone broken by desert plains, mountain ranges, cold, and drought. Separated by the Himalayas from this northern route lay the second path, which led through tropical India into Southeast Asia. Here the ecology was warm, moist, and heavily forested. The third route followed the marine shoreline from East Africa to island Asia around the littoral of the Indian Ocean.

Humans were not the only migrants using these three routes. Mammals large and small, birds, insects, and microörganisms all moved back and forth along these routes, with some species moving west to east out of Africa, and others moving the opposite direction. In the northern steppes, humans encountered the cold-adapted grazing animals, including sheep and goats. Along the tropical mainland route, they encountered predators like the leopard, and small mammals that were their prey, like monkeys. Migrants around the Indian Ocean shoreline would have learned to incorporate marine animals like turtles and crustaceans into their diet. Thus, by the time human populations became established in mainland Asia, island Asia, and the Pacific, they would have passed through markedly divergent ecologies, and would have become part of markedly different coevolved life systems.

At first, human populations moved into and across land inhabited only by other species. With increasing frequency, however, they encountered other human populations as well. Thus, for more than one hundred thousand years, humans have been initiating and participating in what ecologists call "biological invasions" (when a species enters a region where it was absent before). As Rob Hengeveld points out, "Invasions are not exceptions, but the rule. They are not isolated and incidental phenomena disturbing the order of ecological communities; they exhibit the dynamics inherent to any species."[49]

Biogeographers describe the dynamic of biological invasions with the "advancing-wave" model, which portrays spatial diffusion of the intruding species (or set of species) as it moves across the landscape behind a line that marks the leading edge of the "wave." Behind this advancing edge, the population of the invading species grows logistically; that is, growth is slow at the beginning of the invasion, accelerates to exponential rates as the invasion matures, and slows down again as the resources supporting the invasion decline (at least on a *per capita* basis). The speed and direction of the advancing wave are shaped by a number of factors: the relative density of the invading and indigenous populations, the availability of vectors or other transport resources, the ability of the indigenous populations to resist the invasion, and changes in the gene pools of invading and indigenous systems. Neither the invaders nor the natives constitute single species, but rather systems of coevolved species. The relative ability of each system to mobilize, channel, use, dissipate, and preserve energy may well decide the outcome of the invasion.

Every continent has a biosphere that reflects its many invasions and subsequent alterations.[50] New arrivals to any region seldom represent simple additions to the ecosystems. Both invaders and natives face novel genetic challenges. No organism can be expected to have evolved genetic defenses against threats its ancestors never faced, so when confronted with new challenges, an organism could follow one of three paths: (1) its genes were sufficiently adaptable to protect the organisms adequately without changing; (2) by means of natural selection, minor modifications were introduced that enabled populations to survive by adapting; or (3) the population became extinct. The history of biological invasions shows that native organisms were not protected by their size (large animals were just as vulnerable as small) nor by their antiquity (life systems that had flourished for millennia were in some instances swept aside in a matter of a few centuries).

Scholars are gradually piecing together the story of humankind's earliest migrations with the constant discovery of fresh archeological evidence. In broadest outline, we now believe that *Homo sapiens* left East Africa between 100,000 and 200,000 years ago, reaching Europe between 35,000 and 40,000 years ago, Australia between 40,000 and 60,000 years ago (although much earlier dates are not impossible), and East Asia about 60,000 years ago (see figure 2.4)[51]. While many scholars believe that Asians first crossed the Bering land bridge into the Western Hemisphere about 15,000 to 35,000 years ago, new discoveries suggest other possibilities: that people with "Europeanlike" features entered the Americas long before Asians; that the initial passages were made long before 30,000 years ago; and that at least some of the migrants may have come by boat along the coast.[52]

As a result of these lengthy migrations, by about 10000 B.C. the world population had reached the planet's more or less natural (that is, without technology) carrying capacity of 4 to 6 million.[53] The consequence was the Neolithic Revolution and the creation of the world's first bulk-flow systems.[54] Humans could not have populated the world in any appreciable numbers beyond this natural limit without devising ways of increasing, regularizing, and carrying their food. Woven baskets and pottery appeared as containers in which harvested crops could be collected and transported, and canoes and sledges began to be used to move cargo across water or land. Domesticated animals were part of a bulk-flow system for the transport of food energy. Pastoral nomadism was simply a way of moving a population's food supply "on the hoof," so that their animals' meat, milk, and blood could be consumed by the herders as they moved.

From about 8000 B.C. on, human populations began to gather in villages and then cities. The advent of the first bulk-flow technologies made possible population densities that had previously been both inconceivable and unnecessary. From about 3000 B.C. on, the process of urbanization reached such a level that human

Figure 2.4   Probable Expansion Routes of Modern Humans, with Probable Arrival Dates

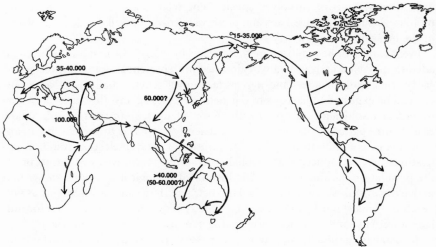

Source: Luigi Luca Cavalli-Sforza and Francesco Cavalli-Sforza, *The Great Human Diasporas: The History of Diversity and Evolution*, trans. by Sarah Thorne (Reading, Massachusetts: Addison-Wesley, 1995), Fig. 5.5, p. 122. © Arnoldo Mondadori Editore S.p.A. Reprinted by permission.

populations could be sustained only by the bulk-flow technologies that characterized the next phase of globalization: wheeled vehicles; irrigation systems to lift and transport large quantities of water to supply fields and carry human waste away from urban areas; horse collars and other harness technologies that made it possible for domesticated animals to pull plows and carts; slave labor to work the fields; and maritime technologies (sails, rudders, navigation, and the like) that made possible the Bronze Age civilizations of the eastern Mediterranean.

Until the Neolithic Revolution, the world's life systems had evolved in relative isolation from one another. Though archaic trade networks were extensive and complex, humans for the most part still lived in very low densities, and had limited contact with each other or animals. Plants, animals, and diseases had all evolved, as had human beings, separated by the biogeographical dividing lines that Alfred Crosby calls "the seams of Pangaea."[55] With the Neolithic Revolution, human beings intensified their contacts by carrying, accompanying, and being accompanied by, other life systems across these population, food, and disease gradients.

The next episode in globalization, from 100 B.C. to 1400 A.D. was marked by what William McNeill calls the "closure of the Eurasian ecumene."[56] The camel caravans of the Silk Road and Indian Ocean trade routes operated by Arab traders brought into contact for the first time the great civilizations on the fringes of the Eurasian steppes: Rome, the eastern Mediterranean, East Africa, the Near East, India, southeast Asia, China, and Japan. These changes wrought the beginning of the first "proto-global" life systems. As human populations began to move over greater distances, food and diseases also began to flow as well.

Many people date the beginning of truly global life systems from that fateful morning in 1492 when Europeans and Amerindians first laid eyes on one another. The transfer of humans, plants, animals, and diseases back and forth between the Americas and the Old World, known as the "Columbian Exchange," altered the global distribution of living organisms to a degree that had no precedent as far back as the end of the last Ice Age.[57] Europeans brought to the Americas Old World crops (wheat, rice, sugar, coffee), animals (cattle, horses, pigs, sheep), and diseases (smallpox, measles). For more than three hundred years, Europeans themselves came in small numbers, but they imported large populations of African slaves. The Africans were needed in the Americas, particularly in the tropics, because European diseases had virtually decimated the indigenous population;[58] and the cultivation of crops for sale in Europe needed huge amounts of slave labor. Begun by the Portuguese in 1531,[59] the slave trade became the first example in history of the large-scale movement of human beings over long distances.[60] By the close of the trade in the 1870s, more than 10 million Africans had been forcibly moved to the Americas; a century later, their descendants were nearly five times that number.

The Americas' most significant biological gift to the rest of the world was its two key food staples, maize and potatoes, foods that enabled the European population to leap forward in the nineteenth century at just the time when the Industrial Revolution had engendered a need for more labor.[61] The population pressures in Europe stimulated the second great demographic wave, the massive emigration of Europeans to the Americas and Australia between the 1840s and World War I.[62] In all, some 50 million Europeans came to the Americas during this period, mostly from Britain, Ireland, and Italy. This flood of immigration was greatly facilitated by fossil fuel energy in general, and by the steam engine in particular. The steamship and the railroad changed forever the distribution of the world's human population by facilitating the movement of people in greater numbers and at greater speeds than had previously been conceivable.[63]

Since 1960, the global movement of people has continued to grow in every dimension: numbers moved, their speed, and distances covered. The spread of manufacturing to virtually every corner of the world, the availability of large-scale air travel, and the global diffusion of information technology and the communications media have produced a truly global economy and culture. Most of the products we consume have been assembled by a global work force at sites around the world from component parts that have themselves come from other distant locations.[64] Virtually every piece of the manufacturing system—capital, labor, energy, technology, component parts, finished products, waste materials—now flows relatively freely around the world, unobstructed by technology, tariff barriers, cultural differences, transport costs, or markets. A global culture is taking shape as well.[65] The agent of this transformation is the "culture industry," a group of commercial enterprises dedicated to the creation, distribution, and sale of cultural objects, whose principal sectors include media (entertainment, film, recorded music, news), fashion, sports, celebrities, knowledge, and the arts.

Manufactured goods and information are not the only things being moved in bulk, however. Tourists, business travelers, refugees, and immigrants are on the move in numbers, over distances, and at speeds that are unprecedented. Each day, some 2 million people cross an international border. Annual international tourist arrivals now equal about 10 percent of the total world population; and global refugees fleeing from war, environmental crises, or economic collapse are at an all-time high of about 48 million. The United States alone receives nearly 1 million new immigrants each year (not counting those who enter without documentation), and the flow shows no signs of abating.

We do not yet understand or appreciate the long-term consequences of so many people traveling so far from their place of birth and staying on to form new homes and new biological attachments, but they surely will not be trivial. Without fully realizing it, we have reached the stage of total global "hominization" as described by Pierre Teilhard de Chardin some four decades ago when he wrote of our great biological adventure:

> Several hundred thousand years had been spent on the mere *preparation*, mainly in Africa, of a human planetary invasion. Some thirty thousand years more had been required for the actual *occupation* of the extra-African lands. Approximately ten thousand years . . . were necessary before a preliminary *consolidation* of the human envelope had been realized all around the earth. But today, after so many eons of hominization, the great accomplishment pursued by life since its first emergence on earth two or three billion years ago is over; namely, the achievement of an unbroken, co-conscious organism, coextensive with the entire area of the globe. Definitely cemented on itself in the course of the last century by the powerful forces of industry and science, the newborn noösphere is now spread right before our eyes and is caught already in the first grip of an irresistible *totalization*.[66]

NOTES

1. Carl Sauer, "The Agency of Man on the Earth," in *Man's Role in Changing the Face of the Earth,* ed. William Thomas (Chicago: University of Chicago Press, 1956), p. 50.

2. Suggested by an article by Alan Cutler, "How Old Is Earth, and How Do We Really Know?" *Washington Post,* March 12, 1997.

3. Colin Tudge, *The Time before History: 5 Million Years of Human Impact* (New York: Simon & Schuster, 1996), p. 119.

4. Tudge, *Time before History,* pp. 120–30.

5. Robert Wesson, *Beyond Natural Selection* (Cambridge, Mass.: MIT Press, 1991, 1997), chapter 8.

6. Tudge, *Time before History,* pp. 166–70.

7. Of the abundant literature on human origins, the following general works are particularly useful: Richard Leakey, *The Origin of Humankind* (New York: Basic, 1994); Roger Lewin, *The Origin of Modern Humans* (New York: Scientific American Library, 1993); Donald Johanson, Lenora Johanson, and Blake Edgar, *Ancestors: In Search of Human Origins* (New York: Villard, 1994).

8. The following are a sample of press accounts of recent discoveries that have called into question existing paradigms about human origins. John Noble Wilford, "2.3-Million-Year-Old Jaw Extends Human Family," *New York Times*, November 19, 1996; John Noble Wilford, "3 Human Species Coexisted on Earth, New Data Suggest," *New York Times*, December 13, 1996; Curt Suplee, "Fossils May Be Older Ancestor Common to Humans, Apes," *Washington Post*, April 18, 1997; John Noble Wilford, "Fossils Called Limb in Human Family Tree," *New York Times*, May 30, 1997.

9. Jonathan Kingdon, *Self-Made Man: Human Evolution from Eden to Extinction?* (New York: Wiley, 1993), chapter 1.

10. Yves Coppens, "East Side Story: The Origin of Humankind," *Scientific American* 270 (5) (May 1994): pp. 88–95. For a different scenario, see James Shreve, "Sunset on the Savanna," *Discover* (July 1996): pp. 116–25.

11. Lewin, *Origin of Modern Humans*, pp. 21–22.

12. Nicholas Wade, "Neanderthal DNA Sheds New Light on Human Origins," *New York Times*, July 11, 1997.

13. Nicholas Wade, "To People the World, Start with 500," *New York Times*, November 11, 1997.

14. "Ideas on Human Origins Evolve at Anthropology Gathering," *Science*, vol. 276 (April 25, 1997): 535–36.

15. Clive Ponting, *A Green History of the World: The Environment and the Collapse of Great Civilizations* (New York: St. Martin's, 1991), pp. 10–11; Kingdon, *Self-Made Man*, chapter 2.

16. Kingdon, *Self-Made Man*, p. 70.

17. Rick Potts, *Humanity's Descent: The Consequences of Ecological Instability* (New York: Morrow, 1996), esp. chapter 4.

18. Potts, *Humanity's Descent*, p. 89.

19. Tudge, *Time before History*, pp. 304–07.

20. R. E. Passingham, "The Origins of Human Intelligence," in *Human Origins*, ed. John Durant (Oxford: Clarendon Press, 1989), chapter 8.

21. Vaclav Smil, *Energy in World History* (Boulder, Colo.: Westview, 1994), p. 15.

22. Massimo Livi-Bacci, *A Concise History of World Population*, trans. Carl Ipsen (Cambridge, Mass.: Blackwell, 1989), pp. 2–4, fig. 1.1.

23. Jeffrey Wicken, *Evolution, Thermodynamics, and Information: Extending the Darwinian Program* (New York: Oxford University Press, 1987), chapter 13.

24. Michael Kremer, "Population Growth and Technological Change: One Million B.C. to 1900," *Quarterly Journal of Economics* 108 (3) (August 1993): table 1, p. 683.

25. Edward Deevey, "The Human Population," *Scientific American* (September 1960): p. 201.

26. Kingdon, *Self-Made Man*, p. 311.

27. Roy Anderson and Robert May, *Infectious Diseases of Humans: Dynamics and Control* (Oxford: Oxford University Press, 1991), pp. 653–54.

28. Livi-Bacci, *Concise History*, esp. fig. 2.1, p. 43.

29. Boyce Rensberger, "In Death, Ancient Peoples Offer Evidence that 'Progress' Often Shortened Life," *Washington Post,* May 13, 1998.

30. Peter Bogucki, *Forest Farmers and Stockherders: Early Agriculture and Its Consequences in North-Central Europe* (Cambridge: Cambridge University Press, 1988), pp. 97–100.

31. Charles Westoff, "Marriage and Fertility in the Developed Countries," *Scientific American* 239 (6) (December 1978): pp. 51–57.

32. Livi-Bacci, *Concise History,* chapters 4, 5.

33. John Caldwell and Pat Caldwell, "High Fertility in Sub-Saharan African," *Scientific American* (May 1990): 118–25.

34. Barbara Crossette, "World Is Less Crowded than Expected, the U.N. Reports," *New York Times,* November 17, 1996.

35. Clive Gamble, *Timewalkers: The Prehistory of Global Colonization* (Cambridge, Mass.: Harvard University Press, 1994), chapter 6; Michael Little and Paul Baker, "Migration and Adaptation," in *Biological Aspects of Human Migration,* ed. C. G. N. Mascie-Taylor and G. W. Lasker (Cambridge: Cambridge University Press, 1988), p. 167.

36. Niles Eldredge, *Reinventing Darwin: The Great Debate at the High Table of Evolutionary Theory* (New York: Wiley, 1995), pp. 64–65.

37. Potts, *Humanity's Descent,* pp. 211–13.

38. Tudge, *Time before History,* pp. 209–13.

39. Steven Vogel, *Vital Circuits: On Pumps, Pipes, and the Workings of Circulatory Systems* (New York: Oxford University Press, 1992); Robert Clark, "Bulk Flow Systems and Globalization," 1996 meeting on the Political Economy of the World System (PEWS), Kansas State University, Manhattan, Kansas, reprinted in Paul Ciccantell and Stephen Bunker, eds., *Space and Transport in the World-System* (Westport, Conn.: Greenwood, 1997), chapter 10.

40. Robert Clark, *The Global Imperative: An Interpretive History of the Spread of Humankind* (Boulder, Colo.: Westview, 1997).

41. Kingdon, *Self-Made Man,* chapter 1.

42. Leakey, *Origin of Humankind,* pp. 54–55.

43. Richard Potts, *Early Hominid Activities at Olduvai* (New York: Aldine de Gruyter, 1988).

44. Kingdon, *Self-Made Man,* p. 286; Livi-Bacci, *Concise History,* table 1.1, p. 27; Gamble, *Timewalkers,* pp. 108–10; Lewin, *Origin of Modern Humans,* p. 150.

45. Smil, *Energy in World History,* p. 17.

46. Gamble, *Timewalkers,* passim.

47. W. S. Laughlin and A. B. Harper, "Peopling of the Continents: Australia and America," in *Biological Aspects,* ed. Mascie-Taylor and Lasker, chapter 2; Kingdon, *Self-Made Man,* pp. 285–86.

48. Kingdon, *Self-Made Man,* pp. 77–82.

49. Rob Hengeveld, *Dynamics of Biological Invasions* (London: Chapman and Hall, 1989), p. 115.

50. Kingdon, *Self-Made Man,* pp. 82–84.

51. Lewin, *Origin of Modern Humans,* chapter 3; Luigi Luca Cavalli-Sforza and Francesco Cavalli-Sforza, *The Great Human Diasporas: The History of Diversity and Evolution* (Reading, Mass.: Addison Wesley, 1995), chapter 5; Ian Tattersall, "Out of Africa Again . . . and Again?" *Scientific American* 276 (4) (April 1997): 60–67.

52. John Noble Wilford, "Clue to Earliest Americans in 11,700-Year-Old Campsite," *New York Times,* March 25, 1993; Kathy Sawyer, "Asian Fossils Suggest Early Migration,"

Washington Post, November 16, 1995; Karen Freeman, "More Recent Migration of Humans from Africa Is Seen in DNA Study," *New York Times*, June 4, 1996; John Noble Wilford, "In Australia, Signs of Artists Who Predate Homo Sapiens," *New York Times*, September 21, 1996; Karen Freeman, "9,700-Year-Old Bones Back Theory of a Coastal Migration," *New York Times*, October 6, 1996; Thomas Dillehay, "The Battle of Monte Verde," *The Sciences* (January/February 1997): 28–33; Curt Suplee, "Find May Rewrite Americas' Prehistory," *Washington Post*, February 11, 1997; Curt Suplee, "Artifacts May Push Back Human Residency in Siberia by 300,000 Years," *Washington Post*, February 28, 1997; Boyce Rensberger, "Putting a New Face on Prehistory," *Washington Post*, April 15, 1997; Scott Elias, "Bridge to the Past," *Earth* (April 1997): 50–55.

53. Livi-Bacci, *Concise History*, pp. 37–44; Ponting, *Green History of the World*, chapter 4.

54. V. Gordon Childe, *Man Makes Himself* (New York: New American Library, 1951), chapter 5.

55. Alfred Crosby, *Ecological Imperialism: The Biological Expansion of Europe, 900–1900* (New York: Cambridge University Press, 1986, 1993).

56. William McNeill, *The Rise of the West: A History of the Human Community* (Chicago: University of Chicago Press, 1963, 1991), chapter 7.

57. Alfred Crosby, *The Columbian Exchange: Biological and Cultural Consequences of 1492* (Westport, Conn.: Greenwood, 1972).

58. W. George Lovell, "'Heavy Shadows and Black Night': Disease and Depopulation in Colonial Spanish America," in Karl Butzer, ed., *The Americas before and after 1492: Current Geographical Research*, Annals of the Association of American Geographers 82, no. 3 (September 1992): 426–43; William Cronon, *Changes in the Land: Indians, Colonists, and the Ecology of New England* (New York: Hill & Wang, 1983), chapter 5; Timothy Silver, *A New Face on the Countryside: Indians, Colonists, and Slaves in South Atlantic Forests, 1500–1800* (Cambridge: Cambridge University Press, 1990), pp. 74–83. While scholars agree that European diseases were devastating to the native population, there is debate over the timing and exact mechanisms by which smallpox or the plague reached the Western Hemisphere; see Heather Pringle, "The Plague that Never Happened," *New Scientist* (July 20, 1996): 32–35.

59. D. W. Meinig, *The Shaping of America: A Geographical Perspective on 500 Years of History*, Volume 1: *Atlantic America, 1492–1800* (New Haven: Yale University Press, 1986), p. 23.

60. Philip Curtin, "Africa and Global Patterns of Migration," in *Global History and Migrations*, ed. Wang Gungwu (Boulder, Colo.: Westview, 1997), chapter 3.

61. Alfred Crosby, "The Demographic Effect of American Crops in Europe," in *Germs, Seeds and Animals: Studies in Ecological History* (Armonk, N.Y.: Sharpe, 1994), pp. 148–66.

62. Livi-Bacci, *Concise History*, pp. 123–29; Ewa Morawska and Willfried Spohn, "Moving Europeans in the Globalizing World: Contemporary Migrations in a Historical-Comparative Perspective (1955–1994 vs. 1870–1914)," in Wang, *Global History*, chapter 2.

63. Aristide Zolberg, "Global Movements, Global Walls: Responses to Migration, 1885–1925," in *Global History*, ed. Wang, pp. 282–83.

64. Nigel Harris, *The End of the Third World: Newly Industrializing Countries and the Decline of an Ideology* (New York: Penguin, 1986); Robert Ross and Kent Trachte, *Global Capitalism: The New Leviathan* (Albany: State University of New York Press, 1990); William Greider, *One World, Ready or Not: The Manic Logic of Global Capitalism* (New York: Simon & Schuster, 1997).

65. Herbert Schiller, *Culture, Inc.: The Corporate Takeover of Public Expression* (New York: Oxford University Press, 1989); Richard Barnet and John Cavanagh, *Global Dreams: Imperial Corporations and the New World Order* (New York: Simon & Schuster, 1994), part 1. The fact that a global culture seems to be emerging does not mean the extinction of numerous distinctive cultural identities around the world. In fact, the opposite seems to be happening; see Benjamin Barber, *Jihad vs. McWorld* (New York: Random House, 1995).

66. Pierre Teilhard de Chardin, "The Antiquity and World Expansion of Human Culture," in *Man's Role*, ed. Thomas, p. 106. Emphasis in the original.

Chapter Three

Food

To become a global species, humans needed much help from other living organisms, which also had to become global to provide the food energy and mobility we needed to complete our journey. Why this link between humans and their food supply should be so critical to globalization is rooted in the nature of human anatomy. As a result of our large body size, large mammal reproductive strategy, the need to maintain a constant body temperature, physical mobility, and brain size and complexity, *Homo sapiens* is an energy-intensive organism. Yet our gut physiology severely limits what we can digest, making us restricted omnivores (i.e., we can eat a very limited number of samples of almost everything). This condition, plus energy losses across the food chain, meant that nature could not provide a large, densely concentrated population of humans with the energy they needed; so humans evolved for more than one hundred thousand years in small groups widely scattered across the landscape and more or less constantly on the move. To survive, our ancient ancestors evolved food acquisition systems based on foraging, scavenging, hunting, and gathering.

After 100 or so millennia of living this way, humans reached the natural carrying capacity of the Earth (four to six million), or about one person per two square kilometers. To grow beyond that density, it was necessary to devise ways to squeeze more food energy out of a given unit of land. The result was the Neolithic Revolution. Since that time, the human population and the plants and animals on which we depend for food have all become global more or less together.

The selection of foods for domestication was greatly complicated by a number of factors. Human anatomy was of central importance, since it dictated how much energy we needed and how many different kinds of plants and animals we could digest to acquire it; and the energy loss in the food chain was also critical, since it set ultimate limits on how much of the sun's energy we could eventually tap. Another factor was the resistance of most species to domestication—of all

55

the thousands of plants and hundreds of animals that are edible, we have been able to domesticate only a very small number. Equally important was the fact that no single food type was found everywhere. There were no global food sources at all until after the sixteenth century, so all human diets until very recently had to be fashioned from what was available more or less locally.

Finally, we must take into account the complex web of causes (culture, biology, etc.) that yields food preferences and aversions.[1] After all, the choice of plants and animals to eat or to avoid carried with it many implications that went far beyond the simple matter of energy:

> The way that animals live, how they spend their days, and the extent to which they socialize, is largely determined by what they eat. Committed herbivores need to eat more or less all day (or all night) if they are to find enough, while big predators eat only occasionally. . . . Some creatures need to be sociable in order to feed efficiently. . . . Other animals . . . need to be more or less solitary if they are to find enough to eat. Clearly, too, diet determines ecological impact: predators stand higher on the food chain than herbivores do, but in general are less numerous than herbivores.[2]

ENERGY AND FOOD

The food energy web within which we live appears to us so natural that we take it for granted, unaware that there was a time when Earth's biosphere did not process and channel solar energy the way it does today.[3] Before the Permian period, which began some 290 million years ago, there were no creatures capable of eating and digesting living photosynthesizing plants—no herbivores, in other words. The sun's energy was received by plants, which converted a portion of it to their own tissue, where it resided until their death and decay. Terrestrial animals were either insects, which ate the detritus of decayed plant matter on the forest floor and each other, or vertebrates, which ate the insects and each other. The plant life of the Earth, with no natural enemies to graze or browse upon it, flourished and spread profusely.

By some 255 million years ago, a number of four-legged herbivores, mostly reptiles, had come into existence, and had radiated widely across the landscape. These creatures of the Permian changed fundamentally the relationship between plants and animals and the way the biosphere channels the sun's energy. The lives of large animals now became inextricably connected to that of the plants around them. Plants evolved defenses to keep most herbivores at a distance; but about 125 million years ago, seed plants made their appearance, so some animals were permitted (and even encouraged) to come closer to aid in the dispersal of the plant's seeds. Thus, herbivores became the essential link between the sun's energy and photosynthesizing plants on the one side, and carnivores on the other. Species came and went; the continents broke apart and drifted away from each other; and the planet cooled and warmed many times. But the basic pattern of energy processing through the biosphere remained much the same as it was 250 million years ago.

All living organisms confront an imperative: to capture energy from the environment and convert that energy into self-maintenance and the production of progeny.[4] All of an organism's metabolic processes evolve to serve these needs. How well the organism achieves these goals defines its survival-reproductive efficiency. In general, the organisms's energy can be expended in three ways: behavior (energy procurement, predator avoidance, reproduction); metabolism (growth, biosynthesis, homeostasis, physiological operation); and waste (the unused portion of ingested energy).

Living organisms face a zero-sum game. Since the three uses of energy are interdependent, spending more on one function forces reductions and economies in the others. Energy exists in the environment in different packages, each with its own set of metabolic requirements. Each species adapts to this setting by evolving a metabolic strategy that uses some forms of energy and avoids or rejects others. If an organism evolves a metabolic strategy that diminishes the energy it spends on biosynthesis, then it must establish relationships with other organisms that will do the biosynthesizing for it. There are obvious behavioral implications from such choices, as Jeffrey Wicken explains: "Nature does not provide its fruits *gratis*. For the jettisoning of metabolic machinery to be adaptively successful, it must be compensated by appropriate behavioral modifications that provide for the exploitation of the metabolic labors of other organisms."[5]

How a species adapts to these exigencies determines the niche it occupies in a given ecosystem and how it interacts with other organisms in that system.[6] Because energy is stored and made available in our environment in many different forms, evolution has produced a great diversity of organisms to tap those diverse energy sources. Not all evolution leads to greater and greater thermodynamic efficiency. Reptiles, for example, produce less entropy (less energy dissipated as heat) than do the mammals that evolved from them. Yet homeothermy ("warm-bloodedness") emerged as a metabolic strategy to endow certain species of animals with the mobility and vigor that come from internal temperature regulation. Those attributes, in turn, enabled homeothermic animals to reach into energy niches that had previously been inaccessible and unexploited. Likewise, coevolution (of the mutualistic variety) becomes a reasonable strategy when a given species can get other organisms to do their metabolic work for them, and can expend less energy on maintaining the mutualism than they would otherwise have spent on energy collection and biosynthesis.

Mobility, or behavioral range, is one of the key variables in these metabolic strategies. Plants possess very little mobility, but they do not need much since they absorb nutrients from their chemical surroundings via systems of roots, leaves, and supports. Animals, particularly predators, have sacrificed this kind of metabolic autonomy in the interest of behavioral range. Mammals in particular have lost through evolution the ability to synthesize in their own bodies a wide range of amino acids, which they must now ingest by eating other organisms that have done this synthesizing for them (or by taking manufactured vitamins, as many humans do). But the exchanges forced on living organisms by evolution are unforgiving. Every gain in locomotion or a large and complex brain must be paid for by increased efficiencies in resource capture.

The metabolic rate of homeothermic animals is directly related to their size.[7] The amount of heat generated by an animal is related to that animal's mass or volume, but the amount of heat dissipated to the environment is related to its surface area. Small animals have a high ratio of surface area to mass, so they dissipate heat relatively quickly; large animals have a low ratio of surface to mass, so they radiate heat slowly. It follows that small animals must metabolize food more quickly than large animals to maintain body temperature above that of the surroundings. The metabolic rate of a mouse, for example, is a thousand times greater than that of an elephant.

Because of their high metabolic rate, small homeotherms such as rodents must base their diet on high energy foods such as insects or worms. But large homeotherms such as elephants can afford to eat foods with less energy per unit of volume, such as the green leaf. This ability has worked to the great advantage of large animals, since green leaves are by far the most abundant food on land. An abundance of green foliage has produced large homeothermic herbivores, which have in turn produced large colonies of predators, including *Homo sapiens*.

The problem with depending on green leaves for food is that the energy is in the form of fiber, made up largely of cellulose, and no large animal is able to produce the enzymes that digest cellulose. The panda, for example, has no way to digest cellulose and subsists on bamboo leaves by living mostly on the sugar they contain and by expending very little energy in a lethargic lifestyle. All other large herbivores tap the food energy in green plants with the help of bacteria and other microbes that live in their gut and do the digesting for them. Elephants, rhinos, and horses have these bacteria near the end of their gut, in the colon or below, so they are known as hindgut digesters. Kangaroos, camels, and ruminants such as cattle, sheep, and goats do their digesting high up in the gut, so they are known as foregut digesters. Foregut digestion tends to be more thermodynamically efficient than hindgut, since the food is acted upon virtually the entire length of the digestive system. For very large animals, these advantages diminish, so the hindgut herbivores tend to be the largest land animals. These are also the least desirable food for carnivores, however, because their flesh contains less accessible energy. Midsize herbivores such as cattle and sheep are foregut digesters, highly desired as food for carnivores because of the relatively higher proportion of energy in their flesh.

In addition, there is a difference in the digestibility of leaves that grow on trees and shrubs, on the one hand, and grass, on the other. Animals that eat the former are browsers; those that eat the latter are grazers. Browse is easier to digest and usually relatively energy rich, but grass is much more abundant and easier to obtain. Browsing animals that have evolved to eat from trees and shrubs, like the giraffe, are highly selective in their diet, but grazers like cattle and sheep eat virtually everything green in their reach. As climatic changes shifted the balance of the photosynthesizing part of the biosphere from trees to grassland, the balance of animals shifted as well from browsers to grazers. This is an additional reason why climatic changes worked to the advantage of our earliest ancestors, the australopithecines, as they made the transition from living in trees to walking on the ground. It also helps explain why we would find cattle and sheep so much more helpful to us thermodynamically than giraffes. Moreover, since grazers operate in the much more open and expansive grasslands, they tend to be the more social (or herd) animals, like cattle and sheep, compared to the browsers like roe deer, which are more solitary feeders. When humans turned to herding and animal husbandry, they would find this herding attribute of special importance in determining which animals they would domesticate successfully, and which they would continue to hunt as wild game.

Our choice of which part of the biosphere to eat and which to leave alone was not unlimited. On the contrary, we were restricted by a wide range of factors, not the least of which was the size and shape of our digestive system.[8] As *Homo erectus* evolved with a relatively large and complex brain, there were implications for other organs of the body. The metabolism needed to grow and operate a larger brain had to be taken from some other part of the body. Other organs that are high energy consumers, such as the heart or liver, are too vital to be robbed, but the intestines are not as important, so it was here that economies were achieved. Thus, unlike the gut of pure herbivores, which tends to be long and large, that of humans is small and metabolically cheap to maintain, like most carnivores. Adding meat to the diet may thus have had several important consequences: in addition to giving our ancestors many more food sources from which to choose and providing an increased density of food resources, carnivory may have altered our gut size and structure and thus freed up some metabolized energy to divert to brain growth and functioning.

As restricted omnivores, modern humans can eat virtually every class of plant or animal, but only a few members of each class. For example, of the 250,000 plant species known to humankind, only about 30,000 are edible, only 120 are cultivated for food today, and only three—wheat, rice, and maize—account for more than half of human food intake from plants.[9] But the balance between animal and plant sources for human food supply has varied greatly across the millennia.

The expansion of the human diet was tied closely to humans' global migration.[10] As our ancient ancestors moved into new ranges and new habitats, they encountered new flora and fauna and new climates. They responded by changing their diets and themselves physically, laying the foundation for many food-related cultural preferences that are still with us today.

Wherever they found themselves, humans' choices of food would have been shaped by four forces: their own nutritional needs and physiological limitations; the range of plants and animals available in any given range at any given time;

the defenses erected by the plants and animals, and other constraints imposed by the local ecology (e.g., diseases, predators, direct competition from other animals); and the technologies available to humans. But the dynamics of coevolution meant that the choice of food was not without its consequences as well. For example, in many spots human migrants subsisted by following migrating herds of herbivores, but these large and hungry animals in turn often laid waste to the landscape by their widespread grazing or browsing. Indeed, the pathways chosen by early migrants usually followed the open spaces beaten through the forest or jungle or across the grasslands by migrating herds of large herbivores. There is also much evidence that human hunters overhunted the array of large mammals, driving many of those species to extinction during the Pleistocene and altering the ecology of every continent in fundamental ways. By removing the large herbivores like mammoths and horses from North America, humans altered an ecological balance that had evolved over many hundreds of millennia.

Meat has constituted a significant part of our diet for several million years. Australopithecines 3.5 million years ago derived probably 10 percent of their dietary requirements from meat; and our immediate predecessors, *Homo erectus*, probably 20 percent.[11] While this may seem low to us, meat was certainly more than a marginal part of Lucy's diet.

Nutrition experts disagree about whether meat is essential to the human diet. Some argue that combinations of cereal grains and legumes provide all the amino acids we need;[12] and there are historical instances of large populations living healthy lives with little or no meat in their diet. The Aztecs apparently lived well on a diet composed largely of maize, beans, and squash;[13] and the dependence of the Irish on a diet of potatoes and milk in the nineteenth century is well known.

There are those who believe, however, that meat protein is of higher quality than plant protein because it contains all the essential amino acids in the ratios humans need, as well as minerals difficult to obtain from plant food. In a changing environment, animals and plants tend to be easier to take, or are more accessible, at different times; so an omnivore has a diet that is adequate regardless of the changing circumstances. Finally, meat eating tends to be a more social kind of feeding than herbivory, so the inclusion of even a small amount of meat in the diet encouraged cooperation and social life. Thus, by incorporating a small amount of meat into their diet, even the earliest bipeds extended their range significantly.

But humans are carnivorous in a way that no other meat-eating species can match.[14] Ecologists believe that the population, size, and range of a species are related to its diet. The larger the animal, and the more there are of them, the more territory they need to survive. Territorial requirements are much greater for carnivores than for herbivores because of the loss of energy across the food chain.

The surface of the Earth is bathed constantly by a flood of solar energy. Different regions of the Earth receive varying quantities of this energy, but we know that a typical field of corn in Illinois receives in one summer day more than two million calories per acre, or about five hundred calories per square meter.[15] Given our own energy requirements, usually between 2,000 and 2,700 calories per day,[16] this ought to provide a supply sufficient to support a human population much larger than what the Earth now supports.

The problem is that we can capture only a very tiny portion of that energy to metabolize for our uses (see table 3.1). Photosynthesizing plants capture the solar energy (convert energy into plant tissue)[17] striking a given area with an aver-

Table 3.1   The Energy Cascade: Energy Flow from Sunlight to Humans

	total	as percent of initial
sunlight reaching the top of Earth's atmosphere	340	100
reflected by water, snow, atmosphere	−100	
	240	70
reflected by clouds, dust, gases	−70	
	170	50
infrared photons, too weak to stimulate photosynthesis (57 percent of received)	−96	
	74	21
light waves not tuned to frequency of plant's chlorophyll molecules (20 percent)	−14	
	60	17
energy lost due to inefficiency when photons incorporate one carbon atom into a molecule of sugar (approx. 70 percent)	−42	
	18	5
energy lost due to inefficiency of certain photosynthesizers (e.g., wheat, rice) in incorporating carbon into organic molecules (approx. 20 percent)	−4	
	14	4
plant's expenditures on its own metabolism and structures (50 percent)	−7	
	7	2
inefficiency due to water stress (50 percent), seasonal dormancy (20 percent), maximum absorption of real vegetation (15 percent), nutrient limitations (70 percent)	−6.3	
	0.7	0.2
reductions for land without vegetation	−0.4	
	0.3	0.1

Notes: "Total" refers to the rate of energy flow averaged over a year and over the entire planet, measured in watts per square meter. After the energy has been converted into plant tissue, herbivores eating plants capture only about 10 percent of the plants' energy, and more than 90 percent of that is used for the herbivores' own metabolism. Carnivores, in turn, capture only about 10 percent of the energy stored in herbivore tissue. Thus, the total loss across these levels of the food chain is an additional 99.9 percent.

Source: Tyler Volk, *Gaia's Body: Toward a Physiology of Earth* (New York: Springer-Verlag, 1998), Chapter 6.

age efficiency of between 0.1 and 0.5 percent.[18] Although we view the tropics as "sun-drenched" and "covered with lush vegetation" the reality is that the humid tropics cannot compete with the temperature zones in food production. Dense cloud cover in the monsoonal regions reduces insolation to such a degree that most of the Brazilian Amazon, for example, receives less sun light than Kansas, and Indonesia resembles northern France and southern England in solar energy received. In addition, the tropics experience elevated night temperatures, which promote moisture losses through high respiration rates, low fertility soils, and conditions that favor the spread of pests and parasites.[19] Moreover, in many forest ecosystems, either tropical or temperate, much of the energy is locked up in tree trunks, branches, and root systems that are not digestible by humans.[20] Even richly productive crops grown in the richest farmland in the world and given constant care and attention still can attain only 1.5 to 2.0 percent efficiency.[21]

These limits are imposed by certain immutable biochemical properties of photosynthesis.[22] First, only about half the light that shines on a plant has an effect on the plant's chemistry. The other half comes in the red end of the spectrum, and radiations of infrared light are not sufficiently strong to stimulate photosynthesis. Second, plants convert energy at an optimum rate (that can get as high as 8 percent) only when the intensity of the light is intermediate between dim and bright. At very dim levels, plants are highly efficient but not very productive because of the low light levels. With very bright light, both efficiency and productivity fall off. The best productivity comes with moderate light.

Another important constraint on plant productivity is the subject of much current controversy: the concentration of carbon dioxide (CO_2) in the atmosphere. CO_2 is critical to the photosynthesis process because it activates an enzyme that catalyzes the first step in the process. CO_2 is present in the atmosphere at an average concentration of only 0.03 percent by volume (310 to 360 ppm). Most plants evolved at a time when CO_2 concentration was somewhat higher; so at this level (350 ppm), the enzyme works at only about three-quarters of its capacity. Even if we could somehow solve the light problems cited above, the atmosphere could still not provide plants with the increased carbon dioxide they need to use this light more efficiently.

It is true that the concentration of CO_2 is rising, principally as a consequence of the combustion of fossil fuels since the Industrial Revolution began (although the exact causes remain disputed). At the current rate of increase, CO_2 concentrations will double to 700 ppm by the year 2050.[23] Some scientists believe that the increase in CO_2 levels will enhance the productivity of wheat, rice, beans, and potatoes, although other plants such as corn and sugar cane will not benefit.[24] The productivity of plants in greenhouses, for example, is enhanced by nearly doubling the level of CO_2 to about 600 ppm. If farmers could adjust to rising gas levels quickly enough, and if plant strains could be bioengineered to withstand increased temperatures, and if water scarcities could also be resolved, then perhaps the much discussed global warming trend could actually benefit agricultural production.

However, there are simply too many unknowns, and too many forces working in opposite directions, to be able to predict such an outcome with confidence.[25]

Moreover, not all of a plant's energy is given over to the production of green leaves. All plants have evolved defenses and dispersal techniques that involve interaction with animals; and these (such as shells around nuts) require a considerable portion of the plant's energy.[26] Herbivores eating the plants capture about 10 percent of the plants' energy, and the great bulk of that goes for the metabolic functions of the herbivore itself. A cow can store only 0.6 percent of the energy it consumes from the grass in a pasture. The carnivores eating the herbivores capture about 10 percent of the energy stored in the herbivores' bodies. By the time the energy has made its way through the food web to the top carnivores, frequently *Homo sapiens*, more than 99 percent has been diverted to other uses.

This loss of energy across the food chain helps explain why *in nature* the higher an organism is in the food chain, the more rare it is. According to Donald and Lenora Johanson,

> In an average African game park . . . only 1 to 2 percent of the animals eat meat. The reason for this lies in the nature of the food pyramid. The occupants of each layer in the food pyramid obtain only about 10 to 20 percent of the total energy of the occupants of the next lower level. By the time we get to the carnivores, who are perched precariously at the very top, the amount of packaged energy available is much smaller than that available to the herbivores they consume. Their numbers must of necessity be lower, to reflect their more limited feeding opportunities.[27]

From the days of *Homo erectus*, hominids have been able to avoid the full impact of this general rule, though not without paying a very high price over the long term. Before the Neolithic Revolution, humans prospered by being more efficient hunters, with greater stamina than most prey, social organization, and the ability to hurl weapons with accuracy. After the transition to farming, it was our partnership with other living organisms—our coevolved life systems—that augmented so dramatically our ability to increase our population and to enter new niches.

COEVOLVED FOOD SYSTEMS

Chapter 1 stressed the importance of mutualism in building the coevolved life systems so crucial to globalization. The emergence of mutualistic relationships involving humans, plants, and animals, as well as human populations cooperating with each other, can be traced in many instances back to several fundamental aspects of human nutrition.[28] Humans have sacrificed nutritional autonomy for other advantages, including mobility and culture. Consequently, we have come to rely on other organisms to provide us with a very diverse array of substances that we need to survive. These include fats, proteins, carbohydrates, vitamins (water soluble and fat soluble), and mineral nutrients.

Proteins provide our bodies with amino acids that we need to build, repair, or replace body tissues, while carbohydrates and fats provide energy. Our basic energy requirements necessary for essential metabolism are a large proportion of our total energy budget—about 1,600 calories, or about 60 percent of a daily requirement of 2,700.[29] These needs must be met before repair and maintenance needs can be attended to. If carbohydrates and fats are insufficient to meet energy requirements, then our body will tap protein supplies to meet current energy needs.

Food itself has a thermogenic effect, meaning that digestion causes the basic metabolic rate to increase. (Metabolism refers to the physical and chemical processes by which our body builds up protoplasm from ingested food, and then breaks down that protoplasm into simpler substances and waste matter, with a consequent release of energy to carry out the body's vital functions.) Proteins raise the metabolic rate the most, fats second, and carbohydrates the least. People living primarily on proteins have a higher metabolic rate than do those whose diet is heavy in fats and carbohydrates; consequently, they have higher minimum caloric requirements as well.

The ideal diet contains portions of all three nutritional sources. Foraging populations, however, were vulnerable to dietary stress during seasons when the game animals they hunted were depleted of their fat reserves. If their supplies of carbohydrate-rich plant foods were depleted at the same time, these populations would have had to devise ways to store foods rich in fats and carbohydrates. Many food scientists believe that we evolved with a strong desire to consume fat, since energy ingested as fat can be stored in the body and thus provide calories to carry us through times of food shortages. In biochemical terms, it is cheaper to store calories from fat than to acquire them from consuming carbohydrates. The reason fat consumption is such a health problem in today's rich countries, however, is that we seldom if ever experience food shortages, so our acquired fat supply tends to become permanent.

An alternative to fat or carbohydrate storage was to exchange something of value for such foods. Thus, the most common mutualistic interaction came to involve the exchange of protein for fats and carbohydrates, a relationship that required that each segment of the population specialize in one food or the other. A second kind of mutualism involved the exchange of any of the three basic foods for farm labor, or for other services such as transportation or defense from predators or attacks.[30]

Eventually, however, humans had to join with plants and animals to form sets of coevolved food systems. The evolutionary logic behind such systems is not readily apparent. Coevolution requires that the changes be beneficial for all the involved species. Yet how could such a system be beneficial for both the grazers/predators (humans) and the host/prey (wheat and sheep)?

Predator-prey (or grazer-host) systems are of two types. If the prey and predators compete (that is, the prey resist and make difficult their role in the system;

the predators try to consume all the prey, and do so violently), then populations of both tend to oscillate out of phase with each other (as one rises, the other falls), so both populations remain more or less stable. If prey and predator cooperate, however—if prey remain docile and submissive, and the predators treat them gently and perform essential functions for them—then the populations of both tend to rise over time. It is for this reason that the populations of humans and cattle have risen over the last ten thousand years, while the tiger population has declined. Such cooperation between prey and predators is not restricted to systems with humans in them; coevolved animal-plant systems that do not involve humans may also combine predation and mutualism. John Thompson reports that the grazing habits of deer and elk among certain plant populations actually stimulated greater flower production and increased seed output, with little or no loss in plant growth.[31]

All plants and animals have to perform two essential tasks if they are to survive in a competitive world: avoid or defend against predators, and disperse their genes in order to reproduce. To accomplish the first task, most plants and animals have evolved defense mechanisms that prevent grazers or predators from finding them (camouflage), eating them (thorns, shells, husks), or digesting them (chemicals).[32] When populations of the same species evolve in widely separated locations and surrounded by different kinds of predators or grazers, they will evolve different kinds of defenses as well.[33] A population that finds itself in environments free from enemies will lose its defenses through natural selection, genetic drift, or a combination of the two. Over evolutionary time, these differences in selection pressures caused by different sets of enemies will create what John Thompson calls "a genetic mosaic in the evolutionary arms race between antagonists."[34]

Susan Grant has written extensively on the coevolution of plants and animals to achieve these essential goals.[35] Plants growing in the wild expend a large portion of their energy on defenses that protect them from being eaten. Some of these defenses work to shield the plants from predators, such as "armor" (shells, husks) or "barbed wire" (thorns, thistles). Some use biting insects such as ants as "bodyguards" that attack would-be predators. In other instances, plants attempt to flee predators by means of an r-strategy of reproduction: they produce large numbers of small, light seeds that are carried by the wind some distance from the parent. Others grow below ground, drop off injured parts after being attacked, or produce huge quantities of seeds at very wide time intervals. Many plants produce chemicals that repel or poison attackers, or hormones that act as contraceptives to inhibit the reproduction of animals that eat them. Finally, some plants grow brightly colored parts that, when joined with some aversive stimulus such as bad taste, advertise to would-be predators that it would be better to leave those plants alone.

In evolving their defenses, plants are confronted with a dilemma. If they make their defenses too porous, they will let in grazers and predators that will feed off them without making any positive contribution to their fitness. If they make their defense filter too narrow, then they will close out beneficial visitors that are essential if plants are to disperse their genes to reproduce. A solution to this challenge—finding and maintaining what Thompson calls "a selective sieve"—is essential if plants are to perform their second task: dispersal of their genetic material.[36]

Plants also face difficulties when it comes to reproduction. To reproduce, they must set their seed, but they must try to do so far enough away so that offspring do not compete with the parents for the local supply of nutrients. To solve this problem, plants have evolved a number of strategies for dispersing their seeds. Some rely on insects such as bees or wasps to carry their pollen, while others have coevolved with animals like birds, bats, or lemurs to disperse their pollen.[37] Many plants use the attractions of sight, scent, and taste to get animals to eat their seeds and carry them in their gut to another site; still others use hooks or sticky surfaces to adhere to the fur of animals to ride to their new home. Many of these latter dispersal strategies were evolved for mammals in general, or for primates in particular, so they were easily adapted to humans as well.

Having the full ability to perform these functions requires that animals and plants do two things: devote much of their energy to defense and reproduction, and achieve maturity. And yet, it was precisely these two factors that humans had to curtail in order to make plants and animals partners in our coevolved food systems. We needed to breed plants and animals that would devote most of their energy to providing us with food, and that would remain juvenile in their behavior even as they grew large. To accomplish these goals, we then had to take over some of the essential functions of domesticated plants and animals. Human farmers and animal herders had to assume responsibility for protection from predators and for assisting in reproduction. In many instances, humans were so effective in managing these functions that their domesticated plants and animals became helpless without their human companions. For example, maize long ago lost its ability to disperse its seeds without human help; and sheep likewise lost their ability to defend themselves from predators without the help of shepherds and sheep dogs. In these ways, humans were forced to evolve culturally as their companion plants and animals evolved biologically.

THE INVENTION OF AGRICULTURE

There is no doubt that the invention of agriculture is of supreme historical importance, but the true significance of food production for humankind and for our planet is still hotly debated.

Agriculture created the dividing line, first identified by the Chinese more than two millennia ago, between "barbarism" (the nomadic life style of pastoralists) and "civilization" (the life of cities made possible by sedentary food production). The transformation from hunting and gathering to farming and animal raising yielded more food energy per unit of land, and so made it possible to support an increase in the number of people not engaged in the direct production of food. This specialization became the basis for all subsequent human cultural and scientific advances. But if the transition to agriculture made possible the rise of civilization, it also placed increasing pressure on the Earth's ecosystems and bred class and gender inequalities, disease, and despotism. Thus, many would agree with Jared Diamond's assessment that agriculture was "the worst mistake of the human race, . . . in many ways a catastrophe from which we have never recovered."[38]

For the biosphere, the transition to agriculture was a turning point of fundamental importance. Paul Colinvaux calls the invention of herding and agriculture "the most momentous event in the history of life" because

> for the first time an animal had adopted a new niche without speciating. . . . It meant that one kind of animal was now able to keep changing its habits in ways that should take the food from others, and it would pay no cost for this in the loss of the old ways—a cost always paid in changing a niche through speciating. People would take away the resources that supported the niches of other animals one by one, constantly adding these resources to their own niche.[39]

But these changes in the Earth's biology were achieved at an extremely heavy price, as Clive Ponting explains:

> Agriculture involves clearing the natural ecosystem in order to create an artificial habitat where humans can grow the plants and stock the animals they want. The natural balances and inherent stability of the original ecosystem are thereby destroyed. . . . The soil is exposed to the wind and rain to a far greater extent than before, . . . leading to much higher rates of soil erosion. . . . Nutrient recycling processes are also disrupted and extra inputs in the form of manures or fertilizers are . . . required. . . . The adoption of irrigation is even more disruptive since it creates an environment that is even more artificial than dry farming. . . .

> [T]he emergence of villages and towns . . . meant that the demand for resources was now more concentrated, and efforts to increase supply would inevitably impose significantly greater strains on smaller areas. New demands arose, especially for construction materials for permanent houses and also for new and more varied goods. Forests suffered most as the requirement for wood to build houses, heat homes and cook food rose steadily. Local deforestation leading to increased soil erosion became a problem around settled areas.[40]

For 250 million years, the Earth's biosphere had received, stored, processed, shared, and ultimately dissipated the energy from the sun in the pattern so familiar to us.[41] Energy flowed into the biosphere where it was captured by photosynthesizing plants. They in turn were eaten by a wide and diverse range of herbivores, which were eaten by a wide and diverse range of carnivores. Control over the system was decentralized. All the participants exerted some control over the others by virtue of their selections of what to eat and what to leave, and by the adaptation of all concerned to the pressures of natural selection.

Hardly anyone lives in such a food energy network today. Such a system is simply too uncertain and too inefficient. Any species that can gain control over the system will certainly strive to do so, and *Homo sapiens* possesses such an ability. For ten thousand years or more, people have constructed and controlled their own food chains to fit their needs. Plants and herbivores that match those needs are retained and encouraged; those that do not fit, as well as all competing carnivores, are discarded. The few plants that we can eat ourselves, such as the cereal grains, we cultivate and promote. Those that we cannot eat, we either destroy or arrange for a few herbivores to eat them, and then we eat the herbivores. Those herbivores that we cannot eat we discard. Competitors and predators we marginalize in zoos and game parks.

The invention of agriculture was humans' way of adapting to an unstable and uncertain food energy system by controlling the selection of who eats, and who or what gets eaten. No longer would we allow these decisions to be made according to the logic of the larger energy system. From that point on, and to an ever increasing degree, the flow of energy through the biosphere has been controlled to serve one single species: *Homo sapiens*.

Experts disagree over the reasons why humans adopted agriculture;[42] but it is well understood now that between ten and twelve thousand years ago, humans began the long transition from hunting, scavenging, and gathering their food to a totally new culture based on the domestication of plants and animals. The selection of plants and animals to eat must have presented early humans with considerable uncertainties. As the earliest long distance traveler, *Homo erectus* would have frequently entered novel food environments, where the decisions about what to eat and what to leave alone could not have been readily apparent.[43] Even relatively sedentary *erectus* would have moved about the local range quite frequently in response to seasonal and climatic changes and to the movement of animals, confronting dilemmas about which foods to eat. And they must have made the wrong choices often: For example, the *erectus* skeleton known as Turkana Boy exhibits evidence of a dietary disease called hypervitaminosis, an overconcentration of vitamin A that comes from eating excessive amounts of the livers of carnivores.

Long before humans took up farming to produce food, they had already acquired the ability to change their surrounding landscape to facilitate the gathering and hunting of their food supply. Ancient hunters set fires deliberately to clear trails and open up spaces in wooded areas to channel the movement of game during the hunt, to drive frightened animals into traps or over cliffs, and to improve pasture or grazing areas to attract animals. Ancient food gatherers also understood the benefits of fire to improve the yield of wild seeds, berries, and nuts.[44]

The transition from food collection to food production was a gradual process that in many instances required several millennia to complete. The change from shifting horticulture to permanent agriculture required numerous cultural changes, including the improvement of tools, the application of natural manure to fields, the burning of sod or soil, the alternation of cropping and grass fallow, and intervention in the pollination process to influence plant genetics.[45] Traditional foraging peoples did not abandon their food collection practices overnight in favor of food production, which must have appeared quite revolutionary to them. Ancient peoples lived for thousands of years in the Oaxaca Valley of Mexico by combining food cultivation and foraging in an integrated strategy for survival.[46] In wet years, when food was plentiful, the people sowed domesticated crops close to home. In dry years, when crops were less reliable, they reverted to the time-tested ways of foraging that often took them far from home. The effect was to achieve food security in an uncertain world. In this instance, as in many others, agriculture was not a dramatic response to a crisis, but the outcome of a very lengthy process by which human beings interacted with, adapted to, and learned to cope with an unpredictable environment.

The coevolutionary perspective enables us to see the transition to food producing as the result of countless daily, commonplace interactions that brought about cultural changes in people and biological changes in plants and animals. One proponent of this perspective, David Rindos, has argued that the invention of agriculture proceeded in three stages.[47] In stage one—incidental domestication—the harvesting, incidental dispersal, and protection of certain plants and animals by humans led to an abundance of some plants and animals over others, as well as to a relocation of plants and animals outside their natural range. Of greatest significance in this stage is this simple but vital fact: humans selected only a very few species within the realms of those plants and animals that were already attractive foods because of certain biological characteristics. Humans enhanced these features through their (mostly) unconscious behaviors, and we continue to live today with the consequences of these ancient food choices.

In stage two—specialized domestication—humans expanded the range of their actions to encourage certain plants and animals and began to modify the environment via burning, clearing, and planting. At this point, the plants and animals began to exhibit morphological changes (e.g., in seed size) in response to these behaviors. Finally, in stage three—agricultural domestication—human actions became systematized in what we would recognize as "farming," plants and animals increased their productivity and homogeneity, and species diversity declined.

Scholars have searched for the reasons why foragers, hunters, and gatherers would have wanted to make the transition from food discovery to food production.[48] After all, farming is more difficult than hunting and gathering, takes more effort and time, and produces a poorer quality diet. Moreover, the costs of food production in terms of energy are very high, and depend on the labor of draft animals (especially horses and oxen) and on irrigation, which requires lifting water against the force of gravity. These innovations, while essential to farming, had high energy costs attached.[49] Yet despite the distasteful nature of farming, farmers persisted and eventually prevailed over foragers for one central reason: increased thermodynamic efficiency. With this advantage, farmers simply outbred foragers, and where they competed for the same ground, the farmers eventually displaced their competitors.

Jared Diamond has identified a number of factors that would have tilted the scale in favor of farmers:

- a decline in the availability of wild foods, at least partly because humans had hunted a number of large mammals to virtual extinction;
- a rise in the availability of domesticable wild plants, occasioned by climate changes in the Middle East and Mesoamerica;
- the accumulation of technologies and techniques for harvesting and storing grains, which reached a critical mass of knowledge in the Fertile Crescent by about 11,000 B.C.;
- demographic pressures that set in motion a positive feedback loop of mutually reinforcing increases in population and food production.[50]

But wherever farming won out over foraging, it was because farmers had available to them a package of domesticable food sources whose combined food energy made it feasible for them to take the risks inherent in such a change in subsistence strategies. In the Fertile Crescent, for example, such a package consisted of three cereals to provide carbohydrates, four animals as the main protein sources, and four pulses to fill in the gaps with additional protein. Thus, the coevolution of systems of humans, plants, and animals was the key to the increased food energy that farmers were able to wrest from the ground.

Plants

The first step in the transition from foraging to farming was the domestication of plants—the transformation of wild, edible plants into food staples such as wheat or rice. Plant cultivation on a very limited scale has probably been practiced for thirty thousand years or more, in settings around the world from tropical rainforests to European alpine meadows.[51] Despite its limited beginnings, people who practiced plant cultivation would have had a slight advantage over those who did not, and the former would have left behind more of their genes and more of their cultural practices than would the latter. They would have also been the more expansive of the two groups, eventually spreading their food production strategies around the world. A commitment to food production as the principal strategy on which people relied first appears in the archeological record some 10,000 years ago, demonstrating that plant cultivation had by that time become economically significant and widespread enough to leave behind traces that we can discern today.

A. J. Legge has summed up the purpose of plant domestication in terms of energy flow:

Studies of the energy capture among hunter-gatherers (in terms of the energy return of calories gained for calories expended in work) tend to show an advantageous return in the order of 1:10. . . . At first sight it would seem that non-mechanised farmers do not do vastly better with a simple technology and manage from about 1:14 to 1:60. The point is that they manage with a very much smaller area. . . . Food collecting is extensive and commonly involves considerably more than 10km² of foraging area per individual. Land use estimates of about 3km² per individual are given even for sedentary hunter-gatherers in very diverse and productive environments.

On the other hand cultivation is intensive and can be seen in terms of hectares per family. After all, the point of cultivation is simply to produce a monoculture of the largest amount of the desired crop in the smallest area and to thus maximise energy capture and minimise the energy cost of its production.[52]

Our search for nourishment began, and remains, fundamentally shaped by plants. As late as the 1950s, humans derived 85 percent of their food energy directly from vegetation. As human populations have grown richer, our diet has shifted toward meat; but plants remain our chief source of directly consumed food energy. And remember that animals entered our diet only as conduits for delivering plant energy, making plants the ultimate source of all food for humans, directly or indirectly.

Humans have been affecting the Earth's plant life, consciously or unconsciously, for hundreds of millennia.[53] Fire and other techniques such as girdling were used to clear forests and woodlands for thousands of years before farming arose. As agriculture took hold, humans transformed the regional flora by clearing the land, irrigation, and pest eradication. Grazing animal herds devastated huge areas of grassland by eating vegetation and hardening the soil with their hooves. Lumbering to provide wood for construction further depleted forest resources. Irrigation, managed flooding, and other water-control practices enabled farming in areas where plants could not grow naturally. The emergence of cities took even more land for human use where plants had once grown unchallenged. There have even been instances of farmers' unconsciously manipulating a plant population to such a degree that a new plant species emerges.[54]

When people began farming, they simply adopted the most successful and adaptable wild plant species and turned them into reliable food staples. The earliest farmers quite naturally favored plants that germinated quickly, grew rapidly, and remained dormant in unfavorable conditions (e.g., cold, drought).[55] These were the attributes, it turned out, that enabled plants to survive in unstable environments. Plants with more food energy per weight, such as nuts, were not selected for a variety of reasons: They grew too slowly, or were too sparsely disseminated, or were too difficult to gather or eat. We preferred weeds: fast growing, hardy under the worst conditions, prolific. So weeds became the foundation upon which the Neolithic Revolution was based: wheat, maize, barley, rice, sorghum, squash, beans, and so forth.

For the earliest farmers, the most favorable spot on Earth to domesticate plants was the Fertile Crescent of the Middle East.[56] The area was blessed with a climate that favored the wild growth of plants that would be most attractive as potential domesticates. The mild, wet winters and the hot, dry summers were conducive to plants that would devote much of their energy to producing large seeds that would survive the dry season and be ready to sprout when the rains reappeared. Such plants put relatively little energy into edible wood or fibrous stems, like trees and bushes, and more energy into seeds, which could be harvested, stored, and then eaten by farmers and their families.

As a result of this climate, cereal grasses grew wild throughout the Fertile Crescent in abundance. Experiments by botanists have shown that harvesting these wild grains can yield up to fifty kilocalories of food energy for each kilocalorie of work expended. Foragers living in this region would have been able to make the transition to cultivation fairly easily while still relying on an abundant wild food supply if the crops failed. (In contrast, the staple food crop in Mesoamerica, maize, descended from a wild plant, teosinte, that devoted much of its energy to a hard shell covering its seed and thus resisted domestication. Mesoamerican farmers must have needed centuries if not millennia to breed something approaching the corn we enjoy today.)

There were, of course, other regions of the world that experienced a climate similar to that of the Fertile Crescent, but compared with these regions, such as Chile or California, the Middle East was privileged in a number of ways. The Fertile Crescent was by far the largest such climatic zone in the world, it possessed a greater range of altitudes, and it experienced a greater diversity of climatic conditions than did any other. As a consequence, it was home to a greater variety of domesticable plants. Of the world's thousands of wild-grass species, fifty-six are considered to hold the greatest potential for domestication because their seeds are so large. Virtually all of them are native to Mediterranean-like climates. The Fertile Crescent was home to thirty-two of these, while in all the Americas there were only eleven, in East Asia six, and in Africa only four. Thus, plant domestication could proceed in the Fertile Crescent on the strength of an abundance of locally available wild plants, which reduced significantly the risks involved in shifting from foraging to food production.

Animals

The abundance of wild cereal grasses and their easily tapped food energy led to the appearance of a greater variety of grazing large mammals, including horses, goats, sheep, and cattle, which yielded yet another advantage for the Fertile Crescent. Humans began their association with animals as what Colin Tudge calls "paleolithic game managers."[57] That is, they were even at this early date manipulating their fellow creatures to favor and encourage the ones they liked and to discourage the ones they disliked or feared. Species that were of the right size (for example, cattle rather than elephants), passive rather than aggressive, social rather than solitary, and juvenile (neotenic), would be herded and protected; those of the other categories would be hunted (in many cases, to extinction). Individual animals that lent themselves to domestication, that "cooperated" in a sense with the humans, would leave behind more of their genes than those that did not. Again, as with plants, such an arrangement gives a huge advantage in thermodynamic efficiency to the humans and their animal companions.

At one time or another over the eons, most large animals have lived nearly everywhere on Earth. We should not draw any conclusions about these patterns at any given time. Zoögeography (the patterns of distribution of animals across the landscape) "expresses no deep pattern," writes Colin Tudge, "but simply reflects the way things happen to be at the moment."

> Most of the groups of large animals have in their time been everywhere (except of course Australia . . .). They have been motivated to move by changing climate and allowed to move by seas that conveniently drained from time to time. . . . Their peregrinations stop only when they run out of habitat. . . . We think that animals belong where we happen to have found them, but usually they are just passing through. . . . [T]hey trek the entire surface of the globe once the opportunities arise: cascades of animals migrating, radiating, moving on or drifting back from whence they came.[58]

Nevertheless, the distribution of large animals around the world ten thousand years ago had an enormous impact on the transition to agriculture and on the subsequent history of the planet's biosphere. While the world of large mammals is extraordinarily diverse, early animal herders concentrated on a single group: the ungulates (mammals having hoofs).[59] The carnivores were of less significance for our story, since they were never serious candidates for domestication for food: for one thing, many of them preyed on humans, so it was dangerous to have them around; for another, they competed with humans for the same food supply since we had both evolved to appreciate the taste of large to mid-sized herbivores; and finally, there were not many of them around, since the food chain cannot support very many meat eaters.

Thus, when humans evolved the practices of animal husbandry, they concentrated their efforts on the ungulates. And not all ungulates, at that, but only on a select subgroup: horses, cattle, sheep, goats, and pigs. Excluded were the large animals that moved too slowly or caused too much damage to the food supply to be raised in large herds: elephants, rhinos, hippos, and the like. Also excluded were the solitary browsers like giraffes. Horses were evolutionarily favored by their improving ability to eat increasingly abundant grass, their large bodies, and their speed.[60] Pigs were favored by the incredibly absorptive power of their digestive systems, which meant they could survive on food that other animals, especially humans, could not eat. But the most successful of all were the ruminants, whose digestive systems permitted them to digest bulk fodder efficiently and thus enabled them to dominate both grasslands and forests. Several kinds of ruminants, primarily deer, were tracked by pastoral nomads and hunted by American natives.

Of much greater significance to food production, however, have been cattle and sheep, domesticated and raised in herds for thousands of years.

Compared to people in other parts of the world, in the domestication of ungulates for food, the inhabitants of Eurasia had a much greater selection of species from which to choose due to the dynamics of the adaptive radiation of mammals—that is, how groups of species spread across, and eventually fill up, a land mass such as a continent or very large island. When a species colonizes a new habitat, variability, diversity, and adaptability become very advantageous.[61] We should expect, then, to find those species that have colonized the most to exhibit the greatest flexibility and adaptability. And it was the animals of Eurasia that colonized new lands the most, that experienced the most frequent changes in their habitat, and therefore had the greatest flexibility.

According to Edward O. Wilson, today's set of mammal species are the product of three great adaptive radiations.[62] Since the breakup of Pangaea more than 200 million years ago, only three continents have been sufficiently large to support mammalian radiation: Australia, the "World Continent" (Africa, Europe, Asia, and North America as far south as southern Mexico), and South America. North America is included in the World Continent because in the distant past it was joined to both Asia via the Bering Straits, and to Europe via Greenland and Scandinavia. South America, however, was joined to North and Central America only about 2.5 million years ago and so is treated as a separate continent.

The animals of Australia are seen by the rest of the world as exotic because they developed in isolation from the World Continent's genetic influences. Likewise, South American mammals are either distinctively different (such as the ground sloth) or are themselves descended from World Continent mammals that entered the continent after the land bridge was established across Panama. In general, two things happened in South America when North American mammals entered: first, where there was competition between similar species, the North American variant usually won out; and second, the fauna of South America became markedly more diverse or heterogeneous.

The mammals of the World Continent prevailed throughout the rest of the world because of the size and diversity of their population, both of which were due to the larger and more diverse habitat within which they evolved.[63] Dominant species occupying large areas are less prone to extinction in any given locale; and they are better able to colonize distant locales, increasing their numbers and decreasing their vulnerability to purely local conditions. Because dominant groups spread farther, they tend to divide into multiple species that inhabit different niches, so they resist better the pressures pushing them toward extinction. Being much larger than either South America or Australia, the World Continent mammals tested more evolutionary lines, built tougher competitors, and perfected more defenses against predators and disease.

An alternative explanation, however, focuses on climatic changes that were occurring at about the same time that North and South America were being joined.[64] About three million years ago, the world was growing cooler and drier, a change that was crucial to the emergence of *Homo* in East Africa. In the Americas, the animals of the north began to move south toward the equator, where they encountered a landscape that resembled that of their origins. The southern animals, however, had no place to turn, since their homelands were being turned from tropical rainforests to grasslands and temperate forests. Deprived of their habitat, the southern species became extinct; and it was into a more or less empty landscape that the northerners migrated in flight from their chilly hemisphere. According to this hypothesis, then, northern animals survived the Great American Interchange not because they were fitter or could out-compete the southerners. The latter would have gone extinct even without the invasion of the northerners, who just happened to be fortunate to find a mostly empty habitat much like that from which they had come.

Whatever the mechanism by which these changes occurred, when *Homo sapiens* began to domesticate animals for food, transport, and other benefits, Europeans and Asians had many more species from which to choose.[65] According to Jared Diamond, ten thousand years ago there were 148 candidates for domestication. To be a good candidate, the animal had to be a big (defined as weighing more than one hundred pounds), terrestrial, herbivorous mammal. Before the twentieth century, only fourteen of these species had been domesticated. Nine of these were important in only limited areas of the world: Arabian camel, Bactrian camel, llama/alpaca, donkey, reindeer, water buffalo, yak, banteng, and gaur. Five others had become global species: cattle, sheep, goats, pigs, and horses.

To be sure, humans succeeded in taming large, herbivorous mammals, such as the elephant, but taming is not the same as domesticating, as Barbara Noddle points out in her discussion of the domestication of cattle and sheep in neolithic Britain:

> The process of taming takes place within the lifespan of an individual, and probably involves considerable close human contact. . . . The process of domestication . . . involves controlling and exploiting the natural behaviour of an animal, including its breeding and feeding activities over a number of generations. Both physique and behaviour may become genetically altered in the course of events, the animal having come under selection pressure exerted by the stress of human contact, restriction of diet and choice of mate.[66]

Of the 148 candidates, argues Diamond, by far the greatest percentage were native to Eurasia: 72, or 48.6 percent. Africa, expansive but less diverse ecologically, harbored 51 species (34.4 percent); the Americas, 24 (16.2 percent); and Australia, only one (the kangaroo). North America may at one time have held more candidate species, but they were hunted to extinction about eleven thousand years ago, when humans began to spread across the continent, taking huge numbers of the available mammal population for food as they went. That something similar did not happen in Eurasia is due, claims Diamond, to the fact that large mammals began to encounter human hunters in Eurasia much further back in time, when human hunting skills and technologies were much more limited. Eurasian animals thus had many millennia in which to adapt to the presence of *Homo sapiens*. In North America, in contrast, human hunters appeared on the scene suddenly and at a much later date, when hunting skills and techniques had evolved to a much higher degree of efficiency. Since the mammals of North America were not given the chance to coevolve with humans, they succumbed to hunting pressures more readily.

But the advantages of Eurasian mammals were not all due to their relatively greater number, for, as Diamond argues, a much greater proportion of Eurasian mammals were domesticated: 18 percent, as against 4 percent in the Americas (the llama), and zero in Africa and Australia. The fact is, to be a good candidate for domestication, a species must possess all of six specific traits, the first of which involves diet. The inefficiencies of the food chain rule out any carnivore, since too much food energy is lost between the photosynthesizing plant and large carnivores. But good candidates for domestication must be able to eat foods that humans cannot digest, such as grass or plant stalks; otherwise, the domesticated animals would compete with the humans within our niche, which would put added stress on the humans' local food supply.

The other five traits of successful domesticated animals involve neoteny: the continuation of the traits of juvenile animals into adulthood. Neoteny implies that certain parts of an animal are retained in the juvenile form even while the rest of the animal continues to grow.[67] This development pattern rests on mutations of regulator genes that control the pace, timing, and sequencing of changes in the body. Neoteny is conducive to innovation in that old body forms can be left behind and new features can be more easily accommodated during evolution. For example, in humans, the growth of the head was allowed to accelerate and continue to occur long after many other body parts had slowed down or stopped growing, thereby making possible our large brain. When humans wished to domesticate other animals, they selected those animals that demonstrated the ability to slow down the growth of disadvantageous traits (such as competitiveness, aggression), and accelerate advantageous ones (such as docility).

Domesticated animals must also grow quickly to adulthood, and they must retain many of their juvenile characteristics as they do so. They must breed relatively easily in captivity, which usually involves their maintaining a childlike, playful attitude into adulthood. They must remain docile and easily controlled in captivity; and they must not panic when exposed to predators (such as the humans seeking to domesticate them). Finally, their social structure must predispose them to easy outside control: they live in herds, they maintain a well-developed dominance hierarchy within the herd, and the herds occupy overlapping territories rather than exclusive home ranges.

The mammals of Eurasia possessed these six traits in greater numbers than did the mammals of the other regions of the world, so Europeans and Asians were the first to domesticate, and thus to globalize, sizable populations of large mammals. According to Stephen Budiansky, there is a direct relationship between long-distance migration of animals and the evolution of neotenic characteristics.[68] Populations confined to a particular range and a limited food supply tend to adopt slower maturation rates, to live longer, and to devote less energy to reproduction. But a population that has migrated to a new, less densely populated range finds more abundant food and adopts high rates of reproduction, faster maturation, and shorter life spans. These conditions favor the retention of juvenile features into maturity, which helps explain why wild sheep living today at a distance from their point of origin show progressively more pronounced neotenic traits the farther away they are. Thus, animals living in regions that facilitated long-distance migration exhibited more neotenic characteristics and were more easily domesticated.

The path of domestication took different routes, depending on whether the animal in question clustered into groups while in the wild. If the animals naturally moved about in herds, the domestication process might have been rather rapid, especially if the animals naturally respected hierarchy, such as sheep. In Eurasia, and elsewhere, the domestication of long-range migratory animals led to the livestock management practice known as pastoralism.

Pastoralism may have its roots in the efforts by early hunters to capture and tame a few animals to use as decoys or bait to attract wild game.[69] Breeding animals in semicaptivity would have been an obvious next step toward the maintenance of a herd. In any event, pastoralism, in which animals are restrained and kept in close proximity to humans, usually means that more animals occupy a smaller space for a longer time than would be the case with natural grazing. Sheep were probably the first animals to be domesticated in Eurasia in large numbers. The domestication of the first sheep took place after people had achieved a certain degree of sedentariness, probably a result of food surplus brought about by plant cultivation and domestication. The first such domestications probably had as their objective the use of animals for ritual and status. Use of the animals for meat, milk, and wool would probably have come somewhat later.

FOOD AND POPULATION

Connections between food supply and the size and growth rate of the population are ambiguous and controversial. Ever since the eighteenth century and the writings of Thomas Malthus, many have thought food supply to be the principal limit on population. According to this view, humans have the tendency to increase their population geometrically, but food supply grows only arithmetically. Eventually, population will outgrow food supply, famine will result, and the rising death rate will bring the population back down to a level that can be supported by the Earth's food-production capacity.

Massimo Livi-Bacci has studied the connections between food supply and population growth in two ways: first, by examining the connection between malnutrition, famines, and death rates; and second, by looking at three nutritional revolutions and their impact on population (with an emphasis on Europe).[70]

With regard to the first issue, Livi-Bacci contends that deaths caused directly by starvation are actually fairly rare. Humans evolved with the capacity to endure very long periods without food, and even longer periods with a minimal food supply (below fifteen hundred calories). Usually, when we read of famine and increased death rates, the deaths are caused by some aspect of social erosion, such as disease, war, or ecological catastrophe.

On the second point: The effects of the first great advance in food production, the Neolithic Revolution, have already been discussed in chapter 2, where we learned that the invention of agriculture had mixed consequences for mortality rates, which generally remained high. Nutrition probably did not improve significantly, and disease and social pathologies (crime and banditry) probably rose. Life expectancy hovered around the mid-twenties, not appreciably better than levels experienced by foraging populations for many millennia previously (see fig. 1). If population grew rapidly after 8000 B.C., it was due principally to a great increase in birth and fertility rates caused by the sedentariness that agriculture made possible.

The second nutritional revolution that Livi-Bacci considers was a very brief one in Europe that coincided with the beginning of the plague cycle in 1348. After several hundred years of rising population in medieval Europe, farmland had become extremely scarce and expensive; but the horrendous death rates over the next century reversed that trend. As vast tracts of land were now switched from plant cultivation to animal grazing, meat consumption in the fifteenth century reached levels not again attained in some parts of Europe until the present. Per capita caloric consumption estimates from this period suggest that even people on the middle rungs of society were eating four thousand or more calories per day; and the elites of course consumed much more than this. Nevertheless, according to Livi-Bacci, while this improved diet was certainly to be welcomed, available data do not allow us to conclude that it was directly responsible for Europe's subsequent population resurgence. Instead, demographic growth was due principally to, first, an attenuation of epidemic crises and, second, an increase in nuptiality and birth and fertility rates. In other words, population grew because European societies were getting their epidemics under control, and European men and women were getting married younger and having more children. Having more food to eat may have contributed indirectly to these changes, but Livi-Bacci can find no direct link between food availability and population growth.

The same picture emerges from the third nutritional revolution, which began in the eighteenth century. The key factors in the improvement in food supply in Europe were the introduction of new crops from the Americas (maize, potatoes), advances in farm productivity, the cultivation of new lands, and (after 1870) the use of steamships to regularize the transport of food from global food sources to European cities. Again, Livi-Bacci asserts that nutritional quality may actually have declined even while population was exploding; Ireland is often given as a case in point. Population growth was due primarily to the conquering of certain diseases rather than to an improvement in food supply. Other scholars, most particularly

Alfred Crosby, argue the contrary position, however: that the arrival of the new American staple crops in Europe made possible the Old World's demographic explosion of the eighteenth and nineteenth centuries, even while Europe was exporting hundreds of thousands of people to North America, Argentina, Brazil, and Australia.[71]

If the connection between agriculture and total population seems a bit tenuous, the connections between food production and urbanization are clearer and more direct. The shift to agriculture made cities possible by concentrating a large food supply within easy reach of an urban population who did nothing to produce this food. There were hidden costs, however, to the concentration of population. Epidemics were touched off by the unnatural proximity of humans to each other and to animals, which were the carriers of many diseases previously unknown to humans. But the history of cities is inextricably connected with the history of agriculture and of food production and distribution.

All cities depend on the capacity of the agricultural production and distribution system to supply them with food. The food supply plays a role similar to that of the supply of petroleum to power automobiles, or of natural gas to heat homes. The larger, more complex, and more densely populated a city is, the farther afield it must spread its network to capture the food energy its people need. All civilizations have eventually confronted the limits of their ecosystems to provide them with food. However, the wealth and technology of the industrial city enabled it to extend its food networks to all corners of the globe and to tap into distant ecosystems to satisfy its enormous food energy requirements. In this way, industrial and postindustrial cities have been able to stave off the inevitable by drawing on the food supplies of the entire planet to feed themselves.

NOTES

1. Marvin Harris and Eric Ross, eds., *Food and Evolution: Toward a Theory of Human Food Habits* (Philadelphia: Temple University Press, 1987).

2. Colin Tudge, *The Time before History: 5 Million Years of Human Impact* (New York: Simon & Schuster, 1996), p. 193.

3. Rick Potts, *Humanity's Descent: The Consequences of Ecological Instability* (New York: Morrow, 1996), pp. 20–23.

4. Jeffrey Wicken, *Evolution, Thermodynamics, and Information: Extending the Darwinian Program* (New York: Oxford University Press, 1987), pp. 140–41.

5. Wicken, *Evolution, Thermodynamics, and Information*, p. 141.

6. Wicken, *Evolution, Thermodynamics, and Information*, pp. 165, 183.

7. Tudge, *Time before History*, pp. 125–29.

8. Katherine Milton, "Primate Diets and Gut Morphology: Implications for Hominid Evolution," in Harris and Ross, *Food and Evolution*, chapter 3; Potts, *Humanity's Descent*, pp. 126–27.

9. "Dwindling Diversity," *Washington Post*, February 15, 1997; Boyce Rensberger, "Nurturing a Cornucopia of Potential," *Washington Post*, October 20, 1993.

10. Jonathan Kingdon, *Self-Made Man: Human Evolution from Eden to Extinction?* (New York: Wiley, 1993), chapter 4.

11. Tudge, *Time before History*, pp. 197–99, 210.

12. Massimo Livi-Bacci, *Population and Nutrition: An Essay on European Demographic History*, trans. Tania Croft-Murray, with assistance of Carl Ipsen (Cambridge: Cambridge University Press, 1991), p. 30.

13. Bernard Ortiz de Montellano, *Aztec Medicine, Health, and Nutrition* (New Brunswick, N.J.: Rutgers University Press, 1990), chapter 4.

14. Tudge, *Time before History*, pp. 254–59.

15. Paul Colinvaux, *Why Big Fierce Animals Are Rare: An Ecologist's Perspective* (Princeton: Princeton University Press, 1978), p. 36.

16. Livi-Bacci, *Population and Nutrition*, chapter 2; Vaclav Smil, *Energy in World History* (Boulder, Colo.: Westview, 1994), p. 11.

17. Vaclav Smil, *Cycles of Life: Civilization and the Biosphere* (New York: Scientific American Library, 1997), pp. 20–23.

18. Edward Deevey, "The Human Population," *Scientific American* (September 1960): 202; Clive Ponting, *A Green History of the World: The Environment and the Collapse of Great Civilizations* (New York: St. Martin's, 1991), pp. 11–12.

19. Vaclav Smil, *Energy, Food, Environment: Realities, Myths, Options* (Oxford: Clarendon, 1987), pp. 82–88.

20. Smil, *Energy in World History*, p. 18.

21. Colinvaux, *Why Big Fierce Animals Are Rare*, p. 36.

22. Smil, *Energy in World History*, pp. 37–44.

23. Yvonne Baskin, *The Work of Nature: How the Diversity of Life Sustains Us* (Washington, D.C.: Island Press, 1997), pp. 127, 191–96.

24. Irwin Forseth, "Plant Response to Multiple Environmental Stresses: Implications for Climatic Change and Biodiversity," *Biodiversity II: Understanding and Protecting Our Biological Resources*, ed. Marjorie Reaka-Kudla, Don Wilson, and Edward O. Wilson, Washington, D.C.: Joseph Henry, 1997), pp. 189–90.

25. Smil, *Cycles of Life*, chapter 4; Smil, *Energy, Food, Environment*, pp. 274–79.

26. William Agosta, *Bombardier Beetles and Fever Trees: A Close-up Look at Chemical Warfare and Signals in Animals and Plants* (Reading, Mass.: Addison Wesley, 1996).

27. Donald Johanson, Lenora Johanson, and Blake Edgar, *Ancestors: In Search of Human Origins* (New York: Villard, 1994), p. 203.

28. Charles Heiser, *Seed to Civilization: The Story of Food* (Cambridge: Harvard University Press, 1990), chapter 3; Livi-Bacci, *Population and Nutrition*, chapter 2; Smil, *Energy, Food, Environment*, pp. 108–45.

29. Livi-Bacci, *Population and Nutrition*, pp. 42–43.

30. Susan Alling Gregg, *Foragers and Farmers: Population Interaction and Agricultural Expansion in Prehistoric Europe* (Chicago: University of Chicago Press, 1988), pp. 48–50.

31. John Thompson, *The Coevolutionary Process* (Chicago: University of Chicago Press, 1994), table 9.2, p. 164.

32. John Thompson, *Interaction and Coevolution* (New York: Wiley, 1982), pp. 26–32; Agosta, *Bombardier Beetles*, passim.

33. Thompson, *Coevolutionary Process*, pp. 161–66.

34. Thompson, *Coevolutionary Process*, p. 165.

35. Susan Grant, *Beauty and the Beast: The Coevolution of Plants and Animals* (New York: Scribner, 1984).

36. Thompson, *Coevolutionary Process*, pp. 183–84.

37. Stephen Buchmann and Gary Paul Nabhan, *The Forgotten Pollinators* (Washington, D.C.: Island, 1996); Deborah Churchman, "How Plants Entice Animals for Sex," *Washington Post*, June 11, 1997.

38. Jared Diamond, "The Worst Mistake in the History of the Human Race," *Discover* (May 1987): 64–66.

39. Colinvaux, *Why Big Fierce Animals Are Rare*, pp. 218–19.

40. Ponting, *Green History of the World*, pp. 68–69.

41. Potts, *Humanity's Descent*, pp. 32–36.

42. C. Wesley Cowan and Patty Jo Watson, eds., *The Origins of Agriculture: An International Perspective* (Washington, D.C.: Smithsonian Institution Press, 1992); Anne Birgitte Gebauer and T. Douglas Price, eds., *Transitions to Agriculture in Prehistory*, Monographs in World Archeology No. 4 (Madison, Wisc.: Prehistory Press, 1992); Mark Cohen, *The Food Crisis in Prehistory: Overpopulation and the Origins of Agriculture* (New Haven: Yale University Press, 1977); T. Douglas Price and Anne Birgitte Gebauer, eds. *Last Hunters, First Farmers: New Perspectives on the Prehistoric Transition to Agriculture* (Santa Fe, N.M.: School of American Research Press, 1995); Ernest Schusky, *Culture and Agriculture: An Ecological Introduction to Traditional and Modern Farming Systems* (New York: Bergin & Garvey, 1989).

43. Kingdon, *Self-Made Man*, pp. 52–61.

44. Omer Stewart, "Fire as the First Great Force Employed by Man," in *Man's Role in Changing the Face of the Earth,* ed. William Thomas (Chicago: University of Chicago Press, 1956), pp. 115–33.

45. H. H. Bartlett, "Fire, Primitive Agriculture, and Grazing in the Tropics," in Thomas, *Man's Role*, pp. 692–720.

46. Potts, *Humanity's Descent*, pp. 247–49.

47. David Rindos, *The Origins of Agriculture: An Evolutionary Perspective* (Orlando, Fla.: Academic, 1984).

48. Tudge, *Time before History*, pp. 268–73.

49. Smil, *Energy in World History*, pp. 39–56.

50. Jared Diamond, *Guns, Germs, and Steel: The Fates of Human Societies* (New York: Norton, 1997), pp. 109–13.

51. Tudge, *Time before History*, pp. 269–70.

52. A. J. Legge, "Milking the Evidence: A Reply to Entwistle and Grant," in *The Beginnings of Agriculture*, ed. Annie Milles, Diane Williams and Neville Gardner (Oxford: Symposia of the Association for Environmental Archaeology No. 8, BAR International Series 496, 1989), pp. 223–24.

53. Edward Graham, "The Re-creative Power of Plant Communities," in Thomas, *Man's Role*, pp. 677–91.

54. Edgar Anderson, "Man as a Maker of New Plants and New Plant Communities," in Thomas, *Man's Role*, pp. 763–77.

55. Potts, *Humanity's Descent*, pp. 249–51.

56. Diamond, *Guns, Germs, and Steel*, pp. 134–42.

57. Tudge, *Time before History*, pp. 270–72, 311–14.

58. Tudge, *Time before History*, pp. 118–19.

59. Tudge, *Time before History*, pp. 144–66.

60. Stephen Budiansky, *The Nature of Horses: Exploring Equine Evolution, Intelligence, and Behavior* (New York: Free Press, 1997).

61. Robert Wesson, *Beyond Natural Selection* (Cambridge: MIT Press, 1991, 1997), p. 211.

62. Edward O. Wilson, *The Diversity of Life* (Cambridge: Harvard University Press, 1992), pp. 120–30.

63. Diamond, *Guns, Germs, and Steel*, chapter 10.

64. Tudge, *Time before History*, pp. 97–102.

65. Diamond, *Guns, Germs, and Steel*, chapter 9.

66. Barbara Noddle, "Cattle and Sheep in Britain and Northern Europe up to the Atlantic Period: A Personal Viewpoint," in Milles, Williams, and Gardner, *Beginnings of Agriculture*, pp. 185–86.

67. Wesson, *Beyond Natural Selection*, pp. 204–6.

68. Stephen Budiansky, *The Covenant of the Wild: Why Animals Chose Domestication* (Leesburg, Va.: Terrapin, 1995), chapter 4.

69. F. Fraser Darling, "Man's Ecological Dominance through Domesticated Animals on Wild Lands," in Thomas, *Man's Role*, pp. 778–87.

70. Livi-Bacci, *Population and Nutrition*, esp. chapter 1.

71. Alfred Crosby, *Germs, Seeds, and Animals: Studies in Ecological History* (Armonk, N.Y.: Sharpe, 1994), chapter 9.

Chapter Four

Disease

Over the last ten millennia, human populations, aided and accompanied by their domesticated plants and animals, have expanded their numbers by three orders of magnitude and staked their claim to most of the planet's land mass. But these two trends have not proceeded evenly across time or space, and they have not been without their biological costs. One of the chief barriers to expansion, and thus one of the leading costs of globalization, has been disease. Indeed, Roy Anderson and Robert May assert that "infectious diseases have surely been the most significant agents of natural selection acting on human populations since the dawn of the agricultural revolution, and possibly earlier."[1] Paradoxically, diseases have also aided the globalization of certain populations, primarily Europeans and Asians, at the expense of other peoples of the world.

Even before the first recorded urban epidemic, in Athens in 430 B.C., the history of globalization frequently turned on the coevolution of humans and diseases.[2] No history of what William McNeill calls the "closing of the Eurasian Ecumene."[3] would be complete without a discussion of the great Eurasian plagues that began in the fourteenth century and continued for several hundred years; nor could a history of the Americas be written without reference to the devastation of native populations by European diseases in the early sixteenth century. Globalization following the Industrial Revolution was accompanied by an increase in life expectancy from twenty-five to seventy-five years between 1700 and 1970, an improvement that "comes mainly from a decline in deaths induced by directly transmitted viral and bacterial infections."[4] Yet diseases have not ceased to be significant in our century. The great influenza pandemic of 1918–1919 caused the deaths of more than twenty million people worldwide within twelve months; and the plague of the latter decades of the twentieth century, AIDS, reminds us of our continuing vulnerability to microbes in a world of mass travel and easy movement of people and lifestyles.

People have long been fascinated by epidemics of infectious diseases, and have recorded their devastating impact almost since writing was invented.[5] Ancient civilizations in Egypt and Mesopotamia were aware of the damage done by internal parasites such as tapeworms, and their medical practitioners used drugs to rid people of these infestations. The Biblical writings made frequent reference to plagues of indeterminate nature and origin, including those produced by "fiery serpents" (worms again?).

What the ancients lacked in order to undertake the scientific study of infections was the germ theory of disease. As far back as Aristotle, some Greek writers expressed the idea that invisible living creatures might be responsible for disease. In 1546, Girolamo Fracastoro hypothesized that diseases were caused by germs that could multiply within the body and be transmitted directly from one person to another or even indirectly over long distances by other contaminated objects. Fracastoro also theorized that these germs might change their virulence, thereby causing epidemics of varying intensity. His ideas were not pursued, however, largely because of the inability of Renaissance scientists to observe the world of micröorganisms directly.

It was not until the late seventeenth and early eighteenth centuries that the manufacture of magnifying lenses made it possible for people to see living organisms through the microscope. One of the pioneers in microscopy, the Dutch scientist Anton van Leeuwenhoek (1632–1723), is credited with demonstrating that micröorganisms exist, which made possible their systematic study. The scientific study of diseases began to register important advances and accumulate them into an expanding body of knowledge: the dissections and anatomical drawings of Andreas Vesalius; Thomas Sydenham's theory that diseases developed like living organisms inside the body; the work of Giovanni Morgani on the component organ systems of the body; and Marie Bichat's focus on diseased tissue within organs as the source of illness.

In 1840, Jacob Henle resurrected Fracastoro's theories and expressed the germ theory of disease as it is known today. This step was followed by the great scientific advances of the latter half of the nineteenth century that are associated with the names of Louis Pasteur, Joseph Lister, and Robert Koch; Koch in particular made a key breakthrough when he identified the specific bacteria that causes anthrax. In the mid-1850s, John Snow conducted the first empirical testing of the germ theory and was able to show the connection between the contaminated water supply drawn by the city of London from the polluted Thames and cholera epidemics that were then ravaging the city. These scientists and physicians were responsible for transforming our knowledge of diseases from the vague superstitious notions of the Middle Ages to rigorous scientific principles that explained the origins of infectious diseases, their structure and transmission, and appropriate remedies and preventive measures.

THE WORLD OF PATHOGENS

Whether an organism is a parasite or a predator depends to some degree on its size relative to its host.[6] Most organisms would probably prefer to be parasitic if they could get away with it, because then they would not have to kill their food supply; they could simply nibble a bit at each meal, leaving the host alive so they could continue to dine on another occasion. Extremely tiny organisms can pursue the parasite option, because they do not have to eat much of their host at one sitting, and, for a bonus, they get to live and reproduce inside the host. As organisms get larger, however, they lose that option. A protozoan or a bacterium can pursue the parasitic option with humans, but this option quickly evaporates as the organisms grow larger to the size of a wolf or a bear, when they have no choice but to kill the host.

Until relatively recently, it was thought that diseases in humans could be caused by three kinds of organisms.[7] The largest, macroparasites, are multicellular organisms such as parasitic worms and insects that are visible to the naked eye. Then there are two classes of microparasites. Bacteria and (most but not all) protozoans, are 100 to 300 times smaller than macroparasites and visible only under optical microscopes. The smallest of all, viruses 100 times smaller than bacteria, are visible only under electron microscopes.

In the last two or three decades, scientists have discovered other infectious entities that do not belong to any of the above categories. One is only about one-tenth the size of the smallest known virus. Called a "viroid," this free strand of RNA has the ability to invade certain plants like tomatoes and, in a process not yet understood, use the plant's enzymes to replicate itself. While such agents have not been detected in any animal, in at least one instance a virus particle that replicates like a viroid has been discovered to be involved in certain hepatitis infections.[8] Another infectious agent, discovered in 1982, is a pathogenic protein molecule called a "prion." Despite its lack of genes of its own, the prion manages to multiply by taking control of the host cell's genes in a manner not yet understood. The prion causes disease by inducing neighboring proteins to take on distorted shapes. It has been identified as the cause of "mad cow disease."[9]

All of these parasites are of extremely ancient lineage. The first multicellular animals entered the fossil record over 600 million years ago, but the emergence of bacteria marks the beginnings of life itself, some 3.5 to 3.6 billion years ago. Infections were already common when more complex organisms began to leave fossilized traces about half a billion years ago.[10]

Stephen Jay Gould contends that bacteria are today, and always have been, the dominant life form on Earth.[11] They are very nearly indestructable, and they inhabit every place suitable for life on Earth, including (in very large numbers) our own body. One person's gut harbors more individuals of the species *Escherichia coli* than the total number of people that now live and have ever lived, and this is only one species of the bacteria that inhabit the normal human digestive system. About 10 percent of our dry body weight consists of bacteria, many of which we have coexisted and coevolved with and found indispensable to our own health and functioning. Other animals too have coevolved with their chosen bacteria; but when we come into intimate contact with *them*, it is a very different story.

The exact origin of viruses is not yet fully understood, but they are clearly ancient organisms, since some forms of pox viruses have evolved using reptiles as their reservoir host, a process of coevolution that must extend back several hundred million years at the least.[12] Some virologists believe that viruses are the surviving descendants of primitive precellular life forms that have become extinct; but the prevailing hypothesis today is that viruses are "footloose genes," that is, pathologically active fragments that escaped or broke away from the cells of higher life forms.[13]

Viruses have carved out their niche in the biosphere by virtue of their structural simplicity, but they achieve this simplicity by relying entirely on the exploitation of their host cells for performing the basic functions of life.[14] Until they enter the cells of their host, viruses lack the structures necessary to manufacture proteins, metabolize energy sources, reproduce, or do the other things we usually ascribe to living organisms. Since they disagree about whether viruses are alive or not, scientists also disagree about the applicability of the theory of evolution via natural selection to viral adaptation or mutation. We know that many viruses are capable of genetic variation or adaptation at a very high rate, thus confounding attempts to destroy or suppress them with drugs. What remains still controversial is the extent to which this rate of adaptation is driven by genetic drift, or random mutations that spread through the population without (or possibly with) the intervention of natural selection.

Microparasites reproduce directly within the infected individual, called the host, usually at very high rates and in very short generation times. Hosts who recover from the infection usually acquire immunity against reinfection, sometimes for life. The duration of the infection is relatively short, and this plus acquired immunity means that microparasitic infections are typically of a transient nature. (There are exceptions to these general characteristics, to be noted in a moment.)

The interaction between microparasites and hosts is best described as the flow of pathogens around and through a host population that is divided into a few well-defined classes of individuals: susceptible (those vulnerable to infection), infected (subdivided into infectious, who can pass the disease to others, and latent, who cannot), and immune (either through recovery and acquired immunity, vaccination, or genetics). Two principles are at the heart of this model. The mass-action principle holds that the rate of disease spread is proportional to the product of the density of susceptibles times the density of infectious individuals, while the threshold principle holds that the introduction of infectious individuals into a community of susceptibles will not give rise to an epidemic outbreak unless the density of susceptible individuals is above a certain critical value.[15]

With microparasites, a minimum population density of hosts is necessary before the infection can take hold in the population and be self-sustaining. For example, cities in North America or Europe appear to require a population of between 200,000 and 300,000 to sustain measles infections at the epidemic level.[16] As the population density rises, the reinfection rate increases rapidly but there is a threshold of population density below which the infection will die out. The important exceptions to this rule are infections transmitted by intimate contact within a well-defined but small group of people, such as sexually transmitted diseases. Here, the reinfection rate is determined by the rate at which new partners enter the system. These parasites, which produce long-lasting diseases that do not confer acquired immunity, have adapted to survive within a small host population whose size and density are for the most part independent of the size and density of the larger population. In these instances, the behavior of the actual and potential hosts is the critical factor in determining disease survival and spread.

When we describe the symptoms of a given disease, we are describing the actions taken by the body's immune system to defend itself from invading cells, which it has defined as "foreign" or "not-self."[17] The immune system consists of organs scattered throughout the body, including the spleen, the thymus gland, lymph nodes, and bone marrow. These organs and others produce white blood cells called lymphocytes, which are carried through the lymph system to the blood, where they circulate, picking up and depositing many cells and particles. Some lymphocytes, called B cells, are programmed to produce antibodies, which are aimed at destroying microbes that float freely in the bloodstream. These cells form the antibody system. Other lymphocytes, called T cells, are programmed to attack pathogens that have invaded specific cells. These cells form the cell-mediated system. Both kinds of lymphocytes carry surface receptors that enable them to recognize and to collect in specific organs.

Lymphocytes have both nonspecific and specific activities. Nonspecific lymphocytes include phagocytes, whose job is to find, identify, and devour (by enveloping) alien cells. The pus that drains from an infected wound, for example, consists of phagocytes that have become filled with dead pathogens. When phagocytes collect in target tissue in sizable quantities, the condition manifests itself as inflammation of that tissue.

While phagocytes can absorb almost any kind of biological debris, B and T cells have more specialized responsibilities in the immune system. They carry out these functions by receiving messages via receptors on their surface called "markers." Each marker is programmed to recognize substances produced by invading pathogens, known as antigens. Collectively, the components of the human immune system can recognize ten million configurations of molecules, including antigens. When a B-cell receptor recognizes a particular antigen, the cell manufactures millions of plasma cells, each of which in turn produces millions of antibody molecules designed to fight off, kill, or expel the intruder in some way. What the antibodies then do to the body we interpret as "being sick": coughing, sneezing, vomiting, diarrhea, skin lesions, fever, joint pain, and much more. Fever, for example, inhibits the growth of bacteria by reducing the availability of iron in the body while simultaneously raising the bacterium's need for iron.[18]

The preceding description is "host-centric" in that it portrays the disease process from the perspective of the infected individual. But pathogens have a perspective as well. For one thing, they are under strong selective pressure to adapt to the body's defense measures and to evolve counter-measures. Moreover, as Jared Diamond reminds us, pathogens provoke the immune system into defenses like skin lesions, coughing, or diarrhea as a way of getting the host's body to assist in moving the pathogen to another potential victim.[19]

In many cases, the antibody system "remembers" the signals sent by antigens and produces antibodies immediately if such an antigen is ever detected again. The cell-mediated system possesses much the same capability. When a pathogen actually invades a cell, the cell displays surface markers that T cells recognize and attack. T cells can remember the foreign protein and keep the cell-mediated system on alert against the possibility of another invasion; we call this condition "immunity." Vaccination was invented in the eighteenth century as a way of artificially creating such a "memory" within the body by injecting dead or attenuated cells of the pathogen into the body and stimulating a very mild immune response. The success of vaccinations against smallpox, yellow fever, whooping cough, and measles raised hopes that a vaccine could be devised for every pathogen, but it has not turned out to be that easy. Vaccines can imprint on an immune system the signals of one strain of, say, the influenza virus; but the virus mutates so rapidly that when it invades the body, it is not recognized for what it is, and the immune system must be mobilized all over again to fight off the attack.[20]

Immunity is essentially a property of individuals, but the degree of immunity within a population can have a great impact on the vulnerability of that population to the spread of disease. Ranchers have discovered that it is not necessary to vaccinate all the animals in a herd against a disease. If a majority are immunized, the disease will disappear just as if the entire herd had been immunized. Once the immunized animals in the herd reach a certain proportion, they protect the non-immunized. The infectious organisms are reduced to such a small population of susceptibles that they cannot sustain themselves, and the disease dies away. This phenomenon, known as herd immunity, also applies to human populations.[21]

The response of the infected individual to an infection varies depending on whether the parasite is a virus, a bacterium, a protozoan, or a macroparasite.[22] As noted earlier, viruses such as measles or HIV must enter a host cell to reproduce. As the virus reproduces, the infection moves to a target organ such as the lungs or the nervous system. The body's immune system mounts a defense by recognizing specific antigens on the surface of the virus and the virally infected cells. The body mobilizes antibodies to attack these cells and either kill them or disrupt their reproduction or interaction. If these antibodies are successful, the infectious agent population ceases to grow and decays, either to extinction or to very low levels. If resistance is unsuccessful, the infection continues to grow, leading possibly to the death of the host. If the host survives, its immune system remembers the antigens and prevents the virus from gaining a foothold again.

Bacteria (for example, cholera, tuberculosis) and protozoa (such as malaria) are larger and more complex than viruses, but, most importantly, they are living organisms in their own right, capable of reproducing and metabolizing energy sources within their own cells. They exhibit more diverse antigens than do viruses, and thus oblige the host body to mobilize more diverse antibodies to counteract the invasion. Since they are alive within the host body, they can be killed without killing the host's cells or tissue, but their defeat does not usually confer immunity. Thus, diseases from these agents are more likely to be chronic and long lasting. They also possess a much greater ability to mutate within the host's body in response to antibodies or medicines.

Much less is known about the ability of humans to develop immunity against macroparasites.[23] Macroparasites such as worms elicit immunological responses from the host, but many macroparasites possess the ability to produce antigens that distract the immune system and pull the antibodies away from the infectious agents, which then continue to grow in number. Immunity to macroparasitic infections, if it exists at all, tends to be partial and short lived. The degree of protection of a given individual seems to depend more on genetic background and nutrition than on the generation of antibodies.

DISEASES, HUMANS, AND COEVOLUTION

Macroparasites exhibit free-living stages, meaning that they can survive outside the host, in some instances for quite a long time. Many of them also possess a certain degree of mobility. Microparasites, on the other hand, face much more difficult challenges. While some microparasites have mastered the art of reproduction, they all need a host for survival (viruses need a host merely to reproduce), and they generally cannot move any appreciable distance unaided.

In their struggle to invade and colonize new hosts before they destroy the old ones, microparasites have relatively few options (see figure 4.1).[24] Some infections can be passed directly from a pregnant mother to her child; this is called vertical transmission, and syphilis and AIDS are examples. A few species can pass from human to human by skin contact (rhinoviruses), in coughed or sneezed vapor droplets (measles, influenza), or by a mingling of body fluids (rabies, AIDS); this transmission method, called direct transmission, is analogous to transport by diffusion. Many microparasites, however, need an equivalent of "bulk flow"—that is, some force in their environment that carries them from host to host; this is known as indirect transmission.

Nature provides several kinds of carriers; human-built technologies supply others. Two kinds of carriers do not utilize other living species: air (influenza) and water (cholera). While winds and flowing rivers can move diseases long distances, there is a price to pay in the form of dilution. Thus, air and water are effective carriers only if the disease is densely packed to start with (as in cough droplets), or if the potential hosts are densely collected around the carrier (as the city of London packed people densely around the Thames).

Other species use living organisms as intermediate infected hosts to carry diseases.[25] These living carriers are called vectors (from Latin for "carrier"). Biting arthropods such as mosquitoes, fleas, flies, and ticks can carry a wide variety of

Figure 4.1   Transmission Routes of Viral Infections in Humans

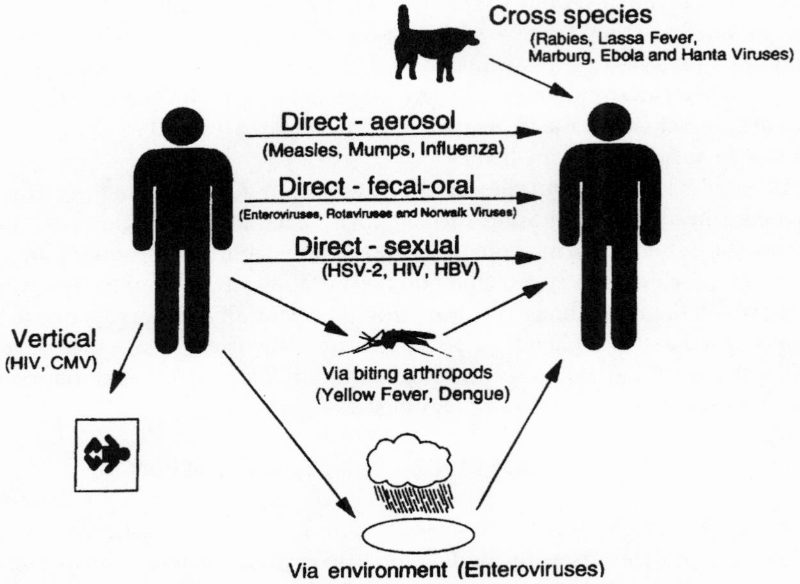

Via environment (Enteroviruses)

Note: Direct transmission can include sexual contact or fecal-oral contact. The sexually transmitted viruses, such as HIV, may also be transmitted by other processes during which blood is
exchanged. Some viruses that are transmitted by fecal-oral contact may also be released into the
environment, which provides a source of infection. The cross-species virus transmission can be from
rodents, from monkeys, or from domestic animals infected by wild animals.

Source: G.P. Garnett and R. Antia, "Population Biology of Virus-Host Interactions," In Stephen
Morse, ed., *The Evolutionary Biology of Viruses* (New York: Raven Press, 1994), Chapter 3, Fig. 2,
p. 54. © Lippincott Williams & Wilkins. Reprinted by permission.

diseases, including viruses known as arboviruses (that is, arthropod-borne viruses).[26] These arthropods have evolved the ability to produce an array of chemical
compounds that can overcome the defenses of the target animal, from blood co-
agulation to inflammation.[27] The large, swarming populations of these vectors can
be a great advantage for the parasites they carry; but this is often offset by their
brief life span (measured in days) and the fact that usually only a small percentage of the population of the carrier will actually be infected with the parasite.
Other living organisms particularly adept at carrying diseases include rodents of
all kinds, bats, and large animals, including humans.

Mosquito-borne parasites must live in at least two, and perhaps three, different kinds of organisms: the infected host, the mosquito vector, and (perhaps) the
reservoir host, where they must reside without causing morbidity, or at least without immobilizing the host.[28] From the perspective of coevolution, parasites that
have evolved to live in two or more species represent the most extreme form of

specialization.[29] Despite the high evolutionary cost of such an arrangement, thousands, if not tens of thousands, of species have evolved such complex life cycles that link species as different as, say, humans and mosquitoes (in malaria), or humans, rats, and ticks (in bubonic plague). Certain viruses and protozoans have evolved to use the transport services of one species (the vector) in order to be able to move between members of the ultimate or destination host (in this case, humans). These pathogens have selected as vectors tiny grazers with piercing mouthparts that can act as mobile hypodermic syringes. The pathogens achieve thereby an unusual degree of mobility that enables them to exploit a larger population of human hosts than would be the case if they were carried by air or water.

Arboviruses and other vector-borne diseases, such as malaria, yellow fever, dengue fever, or the various kinds of equine encephalitis, have been of great significance in history because insects have proven to be such efficient carriers of microparasites from one host species to another. Moreover, unlike human-to-human diseases that can be combated by inducing people to change their behavior, vector-borne diseases are virtually impossible to destroy because of the huge and unmanageable population of organisms that carry the pathogens.

Paul Ewald has coined the term "cultural vector" to refer to "a set of characteristics that allow transmission from immobilized hosts to susceptibles when at least one of the characteristics is some aspect of human culture."[30] "Culture" here has the widest possible meaning, referring to any product of human activity not passed genetically from one person to another. Cultural vectors can move the parasite from an infected individual to a susceptible one, or they can bring the infected and susceptible persons into direct contact with each other. Examples of cultural vectors would include contaminated municipal water supplies (which can transmit cholera); crowded trains or buses (influenza); spoiled or contaminated food (hepatitis, salmonella, shigella); infectious medical personnel, buildings, or equipment such as needles (staphylococcus); or environmental or social upheavals such as warfare (dysentery).

Epidemics occur when pathogenic microörganisms and hosts come into contact with each other for the first time.[31] Since these organisms have not had an opportunity to coevolve, the initial encounter is costly to the host, and perhaps to the pathogen as well, since, if too many of the host population die, the pathogen will also die out. Eventually hosts and pathogens may settle into a symbiotic relationship, although this is not inevitable. Such episodes occur whenever a stable ecosystem is disturbed, large numbers of humans or animals gather together in dense concentrations, or humans or animals are transported across the boundary between disease pools, all of which have taken place frequently as humans have become global.

Infectious parasites exhibit a remarkable ability to mutate very rapidly. It took eight million years for nonhuman primates to change just 2 percent of their DNA to become *Homo sapiens*; by contrast, the polio virus can change 2 percent of its genetic structure in just five days. A given virus may exhibit multiple strains nearly simultaneously, not only within the same host population but also within the same infected individual. Moreover, viruses possess the ability to mutate in ways that enable them to survive drugs or chemicals used to suppress them. New species of microparasites appear and go extinct in very short spans of time compared with other species. Speciation appears to occur with special speed and intensity when a species of microparasite jumps from one host species to another, as, for example, when the HIV jumped from nonhuman primates to humans (or, perhaps, vice versa) sometime during the last several hundred years.

A number of factors contribute to such a high rate of evolution.[32] Microparasites are often adapted for taking advantage of small environments widely separated from each other, and for exploiting critical resources with great efficiency. They are adapted to survive in highly unstable conditions and take great risks in colonizing a new host, since chances of failure and extinction are high; but they have evolved a very high rate of evolution and diversification so they can survive in a very risk-filled environment. Microparasites have evolved to be very proficient at adaptive radiation or at moving from one host to another in search of a more favorable niche; and their speciation apparently does not require geographic isolation, as is the case with larger animals.

The big issue in the coevolution of humans and diseases is whether diseases possess an inherent tendency to evolve toward less virulence. There is considerable controversy over whether micro- and macroparasites evolve in the course of an epidemic, and, if so, in which direction.[33]

Many epidemiologists and biologists believe that diseases facing the pressures of natural selection will over time attenuate, or become less virulent. ("Virulence" means in this context the ability of a parasite to induce morbidity or mortality in infected hosts.) They argue that diseases face a dilemma. If they attack a host too aggressively, they kill off the available host population before the disease can spread. Without a host population, the disease itself dies, having committed "suicide," figuratively speaking. The evolutionary imperative facing micröorganisms, then, is to coevolve with the host population so as to remain sufficiently virulent to infect succeeding generations of hosts, but not so virulent as to destroy the host population. Thus, the forces of natural selection are at work here to select for less virulent strains of a given disease. The task of survival is made much easier when the disease has access to large numbers of vulnerable hosts, especially if succeeding generations do not carry in their immune systems any protection against the disease (the origin of the so-called childhood diseases). For this reason, while harmful micröorganisms have certainly been with us since our earliest days on Earth, the spread of diseases had to await the two cultural achievements that brought humans into close contact with each other and with other animals: agriculture and cities. Before then, the human population was simply incapable of sustaining most infectious diseases for any appreciable period.[35]

A widely accepted paradigm in epidemiology today portrays the parasite as infecting growing numbers of the host population up to a point where the death rate exceeds the rate at which new individuals are entering the population (via birth or immigration), at which point the infection begins to subside.[36] Eventually, the population of susceptibles rises again, whereupon the disease resumes its expansion, only to decline once again as deaths exceed births and immigration. The curve of infection continues its rise and fall, oscillating around a central value but never quite declining to extinction. At some point, the disease comes to be regarded not as exotic or alien, but as native or indigenous, a "normal" feature of a given population, at which point we can say that the disease has been transformed from epidemic to endemic. Natural selection is supposed to be the chief agent here, selecting for survival and reproduction of those parasites that are disposed by genetics to be of moderate virulence.[37]

The case usually cited to illustrate this dynamic involves the spread of myxoma virus through the Australian population of rabbits.[38] To combat an overpopulation of rabbits in Australia, the virus was introduced in 1950, and its progress was closely monitored. Within several years, a clear trend was seen toward moderating virulence, and by the middle to late 1960s, virtually all the cases registered were afflicted with a virus of intermediate virulence. The mechanism of transmission— via mosquitoes taking blood from a skin lesion of an infected rabbit to a susceptible one—selected for the virus strain of moderate virulence, since it was the one that left rabbits with fresh lesions alive longest. More virulent strains killed the rabbits quickly; less virulent strains allowed the lesions to heal quickly; in both cases, these strains were not easily accessible to the mosquitoes. Unfortunately (for those trying to eradicate the rabbit overpopulation), the rabbits also adapted to the virus. Rabbits with genetic resistance to the virus survived, left more offspring, and very quickly came to dominate the rabbit population. In those area where resistant rabbits increased, it was necessary to resort to the most virulent strain of the virus to continue the destruction of the rabbits. Thus, even though the moderate strains of the virus continued to predominate, there was selective pressure toward increased virulence as the rabbits increased their resistance.

The proposition that natural selection works to make diseases evolve toward less virulent strains has been extremely influential in explaining the role of infectious diseases in the process of globalization.[39] Scholars have described this process as the gradual erosion of barriers of terrain and distance that separated human populations into isolated disease pools. Within each population's respective pool (for example, China or Mesoamerica), the population gradually co-evolved with the local pathogens until they reached a *modus vivendi* with each other. In the course of globalization, however, humans crossed these boundaries many times (as in the slave trade between 1600 and 1800), and local populations had to adapt to new pathogens. The adjustment process was extremely painful for these human populations (such as for Europeans in the fourteenth century with the bubonic plague), but eventually they either adapted or perished. In any case, the diseases gradually evolved toward less virulence at the same time that disease pools merged into a single global pool. The AIDS pandemic is the most recent example of this process at work.

Not all biologists accept this paradigm, however. Paul Ewald, for example, argues that there is no inherent reason why diseases should evolve toward a less virulent form, that the interplay of a disease with its host as well as with any intervening vectors is actually extremely complex and involves many different factors, and in fact the trend might go in the opposite direction, toward greater virulence.[40] The paradigm sketched out above works if the transmissibility and duration of infectiousness are entirely independent of virulence, a case seldom seen in the real world. Once the disease begins to interact with many different factors in the environment, however, many coevolutionary paths are possible. For example, for viral infections, there is usually a trade-off between mortality rate and transmission rate such that a slow-replicating virus is less likely to kill its host but also less likely to be retransmitted to another host. Vector-borne diseases frequently evolve toward greater virulence because (1) the vector itself is not affected by the increased virulence, and (2) the disease can immobilize the infected and still rely on the mosquito or tick to help it reach distant potential hosts.[41] Where we do find diseases that were highly lethal in the distant past but are now relatively mild, like measles, they are apt to be transmitted by some method other than a vector. Other interactions between host and parasite that influence the virulence of the latter suggest, as Garnett and Antia argue, that infectious diseases are not unnatural relations between host and parasite but the natural consequence of their coevolution.[42]

The pressure of natural selection on parasites that causes them to evolve to a state in which they do not cause disease in the host is alleged to be the reason why we see micröorganisms that are harmless in their natural hosts (that is, when the product of lengthy coevolution) but lethal when they jump to another species. Some scientists have argued that this must be the case for all parasites that use infected intermediaries to carry them from host to host. For example, the protozoans that cause malaria in humans do not make the mosquitoes that carry them ill. Alphaviruses, however, do cause lesions on the mosquitoes that carry them from host to host, but they do not seem to be evolving toward a less virulent strain since a moderate level of virulence actually improves the chances of the transmission of the virus.[43]

It may well be, however, that both parasites and hosts have been adapting to each other over many generations. Humans adapt to diseases just as diseases adapt to humans. The human genome has evolved to cope with the variety of pathogens to which humans have been exposed around the world.[44] Natural selection works here to reward individuals who possess genes that are associated with phenotype features that resist, ward off, or deceive attacking micröorganisms.

For example, at least five genetic mutations have been identified that protect against malaria.[45] Many West Africans possess a gene that deforms their red blood cells into a sickle shape. While this deformity leads to anemia and thus would be selected against under otherwise neutral conditions, in West Africa it is a positive benefit because it confers protection against malaria on its bearers. Another genetic condition found among West Africans is known as the human leucocyte antigen (HLA), which protects the bearer against malaria by mobilizing the body's immune system. West Africans also have a blood group gene known as Fy Fy, as well as a deficiency trait in the X chromosome, both of which help protect against malaria. This latter condition is also found throughout the tropical Old World, especially in Asia. In Southeast Asia, another genetic buffer against malaria is hemoglobin E.

A second example, just recently discovered, involves a genetic mutation that protects some individuals against AIDS even though they are HIV-positive.[46] This genetic mutation produces a class of cells called macrophages whose surface lacks a protein to which HIV binds in order to gain entry to the cell and infect it. Without this surface protein, HIV cannot infect the cell, and the bearers of these kind of cells are virtually immune to AIDS. This mutant allele is not distributed evenly across the world's population. Native Americans, Asians, and Africans almost never possess it, and African Americans do only very rarely. The gene is fairly prevalent among Europeans and European Americans, however, leading to speculation that long ago Europe's population experienced an epidemic that killed huge numbers of people with the so-called normal gene but spared those with the mutation. These latter then went on to constitute a larger-than-normal proportion of the population. Genetic analysis suggests that the epidemic struck about forty-three hundred years ago, and certainly no more recently than twelve hundred years ago. The center of the epidemic must have been in northwestern Europe, since the incidence of the mutant gene grows significantly as one moves north and west away from the Mediterranean. Other more recent evidence has been interpreted by some researchers to suggest that the bubonic plague that struck Europe in the fourteenth century was responsible for this genetic feature of today's European population.[47]

SOME INFECTIOUS DISEASES OF HUMANS

We do not know exactly how many micröorganisms cause illness in humans, but it would be safe to say that they number in the hundreds. By one count, humans share almost 300 diseases with domesticated animals, and about 100 more with wild birds and animals.[48] More than 500 viruses are carried by arthropods, and nearly 100 of these cause human illness.[49] Mosquitoes alone are the vectors of more than 250 identified viruses, of which at least 80 cause disease in humans.[50] To these we should add bacteria, protozoans, worms, and other multicellular pathogens, and perhaps some other agents such as viroids and prions. Moreover, it is unwarranted to presume that we have already experienced all the infectious diseases our environment is capable of inflicting on us. Prudence dictates that we assume that there are pathogens that have not yet jumped to humans, and that we have yet to feel their impact.

What follows, therefore, is not a complete inventory of the infectious diseases of humans, but rather a very select list that illustrates their range and principal features. While other organizing principles would be possible (such as organs or tissue affected), I have classified them by mode of transmission, since that seems most significant for our understanding of globalization. A few of the more historically significant diseases (influenza, bubonic plague, AIDS, tuberculosis) are discussed elsewhere.

Direct Transmission across Species

For a pathogen to be transmitted directly from another species to a human, the human must have close contact with the other animal. Diseases of this sort were common millennia ago, when humans and their domesticated animals lived close together; but most people today live separated from other animals except their pets, so these diseases have become relatively less significant in industrialized countries. Nevertheless, when they occur, they tend to be especially severe.

Rabies is one of these diseases that we still encounter in contemporary urban life.[51] The rabies virus resides in the saliva of canines such as dogs and foxes, and enters the human bloodstream via a bite from an infected animal. Because of this demanding method of transmission, the virus had to evolve the capability to provoke biting episodes in its hosts. To accomplish this, the virus must seize control of the host's brain, bringing about convulsions and eventually death. In 1996, there were an estimated ten million cases of rabies worldwide, resulting in about sixty thousand deaths.[52]

Hantavirus is another class of pathogen transmitted directly to humans from another animal, in this case rodents.[53] Health professionals first became aware of the disease caused by this virus in the 1950s, when over two thousand U.S. troops serving in Korea came down with what was later named Korean hemorrhagic fever. The pathogen was named the Hantaan virus for the river in Korea near where the epidemic occurred. Since then, several more varieties of the virus have been identified and are collectively referred to as hantaviruses. The pathogens are transmitted via the saliva, urine, and feces of infected rodents such as deer mice. After the mouse droppings dry, the micröorganisms are caught up in the dust and carried by wind currents to nearby hosts who inhale it. The disease exhibits extremely high fever, bleeding, shock, kidney failure, and pneumonia. Varieties of the hantavirus have been discovered all over the world, from Korea to the Balkans, from Baltimore slums to Navajo farms in New Mexico.

Direct Transmission between Humans

Several of the diseases in this category, such as measles, were extremely virulent in ancient populations, but have attenuated in populations that have experienced urbanization and industrialization. Nevertheless, they are capable of resurgence in industrial societies, and they still ravage populations in developing countries today.

Some of these diseases are aerosols—that is, they are transmitted by vapor droplets in the breath of infected persons—and include measles, mumps, and influenza. Measles, also known as rubeola, is a highly contagious fever caused by an airborne virus. The fever is followed by a skin rash and other symptoms such as swollen neck glands and ear infections. Up to the early 1960s, the United States recorded about half a million cases of measles annually; but since 1963, when an effective vaccine became available, the incidence has declined sharply. The disease continues to appear and reappear in American cities, but at much reduced levels. Measles is still, however, a major killer worldwide. In 1996, according to the World Health Organization, there were about forty-two million cases of measles reported, and slightly more than one million deaths were attributed to the disease, making it the eleventh leading cause of death in the world.[54]

A second set of diseases are transmitted from one human to another via an anal-fecal-oral route. A number of parasites are carried in fecal matter from host to host, usually by the water supply, but also by contaminated food handled by an infected person. Although, in theory, vectors of these pathogens need not be very complex, in practice cultural vectors such as a municipal water system are required to move the pathogens in sufficient concentration to sustain an epidemic.

Typhoid is one such disease, caused by a bacterium spread in human fecal matter via the agent *Salmonella typhi*.[55] Of the at least fifteen hundred different strains of salmonella, most are harmless, but a few can bring on the symptoms of typhoid. The disease produces a rash of rose-colored spots on the chest and abdomen, and bloody stool caused by the extensive damage the pathogen inflicts on the gut. A severe case will also exhibit high fever, delirium, and even heart failure. Typically, the cultural vector of typhoid is contamined water used in densely populated urban areas. The force of this disease has been declining steadily as standards of personal hygiene and environmental sanitation, including waste water treatment, have improved worldwide.

Persons carrying this disease may infect others, however, even though they show no outward symptoms of the disease. Typhoid is proving difficult to eradicate because typhoid bacilli migrate to the gall bladder, where they can hide from the body's defenses and linger on in the body of recovering patients. At some point, the disease can emerge again to spread through a population thought to be rid of it. In some patients, the disease never does disappear; one of the most infamous of these cases involved an infected cook named Mary Mallon, who migrated from job to job working in the homes of well-to-do families in the New York–New Jersey area, spreading typhoid as she went. Eventually "Typhoid Mary" was tracked down and detained in isolation for some thirty years until she died of a stroke.

Typhoid takes different forms depending on where in the world it occurs. In temperate zones, the pathogen cannot live for long outside the body, so it has evolved a very invasive strategy of penetrating all the way to the liver and gall bladder, where it can live indefinitely. Since the disease is more invasive, it lingers for a long time and kills a high percentage of its victims. In the tropics, the strains of salmonella can survive outside the body for a longer time and so can remain alive for the time they need to leave one host and be carried by a local water supply to infect others. Thus, in the tropics, salmonella tends to be much less invasive, producing enteric fever instead of typhoid. Survival rates are much higher, and not as many hosts remain infected.

Cholera is another bacterial disease that is carried in fecal matter from infected persons, but unlike typhoid, people carrying cholera who do not exhibit overt signs of infection are usually not infectious.[56] Outbreaks are typically initiated by contaminated water supplies, and they either die out naturally by exhausting the susceptible population or are controlled by the addition of chlorine to the water supply. The cholera bacillus works by secreting a toxin that upsets the delicate balance of the passage of water through the intestinal wall into and out of the bowel. The infected digestive system receives a violent flood of water into the gut, which is subsequently expelled as diarrhea, and the victim begins to become dehydrated. In extreme cases, these attacks may be followed by high fever, cramps, and convulsions.

Since the first recorded outbreak of cholera near Calcutta in 1817, there have been seven pandemics, the most recent of which began in the 1960s and reached the Americas in 1991. A possible eighth pandemic may have already started in eastern India and Bangladesh. Before the introduction of rehydration therapy, the cholera death rate ran as high as 50 percent. In 1996, however, of the 120,000 cases of cholera worldwide, only 6,000 were fatal.[57]

Experts disagree about how long cholera has been present in humans.[58] Paul Ewald believes that cholera is very likely one of the oldest diseases to reach epidemic levels in dense human populations.[59] While we have no direct knowledge of such epidemics, there is considerable indirect evidence that ancient cities in what are today India and Pakistan relied on water systems that could easily have harbored and transmitted cholera. Between 3000 and 1800 B.C., the Harappan civilization constructed cities with water systems based on public wells that had openings just a few inches above street level. Human waste was drained away from dwellings by simple holes in the walls or floor, either directly into drainages or into wastewater pots and then into drains. When water sources lie within or near networks or leaky drainage lines, pathogens from fecal matter are easily recycled back into the drinking water. During periods of heavy rains, when these systems were overloaded, the danger from spreading diseased fecal matter is great. At the beginning of the second millennium B.C., the Harappan cities were effectively abandoned for reasons that remain unknown, but they could have included cholera epidemics that made urban life untenable.

A final method of direct transmission is by the intermingling of body fluids of two people, one of whom is infected. Sexually transmitted diseases (STDs) fall into this category, as do those transmitted by saliva and blood and those passed vertically from a pregnant mother to her unborn child. The most serious threat to public health today in this category comes, of course, from HIV and its disease, AIDS. The other STDs have attenuated, and even though they now cause about 400 million new infections each year, few of these prove to be fatal.[60]

STDs were much more virulent in the past, however, and one of those of greatest historical significance was syphilis.[61] Along with typhus, syphilis is referred to by Arno Karlen as "typical new plagues of the first age of global exploration and conquest."[62] That is, syphilis became a global disease after 1500 as a consequence of enormous changes in warfare, conquest, population growth and movements, clothing, and sexual behavior. In the sixteenth and seventeenth centuries, syphilis swept through Europe, manifesting itself in various stages as, first, minor skin lesions, followed by horrific skin lesions and pustules. In the third and final stage, the disease migrated to the spinal cord and the brain, producing insanity, paralysis, and death. Over time, however, syphilis attenuated to a much less virulent form; and since the 1930s, when penicillin was found to be a powerful cure, the disease has diminished to the level of a widespread but nonfatal illness.

A great controversy rages over the source of syphilis and its method of transmission to Europe and Asia. The disease appeared in Europe for the first time in 1495 and raged like wildfire through what was obviously an unprepared population; the usual interpretation has been that syphilis was unknown in Europe before Columbus's first voyage and was brought back by his crew and/or by the ten natives of Hispaniola whom Columbus took back to Europe. Some scholars have taken issue with this explanation, however, arguing that there are signs that syphilis existed in Europe before 1492; but this evidence is ambiguous and certainly not uncontested.

Indirect Transmission

This category is something of a misnomer, since the vectors are in fact infected hosts that serve as intermediaries, carrying the pathogens between two other hosts (which may or may not be of the same species). One of the principal examples of indirect transmission are the arboviruses (for arthropod-borne viruses).

Malaria is the most serious arbovirus today, killing about two million people worldwide each year, one million in Africa alone.[63] In 1996, malaria was the seventh leading cause of death worldwide, and the fourth leading cause among infectious diseases. It was also the second leading cause of morbidity in the world, infecting between 300 and 500 million people.[64]

Malaria is caused by one of four protozoan species belonging to the genus *Plasmodium*. The infection in humans begins when the parasites are injected into the blood by the female mosquito of the genus *Anopheles*. After migrating to the liver, the parasites mature and reproduce, after which they spread out and invade red blood cells. The disease is then retransmitted to another mosquito as it feeds on the blood of the host, and the cycle begins anew. The parasites remain in the gut of the mosquito for ten days or so and then migrate to its salivary glands, ready to be transmitted to another vertebrate host.

Faced with the imperative to survive in cold climates without a steady population of mosquito vectors to infect, the strains of malaria found in the temperate zones have evolved (or retained) the ability to deposit "sleeping cells" (called "hypnozoites") in the liver of the host and thus to remain alive until warm weather frees them to jump to another host (or cause relapses in the original host). Of the four varieties of malaria, one, *falciparum*, is confined to the tropics; it is also the most virulent.[65] In the tropics, however, *falciparum* never evolved the "sleeping" ability (or lost it) because there are always mosquitoes available to carry the strain from host to host. It is believed that *falciparum* remains especially virulent for two reasons: (1) because it has only recently jumped from other species (birds) to humans and has not had time to adapt to human hosts; and (2) its preferred vector, *Anopheles* mosquitoes, are also resistant to malaria, and the protozoans must literally overwhelm the mosquito in order to infect it.

Malaria manifests itself through bouts of fever, grossly enlarged liver and spleen, and anemia. Recovery does not necessarily bring about immunity, and reinfection can occur. Moreover, genetic variety in the parasite population makes reinfection highly probable. Human hosts can harbor simultaneous infections by different species of malaria or by different strains of the same species, and each will evolve according to a different pattern. The parasite has evolved resistance to antimalarial drugs, the mosquitoes have evolved resistance to insecticides, and the disease even mutates within the host in response to actions taken by the host's immune system. Obviously, this coevolved system involving humans, mosquitoes, and parasites is highly complex, and not easy for epidemiologists to model.

Yellow fever and dengue fever are two other serious arboviruses, killing between twenty thousand and thirty thousand worldwide each year.[66] Yellow fever is caused by a virus transmitted by the mosquito *Aedes aegypti*. An urban form of the disease is carried from person to person, while a jungle form is transmitted between nonhuman primates and occasionally to humans. Today the disease is of much less significance than it was historically, thanks to the development of an effective vaccine, but it is still prevalent in tropical areas of the Americas and Africa. It is endemic in many urban areas but periodically explodes in epidemics in rural areas. Dengue resembles yellow fever closely in its modes of transmission, host species (human and nonhuman primates), and existence in both urban and rural forms. Its symptoms are also similar, but it can also exhibit hemorrhagic fever, meaning that high fever is accompanied by bleeding. Vaccines are not yet available, so control and suppression are based on attacking the vector, the *Aedes aegypti* mosquito.

Environmental Hazards

Some infectious diseases are more correctly seen as environmental hazards, since their parasites reside not in another species but instead in some feature of the environment, such as the soil or the water. Tetanus is one such disease.[67] The tetanus toxin *Clostridium tetani* resides in the soil, and its infectiousness is linked to climate, soil use (agriculture, animal husbandry), and overall level of economic development. It enters the body through open wounds or through unhygienic delivery conditions during childbirth. In developing countries, among newborns the disease is fatal 90 percent of the time, and among adults, 40 percent. In 1996, there were some 385,000 cases of neonatal tetanus reported, 310,000 of which led to death of the newborn;[68] there may have been about 15,000 other deaths caused by tetanus.

DISEASES AND GLOBALIZATION

Were *Homo sapiens* not such a migratory species, we probably would not have had such difficulties with infectious diseases. When humans (or any other species) live for a very long time in a stable environment, they and the local micröorganisms adapt to each other, and a certain disease equilibrium is reached between the two populations. The growth of population, the movement of people into new environments, and the subsequent modification of those environments—all of which happen during globalization—disrupt this equilibrium. Either the newcomers encounter new diseases and new vectors, or they bring their own pathogens with them to infect the natives of their new homeland, or both.[69] Whichever the case, infectious diseases causing massive suffering and death have been part of the price we have paid for globalization.

Plagues afflict us because we have upset the balance of nature; and, observes Christopher Wills, "we have been upsetting this balance for a very long time."[70] The coevolution of diseases and humans has roots that reach back before the existence of *Homo sapiens*:[71] Some four million years ago, the descent of prehominids from trees to the forest floor exposed them to new ecological zones and thus to new pathogens. About two million years ago, *Homo erectus* became carnivorous, thus exposing themselves to pathogens carried in the flesh of other animals. The migration of *Homo erectus* and *Homo sapiens* out of Africa exposed them to new climates, ecosystems, and pathogens.

Relatively little is known of the health conditions of the earliest human populations, but some inferences can be drawn based on our understanding of the size, composition, distribution, and diet of that population. Half the population died before reaching the age of ten, and no more than 20 percent survived past forty; life expectancy may have been about twenty-five years.[72] Diseases certainly played a role in maintaining these population dynamics. Bands of hunter-gatherers living 15,000 years ago would have numbered between 20 and 200 individuals. At that density, most microparasitic infections could not have been maintained, but macroparasites—such as worms—and some microparasites with long-lasting infectiousness—such as hepatitis and the sexually transmitted diseases—could have been. Some other diseases that can be maintained in other host species—or even in the soil—and passed relatively easily to humans would have also been significant, such as tetanus.

About ten thousand years ago, the Neolithic Revolution brought about a major change in the relationship of humans to pathogens.[73] Paleontologists examining skeletons and ancient cultural artifacts from such widely separated sites as

Ecuador, New Mexico, and Illinois have confirmed that the health of local residents grew progressively worse as agriculture spread and population centers grew.[74] Farming as a way of life transformed widely scattered populations that were fairly constantly on the move into densely concentrated, sedentary groups; and both of these changes made the populations more susceptible to the spread of disease. The labor associated with farming brought humans into close contact with their own urine and feces (and later, that of animals) used as fertilizer, with disturbed soil that harbored micröorganisms, and with water used for irrigation and therefore not moving and cleaning itself as a river would. Food production required the destruction of forests, which brought humans into contact with previously stable ecosystems and the micröorganisms they sheltered, and it attracted rodents and other parasites looking for an easily accessible food supply. Reliance on a few stable crops also caused nutritional deficiencies that not only produced their own distinctive pathologies (such as anemia, rickets) but also weakened people and made them more susceptible to invasion by micröorganisms.

Most important, farming brought humans into close contact with animals for the first time, exposing humans to the pathogens they carried. The indirect evidence uncovered in the bones of early farmers shows that the domestication of animals had negative consequences for humans as far as disease is concerned.[75] Recall that farmers had more success domesticating herd animals like cattle or sheep because of their docility and respect for hierarchy and authority. But pathogens like densely crowded animal populations, just as they prefer dense populations of humans in which to live; so when farmers domesticated herd animals they were also bringing into our world the species that harbored the greatest number and variety of pathogens. Today, humans share 65 diseases with dogs (including whooping cough), 45 to 50 with cattle (including smallpox, tuberculosis, and measles), 46 with sheep and goats, 35 with horses, 26 with poultry, and 42 with pigs (including influenza, which also resides in ducks).[76]

Population growth during the ten millennia before the Industrial Revolution proceeded at two dramatically different rates.[77] For the five millennia before the Bronze Age (from 8000 B.C. to 3000 B.C.), population rose twenty-fold, from 5 million to 100 million. During this period, mortality rates rose (because of infectious diseases transmitted from animals), but fertility rates rose even faster. Using data from Catal Huyük, in Turkey, one of the first places where extensive agriculture was practiced, Christopher Wills demonstrates that human populations suffered high rates of infant mortality, losing 40 percent of their number before the age of five years; and virtually no one lived beyond what today is middle age.[78] If a person could survive the diseases of childhood, however, his or her middle years would probably not have presented much of a threat until the stresses of drought, starvation, toil, and accidents began to claim those above the age of forty.

For all but the last 300 years of the next five millennia (from 3000 B.C. to the Industrial Revolution), population grew only fivefold (100 to 500 million), primarily because of an increase in death rates. These increased mortality rates were brought on by two factors: urbanization and long-distance travel.

Urbanization

The crowding produced by urbanization turned cities into graveyards, at least until the technological innovations of the Industrial Revolution could be focused on the purification of water and the disposal of human waste.[79] Some three thousand years ago, the rise of cities brought humans in large numbers into close contact with each other for the first time. In 430 B.C. the city of Athens was laid waste by the first recorded urban plague[80]—one that also marked the first time that disease was transmitted over a long distance. The origin of the plague remains a mystery, but Africa is a likely source. The disease remained in Athens five years, and killed between one-fourth and one-third of the city's population. The effects were horrendous: the victims suffered a maddening fever, followed by bloodshot eyes, vomiting and bleeding, skin lesions, and diarrhea. Death occurred in the huge majority of cases, typically within seven to nine days. The disease spread with ease throughout the city's population, including those attending the sick; but Spartan soldiers besieging the city a few hundred yards away were unaffected. Some of the greatest minds produced by ancient Greece succumbed to the disease, including the great political leader, Pericles. The disease is usually credited with ending the Golden Age of Greece.

Epidemiologists and historians have labored for years to identify the disease that struck Athens.[81] They are hampered by the lack of recorded accounts; the only one left behind is that of the historian Thucydides, who lacked a medical vocabulary to describe the symptoms accurately. Thucydides claimed that the disease originated in Africa south of Ethiopia; and that plus the symptoms have led some researchers to suspect Ebola virus. But Ebola works so swiftly, and ancient transport facilities were so slow, that a virus-carrying monkey and its human handlers would have died long before reaching Athens. Influenza seems a good candidate, but its epidemics last only a few months, not five years. The nature of the skin lesions is not clear from the Greek text, so it cannot be determined if they were blisters, which might suggest smallpox, or some other kind of skin affliction, which might make bubonic plague a possible candidate.

Two millennia later, city life exhibited yet more appalling health conditions. Death rates in seventeenth-century London were in some respects worse than those of Catal Huyük or Bronze Age Athens. Infant mortality was only slightly improved, with one-third of the population dying by age six. A select few could actually look forward to reaching age sixty and beyond; but for the immense majority, life during the middle years, from the teens to age fifty, was a constant struggle against the crowding diseases of urban life: cholera, tuberculosis, bubonic plague, and the like.[82]

The conditions of urban health began to improve as early as the first half of the eighteenth century, however, even before the germ theory of disease, sanitation, or improved public health measures.[83] In London in 1728, infant mortality rates were still as high as they had been for centuries, but more and more adults were living into their forties and fifties. This trend continued through the first half of the nineteenth century, and then accelerated sharply after 1860, when such technologies as indoor toilets, waste-water treatment, and sewers became regular features of urban life. In the early 1850s, John Snow—a British physician/researcher and one of the pioneers in epidemiology—finally uncovered the connection between cholera and contaminated public water supplies.[84] Following this discovery, the British government forced through a number of measures to reform the unsanitary water treatment system serving London, and cholera disappeared from the city forever.

Wills concludes from these data that two factors were working to reduce the incidence and virulence of infectious diseases in urban populations. Improved sanitation and public health measures after 1860 had a significant impact; the trend toward fewer deaths from disease among the adult population had already set in a century and a half earlier; and that, he argues, was because of the attenuation of infectious pathogens as they coevolved with their human hosts.

Long-distance Travel

The second factor that raised death rates was the spread of many infectious diseases into areas where they had never existed before. Since the Neolithic Revolution, each episode of globalization has been accompanied by the spread of devastating diseases. As human populations and cultures followed new land and water trade routes, the Earth gradually became a single gene pool for many diseases. Each round of population expansion was accompanied by lengthy periods of epidemics, as the local population and the pathogens gradually adapted to each other. In some instances, especially where the two came together on islands (the Caribbean, Hawaii, Polynesia), the consequences were so severe that the native population declined to virtual extinction. These processes were so important to the story of globalization that I examine them in greater detail in the case studies that follow.

The first example of a near-global disease pool came with the linking together of the component empires of the Eurasian Ecumene in the first century B.C. Ancient trade routes like the Silk Road brought the bubonic plague to Europe not once but several times. The Black Death swept through Europe in the mid-fourteenth century, having been carried by caravans of traders and nomads out of the Eurasian steppes.

European expansion after 1500 globalized the gene pools of humans, foods, and diseases. In the sixteenth century, the Columbian Exchange brought the catastrophe of European diseases to vulnerable native populations,[85] and destroyed as much as 90 percent of the Amerindians within a century.[86] The slave trade brought African diseases to the Americas, including yaws, which vanished when the slave trade ended, and malaria, which did not.[87]

From about 1800 on, the rise of large industrial cities and the advent of steam transport spread the "crowding diseases" through Europe.[88] The great European migrations of the mid-nineteenth century were afflicted by the horrendous death tolls that accompanied the slow passage across the Atlantic:[89] In the days before steam, it took more than two weeks to make the crossing, and passengers usually had to wait another fifteen days in quarantine before they could disembark; infectious diseases could sweep through a ship's population and inflict great losses. In the cramped quarters of the sailing ships of that period, and with poor hygiene and inadequate medical attention, it was not uncommon for more than half a ship's passengers to die before reaching port. Typhus and dysentery were especially virulent under these conditions. In 1847, for example, of the more than 100,000 emigrants who left the United Kingdom for Canada, 17,000 died during the voyage, and 20,000 more died in Canada within one year of their arrival.

Transport technologies powered by fossil fuels—the steamship, the railroad, and the airplane—have increased by orders of magnitude the possibilities for the rapid spread of communicable diseases. Humans have mounted what defenses they can against these threats, including improved urban sanitary and public health measures and tighter controls over the movement of people across international borders. These measures have reduced the possibility of serious pandemics, but occasionally the pathogens prove too elusive, or some human agency lets down its guard, and a global disease is the result.

One of the worst of these episodes—probably *the* worst, if measured in terms of deaths produced—was the great influenza pandemic of 1918–1919.[90] This global epidemic killed an estimated twenty-one million victims worldwide, but the real statistics can never be known and were probably considerably higher than this. (One observer reported that the death toll in the Indian subcontinent alone was twenty million.) Alfred Crosby estimates that in the United States, 675,000 died of the flu and its related companion, pneumonia, between September 1918 and June 1919. The disease spread around the world in three more or less distinct waves, all of which came and went in less than a year. The first wave was a mild strain of flu that originated on U.S. military bases and was carried abroad on American troop ships bound for European ports like Brest, in France. As the disease spread through Eurasia, Africa, and the Pacific islands, it rapidly mutated so that when it began its second wave, in August 1918, it had become much more virulent. Although it remains the subject of much conjecture, many observers believe that the disease became extremely virulent as it passed through the ranks of troops living in trenches under very difficult and nonhygienic conditions.

Accompanied by pneumonia, the epidemic hit especially hard at healthy young adults between ages twenty and forty, apparently because their immune systems responded so vigorously to the infection that their lungs filled with blood and they literally drowned in their own disease. The disease was indiscriminate, striking the humble as well as the exalted. President Woodrow Wilson and the French premier, Georges Clemenceau, were both victims of the disease while attending the Paris Peace Conference that drew up the terms of the end of World War I. Despite a massive research effort, the cause of the influenza, a virus whose natural home is in swine, was not isolated until 1933.

In the first half of the twentieth century, successes in antibiotics, immunizations, public health measures, water purification, and sewage disposal led to a popular belief that epidemics were conquered. Since the 1960s, however, there has been a series of epidemics of diseases, viral and otherwise, some previously known and others not. Six factors have been identified as possible causes: breakdown of public health measures, economic development and land use, international trade and travel, technology and industry, human demographics (population growth, increased urban density) and behavior, and microbial adaptation and change.[91]

The emerging infectious diseases of the 1980s and 1990s are the result of a number of complex social trends, including global travel and the drive to push back the edges of tropical rainforests in search of new land for food production. The rapid movement of people, products, and news around the world means that we now confront the globalization of crises and hazards. Diseases like AIDS or influenza can spread around the world at unprecedented speeds. As Richard Preston put it, "A hot virus from the rain forest lives within a twenty-four-hour plane flight from every city on earth. All of the earth's cities are connected by a web of airline routes. The web is a network. Once a virus hits the net, it can shoot anywhere in a day—Paris, Tokyo, New York, Los Angeles, wherever planes fly."[92]

NOTES

1. Roy Anderson and Robert May, *Infectious Diseases of Humans: Dynamics and Control* (Oxford: Oxford University Press, 1991), p. 641.

2. An "epidemic" is a disease event that causes morbidity far beyond its normal levels or limits but that is still confined in time and space. A "pandemic" is an epidemic of continental or even global scope. A "plague" is an epidemic or pandemic accompanied by high death rates. For more, see Christopher Wills, *Yellow Fever, Black Goddess: The Coevolution of People and Plagues* (Reading, Mass.: Addison Wesley, 1996), p. 8.

3. William McNeill, *The Rise of the West: A History of the Human Community* (Chicago: University of Chicago Press, 1963, 1991), chapter 7.

4. Anderson and May, *Infectious Diseases of Humans*, p. 3. See also Roy Anderson, "Directly Transmitted Viral and Bacterial Infections of Man," in Anderson, *Population Dynamics of Infectious Diseases: Theory and Applications* (London: Chapman and Hall, 1982), pp. 2–3.

5. Paul Ewald, *Evolution of Infectious Diseases* (Oxford: Oxford University Press, 1994), chapter 10.

6. Ewald, *Evolution of Infectious Diseases*, pp. 59–60.

7. Anderson and May, *Infectious Diseases of Humans*, chapter 2; Roy Anderson and Robert May, "Population Biology of Infectious Diseases: Part I," *Nature*, vol. 280 (August 2, 1979): p. 362.

8. Ann Giudici Fettner, *The Science of Viruses* (New York: W. Morrow, 1990), chapter 3.

9. David Brown, "At Cow Scare's Core: An Odd Protein," *Washington Post*, April 8, 1996.

10. Arno Karlen, *Man and Microbes: Disease and Plagues in History and Modern Times* (New York: Putnam, 1995), pp. 13–17.

11. Stephen Jay Gould, *Full House: The Spread of Excellence from Plato to Darwin* (New York: Harmony, 1996), pp. 176–95.

12. Frank Fenner and Peter Kerr, "Evolution of the Poxviruses, Including the Co-evolution of Virus and Host in Myxomatosis," in *The Evolutionary Biology of Viruses*, ed. Stephen Morse (New York: Raven, 1994), table 1, pp. 274–75.

13. Stephen Morse, "Toward an Evolutionary Biology of Viruses," in Morse, *Evolutionary Biology of Viruses*, pp. 2–7.

14. G. P. Garnett and R. Antia, "Population Biology of Virus-Host Interactions," in Morse, *Evolutionary Biology of Viruses*, p. 51.

15. Anderson, "Directly Transmitted Viral and Bacterial Infections," p. 1.

16. Anderson, "Directly Transmitted Viral and Bacterial Infections," p. 6.

17. Fettner, *Science of Viruses*, chapter 4; Mark Caldwell, "The Dream Vaccine," *Discover* (September 1997): 85–88.

18. Ewald, *Evolution of Infectious Diseases*, pp. 16–19.

19. Jared Diamond, *Guns, Germs, and Steel: The Fates of Human Societies* (New York: Norton, 1997), chapter 11.

20. Ewald, *Evolution of Infectious Diseases*, pp. 207–12.

21. Wills, *Yellow Fever, Black Goddess*, chapter 11.

22. Anderson and May, *Infectious Diseases of Humans*, chapter 3.

23. Anderson and May, *Infectious Diseases of Humans*, chapter 15.

24. Garnett and Antia, "Population Biology," pp. 53–54.

25. Fettner, *Science of Viruses*, chapter 16.

26. Anderson and May, *Infectious Diseases of Humans*, chapter 14; Karlen, *Man and Microbes*, pp. 156–61.

27. Cynthia Mills, "Blood Feud," *The Sciences* (March/April 1998): pp. 34–38.

28. Thomas Scott, Scott Weaver, and Varuni Mallampalli, "Evolution of Mosquito-Borne Viruses," in Morse, *Evolutionary Biology of Viruses*, p. 293.

29. John Thompson, *The Coevolutionary Process* (Chicago: University of Chicago Press, 1994), pp. 103–11.

30. Ewald, *Evolution of Infectious Diseases*, p. 68.

31. Karlen, *Man and Microbes*, pp. 18–19; William McNeill, "Patterns of Disease Emergence in History, in *Emerging Viruses*, ed. Stephen Morse (New York: Oxford University Press, 1993), chapter 3.

32. Scott, Weaver, and Mallampalli, "Evolution of Mosquito-Borne Viruses," pp. 304–09.

33. Anderson and May, *Infectious Diseases of Humans*, chapter 23, esp. pp. 648–53; Garnett and Antia, "Population Biology," pp. 57–64.

34. Wills, *Yellow Fever, Black Goddess*, chapter 2.

35. Anderson and May, *Infectious Diseases of Humans*, pp. 627–36.

36. Anderson and May, *Infectious Diseases of Humans*, fig. 6.1, p. 124.

37. Morse, "Toward an Evolutionary Biology of Viruses," pp. 16–20.

38. Fenner and Kerr, "Evolution of the Poxviruses," in Morse, *Evolutionary Biology*, chapter 13; Anderson and May, *Infectious Diseases of Humans*, pp. 649–52; Garnett and Antia, "Population Biology," fig. 5, p. 63.

39. Karlen, *Man and Microbes*; William McNeill, *Plagues and Peoples* (New York: Doubleday, 1976).

40. Ewald, *Evolution of Infectious Diseases*, esp. chapter 1. Wills's critique of Ewald is in Wills, *Yellow Fever, Black Goddess*, pp. 44–49 and chapter 10. Ewald's response is in his review of Wills's book in *Scientific American* (May 1997): 112–16.

41. Ewald, *Evolution of Infectious Diseases*, pp. 35–36.

42. Garnett and Antia, "Population Biology," p. 58.

43. Scott, Weaver, and Mallampalli, "Evolution of Mosquito-Borne Viruses," p. 30.

44. Anderson and May, *Infectious Diseases of Humans*, pp. 641–48.

45. Jonathan Kingdon, *Self-Made Man: Human Evolution from Eden to Extinction?* (New York: Wiley, 1993), pp. 247–53.

46. Stephen O'Brien and Michael Dean, "In Search of AIDS-Resistance Genes," *Scientific American* 277, no. 3 (September 1997): 44–51.

47. David Brown, "Black Death May Have Bequeathed Ability to Survive in the Age of AIDS," *Washington Post*, May 8, 1998; Gina Kolata, "Scientists See a Mysterious Similarity in a Pair of Deadly Plagues," *New York Times*, May 26, 1998.

48. Karlen, *Man and Microbes*, p. 39.

49. Karlen, *Man and Microbes*, p. 156.

50. Fettner, *Science of Viruses*, p. 204.

51. Cynthia Mills, "The Deadliest Virus," *The Sciences* (January/February 1997): 34–38.

52. World Health Organization, *The World Health Report: 1997* (Geneva: WHO, 1997), table 2, p. 15.

53. James LeDuc, J. E. Childs, G. E. Glass, and A. J. Watson, "Hantaan (Korean Hemorrhagic Fever) and Related Rodent Zoonoses," in Morse, *Emerging Viruses*, chapter 14; Karlen, *Man and Microbes*, pp. 169–73.

54. World Health Organization, *World Health Report*, table 2, p. 15.

55. B. Cvjetanovic, "The Dynamics of Bacterial Infections," in Anderson, *Population Dynamics*, chapter 2, pp. 48–53; Wills, *Yellow Fever*, chapter 7.

56. Cvjetanovic, "Dynamics of Bacterial Infections," pp. 54–57; Wills, *Yellow Fever, Black Goddess*, chapter 6.

57. World Health Organization, *World Health Report*, table 2, p. 15.

58. Karlen, *Man and Microbes*, chapter 9.

59. Ewald, *Evolution of Infectious Diseases*, pp. 77–82.

60. World Health Organization, *World Health Report*, table 2, p. 15.

61. Wills, *Yellow Fever, Black Goddess*, chapter 9; Karlen, *Man and Microbes*, chapter 8.

62. Karlen, *Man and Microbes*, p. 128.

63. Anderson and May, *Infectious Diseases of Humans*, chapter 14; Joan Aron and Robert May, "The Population Dynamics of Malaria," in Anderson, *Population Dynamics*, chapter 5; Wills, *Yellow Fever, Black Goddess*, chapter 8.

64. World Health Organization, *World Health Report*, table 2, p. 15; table 3, p. 19.

65. Wills, *Yellow Fever, Black Goddess*, pp. 173–85.

66. Anderson and May, *Infectious Diseases of Humans*, pp. 425–29.

67. Cvjetanovic, "Dynamics of Bacterial Infections"; Anderson, "Directly Transmitted Viral and Bacterial Infections," pp. 43–48.

68. World Health Organization, *World Health Report*, table 2, p. 15.

69. Bernice Kaplan, "Migration and Disease," in C. G. N. Mascie-Taylor and G. W. Lasker, eds., *Biological Aspects of Human Migration* (Cambridge: Cambridge University Press, 1988), chapter 8; Wills, *Yellow Fever, Black Goddess*, chapter 1.

70. Wills, *Yellow Fever, Black Goddess*, p. 7.

71. Karlen, *Man and Microbes*, chapter 2.

72. Anderson and May, *Infectious Diseases of Humans*, pp. 653–54.

73. Karlen, *Man and Microbes*, chapter 3; Diamond, *Guns, Germs, and Steel*, chapter 11.

74. Boyce Rensberger, "In Death, Ancient Peoples Offer Evidence that 'Progress' Often Shortened Life," *Washington Post*, May 13, 1998.

75. Massimo Livi-Bacci, *A Concise History of World Population*, trans. Carl Ipsen (Cambridge, Mass.: Blackwell, 1992), chapter 2.

76. Karlen, *Man and Microbes*, p. 39; Diamond, *Guns, Germs, and Steel*, table 11.1, p. 207.

77. Anderson and May, *Infectious Diseases of Humans*, pp. 654–56.

78. Wills, *Yellow Fever, Black Goddess*, figure 3.3, pp. 40–41.

79. Laurie Garrett, *The Coming Plague: Newly Emerging Diseases in a World out of Balance* (New York: Farrar, Straus and Giroux, 1994), chapter 9; Karlen, *Man and Microbes*, chapter 4.

80. Karlen, *Man and Microbes*, pp. 57–58.

81. Anthony Ramirez, "Was the Plague of Athens Really Ebola?" *New York Times*, August 18, 1996.

82. Wills, *Yellow Fever, Black Goddess*, figure 3.2, pp. 37–41.

83. Wills, *Yellow Fever, Black Goddess*, figures 3.4, 3.5, 3.6, 3.7; pp. 42–45.

84. Wills, *Yellow Fever, Black Goddess*, pp. 110–16.

85. Alfred Crosby, *The Columbian Exchange: Biological and Cultural Consequences of 1492* (Westport, Conn.: Greenwood, 1972); Alfred Crosby, *Germs, Seeds, and Animals: Studies in Ecological History* (Armonk, N.Y.: Sharpe, 1994).

86. W. George Lovell, "'Heavy Shadows and Black Night': Disease and Depopulation in Colonial Spanish America," in Karl Butzer, ed., *The Americas before and after 1492: Current Geographical Research, Annals of the Association of American Geographers*, 82, 3 (September 1992): 426–43.

87. Karlen, *Men and Microbes*, pp. 217–18.

88. Karlen, *Men and Microbes*, chapters 8, 9.

89. D. F. Roberts, "Migration in the Recent Past: Societies with Records," in Mascie-Taylor and Lasker, *Biological Aspects of Human Migration*, chapter 3, pp. 45–46.

90. Alfred Crosby, *Epidemic and Peace, 1918* (Westport, Conn.: Greenwood, 1976); Ewald, *Evolution of Infectious Diseases*, chapter 7.

91. Karlen, *Men and Microbes*, pp. 217–28.

92. Richard Preston, *The Hot Zone* (New York: Random House, 1994), pp. 11–12.

Part II

Case Studies

Chapter Five

Agriculture Comes to Europe

"The expansion of food production . . . across Europe over 7,000 years ago," writes Peter Bogucki,

> marked the most radical transformation of prehistoric society in this region since the retreat of the last glaciation. An economy based on non-indigenous cultigens and domestic forms of both local and foreign animal species was established rapidly and successfully across a broad belt stretching from the Ukraine to France and subsequently expanded north to the Baltic and North Seas and south to the Alps. In the course of this process, new environmental zones were exploited for the first time and new ecological adaptations were made by both indigenous and colonizing populations.[1]

The speed with which agriculture came to Europe, and the completeness with which food production replaced food gathering and hunting, raise tantalizing questions about the origins of this new way of life and about how it was brought to Europe. One thing is certain: the impact of the Neolithic Revolution on the biosphere of Europe was as close to total and revolutionary as is possible to imagine.

For many years, writes Royston Clark, "early agriculture in Europe has traditionally been viewed in diffusionist terms, spreading westwards from the Near East."[2] The dominant paradigm held that mixed agriculture (food production by means of both plant harvesting and stock-raising) entered Europe from Turkey or elsewhere in the Near East, and that the entire package of domesticated plants and animals (including the humans who brought it) displaced the local hunter-gatherers and their coevolved life systems.[3] More recently, scholars have been inclined to attribute a less passive role to indigenous populations of hunter-gatherers. The transition to farming and stockherding is portrayed as resulting from the interaction (frequently cooperative) of the indigenous and the invading cultures. It is also possible that very few people actually moved, and that agriculture spread via ideas and technologies rather than via populations (that is, via memes instead of genes). In any case, the spread of agriculture across Europe between 7500 and 3000 bc was one of the earliest examples of the interplay of two sets of life systems as they met and adapted to each other.[4] For this reason, the arrival of the Neolithic Revolution in Europe was one of the most significant biological events in the early history of globalization.

Perhaps the key to sorting out these competing paradigms lies in understanding that Europe is not a single, homogeneous entity, but rather an extremely complex and varied collection of ecosystems; and responses by early farmers and herders to this variety must have been equally diverse. Both the cultural and the natural environments provided varied sets of resources for, and limitations to, the adoption of agriculture. Thus, in all probability, both adaptation and diffusion were at work. Agriculture emerged in Europe as a consequence of both pressure from expanding populations from the outside, and local adaptations to these pressures. As Paul Halstead puts it,

> It is becoming increasingly clear that the inception of farming in Europe was a far from uniform process. The speed and thoroughness with which the new economy ousted the old varied both regionally and locally—as did the reasons for the change—and, in these circumstances, the distinction between immigrant farmers and native foragers may often have been . . . meaningless.[5]

Given such complexity and uncertainty, many scholars have adopted an ecological perspective that emphasizes the entire cluster of social and biological factors that were at work in Neolithic Europe: technology (such as tool manufacture and use), social organization (as in social reproduction, mate exchange, labor exchange), subsistence (for example, land use, food resources), settlement patterns (including group mobility, dispersal, functional variability), and environment.[6] At its core, the Neolithic Revolution signified the production of food with stone tools, but as Julian Thomas explains, it was much more than that:

> It is not the adoption of the odd Neolithic trait or innovation into a Mesolithic lifestyle which represents the onset of the Neolithic; it is a wholesale transformation of social relations which results from adopting an integrated cultural system. Such a system has as its purpose not merely the provision of sustenance, the biological reproduction of the community, but its social reproduction, including the maintenance of power relations, knowledge and institutions. Owning a cow, or an axe, living in a house, or burying one of one's kin in a particular way does not make a person Neolithic. It is the recognition of the symbolic potential of these elements to express a fundamental division of the universe into the wild and the tame which creates the Neolithic world.[7]

While most of these factors will be mentioned, this chapter concentrates on the biological dimensions of this momentous change.

THE MESOLITHIC IN EUROPE

Some 11,500 years ago, temperatures in Europe began to creep slowly upward, and the last of the great glacial ice sheets began to retreat.[8] Within a millennium or two, maximum temperatures averaged 2–2.5 degrees Celsius higher than today. Sea levels rose 60 to 120 meters around the coast of the European continent, taking much of the low-lying land but in return creating new estuaries and other zones rich in sea life. The rising water separated Ireland and Britain from the rest of Europe about 7500 B.C. Dense, mixed forests spread to cover the greater portion of the land. Birch colonized northward first, followed by pine, then hazel, and then the principal forest trees: oak, ash, elm, and linden.

Below the dense canopy afforded by these trees, a vast array of smaller plants flourished in a deep layer of decaying wood and leaves. Giant herbivores of the glacial period began to vanish, and smaller animals like reindeer retreated farther north, following the cold. They were replaced by herbivores better suited to the warmth, such as wild cattle (aurochs), red deer (comparable to the North American elk), roe deer, and wild boar. Much smaller animals—such as lynx, fox, marten, beaver, wolf, and dog—also prospered, as did freshwater fish like pike, carp, perch, trout, and salmon, and numerous bird species, especially water fowl and birds of prey. As climate changes altered the distribution of grazing mammals, humans followed closely behind. An early consequence of the fading of the Ice Age, then, was the movement of foraging populations into new environments.[9]

Although limited to seeds, roots, tubers, nuts, and berries, the plant food available to prefarming peoples would have been abundant. The all-important cereals—such as einkorn or emmer wheat, or barley—and pulses like lentils had yet to appear. And sheep, destined to be so important to the Neolithic Revolution, were not present in significant numbers during the immediate postglacial period but were probably introduced from the Near East about 7000 B.C. Despite these gaps, the increase in exploitable food supply in the wake of the glaciers' retreat offered, in Alasdair Whittle's words, "not major constraints for human activity but abundant opportunities."[10]

Anthropologists have offered several models of how human society might have been organized under the conditions of hunting and gathering that were present in Europe eight to ten thousand years ago. Hoofed animals such as wild cattle and red deer provided the bulk of the food supply. In the coastal areas, shellfish offered additional protein, but fishing and plant gathering were relatively less significant. Settlements were probably transient hunting sites rather than sedentary camps, as the human population followed the migratory animals on which they depended. Few remains of dwellings have been discovered, leading to the conclusion that Mesolithic Europeans lived in temporary shelters made of wood frames and animal skins, which would have decomposed long ago. Nevertheless, enough site remains have been discovered to make it clear that incoming farmers almost certainly encountered indigenous foragers almost anywhere the farmers settled.

The prevailing view holds that prefarming Europeans formed small, mobile, social groups that adapted to fluctuating resources by carefully controlling their group's population. An alternative possibility suggests itself if we assume a richer resource base, as may well have been the case: Mesolithic groups could have maintained much more stable settlements, and therefore more sizable populations, without turning to farming. Still a third possibility was that these earliest Europeans exercised somewhat greater control over food supply by clearing the forests by fire or ax, which would have facilitated the control of animals herds. While these populations had not yet begun the selective breeding of animals, they might have been able to achieve somewhat the same objectives by culling the herds systematically. It is also possible that all three models existed at different times and places.

Whichever of these models proves to be the most accurate explanation, we already have sufficient evidence that across Europe natural vegetation was deliberately altered to a substantial degree by human intervention long before farming arrived. Early foraging populations cleared the land of forests and shrub growth to make space for their settlements, for fire wood, and for materials to construct their dwellings. Their organic refuse and their latrines brought forth new plant growth. Fires from their campsites, or those ignited intentionally to clear land or to control animal herd movements, were an additional factor in land clearance.[11] As Peter Bogucki puts it, "The earliest agricultural communities . . . did not adapt to a completely pristine environment, but one which several millennia of human activity had altered to varying degrees."[12]

Social organization would have varied across these three models. As society became more sedentary, it could have afforded to adopt measures of social differentiation, leading to class stratification, the creation of artisan professions, the emergence of political leaders, the drawing of boundaries between groups, developing rituals to foster group identities, and other divisions of the populations that had not existed before. Which of these models were actually employed would have depended greatly on the available resources, including climate; but Europe's diverse ecosystems suggest that farming peoples entering the continent from the south and east were met by vastly differing conditions the farther they penetrated the region.

The postglacial warming trend continued into the seventh millennium B.C.[13] Winters were warmer than before, and summers wetter. The farther north one went, the more noticeable was the climatic change. Sea levels continued to rise, forest development reached its climax, and soil fertility was at its peak. Archeological evidence from this period reveals the existence of the earliest sedentary settlements. Signs of differential growth suggest that, even at this early date, these populations were beginning to divide themselves along social or economic lines.

THE SPREAD OF AGRICULTURE IN EUROPE

The Neolithic Revolution did not have indigenous roots in Europe but was an import from the Fertile Crescent region of the Middle East. Scholars differ as to the precise date(s) when agriculture entered Europe, or the precise rate(s) at which it spread. But there is general agreement that farming spread in waves from the eastern Mediterranean to southeast Europe and the western Mediterranean, and thence to central, northern, and western Europe (see figure 5.1).

Introduction of Middle Eastern plants such as wheat and barley to the Mediterranean region was easy because of the similarities of climate, rainfall, sunlight, and so forth. In the Mediterranean, as in the Fertile Crescent, crops were planted in the autumn, grew during the mild, wet winter, and were harvested in the spring before the heat and drought of summer could damage the plants. This cycle imitated the natural growth cycle of wild grasses, from which wheat and barley descended.

Figure 5.1   Spread of Agriculture in Europe, Based on Radiocarbon Dating of the Earliest Arrival of Neolithic Cultivators in Various Regions

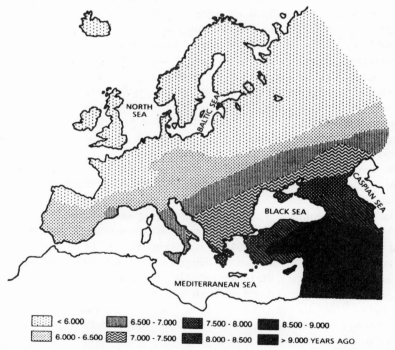

Source: Luigi Luca Cavalli-Sforza and Francesco Cavalli-Sforza, *The Great Human Diasporas: The History of Diversity and Evolution,* trans. by Sara Thorne (Reading, Massachusetts: Addison-Wesley, 1995), p. 135, Fig. 6.5. © Arnoldo Mondadori Editore S.p.A. Reprinted by permission.

From the Mediterranean, agriculture was taken to central Europe, and then on to northwest Europe, the British Isles, and southern Scandinavia. Progress through these northern and western regions was more difficult because of the different growing seasons.[14] In temperate-zone Europe it was winter cold rather than summer heat that threatened plants. As farming spread north and west from Greece, farmers and their domesticated plants and animals encountered a natural environment increasingly different from that to which they were adapted in the Near East and the Mediterranean. Temperatures were cooler, and rainfall occurred in summer rather than winter, even though annual precipitation remained roughly constant. From south to north, cold replaced drought as the leading constraint on plant growth. Livestock could adapt to such changes relatively easily by seeking shelter or alternative sources of water; but Mediterranean and Near East crops, such as wheat and beans, adjusted much less easily to the shorter and inverted growing season. In central and northern Europe, crops had to be planted in the spring and harvested in the fall. To accomplish this change, early farmers had to develop new plant strains and invent new farming techniques. So, while agriculture spread across the Mediterranean in a matter of centuries, it required another millennium or so to move beyond Hungary into central Europe.

Early Neolithic communities were in Greece, particularly in the eastern mainland, by about 7500 B.C. By about 6800 B.C., farming settlements had reached Bulgaria, eastern Yugoslavia, Croatia, and southeastern Hungary. Between 7500 and 4800 B.C., farming settlements were established in many sites around the Mediterranean, from Italy and France to southern Spain.[15] Many of these later sites were built within enclosures of walls or ditches, which some scholars interpret as evidence of their concern for protection from marauding neighbors. (Others see the enclosures as designed to keep livestock in rather than bandits out.) The presence of Mediterranean shells at sites north of the Alps, and of obsidian at Mediterranean sites far from natural deposits, suggests the use of far-flung trade routes by this time.

The spread of early food-producing cultures into northern and central Europe occurred in two phases, identified by Peter Bogucki as the Primary and the Consequent Neolithic.[16]

The Primary Neolithic. The Primary Neolithic spans the period from roughly 5400 to 4400 B.C. Its peoples and their immediate descendants were the pioneer food producers of Europe. By 5400 B.C., a Primary Neolithic farming culture marked by a distinctive linear pottery design known as *Linearbandkeramik* (LBK) had emerged in Hungary, the Czech Republic, Slovakia, southern Poland, northern Austria, most of central and southern Germany, and southeastern Holland.[17] By 4400 B.C., LBK had reached the Alpine Foreland in southern Germany and northern Switzerland.[18] Eventually, this culture would extend as far west as the Paris basin. In addition to a unique pottery style, this culture was also distinguished by architecture (long houses built from heavy oak timbers) and food sources (primarily cereal cultivation, with somewhat less reliance on domesticated cattle and pigs).[19] Domesticated animals were kept primarily for meat, but there is some evidence of their being used for milk and hauling as well. These early farmers did not know the plow, but they used digging sticks, hoes, and other stone tools to work the land and prepare it for planting. The scarcity of animals in this hoe-cultivation system meant there was little animal manure to recycle back into the land, so these farmers had to practice a kind of "slash-and-burn" agriculture that required they regularly shift their fields as the natural fertility of the soil was drained away.

From central and western Europe, agriculture spread to Britain, Ireland, Scandinavia, and interior Iberia by late in the fifth millennium B.C. The earliest farmers to reach Britain were colonists from the western Mediterranean, who at the same time were spreading back eastward through France into Switzerland and Germany.[20] It appears that farming in Britain and the western periphery of Europe was a mixed enterprise virtually from the beginning, combining plant crops with animal husbandry in a system that remains dominant today. Domesticated cattle and sheep were introduced into the British Isles sometime during the fifth millennium B.C. as well. This introduction involved the domestication of wild cattle and boars already in Britain, as well as the transport of domesticated livestock from the mainland either trussed up in skin-covered boats, or by forcing them to swim the English Channel.[21]

During the Primary Neolithic, the connections between agriculture and population size and density were complex. By the time agriculture appeared in Greece, populations were already sedentary and growing.[22] Early villages consisting of mud-brick and post-frame houses contained between 50 and 300 people, and habitation continued on the same spot for several centuries, or even millennia. Farming could supply most of the food needs of a small village on lands no more than five to ten minutes' walk from the settlement, obviating the need to use animals for transport and hauling. However, population growth was such that farming alone could not supply the food energy needs of the people, and subsistence strategies inevitably included foraging and pastoralism as well.

By the time agriculture reached the southern Balkans, farmers had become less densely concentrated and more mobile. Settlements of no more than 50 inhabitants were scattered in long lines along Europe's smaller rivers, where floodplain and watershed configurations produced more abundant alluvial deposits; these settlements left evidence (for example, refuse deposits) of shorter periods of habitation. Such a pattern of dispersal and mobility continued into the LBK culture of central Europe. Here, access to the grazing lands of the broad European plains promoted an increased dependence on livestock, especially cattle. The shift in dwelling architecture from small, round huts to long houses indicates the beginnings of some functional differentiation of buildings.

After 5500 B.C., the zones of agricultural settlement expanded noticeably. In sites uncovered in northern Greece and along the Adriatic coast, houses were larger and contained more rooms, and the number of houses in a settlement grew to as many as 400. The upper limit of settlement size appears to have been about 80 hectares during this period. Between 4800 and 3700 B.C., farming as a way of life became consolidated throughout southeast Europe.[23] Farming settlements began to fill in the previously vacant lands both on the mainland and on the islands of the Aegean. Not only were settlements larger and more densely populated, but for the first time they gave the appearance of having been planned. Settlements possessed some of the basic characteristics of villages, including boundaries, fortifications, a "center" square or plaza, and special-purpose buildings, including temples or shrines. Worked copper and gold artifacts and other examples of artisanry indicate the existence of specialist crafts. The staples of subsistence, however, appear to have changed little during this period, with wheat the principal cereal crop, and the scale of land clearance increased to allow for greater production. Oats, peas, and lentils were still important, but the domestication of other foods such as grapes, olives, and pears began to bring greater variety into the diet. Cattle became the principal animal exploited for food, followed by sheep, goats, and pigs.

In central and western Europe, the LBK period came to a close about 4800 B.C.[24] The exact sequence of changes varied across the great European plain from Hungary to Paris, but in general between 4800 and 4300 B.C., settlements became smaller, more densely packed together, and more sparsely spread across the landscape. Palisades, ditches, banks, and fenced enclosures began to appear with increasing frequency.[25] Food sources exhibited some continuity from earlier periods, but pigs and sheep became relatively more important among the domesticated animals, and barley was sown along with the various strains of wheat. There is some fragmentary evidence of population movements from the continent to the British Isles, and by 4400 B.C. the first of the megalithic sites began to appear there.[26]

The Consequent Neolithic. The second phase, called the Consequent Neolithic, covers the period from 4400 to 3300 B.C. Its peoples included those who continued the process of adjustment to the European environment and who entered zones not colonized by the Primary Neolithic groups, as well as foraging populations that had adopted food production.

The Consequent Neolithic period was one of both continuity with, and change from, the earlier phase of agriculture.[27] Emmer wheat remained the staple grain of the European diet, and livestock continued to be principally cattle and sheep, although in some sites along the north coast, pigs had become more significant as a food source. It is difficult to generalize about settlement patterns during the Consequent Neolithic because of the great diversity in site sizes and densities; but it seems clear that settlements became more dispersed owing to greater population pressure, more extensive resort to agriculture, animal traction, and wheeled vehicles.

A number of major changes occurred in the farming culture of southeast Europe between 4400 and 3300 B.C. that raise the possibility of a second wave of immigrants into the region from somewhere in the Near East or the Eurasian steppes.[28] Many of the innovations involved animal traction and transport; for the first time, the horse was a significant factor in European farming, along with the cart and the plow.

Even though the plow is associated with the arrival of iron tools—that is, after the Neolithic—there is evidence of the use of stone implements to turn the soil before the close of the Neolithic period.[29] Julian Thomas reports that the earliest use of the plow in Britain dates from about 3500 B.C.[30] The working of the soil in this fashion made possible the rudimentary beginnings of the field system of farming—the organization of land into square plots set apart by boundaries. (Because of the ephemeral nature of plowed furrows, scant archeological evidence remains of field agriculture from Neolithic times.) This set of innovations brought about the "secondary products revolution," so that animals like cattle and sheep began to be seen as valuable resources not only for their meat but also for milk, wool, leather, and traction (especially in the case of cattle and horses).

The use of animals to draw tools to turn the soil led to numerous important changes in the way agriculture was practiced in Europe and eventually throughout the world.[31] (In chapter 7, we will see how these farming practices affected the biosphere of eastern North America more than five millennia later.) The plow enabled the farmer to prepare more land than could be planted and harvested in one season, so the practice of fallowing evolved much later to permit the land to recover. Fields lying fallow could be turned into open pasture for the seasons when they were not under cultivation. The plow required the clearing and leveling of larger expanses of land, which led to increased loss of topsoil from wind and water erosion. Where hoe agriculture was practiced, mixed crops were the rule; but the wide stretches of plowed fields lent themselves to single crops such as wheat or barley. The presence of animals in large numbers made more animal waste available to fertilize the fields, so pasture lands lying fallow emerged as a vital element in the field system. All of these changes produced greater yields and induced farmers and their families to become more sedentary, but these changes in turn made greater populations possible and generated even more pressure on Europe's forest lands.

It is tempting see these radical changes as the product of an invasion (or several waves of invasions) of Indo-European-speaking peoples from the east.[32] Certainly the routes of communication and commerce between southeastern Europe and the Near East were well established by this time, so the infrastructure was available to support such a transformation. Some scholars, such as Alasdair Whittle, are more cautious in interpreting the causes of these changes. The linguistic evidence, they assert, is contradictory and unconvincing, and moreover, the resources for such changes were already available in rudimentary form at the local level. Thus, the changes in European farming after 3500 B.C. could be seen as having evolved from local sources just as easily as they could have been brought in from the outside.

Regardless of the source of these changes, it is clear that food scarcities were much more critical during this phase of the Neolithic Revolution. After 4400 B.C., Britain was the scene of important developments that led to the construction of huge fortresses such as that at Hambledon Hill.[33] The construction of palisades, fences, and ditches reveals great concern for defense and security. In central Europe, the Consequent Neolithic period offers the first evidence of the use of warfare to resolve crises of food shortages.[34] There is also evidence of forest decline, suggesting widespread clearance to accommodate farm plots and animal enclosures.

Across Britain and a broad swath of western Europe, farming peoples began to erect megalithic monuments composed of stones of extraordinary proportions.[35] The purposes of these monuments have been the subject of considerable controversy, with guesses ranging from fortresses for defense to ritual sites for burials to astronomical observatories. The more or less simultaneous appearance of such unusual structures at many different sites argues for the broad movement of peoples and cultures back and forth between Britain, Scandinavia, and the continent. The need of these societies to support the masses of laborers needed to quarry, move, and erect such enormous stones suggests yet another reason why there would have been so much pressure on food supplies. At least one expert, Julian Thomas, has dissented from this view, however, arguing that there is no reason why the construction of such large and complex monuments has to be tied to sedentary agriculture, fixed fields, and staple crops.[36] Foraging peoples, he asserts, have many hours of spare time when they are not engaged in productive labor that could be dedicated to monument building. The construction of the huge mounds at Cahokia on the Mississippi River in the first millennium A.D. was achieved by a society that practiced maize and squash horticulture in small gardens; so it is clear that monument building need not be sustained by agricultural surplus. Nevertheless, once Neolithic Europeans determined to shift from foraging to food production, they were locked into a cycle of rising production and consumption from which there was no easy exit.

THE AGRICULTURAL TRANSITION: ADAPTATION OR DIFFUSION?

In the beginning, the Neolithic Revolution was a local phenomenon. Domesticated plants and animals remained within the habitat of their wild ancestors.[37] Eventually, however, farmers took their domesticated species from their original habitat and transported them to a neighboring site. One way for this to occur was for farmers to prepare the new land to receive its newest species. This they accomplished by cutting timber, clearing brush, constructing shelters, and so forth. Another way was to select domesticants that were adaptable, and to carry them into a virgin, unprepared environment, to which they subsequently adapted. The adaptation would be mutual, however, since the new habitat would change as well.

Grazing animals changed the local ecosystem by what they ate, how they walked across the land surface, how they attracted predators, and how they deposited their waste. Once mixed farming began in Europe, then, it was inevitable that the European biosphere would be transformed.

After the Neolithic transformation, virtually nothing remained of Europe's Mesolithic people, or at least of their culture. Several paradigms have been offered to explain this momentous change. These models are classified according to whether they emphasize the movement of ideas or the movement of people in the spread of the agricultural way of life.[38] The models differ in the way they treat the respective roles of indigenous and invading peoples, the nature of their interactions, and the degree to which the genes of the invading populations mixed with or replaced the genes of the indigenous peoples.

One way mixed agriculture could have spread across Europe was for the meme of food production to be transported by cultural transmission, along with all of the plants and most of the animals that made up the Fertile Crescent package. This "indigenist" model contends that what moved were the ideas—the culture—of farming and animal husbandry, and that the people themselves actually moved relatively little. If this paradigm is correct, then the indigenous peoples are still living in Europe in the form of their genetic material.

Another possibility, called the "diffusionist" model, sees the movement of people as the agent of agricultural expansion. That is, farming practices moved along with the people who practiced them. One version of this model, known as "colonization," argues that invading farmers from the Near East were fitter in a Darwinian sense, and succeeded in driving indigenous populations out of the area. A second version of the "diffusionist" model, called "adaptation," places greater emphasis on the ability of indigenous peoples to compete and cooperate with the invaders, and thus to remain in place to blend with the new arrivals.

It is also possible that both methods operated, but at different times and places. After all, we are considering here an extremely complex dynamic that affected all of Europe across a span of more than four thousand years. It is possible for scholars to embrace variations of each of these models, depending on the times and places in question. For example, some believe that farming was adopted by indigenous peoples very early in the process in the Balkans, and very late in Denmark, coastal Holland, and southern Scandinavia. Mid-way in the transformation, however, in north and central Europe, invading peoples were the primary agents of change.[39]

The evidence for the diffusionist model is based largely on radiocarbon dating of remains gleaned from Neolithic sites. The earliest dates for domesticated plants and animals—as well as for some of the bulk-flow technologies associated with the package, such as ceramics—have much earlier radiocarbon dates in the Near East than in Europe. The general pattern of radiocarbon dates for the spread of the package into Europe shows a westward movement, with later dates as one goes farther west and north across the continent. The dominant characteristics of the

LBK culture, such as pottery style, animal husbandry, and dwelling architecture, replaced their predecessor culture so rapidly that swift colonization by agriculturalists is the most convincing explanation of what happened.[40] And the genetic material of today's Europeans (to be discussed more thoroughly below) reveals clear gradients rippling out from the Near East, across the Balkans, thence across central Europe, reaching Iberia, the British Isles, and Scandinavia last of all.

Dissenting scholars have argued that diffusionists have been too much influenced by examples in the last 500 years or so of the spread of colonial movements into the lands of indigenous peoples, who were overwhelmed by the colonists' superior technology. Advocates of a different perspective believe that the European hunter-gatherers of six to eight millennia ago adapted much more successfully to the arrival of the agricultural package, and that their genes are still very much present in today's Europeans. Indigenous paleolithic populations had already demonstrated their adaptability simply by enduring the harsh climate and changing resource base in Europe following its change thirty-five thousand years ago. Adaptive strategies such as the herding of reindeer and the exploitation of coastal and estuarine resources had been amply developed in Europe long before the first farmers appeared from the Near East.

In evidence, adaptationists argue that in some parts of southeastern Europe (Greece, Bulgaria) and northern Africa, einkorn wheat could have easily evolved from wild strains instead of being introduced from the Near East.[41] In some parts of western Europe, particularly the western Mediterranean and in Britain, domesticated sheep evolved from wild sheep rather than being introduced by colonists. In central Europe, wild cattle bred with domesticated cattle either naturally in the wild or due to the intervention of stock breeders. In many early locations, domesticated animals were valuable for ritualistic or status reasons, and perhaps secondarily for traction, and only quite long afterwards as a source of food. This latter fact suggests that the earliest European hunter-gatherers had domesticated dogs, sheep, and cattle long before outside farmers introduced them for their meat and milk.

One important element in the adaptationist model involves the limitation and management of population growth. As indigenous populations became more Neolithic, they shifted their dependence from herds of animals that migrated long distances (elk, reindeer) to more sedentary animals (sheep, pigs, and cattle). This change required that the humans also become more sedentary, occupy smaller territories, and establish clear boundaries to their land. The same territory could then accommodate greater populations as the people became more closely packed together. There is little evidence, however, of massive population increases of the sort seen in areas of early domestication such as the Near East. Almost certainly, the European groups relied on cultural practices like abortion and infanticide to maintain a supportable population level.

In addition, prefarming European peoples would have practiced a number of strategies intended to minimize the risks they ran from resource instability or unpredictability.[42] Many of these risk-management practices would have led more or less directly to the adoption of agriculture. For example, the devotion of increased time and energy to the manufacture of increasingly diverse stone tools would have yielded a specialized craft or artisan class whose members could have been called upon to fashion the sophisticated tool kits necessary to support the cultivation and harvesting of cereal crops. A second practice detected in the archeological record is direct food storage, which involves setting aside food from current production for future consumption and would have required a sedentary lifestyle as well as the first bulk-flow systems (probably containers made of hides or wood) in which food could be stored. Prefarming peoples were also learning how to store food energy for future use by feeding animals, a lesson that would help them domesticate animals later on. In addition Mesolithic peoples traded surplus food for later considerations, thus learning how to spread the available food resources across the population more evenly.

Perhaps of greatest importance, institutions must have evolved within Mesolithic populations with the purpose of sustaining these and other risk-management strategies, so that the entire process of early adaptation engendered a rather rudimentary form of social differentiation that we ordinarily associate with the advent of agriculture. When hunter-gatherer groups are subjected to stresses from either population growth or climate changes, and they cannot for some reason separate and send one segment of the group to other lands to live, they must develop some kind of hierarchical arrangement by which the labors of the group can be turned systematically to the production of increased food energy. The emergence of such hierarchies engenders a positive feedback loop: the more people released from the daily chores of hunting and gathering, the more intensively must the labor force (and other resources) be exploited to feed the population.

Even after farming took hold in Greece, the Balkans, and central Europe, unexpected fluctuations in weather, crop yields, and labor supply would have still caused considerable anxiety as early farmers confronted the need to feed a growing population. The longevity of early farming villages and their clustering around a central hearth suggest to some scholars that many of the social strategies developed by prefarming peoples to manage food supply were retained into the early Neolithic period. In addition, early farmers traded between villages to secure a more stable and reliable food supply and to even out food resources in times of fluctuations.[43]

Peter Bogucki has described how Primary Neolithic peoples might have managed the risks inherent in their dual procurement strategies: on the one hand, reliance on grain crops required that they live in stable settlements; on the other, the fodder requirements of their large herds of cattle required some degree of mobility to avoid overgrazing a given site.[44] The unpredictability of crop yields, the vagaries of the weather, the potential for diseases affecting both plants and animals, and the possibility of predator attacks or theft by other farmers—all raised the specter of serious food shortfall in any given year.

To counter these risks, to some degree buffer food supplies could be stored either in containers or in the bodies of the livestock, and the flexible exploitation of diverse food sources would have shielded farmers from all but the most devastating crises. But early farmers must also have developed other strategies of risk management that, says Bogucki, would have involved "social options"—protecting themselves as much through social institutions and behavioral choices as through the manipulation of food supplies. Viewed in these terms, the Neolithic colonization of central Europe represented the occupation of a new ecological niche that tied together human populations and their cultures with land, water, plants, animals, capital, space, time, and information in a complex system.

Some of the social options available to Primary Neolithic peoples involved their interaction with indigenous foragers.[45] Upon the arrival of farmers to a new region, the foraging populations would have clustered their settlements more densely together to compensate for the reduced food supplies available to them. In the short run, there was probably conflict between the two populations over finite land and food resources, and whenever farmers entered land occupied by Mesolithic groups, the two populations probably either avoided each other or were actively hostile.

Some scholars believe that eventually, however, foragers and farmers would have entered into collaborative arrangements to exploit the same territory by sharing its resources.[46] Foraging peoples the world over have demonstrated a willingness to alter their subsistence strategies if they see it to be to their advantage; and new farming communities would have seen it to be in their best interests to ensure good relations with Mesolithic groups, since the latter had far superior knowledge of the local landscape, climate, flora, and fauna. Through exchange, each population could have provided the other with food, labor, firewood, building materials, and other valuable resources. Perhaps even mates were exchanged via intermarriage, in which case the two gene pools would have become intermixed. Such population mixing would help explain how the indigenous foraging culture of pre-Neolithic Europe disappeared so rapidly.

Susan Alling Gregg identifies four possible styles of interaction between indigenous foraging peoples and intruding farmers.[47] Three of these form part of the traditional paradigm of forager-farmer interaction. *Expulsion* was thought to occur when Neolithic populations grew rapidly, forests were cleared for crops, and foraging peoples were forced to move elsewhere. *Acculturation* represented another Mesolithic response, wherein foraging peoples adopted agriculture because of its obvious superiority to hunting and gathering—if not in quality and quantity, at least in reliability. A third possibility was *avoidance*, where both populations kept to themselves and had little contact. Gregg finds problems with all three of these models, so she advances a fourth: *mutual cooperation and coexistence*. Her analysis, based largely on food-energy requirements, identifies the conditions under which foraging and farming together produce an optimal yield of such energy. On the basis of simulations of the food-energy results of various subsistence strategies, Gregg concludes that when fish and other wildlife were scarce, farmers would attempt to offset this with increased herds of livestock, which in turn required that they plant more land with wheat for winter fodder. But increased planting required increased labor, and foragers were often the only source of such short-term labor. In return, farmers could provide foragers with increased grain, meat, and milk during the late winter and early spring—precisely the times when wild game would have been at a low point. Out of these mutually beneficial connections, Gregg argues, would have emerged the mutualistic interactions that tied farmers and foragers together.

If, after all their social options had been exhausted, Primary Neolithic peoples still faced impending food shortages, they had only one last resort: migration to new lands.[48] The "wave-of-advance" model of colonization proposed by Ammerman and Cavalli-Sforza calls forth images of gradually increasing population pressures followed by steady, even, and gradual movements of the frontier north- and westward.[49] Some archeological evidence, however, such as pottery styles, indicates that population migrated in irregular spurts and over shorter distances. The image here is of settlements facing unpredicted and irregular food shortages, the solution to which is the departure of a number of their members to nearby sites to exploit fresh land and food resources. Thus, the colonization of Europe may have occurred in a more punctuated and irregular fashion than the "wave" paradigm describes.

As the Consequent Neolithic culture spread across central and northern Europe, social options remained central to the management of risk from food shortages, but the nature of some of the options changed rather fundamentally. Animal husbandry replaced crop cultivation as the primary source of food supply, and the dispersal of settlements became greater, suggesting less need for community-based strategies for buffering the population against food shortages.[50] Since livestock are a more reliable source of food than crops, families in later stages of the Neolithic transition could afford to be more independent and thus more dispersed. Kinship exchanges beyond the individual household would have taken on an added importance, and for the first time there are in the archeological record signs of armed violence, even warfare, presumably with food supplies as the principal objective.[51]

Foraging and farming populations became more tightly interconnected through the Consequent Neolithic period, at least partly because of climatic changes. Between 4400 and 4100 B.C., the weather in central and northern Europe worsened considerably, winters turned markedly colder, and rainfall levels fluctuated widely. In addition, the advancing cultivated fields of the new farmers began to attract wild animals, making them easier to hunt and concentrating this valuable food resource in fewer and fewer areas. The increased presence of sedentary communities and population increases among the farming communities intruded even more into the world of the foragers. Confronted by these developments and caught in the cycle that commits a group to agriculture once it begins to rely on domesticated plants and animals, Europe's foraging peoples completed the transition to farming fairly rapidly.[52]

BIOLOGICAL CONSEQUENCES OF EUROPE'S NEOLITHIC REVOLUTION

Once food production replaced food collection across Europe, the continent's biosphere was altered forever. Some changes involved the removal of pre-agricultural species that were obstacles to cultivation or animal husbandry. Some of these happened fairly quickly, such as deforestation of wide areas, but others, such as the hunting of wolves to virtual extinction, were not completed until recently. To the degree that agriculture was spread by migrating farmers rather than by migrating memes, these changes included the elimination of foraging populations as well.

Another kind of change involved the transformation of native European species to make them more supportive of food production. Where agriculture was adopted by indigenous foraging peoples as they became farmers, this category included humans as its principal component. In addition, three animal species native to Europe could be domesticated: the wild mouflon sheep; the wild boar, which evolved into the pig; and the wild aurochs, from which cattle are descended. (The pig we know in today's diet is a cross of European and Chinese varieties, bred 150 years ago in England.)

The remaining animal domesticants, and virtually all the plant domesticants, constituted a third change: species introduced into Europe from outside. These included dogs, other varieties of sheep, horses, and goats, as well as all the food crops: cereal grains, pulses, fruits, and vegetables. Some of the new species were introduced into Europe as early as 7500 B.C. from the Near East, others were late-comers from Asia or Africa and arrived only during the first and second millennia B.C. (To be complete, we should also cite here the important Western Hemisphere foods introduced into Europe after 1492: maize, the potato, and various other fruits and vegetables.)

"Perhaps the greatest single factor in the evolution of the European landscapes," writes H. C. Darby, "has been the clearing of the woods that once clothed almost the entire continent."[53] Long before farmers arrived, human activity had begun to alter Europe's indigenous life systems, primarily through the planned and systematic burning of woodlands and ground cover.[54] Burning increased the quantities of food resources available to foragers by stimulating the growth of desired plants, raising the food supply of grazing animal herds, promoting the growth of animal populations, and improving hunting conditions. Thus, when agriculture arrived in Europe, it met not a pristine natural environment but one that had already felt the hand of human beings for millennia.

"The earliest Primary Neolithic populations of central Europe," writes Bogucki, "entered an environment which was unlike anything they or their ancestors had previously encountered."[55] Deciduous forests, different species of wild plants and animals, new soil types, new climatic characteristics, new landforms, and indigenous foraging bands all had to be incorporated into the perspective of farmers arriving from the Near East.

Across southeastern and central Europe, early farmers had to clear woodlands for crops and animal grazing. The polished stone ax became an indispensable tool for these earliest Neolithic peoples.[56] The steppes of the eastern European plain, for example, are a relatively recent feature of the landscape, a product of human intervention in the local plant life. Pollen evidence suggests (although not conclusively) that extensive clearance of land began as early as the seventh millennium B.C. Around 4000 B.C., the extensive stands of elm trees across northern Europe went into sharp decline, with some forests losing as many as half of them.[57] Many theories have been advanced to explain these losses, including climatic change and disease, but several plausible explanations focus on human intervention, including land clearance for crops, extensive pruning of trees to provide fodder for animals, and the widespread clearance of vegetation on the forest floor to facilitate the control of animal herds. Clearance of woodlands would have been essential for farming systems that included grazing animals like cattle or sheep, while pigs could be turned out into dense forest to forage for themselves.

Despite the uncertainty of their productivity in the earliest days of the Neolithic, plants still provided most of the food energy for the population.[58] Wheat of either the einkorn or emmer variety was by far the dominant plant food.[59] According to Gregg, annual yields of these two cereals would have ranged between 645 and 1,045 kilograms per hectare, a figure that would have likely been reduced some 200 kilograms per year due to losses from pests and diseases.[60] Since a kilogram of wheat supplies about 3,000 calories of food energy, the food grown on a single hectare could have supported one adult for a year, even given rather pessimistic estimates of crop yield.[61] Thus, a village of some 300 persons could have been fed adequately from the yield of plots of arable land that would have fit easily into a circle with a radius of less than two kilometers. Gregg's simulations of the food needs of a typical Neolithic village of thirty-four persons suggest that cereals could have easily supplied 60 percent of their annual needs.[62]

Archeological evidence from Primary Neolithic sites in Greece and the Balkans shows the systematic planting and harvesting of emmer, einkorn, and bread wheat, barley, peas, and lentils. Pulses (annual legumes cultivated for their seed) such as lentils and peas were essential companion crops because of their ability to fix nitrogen in the soil, which cereal grains cannot do. The same array of crops is evident in the LBK sites, but only emmer and einkorn are ubiquitous. Where these cultigens proved inadequate to sustain the population, early farmers augmented their food supply with foraging, hunting, fishing, and gathering. Other plant foods, such as acorns, olives, and fruit were exploited in their natural state.

In addition, where farmers intervened to cultivate plant food, there also emerged a "weed association"—that is, sets of weeds that grew more or less naturally wherever wheat was cultivated.[63] In Primary Neolithic sites in Germany, researchers have found evidence of a weed association that included inedible plants like chess, nipplewort, goosefoot, black bindweed, sorrel, meadowgrass, and coarse vetch. These plants were attached to, and selected for, fields of wheat by virtue of their height (which caused them to be "harvested" more or less randomly along with the wheat) and/or their ability to climb along the wheat stalk. Plants with shorter stalks, or unable to exploit the wheat stalks, would have been crowded out by wheat cultivation, and thus would have declined as farming advanced across central Europe.

Agriculture had a great impact on Europe's animal population as well.[64] For many years, scholars believed that stockherding played a minor role in Europe's Primary Neolithic phase. After all, they reasoned, animals are higher up in the food chain and thus less productive than plants per unit of land exploited. We now know, however, that the introduction of cereals such as wheat, barley, and rye, and pulse crops to the alien climate of central Europe must have, in Paul Halstead's words, "entailed a reduction in the reliability of yields and an increase in the spatial scale of failures."[65] Fish and other marine life could never have satisfied more than a small portion of nutrition needs: As Whittle points out, 52,000 oysters are needed to match the food value of one red deer.[66] Europe's early farmers coped with this increased level of risk by, among other strategies, a more intensive management of livestock. Bogucki asserts, for example, that stockherds for both meat and milk were an important part the subsistence base for Primary Neolithic populations.[67] If this was the case, then from the earliest times, Europe's farmers were actively intervening in local gene pools of coevolved animal species. By the time of the Primary Neolithic in central Europe, wild animals played a limited role in food supply. By the end of the fourth millennium B.C., between 80 and 90 percent of faunal remains were made up of domesticated stocks; and by the middle of the third millennium, that figure had risen to 95 to 98 percent.[68]

Sheep and goats were the first species to be domesticated for food. There were some 400 breeds of sheep available for domestication, and different breeds proved to be more suitable to different climates and landscapes. Many varieties were introduced from the Fertile Crescent, while others (the mouflon, in particular) were native to Europe. Goats were introduced almost entirely from the Near East. Cattle and pigs also appear in the early archeological record; they were both domesticated from native European breeds as well as introduced from outside. Dogs were domesticated, probably as hunting companions; and the horse was introduced from its native habitat, the Ukraine, after 4000 B.C. Wild species such as red deer were also exploited. In Greece and through the Balkans, sheep were the dominant species represented in the archeological evidence. In the LBK sites in central Europe, however, cattle were the dominant species, and pigs began to appear more frequently in the remains. The increased reliance on cattle would have opened up large expanses of woodlands and other marginal lands for exploitation. At later sites in the Alpine region, cattle became even more important, and the slaughtering patterns suggest a use of cattle somewhere between the extravagant "meat" strategy and the conservative "milk" strategy.

In Britain, the domestication of animals followed a dual strategy: by transporting already domesticated animals from the mainland, and by domesticating wild animals that were native to Britain.[69] Skeletal remains of wild oxen have been found in a number of sites in Britain, although none date from later than the Bronze Age, suggesting that domestication had rather completely transformed the species by 2500 B.C. Sheep were not native to the British Isles, so they must have been imported from continental Europe. Sheep spread across Europe in two directions. Long-tailed woolly sheep were installed around the Mediterranean, while the species taken into northern and northwestern Europe had less wool. It was this latter species that was taken to Britain.

The predominance of juvenile remains among the bones of slaughtered animals has led scholars to conclude that early herders were interested primarily in meat, and rather less so in milk, although Bogucki argues for the importance of a dairy economy in the Primary Neolithic period.[70] It would have been during this time that northern and central Europeans evolved an ability to digest lactose as adults, something that sets them apart from most of the world's peoples. Somewhat later, during the Consequent Neolithic, farming settlements began to exploit livestock for other purposes, including milk, wool and hides, and traction to pull carts and plows.

Europe's earliest farmers practiced a variety of techniques to manipulate, control, and protect their livestock. Herds were moved systematically from one grazing area to another to minimize overgrazing and to protect the animals from cold weather. Farmers and dogs early on formed a team to watch over their animals, particularly sheep, which became increasingly vulnerable to predators as they became more dependent on their human protectors.

One of the first techniques developed by early animal breeders to manipulate the gene pool of their herds was the castration of a large percentage of the young males in the herd, which made the castrates more docile and easy to handle and caused them to grow faster so their meat supply could be exploited sooner. In addition, it reduced possibly disruptive competition between young males for sexual access to the females in the herd; and it ensured that only genes from the "fittest" (in the context of local agricultural needs) animals would be passed on to the next generation.

It is difficult to estimate the optimal size of a herd of cattle in Neolithic Europe.[71] Any given herd of animals would have contained a certain percentage of males (castrates, immature, and mature) and females (immature and mature). The maintenance of such a herd, and the self-sustaining exploitation of the animals for meat and milk, required careful management to ensure that, for example, there were not too many mature males or too few females. Ten or twenty animals drops the herd below a self-sustaining size; even fifty animals may be too small if the herders rely on them for a milk supply. Gregg's simulations shows that a Neolithic village of twenty-five people living in six houses would have required some six square kilometers of territory to support their food resources. About 13 hectares would be required for wheat cultivation, but the 40 head of cattle and the 40 sheep and goats would have needed 18 hectares of pasture, 20 hectares of natural meadows, and 2.6 square kilometers for forest browse. Thus, by far the greatest part of the village's land would be given over to the livestock for grazing and foraging purposes.[72]

Finally, we consider the impact of agriculture on Europe's human population. Here scholars are in considerable disagreement. One school holds that agriculture was the *cause* of population growth and the consequent expansion of settlements; a second, that it was the *response* of a growing population to the pressures of their increased numbers on the land. Still others see the connection as much more coincidental, however, with crop yields more the product of land fertility, and increased agricultural production simply the companion of population growth, rather than its cause or consequence. As Whittle puts it, "That agricultural communities were expansive provides ultimately more insight into the nature of their social relations than into their subsistence basis."[73]

The study of Europe's Neolithic population is hampered by a scarcity of empirical data, but scholars seem to agree on two things: that Europe's population grew at unprecedented rates during the Primary Neolithic period, and that this demographic surge resulted in the movement of a human "wave" across the continent.[74] While exact growth rates are beyond the reach of our data, some scholars have speculated that net annual increases might have approached modern rates, a level that, "while phenomenally large, is not entirely unreasonable."[75] The work of Ammerman and Cavalli-Sforza, to be discussed in a moment, assumes that Neolithic population growth was exponential, that settlements very quickly reached the level where they overloaded the available resources, and that excess populations fissioned off, creating new settlements nearby. In this way, the leading edge of the population wave moved across Europe from southeast to northwest at an average rate of twenty-five kilometers each generation.

Despite a high rate of population growth, whole settlements and individual households quickly discovered that labor shortages were an obstacle to large-scale food production.[76] High birth rates meant that many young children had to be fed long before they could be productive workers, and in addition Neolithic agriculture was hugely labor intensive. Facing labor scarcity, early farming peoples would have adopted social strategies to maximize their labor resources. Farmers would have recognized their need for peaceful relations with foraging populations, who could have supplied them with temporary labor during periods of peak needs. Departing members of the community, leaving to find new, fresh resources, would have been encouraged to remain "in the neighborhood" so that extended kin groups could be tapped for labor when necessary.

Through the analysis of Europe's genetic history, scholars have sought to determine which of the models most accurately describes the actual process of expansion. If the colonialist model is correct, and Europe's indigenous peoples were driven out or killed before they could breed with the invaders, then Europe's gene map should look uniform and resemble that of the origin population in the Near East. If indigenism is the correct perspective, and agriculture spread by ideas and not by people, the genetic map of Europe should be uniform but clearly different from that of the Near East. If the adaptationist model is correct, and indigenous peoples blended with the invaders, then Europe's gene map should show diversity. Gradients of change should spread out from the Near East, with the genetic differences from the original population increasing as land distance increases. Moreover, these genetic gradients should correspond to the chronologies of the spread of farming across Europe as established by other means (such as radiocarbon dating of seeds).

The research of Ammerman and Cavalli-Sforza suggests that this adaptationist model most closely resembles the actual genetic map of Europe[77] (see figures 5.2 and 5.3). Their "wave of advance" model shows that agriculture spread by both people and ideas, as foragers and farmers encountered and mixed with each other across Europe. The findings of Price, Gebauer, and Keeley lead to other conclusions, however.[78] In southern Scandinavia, farming spread by adoption by indigenous peoples, in-migration by outsiders was limited, and the local genotype remains relatively homogeneous and unique. Finally, in central and western Europe, where LBK peoples encountered Mesolithic foragers, the latter were virtually

Figure 5.2   Europe's Genetic Landscape

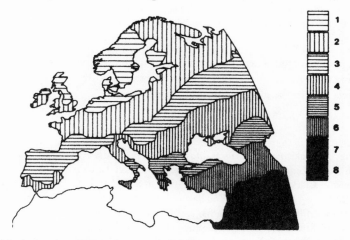

Note: This map portrays the genetic landscape for Europe, depicting the frequencies of 95 genes. The distribution of genes reflects the spread of agriculture in Neolithic times. (The scale of 1 to 8 is arbitrary.)

Source: Luigi Luca Cavalli-Sforza and Francesco Cavalli-Sforza, *The Great Human Diasporas: The History of Diversity and Evolution*, trans. by Sara Thorne (Reading, Massachusetts: Addison-Wesley, 1995), p. 149, Fig. 6.10. © Arnoldo Mondadori Editore S.p.A. Reprinted by permission.

Figure 5.3   Genetic Frequency Map for Rh- Individuals in Europe

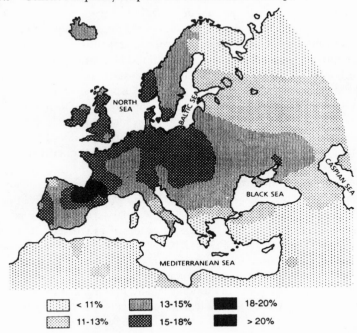

	< 11%		13-15%		18-20%
	11-13%		15-18%		> 20%

Source: Luigi Luca Cavalli-Sforza and Francesco Cavalli-Sforza, *The Great Human Diasporas: The History of Diversity and Evolution,* trans. by Sara Thorne (Reading, Massachusetts: Addison-Wesley, 1995), p. 145, Fig. 6.9. © Arnoldo Mondadori Editore S.p.A. Reprinted by permission.

completely eliminated. Farming spread here by genes as well as by memes, and the colonization model gives us the most accurate picture of what transpired in this earliest step in the globalization of life systems.

NOTES

1. Peter Bogucki, *Forest Farmers and Stockherders: Early Agriculture and its Consequences in North-Central Europe* (Cambridge: Cambridge University Press, 1988), p. 1.

2. Royston Clark, "Towards the Integration of Social and Ecological Approaches to the Study of Early Agriculture," in *The Beginnings of Agriculture,* BAR International Series 496, ed. Annie Milles, Diane Williams, and Neville Gardner (Oxford: Symposia of the Association for Environmental Archaeology No. 8, 1989), p. 3.

3. Karl Narr, "Early Food-producing Populations," in *Man's Role in Changing the Face of the Earth,* ed. William Thomas, et al., (Chicago: University of Chicago Press, 1956), pp. 136–37.

4. Many of the studies upon which this chapter draws use dates based on radiocarbon dating (signified by the lower case "bc"). In this chapter, these dates have been replaced by their estimated equivalents in Western calendar dates. These calendar dates, signified

by "B.C.," are generally between 20 and 30 percent more distant in time from the present. Thus, 4000 bc = 4845 B.C., 2000 bc = 2520 B.C. Where the equivalents were not given in the original source, I have estimated the equivalent date as 25 percent more distant. See Alasdair Whittle, *Neolithic Europe: A Survey* (Cambridge: Cambridge University Press, 1985), table 3.2, p. 38, and table 7.2, p. 266. For more on radiocarbon dating, see Luigi Luca Cavalli-Sforza and Francesco Cavalli-Sforza, *The Great Human Diasporas: The History of Diversity and Evolution*, trans. Sarah Thorne (Reading, Mass.: Addison Wesley, 1995), pp. 32–34.

5. Paul Halstead, "Like Rising Damp? An Ecological Approach to the Spread of Farming in South East and Central Europe," in Milles, Williams, and Gardner, *Beginnings of Agriculture*, p. 24.

6. Bogucki, *Forest Farmers and Stockherders*, pp. 5–8.

7. Julian Thomas, *Rethinking the Neolithic* (Cambridge: Cambridge University Press, 1991), p. 13.

8. Peter Rowley-Conwy, "Stone Age Hunter-Gatherers and Farmers in Europe," in *People of the Stone Age: Hunter-gatherers and Early Farmers*, ed. Göran Burenhult (New York: HarperCollins, 1993), pp. 59–77; Whittle, *Neolithic Europe*, chapter 2; Bogucki, *Forest Farmers and Stockherders*, chapter 2, esp. pp. 27–32.

9. Narr, "Early Food-producing Populations," pp. 134–35.

10. Whittle, *Neolithic Europe*, p. 12.

11. Narr, "Early Food-producing Populations," p. 136.

12. Bogucki, *Forest Farmers and Stockherders*, p. 41.

13. Bogucki, *Forest Farmers and Stockherders*, fig. 2.1, p. 19; Whittle, *Neolithic Europe*, chapter 3.

14. Rowley-Conwy, "Stone Age Hunter-Gatherers," pp. 74–75.

15. Whittle, *Neolithic Europe*, pp. 95–113; Narr, "Early Food-producing Populations," pp. 138–41.

16. Bogucki, *Forest Farmers and Stockherders*, pp. 11–17, chapters 4–6.

17. Whittle, *Neolithic Europe*, pp. 76–95.

18. Halstead, "Like Rising Damp?," fig. 1, pp. 26–28.

19. Bogucki, *Forest Farmers and Stockherders*, pp. 61–69.

20. Estyn Evans, "The Ecology of Peasant Life in Western Europe," in Thomas, *Man's Role*, p. 223.

21. Barbara Noddle, "Cattle and Sheep in Britain and Northern Europe up to the Atlantic Period: A Personal Viewpoint," in Milles, Williams, and Gardner, *Beginnings of Agriculture*, pp. 179–202.

22. Halstead, "Like Rising Damp?" pp. 28–32.

23. Whittle, *Neolithic Europe*, chapter 5.

24. Whittle, *Neolithic Europe*, chapter 6.

25. Bogucki, *Forest Farmers and Stockherders*, pp. 69–72.

26. Göran Burenhult, "The Megalith Builders of Western Europe," in Burenhult, *People of the Stone Age*, pp. 79–101.

27. Bogucki, *Forest Farmers and Stockherders*, chapter 6.

28. Whittle, *Neolithic Europe*, pp. 208–39.

29. Evans, "Ecology of Peasant Life," p. 226.

30. Julian Thomas, *Rethinking the Neolithic*, p. 20.

31. Gottfried Pfeifer, "The Quality of Peasant Living in Central Europe," in Thomas, *Man's Role*, pp. 249–53.

32. Whittle, *Neolithic Europe*, pp. 179–83.

33. R. J. Mercer, "A Neolithic Fortress and Funeral Center," *Scientific American Special Issue: Ancient Cities* (1994), pp. 100–07.

34. Bogucki, *Forest Farmers and Stockherders*, pp. 201–7.

35. Whittle, *Neolithic Europe*, pp. 227–39; Rodney Castleden, *The Making of Stonehenge* (London and New York: Routledge, 1993).

36. Julian Thomas, *Rethinking the Neolithic*, pp. 19–20.

37. Narr, "Early Food-producing Populations," pp. 137–38.

38. Cavalli-Sforza and Cavalli-Sforza, *Great Human Diasporas*, chapter 6; Albert Ammerman and Luigi Luca Cavalli-Sforza, *The Neolithic Transition and the Genetics of Populations in Europe* (Princeton: Princeton University Press, 1984), pp. 6–7.

39. Bogucki, *Forest Farmers and Stockherders*, pp. 49–51; T. Douglas Price, Anne Birgitte Gebauer, and Lawrence Keeley, "The Spread of Farming into Europe North of the Alps," in *Last Hunters, First Farmers: New Perspectives on the Prehistoric Transition to Agriculture*, ed. T. Douglas Price and Anne Birgitte Gebauer (Santa Fe, N.M.: School of American Research Press, 1995), chapter 4.

40. Whittle, *Neolithic Europe*, pp. 76–95; Price, Gebauer, and Keeley, "Spread of Farming."

41. Whittle, *Neolithic Europe*, pp. 54–58.

42. Clark, "Towards the Integration," pp. 5–7.

43. Whittle, *Neolithic Europe*, pp. 63–65.

44. Bogucki, *Forest Farmers and Stockherders*, pp. 90–114.

45. Bogucki, *Forest Farmers and Stockherders*, pp. 105–10, 173–77.

46. Price, Gebauer, and Keeley, "Spread of Farming," pp. 100–03.

47. Susan Alling Gregg, *Foragers and Farmers: Population Interaction and Agricultural Expansion in Prehistoric Europe* (Chicago: University of Chicago Press, 1988), chapter 1.

48. Bogucki, *Forest Farmers and Stockherders*, pp. 114–17.

49. Ammerman and Cavalli-Sforza, *Neolithic Transition*, chapter 5.

50. Halstead, "Like Rising Damp?" pp. 39–41.

51. Bogucki, *Forest Farmers and Stockherders*, chapter 7.

52. Bogucki, *Forest Farmers and Stockherders*, pp. 173–75.

53. H. C. Darby, "The Clearing of the Woodland in Europe," in Thomas, *Man's Role*, p. 183.

54. Bogucki, *Forest Farmers and Stockherders*, pp. 38–41.

55. Bogucki, *Forest Farmers and Stockherders*, p. 101.

56. Evans, "Ecology of Peasant Life," p. 225.

57. Bogucki, *Forest Farmers and Stockherders*, pp. 32–34.

58. Gregg, *Foragers and Farmers*, chapter 4.

59. Daniel Zohary and Maria Hopf, *Domestication of Plants in the Old World*, 2d ed. (Oxford: Clarendon, 1994); John Noble Wilford, "New Clues Show Where People Made the Great Leap to Agriculture," *New York Times*, November 18, 1997; Bogucki, *Forest Farmers and Stockherders*, table 4.1, p. 54.

60. Gregg, *Foragers and Farmers*, pp. 72–73, table 3, p. 74.

61. Whittle, *Neolithic Europe*, pp. 59–60.

62. Gregg, *Foragers and Farmers*, table 43, p. 155.

63. Gregg, *Foragers and Farmers*, pp. 79–94; Bogucki, *Forest Farmers and Stockherders*, p. 56.

64. Sonia Cole, *The Neolithic Revolution* (London: British Museum of Natural History, 1970), chapter 3; Ronnie Liljegren, "The Domestication of Animals," in Burenhult, *People of the Stone Age*, pp. 68–69; Gregg, *Foragers and Farmers*, chapter 5.

65. Halstead, "Like Rising Damp?" p. 23.

66. Whittle, *Neolithic Europe*, p. 123.

67. Bogucki, *Forest Farmers and Stockherders*, pp. 85–90.

68. Bogucki, *Forest Farmers and Stockherders*, fig. 4.2, pp. 57–59, table 6.1, p. 136.

69. Noddle, "Cattle and Sheep in Britain."

70. Bogucki, *Forest Farmers and Stockherders*, pp. 79–90.

71. Bogucki, *Forest Farmers and Stockherders*, pp. 85–90.

72. Gregg, *Foragers and Farmers*, pp. 165–67.

73. Whittle, *Neolithic Europe*, p. 62.

74. Bogucki, *Forest Farmers and Stockherders*, pp. 94–100.

75. Bogucki, *Forest Farmers and Stockherders*, p. 95.

76. Bogucki, *Forest Farmers and Stockherders*, pp. 117–22.

77. Ammerman and Cavalli-Sforza, *Neolithic Transition*, chapter 6. See also Cavalli-Sforza and Cavalli-Sforza, *Great Human Diasporas*, chapter 6, for a series of maps that portray the wave of advance. For a more technical discussion of this and related issues as regards European genetic history, see Luigi Luca Cavalli-Sforza, Paolo Menozzi, and Alberto Piazza, *The History and Geography of Human Genes* (Princeton: Princeton University Press, 1994), chapter 5.

78. Price, Gebauer, and Keeley, "Spread of Farming."

Chapter Six

The Biology of the Silk Road

A feature of the landscape such as a desert, river, or mountain can be a barrier to movement or a corridor that channels and facilitates traffic. How this feature is used depends on many factors. The technology available to travelers may enable them to leap over, go around, or tunnel through some barrier. Knowledge of whether there is hospitality or danger over the horizon encourages or dissuades the continuation of a journey. Travelers may depend on the tolerance or active collaboration of people living along the route. Political and military control may make local cooperation possible, but the natives might just as readily oppose foreigners crossing their land. Then there is the motivation driving the travelers: How badly do they want to get to their destination? Are they making the trip under duress as refugees, are they on a religious pilgrimage, or are they on a trade mission that will make them wealthy? And what about opportunity costs? Where else, and in what other endeavors, could the travelers be investing their time, money, and energy? And are there other ways for them to achieve their goals, other routes that would take them where they want to go?

To the casual observer, the five thousand-kilometer-long stretch of windswept steppes and oasis-studded deserts that lie between the eastern Mediterranean and central China might look barren and forbidding, more a barrier to movement than a welcoming corridor. Nevertheless, for more than three millennia, a complex network of routes known collectively as the Silk Road channeled merchants, pilgrims, immigrants, smugglers, refugees, soldiers, and adventurers across this land. In the process, the routes connected the ancient empires that made up what William McNeill called the "Eurasian ecumene."[1]

That the dry belt of Asia was a corridor and not a barrier was due in part to all of the above: economics, technology, political control, knowledge of the terrain, motivation, and so on. But in this chapter, I want to highlight the role of coevolved life systems—humans, plants, animals, and diseases—in shaping the Silk Road and its consequences. Living organisms provided the chief economic motivations (silk worms and mulberry trees, horses and sheep, grapes and wine, pepper and other spices), the chief mode of transport (camels, horses, donkeys), and the chief long-term consequence (the unification of the previously separated Eurasian disease pools, especially the bubonic plague).

THE GEOGRAPHY OF CENTRAL ASIA

The Old World's three continents are split by a huge horizontal belt of arid land that extends from the northwest hump of Africa to northern China.[2] North of the belt, bracketed by the desert below and the frost line above, lies the broad expanse of Eurasian forests and steppes that run from the Atlantic and the Mediterranean to Siberia. To the south lie Africa below the Sahara, and monsoon Asia from the Indian subcontinent to Australia and the Pacific Islands.

The dry belt in between actually consists of two features: a trade-wind section that extends from the Atlantic coast to Arabia, and a continental section that spans the distance from southern Russia and Iran to Mongolia. Even though the two together present a seemingly unbroken desert belt today, they have had quite different ecological histories. The trade-wind section was less arid during the last Ice Age than it is today, and so would have presented less of a barrier to human and animal migration prior to ten thousand years ago. The continental section, in contrast, was in prehistoric times about as dry as it is today, and would have been just as daunting to the earliest human migrants as it was to travelers only several thousand years ago.

This history helps explain the different routes used by migrants out of Africa from about one hundred thousand years ago.[3] Leaving Africa by crossing the trade-wind section of the dry belt (that is, through Egypt and the Middle East) would have presented fewer difficulties in the distant past. Once into Eurasia, however, long-distance travelers would have been channeled north onto the steppes of the great "world island," where they could turn either west into Europe, or east toward Siberia and, eventually, the Americas.

For the earliest migrants, the mountain ranges and deserts of the dry belt would have been a barrier to movement. But long before the first humans started making their way across the Eurasian grasslands, the climate and terrain were already shaping the flora and fauna of the region. Climatic factors of temperature and rainfall selected for a certain kind of vegetation, and these factors in turn selected for a certain array of large mammals. Some of these animals, most notably the horse, evolved to take advantage of their speed across the open expanses of the steppes. Some, such as sheep and goats, evolved to defend themselves against the cold by growing heavy coats of fleece; others, especially the camel, evolved to survive in an arid environment. They all evolved as grazers or herd animals to make maximum use of the region's food supply stored in the abundant grasslands.

The dry belt, as Hermann von Wissmann observed long ago, consists of three subregions, each with its own climatic features and agricultural history.[4] The southern belt across the Sudan and the Arabian peninsula does not concern us here. The middle belt from Spain and Morocco to northern China features long, hot summers and short winters. Here, farming could prosper if water could be found and either tapped from oases or transported by irrigation from nearby rivers or distant snow melt. The northern belt extends from central and eastern Europe across Russia to northern Mongolia and Manchuria. This belt begins as a rather wide swath in Europe, and narrows steadily as it reaches Siberia. Here, summers are too short and winters too cold to make irrigation farming worth the effort. Farming here was based on the hardy, large-seeded winter cereals, including wheat and barley, that spread out of the Fertile Crescent.

Since farming across this northern belt was precarious, livestock herding became a much more reliable way to bolster the food supply. The biological and cultural package of grazing livestock and wheat entered central Asia from the west, probably from Iran and its surrounding area, and traveled along the chain of oases through Sinkiang and Kansu. The principal carriers of this food system were Indo-European peoples from northwest India and Iran. They were nomadic while shifting from oasis to oasis; but once they located a favorable site, they became steppe farmers, albeit without completely divesting themselves of certain features of nomadism (such as placing a low value on accumulating a large stock of material goods and comforts).

Von Wissmann identified three zones across the northern belt that offered different prospects for herding peoples: wooded steppes, good for both agriculture and pasture; open steppes, good for pasture but marginal for cultivation, and too vulnerable to fluctuating rainfall totals; and desert or semidesert steppes, with only meager pasture. These last two zones supported tribes of shepherd nomads who shaped the Silk Road for several thousand years.

These climatic divisions and their respective cultures of food production have influenced Chinese history for millennia. China south of the Yangtze River adopted a more sedentary food-production system based on rice cultivation and the domestication of pigs. Eventually, such a system became the foundation for a more inclusive Chinese social order. To the north and west, however, lived the nomadic peoples of the steppes, with an agrarian economy based on grazing livestock (especially horses and sheep) and the winter cereals. Much of Chinese history has turned on the struggle between the "civilization" of the sedentary farmers and their cities in China proper, and the "barbarism" (as the Chinese called it) of the nomadic pastoralists of the steppes.

THE SILK ROAD IN OPERATION

The Silk Road was not a single road but a complex network of land and water routes that connected China with the eastern Mediterranean and most of the empires in between (see figure 6.1). Although the date usually given for opening the main Silk Road is the second century B.C., parts of the network were open at

Figure 6.1   The Silk Road Network

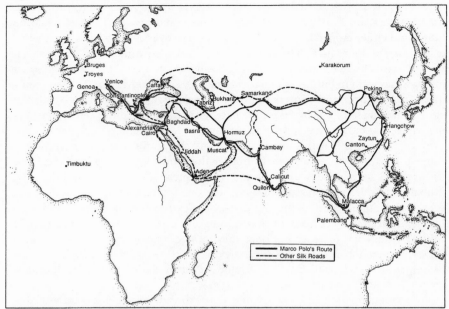

Source: Christopher Chase-Dunn and Thomas Hall, *Rise and Demise: Comparing World-Systems* (Boulder, Colorado: Westview, 1997), p. 165. © Westview Press. Reprinted by permission.

least two thousand years before that.[5] Different sectors of the road varied in importance across the centuries, and there were long periods when some sections were closed completely due to political instability, disease epidemics, environmental crises such as famine or drought, or the loss of control by one of the great empires that lay along the route. What follows, then, is a simplified description of the Silk Road in its entirety: the principal overland routes and the connecting secondary routes between them, the land routes that branched off from the main road and turned south into India or north into Russia and eastern Europe, and the sea routes between China and the Mediterranean that were an important complement to the overland roads.

Silk Road travelers heading west out of China began their journey in the Han Dynasty capital, C'hang-an (today known as Xi-an).[6] Already by 210 B.C., C'hang-an was a large and important capital city; by the seventh century A.D., it had an estimated population of about two million. By the eighth century, it was, in Michael Wood's words, "one of the greatest cities in the world, rivalled only by Baghdad and Constantinople."[7] One of the world's earliest planned cities, C'hang-an was laid out in squares like a huge chess board. By the time of the T'ang dynasty, in the eighth century, the city's western quarter had become an enclave of foreigners, trade diasporas, from all along the Silk Road:[8] from Syria and Iraq, from Persia and central Asia, from India and Turkey. Wall paintings in excavated tombs depict young aristocrats playing polo, a game imported from central Asia along with the horses they rode. In time, the T'ang dynasty would fall to be replaced by others, and the capital city would be moved north, to Loyang and then Beijing. But C'hang-an would never relinquish its celebrated status as the origin of the Silk Road.

For the first one thousand kilometers or so, the route lay through the Kansu Corridor, a narrow strip of land between the Gobi Desert to the north and the Nan Shan Mountains to the south. Control over this land was often hotly contested with the nomadic tribes from the northern steppes, and the western half of this portion of the route lay inside the Great Wall for protection from raiders and bandits.

Leaving the Kansu Corridor, westbound travelers entered the huge expanse of what today is China's Xinjiang Uighur Autonomous Region. The central feature of Xinjiang is the Taklamakan Desert, bounded on the south by the K'unlun Shan Mountains and on the north by the T'ien Shan Mountains. At the entrance to Xinjiang, near the strategic town of Tunhuang, the road forked, offering travelers three options: a southern route between the K'unlun Shan and the Taklamakan, a middle route between the Taklamakan and the T'ien Shan, and a northern route that ran north of the T'ien Shan.

Each route had its advantages and costs. The most northern route was the most comfortable during the scorching summers, but it was the most vulnerable to raids by nomads and bandits. The central and southern routes took travelers over blistering deserts with some of the most desolate landscape on Earth. The feature that made it possible to take the southern or middle route was the string of oasis towns in the foothills of the two bordering mountain ranges: Tunhuang (Dunhuang), where the road forked;[9] Turfan (Turpan), Korla, Kucha, and Aksu north of the desert; and Khotan and Shan-Shan to the south. The rivers and the melting snow from the mountains fed oases that supported rich farmlands and the towns built around the precious water supplies. These oasis towns supplied camel caravans with food and water, and at the same time became important trading centers in their own right.

> The oases depended heavily on trade for their economic survival, and they quickly accommodated the needs and interests of the merchants whom they hosted. They became centers of high literacy and culture; they organized markets and arranged for lodging, care of animals, and storage of merchandise; and they allowed their guests to build monasteries and bring large contingents of Buddhist monks and copyists into their communities.[10]

Some of the travelers on the northern route turned south along an auxiliary road to rejoin the main road after it had left the Taklamakan, but others continued north and west, skirting the Caspian and Black Seas to connect with European networks at Byzantium (Constantinople) or farther north into Europe proper. The central and southern routes came together and emerged from the Taklamakan at Kashgar, just before crossing the Pamir Mountains. Here the road entered the easternmost extension of the empire of Alexander the Great, but by Han times the region was under the control of the smaller kingdoms of Ferghana and Sogdiana.

From this point, the road offered several options for crossing the Iranian Plateau between the Elburz Mountains to the north and the Zagros Mountains to the south. Seven hundred kilometers to the west, the road reached the trading cities along the Tigris and Euphrates rivers, from where it turned northwest toward the city of Palmyra in Syria. The road branched at this point, with one route turning west toward the Mediterranean ports, and the other route continuing northwest into Turkey. Either way, the travelers were now at the doorstep of the Roman Empire.

Other land routes connected this main road with markets in Russia and the Balkans, India, Burma, and the rest of southeast Asia. To the north, the Eurasian Steppe Road skirted the Altai Mountains, turned west until it reached the Volga River, and then angled southwest to the Black Sea port city of Kaffa (a site of great importance to the biological consequences of the Silk Road, as we shall soon see). The southern branch, called the Indian Grand Road, left the main route just west of the Pamirs, turned southeast through the Hindu Kush to the broad Indian plain, and ended at the mouth of the Ganges River, where it connected with maritime routes across the Bay of Bengal. At Palmyra, in Syria, the road connected with a route that headed south and west toward the Mediterranean ports of Tyre and Sidon, and beyond to the spice and incense trade routes through the Red Sea and across Arabia.[11] At the terminals of these routes, merchants connected with maritime trade routes across the Indian Ocean to India and Southeast Asia.

Land routes were not the only option for travelers between Mediterranean Europe and the Orient.[12] Already by Han and Roman times, sea routes connected southern China with Burma and India, across the Arabian Sea through the Red Sea and the Persian Gulf, and then by land to the Mediterranean. Beginning about 300 B.C., India and China had established trading connections by water with Greece, and later with Rome. Rome's main trade diaspora reached as far as southern India by about 100 B.C.; the first Roman traders to arrive in China came by way of the ocean. From India, the goods were carried by Arab traders through the Indian Ocean to the Red Sea or the Persian Gulf, then overland to the Mediterranean, and then on to European ports.[13]

Before the age of steam power, trade across these sea routes was shaped largely by the seasonal winds. East-west travel across the Indian Ocean was limited by the ocean monsoons, which blow from the southwest during the summer and from the northeast during the winter. At either end of the network, where travel turned along north-south axes, seasonal changes in wind direction imposed similar limitations, blowing mostly north-to-south in the winter and the reverse in the summer.

For the western half of the maritime trading network—from India west to the Mediterranean—the Red Sea route would seem to have held the advantage over the Persian Gulf, since the portion given over to land travel was by far shorter. However, prevailing winds in the northern half of the Red Sea are from the north, so merchants going from east to west had to sail against the wind for that part of the voyage. Even with the lateen sail, an Arab invention, sailing into the wind was not easy, so merchants usually halted their voyages half way up and transferred their goods to camel, either for further transshipment to Nile River boats or to be carried straight through to the Mediterranean via Arabia.

In the eastern half of the network—from India across the Bay of Bengal and the South China Sea—maritime trade began to flourish as early as it did farther west. The Chinese city of Guangzhou was an important trading city during the Han Dynasty, and Chinese merchants were trading regularly with India by the first century of the Christian era. For the South China Sea portion of the network, the Chinese dominated trade; for the Bay of Bengal segment, it was the Indians. A small portion of the trade moved by water through the Straits of Malacca, but in the early days, most goods were transshipped across land at the narrow Kra isthmus between Malaysia and Thailand. Trading settlements of Indian intermediaries brokered the trade there, just as did the traders in the oasis towns and cities along the land routes.

THE SILK ROAD: A BRIEF HISTORY

William McNeill refers to the establishment of the earliest global system as the "closure of the Eurasian ecumen," a transformation essentially completed by about 200 A.D.[14] From this time until 1500, the world system consisted of the Eurasian land mass, with the northern steppes at the center; arrayed around the periphery were the successive states in Europe, the Middle East, India, China, and somewhat later Japan. Beyond the fringes of this ecumene lay lands still largely unknown to Eurasians: the Western Hemisphere, Africa below the Sahara, and Australia and the Pacific Islands.

Half a millennium before the beginning of the Christian era, the Bronze Age societies of Greece, Egypt, and the Middle East had established the technologies and the market institutions necessary to carry on a flourishing trade across the eastern Mediterranean.[15] Within the next five hundred years, other societies across Eurasia followed suit. Alexander the Great led his armies into the lands of the Fertile Crescent to establish Greek outposts as far east as the western fringes of central Asia. The Persian Empire had already established an internal trading network via their Royal Road; and Alexander's conquests enabled this network to be linked to the Greek trading system by the latter part of the fourth century B.C. In the Indian subcontinent, the Maurya Empire arose in the third century B.C., providing a political consolidation of the homeland of Buddhism. Soon, Buddhist monks would begin to travel east along the Silk Road to carry their faith to China, where it thrived long after it had declined in its homeland. The fifth century B.C. teachings of Confucius found political expression in China's Han Dynasty in the third century B.C., and a newly unified China began to take its place as one of the leading political and trading centers of the world.[16]

For many centuries, these empires were separated by mountains, steppes, and deserts, not to mention bandits and hostile nomadic tribes. Contact by land was sporadic and dangerous; ocean travel via the Persian Gulf and the Indian Ocean was possible, but navigation limits restricted this route to short trips between neighboring ports; true long-distance commerce over water was still some centuries into the future.

In one form or another, the Silk Road connected China, central Asia, Mediterranean Europe, the Middle East, and India for nearly two thousand years. To summarize such a long and complicated history in a few pages requires that we concentrate on the three periods during which the power of the empires of the Eurasian ecumene was adequate to keep the road open to commerce and cultural exchange.[17] The first period, from 200 B.C. to 400 A.D., was dominated by China's Han Dynasty and the Roman Empire. During the second, from 600 to 1000 A.D., China's T'ang Dynasty anchored the eastern end of the road, and the Abbassid caliphate of Baghdad and the Byzantine Empire secured the western end. And in the third, from 1000 to 1350 A.D., the route was under the control of the nomadic empires, the Turkish empires in India and Anatolia, and the Mongol Empire, known as the Yüan Dynasty in China.

The growth of imperial power into and through central Asia stimulated contacts in two ways. As the empires expanded, they sent out soldiers, administrators, and diplomats to manage their increasing contacts with border or frontier regions and peoples. As the regions under political control grew, merchants followed closely behind in search of new products and new markets, and farmers arrived to claim abandoned agricultural lands.[18] While these powerful empires were in control, the bandits and nomadic tribes were kept at bay, and traders and pilgrims made their way more or less unmolested across Eurasia. When these regimes declined and collapsed and were succeeded by weak or fragmented ministates, trade was interrupted. Not infrequently, epidemics of diseases such as the bubonic plague or measles also contributed both to the interruption of commerce and to the collapse of empires.

The Silk Road routes evolved from the uniting of Chinese, central Asian, Indian, Persian, and Greco-Roman networks several centuries before the beginning of the Christian era.[19] These connections were made possible by the power of the Chinese and Roman empires, the collaboration and tolerance of the nomadic peoples who lived along the routes, and the services of numerous traders and merchants who brokered the trade and supplied markets, camels, and guides.

But regular caravan operations could not be established and maintained until the trading partners had consolidated their control over the land routes. For the Chinese, this required being able to control the Kansu Corridor just to the south of the Gobi Desert. This corridor marked the western end of the Great Wall, which the Chin Dynasty had begun building to protect China from incursions by the nomadic tribes to the north (from what is today Mongolia). Control over this land corridor was finally established by the Han Dynasty in 154 B.C.;[20] but it was from the beginning a shaky kind of control that depended on the cooperation of the steppe nomads.

Ever since the time of the Shang Dynasty in the second millennium B.C., the steppe nomads had presented the Chinese with a difficult challenge. On the one hand, the nomads were an important market for Chinese goods, especially food and silk; but on the other, the nomads were often violent and aggressive, and they came increasingly to covet China's rich lands to the south.

During the years of the Han Dynasty (206 B.C. to 220 A.D.), one nomadic tribe in particular, the Hsiung-nu, emerged as the principal threat.[21] The Hsiung-nu, or the Huns as they were later called when they reached Europe, were a Turkish-speaking people who had arisen in the area between ancient China and the Mongolian Desert. In the last three centuries before the Christian era, they had absorbed a number of elements of the culture of the nomadic North Iranians, including the use of horse cavalry. In the second century B.C., they were united in a confederacy reaching from the Aral Sea to eastern Mongolia.

Living on land too poor for year-round pasturing and in a climate too cold to permit irrigation agriculture, the Hsiung-nu could survive only through reliance on herds of grazing animals that could be moved from one pasture to another as conditions warranted. Thus, the ecological frontier between the Chinese to the south and the Hsiung-nu to the north became a zone of fierce competition as both groups struggled to establish their control over the region.

At first, the Chinese tried to buy the cooperation of the nomads by arranging dynastic marriages or paying tribute or ransom, but the nomads frequently attacked caravans anyway. Eventually the Chinese grew weary of these arrangements and deployed troops at key points along the frontier. Early in the first century B.C., Chinese armies seized numerous Hsiung-nu strongholds, dispatched farmers and land-reclamation teams into central Asia, and gradually consolidated their control over the Silk Road corridor. From about 60 B.C. on, the Chinese were able to exert a certain level of control over the corridor, even if they had to continue the payment of tribute in addition to their military presence.

In 139 B.C., the Han emperor sent an ambassador west to make contact with the nomads. The envoy, Chang Ch'ien, and his retinue disappeared for thirteen years, ten of which they spent as captives of the Hsiung-nu. Eventually freed, the envoy made his way as far west as northern Afghanistan to an area known as Bactria, an outpost of Greek culture since the time of Alexander the Great. Thus, Chang Ch'ien made the first enduring contact between China and Mediterranean Europe. The envoy's return to China sparked great interest in the lands to the west and to the south as well, for he brought back news of another great kingdom to the southeast of Afghanistan, a land that was said to be "hot and damp. The inhabitants ride elephants when they go into battle. The kingdom is situated on a great river." Chang Ch'ien had learned of India; and land routes would soon connect it with China as well.[22]

Even before Chinese traders began to travel the Silk Road, demand for Chinese silk had created markets throughout the ecumene empires.[23] Some scholars speculate that silk given to the Hsiung-nu as tribute payments eventually made its way to India, Persia, and Rome; others believe that ocean routes brought silk to the attention of the peoples of these distant lands. In any event, as soon as China had secured the trade routes across central Asia, merchants and traders moved quickly to exploit the huge demand for this exotic and highly prized cloth.

The first caravan to travel straight through to Persia (or Parthia, as it was then known) left China in 106 B.C., but in these early days it was surely an exceptional case. Little of the trade was conducted directly by Chinese agents, but rather by intermediaries who brokered the trade at several points along the route. Chinese merchants reached as far as central Asia, and Indian and central Asian merchants carried their goods deep into China; but few individuals ever made the entire round trip. Instead, the oasis towns and other strategically situated cities along the route became transfer points and grand bazaars where goods and cultures were freely exchanged. Half a century later, after the Romans had captured Palestine (the natural western terminus of the route), Chinese silks were being traded in Rome itself. Since the Romans had little the Chinese wanted except for gold, there emerged a trade of Mediterranean bullion for Chinese silks. The emperor Tiberius soon found it necessary to prohibit the wearing of silk because of the drain on the empire's gold reserves.

For centuries after the beginning of the Christian era, there was no more significant factor than the Silk Road in promoting what would have been considered at the time a "global" economy and culture. Not only goods and raw materials but also ideas, knowledge, and skills (in a word, culture) were spread throughout Europe and Asia by the route.[24] Political ideologies, religious faiths, techniques of production, arts, and fashions were all exchanged along its length and breadth. Thanks to the Silk Road, Buddhism emigrated from India to China, and later to Korea and Japan; and Islam was spread from Arabia to Turkestan and India. The Chinese received glass, grapes and wine, wool, cotton, ivory, large horses, and papyrus; and in return, Europeans received silk, jade, tea, apricots, peaches and pears, paper making, porcelain, jewelry, art objects, and precious spices (pepper, cinnamon, ginger, and cloves).

Over the long term, commercial activity along the Silk Road rose and fell as a function of the stability of the empires at either end, and of the willingness of nomadic tribes along the route to let the travelers pass.[25] From 200 B.C. to 400 A.D., trade grew steadily, carried mostly by camel caravans across Asia. With the collapse of the Han and Roman empires and the consequent increasing disorder, turmoil, and instability across the breadth of Eurasia, trade declined sharply for the two centuries between 400 and 600 A.D. Even the Hsiung-nu confederation fell apart, and for a time it seemed that order would never be restored.

But through these centuries of instability and isolation, the impetus to continue commercial exchanges persisted. Following the rise of the silk industry in Byzantine territory after 600 A.D., there was a decline in the importance of the silk trade along the road. Other products were in great demand, however, and during the next 400 years to about 1000 A.D., there was a resurgence of commercial contacts along both land and sea routes, stimulated in large part by the entry of Arabs into maritime trade between eastern Africa, India, and the Mediterranean.

After 600, two major military and political changes, one at either end of the Silk Road, enabled trade to resume at even higher levels than had been the case in ancient times. The first was the rise of Islam, which began in 622. One of the important consequences of the emergence of an Islamic state was the consolidation of a new geopolitical entity that reached from Morocco and Spain, in the west, to Persia and central Asia, in the east. After 750, the Abbasid empire ruled in Baghdad until about 1000 A.D., a time usually considered the golden age of Islam.

The second major change occurred in China, where the T'ang dynasty brought order and peace to the country after centuries of war and disunity.[26] The T'ang period, from 618 to 907, is thought of as one of the most prosperous and creative in Chinese history. It was also a period of expansion, as China established control over Mongolia, Turkestan, Tibet, and as far west as northern Afghanistan, where it met the eastern frontier of the Abbasid empire. It was during this time that C'hang-an became one of the premier cities in the world. Throughout most of T'ang rule, foreigners were welcomed and encouraged to visit China, as the Chinese had acquired a taste for the exotic, and foreign luxury goods were highly prized. Trade brokers from all parts of Eurasia streamed into C'hang-an, although they were segregated in residential enclaves and forbidden to have contact with Chinese women.

"The simultaneous power of the Abbasids and the T'ang," writes Philip Curtin, "made it comparatively easy for long-distance traders to make the whole journey across Asia and North Africa, in effect from the Atlantic to the Pacific."[27] What was novel about the seventh and eighth centuries was not only the political and military consolidation of the Silk Road and its auxiliary routes, but also the existence for the first time of one group, the Radanites, who could operate across the entire trading system. For more than a century, this key group of Jewish merchants constituted a single trade diaspora with a shared culture that could offer customers a trade network from Europe and North Africa to the Pacific Ocean. It was also during this time that the Silk Road became a highway for refugees, as Christians from Persia and Turkestan fled east to escape the growing power of Islam.[28]

Another key group were the Uighurs, a nomadic people from the steppes north and west of the Taklamakan Desert, who allied themselves with the T'ang dynasty during the seventh century. Based on this alliance, the Uighurs became the dominant steppe tribe during this period. They were able to exploit their strategic location and strength by extracting favorable commercial terms from China, and the silk they received they bartered with neighbors farther to the west. Much of this silk eventually ended up in Persian and Byzantine markets.

The trading patterns of this second phase lasted for several centuries. But eventually, the xenophobia of the T'ang leaders, the weakening of the Abbassid empire, and the assaults by restive nomadic tribes spelled the end of this arrangement and laid the foundation for the third and final phase of the Silk Road in the three centuries after 1000, during which the Eurasian trading system achieved a level of regional integration that was unprecedented.[29] The nomadic empires built by the Turks in the west and the Mongols in the east pacified vast territories and encouraged the rapid growth of long-distance travel overland. Important developments in maritime technology emanating from China and the Arab world facilitated long-distance sea travel as well, unifying the Indian Ocean into a single system from eastern Africa to the South China Sea. Finally, the growth of European economic and political power brought western Europeans into the emerging global system to a degree that far surpassed the integration of the eastern Mediterranean in earlier periods.

The Silk Road reached the height of its importance in the thirteenth century. From the 1240s, when the Mongols first invaded Europe, European merchants visiting China and the Far East were protected by the Mongol leaders, the Great Khans. Contacts between Europeans and Mongols increased for both religious purposes and for trade in silk, porcelain, and spices. Marco Polo left Venice in 1271 to accompany his father and uncle on their famous commercial expedition to China. In 1294, however, Kubilai Khan died and the Mongol empire, known as the Yüan Dynasty, began to decline. In 1368, the Mongols were driven from China, the successive Ming dynasty eventually plunged China into an era of isolation, and European merchants lost their privileged access to Chinese markets. The devastating effects of the bubonic plague in the mid-fourteenth century also severely damaged trade between Europe and the East. The fall of Constantinople to the Ottoman Turks in 1453 sharply reduced access to the road and forced European traders to seek ocean routes to the Orient. When, on May 20, 1498, the Portuguese explorer Vasco da Gama dropped anchor in the harbor of Calicut and thus opened a direct sea route from Europe to the riches of Asia, the decline of the Silk Road was complete.

THE BIOLOGY OF THE SILK ROAD: PLANTS AND ANIMALS

To the merchants and pilgrims traveling the Silk Road, the mountain ranges and deserts of the dry belt must have presented enormous obstacles that could be overcome by only the best organized and the most highly motivated. Living organisms, however, found movement across Eurasia significantly easier than across the other continents. The reason, asserts Jared Diamond, lay in the long axis of the Eurasian land mass.[30]

All the Earth's land masses contain features that make movement difficult, but the prevailing long axis of each continent facilitates or blocks travel to different degrees. In the Americas and Africa, the north-south long axis channels travelers across a number of different climatic zones that force repeated adaptation to changing growing conditions. The east-west long axis of Eurasia, however, ensures that migrating organisms will encounter much the same conditions of life: day length, seasonal variation, temperature, rainfall, vegetation, and micröorganisms.

The key to the Eurasian advantage lies in plant adaptation. Seasonal changes, particularly in the length of periods of daylight, signal plants to germinate, grow, develop flowers, seeds, and fruit; or to become dormant. Plant populations evolve genetic programs that are suitable for their respective climates. These growing environments vary greatly with latitude, although other factors are also influential. Plants that have evolved to prosper in tropical zones at the equator will not survive in a temperate zone at, say, 30 degrees north latitude because they will not have acquired a strategy for getting through a cold, dark winter. This is why the plants of the Fertile Crescent, particularly emmer and einkhorn wheat, barley, and millet, spread relatively easily east and west from one end of Eurasia to the other.

Where plants went, the animals that depended on them followed. The spread of wheat and other cereal grains across Eurasia was accompanied by the grazing animals that were nourished by their food energy: horses, cattle, and sheep. And these animals were followed by rodents and other small animals, by microparasites, and by the top carnivore that survived on the milk, meat, blood, and flesh of herbivores: *Homo sapiens*. By the beginning of the Christian era, the package of temperate-zone coevolved life systems—farmers, herders, cereals, grazing herd animals, and their parasites (rodents, fleas, and so forth)—had occupied the entire Eurasian land mass of some sixteen thousand kilometers from the Atlantic coast of Ireland to the Pacific coast of Japan.

Living organisms, or the products manufactured from them, made the Silk Road profitable as well as possible. Some of the luxury goods that moved along the Silk Road, such as jade or porcelain, were not biological. But most of the goods in great demand in the markets served by the road were either the products of living organisms, such as silk and wine, or were the organisms themselves: fruit (oranges, peaches, pears), spices (pepper, sesame, safflower), flowers (roses, azaleas, chrysanthemums), and, of course, horses. Moreover, the road was made feasible by two beasts of burden, the camel and the ass, which made possible long-distance travel across the desert.

The Silkworm and Its Industry

The nineteenth-century German explorer and geographer Baron Ferdinand von Richthofen coined the term *die Seidenstrasse*, the Silk Road, by which future scholars would call the trans-Asian highway; but apparently Byzantine-empire traders had a similar name for it because Chinese silk played such a vital role in the transactions along the route.[31] Silk is one of the oldest known textile fibers.[32] It comes from the fiber woven into the cocoon of the mulberry silk moth, commonly known as the silkworm. The silkworm is not a worm at all, however, but a caterpillar, and like many other insects it spins a cocoon within which the cater-pillar transforms itself into a moth; but only the fibers from the cocoon of the mulberry silk moth and a few closely related species are fine enough to be used in commercial silk manufacture. In this controlled process, the adult female silk-worm deposits 300 to 400 tiny eggs, which hatch after ten days or so. The larvae are given mulberry leaves to eat, which they do almost constantly for about six weeks, after which they begin spinning their cocoons. The typical cocoon may contain from 300 to 900 meters of continuous fiber. Since the emergence of the adult moth tears the cocoon fiber, most of the moths are killed by heat before they mature. Only enough individuals to perpetuate the species are kept alive to ma-turity. Having been domesticated for many centuries, silkworms have ceased to exist in the wild and owe their continued existence to human caretakers. The spe-cies was native to China, but was introduced into western Asia in the sixth cen-tury A.D., and into North America in the eighteenth.

Two other species are important components of the silk production system. One is the white mulberry—cultivated in China for many centuries—whose leaves alone yield the continuous fibers so prized in the making of silk. The other spe-cies was the shellfish that produced the dyes applied to the finished fabrics. One of the reasons Chinese silk was so highly prized was its receptiveness to fine dyes, the most highly valued of which were the rich purple dyes produced by Phoenicians from glandular liquid extracted from a species of shellfish that lived in the waters of the eastern Mediterranean. (The name of the Phoenicians comes from the Greek word for purple, *poeni*.) The extraction of this liquid was diffi-cult, time consuming, and could only be performed at certain times of the year, all of which made purple silk extremely expensive. It is from these origins that we associate purple with royalty even today.[33]

Chinese legend and tradition date the knowledge of silk manufacture from the twenty-seventh century B.C. Making silk requires great skill, knowledge, timing, patience, and delicacy. These skills were preserved as a secret known only to the Chinese for three millennia, until about 300 A.D. So important was silk manufac-turing that virtually every family contained at least one person skilled in the tech-nique, and a certain segment of each garden or farm was set aside for mulberry trees. Taxes were payable in silk, so a family's skill in sericulture was critical to their economic fortunes.

How people in the West learned of silk remains a mystery,[34] Prior to 200 B.C., there was already an active trade between China and the Mediterranean, and silk may have passed through the hands of brokers at many sites along the route. By about 200 B.C., the Han Dynasty had built up a lucrative trade in silk with the West, particularly Rome. Persian intermediaries brokered the trade between China and the Mediterranean.

Roman leaders were impatient with this arrangement, since it cost them so much in trade; but they could not for centuries penetrate the Chinese secret. Ac-cording to one account, in 550 A.D. the Roman emperor Justinian I sent two Nestorian Christian monks to China to obtain the secret of silk production. The monks got as far as the central Asian oasis city of Khotan, where they encountered silk production being carried on outside direct Chinese control.[35] The monks managed to escape with both mulberry seeds and silkworm eggs, and the Chinese monopoly was broken. Silk production became a commercial success from Persia to Italy, and the Silk Road was no longer needed for its importation.

Innovations in textile manufacture did not flow in only one direction. Just as the Romans coveted silk, the Chinese were eager to import rare and (to them) exotic cotton goods from India. If the Romans found it hard to believe that silk came from an animal, the Chinese were equally incredulous about cotton's origins from a plant. They believed that the fiber came from a "vegetable lamb," a strange animal that was planted in the ground. There is evidence that cotton was grown in central Asia as early as the second century A.D., but the secret did not penetrate China proper for another millennium.[36] It was not until the time of Mongol rule that a Chinese envoy to the Uighur Turks discovered cotton growing in the area around the town of Almalik, on the north slope of the T'ien Shan Mountains, and carried the truth about the fabric back to China.[37]

Food Products

So many food products were exchanged along the Silk Road that we can do no more here than simply acknowledge a few of them. Wheat, for example, was carried from its southwestern Asian origins into China sometime around the end of the second millennium B.C. along routes that passed through central Asia; and rice was introduced into Persia along the same route about the middle of the first millennium B.C.[38] Many varieties of fruit and vegetables were also exchanged along the road. For example, in the seventh and eighth centuries A.D., a trading people known as the Sogdians fled eastward into central Asia to escape an expansionist Islamic state. They brought with them a method of underground irrigation by means of tunnels that had been invented by the Persians.[39] With irrigation, central Asian land that had previously been arid and worthless now bloomed with crops of figs, cucumbers, spinach, walnuts, peaches, melons, and other fruits and vegetables brought from the West or from India.[40] The Sogdians also brought a new variety of grape, juicy and succulent, and a love of the fine wine it produced.

It is not known for certain when or from where grapes in general were brought for the first time into central Asia.[41] Some sources assert that they were introduced by the Greeks at the time of Alexander the Great, while others suggest they came from Egypt and Persia about the beginning of the Christian era. Grapes and their chief byproduct, wine, became known to the Chinese when the Han Dynasty envoy, Chang Ch'ien, encountered them in the Pamirs' empire called Ferghana. The land and climate around the oasis towns proved to be excellent for viniculture, and by the ninth century A.D. the city of Turfan (Turpan) in the foothills of the T'ien Shan Mountains had become known as the best grape region of central Asia. The city is still famous for its grapes and their products, raisins and wine.

Large Mammals

The silkworm was not the only significant animal in our story. Large mammals were also important in the biological package associated with the Silk Road, and none was more significant than the horse.

Horses

The domestication of horses must surely rank as one of the most important biological events in the history of globalization, for it increased the mobility of humans to a degree unmatched by any other living creature.[42] No other animal capable of carrying a human can match the speed of a horse's sustained gallop of seventy kilometers per hour; and even smaller animals capable of faster speeds, such as the cheetah, can sustain their top speed for only a few hundred meters. Despite its size, the horse's nutritional needs are easily met, since they have adapted to eating the poorest quality forage with the lowest concentration of protein of any large herbivore. Because the horse is a hindgut digester, it passes enormous volumes of food through its digestive system rather quickly, and it can extract greater nutritional value from forage per unit of time than can a cow. Indeed, the horse can thrive on grasses that would be a starvation diet for a cow. For these reasons, the horse ranks along with the lateen sail and the steam engine for its contribution to the spread of humankind across the Earth.

Because of their great mobility, strength, and endurance, animals of the genus *Equus* have been significant factors in globalization for more than six millennia. Donkeys were domesticated from wild asses in the upper Nile region, and soon were widely used as beasts of burden throughout the eastern Mediterranean coast, the Fertile Crescent, and on the Iranian Plateau.[43] Before the domestication of the camel, donkeys were the mainstay of the central Asian trade caravans.

Sometimes before 4000 B.C., horses were domesticated by nomadic peoples living in the Ukrainian steppes north of the Black and Caspian Seas;[44] archeological evidence suggests that they were domesticated principally for their mobility, as the horse is an inefficient producer of food energy. Horses were used to pull four-wheeled carts in Mesopotamia as early as 3500 B.C., heavy two-fighter war chariots by 3000 B.C., and lighter one-person chariots by about 2000 B.C. About this same time, nomads from central Asia developed a powerful compound bow, and the combination of archers and horse-drawn chariots proved to be unstoppable.[45] In the second and first millennia B.C., the peoples known as Indo-Europeans left their homelands around the Black and Caspian Seas and began to spread out in all directions in waves of expansion borne largely by horse-drawn vehicles.

The first peoples to develop the art of fighting on horseback, probably about 1300 B.C., were from the mountainous region of northwest Iran.[46] Since these people were sedentary farmers, it seems that horses first demonstrated their great value in warfare rather than for the mobility of nomads. By about 900 B.C., steppe nomads were experimenting with calvary formations and tactics for mounted warfare, and the chariot gradually became obsolete. Only somewhat later did stock herders discover how horses could be used in population movements. The first steppe peoples to use the horse this way were the steppe-farmer Scythians from northern Iran, who gave up their crops to devote themselves completely to stock breeding of herd animals, especially horses.

Sometime about the eighth century B.C., these nomads began to work their way across the northern Eurasian steppes, pushing ahead of them the poorer farmers and hunters. Their use of the horse gave them such great military superiority that no farming people could withstand their onslaughts. Von Wissmann refers to them as a "plague" that enlarged the empty spaces of the dry belt by destroying steppe-farming communities and weakening oasis civilization. Eventually, the tribes of the central T'ien Shan Mountains adopted the life of horse nomads, as did the steppe farmers of Mongolia. These peoples finally reached China itself in the person of the Hsiung-nu, who engaged in centuries of fierce warfare with the Chinese.

In the early days of the Silk Road, Chinese leaders were interested primarily in acquiring herds of horses for use against the Hsiung-nu and other steppe nomads. The return of envoy Chang Ch'ien to China brought news of large, powerful horses living in huge numbers in the kingdom of Ferghana, an area that is today in the states of Kazakstan, Uzbekistan, and the Kyrgyz Republic. In a four-year campaign at the turn of the first century B.C., the Han emperor sent some thirty thousand troops into Ferghana to obtain large numbers of these horses.[47] During the Han dynasty, horses from western Asia were crossbred with Chinese horses to produce animals with exceptional strength, agility, and endurance.

Much later, during the seventh and eighth centuries A.D., trade relations between the Uighur people and the T'ang dynasty centered on the exchange of silk for horses. On the steppes, a horse would cost a single roll of silk; delivered in C'hang-an, however, the price of even an old and tired mount rose to forty rolls of the precious fabric.[48] During the T'ang dynasty, the horse herds under government control alone contained more than seven hundred and fifty thousand animals.

Camels

The horse may have been the animal in prime demand in the markets served by the Silk Road, but extensive overland trade between Europe and China would have been impossible without the domestication of beasts of burden, especially the camel.[49] The Persians are credited with inventing the camel caravan, the institution by which trade with China was conducted. The ability of camels to survive for long periods without water is well known, but they also need very little food and can subsist for long stretches of time on the rough and sparse desert scrub that grew along the Silk Road. They are also very powerful animals capable of carrying loads of up to 200 kilograms across the most difficult terrain.

The two varieties of camel are distinguished by their hump. The Arabian camel has a single hump; the Bactrian camel has two. Both have great endurance and are endowed with features that equip them for desert survival, including heavy, double-lidded eyes, the ability to close their nostrils, and an extraordinary sense of smell and sight. They are both nasty, mean-tempered animals that are difficult to train and control, but a number of features distinguish the two varieties and adapted them to different segments of the Silk Road.

The Arabian camel is a desert animal, better suited for hot weather and relatively useless in rough or rocky terrain. These animals were domesticated by Arabian peoples between 3000 and 2500 B.C. for use in desert warfare; but their service as beasts of burden was delayed until about the middle of the first millennium B.C.[50] In time, however, camel caravans became as essential to the commercial life of the desert societies at the western end of the dry belt of Asia as they had already become to the traders who traveled the Silk Road farther east.

The Bactrian camel originated in central Asia and was domesticated in Persia by about 2000 B.C. The Assyrians brought the animal to Mesopotamia by about 1000 B.C. With a heavy winter coat that it sheds in clumps every spring, the Bactrian camel was well suited for cold weather and mountainous terrain. It was used exclusively as a pack animal until sometime between 500 and 200 B.C., when the camel saddle came into use[51] and camel shoes made from copper or leather were invented. By this time, the camel had become the dominant animal of the Silk Road trade. Camels were often part of tribute sent to rulers, and they are even represented in wall sculptures found in excavated Persian palaces.

THE BIOLOGY OF THE SILK ROAD: DISEASES

Products and ideas were not the only things spread by the commercial contacts of the Silk Road, nor were plants and animals the only living organisms transported across Eurasia along these ancient trade routes. Micröorganisms causing measles, smallpox, diphtheria, and plague were carried to new lands as well:

> When . . . travel across the breadth of the Old World from China and India to the Mediterranean became regularly organized on a routine basis, so that thousands of individuals began to make a living by traveling to and fro, both on shipboard and by caravan, then conditions for the diffusion of infections among the separate civilizations of the Old World altered profoundly."[52] . . . [W]ithin the circle of Old World civilizations, a far more nearly uniform disease pool was created as a byproduct of the opening of regular trade contacts in the first century A.D.[53]

Many episodes of disease were required before the Eurasian ecumene achieved some rough kind of balance between its human population and the pathogens that afflicted them. As the great empires on the periphery of central Asia were integrated into a single biological system, a process that lasted between fifteen hundred and two thousand years, their populations endured repeated epidemics and plagues when humans and pathogens encountered one another in new settings. We have no precise figures for the number of deaths caused by these infectious episodes, but it could well have been in the tens of millions.

One such episode stands out above all others as virtually synonymous with epidemics: the bubonic plague. Beginning in 1347, the "Black Death" (as it later became known) inflicted on Europeans a degree of suffering and death that has had few equals in world history. The loathsomeness of the disease, the speed and cruelty with which it worked, and the horrible randomness and reach of the epidemic that spared few families or towns—all left an indelible mark on Europe's culture and institutions. In paving the way for the great transformation of Europe after the Middle Ages, the plague was a pivotal episode in global history.

There have been only three occasions in recorded history when outbreaks of plague reached pandemic proportions.[54] The first was the so-called plague of Justinian, named after the Roman emperor during whose reign the disease struck. This plague arrived in Europe in 542 A.D., and by 600 it had killed nearly half the continent's approximately 22 million people.[55] The second was the Black Death, which struck China in the 1330s and reached Europe through the Crimea in 1347. By 1349, when its initial wave (there would be many others over the next 300 years) finally had run its course, the plague had killed an estimated one-third of Europe's population. The third pandemic began in southwestern China in the eighteenth century, spread out of China in the late nineteenth century, and followed shipping routes as far as San Francisco and Glasgow. This third wave lasted well into the twentieth century, and indeed there are still a few remnants of it in the Rocky Mountains and other remote regions of western North America.

In general usage, the word "plague" refers to any epidemic or pandemic with high death rates. In modern biomedicine, however, "plague" is the specific disease caused by the bacillus *Yersinia pestis* (sometimes called *Pasteurella pestis*).[56] Plague primarily affects small burrowing or ground-dwelling animals, especially rats of many varieties, marmots, prairie dogs, rabbits, voles, and shrews. In all, more than 200 species of rodents can serve as vectors for strains of plague that are harmful to humans. The bacillus lives among populations of these animals in the wild in well-defined geographical areas called "natural plague reservoirs." Most of the animals in these reservoirs are naturally resistant to the bacillus, but they carry in their hair or fur tiny fleas called rat fleas, which feed off their blood and in so doing can sustain the plague for a very long time. A flea no longer than one millimeter can carry in its gut several hundred thousand bacilli. When a host animal carrying these fleas dies, the fleas jump to another carrier and feed from its blood. The flea's gut provides an ideal growth medium for the bacilli, and they quickly multiply to block the flea's digestive system. As the flea feeds, then, it regurgitates blood back into its host, injecting the bacilli into the host as it does so. If significant numbers of these new hosts prove to be susceptible, the disease becomes wide spread.

It is not easy for *Y. pestis* to migrate from an infected rat to a human. Direct transmission is possible but extremely rare, since it requires that the human actually handle the infected rodent so that the bacillus can enter through a break in the skin. By far the most usual method of transmission is via infected fleas that jump from a dead or drying rodent onto a nearby human. Humans come into contact with infected fleas and their hosts when they enter an area where the plague is established, or when animal hosts enter human settlements. Rats normally do not travel more than 200 hundred meters from their nest;[57] but infected animals have left their natural reservoir to enter human settlements either when carried by traveling humans (most often, traders, smugglers, or soldiers) or when driven from their habitat by ecological disasters such as earthquakes, drought, famine, or floods.

Fleas cannot travel far by themselves. Although the typical flea can jump a distance some 150 times its own length, the average distance of such jumps is only about fifteen centimeters horizontally or ten centimeters vertically.[58] For long-distance mobility, fleas must be transported by other, more mobile animals, such as birds, rabbits, and predators that feed on dead rodents. Humans are also good carriers, principally through modes of transport such as wagons, boats, or camel caravans. Rats and fleas are easily carried in many different commodities, including animal hides, cotton, wool, or grain, or in packaging materials such as jute or hemp bags. Bubonic plague thus tended to follow long-distance trade routes, and the spread was facilitated by trade between growing, densely populated cities.[59] Once *Y. pestis* has entered a human population, transmission from human to human can take place if the bacteria enter the lungs and are coughed up as vapor droplets or blood. It is also possible, but rare, for the bacillus to enter directly into the bloodstream.

Plague takes different forms in humans depending on its mode of transmission.[60] If it is transmitted via a flea bite from an infected rodent, the bacteria migrate to the portion of the lymphatic system nearest the point of entry: if the lower extremities, to the groin; if the upper body, the armpits or neck. There, they cause swelling of painful lumps called "buboes," hence the name "bubonic plague." (The term comes from the Greek word for groin, *boubon*.) Other symptoms include high fever, delirium, vomiting, and headaches. Today, treatment by antibiotics is usually effective in saving the victim's life; but in earlier times, bubonic plague caused death in 60 to 90 percent of the cases, and usually within five days. If the bacillus is transmitted directly via coughed droplets of blood, the disease is called "pneumonic plague," which strikes much more quickly, usually within three days, and is almost always fatal. Transmission via the bloodstream is much more rare; it is called "septicemic plague."

While informed speculations are possible, it is virtually impossible to ascertain with certainty the origin of any plague pandemic or the exact means by which the bacillus was carried from its natural reservoir into human settlements. By their very nature, natural reservoirs are remote places where humans seldom ventured, so it was not easy to record, or even observe, the events leading to the break-out of the disease. Early observers lacked the medical terminology to describe symptoms accurately or the germ theory of disease to inform their observations, so their descriptions were often vague and impressionistic. Until the late nineteenth century, for example, there was not even a word for "plague" in Chinese. Too often, then, historians have had to rely on records or accounts left behind by travelers, religious officials, or local bureaucrats that leave much to the imagination.

Epidemiologists and medical geographers have developed three models that describe the patterns of disease diffusion.[61] "Relocation diffusion" refers to the process by which a disease jumps from one region to another without affecting the space in between; long-distance transport is its means. Today, such means are mechanized: air, rail, or highway; in earlier times, such transport usually followed rivers or trade routes, where the inhabited areas were few and distant from each other. With "urban-hierarchical diffusion," the disease spreads from one inhabited area to another along transportation routes. An infection entering a large urban area cascades down to the city's hinterland via highways or rail in a systematic fashion. With "contact (or expansion) diffusion," the disease spreads outward from a central focus in even waves without being concentrated along any specific transport route.

Where a plague comes from, and how it spreads, matter a great deal to historians trying to determine its morbidity and mortality rates. Some scholars have argued that the bubonic plague required a minimum population density of rats to be sustained; that in fourteenth century Europe such a rodent population existed only in larger cities connected by trade routes; that the disease spread by urban-hierarchical diffusion; that the great majority of the population lived in rural areas, and thus were spared; so the net demographic impact on Europe was not severe. Others believe that the disease spread by contact diffusion, so all areas, rural as well as urban, were hard hit, and the demographic cost extraordinarily high. Carol Benedict believes that a vector-borne disease like plague actually exhibits all three kinds of diffusion patterns in combination and in sequence, so all the spaces within a regional-city trading system eventually are affected, and the death rates extremely high.[62]

The second plague pandemic in recorded history began when the bacillus *Y. pestis* was carried out of its ancient home, the Himalayan foothills in the border region between China, Burma, and India, to the Eurasian grasslands.[63] The carriers were Mongol cavalry, who invaded the region in 1252–1253. Following the campaign, terminated prematurely at least partly because many soldiers were struck down by a previously unknown disease (which may well have been plague), the Mongols withdrew to their steppe homelands, carrying the fleas and the bacillus with them.

Europeans had heard rumors as early as 1346 of a terrible plague sweeping out of China, through central Asia to India, Persia, and eventually all of the Middle East. India was reported to be depopulated, and the overall death toll was said to be more than twenty million (although there was no way to accurately confirm these figures then, nor is there today). We now know that the plague arrived in China perhaps as early as 1331, but certainly by between 1342 and 1345. The epidemics coincided with, and probably contributed to, the decline and eventual collapse of the Mongol empire. The population of China, about 123 million in 1200, declined by nearly half, to 65 million, by 1393.

From China, the disease gradually worked its way west along caravan routes, following traders and invading Mongol armies. By 1346, it had arrived along with Mongol soldiers at the Black Sea port of Kaffa (now called Feodosiya), which is situated on the Crimean Peninsula. Kaffa at the time was operated as a trading center by merchants from Genoa. The Mongols besieged the city, but were unable to drive the Genoans out, who were able to resupply the city by ship. The Mongols then began to catapult over the city walls the cadavers of their troops who had succumbed to the plague, a macabre early form of germ warfare. Whether the rain of dead bodies on the city carried the disease into Kaffa as well is unknown; but the Genoans soon fled the city and headed by ship back to Italy, thus carrying rats and fleas harboring *Y. pestis* into western Europe for the first time since the plague of Justinian.

The ships carrying the Genoans and their deadly companions arrived at the Sicilian port of Messina in October 1347, and the plague followed them ashore almost immediately. The townspeople drove the infected sailors back onto their ships and out of the port, but it was too late. The plague was already among them. By their actions, all they accomplished was to ensure that the ships would continue westward through the Mediterranean, carrying the plague on to French and Spanish ports as well.

The plague entered the mainland of Europe via both Marseille and Constantinople by the end of December 1347.[64] Within six months, the epidemic had covered all of Italy, France as far north as Paris, and the eastern one-third of Spain. From the French coastal ports, the disease crossed into England, probably via the port at Bristol, during the summer of 1348. Perhaps by autumn, but by winter at the latest, it had reached London, and raged throughout the British Isles for most of 1349. From England, the disease re-entered the European mainland, reaching Scandinavia by late 1349 or early 1350. By about 1350, this particular wave of the plague had spent itself, but it would return to Europe again and again for the next 300 years. In England, the plague of 1545–1546 was especially severe; and the Great Plague of London of 1665–1666 has gone down in history as one of humankind's worst urban epidemics.

Scholars can only estimate the number of deaths caused by the plague. Mortality rates varied widely, depending on whether the areas were urban or rural, hinterland or port city, but no other dividing lines seemed to matter much. The poor and the rich fell in more or less similar measure; well-fed monks and priests in secure monasteries suffered more or less the same death rates as the urban poor or rural farm workers. Some cities, like Milan, were surprisingly spared, while others, like Siena, lost perhaps half their total population. After a review of much of the evidence, one of the plague's leading chroniclers, Philip Ziegler, confirms the consensus assessment of mortality rates:

> As a rough and ready rule-of-thumb, . . . the statement that a third of the population died of the Black Death should not be too misleading. The figure might quite

easily be as high as 40% or as low as 30%; it could conceivably be as high as 45% or as low as 23%. But these are surely the outside limits.[65]

Europe was never the same again once the plague had passed across the land; but historians debate whether the epidemic was the prime mover in these changes, or whether it simply accelerated changes that were already under way. The depletion of rural labor, for example, made life somewhat better for the survivors and their offspring, with land more readily available, jobs and income more secure, and diet improved. Indentured rural laborers now broke free from their bondage, forcing landowners to improve agrarian productivity. Religious orders were decimated, and numerous convents and monasteries were closed for want of personnel. Political and economic conflicts seemed to be less intense, and governments took advantage of the lull to strengthen their ability to manage and resolve disputes by means other than brute force. Perhaps above all, the poor now found a solution to their poverty in the mobility made possible by the decline in population. "No paradigm shift had brought these things about," summarizes Colin Platt, "no sudden conviction of slavery's wickedness, no conversion on the road to Damascus. Behind every change was a labour shortage, and at the back of each shortage was the Black Death."[66]

The Silk Road, trade, and the plague were intertwined in a single social and biological system. The road channeled trade among the Eurasian empires that reached their height in the three centuries after 1000 A.D. Along with horses, camels, pepper, and silk, these trading connections also moved rats, fleas, and the plague bacillus. By the time this last organism had spread successfully from C'hang-an in the east to Bristol, England, in the west, it had so thoroughly disrupted social ties and economic exchanges that trade virtually ceased. "Indeed," as Jerry Bentley observes, "the plague ranks as the most important single agent in bringing down the complex system of interregional trade that developed during the thirteenth and early fourteenth centuries."[67]

After the devastation of the plague at both ends of the Silk Road, and at many points in between, the empires of the Eurasian ecumene rested a brief while before launching a remarkable series of expansionist steps that marked a turning point in global history.[68] During the fifteenth century, the civilizations of China, Islam, and Europe all sought to rebound from the collapse of the preceding century and a half. Because the Silk Road had fallen into disuse, and because the technologies of long-distance maritime travel had improved, these expansionist moves were undertaken by naval expeditions and radiated outward, away from Eurasia, rather than inward. During the first half of the century, the Chinese treasure fleets would embark on a series of remarkable voyages that would take them into the Indian Ocean, all the way to the Straits of Hormuz and the east African port cities. From the other direction, the Portuguese sought a way to connect Europe and Asia by water around the tip of Africa, a search that culminated in the voyage of Vasco da Gama in 1498. Elsewhere in Iberia, the rulers of Castille decided to support Columbus's expedition to reach Asia by heading west. What lay ahead was the next step in the globalization of life systems: the arrival of Europeans, Africans, wheat, horses, and smallpox in the Western Hemisphere.

NOTES

1. William McNeill, *The Rise of the West: A History of the Human Community* (Chicago: University of Chicago Press, 1961, 1993), chapter 7. The word "ecumene" is used here to refer to "the known world" (that is, the world known to Eurasians).

2. Hermann von Wissmann, "On the Role of Nature and Man in Changing the Face of the Dry Belt of Asia," in *Man's Role in Changing the Face of the Earth*, ed. William Thomas (Chicago: University of Chicago Press, 1956), pp. 278–99.

3. Jonathan Kingdon, *Self-Made Man: Human Evolution from Eden to Extinction?* (New York: Wiley, 1993), pp. 77–83.

4. Von Wissmann, *Man's Role*, pp. 287–92.

5. Irene Franck and David Brownstone, *The Silk Road: A History* (New York: Facts on File Publications, 1986), chapter 1. The Silk Road route remains in active use today, as described in these reports: Michael Specter, "Opium Finding Its Silk Road in the Chaos of Central Asia," *New York Times*, May 2, 1995; Brian Killen, "Part of Ancient Silk Road Is Now Opium Road," *Washington Post*, October 3, 1996; John Lancaster, "Iran Offers New Wrinkles for Old Silk Road," *Washington Post*, December 10, 1996.

6. Franck and Brownstone, *The Silk Road*, chapter 2; Che Muqi, *The Silk Road, Past and Present* (Beijing: Foreign Languages Press, 1989), chapter 3.

7. Michael Wood, *Legacy: The Search for Ancient Cultures* (New York: Sterling, 1994), p. 109.

8. See Philip Curtin, *Cross-Cultural Trade in World History* (New York: Cambridge University Press, 1992), pp. 1–3, for a definition of "trade diaspora."

9. Neville Agnew and Fan Jinshi, "China's Buddhist Treasures at Dunhuang," *Scientific American* 277, no. 1 (July 1997): 39–45.

10. Jerry Bentley, *Old World Encounters: Cross-Cultural Contacts and Exchanges in Pre-Modern Times* (New York: Oxford University Press, 1993), p. 48.

11. John Noble Wilford, "Ruins in Yemeni Desert Mark Route of Frankincense Trade," *New York Times*, January 28, 1997.

12. Curtin, *Cross-Cultural Trade*, pp. 96–103.

13. Lionel Casson, *Travel in the Ancient World* (Toronto: Hakkert, 1974), chapter 6.

14. McNeill, *Rise of the West*, chapter 7; Christopher Chase-Dunn and Thomas Hall, *Rise and Demise: Comparing World-Systems* (Boulder, Colo.: Westview, 1997), chapter 8.

15. Franck and Brownstone, *The Silk Road*, chapters 3, 4; Ahmad Dani, "A Silken Bond between East and West," *The Unesco Courier Cross-Cultural Trade*, 42 (March 1989): 4–10.

16. Curtin, *Cross-Cultural Trade*, chapter 5.

17. Bentley, *Old World Encounters*, passim; Curtin, *Cross-Cultural Trade*, chapter 5.

18. Che Muqi, *Silk Road, Past and Present*, chapter 14.

19. M. G. Lay, *Ways of the World: A History of the World's Roads and of the Vehicles that Used Them* (New Brunswick, N.J.: Rutgers University Press, 1992), pp. 45–48; Norma Martyn, *The Silk Road* (North Ridge, Australia: Methuen Australia, 1987); Casson, *Travel in the Ancient Road*, pp. 123–24.

20. Bamber Gascoigne, *The Dynasties and Treasures of China* (New York: Viking, 1973), chapter 3.

21. Franck and Brownstone, *The Silk Road*, pp. 86–88.

22. Ying-shih Yü, *Trade and Expansion in Han China: A Study in the Structure of Sino-Barbarian Economic Relations* (Berkeley: University of California Press, 1967), pp. 135–38; Franck and Brownstone, *The Silk Road*, pp. 92–100; McNeill, *Rise of the West*, p. 295.

23. Ma Yong, "A Silken Highway from East to West," *The Unesco Courier* 37 (June 1984): 22–24.

24. Bentley, *Old World Encounters*, chapter 2.

25. Sechin Jagchid and Van Jay Symons, *Peace, War, and Trade along the Great Wall: Nomadic-Chinese Interaction through Two Millennia* (Bloomington: Indiana University Press, 1989).

26. Che Muqi, *Silk Road, Past and Present*, chapter 13.

27. Curtin, *Cross-Cultural Trade*, p. 105.

28. Franck and Brownstone, *The Silk Road*, pp. 190–94.

29. Bentley, *Old World Encounters*, pp. 114–15.

30. Jared Diamond, *Guns, Germs, and Steel: The Fates of Human Societies* (New York: Norton, 1997), chapter 10.

31. Franck and Brownstone, *The Silk Road*, p. 2.

32. Franck and Brownstone, *The Silk Road*, pp. 45–47, Che Muqi, *Silk Road, Past and Present* pp. 3–4, 287–89; William Agosta, *Bombardier Beetles and Fever Trees: A Close-up Look at Chemical Warfare and Signals in Animals and Plants* (Reading, Mass.: Addison Wesley, 1996), pp. 115–18.

33. Franck and Brownstone, *The Silk Road*, pp. 71–74.

34. Franck and Brownstone, *The Silk Road*, pp. 78–81.

35. Franck and Brownstone, *The Silk Road*, pp. 157–59.

36. Che Muqi, *Silk Road, Past and Present*, pp. 240–41.

37. Franck and Brownstone, *The Silk Road*, p. 225.

38. Franck and Brownstone, *The Silk Road*, pp. 37, 67, 80.

39. Che Muqi, *Silk Road, Past and Present*, pp. 190–91.

40. Che Muqi, *Silk Road, Past and Present*, pp. 7–8, 36, 48, 210, 236; Franck and Brownstone, *The Silk Road*, pp. 134–35, 145, 193.

41. Franck and Brownstone, *The Silk Road*, p. 93; Che Muqi, *Silk Road, Past and Present*, pp. 184–87.

42. Stephen Budiansky, *The Nature of Horses: Exploring Equine Evolution, Intelligence, and Behavior* (New York: Free Press, 1997), chapter 1.

43. Franck and Brownstone, *The Silk Road*, p. 39.

44. Budiansky, *Nature of Horses*, chapter 2.

45. Franck and Brownstone, *The Silk Road*, pp. 50–51.

46. Von Wissman, "Role of Nature," pp. 292–96; Franck and Brownstone, *The Silk Road*, pp. 56–57.

47. Franck and Brownstone, *The Silk Road*, chapter 5; Che Muqi, *Silk Road, Past and Present*, pp. 32–33, 76–78, 151, 246.

48. Bentley, *Old World Encounters*, p. 75; Che Muqi, *Silk Road, Past and Present*, p. 194.

49. Franck and Brownstone, *The Silk Road*, pp. 48–50.

50. Casson, *Travel in Ancient World*, pp. 54–55.

51. Richard Bulliet, "How the Camel Got Its Saddle," *Natural History* 92 (July 1983): 52–59.

52. William McNeill, *Plagues and Peoples* (New York: Doubleday, 1977), p. 97.

53. McNeill, *Plagues and Peoples*, p. 129.

54. Carol Benedict, *Bubonic Plague in Nineteenth-Century China* (Stanford, Calif.: Stanford University Press, 1996), "Introduction"; Philip Ziegler, *The Black Death* (New York: John Day, 1969), p. 25.

55. Christopher Wills, *Yellow Fever, Black Goddess: The Coevolution of People and Plagues* (Reading, Mass.: Addison Wesley, 1996), pp. 55–59; Arno Karlen, *Man and Microbes: Disease and Plagues in History and Modern Times* (New York: Putnam, 1995), pp. 74–78.

56. Benedict, *Bubonic Plague*, pp. 4–5.

57. Colin Platt, *King Death: The Black Death and Its Aftermath in Late-medieval England* (Toronto: University of Toronto Press, 1996), p. 33.

58. Charles Mee, "How a Mysterious Disease Laid Low Europe's Masses," *Smithsonian* (February 1990): 69.

59. Carol Benedict, "Bubonic Plague in Nineteenth-Century China," *Modern China* 14, no. 2 (April 1988): 111.

60. For a graphic and detailed description of the impact of *Yersinia pestis* on humans, see Charles Gregg, *Plague: An Ancient Disease in the Twentieth Century*, rev. ed. (Albuquerque: University of New Mexico Press, 1985), chapters 57, 10. Also, R. Pollitzer, *Plague* (Geneva: World Health Organization, 1954), chapters 4, 8.

61. Benedict, *Bubonic Plague*, pp. 73–76.

62. Benedict, *Bubonic Plague*, pp. 76–78.

63. McNeill, *Plagues and Peoples*, chapter 4.

64. Rosemary Horrox, trans. and ed., *The Black Death* (Manchester: Manchester University Press, 1994), pp. 8–11; Ziegler, *The Black Death*, map on pp. 104–5.

65. Ziegler, *The Black Death*, p. 230.

66. Platt, *King Death*, p. 189.

67. Bentley, *Old World Encounters*, p. 163.

68. Bentley, *Old World Encounters*, chapter 5.

Chapter Seven

The Biological Impact of Europeans on Eastern North America, 1600–1800

Although Europeans began to visit North America only a few years after Columbus's first voyage, they did not appear in large numbers with the intention of staying until the early seventeenth century.[1] In 1497, Giovanni Caboto (known to the English as John Cabot)—a Genoese sailing out of Bristol, England—explored the coast of Newfoundland and thus became the first European to touch North American shores since the epic Norse adventurers half a millennium earlier. Another Italian, Giovanni da Verrazano, sailing for the king of France, traveled the east coast from Florida to New England in 1524. Spanish explorers—including Vásquez de Ayllón, Pánfilo de Narváez, and Hernando De Soto—traveled through the southeastern region of the continent in the first half of the sixteenth century; and the French explorers Jacques Cartier and Samuel de Champlain explored the northeastern region in their respective expeditions between 1534 and 1604. The English arrived later, establishing their ill-fated colony on Roanoke Island in 1584, and their first lasting settlement at Jamestown, Virginia, in 1607.

Upon their arrival, Europeans found a fairly large and stable population of natives who were part of a set of coevolved life systems that had existed in North America for millennia.[2] Despite its longevity, however, this local system of humans, plants, and animals (and very few pathogenic microörganisms) proved to be remarkably fragile, and within three hundred years (much less in some places) the native system had been transformed by the intruders—but not destroyed, since what replaced the Indians' life system was a biological amalgam that was both indigenous and foreign.

Eastern North America was a far different place in 1800 from what it had been when Europeans first laid eyes and hands upon the land. But, as William Cronon reminds us, we must be careful not to see the changes as simply the consequence of European culture or of global economic systems.[3] The differences between North America in 1600 and in 1800 were the product of the interaction of two

sets of life systems in a dynamic that was driven and constrained as much by biology as it was by culture, politics, or economics.

NATIVE LIFE SYSTEMS IN NORTH AMERICA

The number of people living in the Americas in 1492 has been the subject of much
controversy for years. Until rather recently, the prevailing belief was that the Western Hemisphere was relatively empty, but more recent scholarship now suggests
that early censuses seriously underestimated the native population. By the time
Europeans turned their attention to counting the native populace, diseases had
already decimated local populations, and census takers were misled into thinking
that the hemisphere had hardly known a human population before Columbus.

Researchers now believe that at the time of the arrival of Europeans, the Western Hemisphere was home to between 40 and 80 million people, with a figure of
100 million not impossible. One leading scholar in this field, William Denevan,
argues for a figure of 53.9 million in 1500, with a range of 43 to 65 million being
most probable. Of the nearly 54 million, Denevan estimates, about 3.8 million
lived in North America.[4] By 1800, this population had been reduced to about 1
million, a decline of 74 percent in 300 years.

Geoffrey Turner estimates that the native population of the northeastern quarter of North America (approximately the lands north of the Ohio River and east
of the Mississippi) amounted to about 233,000, divided into 31 nations or tribes;
and in the southeastern quarter there were about 102,000 people divided into 19
tribes.[5] Most of these tribes contained 5,000 people or fewer, and some had fewer
than 1,000; but a few numbered in the tens of thousands. The largest were the
Algonquians (55,000), the Ojibwa (33,000), and the Cherokee (22,000).

In New England in 1610, with European colonization just over the horizon, the
indigenous population probably totaled about 76,000, divided into about a dozen
tribes or confederations of tribes[6] (see figure 7.1). In northern New England, what
is now Maine, about 11,900 people of the Abenaki tribe lived at a density of about
0.2 persons per square kilometer, while in southern New England about 64,000
people lived more densely concentrated, about two persons per square kilometer. In the South Atlantic region, from the Potomac River and the Chesapeake Bay
south to northern Florida, the native population probably numbered in excess of
70,000: 33,000 in Virginia (including 9,000 Powhatan—see figure 7.2) and Maryland; 7,000 or more in coastal North Carolina; 30,000 or more in the Cherokee
lands.[7]

Although early European settlers tended to describe the natives as impoverished
and living in misery, they were certainly adequately provisioned as far as food was
concerned. Carolyn Merchant estimates that during the seventeenth century, the
Indian population of New England consumed on average 2,500 calories of food
energy per day.[8] About 20 percent of their food supply came from animal products (all from hunting and fishing) and 80 percent from vegetable products
(mostly cultivated maize, beans, and squash, augmented by gathered foods such

Figure 7.1   Southern New England, Showing Locations of Indian Tribes, ca. 1636, and Colonial Boundaries, ca. 1660

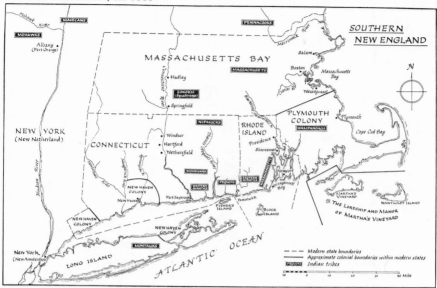

Source: Francis Jennings, *The Invasion of America: Indians, Colonialism, and the Cant of Conquest* (New York: W.W. Norton, 1976), p. 200, Map 1. © 1975 by the University of North Carolina Press. Used by permission of the publisher.

as berries and nuts). Women were responsible for procuring about 85 percent of their food energy.

What Europeans found surprising, however, was the Indian practice of storing relatively little food to tide them over the winter months.[9] In a land of such obvious abundance, a rational person would never knowingly choose to go hungry even for a day, even if it meant harvesting more food in the autumn. Yet the Indians lived, as the English put it, "from hand to mouth," rarely storing up enough to feed themselves over long periods of food shortages. The Indians of New England were not averse to going without food for a week at a time during the winter—something the Europeans could not fathom—but the ecological rationality of such a choice is obvious in retrospect. By deliberately limiting their food supply during the winter, Indians also limited their population, either consciously or unconsciously, and thereby reduced the load they put on their environment. In other words, the Indians had coevolved so well with their surrounding life systems that the whole package had existed for millennia in a rather precarious equilibrium that depended on the self-restraint of the human population.

To the eye of the European, already accustomed to the homogenizing forces of several millennia of agriculture, North America offered a spectacular diversity of flora and fauna. In their descriptions of this new world, the first European explorers marveled at the life forms they encountered, in some cases because what

Figure 7.2   The Powhatan Empire

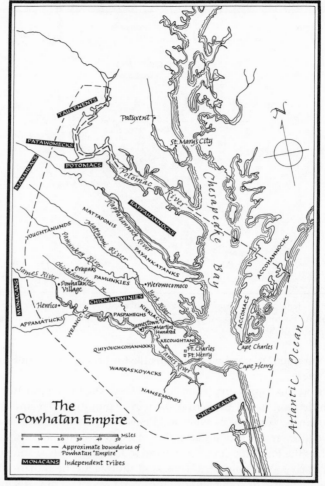

Source: James Axtell, *The Rise and Fall of the Powhatan Empire: Indians in Seventeenth-Century Virginia* (Williamsburg, Virginia: Colonial Williamsburg Foundation, 1955), p. 2. Drawn by Richard Stinely. © James Axtell. Reprinted by permission.

they found was to their eyes so exotic or bizarre (the opossum, for example), but mostly because of its abundance, size, and variety: flocks of land and sea birds so thick they covered the land or blocked out the sun, and could be taken fifty at a single shot; fish in schools so dense the colonists imagined they could walk to shore over the fishes' backs; wild turkeys weighing fifty pounds or more; sturgeon nine feet long; oysters so large they had to be cut into three pieces before being swallowed.[10]

What Europeans also found remarkable was the intimate connections the Indians had to the living things that surrounded them. Most of the native cultures felt a deep kinship with the animals with which they shared their territory.[11] In many instances, the Indians assumed they had descended from animals such as the groundhog, and they believed that all living things came from a common earth mother. Animals were not resources to be exploited for profit, but companions in an integrated natural world. Thus there had evolved a set of rituals and taboos that limited the killing and disposal of the remains of game animals that had given up their lives to sustain humans.

In New England, one of the most important mammals was the beaver, whose engineering skills made it an active participant in reshaping the landscape.[12] Beaver dams retained water, soil, and sediment from hillsides, and the ponds behind them became habitats for a great variety of birds, fish, and plants. Over time, these ponds grew to large lakes, operating like irrigation works and reservoirs to preserve watersheds but also to capture sediment and debris and increase the fertility of the lake floor. Once beavers had exhausted their food supply and moved on, the abandoned dams released their water, exposing the vast fields of rich nutrients that gradually helped create "beaver meadows," which were highly prized as land where a farm's crops could take hold quickly. Farther south, in Virginia and the Carolinas, beaver were much admired for their imputed "social organization" and work habits. The warmer climate inhibited the growth of a thick fur coat, however, which made them less desirable to hunters and trappers and delayed their eventual demise for sometime longer than their northern cousins.[13]

"A central fact of temperate ecosystems like those of New England," writes William Cronon, "is their periodicity."

> Each plant and animal species makes its adjustments to these various cycles, so that the flowing sap of trees, the migration of birds, the spawning of fish, the rutting of deer, and the fruiting of plants all have their special times of the year. . . . Because animals, including people, feed on plants and other animals, the ways they obtain their food are largely determined by the cycles in which other species lead their lives.[14]

To adapt to the seasonality of their surrounding life systems, Indians moved about frequently. The Indians were a mobile foraging people, but they were not nomadic in the same sense as the people of the Eurasian steppes. The village was the core social unit, but it was not a fixed set of buildings and farms. Instead, the village could be disassembled and moved easily to another site as the seasons and land fertility dictated. All aspects of Indian life turned on this reality, and houses were designed to be taken apart and moved in a matter of hours. Food-storage sites were few in number and mostly hidden below ground, away from animals and the inhabitants of other villages. Material property consisted solely of a few tools, weapons, and clothing, all light-weight and easily movable.

New England Indians had evolved a system of land clearing and plant cultivation that was more horticultural than agricultural, a system that mimicked natural patterns instead of attempting to dominate and destroy them.[15] This system was not indigenous to the area but rather had migrated north from its origins in Mesoamerica some six to seven millennia earlier. Near the end of the first millennium B.C., gourds and squash arrived in the southern Atlantic region from Mexico, and maize was cultivated in the south by 200 B.C. A far superior strain of maize, known as eastern flint, which originated in the Guatemalan highlands, was under cultivation in the south by 1200 A.D.[16]

Scholars debate the dominant type of agriculture employed by Indians in eastern North America.[17] Some describe the native system as shifting, swidden, or slash-and-burn agriculture, characterized primarily by the frequent movement of settlements as the land became drained of nutrients.[18] Since the Indians had no domesticated animals except the dog, they had little animal waste available except food residues like fish heads. Therefore, they seldom used fertilizer and usually farmed an area until the land's fertility was exhausted, at which time they moved on to another site. Lacking draft animals and the plow, the Indians had no need for meticulously groomed, level, cleared lands; and so their fields frequently impressed the English as a jumble of overgrown vegetation with no order or pattern. Their principal field implement was the digging stick, and planting and harvesting were slow, laborious processes, so fields remained small and (by European standards) relatively unproductive. Farming was the province of women and children; men were employed in hunting and fishing. Once a site was exhausted and abandoned, vacated land was available to any other group that wished to occupy it. Land ownership did not reside in the individual or the village, but in the tribe (or its paramount chief).

Some scholars, however, pointing to the discovery of the remains of raised and ridged fields, and to observations made by early European travelers, believe that some Indian groups used a much more intensive agricultural system that involved complete land clearing, long periods of cultivation, large fields, and short fallows. In these instances, in late winter or early spring, the land was claimed from the forest by fire. After stripping the bark from trees to kill them, Indian women burned the trees and spread the ashes across the soil to recycle the nutrients. They then mounded soil into hills and planted maize and beans together so that the vines of the beans would twine around the corn stalks. In the spaces between hills, squash and pumpkins were planted, producing a three-tiered system in which each species helped the others.

Accustomed to the monocultural fields of their homeland, Europeans thought the natives' fields a tangled jungle and failed to understand the rationality behind them. The maize provided a support frame for the beans, the beans fixed nitrogen in the soil, and the squash leaves sheltered the soil from excessive sun and rain. The resultant polycultural system reduced weeds and insect pests as well. Moreover, the nutritional effects were positive, since beans supplied the amino acids that the maize lacked. After eight to twelve years of such production, the soil's nutrients were exhausted, so the village moved on to other land, allowing the forest to reclaim the original plot and soil fertility to be restored through natural processes.

Maize was the foundation upon which the native diet was based, supplying about two-thirds of the calories in the typical New England Indian diet. But beyond this biological dependence, the Indian culture celebrated maize as the source of meaning for the society.[19] Maize was believed to be the gift from a mythical "Corn Mother," the original female from whose body the first maize had come. Such beliefs were found not only in the Indian cultures of New England but indeed throughout the east, including southern tribes like the Cherokee and Creek. The natural cycle of maize planting, ripening, harvesting, and consumption was embedded in the calendar of Indian rituals. Since horticulture was the domain of women, a diet of maize defined the role and status of women in Indian society. It was women who prepared the fields and planted the seeds, so it would have been women who selected the types of seeds for planting, thus performing a key role in the coevolution of maize and humans.

On the eve of colonization, about 95 percent of New England was covered by forest. Farthest to the north, in northern Maine, New Hampshire, and Vermont, were the coniferous forests of spruce and fir, and hardwoods such as aspen and red maple. To the south was a band of hemlock, oaks, hickories, and American chestnuts, as well as the famous white pines, trees of such magnitude (four to six feet in diameter, 100 to 200 feet tall) that their like had never been seen by the English. Then came the hardwood forests of southern New England: oaks of many different varieties, ash, maple, and birch. Over the millennia since the retreat of the glaciers, these forests had coevolved with numerous woodland animals including deer, beaver, and the passenger pigeon. Humans also left their mark in them, for the Indians had carefully cleared away the underbrush below the trees to facilitate the hunting of deer as well as the cultivation of the surrounding soil. In southern New England, much of the land reminded Europeans of parks, so easy was it to stroll beneath the trees. All these species played their part in maintaining a dynamic equilibrium and creating their own distinctive landscape.[20]

In the south, forests were equally extensive but comprised many different varieties of trees.[21] Along the southern coastal plain, forests of mixed hardwoods included magnolia and palmetto trees, live oaks and beech, holly and hickory. Farther inland, the swampy wetlands promoted the growth of cypress and the giant white cedars that towered fifty to eight feet above the ground. Farther still, throughout the inner coastal plain, was the tree that most typified the south, the great pine. Well adapted to the southern heat, the pine in its numerous varieties dominated the landscape from Virginia to Texas.

The one kind of living organism that the American natives seemed to have little of proved to be their eventual undoing: pathogenic micröorganisms. John Verano and Douglas Ubelaker have cautioned against a stereotype that portrays pre-

Columbian Indians as living in a disease-free paradise.[22] Analyses of Indian skeletal remains and Indian art suggest that many indigenous populations suffered from infestations of macroparasites like hookworms, lice, and pinworms. Numerous archeological finds, particularly in South America, attest to the presence of tuberculosis before the arrival of Europeans. And most scholars accept the hypothesis that syphilis was spread from Amerindian populations to Europeans, who promptly imported the disease to Europe in a series of epidemics after 1500. Life expectancy at birth for indigenous populations was between twenty and twenty-five years, and adult age at death averaged in the mid-thirties. In the more settled, sedentary populations such as the Aztec centers like Tenochtitlán, mortality rates resembled those of European cities of the same period.

But the most significant feature of Amerindian health was that they had no experience with, and no immunity to, diseases introduced from Europe during the sixteenth century. The distant ancestors of all Amerindians had reached the Western Hemisphere twenty to thirty millennia before, having crossed the Bering Straits land bridge during the last Ice Age. Perhaps the diseases of the Old World were defeated or left behind during this most arduous journey; or perhaps the low population density of the Indians or their lack of domesticated animals allowed diseases to become extinct. Whatever the cause, American Indians had had no contact with the diseases that Europeans took for granted (measles, chicken pox) nor with the much more devastating organisms like smallpox, influenza, plague, and so forth. When European explorers first ventured into the Gulf Coast, they were tormented by clouds of mosquitoes that swarmed about them. As annoying as these pests were, they were not yet the carriers of deadly disease that they would become, since malaria had not yet been introduced via the body of an infected European.[23] Never having encountered these diseases, Indian mothers could not pass on their antibodies to their children as protective shields. When the Europeans arrived with their tiny but deadly companions, the result was catastrophic.

Such a disaster had already befallen the southern North American natives long before the English arrived to establish their permanent colonies.[24] The Spanish explorers De Soto and Vásquez de Ayllón had passed through the south in the early sixteenth century, leaving behind a trail of infections that wrought such damage that the indigenous people and their culture were reduced to a state of primitiveness and poverty that misled the seventeenth-century European explorers into thinking that that was their natural condition. Of the few remaining natives in the interior south, none could recall who had built the monumental mound cities, or why. Memories of the diseases brought by the invaders had also faded, so that when the English arrived with their pathogens to the Carolinas and began to spread a new round of European diseases, not even the oldest Indians could recall a similar episode.

A similar scenario was played out in Virginia as well. The English colonists who anchored at Jamestown in 1607 were not the first Europeans to visit eastern

Virginia or the Chesapeake Bay. The Spanish had visited there on several occa-sions, usually in search of slaves, and other English ships had passed through the area on reconnaissance missions. During these visits, the Europeans had undoubt-edly passed on their diseases to the indigenous population. Thus, the estimated 14,000 Algonquian-speaking Indians who inhabited Virginia in 1607 were cer-tainly a much reduced remnant of the original population. This would explain the comment of the Indian chief Powhatan to the Englishman John Smith that "he had seen the death of all his people thrice."[25]

Perhaps the most telling summary analysis of the true nature of Amerindian civilization on the eve of European arrival is that provided by Francis Jennings, who asserts in his book *The Invasion of America* that the depiction of America as a "virgin wilderness" is a myth.[26] The indigenous peoples of North America had established stable populations and maintained them in the face of food uncer-tainties and changing climatic conditions for several thousand years. And it was fortunate for the Europeans that such was the case, because England, Spain, and France could never have established their colonies and maintained them over such vast expanses of ocean without drawing substantially on the resources already developed by the Indians. A century and a half—or more—would be required to complete the transport of European genes and memes across the Atlantic in such numbers as to be self-sustaining. In the meantime, the advance guard at Jamestown, Plymouth, and elsewhere, relied heavily on the food crops and the cleared land provided them by the native peoples. "European explorers and in-vaders," writes Jennings,

> discovered an inhabited land. Had it been pristine wilderness then, it would possi-bly be so still today, for neither the technology nor the social organization of Eu-rope in the sixteenth and seventeenth centuries had the capacity to maintain, of its own resources, outpost colonies thousands of miles from home. Incapable of con-quering true wilderness, the Europeans were highly competent in the skill of con-quering other people, and that is what they did. They did not settle a virgin land. They invaded and displaced a resident population.[27]
>
> Jamestown, Plymouth, Salem, Boston, Providence, New Amsterdam, Philadel-phia—all grew upon sites previously occupied by Indian communities. So did Que-bec and Montreal and Detroit and Chicago. The so-called settlement of America was a *resettlement*, a reoccupation of a land made waste by the diseases and demoral-ization introduced by the newcomers.[28]

INTRUDING LIFE SYSTEMS IN NORTH AMERICA

"Demographically," Alfred Crosby has observed, "the eighteenth and nineteenth centuries are among the most amazing of all centuries."[29] For one thing, the total world population soared at rates that had seldom been recorded before. But what was truly unprecedented, argues Crosby, was the virtually complete replacement of one gene pool (Amerindians) by two others (Africans and what Crosby calls the neo-Europeans).[30] Prior to 1492, global migrations had been slow and gradual episodes involving relatively few people at a time, and the receiving indigenous populations had always had time and space necessary to adjust to the intruding life systems. Such was not to be the case in the Americas.

The replacement of Indians by Europeans and Africans was at first a slow process that began to pick up momentum only in the latter half of the seventeenth century.[31] In 1638, there were only 30,000 English in North America, but from 1650 to 1700 their population surged forward at an average rate of nearly 3 percent annually. Population growth was accelerated by heavy emigration from England (more than 375,000 total by 1700), especially by women of reproductive age in disproportionately large numbers. By 1700, the English population numbered more than a quarter of a million, mostly living in New England, Pennsylvania, and around the Chesapeake Bay. In 1700, Virginia, a prosperous colony, had a European population of 56,000 and an African population of 5,000; in much poorer North Carolina, Europeans numbered fewer than 10,000 and Africans fewer than 500. By 1750 the total number of non-natives had risen to 1.3 million (both Europeans and Africans), and Philadelphia was the second most populous English-speaking city in the world, after London. There were still only small pockets of settlements of Europeans and Africans outside a coastal belt stretching from New England to northern Florida; but as the native population died away from disease, starvation, and warfare, the populations of Europeans and Africans grew steadily, especially from the late eighteenth century onward. By 1767, North Carolina's European population had grown to 124,000, its African population to 41,000. While such growth seems modest by human standards, in ecological terms it was blindingly fast given the degree of change that native life systems had to absorb.

In some respects, particularly in terms of climatic cycles, English and Indian agricultures paralleled each other. The spring thaw was the time for both to begin to work and plant the land, August to October was the period set aside for harvest, summer and late autumn brought wild game, fish, and migratory birds into their diets, and the winter months were spent indoors, repairing tools and living off the food collected earlier. Despite these important similarities, indigenous and European food systems were so different that the arrival of the latter in the seventeenth century marked the greatest change ever experienced by the biosphere of North America.[32]

Europeans brought more than new life systems to North America, however; they also brought new cultural rules to govern the relationships between humans and other living organisms. Native cultures were not without the notion of private property, but it was restricted to those objects made for one's own use, such as a tool or an article of clothing. Europeans brought the idea that one could possess the land and its products as well, including the rights to enjoy monetary profits from these resources and to keep others from using them. Europeans and

Indians also clashed over the concept of animals as private property. For the Indians, animals like deer and elk were companions in nature, but the English considered their cattle and hogs property just as much as their houses and clothing. Whereas Indians had allowed the soil to restore its fertility naturally through long-term fallow, the colonists replenished the soil's depleted nutrients by means of fertilizers like lime and niter. Europeans used maps to depict graphically what belonged to whom, written contracts (that the Indians could scarcely understand) to support the legal authority of such relationships, and fences to translate those boundaries into physical barriers to the movement of people and animals. The crucial role of native women in the production of food was replaced by the Europeans' male-dominated cultivation system. Christianity and the Bible took the place of animistic religious visions that had been carried across the generations by an oral tradition.

The most visible impact of Europeans on New England's life systems came from humans and the large animals they brought with them. For some years after their arrival, the colonists continued to live from the same plant foods as the natives, especially maize. But domesticated grazing animals and their associated technologies—particularly fences and plows—altered forever the relationship of humans to the land in New England and the south.

The animals' feeding habits were disruptive in themselves. Pigs rooted for forage in the woods, and cattle, horses, and sheep chewed up endless acres of native grasses.

But it was the humans' use of animals that brought about the greatest change in land use. The energy dynamics of meat production from domesticated livestock were such that Europeans needed much of the settled agricultural land to grow food for their cattle and horses, land that Indians had used to grow maize and beans for themselves. The meat supply of the Indians had been satisfied by hunting wild animals in the uplands and forests; but the colonists altered the land-use balance and in so doing drove the Indians farther and farther away from the coastal and riverside lands they had occupied before 1600.

For example, in 1539, De Soto brought with his expedition thirteen hogs and bred them on the march. By the time his expedition left North America in 1542, the number had risen to 700, which were all left behind to thrive and grow huge (and wild) in the lush climate of the Gulf Coast.[33] This particular biological gift from the Old World remained isolated from the coastal English settlements for a century or more.

European livestock were introduced to the English colony at Jamestown in 1611, and soon became a crucial part of the colonists' diet.[34] In the English colonies during the first half of the seventeenth century, livestock were so scarce and in such great demand that ships arrived frequently from Europe carrying up to fifty animals at a time. But by mid-century, Virginia herds had grown so extensive that meat was being exported to as far away as the West Indies, and cattle were being driven from the inner coastal plain to the seaports such as Norfolk and Philadelphia. Beef was by far the most popular meat in the English colonies, but pork was not far behind, and Virginians quickly developed a reputation for salting and curing hams that they continue to enjoy today.[35]

Each European species brought its own peculiar virtues. In addition to their ability to reproduce in large numbers, hogs could defend themselves against wolves and could eat virtually anything, so they were turned loose to forage for themselves in the woods until the time came to capture and slaughter them for winter food supplies. Cattle could also be left relatively unattended and provided meat, leather, milk, and dairy products. Oxen provided the traction needed to pull plows, which enabled the tilling of larger expanses of land and the production of surplus food; they could then haul wagons to move that surplus to market. Horses were superior for traction purposes but were in much shorter supply owing to their important military purposes. Sheep supplied the colonists' clothing in the form of wool, but they needed constant attention because of their vulnerability to predators and the wear they imposed on grazing lands.

The colonists' heavy dependence on their livestock brought them into direct conflict with another member of the native life system: the wolf.[36] Wolves found sheep and cattle to be easy prey and attacked them frequently, causing the colonists to wage war on the predators. Townships paid bounties for the heads of wolves, and ingenious methods of hunting the animals were devised, including poisons, traps, and rifles set with tripwires. In Virginia, Indians were pressed into service to hunt for wolves and were rewarded with trade goods. By the first third of the eighteenth century, wolves and bears had ceased to be much of a threat to southern colonists: A traveler to North Carolina in 1738 reported that wolves had virtually disappeared. In much less than 300 years, the New England wolf had been virtually hunted to extinction.

Bear in mind, however, that European animals, especially hogs, were also consumers themselves. They had an annoying habit of wanting to graze on the colonists' carefully laid-out crops, so miles-long barriers to animal movement were constructed across landscapes that had never been divided artificially before. The interactions among cultivation systems, domesticated grazing animals, fences, and English property rights had the effect of segregating the uses to which land could be put, and thus altered profoundly the ecological relationships between humans and the land they occupied. European grazing animals also altered the economy of New England. Whether sold fresh to nearby city markets, or salted for shipment to Caribbean plantations, New England meat was a major source of cash income for the colonists.

Grazing animals were one of the keys to making commercial agriculture successful in New England, but they exacted a huge price from the ecosystem. The broad roadways carved through the forests to drive the cattle to Boston or Providence laid waste to countless acres of pristine woodland, as did the land-clearing undertaken to control the animals' grazing. Pasturing animals close to growing towns quickly became unfeasible because of the extensive land they required. Grazing cattle and sheep quickly destroyed the native grasses, unaccustomed to the heavy demands of pastoralism, and the so-called English grasses, bluegrass and clover, soon replaced them. And where the imported grasses went, they were followed by European weeds like the ragweed and the dandelion.[37]

Livestock reshaped New England forests as well. To facilitate the grazing of cattle and sheep, colonists burned the forest undergrowth at frequent intervals, much as the Indians had done for centuries. But because English livestock grazed more closely and more continuously, and were kept in much denser concentrations than the native deer or elk, English pastoralism had the effect of altering the forest ecosystem permanently. Cattle grazing encouraged the expansion of thorny undergrowth that they could not eat and that had to be removed by hand. Certain tree species, like oak and birch, could return to cleared land if pasturing ceased for several decades, but other species, like white pine, thrived where cattle grazed, since pasturing kept down the growth of plants that blocked needed sunlight from pine seedlings.

Much the same kind of ecological impact was felt on the ground cover as well. Wherever livestock grazed, their small hooves and heavy weight compacted the land, increasing water runoff and destroying the very plants on which the animals depended. Land worked by plows pulled by European animals stirred up soil much more deeply than had been done by Indians, and native plants were destroyed in the process. Wind and water erosion began to strip off the ground cover, and, with the land losing its ability to retain water, there was more flooding. Rivers carried greater and greater quantities of topsoil downstream, where much of it contributed to the silting up of coastal harbors and ports.

If European animals made their impact felt on forests and fields, the English approach to farming was the final blow to the indigenous ecosystem. To be sure, the Indians had also faced soil exhaustion and had responded by moving their fields from site to site as local nutrients were drained. But the English practiced a different sort of plant husbandry, and the effects were devastating to the soil. At first, the colonists adopted maize as their staple crop, but they didn't adopt the precautions taken by the Indians. Maize is second only to rice in the food energy it yields, but it also drains nutrients from the soil in heavy quantities. Indians compensated for this by planting maize alongside beans and squash, and by cultivating small plots intensively with the hoe. The English practiced monoculture, planting maize by itself, and tried to use plow agriculture, suitable for wheat and barley but inappropriate for maize in the New England setting. Since the colonists allowed their cattle to graze freely across the land and didn't house them in barns at night, there was no manure to collect and thus its nutrients weren't recycled into the soil. Lacking animal waste, the colonists turned to fish fertilizer to regenerate their fields, but this solution had its drawbacks as well, and in any event the construction of dams, mills, and canals effectively destroyed the river population of fish like salmon by the end of the eighteenth century. Another solution, the application of ashes to the soil, simply substituted the destruction of the forests for the ruining of the fields.

For both human and animal food supplies, Europeans eventually determined that native New England plants would not do, and soon introduced European foods with which they were familiar. In place of the Indians' maize and beans, the Europeans brought their grain crops (rye, barley, oats, and wheat), root crops (carrots, radishes, and turnips), vegetables (cabbage, lettuce, garden beans), herbs (parsley, thyme), and garden plants (ivy, roses). At first, European animals lived off of native grasses, but as it became evident that these plants lacked sufficient nutrients for their bulk, the colonists planted European grasses.

Unfortunately, not all the flora Europeans brought to New England were useful. Uninvited stowaways also made the trip, seeds hidden in food supplies or on the clothes of colonists. Dandelions, thistles, stinging nettles, and other European weeds soon made their appearance and grew like wildfire across the landscape. "Where a European had walked," wrote one observer, weeds "grew in his footsteps."[38] "Animal weeds" also made their appearance: the "Hessian fly" (so-called because it was allegedly brought by Hessian mercenaries in their straw mattresses during the Revolutionary War) laid waste to the wheat crops of New Jersey and Connecticut; the black fly and cockroach successfully made the Atlantic crossing to annoy generations of North Americans just as they had Europeans for centuries; and the brown rat and house mouse arrived in New England ports in shipments of grain from Europe.

In the south, all of the other abuses inflicted by the English on the soil were aggravated by the extensive cultivation of tobacco, grown primarily for export back to England. European explorers had encountered tobacco on their earliest voyages to the Americas, and its use became widespread throughout Europe during the sixteenth century.[39] In 1612, John Rolfe, a leader of the Jamestown colony (and future husband of Pocahontas), planted the seeds of a West Indies variety of tobacco that proved to be much more popular to European tastes than the tougher variety grown by the Algonquin Indians. Before long, tobacco exports to England began to increase rapidly, from 20,000 pounds in 1618, to 60,000 in 1622; 500,000 in 1627; and 1.5 million in 1629. In 1634, the colony of Maryland was founded, and tobacco became its principal crop as well. In 1707, the Act of Union brought the kingdoms of Scotland and England under a single monarch, thus removing the prohibitions against Scottish firms becoming engaged in English colonial commerce. Before long, Scottish merchants had set up tobacco warehouses and transshipment services in Virginia ports, especially Alexandria. These merchants were intermediaries who brokered the sale of Virginia tobacco to the European continent, thereby opening up huge new markets for the Virginia leaf.[40]

Tobacco probably was the salvation of the Virginia colony because it provided a profit incentive to the English backers to continue their support of Jamestown. So extensive was tobacco cultivation that it threatened to crowd out all other agriculture, and the governor of Virginia was forced to order each tobacco planter to plant two acres of maize to support their families and slaves. But the long-term political and social consequences of the crop were definitely negative, and the ecological impact was nothing short of catastrophic.[41]

Just as with maize, the colonists tried to cultivate a native crop using European practices, with disastrous results:

> Tobacco requires eleven times the nitrogen and thirty-six times the phosphorous of a food crop and therefore exhausts the nutrients in the soil very quickly. Farmers growing tobacco found that the second crop on newly cleared ground was the best. After another one or two seasons its cultivation had to be abandoned in favour of maize or wheat, but even these crops could not be grown for long in the severely depleted soil. Land was abandoned and the ruined soil was easily eroded away by wind and rain. . . . By 1685, . . . Virginia was already suffering severe flooding brought about by deforestation. . . . By 1780 the Chesapeake area was experiencing severe soil erosion caused by exhaustion following tobacco cultivation and water run-off rates were twenty times higher than natural levels.[42]

The presence of Europeans in North America was also felt in the dense forests that had stood in the region for millennia.[43] More than most products, wood appeared to be free for the taking, a gift of nature, so to speak. Much of the clearance of woodlands was to produce a commodity that could be exported to Europe to repay the debts to the backers of the original settlements. For example, when the Pilgrims sent their first shipment of New England products back to England in 1621, the bulk of it was in clapboard. As the years went on, wood came to be a highly valued product by which one region of the New World enriched the Old.

Europeans' commercial exploitation of New England lumber began in the 1640s, when Massachusetts Bay merchants bought land from the Maine Indians and started exporting pine lumber to England. A number of English settlements were founded at the mouth of rivers along the Maine and New Hampshire coast, where pine trees could be cut, milled, and prepared for export. Sawmill owners reaped large profits from this trade and soon expanded their enterprises into other fields, such as general stores and gristmills. The English fleet of ships for commerce, fishing, and war demanded huge quantities of wood, and the colonies were ideally suited to meet that demand. After war with the Dutch closed off the Baltic supply lines to England in 1654, the American colonies became an essential source of wood for ship construction. White oak was ideal for the planking of ships and for barrel staves, while black oak was used for ships' timbers below the water line because it resisted the boring of tropical worms. White pines were highly prized for their long, straight trunks, which were easily converted into ships' masts.

There were other export markets to service as well. Sugar plantations in the West Indies and wineries in the Madeiras needed barrels to ship their products to Europe and wood to burn for the distillation of their raw materials; once the plantation owners had destroyed Caribbean and Atlantic forests, they turned to North America for their wood. Near the end of the eighteenth century, the introduction of iron furnaces in New England raised fuel consumption considerably. As Cronon reports, each ton of iron required the burning of more than 750 cubic feet of wood, and since a single furnace could produce over 500 tons of iron a year, the growth of the iron industry increased the rate of local forest destruction.[44]

The timber trade had devastating effects on New England's environment. Much timber was wasted in the colonists' drive to exploit such a valuable resource; one favorite method of clearance involved notching many smaller trees and then felling a single large one on top of them. This technique saved labor and cushioned the fall of the large, valuable tree, but it was extremely wasteful. Neither white pine nor white cedar had ever been abundant in New England; once removed they tended not to grow back and were replaced by other species. The large-scale removal of trees by the timber trade altered the forest microclimate, its soils, and its ability to retain water. Deforestation and farming warmed and dried the soil in the summer, and cooled it in the winter. Winter cold froze the ground to deeper levels than normal, and spring runoff of water began earlier and occurred at a faster rate. Water tables fell and flooding became more common. Removal of large stands of timber disrupted the foraging habitats of large mammals like deer, elk, and moose; and the numerous sawmills dammed streams and polluted waters where fish ran and spawned. As Cronon puts it, "the disappearance of deer, turkey, and other animals thus betokened not merely a new hunting economy but a new forest ecology as well."[45]

Notwithstanding the consequences of the timber trade, it was the farmer, not the lumberer, that was, as Cronon puts it, "the chief agent in destroying New England's forests."[46] At first, colonists cultivated already cleared lands such as river bottoms and beaver meadows, followed by lands that had been abandoned by Indians. Eventually, however, they ran out of cleared land and began to move into nearby forests. Trees that maintained moist forest conditions, such as hickories and maples, produced a rich humus on the forest floor, which settlers interpreted as a sign of soil fertility that would yield good agricultural land. These trees were usually felled first. In a short time, the farmers realized their error—that a forest cleared of its trees has little residual fertility—and were forced to move on in search of good farm land. To clear the land, colonists imitated the Indians' use of fire, but with a major difference: whereas the Indians used fire to clear the underbrush only, the Europeans burned the entire forests, trees and all.

Lumbering also took its toll in the south, where pines were the principal tree.[47] Pine wood could be boiled to produce a thick sap that the English called turpentine or resin. Spirits of turpentine had a wide variety of medicinal uses, and could even be taken internally in small doses as a laxative. Resin, the solid part of the sap, could be made into candles or combined with lye to make soap. But the English most valued pines for a sticky, black tar called pitch, from which valuable naval stores could be made. Ropes used as ships' rigging would resist fraying better if coated with tar, and pitch was used to cover the hulls of wooden ships below the water line. The pine trees of Virginia were only marginal for the production of pitch; those of the Carolinas proved to be far superior. The settlement of those colonies in the latter seventeenth century coincided with the interruption of the flow of pitch from the Baltic, which had been the chief supplier of the Royal Navy, so the manufacture of naval stores soon became a thriving commercial enterprise in the colonies. By 1715, the colonies were supplying half the English demand for such products.

The destruction of pine forests proceeded at varying rates, depending on the extraction techniques used and the final products desired. Lighter products like resin and turpentine could be gathered by slashing the trees and allowing the sap to drain out, not unlike the technique used to collect maple sap farther north. Heavier products such as tar and pitch required the complete removal of the bark to a height of eight feet or more, or, if the colonist were in a hurry, the burning of the timber under controlled conditions. No matter the technique, the production of naval stores laid waste to thousands of acres of Carolina woodlands. By the mid-eighteenth century, to export tens of thousands of barrels of pitch and tar to England, North Carolinians were consuming about 75,000 cords of wood a year, equivalent to a stack of wood four feet high, four feet wide, and 113 miles long. One colonist with ten slaves could exhaust a thousand acres of suitable pine trees in as little as three years.

Lumbering set in motion a series of events that reinforced the exploitation of the woodlands. Sawmills arose along rivers that ran through wooded areas, and these mills (which also ground grain) attracted settlements. These villages needed numerous wooden structures, including houses, churches, barns, and other farm outbuildings. Building styles changed away from the Old World preference for stone to the use of more wood throughout the homes and other buildings (at least until fires became a serious problem in growing cities like Philadelphia, New York, and Boston, where wooden homes were eventually banned). Even where bricks replaced lumber, wood was needed in large quantities to fire the clay. Fences were constructed largely of wood cut into rails or pickets, and usually in a style that was wasteful and subject to rotting. Finally, New Englanders consumed huge quantities of wood to heat their homes and other buildings. It was not only the fierce New England winters that caused this consumption, but also the colonists' practice of burning wood in open fireplaces that were much more wasteful than the closed cast-iron stoves used by the Germans of Pennsylvania. Cronon reports that the typical New England household probably burned thirty to forty cords of firewood per year, and that New Englanders overall probably consumed more than 260 million cords of firewood between 1630 and 1800.[48]

As great as were the effects of large animals and plants, it was the invisible life forms that accompanied Europeans that had the greatest long-term impact on North America's native population. European diseases flowed effortlessly into a region of the world that had scarcely known Eurasian pathogens before.[49] Rats were observed leaving European ships for dry land as early as Champlain's voyages of 1603–1606, and where rats were, there one would also find fleas and the plague. Fur traders carried various intestinal and respiratory ailments as well as tuberculosis, and smallpox came ashore with people and their cattle. In northern New England, the first epidemic (probably either chicken pox, smallpox, or the bubonic plague) swept through the Abenaki population in 1616, killing about two-thirds of the tribe by the time it ran its course in 1619; in some villages, only a single inhabitant survived. A smallpox epidemic in 1638 essentially completed the destruction of a tribe that had once numbered nearly 12,000. A similar fate befell the tribes of southern New England. The epidemic of 1616 virtually destroyed the native populations living near Massachusetts Bay and Plymouth colonies, and smallpox had the same effect on Indians in the Connecticut Valley in the winter of 1633, when 950 of the 1,000 or so Indians living near Hartford died. In all, the Indian population of New England declined from 70,000 to 12,000 between 1600 and 1675.

Smallpox was introduced into Virginia by an infected sailor in 1667, and the disease followed white traders inland.[50] Between 1696 and 1783, there were at least five major epidemics across the South, each lasting three to five years. Epidemics of measles swept through native populations four times during the eighteenth century, and typhus and influenza were also rampant. The native population in coastal Virginia and Maryland, estimated at more than 30,000 at the time of the arrival of Europeans, declined to 3,000 by 1685, and to fewer than 300 by the end of the eighteenth century. Indians in the Carolinas fared equally poorly; the two populations in the piedmont and along the coast dropped from 10,000 each to about 300 each by 1800. Tribes farther inland—the Creeks, the Choctaws, and the Chickasaws—fared somewhat better, perhaps because of their relative isolation from Europeans. Still, their populations were reduced by half between 1600 and 1800.

Social disorganization added to the miseries of disease. Populations weakened by illness were unable to complete tasks that were crucial to survival, such as planting crops or hunting, so hunger and even starvation intensified the suffering. Other diseases that Indians had never known, such as tuberculosis, measles, typhus, and influenza, swept into the villages that had been weakened by smallpox or plague. Networks of kinship and authority were disrupted, and people began to lose faith in the religious vision that had inspired them for millennia. The depopulation of Indian villages left their lands vacant and untended, and their farms were soon either reclaimed by weeds and forest or taken over by Puritans, who saw the epidemics as God's way of clearing the land for their occupation.[51]

GLOBAL LIFE SYSTEMS AND NORTH AMERICA

"It is tempting," writes Susan Alling Gregg,

> to draw parallels between the rapid spread of wheat farming in Neolithic Europe and in historic North America. There are, however, critical differences. The introduction of wheat farming into and subsequent spread throughout the New World was

stimulated in part by a growing global economy. Colonies were initially founded and financially supported by European companies with the express intent of providing Europe with much needed furs and raw materials for their manufacturing centers and an outlet for their finished goods. The spread of European populations throughout North America was subsequently stimulated, at least partially, by the need to provide eastern industrial centers with food and raw materials. The destruction of the environment and depletion of the wild game throughout North America was primarily a function of the scale of the population movement, the insatiable demands of eastern industrial cities, and trade relations with Europe.[52]

As Carville Earle makes clear, global forces began to affect the future of eastern North America well before the first European colonist came ashore.[53] The return of the explorer Francis Drake to England in 1580 with the riches he had plundered from Spanish shipping astounded the English and convinced Queen Elizabeth that North America offered the wealth England needed to finance the heavy consumption needs engendered by the growth of its population in general and its burgeoning landlord class in particular.[54]

From then on, lands were chosen for English colonization on the basis of two criteria: the choice lands would be in the same latitudes as the Mediterranean (on the mistaken assumption that latitude was the chief factor in determining land fertility), and they would be lands drained by a river that offered the best prospect of a passage through the continent to the Pacific and Asia. On the basis of these criteria, Virginia and Maryland were identified as the optimal colonies and were assigned to friends of the Crown for exploitation. The Carolinas were seen as somewhat less than optimal and were given to later waves of royal friends and associates. New England and Pennsylvania were seen as distinctly marginal and thus were reserved for the dissenters such as Puritans and Quakers to colonize.

What Carolyn Merchant calls the "colonial ecological revolution" in New England was the product of both natural selection (as in cattle and hogs replacing bears and deer) and cultural selection (the Europeans and Africans replaced Indians; Christianity and fences replaced animistic religions and open fields).[55] The transformation involved the replacement of one set of coevolved species (Indians, beaver, deer, maize, beans, squash, and so forth) by another (Europeans, Africans, horses, cattle, wheat, smallpox, and others).

What resulted in the short term was an amalgamation of these two packages of living organisms. For example, colonial farmers in the inland areas of New England adopted a synthesis of native and European methods of agriculture that combined the Indian method of clearing the land by girdling trees and fire; the Indian polyculture of maize, beans, and squash; the medieval European three-field crop rotation system; and upland pasturing of animals, also a European invention.[56] These elements of subsistence agriculture endured until the late eighteenth century, when they were gradually replaced by a more market-oriented farming system clearly dominated by the genes and the values of the intruders. Eventually, what remained of the native culture was either eliminated entirely or reduced to the status of a museum relic, although certain components of the native life systems (squash, maize, beans, turkeys) remained and were absorbed into the colonists' life system.

The agent that produced this transformation was the entry of mercantile capitalism into the eastern United States via the commodification of land and its products such as tobacco, fur, and pine tar. Under the pressure of these global forces, the native ecosystem gave way to subsistence farmers in New England and the South, who in turn were compelled to shift to extensive, market-oriented farming techniques or to sell out to someone who would.

It was a global system that brought Europeans to North America in the first place; and by the late sixteenth century, it was the global system that contributed to the eventual demise of the native life forms. Although not unique, the fate of the New England beaver is a good example of this dynamic at work.[57]

In Europe in the Middle Ages, the wearing of animal fur on one's garments became a mark of social status: royalty wore clothes decorated with ermine; lesser nobles wore sable; lower class artisans wore fox and rabbit; the poorest wore sheepskin. In the late sixteenth century, however, popular tastes began to shift to more staple fur, and it was the fate of the beaver that its pelt was the best for producing this kind of fur. In the 1580s, hats made of imported beaver fur appeared in England; and by the 1620s, women began to wear large beaver hats that imitated those of their husbands. Until the late nineteenth century, beaver hats symbolized the financial success of the growing commercial middle class in Britain. In the face of such demand in Europe, commercial interests in colonial North America responded by expanding the trapping and export of beavers.

Long before the arrival of Europeans, fur was exchanged between Indian villages as a part of a trade network that moved food items such as shellfish and chestnuts from regions of plenty to regions of scarcity. It was natural, then, that the natives began to trade furs with Europeans from the earliest days of a European presence in North America. Indians traded beaver and deer pelts with the cod fishers from England and France, as well as with early explorers like Cartier and Verrazano. The exchange brought new European technologies into the Indian world, as iron and copper goods (such as fish hooks, arrow heads, kettles, knives) and woven cloth began to replace objects crafted from bone, wood, and tree bark. These earliest exchanges thus began the gradual erosion of Indian self-reliance as they came to depend increasingly on clothing, utensils, tools, and weapons made outside their lands.

With the rise in demand for beaver hats after 1580, the Europeans launched systematic efforts to engage the Indians in the more intensive exploitation of, and commerce in, beaver pelts. European fur traders realized early on that they had to have the help of the Indians if they were to trap the beaver in large numbers, since the natives' hunting skills were obviously far superior to, and more efficient than, those of the Europeans. Samuel de Champlain visited the New England coast in 1604, 1605, and 1606, offering to trade for beaver pelts with the Penobscot Indians. The English began their ventures in earnest in 1605 with George Weymouth's expedition to the Maine coast. In the 1620s and 1630s, Dutch traders took out thousands of pelts from the lower Connecticut Valley.

For the first several decades of the seventeenth century, the principal traders in beaver pelts were the Abenaki Indians of Maine. When their population was virtually wiped out by a series of epidemics between 1616 and 1638, the fur trade was taken over by the Plymouth Pilgrims, who needed a local resource of value to exchange for European merchandise. As the fur trade expanded inland, the Pilgrims became essential intermediaries between European traders and Indian trappers. The Pilgrims built trading posts on the Kennebec River, where by 1633 as many as 100 Indians would gather at a time to exchange beaver, otter, deer, and bear pelts for food and tools. By this time, the Indians also needed food from the Europeans to make up for their own lost production and before long were even trading furs for maize, a crop they had cultivated for millennia. Eventually, the Indians began to cede trapping and hunting rights on their land, and finally gave up their land rights altogether via a legal and land tenure system that they barely understood.

Through the first seven decades of the eighteenth century, the trapping and export of beaver pelts grew steadily. Between 1700 and 1775, beaver skins made up half of England's fur imports. New England's share of English fur imports was about 15 percent in 1700, but declined steadily as the supply of beaver became exhausted. British merchants in turn reexported beaver hats back to the American colonies, where beaver hats were just as symbolic of financial success as they were in the homeland. By 1800, most game animals had disappeared from New England; by 1808, the fur trade had virtually ceased; and by 1818, the Abenaki Indians had abandoned the last of their trapping grounds to outsiders.

The loss of the beaver meant ecological devastation to New England and its native population. With the beaver went the beaver ponds, the beaver meadows, and all the life systems they had supported: mink, otter, muskrats, raccoons, moose, deer, black bears, rabbits, hares, red foxes, and many others. The gradual disappearance of deer and moose meant that cougars and wolves turned for food to cattle and sheep, which in turn stimulated humans to hunt the predators to extinction. The last wolf was killed in Connecticut in 1837. "In colonial America," concludes Carolyn Merchant, "few tears were shed over the demise of the wild. A nineteenth-century New England chronicler noted proudly that, where the shrieks of the "wild panther" had once rent the night now resounded Sunday hymns and the busy hum of machines."[58]

But there was more at stake in the fur trade than just New England's ecosystem:

> The fur trade was . . . far more complicated than a simple exchange of European metal goods for Indian beaver skins. It revolutionized Indian economies less by its new technology than by its new commercialism, at once utilizing and subverting

Indian trade patterns to extend European mercantile ones. European merchants created an expanded regional economy in New England by shuttling between several different trading partners. . . . Trade linked these groups with an abstract set of equivalent values measured in pelts, bushels of corn, fathoms of wampum, and price movements in sterling on London markets. The essential lesson for the Indians was that certain things began to have *prices* that had not had them before.[59]

There was, of course, much more involved in the transformation of eastern North America than simply the intrusion of Europeans and of the global capitalist systems of which they were a part.[60] The impact of the diseases that devastated Indian populations was at least partly a function of the biological isolation of North America from the Old World for millennia, and would have occurred no matter how the Europeans' economic systems were organized. Likewise, the damage done by European livestock cannot be attributed solely to global capitalism; after all, grazing animals have been laying waste to the land since the invention of pastoralism four to five thousands years ago. Moreover, we should not see the natives as passive in the face of the European intrusion. Many tribes carried on a spirited resistance against the European intruders for generations before being overwhelmed.[61] The Indians also made choices about their responses to the threats to their way of life that shaped the overall impact of those threats.

However, European fur traders and livestock would not have come to North America in such numbers, and would not have spread their disease and their environmental damage so far or so fast, in the absence of global economic pressures. North America's land and water had felt the hand of human beings for millennia before Europeans arrived. The impact of Europeans was felt so strongly on North America not because they ravaged a previously pristine landscape, but because they turned the land and its products into commodities for which distant markets would pay handsomely.

Despite the complexity of the transformation process, after less than half a century of the European presence in New England the outcome was clear, even to the Indians. In 1642, the Narraganset leader, Miantonomo, predicted his peoples' fate in these words:

Our fathers had plenty of deer and skins, our plains were full of deer, as also our woods, and of turkies, and our coves full of fish and fowl. But these English having gotten our land, they with scythes cut down the grass, and with axes fell the trees; their cows and horses eat the grass, and their hogs spoil our clam banks, and we shall all be starved.[62]

NOTES

1. D. W. Meinig, *The Shaping of America: A Geographical Perspective on 500 Years of History*, Vol. 1, *Atlantic America, 1492–1800* (New Haven, Conn.: Yale University Press, 1986), pt. 2; John Allen, "From Cabot to Cartier: The Early Exploration of Eastern North America," in Karl Butzer, ed., *The Americas before and after 1492: Current Geographical*

Research, *Annals of the Association of American Geographers* 82, no. 3 (September 1992): 500–21; Samuel Eliot Morison, *The Great Explorers: The European Discovery of America* (New York: Oxford University Press, 1978); John Bakeless, *America as Seen by Its First Explorers: The Eyes of Discovery* (New York: Dover, 1989).

2. James Malin has warned us against assuming that North American Indians living as hunters and gatherers were in balance with the land, and that they (and their land) were corrupted by invading European farmers and herders. Writing about the Indians of the Great Plains, he observed that through fire and deforestation these Indians had already greatly abused the land, and their "cultures were already off-balance and were running into trouble prior to any definite 'pressure' being placed upon them by the actual invasion of the area and their displacement by white men." James Malin, "The Grassland of North America: Its Occupance and the Challenge of Continuous Reappraisals," in *Man's Role in Changing the Face of the Earth*, ed. William Thomas (Chicago: University of Chicago Press, 1956), p. 355.

3. William Cronon, *Changes in the Land: Indians, Colonists, and the Ecology of New England* (New York: Hill and Wang, 1983), chapter 8.

4. William Denevan, "The Pristine Myth: The Landscape of the Americas in 1492," in *The Americas before and after 1492*, ed. Butzer, pp. 370–71.

5. Geoffrey Turner, *Indians of North America* (New York: Sterling, 1992), chapters 2, 3.

6. Carolyn Merchant, *Ecological Revolutions: Nature, Gender, and Science in New England* (Chapel Hill: University of North Carolina Press, 1989), table 2.1, p. 3.

7. Timothy Silver, *A New Face on the Countryside: Indians, Colonists, and Slaves in South Atlantic Forests, 1500–1800* (Cambridge: Cambridge University Press, 1990), pp. 38–39.

8. Merchant, *Ecological Revolutions*, table 3.1, p. 75.

9. Cronon, *Changes in the Land*, pp. 40–42.

10. Cronon, *Changes in the Land*; Bakeless, *America as Seen by Explorers*.

11. Merchant, *Ecological Revolutions*, pp. 44–50.

12. Merchant, *Ecological Revolutions*, pp. 36–38. For a discussion of the earth-shaping activities of beavers, see Yvonne Baskin, *The Work of Nature: How the Diversity of Life Sustains Us* (Washington, D.C.: Island Press, 1997), pp. 162–63.

13. Silver, *New Face on the Countryside*, pp. 97–98.

14. Cronon, *Changes in the Land*, p. 37.

15. Merchant, *Ecological Revolutions*, pp. 74–81; Cronon, *Changes in the Land*, pp. 41–50.

16. Silver, *New Face on the Countryside*, p. 37.

17. Silver, *New Face on the Countryside*, pp. 46–51; William Doolittle, "Agriculture in North America on the Eve of Contact," in *The Americas before and after 1492*, ed. Butzer, pp. 392–96.

18. Helen Rountree, *Pocahontas's People: The Powhatan Indians of Virginia through Four Centuries* (Norman, Okla.: University of Oklahoma Press, 1990) chapter 1; James Axtell, *The Rise and Fall of the Powhatan Empire: Indians in Seventeenth-Century Virginia* (Williamsburg, Va.: Colonial Williamsburg Foundation, 1995).

19. Merchant, *Ecological Revolutions*, chapter 3; Silver, *New Face on the Countryside*, p. 41.

20. Cronon, *Changes in the Land*, pp. 24–30.

21. Silver, *New Face on the Countryside*, pp. 13–84.

22. John Verano and Douglas Ubelaker, "Health and Disease in the Pre-Columbian World," in *Seeds of Change*, ed. Herman Viola and Carolyn Margolis (Washington, D.C.: Smithsonian Institution Press, 1991), pp. 209–23.

23. Bakeless, *America as Seen by Explorers*, pp. 128–29.

24. Silver, *New Face on the Countryside*, pp. 70–71.

25. Rountree, *Pocahontas's People*, p. 25.

26. Francis Jennings, *The Invasion of America: Indians, Colonialism, and the Cant of Conquest* (New York: Norton, 1976), chapter 2; see also Stephen Hyslop, "Life in America 400 Years Ago," *Washington Post*, June 14, 1995.

27. Jennings, *Invasion of America*, p. 15.

28. Jennings, *Invasion of America*, p. 30 (emphasis in original).

29. Alfred Crosby, *Germs, Seeds, and Animals: Studies in Ecological History* (Armonk, N.Y.: Sharpe, 1994), p. 62.

30. Alfred Crosby, *Ecological Imperialism: The Biological Expansion of Europe, 900–1900* (Cambridge: Cambridge University Press, 1986).

31. Carville Earle, "Pioneers of Providence: The Anglo-American Experience, 1492–1792," in *The Americas before and after 1492*, ed. Butzer, pp. 478–99, esp. pp. 485–86; Meinig, *Shaping of America*, pt. 1; Denevan, "Pristine Myth," p. 371; Silver, *New Face on the Countryside*, pp. 166–68.

32. Cronon, *Changes in the Land*, chapters 4, 7.

33. Bakeless, *America as Seen by Explorers*, p. 47.

34. Silver, *New Face on the Countryside*, pp. 172–74.

35. Audrey Noël Hume, *Food: Colonial Williamsburg Archaeological Series No. 9* (Williamsburg, Va.: Colonial Williamsburg Foundation, 1978).

36. Silver, *New Face on the Countryside*, pp. 175–77.

37. Crosby, *Ecological Imperialism*, chapter 5.

38. Merchant, *Ecological Revolutions*, p. 86.

39. Susan DeFord, "Tobacco: The Noxious Weed that Built a Nation," *Washington Post*, May 14, 1997.

40. Meinig, *Shaping of America*, pp. 157–58.

41. T. H. Breen, *Tobacco Culture: The Mentality of the Great Tidewater Planters on the Eve of Revolution* (Princeton: Princeton University Press, 1985).

42. Clive Ponting, *A Green History of the World: The Environment and the Collapse of Great Civilizations* (New York: St. Martin's, 1991), p. 259.

43. Cronon, *Changes in the Land*, chapter 6; Merchant, *Ecological Revolutions*, pp. 57–58.

44. Cronon, *Changes in the Land*, pp. 155–56.

45. Cronon, *Changes in the Land*, p. 108.

46. Cronon, *Changes in the Land*, p. 114.

47. Silver, *New Face in the Countryside*, pp. 121–29.

48. Cronon, *Changes in the Land*, pp. 120–21.

49. Merchant, *Ecological Revolutions*, p. 56; Cronon, *Changes in the Land*, chapter 5.

50. Silver, *New Face in the Countryside*, pp. 74–83.

51. Crosby, *Germs, Seeds, and Animals*, chapter 7.

52. Susan Alling Gregg, *Foragers and Farmers: Population Interaction and Agricultural Expansion in Prehistoric Europe* (Chicago: University of Chicago Press, 1988), pp. 29–30.

53. Earle, "Pioneers of Providence."

54. Michael Farquhar, "England's Pirate Base in America," *Washington Post*, April 9, 1997.

55. Merchant, *Ecological Revolutions*.

56. Merchant, *Ecological Revolutions*, p. 155.

57. Merchant, *Ecological Revolutions*, pp. 41–43, 52–68; Cronon, *Changes in the Land*, pp. 91–103.

58. Merchant, *Ecological Revolutions*, p. 67.

59. Cronon, *Changes in the Land*, p. 97 (emphasis in the original).

60. Cronon, *Changes in the Land*, chapter 8.

61. Wilma Dunaway, "Incorporation as an Interactive Process: Cherokee Resistance to Expansion of the Capitalist World-System, 1560–1763," *Sociological Inquiry* 66, no. 4 (fall 1996): 455–70.

62. Quoted in Merchant, *Ecological Revolutions*, p. 89.

Chapter Eight

Feeding Industrial Cities

Cities are not natural habitats for humans. We did not evolve to live in such dense concentrations; massive bulk-flow technologies and complex institutions have been necessitated to make the urban environment fit for human habitation. The problem, as Lester Brown and Jodi Jacobson point out, is:

> Cities require concentrations of food, water, and fuel on a scale not found in nature. Just as nature cannot concentrate the resources needed to support urban life, neither can it disperse the waste produced in cities. . . . As urban material needs multiply . . . , they eventually exceed the capacity of the surrounding countryside, exerting pressure on more distant ecosystems to supply resources.[1]

In *The City in History*, Lewis Mumford addressed the dilemma posed by the entropic tendencies of a concentrated human population:

> All organic phenomena have limits of growth and extension, which are set by their very need to remain self-sustaining and self-directing: they can grow at the expense of their neighbors only by losing the very facilities that their neighbors' activities contribute to their own life. Small primitive communities accepted these limitations and this dynamic balance. . . . Urban communities, engrossed in the new expansion of power, forfeited this sense of limits.[2]

Mumford believed that cities need not have chosen this route. There was a time, he argued, early in their development, when urban populations could have opted for another model, more restrained, more respectful of their limits:

> Two ways were . . . open for the development of human culture, once it had passed beyond the stage reached in the neolithic community: . . . the symbiotic and the predatory. They were not absolute choices, but they pointed in different directions. The first was the path of voluntary co-operation, mutual accommodation, wider

communication and understanding; its outcome would be an organic association of a more complex nature. . . . The other was that of predatory domination, leading to heartless exploitation and eventually to parasitic enfeeblement: the way of expansion. . . .

As a city's population grew, it was necessary either to extend the area of immediate food production or to extend the supply lines, and draw by co-operation, barter, and trade, or by forced tribute, expropriation, and extermination, upon another community. Predation or symbiosis? . . . A power myth knows only one answer.[3]

This choice confronted cities from the beginning. The earliest cities, such as the Minoan city of Knossos, were small and compact and lived largely off the produce of a hinterland no more than several tens of kilometers across.[4] But already by the first millennium B.C., cities had grown to such proportions that they relied on food and other raw materials imported from fields and mines hundreds and even thousands of kilometers away.[5] Despite extensive trade connections, many cities still failed to supply their populations and were eventually abandoned; but the trend through the centuries was for cities to continue to grow and to deepen their reliance on imported food, fuel, and fiber.

In the nineteenth century, the industrial cities of Europe and North America fed themselves by drawing on the temperate-zone grasslands of the entire planet. The wheat of Kansas and Nebraska fed Chicago and New York in a system that was merely regional or continental. But when the grasslands of Argentina and Australia were pressed into the service of London and Manchester, the food system became truly global. In the process, indigenous species were swept aside, replaced by the European life system: farmers and pastoralists were tied to distant markets by commercial intermediaries and industrial technologies by the products of their land (wheat, cattle, sheep, and pigs), and by their other attendant species (horses, dogs, rodents, and microparasites).

STEAM, REFRIGERATION, AND THE GLOBAL FOOD SYSTEM

Farming can be seen as an exercise in managing energy flow to maximize thermodynamic efficiency. Farmers invest energy in the ground in the form of their own labor, the labor of their farm animals, the fertilizers they spread over the soil, the seeds they plant and the fuel they use to run their equipment; and they extract energy from the ground in the form of food, some of which humans eat directly, and some of which is fed to animals and then eaten indirectly by humans as it passes through the flesh, eggs, or milk of the animals.

For millennia, farmers extracted food energy from the ground with only their own muscles and the assistance of cattle, oxen, and horses; they could transport food to consumers only with draft animals, canal barges, and sailing vessels.[6] Anthropologists and ecologists have estimated that the earliest traditional farming societies using only muscle power, wind, and moving water reaped a return of ten to twenty calories of food energy for each calorie they invested in producing food. On the negative side, these societies typically invested 90 to 95 percent of human energy in producing their food.

Before the age of fossil fuels, early farming peoples could never invest in farming more energy than they got out of the land in return.[7] The ability to exploit the stored energy in fossil fuels, what Ernest Schusky calls the "Neocaloric Revolution,"[8] meant that early industrial societies could feed themselves with an investment of as little as 15 percent of their available human energy.

> Despite this drop in percentage, overall energy use in food production reaches revolutionary new heights. . . . [T]he modern grain farmer using an array of machinery, fertilizers, and pesticides expends about eight calories for every one calorie that is produced. In an energy-short world such "production" makes no sense, but in a world where fossil energy is cheap and seemingly unlimited it is highly profitable. Of course, the direct use of fossil energy on the farm is only the beginning of the food system. Even more calories are expended in the transportation, storage, and processing of food, and most estimates agree that once food reaches a modern kitchen, another eight fossil calories are expended to prepare one calorie for eating.[9]

The Neocaloric Revolution did not affect farming operations and food production and delivery uniformly because the power that lay in fossil fuel could be applied more easily to some sectors of the emerging global food system than to others. Coal and steam enabled the movement of food across greater distances via steamship and railroad, and thus made possible the exploitation of distant lands and waters for food consumption in Europe. Steam power was also widely used in factories and mills that processed food and fiber for individual consumption. But the application of steam power to the actual production of food was a different matter.

In some ways, steam power increased enormously the productivity of farm workers.[10] The first farm to use steam power was in North Wales in 1798, and by the 1850s steam pumps were used to drain wetlands and lift water for irrigation. In 1849, a small, portable steam engine was invented to thresh grain, and a steam plow was devised shortly after the American Civil War. But the problems of designing the accessory technologies for high-pressure boilers delayed the full application of the steam engine to farming until about 1870. By that time, chain drives and gear assemblies had been invented that made it possible to connect steam power to machines for specialized farm tasks like threshing, cultivating, plowing, ginning cotton, crushing sugar cane, and digging drainage ditches. A steam tractor made its appearance around the turn of the century, and there were some five thousand such tractors in use on American farms by early (pre-WWI) in the twentieth century.

For decades, however, numerous obstacles prevented the full application of steam to farming itself. The steam tractor's weight packed the soil, and sparks from the boiler caused fires. Steam also required teams of men and horses to haul water and fuel, so the use of fossil fuel remained tied to animal and human power.

The horse remained an economically competitive alternative source of energy through most of the nineteenth century. In the 1830s, John Deere began to experiment with steel plowshares, and by 1857 his factory in Moline, Illinois, was producing 10,000 plows a year. About the same time, mechanical seed drills and harvesters also appeared. But all of this new equipment was designed to be pulled by teams of horses, and would not be connected to fossil fuel power until the perfecting of the internal combustion engine in the 1890s.

As important as steam power was in working the land, where steam really made a difference was in transport.[11] By increasing human mobility exponentially, the steam engine transformed the human condition in two ways: it made possible cities of unprecedented size, density, and complexity; and it extended the food-supply system of cities many times over, resulting in dramatic improvements in food quality, variety, and reliability. Steam-powered transport set in motion a series of positive feedback loops that increased city populations, productivity, and consumption—more or less simultaneously.[12] Lewis Mumford refers to these changes as "a process of up-building,"

> with increasing differentiation, integration, and social accommodation of the individual parts in relation to the whole . . . : an articulation within an ever-widening environment was taking place within the factory, and indeed within the entire economic order. Food-chains and production-chains of a complicated nature were being formed throughout the planet: ice travelled from Boston to Calcutta and tea journeyed from China to Ireland, whilst machinery and cotton goods and cutlery from Birmingham and Manchester found their way to the remotest corners of the earth.[13]

The important role of the steam engine in globalization derived from two nineteenth-century inventions: the railroad and the steamship.[14] The steam engine made its appearance in Britain in the eighteenth century, principally to power pumps to lift water out of deep coal mines. In 1804, a Cornish mining engineer named Richard Trevithick installed a high-pressure steam boiler on a rolling platform to move heavy loads around an iron works in South Wales, and the age of steam transport was born. The Stockton and Darlington Railway opened public transport via steam locomotives in 1825; and by mid-century, Britain was served by a rail system of more than 11,000 kilometers. The eastern United States had its own rail service by the 1830s, and the first rail line across North America was completed in 1869. In the 1850s and 1860s, other expansive countries followed suit, especially Canada, Argentina, and Australia. Many of the countries that invested heavily in extensive rail networks were located in the temperate zones, where vast grasslands offered the best prospects for the export of grain and meat to urban markets.

Globalization was also greatly accelerated by the application of steam power to ocean transport. Robert Fulton demonstrated the first successful steamboat on the Seine River in 1803; his famous *Clermont* was offering regular trips on the

Hudson River between New York and Albany by 1807, and steamboat service on the Ohio River began in 1811. The steam-powered *Savannah* crossed the Atlantic in 1819, although most of its run was completed under sail since it exhausted its fuel supply early in the voyage. In 1838, a vessel powered completely by steam, the *Sirius*, crossed the Atlantic westbound, and regular service between Europe and the United States was established in 1840, and between Europe and Asia in 1842. The sailing vessel struggled to compete with steam for mercantile shipping, but by the 1870s and 1880s steam vessels had demonstrated their superiority.

Through the eighteenth century, steamships both grew in size and increased their speed. In 1838, the *Great Western*, slightly larger than 1,000 tons, crossed the Atlantic in just under 400 hours, only marginally better than a vessel under sail. By 1890, the *Lucania*, at about 15,000 tons, accomplished the same trip in about 125 hours.[15]

Food Preservation Technologies

Before the global movement of food could be reshaped by the steamship, however, a way had to be devised to preserve meat during long, transoceanic voyages. Until the nineteenth century, the only methods available for preserving meat were salting and smoking, neither of which was entirely practical, since people using these techniques were not able to process large quantities or to preserve them for very long. Semi-isolated populations such as plantations in the American South could sustain themselves on smoked or salted meat, but meat was a rarity for the populations of large cities, who were sustained on grains and seasonal vegetables.

Early in the nineteenth century, scientists began to experiment with ways to store large quantities of food for long periods.[16] Initially, the prime motivation was military: the huge armies raised by Napoleon, and eventually by other European states, made obsolete the traditional strategy for feeding an army by foraging off the land, as Napoleon's forces were simply too large to be sustained in this way. In June 1800, at the battle of Marengo, Italy, Napoleon was nearly defeated by the Austrians because most of his troops had been dispatched to forage for food and returned to turn the tide only when the battle had been almost lost.

Upon his return to France, Napoleon offered a financial prize to anyone who could devise a way to feed his armies; and one of the first winners was an expert in wine and champagne named Nicholas Appert. Appert had been experimenting with ways of preserving food for some time, and eventually hit upon sterilization by heat. He placed a variety of foods in thick champagne bottles, corked them, and immersed them in boiling water. In 1807, the French Navy took a supply of preserved vegetables on a trial run to the Caribbean and reported excellent results. Eventually, Appert's method would be used to store not only a variety of vegetables but also fruit like peaches and prunes.

When the Appert method was transported to England, the container of choice was not glass bottles but tin cans, because the tin-plate industry, although nonexistent in France, was quite advanced in England. In 1814, the Royal family was offered a taste of beef preserved in tin and gave their approval; in the next two years, British naval expeditions to the Arctic and in search of the Northwest Passage carried canned food. By 1830, the first cans of food were being offered for sale in shops. Tinned beef and mutton were imported from Australia as early as 1848; but the gold rush to Australia after 1851 raised the price of meat there so that none was exported to Britain again until the mid-1860s. The American Civil War interrupted meat exports from the United States to Britain, and tinned meat from Australia, New Zealand, and Argentina flowed in to fill the vacuum. In 1871, Britain, faced with a food crisis brought on by an epidemic of cattle disease, imported 11,000 tons of canned mutton and beef from Australia.[17] In 1880, with the crisis past, British imports of canned meat from the Southern Hemisphere still amounted to 8,000 tons.[18]

After this initial burst of enthusiasm for canned and bottled food, by mid-century the industry encountered three serious obstacles. The first was economic: the cost of canning was so high that individual consumers could not afford the food products. The second was technological: a satisfactory method had not been discovered for opening the cans once they had been sealed. And the third was a shortcoming in the processing of the cans. In 1855, canned food destined for British troops in the Crimea arrived already spoiled. People believed that the cans had leaked so that germs could get into them, but the real reason—that the cans had been heated insufficiently to kill all their microörganisms—would not be understood for another decade, after the work of Louis Pasteur became known.

For some time after the Crimean incident, Europeans continued to rely on canned food simply because there was no alternative. Canned vegetables were at least palatable; and once mechanical harvesters brought down the cost of gathering them, canned vegetables like peas were competitive with the fresh variety. But canned meat still too often reached the market spoiled or otherwise unfit for consumption.

To meet the demand for meat in industrial cities, scientists and inventors began experimenting with another technique for food preservation: mechanical refrigeration. Before the middle of the nineteenth century, four kinds of refrigeration existed that did not depend on mechanical devices.[19] One technique had been in use since ancient times: porous pots made of unglazed clay, filled with water, and placed in the open air over night. With cool temperatures and a brisk wind, some of the water would vaporize, drawing off considerable heat and lowering the water temperature sufficiently to change it to ice. Such a technique was used in Egypt in the second century A.D. and in India in the fourth century B.C.[20] Another simple technique was the storage of perishable food supplies in cool cellars or caves. These storage sites ranged in complexity and size from the cellars in the family home to huge, multistoried cellars used by many breweries. A third approach was to lower the temperature of water by mixing it with salts like ammonium nitrate or saltpeter. As the salt turned from solid to liquid, heat was absorbed and the temperature of the mixture dropped, often to the point where it could freeze containers of water submerged inside the mixture.

A fourth type of refrigeration involved the harvesting, preservation, and transport of natural ice—that is, ice cut from rivers or lakes during winter for later use during warm months or in distant cities. Wealthy Romans imported ice and snow from distant mountains to cool their food, drink, and homes; Greeks built icehouses as early as the times of Alexander the Great; and the remains of an icehouse have been discovered in China dating from the seventh century B.C.[21] The harvesting of ice became a large commercial enterprise, and natural ice was the most significant refrigeration technique in Europe and North America as late as 1870. Boston firms sent ice to ports as far away as Calcutta. Restaurants in southern cities, breweries, and meat packers serving large eastern markets became dependent on natural ice. Since animals lost so much weight when they were driven on the hoof from midwestern prairies to urban markets, there arose a demand for slaughtering and packing facilities located closer to the grazing lands. Chicago in particular owed much of its growth to the meat-packing industry. The first ice house for dressed beef was introduced in the United States in 1858, and the first patent for an ice-cooled railroad car was issued in 1867. The long-distance, transoceanic transport of chilled meat began in the 1870s using natural ice.

By mid-century, the reliance of the food industry and of urban markets on expensive natural ice helped drive the search for a mechanical substitute.[22] Three technologies competed in the market: air expansion, ammonia absorption, and vapor (ammonia) compression.[23]

Early air-expansion devices owed much to the work of a Florida physician named John Gorrie, who was looking for a mechanical way to cool the ward of his hospital where patients suffered from malaria. In the mid-1840s, he found the answer by using the principle that compressed gases that expand rapidly in a cylinder absorb heat from a surrounding bath of brine. Unfortunately, Gorrie's principal investor died, and he was unable to find financial backing for his ice-making machine.

In the early 1850s, Gorrie had predicted that his invention would be used aboard ships to preserve food, and in 1869—using the air-expansion system on board a steamship, a Texan named Henry Howard delivered a load of frozen beef by ship from Texas to New Orleans. A New Orleans newspaper observed that the apparatus "virtually annihilates space and laughs at the lapse of time; for the Boston merchant may have a fresh juicy beefsteak from the rich pastures of Texas for dinner, and for dessert feast on the delicate, luscious but perishable fruits of the Indies."

Gorrie died in 1855, thinking himself a failure; but other inventors continued working on refrigeration by means of air expansion. In 1877, in Glasgow, Scotland, a chemical engineer, James Coleman, and two brothers, James and Henry Bell, registered a patent on a cooling machine based on the air-expansion principle. They installed their first machine on the steamship *Circassia*, then carrying chilled meat from the United States to Britain. It was a Bell-Coleman machine that refrigerated the first meat shipment from Australia to Britain in 1880.[24] For years after 1880, refrigeration machines installed on board many ships were based on air expansion because of the fear of the hazardous substances used in the other technologies.

In the 1860s, air expansion was challenged by ammonia absorption as the dominant technology for mechanical refrigeration. The removal of heat from the refrigerator area was performed by vaporized ammonia, which was then drawn off by absorbing it into water (hence the name, ammonia absorption). The water and ammonia mixture was next recirculated back through the system, where heat was added. The ammonia was then released from the water and directed into a condenser to be vaporized, whereupon the cycle would begin again.

By 1860, Ferdinand Carré of France had produced an ammonia-absorption ice-making machine that became the world standard for the next decade. His device was exhibited at the Crystal Palace Fair in 1862; and in 1867, the largest Carré machine could produce 200 kilograms of ice per hour. The Carré system had its drawbacks, however, chief of which were the large amount of heat that had to be added to the system to liberate the ammonia from the water, and the complexity of the process. For these reasons, when mechanical refrigeration entered its scientific phase after 1870, the simpler vapor-compression technology was able to challenge the ammonia-absorption devices and eventually came to dominate the market.

Meanwhile, in Britain the government became increasingly concerned about the possibility of mass starvation in the face of rising urban population.[25] In the 1850s, domestic meat production (beef, mutton, and pork) in Britain averaged 910,000 tons annually, which was supplemented with a small quantity of imported livestock. From that point on, domestic meat production increased only slightly, to 1,036,000 tons per year in the 1860s, and to 1,090,000 tons in 1882; but imported meat (still largely in the form of livestock) rose to 131,000 tons annually in the 1860s, and to 654,000 tons in 1882. Between 1860 and 1870, food consumption rose by 25 percent, while a series of bad growing seasons and livestock epidemics inflicted much damage on British agriculture.[26] Along with the rise in the population of the United Kingdom from 28.2 million (annual average) in the 1850s to 35.6 million in 1882, per capita annual meat consumption also increased, from 34 kilograms (75 pounds) in the 1850s to 50 kilograms (110 pounds) in 1882, 40 percent of which was imported.[27]

Thomas Mort is credited with having the idea of exporting frozen meat from Australia to Great Britain. In 1861, Mort established the world's first meat-freezing plant in Sydney, a plant that employed ammonia-compression technology. At a luncheon in 1875 (a meal made entirely from frozen foods), Mort articulated his vision of a global food system:

> That time has arrived . . . when the various portions of the earth will each give forth their products for the use of each and of all; that the over-abundance of one coun-

try will make up for the deficiency of another . . . for cold arrests all change. . . . Climate, seasons, plenty, scarcity, distance, will all shake hands, and out of the commingling will come enough for all. . . . God provides enough and to spare for every creature He sends into the world; but the conditions are often not in accord. Where the food is, the people are not; and where the people are, the food is not. It is, however, . . . within the power of man to adjust these things.[28]

The next year, 1876, Mort installed an ammonia-compression machine on the sailing ship *Northam* in Sydney harbor and loaded it with frozen beef bound for London. While the ship was still in the harbor, however, ammonia leaked into the freezing compartment, and the meat had to be removed. The failure was a severe blow to Mort, who died shortly thereafter.

Another pioneer in meat export was a Scotsman named James Harrison, who had emigrated to Australia in 1837. In 1850, Harrison opened an ice factory in Australia to service a local brewery, and eventually provided frozen meat, poultry, and fish to local markets. He designed a refrigeration device that worked by compressing a refrigerant, usually ammonia, in a cylinder. The advantage of the ammonia-compression system was the low temperatures that could be achieved. The chief drawback was the danger in the system: Leaking ammonia was highly toxic, and other possible alternatives, such as diethyl ether, were either poisonous or flammable.

Harrison returned to Britain, where he collaborated with a London engineering firm, Siebe Bros., to produce the Harrison-Siebe vapor-compression machine, which became the industry standard for the production of ice. Their large machines were capable of manufacturing three tons of ice each twenty-four hours. Before long, the Harrison-Siebe machine was being manufactured in Australia. In 1873, the first shipment of twenty tons of mutton and beef frozen by ice from Harrison's ice factory departed for England, but en route the system developed a leak and the shipment spoiled.

In 1877, a steamship, the *Paraguay*, equipped with ammonia-compression machinery delivered a shipment of frozen meat from Argentina to Le Havre, France. A group of Queensland sheep herders heard of the *Paraguay* achievement and mounted their own effort, using machinery of the Bell-Coleman air expansion design. In early December 1879, a load of forty tons of frozen beef and mutton departed Melbourne on the S. S. *Strathleven*, arriving in London in February 1880. This first frozen meat from Australia was delivered to Queen Victoria, who dined on some lamb from the shipment.[29]

In 1870, a German mechanical engineer named Carl Linde began working on a system to refrigerate beer.[30] He used the ammonia-compression system, arranging several of the compression cycles in a cascade so that each would withdraw part of the heat left after the preceding step. Two key differences contributed to Linde's success: he was the first person to use the science of thermodynamics to design his machines; and he was heavily supported by the German brewing industry, desperate for a means of keeping their product cool. By 1891, Linde had sold some 12,000 refrigerators in Germany and the United States, all using essentially the same system that we still find in home refrigerators today.

By the end of the century, Australian (and New Zealand) grasslands and London kitchens had become connected by a vast network of animals, plants, technologies, and institutions. By 1910, there were in service around the world 251 refrigerated ships with a combined capacity of 1.2 million cubic meters (43.9 million cubic feet), or enough to carry between 14.6 and 17.5 million sheep carcasses at one time.[31] Australian sheep runs, slaughter houses, meat freezing plants, meat inspectors, commercial brokers, harbor facilities, insurance underwriters, and other financial institutions were connected by these ships to London docks, dockside refrigerated warehouses, and retail marketing and distribution outlets that reached as far as Scotland and Wales.[32]

FEEDING CITIES IN THE NINETEENTH CENTURY

In 1800, between 2.5 and 5 percent of the world's 800 million people lived in cities; no one city's population surpassed one million inhabitants, although some (London, Peking) came close. One century later, the world's population had doubled to about 1.6 billion; the percentage living in cities had risen to between 10 and 15 percent, and nine cities had populations of greater than one million.[33]

These trends of population growth and rapid urbanization were concentrated in Europe, Australia, and North America; by 1900, two-thirds of the world's city dwellers lived in these three areas. Britain was the first country to experience these wrenching changes. In 1800, two million Britons lived in cities; by 1900, thirty million did. Its rising industrial centers included London and Manchester, the latter of which saw its population increase by nearly an order of magnitude in two generations, from 29,000 in 1774 to 228,000 in 1831.[34] Similar growth was registered in cities in Belgium, northern France, the Ruhr valley, and the United States.

Until the nineteenth century, cities managed to live mostly off the food produced in their hinterlands, although to do so depended on maintaining a rough balance of population between natural growth and periodic declines due to emigration, wars, epidemics, and starvation. The population increases associated with the Industrial Revolution destabilized this balance. Even in England, with one of the most productive agricultural systems in the world at the time, population growth averaging 1 percent annually threatened to outstrip food supply after 1780. For a time, relief was sought from local resources: new land was brought under the plow, fallow land was reduced, and new crops from the Americas—the potato and maize—were introduced into parts of Europe where wheat and barley could not be grown efficiently.[35] Across industrializing Europe, however, it was quickly recognized that long-term solutions to the tension between population and food lay abroad: either the food had to be imported from overseas, or the people had to emigrate, as the Irish did in the middle of the nineteenth century.

From 1860 on, three factors made it possible to feed the cities of the industrializing world.[36] First, between 1860 and 1920, a billion acres of new land were brought into food production—mostly in the corn belt of the United States (about 40 percent of the global total), southern Russia (another 20 percent), and the pampas of Argentina, Australia, and South Africa. Second, the mechanization of agriculture and the application of increased energy through fertilizers, pesticides, and herbicides raised the productivity of the agrarian work force while at the same time freeing up millions of new workers for factories and urban service jobs. Finally, the new transportation and food-preservation technologies facilitated the flow of food products from the Southern Hemisphere to Europe and North America. As Carl Sauer put it, "The industrial revolution was made possible by the plowing-up of the great non-tropical grasslands of the world."[37]

For Britain, the turning point in feeding its people was the repeal in 1846 of the Corn Laws, which had blocked the importation of grain. In the 1840s, about 5 percent of Britain's food was imported; by 1900, imports accounted for 80 percent of the grain for human consumption, 40 percent of the meat, and 72 percent of the dairy products.[38] During the period 1904 to 1910, the United Kingdom imported 46 percent of its food and fiber supply (by value), including 24 percent of its fruit and vegetables, 36 percent of its meat, and 84 percent of its wheat and flour. In the 1830s, London satisfied most of its food needs from British sources or, at the most distant, from the Baltic. By 1910, the city was importing its basic food supplies from the United States, Canada, Argentina, Australia, and New Zealand. Between the periods 1831–1835 and 1909–1913, the average distance traveled to London by fruit and vegetables increased from essentially zero to 3,000 kilometers (1,880 miles), by meat from 3,200 to 10,000 kilometers (2,000 to 6,250 miles), and by wheat and flour from nearly 3,900 to more than 9,500 kilometers (2,430 to 5,950 miles).[39] In 1910, the United Kingdom imported slightly more than 600,000 tons of meat; New Zealand was the chief source of mutton and lamb (about 105,000 tons), followed by Argentina and Australia (about 81,000 tons each). Argentina was the principal source of beef (about 254,500 tons), followed by Australia (slightly less than 53,000 tons) and New Zealand (slightly less than 27,000 tons).[40]

The need of Europe's industrial cities to tap more distant and more dependable food supplies was made painfully evident by what John Post calls "the last great subsistence crisis in the Western world".[41] The European food crisis of 1816–17 stemmed from increased volcanic activity which threw huge quantities of ash and soil into the atmosphere, creating stratospheric dust veils that encircled the Earth. Surface temperatures dropped across the Northern Hemisphere through the critical spring and summer planting and growing seasons. Cereal crops failed or were harvested at record low levels. Much of the food that could be harvested was spoiled by mold or blight; and draft animals died of hunger or had to be slaughtered to replace the missing grain in the peasants' diet.

Across Europe, the result was massive social upheaval. Death rates, which had been steadily dropping for two generations, rose again, and marriage and birth rates dropped, causing the population to decline. Since agriculture was still the most important sector in the economies of Europe, the disaster spread until it affected nearly every working person. Beggars and vagrants appeared in historic numbers, and marauding mobs of food scavengers roamed the country. Public health measures failed, and infectious diseases reached epidemic proportions.

Many factors contributed to starting the food crisis and to aggravating and maintaining it once it began, but transport limitations and rigidities played a key role in preventing governments from replacing lost food with imported staples.[42] Europe's leaders desperately searched the world's grain stocks for relief; but food supplies could be transported only by sailing vessels, and Europe lay completely at the mercy of the prevailing winds. The famine of 1816–1817 would be the last time, however, that Europe as a whole would experience such a crisis in feeding its population. Within a generation, the advent of steam transport meant that Europe could now tap distant food supplies and move staple crops quickly to urban markets.

Case Study: Manchester

There is no better illustration of the impact of steam power on the feeding of an industrial city in the nineteenth century than that provided by Manchester, England.[43] Steam-powered transport came early to Manchester, and was critical to the city's commercial success.[44] Manchester lay nearly fifty kilometers from Liverpool, the nearest seaport, and the city's trade suffered from the delays encountered in transporting goods to and from the port; sometimes it took longer to transport a cargo of cotton from Liverpool to Manchester than to bring it across the Atlantic in a sailing ship.

About 1825, the leading merchants of Liverpool and Manchester organized a company to construct a railway between the two cities, which was completed in 1828. Once the locomotive was chosen, rail service was begun on September 15, 1830, and in 1831, Manchester opened the world's first railroad station.[45] The Liverpool-to-Manchester line was a huge success from the beginning, and the railway became the model against which all subsequent rail service in Britain would be measured.[46]

This service got in place just in time, for, as noted earlier, the population of Manchester increased sharply through the nineteenth century.[47] The city's demand for food was driven by sharp increases in population coupled with steadily rising family incomes. The relative economic comfort of Manchester's population made possible a diet that exceeded today's recommendations: a per capita daily caloric intake of about 2,600, and levels of protein, iron, and vitamin C well beyond what an adult needs.[48]

The effects of steam power on Manchester's food supply were not felt overnight. Until the early 1840s, the city continued to draw most of its food from traditional nearby sources. But after 1830, Manchester's merchants began slowly to tap more distant markets; and in the period 1850 to 1870 the city's food network became truly global.

Livestock began to be imported from Ireland for Manchester markets soon after regular steamship service was established between Britain and Ireland, with more than 420,000 cattle, sheep, and pigs brought from Ireland through Liverpool in 1852.[49] American bacon and ham were imported through Liverpool at the rate of 9,000 tons each year. The transport of milk by railway began in 1844, and by the 1860s had supplanted the use of roads and canals to bring milk to the city. Imports of butter from Ireland nearly doubled between the 1820s and 1850, and cheese was imported from the United States after the 1860s. The use of rail services in the 1840s to transport fruit and vegetables to Manchester transformed completely the traditional networks on which the city had relied and increased the importance of other regions of Britain as sources of food for the city.

After the mid-1840s, rail transport of iced fish also introduced major changes in Manchester's diet. The city became dependent on fishing ports on Britain's east coast, from which the cod fleet sailed to fish the North Sea. Then, between 1880 and 1920, fish and chips—the mainstay of the diet of the English working class—could tie its popularity directly to the steam-powered fishing trawler and the railroad, which together extended England's food network to Icelandic waters and even to Canada for new supplies of white fish such as haddock. Potatoes came from Germany, Belgium, and Holland when local crops failed to meet demand. The oil in which fish and chips were prepared came from Egyptian and American cotton seeds as well as Argentinian beef drippings. Thus, the railroad and steamship transformed Britain's internal food-supply network. The country's industrial cities were supplied from a few large port cities, leaving many of the old farming and fishing villages bypassed and abandoned.[50]

The global spread of Manchester's trade networks via the railroad and steamship made possible four major changes in the city's diet:[51] supply was made more reliable; quality was improved; a wide variety of food items were now available throughout most of the year instead of only on a seasonal basis; and the price of food staples stabilized so that the people of Manchester could remain blissfully unaware of the state of harvests, either local or global. In this way, steam and refrigeration removed food scarcity from the list of troubles weighing on the minds of Britain's industrial working class.

THE "NEW EUROPES": AUSTRALIA AND NEW ZEALAND

By the 1880s and 1890s, wool, refrigerated meat, grain, vegetables, and fruit were being shipped long distances, from the prairies of what Alfred Crosby calls the "neo-Europes" to the rapidly growing cities of the industrializing world.[52] The emergence of a global food system affected many regions of the world, especially the temperate-zone grasslands of the Southern Hemisphere. With scant regard for what they would do to their new habitat, dozens of exotic species were transported (some unintentionally and unknowingly) from Europe to these regions. These new species included grazing animals (cattle, sheep, goats, horses, pigs), plants that were food for humans (wheat) and animals (turnips, English grasses, clover), animal and plant pests (rabbits, thistle, daisy), species transported for "cultural" reasons—to give the new lands the "feel" of home (game animals like deer)—and diseases (measles, smallpox, and influenza).

For want of space, our discussion here will focus on two of these "new" Europes: Australia and New Zealand.[53] As these Southern Hemisphere countries were drawn into the worldwide food-and-fiber network, their indigenous life systems underwent a dramatic transformation. While many species were involved in shaping this transformation, our emphasis here will be on the most numerous of these, and the one with the greatest impact on the land: sheep.

In virtually every instance where European grazing animals were introduced to non-Eurasian, temperate-zone grasslands, it was for reasons other than to provide food for European cities. Initially, the primary purpose in most cases was to provide the nonperishable parts of grazing animals (leather and wool) for European markets; the secondary purpose was to provide meat and dairy products for either internal markets or external markets close enough to be reached by sailing vessels (meat exports from New Zealand to Australia). By the mid-nineteenth century, before refrigerated steamships, the population of grazing animals had already exploded in both Australia and New Zealand. After 1880, when mechanical refrigeration became available, the export of meat to Europe came to be just as important to the pastoral industry as wool and leather. The shift to long-distance meat exports simply added more pressure to already stressed ecosystems.

To the newly arrived European farmers and herders, the grasslands of the Earth's temperate zones must have appeared not only bountiful but also indestructible. The combination of climate, a sparse human population who lacked advanced or complex technologies, and an absence of natural predators for European animals and crops invited them to transport their agricultural system more or less intact from Britain and northern Europe. In the eyes of the invaders, the enormous stretches of prairie that had obviously existed for countless millennia possessed such strength and resilience that it could absorb whatever assault that system could inflict on them.

In their assessment of the biological wealth of these grasslands, the invaders were correct: Eventually, the state of Kansas, New Zealand's South Island, Australia's New South Wales, and the pampas of Argentina and Uruguay supplied the world with wool and leather, then with wheat, and finally with frozen beef and lamb.

As for the indestructible nature of these lands, however, they were seriously wrong. Because the Neolithic Revolution had not yet reached the temperate-zone grasslands outside Eurasia, the plants growing there were for the most part of no direct use to humans.[54] The energy in these lands could be tapped directly in only two ways: by converting the indigenous plants into animal protein by grazing cattle or sheep on the land, or by burning or plowing up the native vegetation and replacing it with European crops. Plowing ripped the earth apart, exposed the roots of perennial grasses, weakened the soil, and made it more susceptible to wind and water erosion.[55] The sharp incisors of vast herds of grazing ungulates stripped off the vegetation, and their hard hooves beat and compacted the soil, turning grass into bare earth. Unwanted and unintended exotic plants and small animals, such as rabbits and wild goats, invaded the land and became nuisances or worse. Farmers and herders hunted and trapped many indigenous species to virtual extinction, leading to a population explosion of rodents like gophers and prairie dogs, which inflicted their own kind of pressure on the soil.

The net effect of these and related changes, as Andrew Clark pointed out, was "the large-scale obliteration of the original grasslands as such."

> In each case, the invasion precipitated large-scale displacement of the pre-European peoples and their culture. Native grazing fauna were considerably altered; the principal grazing animals in the largest of the areas were all but obliterated. Millions of horses, cattle, sheep, and goats were introduced. Animals were imported for sport, or by accident, and became noxious pests. There were weeds and birds, with bacteria and viruses in train. Fences appeared as well as hedges and groves of exotic trees; wells were sunk and windmills were erected to pump them; irrigation channels and stockwatering races were etched in the surface of plain, terrace, or river flat. And there were houses, villages, and towns; trails, roads, and railroad lines; dams and power lines.[56]

Australia

With a land area of 7.7 million square kilometers (nearly three million square miles), Australia is the sixth largest country (but the smallest continent) in the world. Its climate ranges from the humid tropics to temperate zones, but the country's insularity and lack of striking physical features contribute to a climate without great extremes.

The interior of the country is dominated by a great plain or central basin, where the richest pastoral land lies. This region is crossed by a network of rivers that flood the low-lying countryside in the rainy season but are reduced to a mere trickle in the dry season. However, great expanses of the interior (amounting to about one-third of the country's total land area) lie atop vast underground water reserves that are tapped by drilling to provide water for livestock.

Australia possesses distinctive flora and fauna not found elsewhere in the world. Coastal areas along the eastern and northeastern coast are heavily wooded with eucalyptus trees. Much of the land would be desert if not irrigated; but substantial tracts of land are given over to native grasses that lend themselves to forage crops for livestock. Most native mammals are marsupials, including some fifty varieties of kangaroo, the wallaby, and the opossum.

Despite its biological wealth, Australia never experienced its own Neolithic Revolution. The principal reason for this, argues Jared Diamond, is that only a very few species of plants and animals can be domesticated, and none of these were native to the country. Moreover, because of Australia's isolation from the Asian mainland, none of these plants and animals could migrate there without being transported by the bulk-flow technologies of transoceanic shipping.[57]

Australia's current population of slightly more than eighteen million is virtually entirely European. Prior to 1940, 90 percent were of British origin, but following World War II about two million Europeans from the continent immigrated, adding diversity to the population. The proportion of people of Asian origin has also been increasing since the country abandoned its restrictive immigration policies in 1973.

Australian Aborigines (sometimes referred to by ethnologists as Australoids, because they are not connected to any other racial group) constitute 2 to 3 percent of the population. The Aborigines have lived in Australia for about 60,000 years. Their population in 1788, at the time of the first European settlement, is unknown, but some estimates ran as high as 1.5 million, with most between 150,000 and 300,000.[58] After 1790, the native population declined significantly because of a lack of resistance to European diseases, most notably smallpox, influenza, and measles, and disruption of the aboriginal way of life; two smallpox epidemics, in 1789 and 1830, were particularly devastating. In addition, since the Aborigines had retained the foraging lifestyle, they were steadily marginalized by the European farming culture. Significant numbers were also killed by Europeans, the last massacre of indigenous people occurring in 1928. By 1921, the aboriginal population had declined to about 60,000.[59] Since the 1970s, the aboriginal population has been growing, and is now estimated at 400,000 to 500,000.

Many white Australians have become increasingly aware of the damage done to both the lands and the culture of the Aborigines by the introduction of European agriculture, technology, and lifestyle. In the 1990s, two issues regarding Aboriginal rights became very controversial. The first stemmed from a series of land claims brought by an Aboriginal group known as the Wik. A 1997 ruling of the Australian High Court found that the Wik had legal standing to sue for the restoration of native lands that had been seized by Europeans for grazing, a decision that potentially opens up nearly 80 percent of the entire country to native claims. The second issue involves some one hundred thousand Aborigine children who were removed from their homes between 1910 and 1970 and placed in foster homes with white families, supposedly out of concern for their well-being in light of what the whites believed was the impending demise of the Aborigine culture and people. In the 1990s, some Australian leaders began to urge the government to admit that these policies were nothing other than cultural genocide and to make restitution to the Aboriginal people for the damage done to them by this policy.[60]

Colonization

Distant from the shipping lanes of the fifteenth and sixteenth centuries, Australia was the last continent to be colonized by Europeans. The first Europeans to explore the Australian coast were the Dutch, operating out of their ports in Indonesia. In 1642, Abel Tasman discovered the island that bears his name off southern Australia (Tasmania). The British launched two expeditions to the region, in 1687 and 1699, but they returned with a rather dismal assessment of the potential for acquiring valuable resources, and European interest in the country waned.

Britain's expansion as a maritime power in the eighteenth century led to further exploration, most notably James Cook's voyage to Australia and New Zealand in 1768–1769, and to Britain's claiming of the two countries in the 1770s. After the American Revolution, when the United States refused to accept British convicts, Britain established a penal colony in Australia. Between January 1788, when the first shipload of convicts arrived, and 1841, some 83,000 persons were sent as convicts to the Australian colonies. There was a second tide of emigration (about 93,000) from Britain in the 1830s, mostly of impoverished urban dwellers driven by Britain's desperate economic situation; and a third in the 1850s, lured by the discovery of gold in Australia.

The Sheep

Australia's pastoral industry was founded in the early days of British settlement.[61] The first sheep of any kind—an African variety of sheep from the area around the Cape of Good Hope—were introduced into the New South Wales region of Australia in 1788. For nearly a decade, sheep were brought from southern Africa and from India, but they met only limited success in the Australian climate. Merino sheep were introduced to Australia in 1797 and gradually became the country's major economic resource, more for their fine wool than for the meat. The Merino breed, known in Spain from the twelfth century, was distinguished by its ability to thrive in arid climates and on scarce fodder. Difficult to raise in England because they did not take well to close confinement, the Merino were ecologically at home on the vast plains of New South Wales. In 1813, colonization of the interior plain began; and by 1830, sheep grazing had been established across vast stretches of the plateau in order to meet the growing demand for Australian wool by Britain's textile industry. Between 1830 and 1850, wool exports from Australia rose twentyfold, and colonists established huge sheep runs throughout the interior. By 1850, there were twelve million Merinos in the province, virtually all descendants of the 10,000 there in 1821. With the introduction of refrigerated steamship service to Britain in the 1870s, it was natural to convert the country's resources to the export of beef and mutton as well as wool.

Other Industries

Although agriculture is important to Australia's economy, especially in wheat and fodder crops, only 6 percent of the total land area is given over to crop cultivation. Today, the country has about 23.5 million head of cattle, about 1.5 head per person. Australia leads the world in both the production of raw wool and in its export (about 900,000 and 700,000 metric tons, respectively), slightly more than half the world's raw wool exports. Australia is second in the world in the export of red meat (about 1.1 million metric tons annually). It is seventh in the world in beef production (about 1.5 million metric tons), but first in the world in beef exports (about 900,000 metric tons).

The Impact

The replacement of indigenous Australian flora such as eucalyptus trees by imported species like wheat and pasture grasses has in less than a century threatened to upset a delicate ecological balance, particularly in the southwest near the city of Perth.[62] Here, about 90 percent of all native scrub and woodland habitat has disappeared, replaced by plowed fields and sheep pastures. The area has become one of Australia's premier farming areas, producing nearly $3 billion worth of wheat and wool each year on fifteen million hectares of land.

After decades of success, the region's productivity seems to have reached its limit, and moderate to severe soil deterioration has set in because of, among other things, soil erosion and salt intrusions or salinization. When the dominant species of plants here were the indigenous evergreen trees and shrubs, they had evolved a system of roots, trunks, stems, and leaves that captured, drew in, and breathed out again virtually all the moisture that fell across the seasons. There was a balance between soil, water, and plant life. European plants, wheat and field crops, are annuals that take up and transpire water only during the growing season, four to five months long. Rain that falls at other times cannot be absorbed by the plant life, so some of the rain filters into the water table, which is steadily rising, pushing up salt deposits as it does so; some of it simply runs off, carrying valuable topsoil with it.

New Zealand

New Zealand is much smaller than Australia, with only 268,000 square kilometers (103,000 square miles, about the size of the state of Colorado). New Zealand's land area is divided into two large islands (North Island and South Island) and numerous smaller islands. Although the country is generally mountainous, there are several large regions of plains that lend themselves to pastoral exploitation, particularly on the eastern coast of the islands. The two islands lie entirely within the temperate zone: the climate is mild, seasonal differences are not extreme (temperatures virtually never drop below freezing), and three-fourths of the country lies within the temperature zone required for growing wheat. Settlers from the British Isles found the climate to be quite similar to that of their homeland, but with the added benefit of more days of sunshine.[63] At one time a thousand years ago, the islands were heavily wooded with a species of pine tree; but the first human colonizers, a Polynesian people called the Maori, destroyed most of the woodlands through fire and agriculture.

Native Flora and Fauna

Of New Zealand's 2,000 indigenous species of plants, 1,500 are found nowhere else on Earth. The dominant plant associations consisted of rainforest on the islands' western coast, and "tussock" grassland (bunch grasses interspersed with low shrubs) on the eastern coast. This latter ecosystem was ideal for pasturing live-stock and offered an inviting habitat for exotic pests such as rabbits and wild goats as well. The soil, however, proved to be very thin and deficient in key nutrients, including phosphorous and nitrogen.

With the exception of two species of bat, New Zealand had no indigenous land mammals before the arrival of humans. The islands were, however, home to a remarkable array of birds, including a flightless variety known as the moa, whose species ranged in size from a large chicken to a very large ostrich (10–200 kilo-grams).[64] There were also geese, swans, eagles and other birds of prey, ducks, crows, and others. Evidence points to most of these species becoming extinct fol-lowing the Maori colonization of New Zealand, which began in the tenth century A.D. When Europeans arrived, they found dogs and black rats, which had been imported by the Maori, and little else; within five centuries, the Maori had hunted the moas to virtual extinction, disrupting the entire food chain of the islands.

The fish in New Zealand waters were of many varieties, but they were gener-ally not of the fleshy types that were popular with Europeans, such as cod or salmon, so they did not attract the fishing industry. In contrast, sea mammals, especially seals (known variously as sea lions or sea elephants) were hunted ag-gressively by Europeans, as were whales.

Colonization

New Zealand's population of 3.5 million is about 83 percent European and 9 per-cent (about a quarter of a million) Maori.[65] The first Maori came to the islands in the tenth century, but large-scale migration did not begin until the fourteenth century. At the time of the arrival of Europeans, the Maori population probably numbered about 50,000, of whom only about 10,000 lived on South Island. Their level of technological development resembled that of early Neolithic Britain.

Europeans first saw the islands of New Zealand in 1642, when Dutch Explorer Abel Tasman skirted the western coast. An attempt to put ashore a small landing party was repulsed by Maori in canoes at the cost to the invaders of four lives; and no European set foot on land until January 1770, when the expedition of James Cook went ashore on South Island. For a variety of reasons (the remote location, the aggressiveness of the Maori, and the unsettled situation in Europe), British settlement was slow. Sealing and whaling parties sailed the waters sur-rounding the islands in growing numbers; the stands of timber also attracted the attention of the British, who were consuming vast quantities of wood building and maintaining a maritime empire based on wooden sailing vessels.

During the 1830s, whaling parties began to establish shore facilities to support their hunting, and in 1840, when British sovereignty over the islands was estab-lished, the first attempts at permanent settlements were made. British emigration to New Zealand was fiercely opposed by the Maori, but in 1840 a treaty between Britain and fifty Maori chieftains opened the way to large-scale colonization. There were Maori uprisings in the 1840s and 1860s, but British colonists continued to arrive. After 1882, the export of frozen meat was a powerful stimulant to the economy and to the immigration of more British.

Throughout the nineteenth century, New Zealand attracted mostly the urban poor and unskilled, and speculators drawn by the prospects of a quick and easy fortune in the gold fields. With the exception of a small number of Scottish sheep herders who brought their trained dogs with them, there were very few immigrants who possessed farming skills or knowledge, which caused their impact on the indigenous ecosystem to be harsher than it might otherwise have been.

Sheep were introduced to New Zealand by Captain Cook on his second voyage in 1773, but the animals, already sickened by the long ocean journey, did not adapt well to their new home and died without producing a next generation of lambs. Over the next six decades, small numbers of sheep, along with cattle, pigs, and goats, were brought to New Zealand by sealers, whalers, traders, and the tiny groups of early colonists. The earliest land settlement schemes did not include the running of sheep and the export of wool in their plans; but by the 1840s, the sheep industry had successfully migrated from Australia to New Zealand. In one province (Otago) of South Island, the 1855 census recorded 3,436 people and 75,474 sheep—a ratio of 22 to 1.[66]

During the last half of the nineteenth century, the New Zealand economy fell on hard times. The world demand for wool declined as wool clothing was replaced by cheap cotton goods. At the same time, the islands' population exploded following the gold rush of the 1850s, all in all leading to high unemployment and a depressed economy. Refrigeration helped save the New Zealand economy by stimulating milk and dairy product exports to Britain and other distant ports. But there was a price to pay, and it came in the transformation of the country's pastoral industry. The vast acreage of sheep grazing runs were replaced with much smaller and more intensively grazed farms that were connected with meat packing and freezing plants in the port cities. The social consequence was to replace the small number of large landowners with a much more numerous group of small holders who used the land more intensively. The ecological consequence was to put even greater pressure on the available prairie land.[67]

Today, New Zealand's sheep number about 65 million, or about 18.5 sheep per capita. In addition, the country has more than eight million head of cattle, more than two per person. New Zealand exports about 800,000 to 900,000 metric tons of red meat (beef, pork, and mutton) each year; it is fourth in the world in red meat exports and first in the export of mutton and lamb carcasses. Plus, it is second in the world in the export of raw wool (about 300,000 metric tons annually) and third in total production. New Zealand accounts for about one-fourth of world raw-wool exports.

Ecological Impacts

Whether the complex ecological impact of sheep grazing in New Zealand has been destructive or not depends largely on one's perspective. Where the sheep were allowed to graze on indigenous grasses, one effect was to thin out the dominant native varieties, which were then replaced by a combination of other native species and some imported "weeds" such as gorse. Invading animal pests like rabbits and wild deer added their pressures to these lands as well. In many other instances, however, native grasses were deemed inadequate to support a dense sheep population, especially after meat exports became the chief product of the pastoral industry; so the prairies were plowed under, the indigenous grasses burned off, and English grasses (chiefly the so-called Kentucky bluegrass) planted to take their place. Overall, however, these grasslands have remained rather similar to what had existed before Europeans arrived.

The really severe impact of humans on the non-Eurasian temperate zone grasslands stemmed from the plowing of native species and their replacement with food crops like maize and wheat. Where these lands were used for animal grazing instead, they remained essentially grasslands, albeit with major changes in the kinds of life systems living on them. These findings led Andrew Clark to conclude that, "judged in terms of long-range economic benefits, and in terms of technologies available in their . . . centuries of use, the invasions may have been clearly a net gain."[68]

THE THIRD PLAGUE PANDEMIC

Steamships carried more than frozen beef and mutton. They also transported what Charles Gregg calls "the unholy trinity" of *Yersinia pestis*, fleas, and rats across greater distances and at greater speeds than had ever been the case before.[69] Widespread use of steamships to move the world's cargo can be dated from the 1870s or early 1880s. By the beginning of World War I, only a generation later, this new bulk-flow technologyhad carried the plague out of its natural reservoir in China to ports as far away as San Francisco; Alexandria, Egypt; and Callao, Peru.

The world's third epidemic of plague had its beginnings in southwestern China in Yunnan Province in the late eighteenth century.[70] The disease had been endemic in Yunnan since well before 1800, and there are records of epidemics of undetermined nature that clearly could be plague from the last two decades of the eighteenth century. Carol Benedict has assembled material showing that epidemics raged across Yunnan from 1787 until about 1830. At the time, Yunnan had experienced more than a century of immigration as landless farmers from other parts of China streamed in to take advantage of newly opened agricultural areas. The combination of new farms encroaching into what had been a remote wilderness, and the growth of nearby cities, created the conditions necessary for the *Yersinia pestis* bacillus to break out of its natural reservoir and spread through the closest human population. Exact data on deaths are not known, but impressionistic accounts clearly describe epidemics with high mortality rates.

The epidemic grew in intensity in the early part of the next century but subsided, and was virtually unknown for more than two decades. Then in 1854 another series of epidemics began in Yunnan, lasting until the 1880s. The spread of the disease was aggravated by a civil war in Yunnan known as the Moslem Rebellion, which lasted from 1854 to 1873. The high death rates associated with the war, the disruption of the area's food supply, the movement of large numbers of troops and refugees, and the general social dislocation in the war's wake, all contributed to a worsening of the conditions that foment plague and other epidemics. The population of Yunnan declined by more than half, from 7.5 million in 1855 to 2.9 million in 1884, although it is not known how many of these deaths were the result of disease.

Unlike earlier episodes of the plague, this time the disease spread east to Guangxi and Guangdong provinces. The exact mechanism of its spread is unknown. The "cultural vectors" could have been returning troops or fleeing refugees, but Benedict believes the most likely carriers were merchants and opium smugglers operating throughout southern China. Most of the commerce in this region traveled along river routes that were dangerous and difficult, and traders had to contend with pirates and other obstacles. Only the opium trade would have been lucrative enough to justify such efforts.

The plague reached the coastal city of Beihai as early as 1867, but did not begin to travel up the coast until the advent of coastal steamship service in the late 1880s. Hong Kong experienced a full-blown epidemic in 1894, and Macao was affected a year later. From Hong Kong, the disease spread up the Chinese coast, reaching Shanghai in 1908, and across the Taiwan straits, reaching Tainan in 1901. Once established in coastal cities, the disease was carried back inland to smaller cities upriver. By the early twentieth century, the plague was firmly established across southern China, and outbreaks continued to occur into the 1950s. Again, exact data are not available, but estimates are that each epidemic killed between 2 and 7 percent of a given city's population.

From Hong Kong, steamships carried the plague bacilli via rats and/or fleas to major seaports around the world. There has been considerable debate over the exact mechanism of transmission.[71] There is no doubt that infected fleas played a key role in carrying the bacillus; but it is doubtful that fleas alone, unaccompanied by infected rats, could have survived the long journeys across the Pacific or Indian Oceans. Therefore, the passive transport of infected rats in the baggage compartments of steamships seems the most likely avenue by which the third plague pandemic began.

At first, the spread was confined to Chinese coastal cities, but it soon reached other Asian ports and eventually affected cities around the world.[72] In 1896, the plague reached India via Bombay and spread throughout the country. Between 1898 and 1948, more than twelve million people died from the plague in India. In 1899, Egypt was infected via Alexandria (by a ship from Bombay); Algeria, via the port of Philippeville; Hawaii, via Honolulu; and Brazil, via Santos and then other ports. Paraguay was infected via Asunción, as the disease was carried up the Paraná River by infected river steamer. From here, the disease spread back into Argentina.

In 1900, the epidemic reached South Africa via forage imported from infected South American ports to supply horses during the Boer War. San Francisco experienced its first epidemic, from which the bacillus was carried inland to become endemic in wild rodents throughout the western United States, especially in New Mexico. In 1903, Uganda was infected by workers brought from India to construct a railroad, and then Tanganyika was infected from Uganda. Peru was infected via the port of Callao. In 1904, the disease reached Thailand via Bangkok; and in 1906, Kenya from an unknown source.

In 1907, Indochina (South Vietnam) was infected via Saigon and later other ports; Tunisia, via Tunis (by ship from Marseilles); and Seattle. Also in 1907, San Francisco experienced its second epidemic in the wake of the destruction by its famous earthquake. In 1908, the pandemic reached the Azores; Venezuela, via La Guaira; and Ecuador, via Guayaquil; in 1909, Morocco; and in 1911, Indonesia (Java), via Surabaya. In 1914, it was the turn of French West Africa (infected from Casablanca) and New Orleans; and in 1917, Malta.

After World War I, the plague continued its global march, reaching Pensacola, Florida, and Beaumont, Texas, in 1920; Madagascar, via the port of Tamatave, and Bolivia, from Argentina, in 1921; Los Angeles (probably from wild rodents overland) in 1924; Bechuanaland, from South Africa, in 1928; Basutoland, also from South Africa, in 1935; the Belgian Congo (probably brought by truck from an unknown source), in 1938; and Canada, via infected squirrels from the United States, in 1939.

With a few exceptions, such as in India, the death rates from the third pandemic were not as high as in the two earlier pandemics. Fortunately, by then medical science had discovered the cause of the plague as well as the mechanism by which it spread.[73] In 1894, when the plague reached Hong Kong, a Swiss doctor and scientist named Alexander Yersin raced there from Vietnam where he had been working with plague victims. He succeeded in culturing the bacillus from a number of infected patients, and upon returning to France he injected his bacillus into horses to produce an antiserum. In 1896, when the plague broke out again in Hong Kong, Yersin returned and cured several victims with his new serum, the first successful treatment for plague in history. In honor of his having discovered the microörganism, the bacillus was named *Yersinia pestis*. In 1898, a French doctor working in Bombay named Paul Simond proved that rat fleas transmitted the bacillus from rodents to humans, and the medical community now understood the disease's origins, mode of transmission, and effective treatment. Nevertheless, in India the plague caused some six million deaths between 1898 and 1908, and the epidemic continued well into the twentieth century.[74]

Gregg believes that the third pandemic did not end until 1959,[75] and regional epidemics continue to occur. One of the worst epidemics occurred in Vietnam between 1964 and 1974, affecting between 100,000 and 250,000 people. Cases continue to appear today, and the bacillus continues to reside in rodent populations around the world. In the western United States, particularly New Mexico, the bacillus long ago jumped from rats to squirrels and groundhogs, ensuring that human plague would continue to break out there for the foreseeable future.

NOTES

1. Lester Brown and Jodi Jacobson, "The Future of Urbanization: Facing the Ecological and Economic Constraints," *Worldwatch Paper 77* (Washington, D.C.: Worldwatch Institute, May 1987): 35.

2. Lewis Mumford, *The City in History: Its Origins, Its Transformations, and Its Prospects* (New York: Harcourt Brace & World, 1961), pp. 52–53.

3. Mumford, *City in History*, p. 89.

4. Peter Warren, "Minoan Palaces," *Ancient Cities: Scientific American Special Issue* (1994): 46–56.

5. Peter Garnsey, *Famine and Food Supply in the Graeco-Roman World: Responses to Risk and Crisis* (New York: Cambridge University Press, 1988).

6. Vaclav Smil, *Energy in World History* (Boulder, Colo.: Westview, 1994), chapter 3.

7. Eugene Ayres, "The Age of Fossil Fuel," in *Man's Role in Changing the Face of the Earth*, ed. William Thomas (Chicago: University of Chicago Press, 1956), pp. 367–81; John Harris, "The Rise of Coal Technology," *Scientific American* 231, no. 2 (August 1974): 92–97.

8. Ernest Schusky, *Culture and Agriculture: An Ecological Introduction to Traditional and Modern Farming Systems* (New York: Bergin & Garvey, 1989), introduction to Pt. 2, esp. p. 102, and chapter 6.

9. Schusky, *Culture and Agriculture*, p. x.

10. Schusky, *Culture and Agriculture*, pp. 107–9; Smil, *Energy in World History*, chapter 5, esp. pp. 188–91; Asa Briggs, *Iron Bridge to Crystal Palace: Impact and Images of the Industrial Revolution* (London: Thames and Hudson, 1979), chapter 4.

11. G. N. von Tunzelmann, *Steam Power and British Industrialization to 1860* (Oxford: Oxford University Press, 1978); Asa Briggs, *The Power of Steam* (Chicago: University of Chicago Press, 1982); R. A. Buchanan, *The Power of the Machine: The Impact of Technology from 1700 to the Present* (London: Penguin, 1982), pt. 3; Arnold Pacey, *Technology in World Civilization* (Cambridge, Mass.: MIT Press, 1991), chapter 9; Donald Cardwell, *The Norton History of Technology* (New York: Norton, 1995), chapter 10; T. K. Derry and Trevor Williams, *A Short History of Technology from the Earliest Times to A.D. 1900* (New York: Dover, 1993), chapter 13.

12. Allan Pred, *City-Systems in Advanced Economies: Past Growth, Present Processes and Future Development Options* (New York: Wiley, 1977), pp. 84–97.

13. Mumford, *City in History*, p. 451.

14. Robert Clark, *The Global Imperative: An Interpretive History of the Spread of Humankind* (Boulder, Colo.: Westview, 1997), pp. 90–95.

15. Smil, *Energy in World History*, figure 5.18, p. 197.

16. Susan Thompson and J. Tadlock Cowan, "Durable Food Production and Consumption in the World-Economy," in *Food and Agrarian Orders in the World-Economy*, ed. Philip McMichael (Westport, Conn.: Greenwood, 1995), chapter 3; James Burke, *Connections* (Boston: Little, Brown, 1978), pp. 231–46; Rudi Volti, "How We Got Frozen Foods," *Invention & Technology* (spring 1994): 47–56; Derry and Williams, *Short History of Technology*, pp. 695–99.

17. Reay Tannahill, *Food in History* (New York: Crown, 1988), p. 312.

18. James Critchell and Joseph Raymond, *A History of the Frozen Meat Trade* (London: Constable & Company, 1912), chapter 1.

19. Mikael Härd, *Machines Are Frozen Spirit: The Scientification of Refrigeration and Brewing in the 19th Century—A Weberian Interpretation* (Boulder, Colo.: Westview, 1994), pp. 37–42; Tannahill, *Food in History*, pp. 313–14.

20. Peter James and Nick Thorpe, *Ancient Inventions* (New York: Ballantine, 1994), pp. 323–24.

21. James and Thorpe, *Ancient Inventions*, pp. 320–22.

22. Härd, *Machines Are Frozen Spirit*, pp. 42–49, 56–68.

23. Critchell and Raymond, *History of Frozen Meat Trade*, chapter 27.

24. Critchell and Raymond, *History of Frozen Meat Trade*, chapter 2.

25. Critchell and Raymond, *History of Frozen Meat Trade*, chapter 1.

26. Derry and Williams, *Short History of Technology*, p. 685.

27. Critchell and Raymond, *History of Frozen Meat Trade*, pp. 2–3.

28. Critchell and Raymond, *History of Frozen Meat Trade*, p. 20.

29. Derry and Williams, *Short History of Technology*, pp. 698–99; Tannahill, *Food in History*, p. 315; Critchell and Raymond, *History of Frozen Meat Trade*, pp. 30–32.

30. Härd, *Machines Are Frozen Spirit*, chapters 7, 8.

31. Critchell and Raymond, *History of Frozen Meat Trade*, appendix 8.

32. Critchell and Raymond, *History of Frozen Meat Trade*, chapters 6–15.

33. Clive Ponting, *A Green History of the World: The Environment and the Collapse of Great Civilizations* (New York: St. Martin's, 1991), chapter 14, gives the lower figures. A. J. McMichael, *Planetary Overload: Global Environmental Change and the Health of the Human Species* (Cambridge: Cambridge University Press, 1993), chapter 10, gives the higher.

34. Josef Konvitz, *The Urban Millennium: The City-Building Process from the Early Middle Ages to the Present* (Carbondale; Southern Illinois University, 1985), chapter 4.

35. Alfred Crosby, *Germs, Seeds, and Animals: Studies in Ecological History* (Armonk, N.Y.: Sharpe, 1994), chapter 9.

36. Ponting, *Green History of the World*, chapter 12.

37. Carl Sauer, "The Agency of Man on the Earth," in Thomas, *Man's Role*, p. 65.

38. Ponting, *Green History of the World*, p. 115.

39. J. Richard Peet, "The Spatial Expansion of Commercial Agriculture in the Nineteenth Century: A Von Thunen Interpretation," *Economic Geography* 45, no. 4 (October 1969): 283–301.

40. Critchell and Raymond, *History of Frozen Meat Trade*, appendix 3.

41. John Post, *The Last Great Subsistence Crisis in the Western World* (Baltimore, Md.: Johns Hopkins University Press, 1977).

42. Post, *Last Great Crisis*, pp. 54–58, 151.

43. Roger Scola, *Feeding the Victorian City: The Food Supply of Manchester, 1770–1870* (Manchester: Manchester University Press, 1992).

44. Angus Sinclair, *Development of the Locomotive Engine* (Cambridge, Mass.: MIT Press, 1970), pp. 28–29.

45. Konvitz, *Urban Millennium*, p. 96.

46. Cardwell, *Norton History of Technology*, pp. 231–35.

47. Scola, *Feeding the Victorian City*, table 2.1, p. 19.

48. Scola, *Feeding the Victorian City*, p. 275.

49. Scola, *Feeding the Victorian City*, table 3.1, p. 47.

50. John Walton, *Fish and Chips and the British Working Class, 1870–1940* (Leicester: Leicester University Press, 1992), chapters 1, 2.

51. Scola, *Feeding the Victorian City*, p. 272.

52. Alfred Crosby, *Ecological Imperialism: The Biological Expansion of Europe, 900–1900* (New York: Cambridge University Press, 1986).

53. In focusing our attention on the impact of the global food system on Australia and New Zealand, we must not forget that the system also brought about major changes to the biosphere of Britain, chiefly by its impact on the diet of the British working class, and on the economic fortunes and herd-management practices of British cattle and sheep farmers. See Critchell and Raymond, *History of Frozen Meat Trade*, chapters 24, 25.

54. John Curtis, "The Modification of Mid-latitude Grasslands and Forests by Man," in Thomas, *Man's Role*, pp. 721–35.

55. Evan Eisenberg, "Back to Eden," *Atlantic Monthly* (November 1989): 57–89.

56. Andrew Clark, "The Impact of Exotic Invasion on the Remaining New World Mid-latitude Grasslands," in Thomas, *Man's Role*, p. 738.

57. Jared Diamond, *Guns, Germs, and Steel: The Fates of Human Societies* (New York: Norton, 1997), chapter 15.

58. Jonathan Kingdon, *Self-Made Man: Human Evolution from Eden to Extinction?* (New York: Wiley, 1993), pp. 267–70.

59. Diamond, *Guns, Germs, and Steel*, pp. 319–20.

60. "The aboriginal patterns that haunt Australia," *The Economist* (April 19, 1997): 37–38; Clyde Farnsworth, "Australians Resist Facing Up to Legacy of Parting Aborigines from Families," *New York Times*, June 8, 1997; "Lost Childhood," *The Economist* (June 14, 1997): 44.

61. Bruce Davidson, "The Development of the Pastoral Industry in Australia During the Nineteenth Century," in *Pastoralists at the Periphery: Herders in a Capitalist World*, ed. Claudia Chang and Harold Foster (Tucson: University of Arizona Press, 1994), chapter 4.

62. Yvonne Baskin, *The Work of Nature: How the Diversity of Life Sustains Us* (Washington, D.C.: Island Press, 1997), pp. 75–78.

63. Andrew Clark, *The Invasion of New Zealand by People, Plants and Animals: The South Island* (New Brunswick, N.J.: Rutgers University Press, 1949), pp. 15–23; Crosby, *Ecological Imperialism*, chapter 10.

64. Clark, *The Invasion of New Zealand*, pp. 30–31; Colin Tudge, *The Time before History: 5 Million Years of Human Impact* (New York: Simon & Schuster, 1996), pp. 298–99; Kingdon, *Self-Made Man*, pp. 85–87.

65. Clark, *The Invasion of New Zealand*, chapter 2.

66. Clark, *The Invasion of New Zealand*, p. 101.

67. Clark, *The Invasion of New Zealand*, chapter 3.

68. Clark, "The Impact of Exotic Invasion," in Thomas, *Man's Role*, p. 756.

69. Charles Gregg, *Plague: An Ancient Disease in the Twentieth Century*, rev. ed. (Albuquerque: University of New Mexico Press, 1985), chapter 5.

70. Carol Benedict, *Bubonic Plague in Nineteenth-Century China* (Stanford, Calif.: Stanford University Press, 1996); Carol Benedict, "Bubonic Plaque in Nineteenth-Century China," *Modern China* 14, no. 2 (April 1988): 107–55.

71. R. Pollitzer, *Plague* (Geneva: World Health Organization, 1954), pp. 385–91.
72. R. Pollitzer, *Plague*, chapter 1.
73. Christopher Wills, *Yellow Fever, Black Goddess: The Coevolution of People and Plagues* (Reading, Mass.: Addison Wesley, 1996), pp. 71–89.
74. Gregg, *Plague: An Ancient Disease*, pp. 58–60.
75. Gregg, *Plague: An Ancient Disease*, chapter 13.

Part III

Consequences

Chapter Nine

Global Food Networks
in the Information Age

As the First World made the transition from the industrial to the informational mode of production, some observers expected energy to become less important in information-based systems because the transport of symbols requires less energy than the movement of manufactured products or raw materials.[1] While it is true that energy consumption per unit of output has decreased in Western Europe, North America, and Japan,[2] the predicted decline in the significance of energy in the later stages of globalization has not taken place. Thermodynamic efficiency remains just as crucial in the Information Age as it has been in every episode of globalization from the beginning.

One reason is population growth. Although the rate of population increase is declining, the Earth's population continues to rise by some ninety million each year. Moreover, this population does not live like our predecessors: we live virtually everywhere we wish, at densities three orders of magnitude greater than did our ancestors ten thousand years ago. By the close of the millennium, more than half the world's population was urban, with twenty-one cities of ten million people or more. This population density could not have been achieved, and could not be supported today, without global systems for the production and distribution of food.

Today's population also consumes more food energy indirectly through meat and highly processed foods, and uses more fossil fuel for the generation of electricity, transport, and manufacturing, than has any preceding civilization.[3] A global population of six billion can be sustained only by globalizing the food network, which in turn could only have been achieved through the exploitation of fossil-fuel-based energy supplies and information technologies. The world's food supply has been increased dramatically by the application of fossil fuel to agricultural production, and it is transported thousands of kilometers from fields to urban markets by bulk-flow systems wholly dependent on fossil fuel. The global information network of telecommunications, computers, fax machines, satellite imaging, and other devices connects fields, markets, restaurants, food stores, and the family kitchen in a seamless web barely noticeable to the consumer. Yet this information network is still largely dependent on the burning of fossil fuel to generate electricity, despite attempts to replace coal and oil with nuclear fuel, hydroelectric power, or solar energy.

Today's global cities are virtually totally dependent on food brought from distant fields. The small amount of agricultural land still in use around metropolitan areas is devoted largely to "boutique agriculture," the cultivation of exotic and extremely expensive specialty foods in demand by a very affluent and cosmopolitan population. But the basic foodstuffs needed to support a metropolitan population must all be brought from afar, most from great distances, and many from foreign countries.

Why has this happened? Why should my home, Fairfax County, Virginia, which only a century ago boasted rich fruit orchards, be importing apples from Washington state, peaches from California, kiwifruit from New Zealand, and cranberries from Chile? The answer is not simple. Some of the reasons stem from federal government policies: massive subsidies for irrigation, farm policies and health standards that favor large producers, and a highway system that transfers tax burdens from truckers to other highway users. But local factors affecting land use are also significant. Land on which a shopping mall can be built is too valuable to let it remain under cultivation; and large infrastructure projects like international airports or a sports stadium can displace rich farmland before anyone can really calculate the long-term costs.

The affluence of global cities, and the changes in the eating habits of their residents, have also had a great impact on the global food system. It is true that we eat higher up on the food chain, but it's not only how much we eat that matters but also how and where we eat. With the rise in two-income families in the affluent suburbs, there's less time to spend on food preparation, so families spend more money on home-delivered food and food prepared somewhere (and by someone) else. More than half of all Americans eat at least one meal a day outside the home; and we spend nearly half of every food dollar in a restaurant.

The environmental costs of such a food system are huge. By relying so much on California for food, the cities of the eastern United States have placed increasing stress on western groundwater supplies. Transportation of food has also imposed serious environmental costs not reflected in the ultimate product cost to the consumer because of government subsidies. Huge quantities of animal waste and pesticides drain off into rivers and bays, stimulating the suffocating growth of algae and even in some instances promoting the spread of toxic microbes through local fish populations.

Perhaps we no longer appreciate the importance of thermodynamic efficiency, because the life system that has been the chief protagonist of globalization for 500 years has become the dominant global system.[4] The combination of European and neo-European farmers and livestock managers, Third World farm laborers, intensive cultivation of Eurasian crops (wheat and rice) and Amerindian crops (maize and potatoes), and Eurasian animals (beef cattle, pigs, and sheep) now constitutes a single global pool of genes and memes for the production and distribution of food energy.

Other biological systems remain alive, of course, and occasionally some still constitute a serious threat to segments of the reigning global system. Some species of large animals that could not be absorbed into the human-based food system—carnivorous predators like tigers or uncooperative herbivores like rhinos—are either threatened with extinction or protected by hunting bans, zoos, and game preserves. Countless species of tiny creatures are wiped out by the destruction of forests in the interest of expanded food production, but micröorganisms seem to be multiplying their number and variety at speeds that outpace our best efforts to combat them. Nevertheless, competition between varieties of human-based food systems is now essentially concluded, having resulted in victory for the system that originated in England and northwestern Europe more than half a millennium ago.

GLOBAL FOOD NETWORKS

The life system that dominates the Earth is embedded in, and sustained by, global food networks of production, processing, distribution, and consumption. By means of these networks, virtually all the inputs (that is, seed, livestock, fertilizer, chemicals, technology, capital, labor, and information) and virtually all the outputs (food for both humans and domesticated animals) are transported over greater and greater distances and, to an increasing degree, across nation-state boundaries.[5] Thus, the production of food is rapidly becoming liberated from spatial limitations.

Since the late 1960s or early 1970s, the network of suppliers, processors, and distributors that handle our food has been undergoing a global restructuring, in the process becoming more complex and more universal. As one recent account put it, this restructuring is

> universal not simply because agricultural and food systems are being transformed globally, but also because this transformation implicates industrial, financial, and service sectors. Arguably, the very definition and content of current restructuring involve a fundamental process of intersectoral integration, unconstrained by national boundaries. Accordingly, restructuring redraws economic and political boundaries and transforms the spatial categories with which social scientists work.[6]

As Sara Millman and her colleagues observe, "information plays a central role" in the operation of such a system.[7] The global information infrastructure makes the managers of global food systems aware of projected harvests, impending problems such as regional famines, the state of the world's farmlands, weather patterns, demand forecasts, and price fluctuations. Information networks connect the world's commodity markets with buyers and sellers. Satellite imagery depicts land conditions, environmental problems, water scarcity, and many other factors that shape world food production to help policymakers.

Global television makes huge audiences aware of famine in countries like Ethiopia and Somalia, thus generating popular support for food relief missions. Scholars, agricultural activists, policymakers, and others can draw on a vast literature to learn more about nutrition, food-production technologies, food-borne diseases, and sundry other topics. Institutions with global food concerns, such as the Food and Agriculture Organization (FAO), the World Health Organization (WHO), the World Food Council (WFC), Worldwatch Institute, The Hunger Project, and Food Aid are all actively involved in generating and distributing information to interested publics.

The maritime transport of agricultural inputs and of food across great distances owes much to the navigation technologies available from computers and satellite images; air cargo would be impossible without computer-assisted air traffic controls; and ground transport via rail and truck would be chaos were it not for the computers that track hundreds of thousands of individual shipments around the world.

Global food networks are so complex, so distant, and so expansive that they remain largely unseen, even to many of the people whose labor makes them work. The network for a single food product that connects fields with consumers is unbroken and seamless, but can be loosely broken down into three divisions—production, processing and distribution, and consumption—which, though artificial in their delineations, provide us a simple framework in which to explore an extremely complex reality.

PRODUCTION

Considering the planet's storehouse of tremendous biological wealth and potential food energy, one might assume it would be a straightforward task to feed the world's six billion people. Nevertheless, there are sharp limits to our ability to tap this storehouse for our uses, and today we find ourselves pressing against some of those limits.

The key to the food production capacity of the Earth lies in the carbon cycle, the sequence of chemical reactions by which carbon is taken up by plants and converted to carbohydrates like sugar. The net primary productivity of the biosphere (the net amount of plant matter produced on the Earth in any given span of time is not known with precision. Some recent estimates aided by satellite imagery suggest that the amount of carbon assimilated into plant tissue is around 60 to 65 billion tons annually.[8] Huge areas of the planet's surface are covered by photosynthesizing plants not edible by humans, so converting that land to the cultivation of crops like wheat and maize would more than meet our needs. And then there are the oceans: Surely the green plants (algae) there, and the fish that live off them, would supply a significant portion of the diet of a growing population.

The problem is that the capacity of plants to produce food for humans and other animals is much lower than their overall ability to photosynthesize plant tissue from solar energy. (See discussion of the biological limits to food production in chapter 3.) Plants like wheat and maize have been bred over the millennia to devote more of their energy to the plant tissue that we eat and less to the other functions that we perform for them (defense and reproduction). Despite this, cultivated plants still take up much less carbon per square meter of land than do, say, forests or wetlands.[9] A forest of deciduous trees contains more than three times as much carbon per square meter as a field of potatoes. But what about the oceans? Could we not augment our planet's food production by harvesting aquatic creatures more intensively? Actually, the food-producing capacity of the oceans is so diluted that a square meter of land is four times as productive as a cubic meter of ocean; and the land produces 40 percent more carbon each year than the oceans. Even though sea water covers three-fourths of the Earth's surface, plants in the ocean account for only one-quarter of the calories fixed by living organisms from the sun's energy.[10]

Within these limits, our planet has produced, and continues to produce, enough food energy so that each of the 6 billion of its inhabitants should be able to enjoy a daily diet equal to, or better than, the 2,600 calories recommended as a minimum by the World Health Organization. Many in our population do not consume this much energy, however, due to the unequal distribution of food and of the income necessary to purchase food in the marketplace. Of course, many people consume much more than 2,600 calories. In the richer countries of Europe (both Eastern and Western), North America, Oceania, and the Middle East, per capita caloric consumption averages between 3,000 and 3,400 daily, and in a few instances goes as high as 3,600. In Latin America and the Caribbean, as well as in China and a few other East Asian countries, per capita consumption is near the WHO standard. In Africa below the Sahara and in south Asia, however, per capita consumption drops to 2,100; and in a half dozen of the most desperately poor countries, such as Haiti and Bangladesh, the intake drops below 2,000.[11]

The rich countries of the world are not only the principal consumers of food; they are also its leading producers. Of the nearly 1.7 billion tons of cereal grains produced in the world each year, Western Europe, North America, and Oceania produce nearly 500 million tons (more than 28 percent), even though these countries hold only 16 percent of the world's population and 24 percent of its land area.[12] The same is true for meat: Of the more than 160 million tons produced annually, the rich countries produce some 70 million (nearly 43 percent). The world's three largest "metro-agro-plexes" (regions containing cities, industries, and large-scale agriculture) occupy most of Western Europe, eastern North America, and East Asia. These regions are home to about one-third of the world's population; but they account for about 75 percent of the world's use of fossil fuels and nitrogen fertilizers, and for about 60 percent of global food production.[13]

The greater wealth of these countries permits much greater investment in food production, particularly in technologies requiring high energy inputs: irrigation, fertilizer, machinery, and research. Because of these greater inputs, agricultural output per farm worker in these countries exceeds $23,000, 50 to 100 times higher than sub-Saharan Africa, south Asia, or China. Equally significant are the government policies in Europe, the United States, and Japan that subsidize agricultural production and protect it from inexpensive imports. In 1990, the total cost of agricultural subsidies (direct payments, cheap loans, guaranteed prices, and protective tariffs)—as reflected in higher taxes and food prices in the industrialized countries—amounted to $260 billion, or about $1,400 per non-farm household. Such subsidies dropped through the early 1990s, reaching $182 billion in 1995 and $169 billion in 1996. This latter sum still represented about 36 percent of total agricultural production.[15]

Between 1900 and 1990, world population grew threefold and per capita food production doubled. To achieve such growth, total crop yields had to increase some six times.[16] How were these unprecedented increases in world food production attained?[17] One thing is certain: more labor was not the answer. In fact, increased food production has been achieved with a reduced investment of human and animal labor. In 1800, for example, each ton of wheat harvested in the United States required about thirty hours of labor; by the late 1970s, labor inputs had dropped to just two hours per ton.[18] In 1910, a ton of maize required more than fifty hours of labor, and there were between twenty and thirty million horses on American farms. By 1980, the same ton of maize required about one and a half hours of human labor, and horses had virtually disappeared from the farming scene.[19]

During the first three-quarters of this century, much of the growth in food production was obtained the way civilizations have done it since the Neolithic Revolution: by bringing more land under the plow. Between 1900 and 1990, the world's cultivated area increased by one-third, with agricultural appropriation of new land occurring in waves. One came during the early 1950s, when the Soviet Union launched its Virgin Lands project, which expanded its cropland by one-fifth. A second wave hit during the 1970s, when grain prices soared and American and Brazilian farmers expanded cropland in response to demand. During the quarter-century between 1950 and 1976, the area planted in cereals, which accounts for two-thirds of the world's cropland, grew from 590 million to 720 million hectares, a 22 percent increase. Since then, however, the area planted in cereals has not grown to any appreciable degree, and in fact has remained below 700 million hectares since 1987. As population has continued to climb, the area per capita devoted to grain production has fallen, from 0.23 hectare in 1950 to 0.13 hectare in 1992.[20]

Of the world's nearly 130 million square kilometers of land area, about one-third is covered by nonproductive features (desert, ice and permafrost, wetlands); another one-third is covered by forests and woodlands, the clearance and cultivation of which are difficult, expensive, and fraught with negative environmental consequences. Of the remainder, about two-thirds (between one-fifth and one-quarter of the total) is given over to permanent pasture, leaving only about one-eighth of the total land area available for arable and permanent cropland. This area can be expanded only with great difficulty and at a heavy price.

Despite these limitations, global food production continues to expand. During the 1980s, food output increased by more than 3 percent annually. (Rising population absorbed most of the increase, leaving per capita production up only 0.5 percent each year.) Producing more food to keep pace with a growing population can occur only through four measures: more irrigation; more fertilizer, which requires the increased production of nitrogen; improved technologies, including the genetic manipulation of plants and animals; and increased use of energy in machinery and transport.

Irrigation

Irrigation has been used to increase agricultural production for millennia, but its use spread slowly around the world until this century. In 1900, some 40 million hectares were irrigated, and world water demand was 579 cubic kilometers per year. Between 1900 and 1990, the extent of irrigated land grew six times over, to 240 million hectares, and world water demand rose more than seven times, to 4,130 cubic kilometers annually.[21] Thanks to the growth of irrigated area after 1950, this factor in agricultural productivity managed to keep pace with population. Between 1960 and 1990, world irrigated area remained steady at about forty-five hectares per thousand people.[22] Table 9.1 summarizes the growth in irrigated land worldwide; these lands now yield about one-third of all the food harvested in the world.

There are signs that the expansion of irrigated land is slowing down. Moving water long distances is expensive, and governments around the world are increasingly reluctant to invest in large irrigation projects. Land that is overwatered eventually loses its productivity due to waterlogging and salt buildup. In addition, much of the water for irrigation has been drawn from underground reservoirs

Table 9.1   Growth in Irrigated Area, by Continent, 1950–1985

Region	Total Irrigated Area, 1985	Growth in Irrigated Area			
		1950–60	1960–70	1970–80	1980–85
	(million hectares)	(per cent)			
Asia	184	52	32	28	8
North America	34	42	71	14	−11
Europe	29	50	67	33	9
Africa	13	25	80	27	13
South America	9	67	20	28	17
Oceania	2	0	100	0	0
World Total	271	49	41	26	8

Source: Lester Brown, "Sustaining World Agriculture," in Lester Brown, et al., *State of the World: 1987* (New York: W.W. Norton, 1987), Table 7.1, p. 125. Adapted from W.R. Rangeley, "Irrigation and Drainage in the World," International Conference on Food and Water, Texas A&M University, May 26–30, 1986.

called aquifers. While these reservoirs contain vast water supplies, they are recharged only very slowly, and tapping them for irrigation has dropped many of them to dangerously low levels.

Moreover, an expanding population has drawn water away from agricultural purposes. For example, growing cities in the American West such as Las Vegas compete with California agriculture for water for urban purposes. Western rivers in the United States now provide more than 40 percent of the water to irrigate the nation's crops.[23] Because of its long growing season, consumers in the East have come to depend on California's Imperial Valley for much of their food; but the region's low rainfall must be supplemented by diverting waters of the Colorado River, more than 140 kilometers away. Roughly one-fifth of the river's annual flow ends up in Imperial Valley irrigation ditches, an amount equal to the water needed to support three million families of five for a year.[24]

Fertilizer

After water, the next significant input enabling increased food production has been fertilizer.[25] The scientific knowledge that underlies the use of chemicals to raise land productivity has been available since the mid-nineteenth century, but the application of artificial fertilizers (manufactured, rather than organic) has been widespread only since the early 1950s. In 1950, world fertilizer usage amounted to only 14 million tons, or about 5.5 kilograms per person.[26] The use of fertilizer grew rapidly, reaching a high of 146 million tons in 1989, or about 28 kilograms per capita. Since that peak, fertilizer application has declined steadily, reaching 126 million tons (22.7 kilograms per capita) in 1993 (see table 9.2).

Table 9.2   World Fertilizer Use, Total 1950–1985

Year	Total	Per Capita
	(million metric tons)	(kilograms)
1950	14	5
1955	18	7
1960	27	9
1965	40	12
1970	63	17
1975	82	21
1980	112	26
1985	130	26

Source: Lester Brown, "Sustaining World Agriculture," in Lester Brown, et al., eds., *State of the World: 1987* (New York: W.W. Norton, 1987), Table 7.2, p. 128. © the Worldwatch Institute. Reprinted by permission of W.W. Norton & Company, Inc.

The increase in fertilizer use stemmed from several sources. Population growth and a leveling off of cultivated land meant that food production per hectare had to be increased, and the vigorous application of water and fertilizer were the most obvious ways to achieve these gains. The Green Revolution in the 1960s (see the technology section) produced seed varieties that were especially responsive to additional fertilizer, so chemical additives to the soil spread beyond their traditional centers in Europe and North America. Many governments in the developing countries subsidized fertilizer usage to achieve self-sufficiency in food, as well as to stimulate the export of agricultural commodities. Since the early 1980s, however, fertilizer application has declined around the world, as farmers and governments have concluded that additional application makes little sense economically or biologically.

Technology

About half the fertilizer used in the world today is manufactured from chemical feedstocks, which illustrates the third general measure to increase food production: the application of technology. In the nineteenth century, chemists began to understand the critical role of certain elements in promoting plant productivity, especially potassium, phosphorous, and nitrogen.[27] While the first two could be obtained fairly readily from nature, nitrogen posed a much more difficult problem.[28] Nitrogen is an essential ingredient in the human diet; we cannot draw it directly from the atmosphere, however, so we must ingest it with our food. With the exception of legumes, which can draw nitrogen directly from the atmosphere by means of nitrogen-fixing microörganisms attached to their roots, most plants are unable to fix nitrogen directly, so it must be added to the soil as fertilizer. Traditional farmers accomplished this by raising legumes such as peas or beans and/ or by adding human and animal wastes to their fields. Such measures were inadequate to provide food for a growing population, however, so scientists began to look for a way to synthesize a fertilizer based on nitrogen. The achievement of this technique is credited to two German scientists, Carl Bosch and Fritz Haber, whose process for synthesizing ammonia from nitrogen and hydrogen was put into production in 1913. The conversion of atmospheric nitrogen into solid or liquid as ammonia made possible the production of synthetic fertilizer.

For economic reasons, the manufacture of ammonia spread very slowly, and world production remained below five million tons until the late 1940s. There was some modest growth of production in the 1950s, but in the 1960s technical innovations reduced the use of electricity in the synthesis and global production soared: to forty million tons by the mid-1970s, and to eighty million tons by 1990. Synthetic fertilizers provide an estimated 40 percent of all the nitrogen taken up by the world's crops. Since these crops provide some three-fourths of all the protein consumed in the world, about one-third of all the protein in our diet depends on synthetic nitrogen fertilizer.

One of the best-known examples of the application of technology to increased food production was the Green Revolution.[29] In 1943, the Rockefeller Foundation sent a scientific mission to Mexico to assist Mexican researchers in their experiments with hybrid strains of wheat and maize. Their efforts were crowned with early success: Mexican wheat yield per hectare more than tripled, and by 1955 Mexico was a wheat-exporting country. By the mid-1960s, similar experiments, with equally impressive results, were being undertaken elsewhere: in the Philippines with rice, in Peru with potatoes, and in India with other strains of wheat. India, in particular, was often cited as an exemplary case, with the country shifting from being a chronic food importer to becoming self-sufficient in wheat by the late 1960s.

The Green Revolution did not increase the thermodynamic efficiency of any plant species, however. There are physical limits to the ability of a plant to take in energy and use it for productive purposes. What the Green Revolution accomplished was to increase the thermodynamic efficiency of the larger life system by causing plants such as wheat, rice, and potatoes to shift an increased share of their energy from defense and reproduction to the creation of tissue, which we and other animals eat. For example, the high-yielding varieties of wheat produced multiple heads with large seeds, but they had to be engineered to have fewer leaves (to conserve energy) and shorter stems (to support heavier grains in the wind). The price for these gains: an increased use of fertilizer and water, to facilitate the absorption of nutrients; the increased use of herbicides and pesticides, to suppress the increased pest population attracted by the lush vegetation; and the increased technological expertise (such as agricultural extension agents) and financial institutions (land-development banks) made essential by the necessary investments.

Energy

All of the preceding measures required heavy energy inputs. The application of fossil fuels opened up hundreds of millions of acres of new land for farming and grazing, connected food sources and markets over greater and greater distances, made possible farm machinery of much greater efficiency and power, brought irrigation to land where rain water was insufficient, and yielded new fertilizers based on petrochemicals. In this century, the key that enabled food production to keep pace with population was a worldwide, eightyfold increase in energy inputs into farming, from 2.5 kilograms of oil equivalent per hectare of harvested farmland in 1900, to about 200 kilograms in 1990.[30]

A century ago, coal was the dominant fossil fuel in food production, delivery, and processing.[31] Coal-powered steamships and railroads connected distant new food sources with growing industrial cities; and coal was the fuel of choice in household stoves. With the important exception of China, which still has tens of millions of coal stoves in use and relies on steam locomotives for internal transport, these uses have disappeared, largely replaced by petroleum for transport and by electricity and natural gas for home cooking. As coal declined in transportation and household markets, however, its use has risen exponentially in electricity-generating plants, which are now the world's largest single consumer of coal. And since information technologies rely on a steady flow of electric current, fossil-fuel energy remains critical to a civilization based on information.

At the turn of this century, farmers were largely self-sufficient in energy, relying on livestock for hauling and plowing as well as for fertilizer.[32] As mid-century neared, farm use of fossil fuel, particularly petroleum, increased, slowly at first and then rapidly after 1950. In 1950, the world's farmers used approximately 276 million barrels of oil equivalent (see table 9.3). Slightly more than 50 percent of this energy went to run the world's fleet of about 5.6 million tractors; about 25 percent was used to manufacture fertilizer; and about 6 percent was used to fuel irrigation construction and operations. By 1985, energy consumption had increased to nearly two billion tons of oil equivalent. Less than 40 percent was used to fuel a tractor fleet of 23 million, while about 30 percent went for fertilizer manufacture and 10.5 percent to irrigation.

As a consequence, today's farmers invest about eight calories of energy in the ground for every calorie of food energy they extract; another eight calories are expended to move the food from field to table.[33] A global food network that expends sixteen calories of fossil fuel energy for every calorie of food energy produced is rational only in the context of virtually "free" energy, which of course has never been the case. Moreover, how much such a system contributes to the process of global warming, soil erosion, the altering of hydrologic patterns, and other environmental damage can only be estimated, but it is surely not trivial.[34]

Global Agribusinesses and Labor

Global food production is big business. The total value of food produced each year in the world exceeds $1.4 trillion, about 8 percent of global Gross Domestic

Table 9.3   Energy Use in World Agriculture, 1950–1985

Year	Tractor Fuel	Irrigation Fuel	Fertilizer Manufacture	Other	Total Energy
		(million barrels of oil equivalent)			
1950	143	17	70	46	276
1960	288	33	133	91	545
1970	429	69	310	162	970
1980	650	139	552	268	1,609
1985	739	201	646	317	1,903

Note: "Other" represents estimates made by the Worldwatch Institute of energy consumption for uses such as pesticide manufacture, equipment manufacture, grain drying, and so forth. Since data were not available for these uses, Worldwatch estimated these uses at 20 percent of the total for tractors, irrigation, and fertilizer.

Source: Lester Brown, "Sustaining World Agriculture," in Lester Brown, et. al., *State of the World: 1987* (New York: W.W. Norton, 1987), Table 7.4, p. 131.

Product. About 40 percent of this sum (about $550 billion) is produced in the highly industrialized countries of Europe, North America, and Oceania.[35] Moreover, the production of food is dominated by a dozen or so huge transnational corporations, many of which integrate all of the steps of food production, from seeds and animals all the way to the distribution of processed food products.[36]

In 1992, the twelve leading food processing companies, all global corporations, had gross revenues from food sales of $174.8 billion,[37] a sum larger than the Gross National Product of all but the nineteen largest national economies in the world at the time. The leading global agribusiness, Nestlé of Switzerland, enjoyed revenues in 1992 of over $37 billion, followed by Philip Morris Companies—parent to Kraft Foods, Post cereals, and Miller Brewing—at $33 billion.

This immense global food production system has a labor dimension as well, for most of the workers engaged in the harvesting, processing, and distribution of food consumed in the First World are from the developing countries. This is true whether the food is grown in Third World fields and is harvested and processed by native labor, or in the fields and orchards of the industrialized countries, where it is handled largely by immigrant labor.

The vital role of immigrant labor in food production begins in the fields.[38] Consumers in the United States now depend heavily on migrant labor from the Third World to harvest the food they eat, but the exact degree of this dependence is a subject of controversy. There is agreement that the total farm work force in the United States is about 2.0–2.5 million, but experts disagree on how many of these are migrants, and what proportion of these are immigrants. A 1994 report issued by the U.S. Department of Labor concluded that there were 670,000 migrant farm workers in the United States, of whom 85 percent were foreign born; but a leading expert in the field, agricultural economist Philip Martin from the University of California–Davis, puts the migrant population at between 800,000 and 900,000. The fact that a sizable proportion, estimated by various sources between 25 and 40 percent, of all farm workers are undocumented immigrants adds to the confusion.

Migrant workers now constitute more than half the total agricultural work force in three sections of the country: the Northeast, 59 percent; the Northwest, 55 percent; and the Southeast, 52 percent. Almost half of them (47 percent) are in the West, which includes the key state of California, where more than half of all migrant workers live. Migrants are of particular importance in the harvesting of vegetables (where 44 percent of them work) and fruits and nuts (34 percent). Of all migrant workers and their dependents (estimated 410,000), 57 percent live below the poverty level. Of those born abroad, 36 percent have no assets other than their personal belongings, and the average worker works only twenty nine weeks a year. Their hourly wage averages just slightly above $6.00, and has been declining steadily for the past two decades. The great majority of them are not unionized and enjoy very few if any fringe benefits.

Although most immigrant farm workers work in California, there is not a section of the country where they have not traveled in search of work. Some 15,000 Mexicans work in Hawaii harvesting pineapples; 20,000 are in Alaska working in fish-processing plants; 45,000 work in Michigan harvesting fruits and vegetables; and 75,000 work in New York state harvesting onions, cabbage, and lettuce. On Virginia's eastern shore, more than 100 migrant camps serve as temporary homes for some 6,000 Hispanic and Haitian workers and their families. Organized into work crews by labor contractors in Florida, these workers travel up and down the East Coast as part of the so-called migrant stream. In Virginia, they find work harvesting tomatoes, cucumbers, and potatoes. Across the continent, in Washington state, 40,000 to 60,000 Mexican workers pick the apples, pears, asparagus, and cherries that fill the shelves of supermarkets in eastern cities. Thus, no matter whether the fruit and vegetables we eat came from local sources or from 3,000 miles away, the chances are high that the hands that picked them belonged to someone from the Third World.

PROCESSING AND DISTRIBUTION

If the global food system means anything to the average consumer, it is that what they eat and drink today can come from virtually anywhere on Earth, almost without regard to the distance it must travel. As Alan Durning puts it, "The typical mouthful of American food travels 2,000 kilometers from farm to dinner plate."[39] The globalization of food supplies means that consumers in the highly industrialized world now consume, routinely and probably unconsciously, wine from Australia, beef from Argentina, potatoes from New Zealand, or cranberries from Chile.[40] Staples such as wheat and sugar have been global food products for several centuries, and meat has been included since the 1880s; but in the past three decades, the global food system has expanded to embrace fresh fruits and vegetables as well.[41]

The export of tomatoes from Mexico to the United States illustrates the globalization of fresh foods.[42] Until the last decade, Florida owned the American tomato market. Under the best of circumstances, the journey of a tomato from a Florida field to a consumer's market takes ten days, but if many intermediaries are involved, it can take from two weeks to a month. Picked green, the tomato is ripened under very carefully controlled conditions (cold temperature, ethylene gas piped into the room), then sent through a network of brokers, wholesalers, repackers, supermarket distribution centers, and retail outlets (supermarkets or restaurants).

Mexican tomatoes were able to obtain some market share in the United States during winter months, but until the 1970s the Mexican produce faced insurmountable nontariff barriers to their export. These barriers began to erode through the 1970s, and Mexico began to increase its share of the U.S. market. In the early 1990s, Mexican growers adopted a technique developed in Israel for growing "vine-ripened" tomatoes, and the resulting improvement in quality made Mexican tomatoes competitive with the Florida-grown, "gas-ripened" product. The drop in the value of the Mexican peso in 1994 made Mexican tomatoes competitive in price as well, even after transport costs were factored in. As a result, Mexican tomatoes quickly came to challenge those from Florida.

Mexico now sends about $800 million worth of tomatoes to the United States each year, mostly for use in processed foods like pizza sauce and ketchup. Since consumers say they prefer the vine-ripened varieties, however, Mexican tomatoes are also beginning to appear in supermarkets. Slightly more than 40 percent of all tomatoes consumed in the U.S. now come from Mexico, compared with 45 percent from Florida and 14 percent from California. In the 1996 U.S. presidential campaign, competition from Mexican tomatoes became a political issue when President Clinton reached an agreement with Mexico not to send cheap produce to the United States. The Republican opposition charged Clinton with announcing the deal simply to improve his chances of winning Florida's twenty-five electoral votes: After all, agriculture is the second-largest industry in Florida, after tourism.

Transportation

These and dozens of similar food networks are made possible by global bulk-flow systems in transport and communications. As we saw in chapter 8, global food systems are not new. But in the last five decades, maritime, rail, and truck transport of food staples in bulk has expanded dramatically both in scope and in volume; and air cargo offers delivery of high-value food items (those that are exotic or perishable) over ever greater distances and literally overnight.

About 95 percent of all international trade (by weight) travels over water for at least part of its journey. In the mid-1980s, the world's commercial shipping fleet numbered more than 74,000 vessels, with a gross weight of more than 350 million tons. In any given year, the cargo they carried amounted to more than 3.5 billion tons, and the service they provided generated revenues of over $200 billion. As a highly industrialized, densely populated island nation, Japan led the world in all these categories: nearly 10,000 vessels, with a gross weight of more than 32 million tons, and more than 600 million tons of cargo unloaded annually.[43] Other major actors in global shipping are either highly industrialized countries, like the United States, or traditional maritime nations, like Greece, whose involvement in shipping reaches back to the Bronze Age.[44]

Between 1980 and 1995, the value of world trade more than doubled, from $2.0 trillion to $4.9 trillion. Much of the increase resulted from expanded trade in machinery, transport equipment, and other manufactured goods, all products whose value is more or less unrelated to their size and weight. Trade in food and agricultural products declined as a percent of the total, from 14.4 percent to 11.5 percent. In terms of value, however, international trade in food grew from $288 billion in 1980 to $563.5 billion in 1995.[45] Many factors contributed to this growth in world trade, but declining transport costs certainly figured prominently among them.

Containerization

For bulk-food commodities, the chief reason for declining transport costs involves the revolution in shipping technologies and organization since the 1950s. In 1955, an American freight magnate named Malcolm McLean devised a technique for detaching a truck body from the cab and lifting it onto the deck of a ship.[46] From this beginning evolved the cargo container, a metal box that can be moved from trucks to ships to trains without handling the cargo inside. The invention of the container crane led in the late 1960s to the advent of ships dedicated to nothing but containers. In the mid-1990s, the standard container ship could carry six thousand such boxes; but plans were already under way for the next generation of ships with double this capacity. In 1980, the capacity of the world container fleet was about half a million TEUs (twenty-foot equivalent units); by 1992, it had reached two million; by 1996, three million; and by 1998, four million (projected).[47]

The containerization of cargo led directly to a number of other important innovations in shipping.[48] Intermodal transport systems integrated ships, rail, and trucks in a seamless network that made it possible for goods to be transported from factory to retail outlet with virtually no intermediate handling. Double-stack trains (stacking containers two-high on rail cars) reduced the costs of rail transport by close to half. Specialized firms offering integrated transport services could now monitor the movement of a particular shipment from factory to destination, leading to reduced loss, pilferage, or late arrival. The union of containerization and refrigeration made possible global "cool chains, an integrated system of refrigeration that chills a product within hours of harvest and maintains controlled cool temperatures . . . from the original place of chilling to the delivery to consumers. . . . Without such integrated chains, the present fresh fruit and vegetable system would be impossible."[49]

These changes led to the centralization of shipping infrastructure and to the concentration of shipping through a small number of "superports" or "pivot ports." Ports were no longer the end points of an ocean voyage, but rather a transfer point to steer container flows from water to land modes, and vice versa. Small, inadequately outfitted ports were bypassed, since the large container vessels preferred to limit their stops to a few ports capable of handling the shift of thousands of containers from one mode to another. An earthquake that devastated the port of Kobe, Japan, in January 1995, revealed the degree to which shipping between East Asia and the rest of the world was funneled through this single site.[50] Thousands of exporters and shippers saw their operations disrupted or shut down entirely while the port struggled to repair the damage. One such firm, Monfort, the meat-packing division of ConAgra, located in Colorado, was forced to suspend its weekly shipments of more than 1.2 million pounds of frozen beef and pork into Kobe until alternative routes and cold-storage facilities could be located.

Integrators

Although air cargo carries only a small portion of international trade, it is still a vital part of the global food network because of its ability to deliver high-value products over very long distances in a matter of hours. As recently as three decades ago, air cargo was considered so expensive that it was reserved for emergency shipments such as medicine. With the deregulation of the airlines in the late 1960s, however, conventional freight companies saw their opportunity to incorporate air service into their existing operations. In 1968, Flying Tiger Airlines demonstrated that the high cost of air delivery was less than the cost of long-term warehouse storage, so air cargo paid for itself in terms of inventory reduction and rapid response to changing market conditions. In 1973, Federal Express (now FedEx) began to offer next-day delivery service within the United States, and the time horizons of manufacturers, distributors, and retail outlets began to shorten.

Today's air-cargo firms are called "integrators" to reflect the fact that they offer customers an integrated transport service from "door to door."[51] They combine air, rail, and truck transport with advanced communications technologies to monitor and track shipments, specialized consulting and handling expertise for unusual shipments, and foreign documentation and administrative costs (customs duties) to relieve export and import customers of these onerous burdens. The largest of these firms, United Parcel Service (UPS), has more than 300,000 employees, 119,500 vehicles, and 220 aircraft. Its gross revenues annually are nearly $20 billion. Its principal challenger is FedEx, with 100,000 employees, 31,000 vehicles, 458 aircraft, and annual revenues of nearly $10 billion. In the mid-1990s, UPS handled more than 11 million packages daily, and served 610 airports in 185 countries. The comparable FedEx numbers: 2 million packages daily; 325 airports in 188 countries.[52]

It is no coincidence that UPS is the largest single user of cellular communications in the world,[53] because all of the transport innovations cited above are ultimately dependent on a global computer and communications system that enables vital information to be available around the world in huge quantities and in virtually real time. Fax machines, electronic mail via the Internet, and 800-number, long-distance telephone service connect buyers and sellers worldwide, twenty-four hours per day. Computers, laser-scanned bar codes, and cellular communications using satellite relays enable a shipper to know to within meters where on the Earth a specific shipment is at any moment. Satellite imagery enables fishing boats to find elusive schools of fish and Nebraska ranchers to prepare their livestock for an approaching snowstorm. Thanks to these and other communications developments, the costs of transporting virtually everything have been falling sharply. Compared to 1930, the cost today of sending a ton of ocean cargo has been cut in half, the cost of a passenger flying a kilometer has been reduced more than 80 percent, and the cost of a New York-to-London telephone call has dropped to only 1 percent of what it was six decades earlier.[54]

Food-processing Labor

One of the consequences of this decline in the cost of transport has been the increased flow of immigrants from the developing world to North America and Western Europe. Many of them find work in food-processing plants, where they prepare meat, poultry, and fish for later retail distribution. In her studies of the U.S. meatpacking industry, for example, Kathleen Stanley found that Asian and Hispanic immigrants constituted as much as 60 percent of the work force at any given meat-processing plant; the larger the plant, the greater the proportion of foreign-born workers tended to be.[55] Lourdes Gouveia found that Hispanics in particular were drawn to meatpacking jobs because of the stability of the work (unlike seasonal jobs in the fields), and because they did not need to know English.[56] Immigrant laborers, many of them in the United States illegally, also constitute a significant part of the work force in poultry-processing plants. In 1995 and 1996, raids by agents of the Immigration and Naturalization Service (INS) revealed a smuggling ring that was supplying poultry plants in Maryland with workers from Mexico and Central America. One of the largest poultry processors in Maryland, Allen Family Foods, reported that at least 30 percent of its work force was Hispanic.[57]

Case Study: Seafood

Today's global seafood industry illustrates how these transport and communication technologies and services form a seamless network to exploit one of the Earth's most important food resources. In 1950, the world's fish harvest (made up entirely of fish caught in their natural habitat) was 21 million tons, or about 8.6 kilograms per capita. By 1994, the total fish harvest had reached 109 million tons, or 19.3 kilograms per person.

Today, six countries—China, Peru, Japan, Chile, the United States, and Russia—account for about half of all the fish harvested in the world,[58] and more than one billion people depend on fish as a primary source of protein.[59] Fish provide nearly 28 percent of animal protein consumed in Asia, and 21 percent in Africa. With world population continuing to grow, especially in these two continents, and with fish catches reaching their natural limits, experts expect fish farming to become more important in the next several decades. In 1994, aquaculture produced 18 million tons (or about 15 percent of total fish harvest); by 2010, aquaculture is expected to yield about 39 million tons, or some 27 percent of the total harvest. Fish farming already accounts for more than one-third of all the salmon harvested in the world; and shrimp farms in Asia now produce some 750,000 tons annually.[60]

From the open waters of the Pacific to New York City fish markets, information technology plays a vital role in the global fishing industry.[61] There are about three million fishing vessels operating in the world today, but most of the intensive harvesting of fish on the open seas is carried out by vessels known as factory-freezer trawlers. These ships, many of which can remain at sea for months at a stretch, can harvest, process, and freeze up to thirty tons of fish at a time, bringing the assembly line to the fishing industry. When their freezer compartments are full, their cargo can be transferred to smaller vessels to be ferried back to port. While at sea, these vessels use sonar to detect schools of fish (and even distinguish between species), spotter planes and helicopters to find schools near the surface, radar so they can continue to fish in dense fog, and satellite positioning so they can maneuver precisely to spots where fish are known to congregate and breed.

Once the fish catch reaches land, technology takes on even greater importance.[62] Ports around the Pacific Rim, from Chile to Thailand, are equipped with modern processing plants. The fish are packed in ice in foam-plastic containers, rushed to local airports, and flown to distant markets. Fish can reach New York from Chile by air almost as fast as, and usually less expensively than, they can from Cape Cod by truck—and they are just as fresh upon arrival.

Meanwhile, importers in the wholesale fish business at New York's Fulton Fish Market are working the fax and telephone lines to maintain contact with distant suppliers. Today's seafood brokers must be knowledgeable about international airfreight charges and customs regulations, and they are frequently overseas checking supplies in Chile, Thailand, or China. Thus, while fish harvests in waters off the U.S. coasts continue to decline, reaching $3.6 billion in 1996, the value of imported fish continues to rise, to $6.7 billion.

Many experts believe that the world's wild fish supplies cannot long survive the impact of modern industrial fishing.[63] Fishing technologies and practices such as pair trawling (two trawlers hauling huge nets between them) and fishing lines up to 140 kilometers long enable fishing boats to scoop up as much as 90 percent of the live fish in a school, including many young fish needed for future reproduction. As the continental shelves and shallow waters are scraped clean of their stocks, fishing nets descend to greater and greater depths, seeking out rare species that inhabit waters up to a kilometer deep.[64] The Food and Agriculture Organization (FAO) now classifies virtually every part of the world's oceans as "fully exploited," meaning that fish harvests have reached their biological limit nearly everywhere.[65] Some species have already been fished to exhaustion, such as salmon in the northwestern Pacific and haddock in the northern Atlantic. The breeding population of bluefin tuna in the western Atlantic is less than 10 percent of what it was two decades ago, shrimp have been seriously overexploited in the Indian Ocean, and cod have virtually disappeared from most of the North Atlantic. In less than fifteen years (1981–1995), haddock landings by the Gloucester, Massachusetts, fleet dropped 90 percent (from 21 million pounds to 281,000); and restaurants in New Orleans fly in crawfish from China because local crawfish supplies have become so scarce and expensive.[66]

CONSUMPTION

High rates of consumption of virtually everything are the hallmark of a highly industrialized society, and this is especially true for food. Three inescapable demographic features converge to put an increased burden on the global food supply: population is rising at the rate of about ninety million people per year; a growing proportion of the world's people are experiencing significant improvement in their income, especially in Asia; and, as people become richer, they consume much more energy indirectly through meat and highly processed foods than they do directly through grain and cereal products and unprocessed fruits and vegetables. Moreover, while people with very high incomes have decreased the amount of red meat they consume, they are consuming increased quantities of fresh fruits and vegetables, which require complex and expensive transport and communication networks to connect fields to markets.

Food consumption is not spread evenly around the world.[67] Global diets have three levels.[68] At the bottom are the 630 million impoverished people of the world who are unable to provide themselves the basic ingredients of a healthy diet. Next come the 3.5 to 4.0 billion people whose diets consist largely or entirely of grain and grain products. They typically receive less than 20 percent of their calories from fat and eat very little, if any, animal protein. At the top are the 1.2 billion people whose higher income enables them to afford to eat meat on a regular basis. These affluent consumers receive about 40 percent of their calories from fat, most of which comes from their meat intake.

A rising per capita gross domestic product (GDP) is linked to major changes in diet—not only in the amount of food a population consumes but also in the composition of the overall diet and the way food is processed and delivered to the table.[69] Until per capita GDP reaches about $5,000, a population's diet consists almost entirely of loose unbranded cereals; at about $5,000, increased personal wealth permits the consumption of basic packaged foods; and at $10,000, consumers can begin to enjoy basic frozen foods, including fish and vegetables. At about $15,000, consumers begin to demand popular brand items, pre-prepared meals, and foods with special health or nutrition features; and from $17,500, diets can include fresh foods brought (literally) from the far corners of the Earth.

While in the poorest one-fifth of the world, incomes have stagnated and food demand remains at the lowest level, in the highly industrialized countries of Europe, North America, and Japan, incomes have long since passed the highest threshold of an energy-intensive diet. Rising incomes in the First World have given middle- and upper-income consumers the information they need to make more health-conscious choices regarding diet, and the wealth they need to afford the higher prices of fresh fruits and vegetables. Between 1975 and 1994, for example, American consumption of beef dropped 23 percent, from 37.7 kilograms (83 pounds) per person to 28.9 kilograms (63.6 pounds). Consumption of other meats increased accordingly: per capita pork consumption rose 28 percent, from

17.6 kilograms (38.7 pounds) to 22.5 kilograms (49.5 pounds); and per person chicken consumption increased 88 percent, from 12 kilograms (26.4 pounds) to 22.5 kilograms (49.5 pounds). Per capita consumption of fresh vegetables also rose significantly, from 40.2 kilograms (88.4 pounds) to 51.8 kilograms (113.9 pounds), an increase of 29 percent. Although such a "postmodern" diet may certainly be healthier, compared to the diet of Americans before 1960, it is also just as energy intensive.[70]

Meanwhile, in much of Asia, from India through Indonesia to China, rapidly rising incomes have sparked increased demand for processed foods and meat, leading to major changes in food production and consumption. In Taiwan, by 1991 there were more than 3,000 western-style supermarkets vending all manner of processed foods; and Hong Kong contains seven of the world's ten busiest McDonald's restaurants. Cadbury, the British candy firm, has invested heavily in producing and marketing western-style chocolates in China, as have Nestlé and Unilever for ice cream, Campbell for processed soups, Nabisco for crackers, and Coca-Cola for beverages.[71] Nor have Asian firms been idle. Alone or in concert with American or European companies, food-processing firms in Thailand and Taiwan have begun to handle huge quantities of pigs, chickens, and other energy-intensive meat products, along with the animal feed necessary to supply local industries. The changes have been especially important in China. Since the mid-1980s, China has used more fertilizer, produced more grain, and consumed more red meat than the United States, with pork leading the way.[72]

Beyond the market cost of a diet with so much meat in it, the wealthy quarter of humanity pays for their eating habits in the form of increased heart disease, strokes, and certain kinds of cancer—the "diseases of affluence." According to the National Center for Health Statistics, which uses a measure based on body mass index, 33 percent of all adult Americans were obese (had a body weight more than 20 percent higher than desirable) in 1988–1991. *Prevention* magazine, using height-weight tables of insurance companies, asserts that 68 percent of Americans were overweight in 1995. The health consequences of so much overweight are costly: by one estimate, the United States spends $60 to $80 billion, or almost 10 percent of all health spending, to treat health problems associated with obesity.[73]

The Earth pays for high meat consumption as well. The meat-eating quarter of the population consumes 40 percent of the world's annual grain production, much of it processed through the bodies of herbivores. To produce one kilogram of American beef requires five kilograms of grain, which in turn requires the energy equivalent of 9 liters of gasoline, water for irrigation, pesticides, and fertilizers. The negative environmental consequences include soil erosion, groundwater depletion, and methane emissions from the digestive processes of cattle and sheep. The animal waste from huge farms of hogs, cattle, and poultry has reached critical levels, polluting rivers and streams and killing fish by the hundreds of thousands; today, animal waste in the United States is 130 times greater than human waste, and one large hog farm, for example, can produce more waste than the city of Los Angeles.[74] And consider the environmental effect of a processing plant at Moorefield, West Virginia, which slaughters 340,000 chickens daily: the waste from this processing, plus the 155,000 tons of chicken manure produced annually, are all flushed into the headwaters of the Potomac River, eventually to be carried downstream to the nation's capital.[75]

An affluent population changes not only how much and what it eats, but also when, where, and under what circumstances it eats.[76] A family in which both parents are employed outside the home has become the norm in much of the highly industrialized world. There is simply not enough time for families to prepare much of their own food, so the economy responds by having someone else do it, be it through restaurants, supermarkets, catering services, or home delivery. Increasingly, we expect to eat whenever and wherever we are when we get hungry. Only 24 percent of Americans eat just three meals a day. Fifty-one percent eat four to five times a day (some combination of meals and snacks), and the remainder eat only once or twice a day (including snacks). The locale for eating has become equally varied: homes and restaurants have always been available, but now we also eat in our cars, in fast-food kiosks, in drive-through lanes, and many other places. Even when we buy our food in the supermarket, the chances are high that it has been prepared by someone else. Prewashed vegetables and salad ingredients have become popular with hurried shoppers, and about three-fourths of all U.S. supermarkets now offer home meal "replacements"—that is, food already prepared in delicatessens in the market itself. The trend toward having others prepare one's food has created a huge demand for relatively unskilled workers to work in food-retail services in supermarkets and restaurants. In societies with a stable population and labor force, these workers must be imported. Thus, immigrants working in the retail food sector now constitute a vital part of the global food network operating in the United States and other highly industrialized countries.

But it is not just the quantity of food we consume, or the high proportion of meat or processed foods in our diet, or the circumstances surrounding our eating that characterizes the global food system. Food is more than simply nourishment; it is also a part of a broader culture. The foods that one eats are much more than a way of ingesting energy. As a vital component of our collective identity, the foods we eat help us identify ourselves and differentiate our community from others. Thus, an emerging global culture requires the globalization of food as well.

Benjamin Barber has observed that the world's cultures are simultaneously becoming both more homogenized (what he calls "McWorld") and more fragmented ("Jihad").[77] As the Jacket blurb of Barber's book puts it, the "planet is both falling apart and coming together" at the same time. This apparent paradox has been resolved by David Rieff, who demonstrates that the expansion of global capitalism is the driving force behind both these trends.[78] Global capitalist firms demand homogenization to achieve economies of scale and expand market share, but they also exploit (and thereby encourage) multiculturalism by commodifying ethnic identities.

Since food is a central component of culture, it is not surprising that diets around the world are experiencing these same seemingly contradictory changes. On the one hand, we see familiar U.S. and European brands becoming well-known to consumers in distant markets in East Europe and the developing world. In January 1992, an advertisement for Coca-Cola as a global beverage was broadcast via satellite to millions of viewers in more than 100 countries on six continents. Since then, we have been witnessing the rapid spread of American processed-food products to the far corners of the world: Arby's, Pizza Hut, and KFC battle for market share of the fast-food business in São Paulo; Kellogg's Corn Flakes invade the breakfast market from Latvia to India; Pepsi and Coke compete for the soft-drink market in Venezuela; McDonald goes to court in South Africa to block a local fast-food chain from calling itself "Mac donald's" and selling a "Big Burger" instead of a "Big Mac."[79]

At the same time, diets in the highly industrialized countries are becoming more diverse, more "globalized." The increased income available to western consumers enables them to demand greater and greater diversity in their diets, both in supermarkets and restaurants; and the large and growing immigrant populations from developing countries bring their food preferences with them when they move to American or European cities. In the mid-1990s, one of the hottest trends in food retail from New York to San Francisco was the "global restaurant." One of the most successful of these, World Cafe, in New York, offered its diners, among other dishes, Singapore noodles, eggplant burrito, seared tuna with ginger-wasabi mustard, smoked trout potato latkes, and grilled vegetables with mozzarella.

A similar trend has been seen in supermarkets as well. In Jersey City, New Jersey, Foodmart International opened in 1997, offering 80,000 different food products from around the world: twenty-two kinds of live fish (for Asian customers); an entire aisle just for Philippine products, and another just for foods from Korea; a separate aisle, seventy-two feet long, just for tea; a meat selection that included baby goat, rabbit, pheasant, and veal tails; and virtually every product from Goya brands for their Hispanic customers.[80]

NOTES

1. Manuel Castells, *The Informational City: Information, Technology, Economic Restructuring and the Urban-Regional Process* (Oxford: Basil Blackwell, 1989).

2. Vaclav Smil, *Energy, Food, Environment: Realities, Myths, Options* (Oxford: Clarendon Press, 1987), pp. 60–71. *The Economist* (July 12, 1986, p. 97) offers a graph showing that between 1970 and 1985, Japan's consumption of energy per billion dollars of Gross National Product fell by some 35 percent; that of the United States, by 30 percent; and the entire "non-communist" world (that is, highly industrialized democracies), by 25 percent.

3. John Bongaarts, "Can the Growing Human Population Feed Itself?" *Scientific*

American 270, no. 3 (March 1994): 36–42; William Stevens, "Feeding a Booming Population Without Destroying the Planet," *New York Times*, April 5, 1994.

4. Harriet Friedmann, "Food Politics: New Dangers, New Possibilities," in *Food and Agrarian Orders in the World-Economy*, ed. Philip McMichael (Westport, Conn.: Greenwood, 1995), pp. 17–20.

5. Alessandro Bonnano, et al., eds., *From Columbus to Conagra: The Globalization of Agriculture and Food* (Lawrence, University Press of Kansas, 1994).

6. Philip McMichael, "Introduction: Agro-Food System Restructuring—Unity in Diversity," in McMichael, ed., *The Global Restructuring of Agro-Food Systems* (Ithaca, N.Y.: Cornell University Press, 1994), p. 4.

7. Sara Millman, et al., "Organization, Information, and Entitlement in the Emerging Global Food Systems," in Lucile Newman, et al., *Hunger in History: Food Shortage, Poverty, and Deprivation* (Oxford: Basil Blackwell, 1990), chapter 11, esp. p. 309.

8. Vaclav Smil, *Cycles of Life: Civilization and the Biosphere* (New York: Scientific American Library, 1997), pp. 173–79.

9. Edward Deevey, "The Human Population," *Scientific American* (September 1960): 203.

10. Paul Colinvaux, *Why Big Fierce Animals Are Rare: An Ecologist's Perspective* (Princeton: Princeton University Press, 1978), chapter 9.

11. *The Economist Book of Vital World Statistics* (New York: Random House, 1990), pp. 53, 64–65.

12. *Economist Book of Statistics*, pp. 53, 62–63.

13. Smil, *Cycles of Life*, p. 137.

14. Edward Carr, "Agriculture: The New Corn Laws," *The Economist*; (December 12, 1992): 7.

15. *The Economist* (June 1, 1996): 101; *The Economist* (June 14, 1997): 113. See also "How Subsidies Destroy the Land," *The Economist* (December 13, 1997): 21–22.

16. Vaclav Smil, *Energy in World History* (Boulder, Colo.: Westview, 1994), pp. 188–91.

17. Lester Brown, "Sustaining World Agriculture," *State of the World 1987* (New York: Norton, 1987), chapter 7.

18. Smil, *Energy in World History*, p. 191.

19. Smil, *Energy, Food, Environment*, fig. 1.2, p. 5.

20. Lester Brown, Hal Kane, and Ed Ayres, *Vital Signs 1993* (New York: Norton, 1993), pp. 40–41.

21. "Flowing Uphill," *The Economist* (August 12, 1995): 36.

22. Brown, "Sustaining World Agriculture," pp. 124–27; Lester Brown, Hal Kane, and David Roodman, *Vital Signs 1994* (New York: Norton, 1994), pp. 44–45.

23. "Water in America," *The Economist* (October 4, 1986): pp. 35–38; Peter Rogers, "Water: Not as Cheap as You Think," *Technology Review* (November/December 1986): 31–43; Leslie Spencer, "Water: The West's Most Misallocated Resource," *Forbes* (April 27, 1992): 68–74; Jay Mathews, "Urban, Rural Interests at Odds as California Thirsts for Water," *Washington Post*, June 26, 1990.

24. William Langewiesche, "The Border," *Atlantic Monthly* (June 1992): 91–92; Wade Graham, "A Hundred Rivers Run through It," *Harper's* (June 1998): 51–60.

25. Brown, "Sustaining World Agriculture," pp. 127–30.

26. Brown, Kane, and Roodman, *Vital Signs 1994*, pp. 42–43.

27. Vaclav Smil, "Global Population and the Nitrogen Cycle," *Scientific American* 277, no. 1 (July 1997): pp. 76–81; Smil, *Cycles of Life*, chapter 5.

28. Smil, *Energy, Food, Environment*, pp. 279–86.

29. Ernest Schusky, *Culture and Agriculture: An Ecological Introduction to Traditional and Modern Farming Systems* (New York: Bergin & Garvey, 1989), chapter 7.

30. Smil, *Energy in World History*, figure 5.17, p. 191.

31. Smil, *Cycles of Life*, p. 143.

32. Brown, "Sustaining World Agriculture," pp. 130–32.

33. Schusky, *Culture and Agriculture*, p. 102.

34. Whether the energy costs of global food production are high or low depends to some extent on one's perspective. For example, Lester Brown, "Sustaining World Agriculture," believes the current system to be unsustainable over the long term, while Vaclav Smil, *Energy, Food, Environment*, pp. 97–107, argues that, in the United States, agriculture consumes only 3 percent of the country's total energy budget. There are, he contends, many more areas of wasteful energy usage where savings can be realized with little impact on lifestyle or comfort level.

35. *The Economist Book of Vital World Statistics*, pp. 56–57.

36. William Heffernan and Douglas Constance, "Transnational Corporations and the Globalization of the Food System," in Bonanno, et al., *From Columbus to Conagra*, chapter 1.

37. Martin Giles, "The Food Industry: After the Feast," *The Economist* (December 4, 1993): 1.

38. Philip Martin, "Labor in California Agriculture," *Agriculture and Human Values* 2, no. 3 (summer 1985): 60–67; Eric Schlosser, "In the Strawberry Fields," *Atlantic Monthly* (November 1995): 80–108; "Bad Apples?" *The Economist* (July 18, 1992): p. 29; Peter Kilborn, "Tide of Migrant Labor Tells of a Law's Failure," *New York Times*, November 4, 1992; Evelyn Nieves, "Endless Rows and Hardship on Black Dirt Farms," *New York Times*, July 9, 1996; Sam Dillon, "Job Search Lures Mexicans to Far Corners of U.S.," *New York Times*, February 4, 1997; Seth Mydans, "A New Wave of Immigrants on Lowest Rung in Farming," *New York Times*, August 24, 1995; Lydia Chavez, "More Mexicans, More Profit," *New York Times*, December 9, 1994; Barnaby Feder, "Harvest of Shares," *New York Times*, June 26, 1997; Steven Greenhouse, "As Economy Booms, Migrant Workers' Housing Worsens," *New York Times*, May 31, 1998.

39. Alan Durning, "Asking How Much Is Enough," in Lester Brown, et al., *State of the World 1991* (New York: Norton, 1991): 159.

40. Clyde Farnsworth, "Australia's Other Drink," *New York Times*, May 24, 1997; Anthony Faiola, "The Pampas Challenge the Prairie," *Washington Post*, August 30, 1997; Stephen Stuebner, "Anxious Days in Potatoland," *New York Times*, April 12, 1997; Calvin Sims, "Where Cranberries Are Really an Acquired Taste," *New York Times*, November 22, 1995.

41. William Friedland, "The Global Fresh Fruit and Vegetable System: An Industrial Organization Analysis," in McMichael, *The Global Restructuring*, chapter 7; William Friedland, "The New Globalization: The Case of Fresh Produce," in Bonanno, et al., *From Columbus to Conagra*, chapter 10.

42. Luis Llambi, "Comparative Advantages and Disadvantages in Latin American Nontraditional Fruit and Vegetable Exports," in McMichael, *The Global Restructuring*, chapter 8. Paul Blustein, "U.S., Mexico Reach Tomato Accord," *Washington Post*, October 12, 1996; David Sanger, "President Wins Tomato Accord for Floridians," *New York Times*, October 12, 1996; Carole Sugarman, "It's a Tough Life," *Washington Post*, March 20, 1991; Jerry Gray, "New New Jersey Tomato (Fresh from Tel Aviv)," *New York*

Times, September 17, 1992; Paul Blustein, "The Politics of a Plump, Juicy Feud," *Washington Post*, July 3, 1996.

43. *Economist Book of Statistics*, pp. 116–17.

44. "Beware Greeks Selling Tankers," *The Economist* (November 2, 1996): 63–64.

45. "Schools Brief: Delivering the Goods," *The Economist* (November 15, 1997): 85.

46. "Schools Brief," p. 86.

47. "Schools Brief," p. 86; "Sinking the Container Cartels," *The Economist* (November 2, 1996): 64.

48. John Gulick, "'It's All about Market Share': Competition among U.S. West Coast Ports for Containerized Cargo Throughput, from the Plaza Accord to the Present," in Paul Ciccantell and Stephen Bunker, eds., *Space and Transport in the World System* (Westport, Conn.: Greenwood, 1998) pp. 72–75.

49. Friedland, "The New Globalization, p. 223.

50. Agis Salpukas, "Quake Interrupts Worldwide Trade at Port in Kobe, *New York Times*, January 21, 1995; Nicholas Valéry, "Earthquake Engineering: Fear of Trembling," *The Economist* (April 22, 1995).

51. Marcia Jedd, "Integrators Race for Globalization," *Global Trade* (July 1992): 25–27.

52. John Burgess, "When It Has to Get There Overnight," *Washington Post*, August 5, 1990; Richard Weintraub, "Delivering a Revolution," *Washington Post*, August 28, 1994; Christopher Drew, "In the Productivity Push, How Much Is Too Much?" *New York Times*, December 17, 1995.

53. Jim Kelly, "A Case for Globalism," *Global Finance* (November 1997): 34.

54. *The Economist* (July 30, 1991): 117; "Schools Brief: One World?" *The Economist* (October 18, 1997): 79.

55. Kathleen Stanley, "Industrial and Labor Market Transformation in the U.S. Meatpacking Industry," in McMichael, *The Global Restructuring*, chapter 5.

56. Lourdes Gouveia, "Global Strategies and Local Linkages," in Bonanno, et al., *From Columbus to Conagra*, chapter 6.

57. Amy Argetsinger and Anna Borgman, "124 Arrested as INS Raids Poultry Farm," *Washington Post*, August 29, 1996.

58. Lester Brown, Christopher Flavin, and Hal Kane, *Vital Signs 1996* (New York: Norton, 1996), pp. 30–31; "The Economics of the Sea," *The Economist* (March 18, 1995): 48.

59. "Farming the Waters," *Washington Post*, January 18, 1997.

60. Jon Christensen, "Cultivating the World's Demand for Seafood," *New York Times*, March 1, 1997; Mike Skladany and Craig Harris, "Paneids, Ponds and Perch: The Technoscientific Structure of the Global Fishing Industry," 1996 Conference on the Political Economy of World Systems (PEWS), Kansas State University, Manhattan, Kansas, table 2, p. 10; Claude Boyd and Jason Clay, "Shrimp Aquaculture and the Environment," *Scientific American* 278, no. 6 (June 1998): pp. 58–65.

61. William McCloskey, "To Fish for a Living," *Johns Hopkins Magazine* (June 1990): 20–29; Anne Swardson, "Net Losses: Fishing Decimating Oceans' 'Unlimited' Bounty," *Washington Post*, August 14, 1994; "The Tragedy of the Oceans," *The Economist* (March 19, 1994): 21–24.

62. Molly O'Neill, "Despite the Bad News, the Fishing Is Good," *New York Times*, October 22, 1997; Amanda Hesser, "Now Boarding: The Turbot, a True Fish Out of Water," *New York Times*, June 10, 1998.

63. Carl Safina, "The World's Imperiled Fish," *Scientific American* 273, no. 5 (November 1995): 46–53.

64. William Broad, "Creatures of the Deep Find Their Way to the Table," *New York Times*, December 26, 1995.

65. Swardson, "Net Losses"; "The Tragedy of the Oceans."

66. Steven Pearlstein, "In Gloucester, a Painful Lesson: Net Gains Aren't Forever," *Washington Post*, August 21, 1996; Donna St. George, "Crawfish Wars: Cajun Country vs. China," *New York Times*, May 7, 1997.

67. Smil, *Energy, Food, Environment*, pp. 145–61.

68. Durning, "Asking How Much Is Enough," pp. 158–60.

69. Giles, "The Food Industry," figure 11, p. 15.

70. Friedland, "The New Globalization," chapter 10; Robert Samuelson, "The Trouble with Steak," *Washington Post*, April 2, 1997; "The Age of the Chicken," *The Economist* (December 24, 1994–January 6, 1995): 29–30.

71. Giles, "The Food Industry," p. 16.

72. "China Charges Ahead," *Washington Post*, October 5, 1996.

73. Chip Walker, "Fat and Happy?" *American Demographics* (January 1993): 52–57; Shannon Dortch, "America Weighs In," *American Demographics* (June 1997): 39–45; "That Other National Expansion," *The Economist* (December 20, 1997): 27–28. (Bear in mind that what constitutes "overweight" is a matter of definition, and these definitions can (and do) change; Jane Brody, "New Guide Puts Most Americans on the Fat Side," *New York Times*, June 9, 1998.

74. "Animal Waste Threatening Water Quality," *Washington Post*, December 29, 1997.

75. Eric Lipton, "Poultry Poses Growing Potomac Hazard," *Washington Post*, June 1, 1997.

76. Marcia Mogelonsky, "Food on Demand," *American Demographics* (January 1998): 57–60.

77. Benjamin Barber, *Jihad vs. McWorld* (New York: Random House, 1995).

78. David Rieff, "Multiculturalism's Silent Partner," *Harper's* (August 1993): 62–67.

79. Paul Farhi, "Pitching the Global Village," *Washington Post*, June 14, 1992; James Brooks, "With Brazil's New Prosperity Come Arby's and Pizza Hut," *New York Times*, September 3, 1994; Joseph Treaster, "Kellogg Seeks to Reset Latvia's Breakfast Table," *New York Times*, May 19, 1994; Molly Moore, "Cornflakes Pop Up on India's Breakfast Tables," *Washington Post*, October 27, 1994; Glenn Collins, "How Venezuela Is Becoming Coca-Cola Country," *New York Times*, August 21, 1996; Donald McNeil, "Restoring Their Good Names," *New York Times*, May 1, 1996.

80. Florence Fabricant, "Global Village? Just Check the Menu," *New York Times*, May 18, 1994; Florence Fabricant, "Around the World in 23 Aisles," *New York Times*, December 10, 1997.

Chapter Ten

Emerging (and Re-emerging)
Infectious Diseases

In 1993, the Earth's human population increased by about 88 million persons (about 10,000 per hour) to reach approximately 5.6 billion.[1] Since the mid-1980s, the annual net increase has leveled off at 85 to 90 million, and the annual rate of increase has gradually declined to about 1.5 to 1.7 percent, leading some demographers to hope that world population will stabilize by the middle of the twenty-first century at between 10 and 12 billion. What happens to death rates, and particularly to death rates due to infectious diseases, will have a significant impact on these projections.

The 88 million net increase in 1993 was the product of roughly 139 million births offset by about 51 million deaths. The leading causes of death worldwide were noninfectious diseases that affect the circulatory system; but infectious diseases as a group were responsible for more than 16 million deaths, or about 30 percent of the total.[2] More than 99 percent of the deaths from infectious diseases occurred in the developing countries, where they accounted for more than 40 percent of all deaths. Slightly more than 40 percent of all deaths from infectious diseases affected children under the age of five years; essentially, the deaths resulted from lower respiratory infections and diarrhea (including dysentery). Tuberculosis killed slightly fewer than three million persons; malaria, about two million; measles, slightly more than one million.

Simple death statistics do not tell the whole story, however. To know the overall impact of disease on human health, we must employ a broader concept: the global burden of disease.[3] The global burden of disease (GBD) was developed by Christopher Murray of the Harvard University School of Public Health and Alan Lopez of the World Health Organization to measure the worldwide impact of the loss of healthy life from some 100 diseases and injuries. The GBD combines the loss of life from premature death with the loss of healthy life from disability, and is measured in units of disability-adjusted life years (DALYs). The measure takes into account the duration of life lost due to a death at each age, the value of a healthy year of life lived at each age, and the value of time and of disability discounted for each age and for several degrees of disability. Data for deaths and disability were aggregated for three categories of causes: communicable, maternal, and perinatal diseases (such as measles or malaria); noncommunicable diseases (such as cancer or heart disease); and injuries (such as motor-vehicle accidents, war, or homicides).

Using data from 1990, Murray and Lopez found that the entire human population lost 1,362.1 million DALYs that year. Males lost 713 million DALYs, females, 649 million. The age group hardest hit were children five years of age and younger; they suffered 39 percent of all lost DALYs (530 million). Nearly 90 percent of all DALYs were lost in developing countries: India alone lost 292 million, as did sub-Saharan Africa; China lost 201 million; the rest of Asia and the Pacific Islands, 177 million; Latin America and the Caribbean, 103 million; and the Middle East and North Africa, 144 million. In contrast, the former socialist economies lost 58 million DALYs, and the highly industrialized countries of Europe, North America, and Japan lost 94 million.

An examination of the causes of lost DALYs reveals important differences in health standards and conditions around the world. For the world population as a whole, communicable diseases accounted for 46 percent of all lost DALYs (624 million); noncommunicable diseases, 42 percent (575 million); and injuries, 12 percent (163 million). The age group hardest hit by communicable diseases was, again, children under five, who sustained 62 percent of lost DALYs in this category, while people over sixty had the largest share of DALYs lost from noncommunicable diseases (28 percent).

As a general rule, the poorer a country or region, the more significant were communicable diseases and the less important were noncommunicable diseases as causes of lost DALYs. In Africa, for example, DALYs lost from communicable diseases were nearly four times as great as those lost from noncommunicable diseases (209 million versus 57 million); in the Middle East and North Africa, the ratio was 1.4 to 1.0 (74 million versus 52 million); and in India, the ratio was 1.2 to 1.0 (148 million versus 118 million). In contrast, in the highly industrialized countries of Europe and North America, noncommunicable diseases outweighed communicable by a ratio of eight to one: 73 million DALYs lost to noncommunicable diseases versus 9 million lost to communicable. Murray and Lopez assert that the world is passing through an "epidemiological transition," wherein a rising level of wealth is reducing the burden of communicable diseases and raising the incidence of noncommunicable.[4] Many developing countries are already rather far along this transition. Latin America and the Pacific islands are near parity between the two causes; and in China, noncommunicable diseases are already more than twice as heavy a burden as are communicable ones.

EMERGING (AND RE-EMERGING) INFECTIOUS DISEASES

"Expect the unexpected," advises Stephen Morse in discussing the evolution of emerging viruses.[5] Predicting the future in epidemiology is especially difficult, because the microparasites change so rapidly and the hosts (humans) are so unpredictable. However, the speed with which parasites adapt actually helps us understand the dynamic a little better. Because there have been episodes of disease change of huge historical significance within the time of written records, this information provides helpful evidence in anticipating future epidemics. AIDS was not the first pandemic to explode unexpectedly on the scene. In their own time, bubonic plague, smallpox, cholera, influenza, and many others wreaked havoc across human populations, and their effects were duly recorded for later study.

By the middle of the twentieth century, public-health officials had begun to predict the impending elimination of infectious diseases. New "miracle" drugs, better nutrition, and improved water treatment and sewage disposal were thought to hold the key to a relatively disease-free life, at least in the wealthier parts of the world. By 1977, the World Health Organization claimed victory over smallpox,[6] and many observers thought that similar successes over other infectious diseases were near at hand.[7]

Such predictions proved premature. Already in the mid-1970s, a new variant of influenza, dubbed "swine flu," was spreading around the world; and in Philadelphia in 1976, people attending a convention of the American Legion fell victim to a mystery illness that became known as "Legionnaires' Disease." By the early 1980s, acronyms like HIV and AIDS had begun to enter our language, and from the Third World came disturbing reports of mysterious hemorrhagic fevers that caused massive bleeding through every body opening, and respiratory viruses that drowned their victims in their own lung fluids. A new variant of cholera appeared early in the 1990s to initiate yet another pandemic of this scourge; and some of humankind's oldest enemies, such as influenza, tuberculosis, malaria, and yellow fever, appeared in strains and in places never before observed.[8] In 1917, the American Public Health Association identified thirty-eight communicable diseases in the first edition of its handbook. The most recent edition of the handbook, the fifteenth, lists 280 such diseases.[9]

Stephen Morse has identified two processes that can produce emerging viruses (or, more generally, emerging diseases).[10] By far the less significant is *de novo* evolution—that is, the appearance of new strains or variants of microparasites that previously did not exist. Rapidly mutating influenza, for example, seems to produce a new variant practically every year; and these may correctly be considered emerging diseases. Influenza can present new variants by one of two methods. "Antigenic drift" is the process by which the proteins on the surface of the virus change location, allowing the new strain to reinfect previous hosts because their immune system does not recognize the altered antigen. "Antigenic shift" refers to the introduction of a new gene into the virus, usually from a reservoir host population of ducks or pigs. Antigenic drift is a less dramatic change and produces only epidemics; antigenic shift, in contrast, leads to pandemics.

The overwhelming majority of emerging diseases come from the second process, a process Morse calls "viral traffic." Most examples of viral emergence, he contends, are independent of mutation and are simply preexisting human or animal viruses that have been moved from their reservoir host to a new host. AIDS is the best-known example of this process, but the filoviruses (Marburg, Ebola) and other hemorrhagic fevers (Lassa fever, Machupo, Junin) also figure in such a list. Hantavirus and monkeypox, also good examples, entail a virus that resides naturally in rodents and is transferred to humans via the rodents' feces or urine. Morse believes that viral traffic is a much more important source of new diseases, because the world's fauna harbor thousands of ancient microparasites that have been selected by natural pressures for viability. The very fact they have existed for so long means they are well adapted to living in some remote corner in Earth's biosphere until human activity intrudes into and disturbs their habitat.

Some biologists and epidemiologists, such as Paul Ewald, believe that we have been too quick to generalize about the threats from emerging diseases.[11] Extremely virulent and aggressive viruses like Ebola or other kinds of hemorrhagic fevers attract much press attention when they explode periodically, but these are what Ewald calls "suicidal pathogens": Their pattern is to immobilize and then kill a high proportion of the infected individuals rather quickly, and then to die out equally quickly. If the pathogen in question is attendant borne, such as in a rural clinic, it will spread in a highly virulent way through that site but not far beyond it. These pathogens tend not to be durable in an open environment, so they burn themselves out after a particularly dramatic and aggressive local epidemic. Moreover, contends Ewald, the jumping of a pathogen from one species to another should produce a disease of only low virulence, at least at the beginning.[12] The reason for this is that the ability of our immune systems to block new pathogens should be greater than the ability of those novel pathogens to invade a new host species.

The emerging diseases we do have to concern ourselves with, argues Ewald, are those whose transmission involves an arthropod or a cultural vector (especially needles) and that are durable outside the host. If any of these emerge, they will rival smallpox, tuberculosis, or cholera as a hazard to humankind. So far, the most worrisome pathogens in this category have some connection to HIV and AIDS; human T-cell lymphotropic viruses (HTLV viruses), hepatitis, and pathogens that attack vulnerable AIDS patients in hospitals, such as tuberculosis. Also of great concern are the viruses that are carried by mosquitoes, such as Rift Valley fever or dengue fever. Thus, claims Ewald, what matters is not the "newness" or "oldness" of a pathogen, but how it is transmitted and how well it survives outside the host.

FACTORS PROMOTING EMERGING DISEASES

Many human activities associated with globalization are major contributors to viral traffic: intrusion into, and disturbing of, ancient ecosystems whose animals and parasites have coevolved over very long spans of time; the introduction of large numbers of humans into these previously unknown habitats; and the movement of people, pathogens, and vectors (including food) in unprecedented numbers and at unprecedented speeds between disease pools. Arno Karlen has identified six specific causes of disease emergence:

1. breakdown of public health measures
2. economic development and land use
3. international travel and trade
4. technology and industry
5. human demographics and behavior
6. adaptation of the micröorganisms[13]

Many of these processes are related to globalization, as the following examples illustrate.

Increased Commerce, Tourism, Immigration, Refugees

The globalization of the economy has been made possible by the reduced costs of moving people and goods in large numbers, over great distances, and at great speeds. Every day, an estimated 2 million people cross an international boundary, and with them comes increased international commerce in manufactured goods, services, energy, and information.[14] International tourists now number some 600 million per year; and the number of refugees and persons displaced within their own countries by war, environmental crisis, or economic collapse increased by over 60 percent, from 30 million to 48 million, between 1990 and 1997. Unfortunately, this increased traffic has also brought about the international transfer of health risks.

The most obvious route by which health hazards move across long distances is the movement of people. In earlier times, the slow speeds at which people traveled served as a barrier to the transport of infectious diseases, but today air travel means that infected persons can travel around the world in a matter of hours, long before they or anyone else realizes that they are carrying serious diseases. Highly contagious diseases like influenza or tuberculosis now have the potential to move around the world at the speed of a commercial aircraft.

While world population has been increasing 1.5 to 2.5 percent per year since 1950, the movement of passengers across national boundaries has risen 7.5 to 10.0 percent annually.[15] Total air-traffic volume (measured in trillions of passenger kilometers) has more than doubled since the early 1980s, as has the volume of international tourists. There is a strong correlation between a country's per capita wealth and the propensity of its people to travel by air. As populous countries like China, India, and Indonesia raise their per capita wealth, their rates of travel increase from virtually no air travel to an average of about one air trip per year for each two people by the time their per capita GNP reaches $7,500. From that point on, frequency levels off to about one trip per person.

War and ecological disasters are frequently to blame where disease is spread by immigration, first by disturbing ecosystems, and second by promoting the long-distance migration of large populations under conditions of poor hygiene and nutrition. The impact of war on both the incidence and the virulence of disease is well understood.[16] Before the era of antibiotics and vaccines, disease regularly claimed a greater number of combatants than did combat itself; but today the primary consequence of warfare is felt by the civilian populations caught in the hostilities. When large populations are uprooted from their homes, forced into refugee streams, and made to live densely packed together in camps with poor hygienic conditions, the result cannot be other than epidemics.

Global migration is not only spreading infectious (or "Third World") diseases from developing countries to global cities; it is also spreading the so-called western diseases from Europe and North America to the urban sectors in developing countries.[17] These diseases are not infectious in the sense that microparasites carry them from person to person; rather, they accompany the spread of a particular lifestyle or culture (meme) from one region to another. They stem from changes in diet, work arrangements, family life, economic insecurity, and other sources of stress usually associated with incipient industrialization. These illnesses are well known to any North American or European reader: hypertension, atherosclerosis, coronary heart disease, diabetes, gastrointestinal diseases, a number of different cancers, and psychological disorders. If these changes continue to accompany global migration, the map of world diseases and causes of death will begin to look more nearly uniform, with the diseases of the developing world such as tuberculosis spreading to large western cities, and diseases of the western middle class, such as cancer and heart disease, invading the middle class of developing countries.

Increased commerce provides enhanced opportunities for disease vectors to be transported across long distances. The mosquito that spreads dengue fever was introduced into the United States in a shipment of used tires from Asia through the port of Houston; and a recent cholera epidemic in Peru was started by the discharge of infected bilge water from a freighter into a Peruvian harbor, from where it was taken up by shellfish and then by humans. The increased use of primates in medical research has created a global market for monkeys caught in the wild in Africa, Asia, or the Americas and then transported to Europe or North America for laboratory experimentation. Despite extensive quarantine measures in Europe and the United States, there were six outbreaks of the Asian strain of the Ebola virus between 1989 and 1996, all involving animals captured and sold by Ferlite Scientific Research Inc.[18] The first of these outbreaks was the now well-known incident at a primate importing firm in Reston, Virginia; others have occurred in Texas, Pennsylvania, and in Italy and the Philippines. None of these strains of Ebola proved to be harmful to humans; but given the speed with which viruses can mutate, health officials are concerned that this natural barrier might be breached with future shipments of infected primates.

Ecological Disturbances and Climate Change

Some disease-spreading activities are associated with the disturbing of the land. "The primary cause of most outbreaks of hemorrhagic fever," writes Bernard Le Guenno, "is ecological disruption resulting from human activities."[19] Clearing a forest for cultivation may bring forth a rodent or microörganism population previously not part of our world. Damming streams, storing water in large containers, and irrigating for agriculture give insects new breeding sites, which can increase the spread of arboviruses. Other economic activities, such as logging and mining, also bring humans into contact with parts of the world whose evolved organisms have never known a human presence before.

> Human activity not only disturbs ecosystems, it simplifies them. Even though we come into daily contact with at least as many other living organisms as our remote ancestors did, the number of species is far fewer and the mix is very different. We have deliberately surrounded ourselves with creatures that are friendly to us, like dogs and cattle and wheat and corn. And we have also surrounded ourselves with other organisms that we have not meant to. Our activities have inadvertently helped these other organisms to multiply into enormous numbers. These are creatures like rats, fleas, lice, cockroaches, pigeons, and seagulls, rarer in the prehuman world but now multiplying enormously. And, although they tend to be overlooked, we have also surrounded ourselves with less obvious creatures, like the teeming microörganisms that have invaded the estuaries we have polluted, and the new mix of soil bacteria that is now found in the fields we have cultivated and altered with the addition of pesticides and fertilizers. These new combinations of micro-organisms provide new evolutionary opportunities. Pathogens with which we have previously been coexisting can be catapulted into new, short-term but terrible modes of existence. In short, they can become plagues.[20]

Tropical rainforests in Africa and the Americas are one site where human encroachment into pristine territory brings about contact with new diseases. In the central African country of Gabon, for example, logging operations and gold miners are cutting deep into a rainforest the size of New York state.[21] Small groups of Pygmies have lived in the region as foragers for a millennium, but now they are seeing their ecosystem give way to outsiders in a matter of a few years. The forest's rare tropical hardwoods bring a high price in Europe; hunters are after exotic animals for zoos or monkeys to sell to medical research laboratories; and gold offers a powerful incentive to adventurers. The result has been the spread of the Ebola virus out of its ancient habitat and into the nearby villages in southern and central Africa. It is not yet known where Ebola resides in the wild, or in what species, or by what mechanism it is transmitted to humans. But in one epidemic in Gabon in 1996, the victims had recently eaten chimpanzee meat, considered a local delicacy, which suggests one possible scenario. The Pygmies also reported seeing unprecedented numbers of dead and dying gorillas and chimpanzees in the forest, something never witnessed before outsiders began intruding into the local forests.

Global warming, occasioned by the accumulation of greenhouse gases that result from the burning of fossil fuels, will also have an impact on world disease patterns. In addition to the other feared consequences of climate change, global warming will bring about a redistribution of many disease vectors, especially insects and the micröorganisms they carry.[22] An increase in world temperatures favors organisms that reproduce in large numbers and colonize disturbed environments: weeds, rodents, insects, bacteria, and viruses. Ordinarily restricted to altitudes below 1,000 meters, the *Aedes aegypti* mosquito that carries dengue fever and yellow fever has now been reported in Costa Rica above 1,350 meters and in Colombia above 2,200 meters. Only a slight movement upward in average temperatures would then allow these mosquitoes to survive as far north as New York City.

We already have ample evidence of the links between global warming and the spread of diseases. The El Niño phenomenon is now known to be the cause of upsurges of malaria globally, cholera in Bangladesh and Peru, hepatitis in South America, and equine encephalitis in Massachusetts. El Niño has even been implicated in a 1993 outbreak of hantavirus in the U.S. Southwest. Other linkages are much more direct. In the summer of 1994, for example, temperatures in India soared more than thirty degrees above normal, resulting in increases in vector-borne diseases like malaria, dengue fever, and pneumonic plague that together killed more than four thousand.

Diet and Global Food Supplies

The world's food supply is distributed in a highly unequal manner. People in wealthy countries consume per capita twice the calories of people in poor countries, and the gap between the richest of the rich and the poorest of the poor is even greater. While famine and starvation may be relatively rare events, malnutrition can be expected in a number of countries; and to the degree that malnutrition accompanies or reinforces certain diseases, we can expect global disease patterns to be affected as well.

In a general sense, there is a close relationship between levels of nutrition and infectious diseases.[23] The more poorly nourished a population is, the more susceptible it is to infectious diseases, and the more severe will be the diseases when they occur. Malnutrition lowers a body's defense mechanisms (including the health of the skin and mucous membranes, important entry points for pathogens) and immune system (ability to create and deploy antibodies).

The linkage between nutrition and infectious disease is rather more complex than this, however. The human body is the product of an evolutionary process that exposed our ancestors to food shortages repeatedly over the millennia. We have evolved the physical ability, through the body's ability to store energy in fat, to cope with food shortages that may last as long as six months. While nutrition below subsistence level clearly weakens a person's ability to ward off disease, above that point the benefits from additional food do not increase in a linear manner; clearly, too much food can be just as harmful as too little. Malnutrition is in the overwhelming majority of cases only one element in a syndrome of factors, including poverty, unfavorable environmental and hygienic conditions, and political and social instability, which contribute jointly to rising levels of infectious diseases; and it is usually impossible to separate inadequate food supply as a single cause. Often the causal relationship runs the other way as well; that is, infections inhibit the absorption of essential nutrients, thus aggravating the state of malnutrition. Disease and malnutrition thus are linked in a positive feedback cycle, making it difficult to know which caused which.

Finally, we need to note the different impacts of malnutrition on different kinds of diseases. Low nutrition levels reinforce many diseases, especially if they affect the gastrointestinal tract, such as cholera; yet other diseases, such as yellow fever, seem to be rather unaffected by malnutrition. There are even a few instances where nutritional deficiencies actually work for the patient by interfering with the metabolic or reproductive processes of the attacking micröorganisms.

Another way in which food works to exacerbate disease is through the global transport of foods that are themselves the carriers of diseases. We have already seen how the distance between field and table is lengthening. Consumers living in global cities now routinely eat and drink products that have traveled thousands of kilometers and have been handled by dozens of intermediaries. It would be a miracle if there were not some negative health consequences from such a system. Nichols Fox sums up the challenge this way: "Changes in the ways we produce, process, and distribute food, along with changes in our lifestyle and culture, have created niches for emerging foodborne pathogens."[24]

There are at least three ways in which food can transmit disease, and all of them are aggravated by globalization:

1. The food can itself be spoiled, and can harbor pathogens such as *Salmonella* that attack the consumer.

2. The food can carry disease from the hands of the person who prepared it to the mouth of those who consume it. For example, people infected with hepatitis who work in food processing plants can pass the disease on to those who eat the food products, even though the food has been frozen for periods of up to a year.[25]

3. The food can come from plants or (more likely) animals that were infected with a disease that can jump to humans and cause them to become ill. The so-called mad cow disease scare of 1996 showed how vulnerable the global food system is to such a cross-species transmission of pathogens.[26] Integrated pig-duck farming has been linked to the appearance of new influenza strains by providing opportunities for genetic reassortment within existing strains.

Population Growth, Urbanization, and Poverty in the Developing World

At the most basic level, the rapid growth of the world's population provides an unprecedented opportunity for disease organisms to evolve and mutate. As Christopher Wills puts it, "In most parts of the planet, so far as these organisms are concerned, we are the largest meal around."[27] As the human population grows, so do the populations of pathogens that feed on us. The larger the population and the more rapidly it grows, the more likely that some random mutation will occur, find a niche in the surrounding ecosystem, and grow to become a significant parasite on humans.

The basic mathematical models of disease spread and decline assume zero population growth and only moderate virulence of the so-called childhood diseases (such as measles), which cause widespread illness in the host population but do not kill many of the infected people. In the developing world, such assumptions are contradicted by the facts. Population growth rates, while declining, continue to be high, in some instances between 2 and 3 percent per year; and rates of urbanization are even higher, leading to dense crowding of populations in unsanitary conditions. Moreover, many viral and bacterial infections kill large numbers of children across the developing world, especially where illness is complicated by malnutrition, contaminated water supplies, inadequate public health facilities, and swarming insect populations.[28]

In addition, high fertility rates in developing countries mean that there are large numbers of new members entering the population in any given month or year. For some diseases, newborns receive antibodies from their mother that protect them for some finite period. For measles, for example, the protection lasts from three to twelve months, after which it wanes and the child becomes susceptible to infection. If a vigorous vaccination program is not carried out during this "window" from about one to two years of age, then the children will likely be infected and the disease will be endemic. If complications of other sorts accompany these infections, the consequence will be high death rates from diseases that need not be fatal. Nevertheless, of the some 1 million deaths from measles in the world every year, 900,000 occur in the developing world.

Rapid urbanization, mostly concentrated in the developing countries, is likely to play a major role in rising disease incidence in the coming decades. While natural or vegetative growth accounts for part of the increase in urban population, migration from rural areas to cities is of even greater significance and is one of the most prevalent types of human movement.[29] In 1800, when the world population was about one billion, only some twenty-five million lived in urban areas. By the year 2000, when world population had climbed to six billion, urban population rose to more than three billion, which means that the urban proportion of the population increased some twenty times faster than the population overall. At the turn of the millennium, more than half the human population will live in cities.

The impact of population growth on disease incidence and spread depends on whether the growing population expands spatially or remains confined to a given space. If the city's boundaries expand as the population grows so that density remains constant, the transmission rate of new infections will be only marginally affected. If the growing population is confined to a rigidly maintained urban area, however, the transmission rate will rise significantly. The reality of most city growth is somewhere between these two extremes: city boundaries expand, but not fast enough to allow the luxury of a constant density.

The city is a novel habitat for *Homo sapiens,* and an unnatural one as well. Humans evolved to live in groups of fifty or so; for us to live in populations three to five orders of magnitude greater than this is extremely stressful and takes a huge toll in morbidity and mortality. Until well into the Industrial Revolution (that is, after 1850), cities were considered to be death traps, where the impact of infectious diseases, environmentally induced illnesses, and accidents produced death rates that exceeded birth rates. Had it not been for rural-to-urban migration, cities would not have grown at all until relatively recently.

Between 1750 and 1950, most of the increase in urbanization occurred in the cities of the developed or industrialized world. The combination of improved standards of living in urban areas and pressures to leave rural areas produced these high rates of migration. Moreover, rates of urban mortality due to infectious disease began to decline, largely because of improvements in sanitation, water treatment, and other public health measures. In addition, humans and pathogens adapted to each other sufficiently so as to change diseases like measles from a mass killer to simply a "childhood" illness, an annoyance that caused suffering but did not kill in huge numbers. By 1950, as a consequence, more than half the population of the industrialized world was urban, compared to about one-sixth in the developing world.

After World War II and the decolonization process in the late 1950s and early 1960s, the bulk of urbanization took place in the developing world, and since 1975 more than half of the world's urban population has been in developing countries. Three-quarters of the world's megacities are located in developing countries, where, by the end of the twentieth century, about 40 percent of the total population was urbanized.

Urbanization in the developing world increases the burden of disease in two ways. First, in and of itself, the act of migrating is stressful, and the evidence is that recent migrants suffer from increased incidence of a wide range of stress-induced disorders, including hypertension, coronary heart disease, Type 2 diabetes, and obesity. One of the effects of this stress is a reduced effectiveness of the body's immune system, making migrants more susceptible to infectious diseases, especially those that are associated with crowded populations, such as tuberculosis and cholera. The second consequence of urbanization is the increased exposure of people to these infectious diseases. Of special significance here are diseases associated with inadequate treatment of food and drinking water (cholera), intimate contacts between people living and working in dense concentrations (tuberculosis, AIDS), and vectors like rodents and mosquitoes that find a comfortable habitat in refuse or standing pools of water (malaria, yellow fever, dengue). Eventually, rural-to-urban migrants adapt to the stress and disease patterns of their new city, and migrants who have lived in cities for many years usually exhibit disease profiles similar to those who were born there. But for some time after migration (up to a decade) migrants experience increased morbidity and mortality rates due to infectious and other diseases.

The connections of urbanization to the global burden of disease are clear, since they are two sides of the same coin; that is, as the human population has become more global, it has also become more urban. Globalization requires bulk-flow systems of transport and communication that can only be supported by a dense urban population; and large cities need global systems to keep them supplied with the resources they need to keep running. We can say that cities and global systems have a symbiotic relationship to each other; they are mutually interdependent.

Moreover, when people move across international borders, they are almost always moving from one city to another. Most immigrants to the United States, Canada, or Western Europe are leaving Guadalajara, Karachi, or Nairobi, and moving to Los Angeles, Toronto, or Paris. In the United States, just six cities—New York, Miami, Chicago, Los Angeles, Washington, and Houston—receive more than half of all the immigrants coming into the country each year. Thus, the health problems of cities in the developing world are issues for cities in Europe and North America as well.

Medical Practices, Technology

Prominent on Paul Ewald's list of cultural vectors are the technology and the personnel of hospitals and other institutions that care for the sick.[30] As they attend to patients, doctors and nurses often inadvertently transport pathogens from one patient to another either on their skin, in their clothing, or on the equipment they use, including hypodermic needles. Hospitals and clinics in poor countries are frequently forced to re-use equipment like syringes that in richer countries would be routinely discarded as hazardous waste. (The disposal of this kind of waste constitutes yet another kind of problem that cannot be addressed here.) Particularly vulnerable in hospitals are newborns and AIDS patients, both of whom have weak or poorly functioning immune systems that can easily be overwhelmed by pathogens that healthy people would defeat, which explains how hospital attendants can serve as vectors without becoming sick themselves.

Diseases of the digestive system, which manifest themselves as diarrhea, are especially important here. Attendants helping patients with such diseases by touching the patients themselves and their clothing and bedding run a great risk of retaining the pathogens on their hands. Many of these pathogens remain present and virulent even after repeated washings with disinfectant. The bacterium *E. coli*, which usually has little effect on its human hosts, can mutate into much more virulent strains that can immobilize or even kill infected people. Epidemics of *E. coli* have frequently ravaged hospitals in the United States, and the neonatal wards are usually discovered to be the focal point of transmission.

Gastrointestinal diseases that reach epidemic proportions outside hospitals usually burn themselves out quickly and seldom reach virulence levels that are life-threatening. In these instances, the immobility of the infected individuals and the slowness of transmission work to attenuate disease virulence. But in hospitals, the opposite is the case. Here, the proximity of the infected persons and the ease with which the pathogens are transmitted contribute to a heightened virulence. Epidemics of *Salmonella*, for example, rarely become lethal outside hospitals, but inside hospitals death rates as high as one in three infected individuals have been registered.

Two other kinds of bacteria that can lead to epidemics in hospitals are *Staphylococcus*, which causes skin lesions, breast infections, and a kind of skin affliction in babies that produces the flaking and shedding of skin, and that can be fatal; and *Streptococcus*, which produces infections of the bloodstream and inflammation of the spinal cord. When these diseases occur outside the hospital, they run their course quickly. Inside a hospital or clinic, however, they persist for months or even years, seemingly impervious to even the most determined countermeasures such as the heavy use of antibiotics, as these pathogens have demonstrated a remarkable capacity to mutate and adapt to the medicines.

Looming on the horizon is the threat of pathogens jumping to humans by means of the cross-species transplants of organs.[31] A boom in organ transplants has come at the same time we are experiencing a shortage of human donors. In 1997, more than fifty-five thousand Americans were on waiting lists for organs, but more than three thousand were expected to die while waiting for a replacement organ. With waiting lists growing by 10 percent per year, but donors increasing by only 2 percent, the search for alternative sources has turned to other species. Baboons are considered to be a good source for hearts, and pigs for livers; but the risks of cross-species transplants are substantial. Other species may well harbor micröorganisms that are harmless to them but lethal when introduced into humans. Transplant patients are routinely treated with drugs to suppress their immune system so their body will not reject the new tissue, and this suppression could make them supremely vulnerable to the new pathogens. Once these novel micröorganisms are introduced into humans, the direction they take cannot be predicted.

Adaptation of Parasites or Vectors

Much of the current theory and practice in epidemiology is based on a presumed stability of the parasite in question and/or its vector.[32] It is rapidly becoming apparent, however, that many parasites and vectors such as arthropods possess an unexpected ability to change genetically or mutate in response to drugs or efforts at chemical suppression (such as insecticides). Moreover, micröorganisms such as E. coli exhibit a remarkable ability to borrow genes from other species, including, for example, Salmonella and Shigella, thereby increasing their toxicity and complicating human countermeasures.[33]

In his discussion of the resurgence of the bubonic plague in the twentieth century, Charles Gregg offers the disturbing prospect that all three of the organisms implicated in the plague—the "unholy trinity" of bacillus, rats, and fleas—are evolving genetic resistance to the chemicals that humans have been using in large quantities to control them.[34] For example, the rodenticide most widely used to control rat populations is warfarin; rats that possess genetic resistance to warfarin have been discovered across Western Europe, and in large U.S. cities from Newark, New Jersey, to San Francisco. Similarly, the widespread use of DDT to control insect populations began in 1946, but within four years, DDT-resistant fleas of the kind that carries the plague bacillus were found in locations from Ecuador to Greece to Bombay, India. The bacillus itself, Yersinia pestis, has evolved genetic resistance to most of the drugs used to counteract it, beginning with the sulfa drugs in the 1940s and continuing to the present day with streptomycin, tetracycline, and chloramphenicol. Moreover, Y. pestis appears to possess the ability to acquire drug resistance not only via its own mutations but also by close contact with other organisms, such as E. coli, whose resistance factors exist more or less naturally.

How do drug-resistant micröorganisms emerge? Frequently, when a mutant type of a gene appears to provide genetic resistance of a given parasite species against human countermeasures, it may reside in a very tiny portion of the species population for a long time without expanding significantly. As the drug or pesticide succeeds in suppressing the part of the population without this genetic type, however, the resistant species will suddenly begin to grow exponentially and will quickly come to dominate the population, thereby rendering the countermeasure ineffective. To the human observer, it will look as if the resistant strain of the parasite appeared "out of nowhere," suddenly and unexpectedly, to outwit its human hosts. Ticks have been known to develop resistance against insecticides in less than a year, black flies in five to six years, and some varieties of mosquitoes in a matter of weeks.

Such rapid genetic mutation of parasites and vectors carries some counterintuitive implications. For example, migration of untreated species into the treatment area tends to slow down the emergence of resistance (by keeping fresh the population without the resistant genetic type), so insect control officials may not want to isolate the target population but rather encourage untreated individuals to migrate into it. In addition, by withdrawing the suppressive application of insecticides early, control agents may actually encourage the "back-selection" or the return to dominance of the susceptible genetic type (and, thus, the declining importance of the resistant type).

Resistance to antibiotics and other chemical countermeasures poses major problems in the control of infectious diseases.[35] In particular, malaria and influenza have both demonstrated a remarkable ability to mutate rapidly in response to treatment. Influenza virus spreads quickly through a susceptible population and has a very short generation time. The host population rapidly builds up immunity against one variant of the pathogen in their midst. For such parasites, the ability to change genetically is of great selective value, one which they exploit frequently and with great costs for the host population. Tuberculosis is another disease that is demonstrating increasing resistance to antibiotics,[36] with strains of the disease showing up particularly heavily in urban areas like New York City as well as in developing countries; new replacement drugs do not appear to be forthcoming in the near future. In poor countries that cannot afford expensive healthcare programs, we should expect to see both increased incidence and increased virulence from tuberculosis in the future.

The heavy use of antibiotics to suppress bacterial infections in hospitals and clinics has stimulated the pathogens to evolve variants that are resistant to even the most powerful antibiotics.[37] Outside hospitals, doctors in the United States prescribe antibiotics for patients about 150 million times a year; according to researchers at the Centers for Disease Control and Prevention, more than fifty million of these prescriptions are probably unnecessary.[38] About eighteen million of these prescriptions are for the common cold, which is caused by a virus that is not affected by antibiotics. Other illnesses, such as ear infections, sore throats, bronchitis, and sinusitis are also attacked with antibiotics far beyond what is actually necessary.

AIDS: A "NEW" GLOBAL DISEASE

Most microparasites need large, dense populations to survive and carry their infections from host to host. An important exception to this rule are the sexually transmitted diseases (STDs), which differ from diseases like measles or influenza in three significant ways:

1. STDs can survive in very small populations, because the hosts are in much more intimate contact than are people generally. Unlike the crowding diseases, STDs do not seem to be much affected by the size or density of the larger population so long as the potential host population members remain in intimate contact via either sexual relations or sharing needles.
2. The human carriers are frequently "asymptomatic," meaning they do not exhibit the outward signs of having the disease—sometimes for a very long time, sometimes forever. Often, they may not even be aware that they are carrying the disease until long after they have infected others.
3. Many STDs confer little or no acquired immunity following recovery, so the hosts become susceptible to reinfection again after they have recovered.

In the case of AIDS, we have little knowledge of postrecovery immunity. Remission of infection appeared to be impossible until the mid-1990s, when a new treatment combining three antiviral drugs seemed to give new hope that at least the virus could be held in check more or less indefinitely.[39]

AIDS' Origins

Working backward from fragmentary evidence, researchers have been able to document small numbers of cases of different versions of HIV and of its equivalent in monkey populations (SIV, for Simian) as far back as the 1970s, and a scant handful of speculative cases can be identified as long ago as the late 1950s or early 1960s. However, the virus and its disease manifestations began to appear in large numbers only in the early 1980s.

Between October 1980 and May 1981, in Los Angeles five young homosexual men were diagnosed with a kind of pneumonia usually associated with a depressed immune system, and health-care providers in New York observed an increased incidence of Kaposi's sarcoma.[40] Both were interpreted as signs of the emergence of a new disease. Early in 1982, the U.S. Public Health Service identified sexual transmission as the route by which the disease was being spread, but that same year a noted incidence of the disease among drug users, people receiving blood transfusions, and infants born of infected mothers suggested that blood was also a route of transmission, and that heterosexual contact could also spread the disease. The Centers for Disease Control named the new disease AIDS (for acquired immune deficiency syndrome). In 1983, separate groups of researchers in France and the United States isolated the virus that was causing the disease, and in 1984 it also acquired a name: HIV (for human immunodeficiency virus).

The origin of the virus, its original host species, and the route by which it jumped from that species to humans remain points of speculation and contention.[41] One theory is that the disease originated in nonhuman primate populations in Central Africa, where it has lived for a very long time. HIV and simian versions are so similar that it is virtually impossible to tell from their DNA whether the sample came from a human or a monkey. HIV appears to have evolved from an unknown precursor in the very diverse subfamily called "lentiretroviruses," found also in ungulates such as sheep. Another theory cites evidence that suggests that the virus diverged to enter the primate population as a simian virus several thousand years ago and split into simian and human versions six hundred to twelve hundred years ago; but some researchers believe that the disease jumped the other way—that is, it originated in humans and passed to other primates thousands of years ago.

Yet other evidence places the human virus as being much more recent, suggesting that it may have appeared in human populations no more than 150 years ago. In 1997, a team of researchers at the Aaron Diamond AIDS Research Center in New York published the results of their analysis of a blood sample taken in 1959 from a man in what was then the Belgian Congo (later Zaire, now Congo).[42] The test revealed that the man was carrying HIV. The team's analysis of the DNA of that virus strongly suggested that the seven strains of this particular form of HIV (called HIV-1) all shared a common ancestor as recently as the late 1940s or early 1950s, and that it jumped the species barrier to humans only once—sometime during the ensuing decade or so.

Exactly how the virus may have passed between species is not clear. Sexual activity may be ruled out, and the hunting and eating of one species by another may explain simian-to-human transfer, but not the transmission in the opposite direction or from one nonhuman primate species to another. Some theories posit some sort of biomedical accident, such as the use of monkey tissue to manufacture the polio vaccine; other observers have argued that the virus was introduced into humans by government agents in an attempt to destroy the homosexual population. If the virus is indeed of ancient origin, however, then the only possible explanation would involve some sort of vector like a mosquito feeding on both human and simian hosts.

In any case, the virus remained confined to central Africa until the 1960s and 1970s. AIDS researchers have now concluded that three independent events of cross-species viral transmission took place at about this time, when global dissemination of the disease began. This highly improbable coincidence was due to a combination of factors, including the increased handling of animals occasioned by the rise in animal exportation from Africa for zoos and medical laboratories, the widespread use of needles in association with human and captive monkey vaccination programs, the urbanization of Africa, the rise in long-distance air travel, and the increasing openness of homosexual activity in North American and European cities.

Traits of the Disease

HIV enters the body through intimate contact with the infected fluids of another person, especially blood, semen, or cervical secretions. HIV cells have also been isolated in tears, saliva, and urine. The virus works by penetrating cells in the host's lymphatic system, reproducing itself using the host's own cells, and spinning off viral subunits throughout the immune system. As it destroys these cells, it weakens and subsequently destroys the body's ability to ward off other illnesses. The most severely affected patients will be extremely susceptible to infectious diseases, especially those affecting the lymph nodes, and to cancers.

The appearance of HIV manifests itself rather soon after infection in the form of low-grade fever and other mild symptoms, but these usually disappear within weeks and the host remains unaware of his/her infection. The virus then enters a period of latency that may last many months or even years. During this time, the body's immune system attempts to mobilize its defenses against the virus and succeeds in keeping the disease limited. Nevertheless, the virus is relentless, and eventually the host succumbs to its more serious effects. Throughout the latency period, while hosts manifest no outward symptoms of disease, they are infectious and can (and do) spread the virus to others with whom they have intimate contact.

Infected Populations

Compared with the "old" global diseases that are still active, like tuberculosis, malaria, or influenza, AIDS has not yet begun to produce high levels of mortality, but this is already changing at the turn of the millennium. In 1997, according to the World Health Organization, about 31 million people in the world were living with HIV or AIDS, of which 21 million were in Africa, 6.5 million in Asia, and 1.3 million in Latin America.[43] The worldwide total is rising at the rate of 5 to 6 million each year, the majority of which are in the developing countries. Infection rates have stabilized or are actually declining in North America, Europe, and Australia, but are rising sharply in South, Southeast, and Northeast Asia.[44] At the same time, the disease's social and demographic profile has changed. In the 1980s, the infected population comprised mostly white, middle-class, gay men who transmitted the virus via sexual contact. By the mid-1990s, the groups experiencing the infection were increasingly nonwhites, drug users, and heterosexuals. In particular, its incidence among women and young children has been rising especially rapidly.

Although AIDS was first observed, diagnosed, and labeled in the highly industrialized world, it quickly became apparent that the developing world would not be spared.[45] Within five years of when the disease made its appearance in the United States, the presence of AIDS was recorded in over eighty countries on five continents, especially in Africa and the Caribbean. By 1989, 149 countries reported at least one case; and by 1990, AIDS was a true pandemic, or epidemic of global proportions. Unlike AIDS in Europe and North America, however, in the developing world the host population was principally heterosexual; and prostitution was one of the leading sources of transmission. In Africa and Asia, the disease struck females as much as it did males. Another important source in the developing world was the use of contaminated needles in medical facilities, particularly clinics in poor urban or rural areas.

Writing in the late 1980s, Roy Anderson and Robert May predicted that, with no change in behavior patterns, the incidence of AIDS would peak in the homosexual population some ten to twelve years after the disease was introduced.[46] Indeed, such a leveling off and decline does seem to have occurred in the latter half of the 1990s in some parts of the highly industrialized world—the larger cities in Europe and North America; in other parts of the world, however, such as Thailand or sub-Saharan Africa, the epidemic was still raging; and in a few countries (ominously, China was one), the disease had just been introduced.

Anderson and May also predicted an upsurge of the disease throughout the developing world, especially in densely populated urban areas, among prostitutes and their clients, and through vertical transmission from infected mothers to their babies. Unfortunately, all of these predictions are coming to pass. Although the impact of AIDS would have very diverse impacts on developing countries given the great diversity in patterns of sexual behavior, Anderson and May concluded:

> AIDS will cause major demographic changes in some developing countries over the next two decades. . . . [T]he very high predicted mortality due to a disease which requires repeated hospitalization, perhaps over periods of a few years, and which is thought to enhance morbidity due to other infections such as tuberculosis, will be devastating to already overloaded health-care systems in poor countries.[47]

Evolution of the Disease

More disturbing are the predictions that AIDS may be rapidly mutating into new forms against which existing medications will prove ineffective.[48] While most viruses evolve or mutate slowly compared with the rate at which they spread through the population, HIV is proving to be an exception. HIV belongs to a class of viruses whose genetic information is carried by RNA rather than DNA. Some RNA viruses, known as retroviruses, produce an enzyme (called reverse transcriptase) that can synthesize DNA from its RNA molecule. The DNA thus formed then acts as the viral genetic material. In the course of this complex process, genetic mutations occur with much greater frequency than is the case with other viruses. There is an evolutionary cost to such a high rate of mutation, in that a substantial proportion of HIV in infected cells are so altered that they cannot complete their reproductive cycle. For HIV, however, the cost of this strategy is more than out-weighed by the advantage it confers, since such frequent mutations enable the virus to hide in the body undetected by the immune system for long periods. Such a feature makes treatment and countermeasures highly unreliable, since HIV has demonstrated an ability to evolve resistance to virtually every drug that has been used against it.[49] And things may be getting worse if, as Gerald Myers and Bette Korber have argued, HIV has entered into a process of "fast-forward" evolution and is in "a singularly threatening state of evolutionary disequilibrium."[50]

The evidence for these predictions comes from a close analysis of the genetic evolution of the various forms of the virus. Myers and Korber believe that HIV diverged from its monkey and chimpanzee cousins very recently and has evolved extremely rapidly since then. This pattern of evolution is suggestive of the model known as "punctuated equilibrium," wherein a very long period of genetic sta-bility is followed by a brief period of intense evolutionary change, leading very rapidly to the emergence of one or more new species. This kind of accelerated evolution is frequently associated with environmental upheavals that cause pre-viously isolated species to be brought into violent contact with each other, dis-turbing their respective ecological equilibria. In the case of a virus, the process of mutual adjustment between its ancient host (nonhuman primates), and its new host (*Homo sapiens*) may take quite a long time (as humans measure time) and involve considerable genetic change before the system resumes some degree of equilibrium.

Moreover, AIDS, it is predicted, will not obey the conventional wisdom that diseases are under the pressure of natural selection to evolve toward ever more moderate levels of virulence. Some AIDS researchers now believe that human behavior, in the form of sexual contacts and intravenous drug use, will in the long run prove to be more significant than natural selection, and that we will inevita-bly see the emergence of new and more virulent forms of HIV as time goes on.

Some forces are working at the molecular level to yield that same outcome as well, most significantly the microscopic diversity of HIV within a single host. Indeed, a single host can harbor so many different versions of the same virus that one can speak of "quasi-species" within a single infected individual.[51] The ease and speed with which these different versions can mutate, and the complexity of their combinations and recombinations, all come together to give HIV "many differ-ent lineages, and possibly different evolutionary scenarios, under a variety of se-lective forces."[52] Since each antibody produced by the human immune system can counter only a single variant of the antigens produced by the virus, it is easy to see how human immunities can be overwhelmed by such a microparasite.

While the above scenario is disturbing, two aspects of the AIDS pandemic are of even greater concern. The first is the possibility of the emergence of a new mode of transmission, perhaps via droplets in a cough or sneeze, that will spread the disease far beyond its current at-risk population. The second involves the con-nections between AIDS and the resurgence of tuberculosis resistant to multiple antibiotics, currently the most deadly infectious disease in the world.[53] While these connections are unclear, most researchers believe that there is some relationship and that it is causal, not coincidental. The weakening of the body's immune sys-tem by AIDS has rendered tens of millions of people susceptible to a disease that many thought was under control, at least in the industrialized world. Yet, the ar-rival of AIDS, coupled with the expansion of travel connecting developing coun-tries with the cities of North America and Europe, has stimulated a recrudescence of tuberculosis to become one of the leading killers in the world. The combina-tion of AIDS and tuberculosis is especially powerful in Africa, where one out of every three people is infected with tuberculosis. But tuberculosis has spread in concert with AIDS in Europe and the Americas as well; and we can be certain that the problem of HIV-induced tuberculosis will only get worse.

TUBERCULOSIS: AN "OLD" GLOBAL DISEASE

Tuberculosis (TB) is a disease of global significance that has been around humans for a long time.[54] Cattle and birds are natural reservoirs for the bacteria that cause TB, and the bones of cave bears from prehistoric Europe carry the signs of tu-berculosis or a related disease, brucellosis.[55] There are two main types of tuber-culosis bacilli. The older of the two, *Mycobacterium bovis*, lived in wild cattle many thousands of years ago. When humans domesticated cattle and began to live close to them and consume their milk and meat, they acquired the bacillus. TB prob-ably entered the human population within the last ten thousand years, when *M. bovis* jumped to humans, mutated, and turned into the pathogen that causes tu-berculosis in humans. It was known in the Middle East five thousand years ago, spread to Greece, was common in late Roman times, and remained a virulent threat to human health through the middle of this century.

Today, most tuberculosis is caused by the younger pathogen *Mycobacterium tuberculosis*, one of a group of rod-shaped bacteria that also includes the micro-organism that causes leprosy. The tuberculosis bacillus requires a mammalian host and is aerobic, meaning that it reproduces best in tissues that are rich in oxygen. The bacillus has a unique ability both to persist for long periods in the body and to pass readily from one person to another.

Traits and Transmission

M. tuberculosis resides in the lungs of infected persons and enters the environ-ment suspended in vapor droplets when the host coughs or sneezes. Only a very small percentage of these droplets ever cause illness; some are so large and heavy that they sink to the ground, others so tiny and light that they remain suspended and are exhaled as quickly as they are inhaled. Indeed, most mycobacteria are so light that they remain in the air for weeks, flowing along with air currents. Fortunately, casual contact with them in open environments is unlikely to cause infection. Closed environments, however, such as schoolrooms or energy-efficient buildings, in which stale air is rarely exchanged but simply recirculated, are particularly prone to harbor the bacilli from a cough or sneeze for long periods, and to infect many occupants.

M. *tuberculosis* possesses a waxy outer covering that protects it from the body's immune system countermeasures. Indeed, it manages to survive inside the white blood cells, or macrophages, that normally engulf and destroy invading microörganisms. As the bacilli multiply in the lungs, they are absorbed by the macrophages, which digest them, display some of their distinctive signals on the outer surface of the macrophages, and transport them to the lymph nodes. The lymph nodes respond to these signals by producing messenger chemicals, called lymphokines, that stimulate the macrophages to become more potent, thereby halting the multiplication of the bacilli within them. In 95 percent of the cases, the bacilli become dormant but are not cleared from the body and can live for years inside their host, where they remain inactive until the host's immune system is weakened by fatigue, malnourishment, or diseases like AIDS, or is suppressed by chemotherapy administered as treatment for cancer. An estimated 10 percent of all those infected develop the active form of the disease, after which it can spread with great speed. Instances have been documented in which one infected person spread the bacillus to as many as 400 others.

Infection Rates

In the nineteenth century, tuberculosis was known as consumption, and was thought to be a condition that afflicted primarily authors, poets, artists, and musicians. The Industrial Revolution created the ideal conditions for TB: malnutrition, crowding, and poorly ventilated homes and factories. Even though living and working conditions improved through the nineteenth century and the incidence of TB declined, as late as 1900 the disease killed more people worldwide than any other infection.

The German bacteriologist Robert Koch discovered the cause of TB in 1882, but an effective treatment was unknown until 1943, when the biochemist Selman Waksman identified streptomycin from a culture taken from the throat of a chicken. The discovery that this new medicine killed tuberculosis bacilli led to a burst of research activity that produced eleven new medications by 1967. For several decades after Waksman's discovery, the incidence of TB declined steadily in the United States and in other industrialized countries. The incidence of TB in the United States dropped from 101.5 cases per 100,000 people in 1930 to 18.3 in 1970.[56] In 1953, there were 84,000 cases in the United States; by 1984, the figure had declined to an all-time low of 22,000. A similar decline was registered in

Great Britain (from 52,000 reported cases in 1945 to 5,000 in 1987), and it was commonly believed that medical science was on the verge of wiping out the disease entirely. The optimism was unjustified, however, and tuberculosis has returned in force to both the developing world and the industrialized countries, and in new strains that are resistant to the medicines that had proven so effective in the past.

Beginning in 1985, the incidence of TB worldwide began to rise once again. Between 1985 and 1991, TB increased 12 percent in the United States, 30 percent in Europe, and 300 percent in Africa (where its resurgence is associated with AIDS). In April 1993, the World Health Organization declared TB to be a global health emergency. By 1995, the trend had been effectively halted in the cities of North America and Europe, thanks to heavy increases in spending on tuberculosis elimination programs; in the United States, for example, spending on TB rose from $9 million in 1986 to nearly $120 million a decade later.[57] But in the developing countries, the disease continued to increase.

In 1996, tuberculosis killed an estimated three million people worldwide. It is the second leading cause of death among infectious diseases (following lower respiratory infections), and fourth among all causes (after heart disease and cerebrovascular disease).[58] The bacillus infects between 10 and 15 million people in the United States, and about 1.7 to 2.0 billion people worldwide. Between 7 and 9 million new cases occur annually, 95 percent of them in developing countries. South Africa now has the highest incidence of TB in the world: 350 cases per 100,000 people. In Peru, the rate is 250 cases per 100,000; in India, 204; in Mozambique, 175; in Ethiopia, 154; and in Bangladesh, 150.[59]

About 15 million people today have active tuberculosis, and the WHO estimated that about 50 million more were expected to contract the disease during the 1990s. These new cases will be predominantly in the developing world: 18 million in South and Southeast Asia, 10 million in East Asia and the Pacific, 9 million in sub-Saharan Africa.[60] Especially at risk are HIV-infected individuals (more of them die from TB than from any other cause), children (170,000 die from TB each year), pregnant women, and refugees (half the world's refugees may be infected with the bacillus).

How Did TB Make a Comeback?

The disease returned for several reasons. One reason can be traced to inadequate health care for socially marginalized people, such as drug addicts, prison inmates, or the homeless. A second was the vulnerability of people whose immune systems were not working as they should, including those with HIV or other diseases that attack the immune system; people undergoing chemotherapy for cancer; and victims of malnutrition. HIV victims are especially vulnerable, since HIV damages the immune system and accelerates the speed with which tuberculosis can change from a harmless infection to one that is life-threatening. The reverse is also true:

TB can hasten and aggravate the onset of AIDS from HIV infection. In Africa, at least 3.8 million people are infected with both diseases, and the threat of co-infection in Asia is even greater. There, an estimated 1.1 billion people harbor the TB bacillus, and the spread of AIDS through the region is expected to have serious consequences as these two diseases combine forces. The World Health Organization expected the level of coinfection to rise in Asia some sevenfold during the 1990s.

Another cause of the rise in TB has been the early cessation of treatment. People infected with TB bacilli usually harbor about two billion separate organisms, present in multiple strains. One of the ways these strains differ is in their resistance to various drugs. About 1 in every 100,000 bacilli is resistant to the drug isoniazid, and 1 in 1 million is resistant to rifampin or streptomycin. Ordinarily, health-care professionals will attack these several strains with multiple drugs, which must be taken in combination and for six months without interruption in order for a cure to be effected. Soon after treatment begins, the patient experiences considerable relief from the symptoms, because the strains most susceptible to treatment have been killed. At this point, many patients stop taking the drugs—perhaps out of ignorance, perhaps because the drugs cause unpleasant side effects. By terminating treatment prematurely, however, the patient allows the more resistant strains to survive, and these strains can now grow and multiply much more freely since their principal competitors, the more susceptible strains, have been removed from the host. The disease now returns, but much more virulently, in forms that make it more contagious and much more difficult and expensive to suppress. An estimated 2 to 3 percent of all active TB cases in the United States are of these drug-resistant varieties; but in New York City, they account for 19 percent.[61]

Following a model developed in Denver, Colorado, in 1965, large cities in the United States have tried to cope with the threat of drug-resistant strains by investing huge sums in a labor-intensive treatment (directly observed treatment short-course, or DOTS) that requires that a health-care professional administer the drug personally to the patient each week. Some patients even have to be hospitalized against their will to ensure their compliance. In 1995, the WHO began experimenting with DOTS programs on a worldwide basis, and within two years the organization reported that the TB pandemic had leveled off. A strict application of the surveillance program had cure rates as high as 95 percent, even in the poorest countries where it was tried; and global incidence of TB leveled off in 1997 for the first time in several decades, at an estimated sixteen to twenty million active cases.[62]

Globalization and Evolution of TB

The resurgence of tuberculosis is connected to the globalization process in several important ways. Since 1960, for example, international air travel has increased seventeenfold. In the closed confines of an aircraft, where the air is recycled for hours, the bacilli carried on cough droplets expelled by one host can find their way into the lungs of several hundred passengers.

Increased immigration from developing countries to crowded cities in Europe and North America is another major factor contributing to the resurgence. In Britain, for example, the incidence of TB among residents born in the Indian subcontinent is twenty to thirty times higher than among people of Indian ancestry born in Britain. British residents of Indian, Pakistani, and Bangladeshi origin, plus those from the Horn of Africa, account for half of all identified TB cases.[63] In New York City, which leads the United States in TB incidence, foreign-born patients accounted for 18 percent of all cases in 1992, but 40 percent by 1996.[64] Arlington County, Virginia, a suburb of Washington, D.C., has a TB case rate double the U.S. average and three times the Virginia state average; about 70 percent of all the Arlington cases are foreign born, mostly from Latin America and Asia.[65]

Immigration and tuberculosis are linked by a complex web of factors. Immigrants fleeing urban poverty in developing countries may bring in the disease with them. They tend to cluster together in crowded housing conditions, where the disease is more likely to spread. Immigrants may fear deportation if they admit to having the disease, so they do not seek medical help until the infection has reached an advanced stage. Language barriers often prevent health workers from being able to explain to immigrants what they must do to combat the disease, an especially critical obstacle to the success of the DOTS strategy of treatment.[66]

In recent years, there have been ominous signs that tuberculosis is evolving mutated forms that are either more contagious and faster spreading than previously known strains, or that resist most known drug remedies and treatments.[67] A 1996 study by the Centers for Disease Control and Prevention (CDCP), which focused on TB patients in Arizona, California, New Mexico, and Texas, found that Mexican-born Hispanics in these border states were five times as resistant as U.S.-born whites to the drug rifampin, and that Hispanics born in the United States were 3.2 times as resistant. Both Hispanic groups were about twice as resistant as U.S.-born whites to streptomycin. The study concluded that the failure of many Mexican TB patients to continue their multiple drug treatment for the required six to nine months was causing a rise in drug-resistant strains of the bacillus.

In 1997, the CDCP reported the discovery of a new TB strain that had swept through a small community along the border between Tennessee and Kentucky between 1994 and 1996. The bacillus was apparently brought into a small factory by one of the employees, who then infected 181 of the 264 workers in the plant. This infection rate of 69 percent was three times higher than any rate ever before recorded in Tennessee. Subsequent checks of 461 other contacts outside the plant found 337 cases of infection, a rate of 73 percent. The CDCP found that this strain of the TB bacillus multiplied in the laboratory 1,000 times faster than the typical *M. tuberculosis*. One TB expert described the Tennessee strain as "a tubercule bacillus on steroids."

NOTES

1. Lester Brown, Christopher Flavin, and Hal Kane, *Vital Signs: 1996* (New York: Norton, 1996), pp. 88–89.

2. World Health Organization, *The World Health Report, 1995: Bridging the Gaps* (Geneva: WHO, 1995), table 5, pp. 18–19.

3. Christopher Murray and Alan Lopez, eds., *The Global Burden of Disease* (Cambridge: Harvard University Press, 1996); World Bank, *World Development Report: 1993* (New York: Oxford University Press, 1993), esp. appendix B, pp. 213–25.

4. Murray and Lopez, *Global Burden of Disease*, chapter 5.

5. Stephen Morse, "The Viruses of the Future? Emerging Viruses and Evolution," in *The Evolutionary Biology of Viruses*, ed. Stephen Morse (New York: Raven, 1994), chapter 15.

6. Donald Henderson, "The Eradication of Smallpox," *Scientific American* 235, no. 4 (October 1976): 25–33.

7. Laurie Garrett, *The Coming Plague: Newly Emerging Diseases in a World Out of Balance* (New York: Farrar, Straus and Giroux, 1994), chapter 2.

8. George Armelagos, "The Viral Superhighway," *The Sciences* (January/February 1998): 24–29; Bernard Le Guenno, "Emerging Viruses," *Scientific American* 273, no. 4 (October 1995): 56–64; Lawrence Altman, "Infectious Diseases on the Rebound in the U.S., a Report Says," *New York Times*, May 10, 1994.

9. Andrew Cliff and Peter Haggett, "Disease Implications of Global Change," in *Geographies of Global Change: Remapping the World in the Late Twentieth Century*, ed. R. J. Johnston, Peter Taylor, and Michael Watts (Cambridge, Mass.: Blackwell, 1995), p. 217.

10. Morse, "Viruses of the Future?"; Stephen Morse, "Examining the Origins of Emerging Viruses," in *Emerging Viruses*, ed. Stephen Morse (New York: Oxford University Press, 1993), chapter 2.

11. Paul Ewald, *Evolution of Infectious Diseases* (Oxford: Oxford University Press, 1994), pp. 191–95.

12. Ewald, *Evolution of Disease*, p. 114.

13. Arno Karlen, *Man and Microbes: Disease and Plagues in History and Modern Times* (New York: Putnam, 1995), pp. 217–28.

14. Institute of Medicine, *America's Vital Interest in Global Health* (Washington, D.C.: National Academy Press, 1997), p. 1.

15. Cliff and Haggett, "Disease Implications," p. 209.

16. Ewald, *Evolution of Diseases*, chapter 7.

17. Bernice Kaplan, "Migration and Disease," in *Biological Aspects of Human Migration*, ed. C. G. N. Mascie-Taylor and G. W. Lasker (Cambridge: Cambridge University Press, 1988), pp. 220–42.

18. David Brown and Curt Suplee, "Ebola in Texas Monkeys Similar to Reston Strain," *Washington Post*, April 17, 1996; "Virus at Texas Center Is Harmless to Humans, Officials Say," *New York Times*, April 17, 1996; Curt Suplee, "'The Monkey Farm' Attracts a Media Swarm," *Washington Post*, April 18, 1996; David Brown, "Exporter's Monkeys Tested for Ebola Virus," *Washington Post*, April 20, 1996.

19. Le Guenno, "Emerging Viruses," p. 58.

20. Christopher Wills, *Yellow Fever, Black Goddess: The Coevolution of People and Plagues* (Reading, Mass.: Addison Wesley, 1996), pp. 25–26.

21. Howard French, "An African Forest Harbors Vast Wealth and Peril," *New York Times,* April 3, 1996.

22. Armelagos, "Viral Superhighway," p. 28; Paul Epstein and Ross Gelbspan, "Should We Fear a Global Plague?" *Washington Post,* March 19, 1995; John Tibbetts, "Plagued by Climate," *Earth* (April 1996): 20–21, 76–77; William Stevens, "Warmer, Wetter, Sicker: Linking Climate to Health," *New York Times,* August 10, 1998.

23. Massimo Livi-Bacci, *Population and Nutrition: An Essay on European Demographic History,* trans. Tania Croft-Murray (Cambridge: Cambridge University Press, 1991), pp. 32–39, 40–43, 46–49.

24. Nicols Fox, *Spoiled: The Dangerous Truth about a Food Chain Gone Haywire* (New York: Basic, 1997), p. 19.

25. Lawrence Altman, "153 Hepatitis Cases Are Traced to Imported Frozen Strawberries," *New York Times,* April 3, 1997; Edward Walsh, "Mexican Strawberries Cause U.S. Outbreak of Hepatitis A," *Washington Post,* April 3, 1997; Keith Bradsher, "Strawberry Shortcake Was Culprit," *New York Times,* April 5, 1997; Sandra Boodman, "Forbidding Fruit: How Safe Is Our Produce?" *Washington Post,* Health Section, July 8, 1997.

26. "Mad Cows and Englishmen," *The Economist* (March 30, 1996); Lawrence Altman, "Mad Cow Epidemic Puts Spotlight on Puzzling Human Brain Disease," *New York Times,* April 2, 1996; David Brown, "At Cow Scare's Core: An Odd Protein," *Washington Post,* April 8, 1996; "Those Corrupting Prions," *The Economist* (April 27, 1996): 90.

27. Wills, *Yellow Fever, Black Goddess,* p. 20.

28. Roy Anderson and Robert May, *Infectious Diseases of Humans: Dynamics and Control* (Oxford: Oxford University Press, 1991), chapter 13.

29. Barry Bogin, "Rural-to-Urban Migration," in Mascie-Taylor and Lasker, *Biological Aspects.*

30. Ewald, *Evolution of Diseases,* chapter 6; see also, Kathleen Phalen, "Needlestick Risk," *Washington Post,* Health Section, August 11, 1998.

31. Lawrence Altman, "Cross-Species Transplants Raise Concerns about Human Safety," *New York Times,* January 9, 1996; Sheryl Gay Stolberg, "Animals as Organ Donors? Not Until They're Germ-Free," *New York Times,* February 3, 1998.

32. Anderson and May, *Infectious Diseases of Humans,* chapter 22.

33. Wills, *Yellow Fever, Black Goddess,* pp. 20–21.

34. Charles Gregg, *Plague: An Ancient Disease in the Twentieth Century,* rev. ed. (Albuquerque: University of New Mexico Press, 1985), chapter 20.

35. Carlos Amábile-Cuevas, Maura Cárdenas-García, and Mauricio Ludgar, "Antibiotic Resistance," *American Scientist,* vol. 83 (July–August 1995): 320–29; David Brown, "'Wonder Drugs' Losing Healing Aura," *Washington Post,* June 26, 1995; Nicholas Wade, "Studies Outline Clever Tricks of Viruses," *New York Times,* May 6, 1997.

36. Ewald, *Evolution of Diseases,* pp. 65–66.

37. Ewald, *Evolution of Diseases,* pp. 96–99.

38. Susan Okie, "Experts Urge Steps to Stem Antibiotic Resistance," *Washington Post,* August 26, 1997.

39. David Brown, "Treatment Holds Virus at Bay," *Washington Post,* August 31, 1997.

40. Anderson and May, *Infectious Diseases of Humans*, pp. 236–303.

41. Jaap Goudsmit, *Viral Sex: The Nature of AIDS* (New York: Oxford University Press, 1997; Gerald Myers and Bette Korber, "The Future of Human Immunodeficiency Virus," in *Evolutionary Biology of Viruses*, Morse, ed., pp. 212–15; Anderson and May, *Infectious Diseases of Humans*, pp. 262–63; Ewald, *Evolution of Diseases*, chapter 8.

42. "How AIDS Began," *The Economist* (February 7, 1998): 81.

43. Serge Kovaleski, "Poverty, Drug Abuse Fuel Caribbean AIDS Outbreak," *Washington Post*, January 14, 1998.

44. James Rupert, "Help Least Likely Where Most Needed," *Washington Post*, September 4, 1997.

45. Anderson and May, *Infectious Diseases of Humans*, pp. 261–62, 339–73.

46. Anderson and May, *Infectious Diseases of Humans*, pp. 267–69.

47. Anderson and May, *Infectious Diseases of Humans*, pp. 369, 371.

48. Myers and Korber, "Future of Human Immunodeficiency Virus."

49. Ewald, *Evolution of Diseases*, p. 170.

50. Myers and Korber, "Future of Human Immunodeficiency Virus," p. 211.

51. Myers and Korber, "Future of Human Immunodeficiency Virus," p. 219.

52. Myers and Korber, "Future of Human Immunodeficiency Virus," pp. 222–23.

53. Ewald, *Evolution of Diseases*, p. 66.

54. Mark Earnest and John Sbarbaro, "A Plague Returns," *The Sciences* (September/October 1993): 14–19.

55. Karlen, *Man and Microbes*, pp. 19, 82–85, 141, 208–10; World Health Organization, *The World Health Report, 1995*, pp. 21–23.

56. Thomas DiBacco, "Tuberculosis on the Rebound," *Washington Post*, January 27, 1998.

57. "Tuberculosis Figures Decline, but U.S. Is Unsure if It's a Trend," *New York Times*, May 26, 1994; Charisse Jones, "Tuberculosis Cases Decline 2d Year in a Row, City Says," *New York Times*, March 14, 1995; David Brown, "U.S. Tuberculosis Cases Decline as Disease Increases Worldwide," *Washington Post*, March 23, 1996.

58. World Health Organization, *The World Health Report, 1997* (Geneva: WHO, 1997), table 2, p. 15; table 3, p. 19.

59. Donald McNeil, "In Surprising Study, TB Is Found To Be Rampant in South Africa," *New York Times*, June 26, 1996; Donald McNeil, "South Africa Slow to Battle Spread of Tuberculosis," *New York Times*, October 13, 1996.

60. "TB Returns with a Vengeance," *Washington Post*, August 3, 1996.

61. Peter Kilborn, "Alarming Trend Among Workers: Surveys Find Clusters of TB Cases," *New York Times*, January 23, 1994.

62. Curt Suplee, "Global Tuberculosis Epidemic Leveling Off," *Washington Post*, March 20, 1997; Alan Cowell, "U.N. Agency Is Optimistic On Treatment To Fight TB," *New York Times*, March 20, 1997.

63. "Tuberculosis: Victorian Values?" *The Economist* (November 30, 1996): 58–59.

64. Vivian Toy, "New York City's TB Rate Falls, but Still Leads Nation," *New York Times*, March 23, 1996.

65. Peter Hong, "Health Workers Battle Old Enemy," *Washington Post*, August 12, 1993.

66. Charles Hall, "Health-Care Workers Ease Tough Transition," *Washington Post*, August 3, 1992; Esther Fein, "Language Barriers Are Hindering Health Care," *New York Times*, November 23, 1997.

67. Denise Grady, "New Strain of Highly Contagious Tuberculosis Is Identified," *New York Times*, September 23, 1997; "Hispanic Cases of TB at Border Resist Remedies," *New York Times*, November 30, 1996.

Chapter Eleven

The Loss of Biodiversity

Humans stand accused today of causing one of the greatest waves of species extinctions our planet has ever experienced.[1] The evidence so far is still circumstantial, but this current round of extinctions may not be the first time we have caused such an event. Near the end of the Pleistocene, and for a period that lasted to about ten thousand years ago, a significant number of species of large mammals became extinct.[2] This die-off coincided with our first experience with globalization, the migration of human beings over the last 100 millennia from Africa, through Eurasia, and into the Americas, Australia, and the large islands of the Indian and Pacific Oceans, including Madagascar and New Zealand.[3] According to some scientists, migrating human hunters caused this wave of extinctions by their overkill of numerous Ice Age creatures.

North America was the scene of one of the greatest of these extinctions. One hundred millennia ago, North America was home to forty-five genera of large mammals, including giant sloths, several species of bears, saber-toothed tigers, giant beavers, horses, camels, llamas, mammoths, and others. Today, only twelve of these genera survive, and a number of these, such as bears and deer, have seen the number of their species sharply reduced. Many of the mammals that survived were of Eurasian origin, and thus had become accustomed to being around human hunters. Many of the other survivors were solitary feeders or prone to unpredictable migrations, characteristics that made them difficult to hunt.

South America was even harder hit, losing forty-six of the fifty-eight genera of large mammals that existed as recently as one hundred thousand years ago. If even one of these species—the horse—had survived this great extinction, the history of the Western Hemisphere would have been very different. Australia, invaded by *Homo sapiens* between forty thousand and eighty thousand years ago, had far fewer large mammals than the Americas, yet the proportion of loss was much higher. Today in Australia, only one genus of large mammal—the kangaroo—of the original dozen survives.

Africa and Eurasia present a somewhat different picture, but again the cumulative evidence points to the hand of human beings in the extinctions. In Africa, some thirty-seven genera of large mammals became extinct during the Pleistocene, but the majority of these losses (at least thirty) occurred earlier in the period—that is, at least 130,000 years ago. Unlike Australia and the Americas, Africa retained most of its late-Pleistocene mammals, although even here the losses were significant. Much the same picture emerges in Europe (the fate of Asian fauna during this period is still largely unknown), where there were significant losses of genera of large mammals, but again these extinctions were spread throughout the Pleistocene rather than concentrated in the last forty thousand years or so. Several reasons have been advanced to explain the different experiences of Europe and Africa, but the most convincing seem to be two: (1) humans, by living close to animals for such a long period, had begun to contract their diseases in epidemic proportions, which reduced the human population density; and (2) animals, by living close to humans for such a long period, had begun to adjust to the hunting tactics of these new predators (by, for example, becoming more solitary feeders).

Not everyone accepts the Pleistocene Overkill hypothesis.[4] Climate changes are sometimes put forward to explain a die-off of such huge proportions, but to many biologists this explanation is not completely convincing, since the extinctions seem to cluster among genera of large mammals only, and small mammals seem relatively unaffected. Another possibility is that diseases introduced by dogs, rats, birds, or parasites that accompanied humans in their migrations jumped to vulnerable large mammals, causing massive die-offs of local species. To date, however, only two existing pathogens have been found that could have devastated these animal populations without necessarily harming humans: leptospirosis, a bacteria spread in rat urine; and the rabies virus.

In all probability, we will never have an explanation that satisfies everyone, but the cumulative evidence seems to support these propositions: that *Homo sapiens* began to migrate in large numbers across the Earth some one hundred millennia ago; that where they want, they were aggressive hunters of large mammals; that especially in the Americas and Australia these animals, being unfamiliar with human predators, failed to take adequate measures to survive; and that the consequence was mass extinctions of more than one hundred genera of such animals. This evidence leads many biologists to conclude that humans have the potential for great destruction of other organisms and that large animals are very vulnerable to human predation. With only modest pressure, humans can drive even very large animals such as horses and mammoths to extinction simply by relentlessly hunting them. After all, natural extinction rates are already biased against large mammals because of their necessarily small populations and their K-strategy of reproduction. Human hunting could simply be the last factor that pushes a species over the edge of extinction.

Moreover, hunting is only one of six ways in which humans could have depleted large mammal populations.[5] Others included destroying the habitat (by logging, fire, or draining), introducing predators, introducing competitors, introducing diseases, and causing secondary extinctions (that is, killing off the mammals' food supply). Presumably many of the factors were at work together, magnifying their impact. For example, we know that grasslands in cold, wet climates need grazing animals to stimulate the emergence of young grass shoots and to fertilize the soil with their dung. If ancient hunters began to take a percentage of the megafauna herds, the more lightly grazed grasslands would have begun to give way to shrubs and other plants unpalatable to the grazers, thus setting in motion a feedback loop that would have combined with the hunting to destroy the grazing species.[6]

If our experience with globalization produced the Pleistocene wave of extinctions, our much more recent expansion (dated, say, from 1500 A.D.) threatens to inflict even greater damage on the planet's biodiversity, and to do it in much less time.

THE ORIGINS OF BIODIVERSITY

Why is there so much biological diversity on the Earth, so many different kinds of organisms? One answer would surely involve geographical separation of species. The fact that species evolved on Earth in separated populations has meant that our planet's biosphere is marked by a diversity of unknown (and perhaps unknowable), but surely large, dimensions. Paul Ehrlich writes:

> Varying physical environments subject populations *isolated from one another in different areas* to different selection pressures, which in turn leads to their becoming increasingly different genetically. As organisms in different areas become less and less alike, the communities of which they are a part automatically become more and more different. Differences in the biological communities then feed back on the speciation process by making the environments even more distinct. . . . Eventually, the separated populations become so different that they are no longer capable of interbreeding and must go their own evolutionary ways.[7]

But this answer simply shifts the question back a step: why should there be such diversity in widely separated ecological settings? The answer to this question involves the different ways in which energy is received, processed, and stored on the Earth.[8] When the sun's light reaches the upper edge of Earth's atmosphere, its rays are virtually parallel. As these rays reach the curved surface of the Earth, they strike the surface at an angle. The farther away from the equator, the shallower the angle between the rays and the surface. Shallower angles spread the light over larger areas, so that polar regions receive less light per square meter than do regions at the equator.

The result is a gradient of primary heating. The quantity of energy absorbed by the surface varies as a function of latitude. From 20° south to 20° north latitude, absorption is fairly uniform. But at New York City, at about 40° north, annual absorption of energy is less than 70 percent of the value at the equator, and at St. Petersburg, at about 60° north, it is less than 45 percent. The Earth's oceans and atmosphere do what they can to restore temperature equilibrium by moving heat poleward from the equator via wind and ocean currents; but the sun's effects are relentless and the gradient virtually permanent. Add to this the tilt of the planet, producing seasonal changes, and the Earth's wobbling on its axis, producing climatic changes over much longer spans of time, and we have the bases for widely varying thermodynamic systems. Because of the partially offsetting effects of wind and water currents, however, these varying thermodynamic systems share the same resources: nutrients, essential elements (hydrogen, oxygen, nitrogen, phosphorous, sulphur), and energy as they are carried across the Earth's surface.

The primary-heating gradient has a corresponding species-diversity gradient: there is an increase in the number of species encountered as one travels from the poles to the equator.[9] For example, there are 56 species of breeding birds in Greenland, 81 in Labrador, 118 in Newfoundland, 195 in New York state, 469 in Gautemala, and 1,525 in Colombia. The same is true of butterflies, vascular plants, ants, and beetles. Although the tropical rainforests occupy only 6 percent of the Earth's land surface, they are believed to contain more than half the species of organisms. The differential impact of solar energy on the Earth has a consequence for the planet's biodiversity that can be summed up with what Edward Wilson calls the Energy-Stability-Area Theory (or ESA) of Biodiversity: diversity is positively correlated with (1) the amount of solar energy received, (2) the stability of the climate from season to season and from year to year, and (3) area or space.[10]

In sum, diversity has evolved on our planet because energy supplies are stored in many different places and in many different forms. Different species have evolved with different strategies to occupy different ecological niches, to comprise different thermodynamic systems, and to exploit these various energy supplies (and each other). Species diversity thus ensures that each ecosystem is thermodynamically efficient, so, as Ruth Patrick puts it, "the least amount of entropy accumulates in the system."[11]

Our biosphere would be quite complex just from these energy differences, but some ecologists believe that biodiversity comes also from the special internal arrangements that characterize each ecosystem.[12] Even when sets of similar species occupy similar terrain with similar thermodynamic endowments, they still manage to evolve different strategies for managing these energy resources. This condition obtains, apparently, because nature is not in equilibrium but rather consists of ecosystems that are far from equilibrium. Working from the premises of chaos theory, ecologists have learned that ecosystems have emergent properties—that is, features that cannot be deduced or predicted simply from knowing the system's component parts. Such properties emerge from the interactions of the parts, and these patterns tend to take on unique configurations even when they are rooted in similar surroundings.

THE LOSS OF BIODIVERSITY AND ITS CONSEQUENCES

Biodiversity is defined by Edward Wilson as "all hereditarily based variation at all levels of organization, from the genes within a single local population or species, to the species composing all or part of a local community, and finally to the communities themselves that compose the living parts of the multifarious ecosystems of the world."[13] Before we conclude that we are experiencing (and causing) a loss of biodiversity, we should know at least approximately how many species there are. To say that there is disagreement about what this number is would be an understatement.

To date, between 1.4 and 1.8 million extant species have been identified, named, and described.[14] There are several reasons for the different numbers, including the absence of a central registry for all species and the possibility of duplications. About half of the known species are insects, and another one-sixth are the higher plants. Mammals, and especially large mammals, are a small percentage of the total number of species. Almost everyone agrees that the real number of species is higher, but there is little consensus as to what the real number may be, even as to order of magnitude. Estimates currently range between a low of 3 million and a high of 40 million, with some scientists suggesting the number may be as high as 100 million. If there is a consensus figure, it is probably in the vicinity of 10 million, but this number could be too low by as much as an order of magnitude.

The connections between specialization and coevolution are fundamental to our understanding of the number of species on Earth. Differing assumptions about biological specialization lie at the heart of the controversy over the exact number of species.[15] Specialization, in the words of John Thompson, refers to "a limitation in the number of other species with which a particular species interacts. An extreme specialist is a species that relies upon one or a few closely related other species for survival or reproduction during a major part of its life cycle. . . . The simplest forms of coevolution are between pairs of extreme specialists."[16] Thus, one strategy for estimating the number of species begins with an understanding of how species come to depend on one another. The higher estimates are based on studies that have revealed that a significant proportion of the Earth's species are parasites, competitors, or mutualists that are extreme specialists. Just how large this "significant proportion" may be remains uncertain, however.

Since the early 1980s, ecologists studying tropical forests have determined that the canopies of tropical trees harbor millions of insects specific to particular tree species.[17] In 1982, for example, Terry Erwin, a specialist in beetles at the Smithsonian Institution, reported his findings of a survey of the tropical rainforest in Panama.[18] He found that 955 species of beetle resided on a single species of tree, and that a single hectare of rainforest might harbor as many as 12,448 beetle species. Working from these findings, Erwin arrived at estimates of how many species specialize in each tree species; and since he knew more or less how many tropical tree species there are (50,000), he calculated that there are some 30 million tropical arthropod species and perhaps as many as 1.5 million fungi (only 69,000 have been identified). Such numbers alone would drive up the overall estimate of world species. Other biologists, working from the similar studies on the specialization of fungi and mites, have argued that the estimates of extreme specialization are all much too high.[19] They contend that tropical tree species are too sparsely distributed to encourage specialization by the insects that live on them, so natural selection must work to decrease specialization, not increase it. Clearly the way out of this debate is to conduct numerous empirical investigations of specific tree species; but these are painstaking, time consuming, and expensive. So our knowledge base on this subject has expanded very slowly.

Rates of Extinction

Depending on the time scale one chooses, the disappearance of whole populations of an organism, or even of an entire species, is not necessarily an "unnatural" event. Animals, particularly large mammals, are vulnerable to extinction for reasons that have little or nothing to do with the impact of human behavior: the area of habitat, or the size of an animal's range; the distance their habitat is separated or isolated from other neighboring habitats; the number of other species with which they must share that habitat, and the place of those other species in the food web; the degree of crowding, or the density of population, in their habitat; and climate changes that alter the effects of temperature and rainfall.[20]

To determine the rate of extinction in the distant past, paleontologists have examined the fossil record, particularly of marine invertebrates, and have concluded that in normal times (that is, any periods except those five characterized by the mass extinctions over the past 600 million years), a species typically lasts between 1 and 10 million years.[21] Another way to express this is that, on the average, between 0.1 and 1.0 species per million became extinct in any given year. If there are today on the Earth, say, ten million species, we should expect to see somewhere between one and ten become extinct in any given year. Such a rate is known as the "background extinction" rate.

Estimates of actual extinctions vary, but many biologists believe that birds, mammals, reptiles, frogs, and freshwater clams have been disappearing at the rate of 20 to 200 extinctions per million species per year, a level 20 to 2,000 times greater than the rates observed in the fossil record. To cite one example, a study published by the World Resources Institute asserted that rates of extinction of birds and mammals quadrupled between 1600 and 1950, reaching one species a year in the final century of that period.[22] That rate is at least 100 times faster than the prehistoric rate of extinctions. Extinction rates of unknown species living in remote regions like tropical rainforests may well be significantly higher.

Many prehistoric extinctions occurred because of natural factors such as habitat or climate changes; but ever since observers started keeping reliable historical records of events of extinction, a practice beginning about 1600 A.D., virtually all the recorded extinctions have been associated in one way or another with the hand of humans.[23] Of the approximately 4,200 species of modern mammals, an estimated 63 species and 52 subspecies have become extinct since 1600. Of these 115 categories, 50 were large animals—that is, they weighed more than 44 kilograms. Seventy-three categories went extinct on one of the continents, forty-one were island dwellers, and one (the pelagic whale) lived in the open sea. Of the 8,500 modern species of birds, 88 species and 83 subspecies have become extinct. The overwhelming majority of these (155 of 171) lived on islands. No comparable estimates are available for historic extinctions of reptiles, amphibians, or fish.

It is noteworthy that about three-fourths of all the extinctions between 1600 and 1950 were of island-dwelling species, which were more vulnerable because of their limited range. Today, however, two-thirds of the species at risk are found on continental mainlands, especially in tropical forests.[24]

An accurate assessment of the precise rate and extent of the loss of distinct species today is extremely difficult, because we do not know the number of species present in a complex habitat like a tropical rainforest, and because to witness the death of the last member of a species in a remote area is virtually impossible.[25] In a few well-publicized cases, however, such as that of Lake Victoria in East Africa, the forests of Hawaii, or the Centinela ridge in Ecuador, ecologists have been able to survey the diversity of an ecosystem before and after massive human intrusion; and these cases confirm the devastating losses of species because of such intrusion. Lake Victoria has lost some 200 species of fish since the 1960s, Hawaii's bird species have been cut in half, and the Centinela ridge lost 90 species of plants in less than a decade.[26]

Notwithstanding the controversy surrounding this issue, Edward Wilson has asserted that "there can be no doubt that extinction is proceeding far faster than it did prior to 1800,"[27] and that ecosystems experience a loss of species at a rate 1,000 to 10,000 times faster after human intervention than before. Wilson estimates that reduction in the area of the Earth's tropical rainforests at the current rate will extinguish about half a percent of the species in the forest each year, a rate of extinction unprecedented in the history of life on the Earth.[28]

Since 1960, the World Conservation Union (WCU), through its Species Survival Commission, has kept detailed records on declining populations of threatened wildlife on every continent.[29] Periodically, the WCU publishes its "Red List" of threatened animals to raise public awareness of the magnitude of the problem of species extinction. The 1996 version of the list attracted considerable attention around the world with its grim findings (see table 11.1 for a summary of these findings for vertebrates). Of the 4,355 species of mammals surveyed, nearly 25 percent (1,096) were found to be threatened with extinction; of the 9,615 species of birds studied, about 11 percent (1,107) were similarly threatened. Virtually all the orders of mammals contained threatened species: 330 species of rodents, 231 bats, 152 shrews and moles, 65 carnivores, 96 primates, and 70 ungulates. Nearly half the world's monkeys and apes were on the list, as well as 11 of 18 species of hoofed mammals, including zebras and rhinos. The report also lists 253 reptile

Table 11.1   Conservation Status of Surveyed Vertebrates, 1996

	Category of Vertebrates									
	Birds		Mammals		Reptiles		Amphibians		Fish	
Status	number	%	number	%	number	%	number	%	number	%
Not currently threatened	7,633	80	2,661	61	945	74	348	70	1,323	61
Nearing threatened status	875	9	598	14	79	6	25	5	101	5
Threatened–vulnerable to extinction	704	7	612	14	153	12	75	15	443	21
Threatened–immediate danger of extinction	403	4	484	11	100	8	49	10	291	13

Source: John Tuxill and Chris Bright, "Losing Strands in the Web of Life," in *State of the World: 1998,* Lester Brown, Christopher Flavin, and Hilary French, (New York: W.W. Norton, 1998), Chapter 3, Tables 3.1–3.5, pp. 43–52. Based on Jonathan Baillie and Brian Groombridge, eds., *1996 IUCN Red List of Threatened Animals* (Gland, Switzerland: World Conservation Union, 1996). © World Conservation Union. Reprinted by permission.

(20 percent of the total), 124 amphibian (25 percent), and 734 fish species (34 percent) as threatened with extinction, but it cautioned that a full assessment of all the species in these categories remained to be completed and that conceivably the number could go higher. The report also identified 1,891 species of invertebrates (crustaceans, insects, and mollusks) as threatened, but it emphasized that very few of the species in these categories have been evaluated relative to their immense numbers. In all, some 5,205 species are at risk, and as many as half of these may be gone within a decade.

Patterns of Extinction

When we turn from these global data to some specific regions and species, the threatened loss of biodiversity becomes even more obvious and meaningful. For one thing, species diversity and the impending threat of its loss are not spread evenly across the world's nation-states. According to a report by Conservation International, a private nature-protection organization, at least two-thirds of all known plant and animal species are concentrated in just 17 of the world's nearly 200 nation-states.[30] These homes to megadiversity include seven in the Americas (the United States, Mexico, Venezuela, Peru, Ecuador, Colombia, Brazil), three in Africa (the Congo, South Africa, Madagascar), and seven in Asia and the Pacific (Indonesia, the Philippines, Malaysia, Australia, Papua New Guinea, China, India). Since only two of these seventeen countries are highly industrialized, and the remaining fifteen are all deeply committed to national industrialization and a rising standard of living, we can expect the plant and animal life in those countries to come under increasing pressure. Indeed, Conservation International estimates that as much as 80 percent of the world's most endangered biodiversity is located within one or more of the seventeen megadiversity countries.

The problem is especially severe in the densely populated developing countries, where the combined effects of industrialization and rapid population growth are placing endangered species under heavy pressure. Just four countries—Brazil, China, India, and Indonesia—account for about half the world's human population, but they are also home to an enormous number of plant and animal species as well. Not surprisingly, these countries lead in threatened species. Indonesia, China, and India are the leaders in threatened mammals, while Indonesia, Brazil, and China lead in threatened bird species.

But the highly industrialized countries also experience their particular version of the biodiversity threat. Here, although the fate of individual species has attracted most public attention, the health of entire ecosystems is probably a better measure of biological vitality. In 1995, the National Biological Service, a research agency within the U.S. Department of the Interior, concluded that thirty ecosystems in the United States had declined over more than 98 percent of their area and were considered "critically endangered," fifty-eight such areas had declined by 85 to 98 percent and were classified as "endangered," and thirty-eight others had declined by 70 to 84 percent and were listed as "threatened."[31] Together, these 126 ecosystems covered at least half the area of the forty-eight contiguous states before the arrival of Europeans. Two of the largest critically endangered systems, the Midwestern prairie-savanna and the Eastern forest, together probably covered about 40 percent of the United States before 1620.

A similar study conducted by scientists for the World Wildlife Fund identified 116 large "ecoregions" of North America, such as the coastal temperate rainforests of the Pacific Northwest and the Florida Everglades.[32] Of these large regions, thirty-two contained such great animal diversity that they were the equal of any large ecosystem on the Earth. The report warned, however, that the biodiversity is seriously imperiled in fourteen of these regions, ranging from Hawaiian moist and dry forests, to the coastal forests of northern California, to the tall grasslands of the central plains, to the mixed forests of the southeastern United States.

As these large ecoregions disappear, the numerous species of wildlife within them become imperiled as well. The longleaf pine ecosystem of the southeastern coastal plain, for example, is home to twenty-seven species on the "endangered" list of the federal government, and another ninety-nine species have been proposed for listing. At least 110 of the United States's 20,500 known species of plants and animals have become extinct since the seventeenth century, and 416 more are missing and possibly extinct, according to an analysis by the Nature Conservancy.[33] Hawaii, California, and Alabama have been the states hardest hit by these extinctions, with Hawaii in particular losing as many as 250 species since 1600.

Although most public attention has been focused on the extinction rates of animals, plant life has been under assault as well. One report published in 1990 estimated that about 25,000 of the approximately 270,000 species of plants on Earth were extinct, endangered, or vulnerable.[34] In 1998, however, results of a twenty-year study by the WCU and fifteen other international biological research organizations showed that this number was too low by nearly ten thousand.[35] The Red List for plants documented the threatened disappearance of some 34,000 plant species, about 12.5 percent. Virtually every family of plant life was affected, from yew trees (75 percent threatened) to flowering plants like roses (14 percent) and lilies and irises (32 percent). Even the species of plants we cultivate for food, such as wheat and maize, have been suffering such genetic erosion that a large percentage of their varieties or strains have been lost forever.

The United States seems particularly hard hit by the loss of plant diversity. A 1995 report by the Nature Conservancy found that about 35 percent of all the species of flowering plants in the United States were either extinct, critically imperiled, imperiled, or vulnerable. Figures for conifers were about 30 percent, and for ferns about 24 percent.[36] Overall, the WCU report found that the United States led the world in percentage of imperiled plant species: 29 percent (4,669 out of 16,108 total species).

Why Do We Need Biodiversity?

Aesthetic or moral grounds may certainly be advanced for opposing the continued loss of biodiversity, but there are solid economic, medical, and biological reasons for doing so, as well.[37] Many of the threatened plants and animals may turn out to be valuable foods. Of the 250,000 plant species known today, some 30,000 are edible, but a mere 120 are cultivated for food, and in fact our food supply depends on a mere handful: wheat, rice, maize, potatoes, sugar, and a few more. One of the staple grains of the Inca, the quinua or quinoa, is known to be near extinction, yet it has been identified by food scientists working for the National Aeronautics and Space Administration (NASA) as one of the grains suitable for cultivation in low-gravity hydroponic gardens of the sort that moon or Mars colonies will rely on for their food supply.[38] Of more immediate concern is the loss of genetic diversity among the world's food crops. Domesticated plants and animals need to be able to draw on the gene pool of their wild relatives to maintain or increase yields, to resist pests and diseases, and to adapt to changing environmental features (such as drought and rising temperatures).

Many species of plants and insects also harbor substances that offer the potential for new medicines, either directly or as models for synthesis. Some of our most familiar drugs were derived from plants, including morphine, quinine, and aspirin, as well as a number of lesser known but still important anticancer drugs. The pharmaceutical industry has screened about 50,000 plants and derived about 50 drugs, for a ratio of about one per thousand. If we lose the 34,000 plant species estimated by the WCU, we may lose as many as 34 new drugs as well. Tropical-plant species manufacture toxins to ward off attackers, and these may be used in modern drugs as muscle relaxants. Biting insects manufacture substances that prevent the victim's blood from clotting, and these may be the foundation for anticoagulant drugs to help patients with heart attacks or to facilitate open heart surgery.[39]

The very complexity and interconnectedness of ecosystems argue for caution lest we unknowingly allow a "keystone" species to become extinct and in so doing rip apart some part of the environmental fabric.[40] Many suites of plants and animals have coevolved in such a complex web of interdependence that we may set off a chain of undesired consequences by allowing a single member of a system to vanish. Researchers studying prairies have determined that having more species improves an ecosystem's productivity: The greater the number of species in a parcel of grassland, the more biomass or plant material that parcel produces, and the better it retains nitrogen, its most crucial nutrient. Biodiversity alone is not enough, however; the health and productivity of an ecosystem also depend on which species are present and how they interact. If these important dimensions are held constant across ecosystems, greater species diversity should endow an ecosystem with greater resilience when stressed by drought or other climatic changes.[41]

Ecologists are becoming increasingly aware of the important services that natural ecosystems perform for us more or less "for free" (economically speaking).[42] Some of these services are "output" or "production" services that provide valuable food products for humans and our domesticated animals through the natural process of photosynthesis. Other services are essential "inputs" or "environmental

regulators" that we would have to replace with technology if nature did not provide them. These include the nutrient-cycling services of the oceans, the control
of water runoff by soil filtration, the pollination of plants,[43] the filtration of waste
water and toxic pollutants, and the many intangible benefits humans derive from
unspoiled nature (recreation, spiritual inspiration, and so forth). Some ecological economists have tried to place a dollar value on these natural services;[44] but
the resulting sums reach such daunting and unbelievable levels ($33 trillion in
one well-known instance) that many economists and public policy experts see little
practical applicability of such calculations.[45] In the final analysis, we may wish to
preserve as much of nature's complex interconnectedness as we can for no other
reason than that to do so allows us to retain, in Stephen Budiansky's words,

> a sense of reverence and awe at the sublime process of evolution that has created
> these species over thousands and millions of years. It is that sense of connection with
> the past and with a force much larger than ourselves that is at the core of the con-
> servation ethic. It is that recognition that nature has its own laws that inspires us to
> be humble in imposing our own.[46]

Signs of Hope

We cannot close this section without observing that some species thought to be
near extinction because of human activity have begun to experience a resurgence,
also owing to human intervention. Consider, for example, the tilapia, a species
of fish native to the lakes of East Africa, in particular, Lake Victoria.[47] In the 1960s,
British colonial officials introduced into the lake a carnivorous fish called the Nile
perch, principally for sport fishing to attract tourists. The Nile perch devastated
the tilapia population, which destabilized the entire ecosystem of the lake and its
littoral. The ecological crisis eventually expanded to affect the native fishing populations that lived on the shores of the lake, the woodlands surrounding the lake,
the soil, and numerous other species that had inhabited the area for countless
millennia. The overall crisis still threatens the lake and its ecosystem, but the tilapia itself have been rescued by the growing global demand for fish. Tilapia have
become popular in American restaurants and food markets, but now they come
from huge fish farms in Mexico, Costa Rica, and elsewhere in Central America.

There is also a population resurgence of certain large mammals once thought
to have been virtually exterminated in the eastern United States. Attracted by the
abundant food supplies available in American suburbs (such as lawns, bushes, fruit
trees, restaurant and food-market waste), and protected by hunting bans, animals
such as deer, beaver, and black bears have returned in large numbers. In Maryland, for example, a ban on hunting the black bear was enacted in 1953 after the
population dropped to virtually zero. In 1997, the state's Department of Natural
Resources received over 350 complaints from residents about bears invading the
suburbs around Baltimore, Washington, and other large cities.[48] Deer are also
returning in large numbers, encouraged by the food supply and by the absence

of natural predators such as wolves. Washington suburbs like Maryland's Montgomery County and Virginia's Fairfax County have recorded increases in automobile accidents caused by deer wandering onto roadways, as well as a growing number of cases of Lyme disease spread by ticks that feed on white-tailed deer.[49] Wild turkeys, thought to be near extinction in the mid-1940s, today have grown to an estimated 4.2 million, living in all forty-eight contiguous states—ten more than their ancestors called home. Turkeys have adapted so well to living near farms that, when a farm is abandoned and reverts to forest, the birds lose prime nesting and feeding grounds and have to move elsewhere.[50] Apparently, humans are coevolving with a select group of species toward a rough sort of mutualism that we can sustain without actually domesticating them.

GLOBALIZATION AND THE LOSS OF BIODIVERSITY

The loss of biodiversity is linked to at least three forces that are parts of the process of globalization: mutualism between humans and the species on which we rely for food, which increases the proportion of the biomass given over to our coevolved life system and reduces the proportion devoted to other species; our destruction of the biosphere for food, habitation, and other purposes; and the long-distance migration of human populations and the consequent homogenization of their gene pools.

Coevolution and Mutualism

In one respect, coevolution of life systems involving humans has encouraged biodiversity. As humans and diseases have coevolved, many pathogens have reacted to human countermeasures (such as antibiotics) by diversifying—that is, by evolving new strains that are resistant to medicines.[51] But if coevolution of humans and diseases has encouraged one kind of diversity, coevolution has also meant the decline, and possible extinction, of numerous species of plants and animals. It would appear that humans have been gradually eroding the planet's stock of biodiversity ever since the Neolithic Revolution. Rick Potts sums up the process this way:

> The web of interacting animals and plants was reduced; the wide diversity of species moved aside in favor of a smaller number. And so we come upon still another way in which the development of human-dominated ecosystems repeated an older theme of nature—the displacement and extinction of species. By manipulating the seed beds of the Fertile Crescent, Oaxaca, and elsewhere, humans joined the list of prominent factors disruptive to habitats. As farming intensified, humans became agents of the survival of the generalist. . . . Controlling food production favored colonizers and resilient plant species. It marginalized the delicate and the specialized, which would otherwise fill Earth's bucket of biological diversity.[52]

Most ecosystems contain "keystone" species, pivotal animals and plants whose activities fundamentally shape and reshape the landscape.[53] In the last five to ten millennia, *Homo sapiens* has been the species that has done the most to alter the character and function of the landscape by removing forests, plowing grasslands, filling wetlands, and many other activities. Geomorphologist Roger Hooke of the University of Minnesota has calculated that humans move forty billion tons of earth each year, more than any other force except moving water. Ecologists point out that the aim of all this human earth moving is to simplify our surroundings so as to achieve greater efficiency, predictability, and control over the land and its products. One of the obvious consequences of this activity, however, is to reduce the ecological complexity of the landscape.[54]

The domestication of plants necessarily meant focusing our attention and energies on a very few species. Those few plants we could digest and domesticate we cultivated and harvested; and their numbers grew enormously and continue to grow. Those that we cannot digest we either declared to be "fodder" and fed them to herbivores, or to be "weeds" and attempted to destroy them by burning, applying herbicides, or by other means. Humans now appropriate for their use each year some 40 percent of the Earth's production of energy by photosynthesis (the net primary production of the biosphere).[55] About 3 percent of this energy is consumed directly via domesticated grasses like wheat, or fed to cattle, sheep, pigs, or other herbivores. The remaining 37 percent is "co-opted"; that is, it is consumed in human-dominated ecosystems that differ significantly from natural ecosystems (such as forests converted to grazing land).

The introduction by commercial agriculture of highly uniform varieties of plants has resulted in the loss of numerous traditional strains, with a consequent loss of genetic diversity. This process, known as genetic erosion, makes crops more susceptible to pests and disease and reduces the genetic material available for use in plant improvement. In the United States in the past century, we have lost 95 percent of all cabbage varieties, 91 percent of corn strains, 94 percent of peas, 86 percent of apples, and 81 percent of tomatoes.[56] Wheat would appear to be the very opposite of endangered; in 1994, the species covered about 232 million hectares. But because of genetic erosion, wheat has lost the great majority of its strains and most of its genetic variability. In China, of the nearly ten thousand varieties of wheat that were in use in 1949, only one thousand remained in the 1970s. Of the native wheats of Greece, 95 percent have become extinct.[57]

The same process has occurred with animals. If a herbivore could be domesticated and if it possessed the digestive system that enabled it to eat and process the food energy from a plant that we did not need and could not eat, then we made the animal a part of our food supply. Some animals were domesticated for other reasons: dogs for hunting assistance, horses and oxen for mobility, cats for adornment. But most of the other species, like wolves or foxes, were declared to be "wild" and "ferocious" and were made our enemies, to be hunted and killed, put in zoos, or used for experimentation and research.[58] Today, while numerous feral species are declining, domesticates are experiencing a population explosion: an estimated 10 billion chickens and other poultry; 1.5 billion each of cattle and sheep; nearly 1 billion pigs; about 0.5 billion goats. The meat from these five species now exceeds 150 million metric tons annually. In the early 1990s, reports Vaclav Smil, domesticated animals surpassed wild mammalian vertebrates in mass by an order of magnitude, and the total mass of humanity by a factor of two.[59]

Since the early 1990s, the United Nations Food and Agriculture Organization (FAO) has been operating a program to identify and preserve ancient breeds of animals and strains of plants that are on the verge of extinction.[60] For animals, the aim is to establish banks of frozen sperm and embryos of species in imminent danger, and to seek to breed those thought to have significant economic value. High on the list of targeted species are the Sahiwal breed of cattle in Pakistan and India, the Taihu pig of China, and the Fayoumi chicken of Egypt. Seed banks are also planned for critical plant species, including amaranth from Mexico, the tarwi legume from the Andean highlands, and the oca, a tuber first domesticated by the Incas.

Since coevolution has been a major factor in the globalization of living organisms, it has strongly influenced the loss of species diversity as well. According to Stephen Budiansky, ever since the Neolithic Revolution we have lived in an "age of interdependent forms," that is, a world dominated by species living in mutualistic relationships with one another.[61] The domestication of plants and animals resulted as much from the coevolution of species as it did from human actions. Sheep and dogs adapted *to* humans as much as they were tamed or dominated *by* humans, and the same can be said of plants like wheat or maize.

When animals and their food live mutualistically, their respective populations thrive and grow. Such is the case with the plants and animals that make up our food supply. In contrast, when predators and prey are in competition, their respective populations rise and fall in alternating waves or cycles. Such would be the case for animals that prey on humans, such as lions or tigers, were it not for our technological and organizational superiority. As it is, humans and our interdependent species will inevitably win this competition. The consequence must be the decline and possibly the extinction of those species that cannot for whatever reason adapt to become more cooperative and mutualistic with humans.

One example of this exploitation is the international trade in endangered plants and animals.[62] Despite the Convention on International Trade in Endangered Species (CITES), illegal hunting and killing of, and traffic in, these animals continues, and probable will continue so long as a lucrative market exists for them. The World Wildlife Fund has identified ten such species—eight animals (black rhino, giant panda, hawksbill turtle, tiger, alligator snapping turtle, green-cheeked parrot, mako shark, and beluga sturgeon) and two plant species (goldenseal and big leaf mahogany trees)—which are highly prized as raw materials for food, medicines, fur, or furniture.

The tiger is one of the most visible and dramatic examples of this process. At the beginning of this century, about one hundred thousand tigers lived in the Asian wilderness.[63] Today, they number no more than about five thousand, a population believed to be critically endangered. Three varieties of tiger have gone extinct since the 1940s, and the populations of three other varieties have declined to fewer than one thousand each. The famous Bengal tiger has been reduced to about three thousand in India and fewer than one thousand elsewhere. World tiger populations have been decimated by the loss of habitat and the decline in the stocks of their prey species; but mostly tigers have been driven to the verge of extinction by poachers, who hunt them for the alleged medicinal value of some of their body parts, particularly their bones. The world population of ordinary house cats, in contrast, is estimated at between 150 and 200 million.[64] House cats will "out-compete" tigers because the cat's adaptability to humans makes it fitter in an evolutionary sense.

As we have become global, we have been accompanied by other species with which we have coevolved. Without them, we could not have become global. Some of these organisms are not themselves beneficial to us (diseases), but they are part of the price we pay to enjoy the company of their hosts. The globalization of life systems means that mutually interdependent species are gradually outcompeting more specialized and independent species, and this leads to the latter's decline and even possible extinction. In 1860, according to Budiansky, humans and their domesticated animals accounted for 5 percent of all terrestrial animal biomass (the total weight of all animal life on the continents). By 1990, that figure had reached 20 percent; by 2020, it may reach 40 percent; and by the middle of the next century, if the human population reaches 12 billion, the figure could well have climbed to 60 percent.[65] In this way, the coevolution and globalization of life systems result in the loss of biodiversity.

Destruction of the Biosphere

Paul Ehrlich has asserted that "the primary cause of the decay of organic diversity is not direct human exploitation or malevolence, but the habitat destruction that inevitably results from the expansion of human populations and human activities."[66] Habitat destruction for human residence and food production confronts us directly with the thermodynamic consequences, or the entropic costs, of our own actions, as the following observation by John Curtis makes clear:

> The highest vegetational product of evolution is the tropical rain forest. In the mid-latitudes the climax deciduous forest . . . is the ultimate in complexity, stability, and integration. Large numbers of species grow in intimate relationship, with maximum capture and reutilization of incident energy consistent with the seasonal nature of the climate. Many niches exist, and each has its adapted species with the necessary modifications in nutritional, growth, or photosynthetic habit to enable it to make the most of its specialized opportunities. . . . In the sense that entropy means ran-

domness . . . , the climax deciduous forest may be said to possess a very low entropy. . . . Man's actions in this community almost entirely result in a decrease in its organization and complexity and an increase in the local entropy of the system. Man . . . seems bent on asserting the universal validity of the second law of thermodynamics, on abetting the running-down of his portion of the universe.[67]

Many human activities that have been blamed for the loss of biodiversity are directly related to the destruction of habitat that results from the globalization of life systems.[68] Richard Norgaard, for example, cites three factors that have increased markedly the destruction of habitats by humans, and they are all part of globalization: population growth, technological changes that have polluted the environment, and the transformation of world agriculture "from a patchwork quilt of nearly independent regions to a global exchange economy."[69]

Habitat destruction typically began when humans moved into an area that had had no previous interaction with them. A case in point is the Maori arrival in New Zealand, which altered the balance established in these islands over countless millennia. As the top predator in the food chain, humans began to prey on the local herbivore population, the moas. Human predation always focuses on large herbivores because, as Jonathan Kingdon puts it, "any animal that is sufficiently numerous to contribute significantly to the diet of a burgeoning population of hunters cannot be a trivial component in the local ecosystem."[70] The paradox is that by removing the large herbivores from the food chain, humans disrupted an ecosystem that had endured for thousands of years. The use of fire by new arrivals also dealt a crucial blow to the local flora. Again, Kingdon explains: "A relatively stable relationship between consumer and consumed can only evolve over a very long period. The forces that break that relationship have their own dynamics and, for the new human-induced ecosystems, that usually involved his prime tool, fire; and it takes a specialised plant to cope with being regularly burnt."[71] Further habitat destruction occurred following the arrival of food-producing humans in an area where food gatherers had worked out a relationship with the local ecosystem (for example, the arrival of British settlers in Australia). These biological invasions brought exotic creatures that accompanied humans as they migrated across the Earth.[72] The English settlers of eastern North America did more damage with their cattle, pigs, and sheep than they could have done by themselves.

The Forests

One important area demonstrating the impact of globalization on habitat is deforestation, one of the most dramatic examples of the loss of biodiversity. The loss of the planet's forests is a visible sign of the impact of a global human population as it extends itself into habitats that have not previously felt a human presence. And since the forests are the home of many species of plants and animals not yet even identified by naturalists, when the woodlands disappear so also do the organisms they shelter.

Five thousand years ago, forests covered 50 percent of the Earth's land surface.[73] By 1956, that figure had dropped to 25 percent and by 1978 to 20 percent. No region of the Earth has escaped this decline. Africa has lost nearly 25 percent of its forest cover since 1950; Central America, nearly 40 percent; the Himalayan watershed, more than 40 percent. Germany has lost 50 percent of its forests to acid rain; and in the United States, forests cover only 20 percent of the area they covered in 1620. Southeast Asia was once covered by six million square miles of lush forests; but logging and burning to clear land for crops have destroyed 75 percent of these forests, leaving only a million and a half square miles intact. The raging forests fires that spread over Indonesia and Malaysia in 1997 destroyed another three thousand square miles alone, according to the World Wildlife Fund.[74]

About 50 percent of the remaining forest lands are in developing countries, almost all in the tropics.[75] About 60 percent of these tropical woodlands are densely forested, and more than 50 percent of these so-called closed forests are found in just three countries: Brazil, Indonesia, and the Democratic Republic of Congo. The fact that these countries, as well as nearly all the others that harbor tropical forests, are poor and heavily in debt and have high rates of population growth makes their woodlands especially vulnerable to exploitation for valuable exotic wood such as mahogany or to clearing for agriculture, ranching, or urbanization. In many instances, the people leading the incursion into the forests are poor and landless and cannot permit themselves the luxury of being concerned about vanishing species. In other cases, the exploiters are large multinational firms whose economic activity provides scarce foreign exchange and other revenues to financially strapped Third World governments.

Kent MacDougall has identified five principal causes of deforestation throughout history:[76] clearing the land for farming, livestock grazing, timber supply, firewood, and warfare. To these ancient causes we should add the exploitation of oil, gas, and mineral deposits, and the construction of roadways across forested areas. The spread of raw materials' exploitation into forested lands wreaks havoc on the forests by cutting them into smaller parcels that are not sustainable. By penetrating into these areas, roadways expose forests to what ecologists call the "edge effect"—that is, trees standing at the edge of the forest are hammered by wind and sunlight far beyond what they would experience in the interior of the forest. Latin America in particular can expect to lose broad expanses of its forests in this way, mostly in the tropical belt, as oil and gas exploration penetrates farther and farther into remote areas of countries like Colombia, Peru, and Brazil. As the forests recede, the endangered species within them will be deprived of their habitat, and their extinction is almost sure to follow. In Southeast Asia, the species especially threatened by deforestation include the orangutan, the Asian elephant, the Sumatran tiger, and the Sumatran and Javan rhinos.

Migration and Human Gene Pools

The loss of biodiversity may be affecting more species than just tigers and white rhinos. In the process of globalizing *Homo sapiens*, we may also be reducing our own intraspecific diversity as well, but the consequences of global expansion for the diversity of the human gene pool are not clearly understood.

"Each biological species is a closed gene pool," writes Edward O. Wilson,

> an assemblage of organisms that does not exchange genes with other species. Thus insulated, it evolves diagnostic hereditary traits and comes to occupy a unique geographic range. Within the species, particular individuals and their descendants cannot diverge very far from others because they must reproduce sexually, mingling their genes with those of other families. Over many generations all families belonging to the same biological species are by definition tied together. Linked as one by the chains of ancestry and future descent, they all evolve in the same general direction.[77]

Jonathan Marks asserts that the gene pool stands both apart from, and above, the organisms that are the physical expression of those genes. The gene pool, he writes, is

> the genetic composition of the population, which transcends the specific genotypes of the specific organisms that compose it. . . . Organisms are regarded as simply transient and short-lived packages of heredity; they do the business of ensuring that the genes get transmitted, but are themselves ephemeral. The gene pool thus has greater breadth than any individual organism, and greater longevity (since it endures many generations).[78]

The gene pool that produces and reproduces our species is a product of four more or less interconnected processes.[79] The first is the passage of time. Over time, genes mutate randomly. Some of these changes are harmful for the individuals carrying them, and some are neutral in their effects. These changes tend to be discarded (that is, selected against by nature). A few changes are beneficial to the bearers, and they are retained and passed on to the bearer's progeny. The second process involves the impact of distance. Isolation of a certain population ensures that its members will not exchange genetic material with others from some distance away, and members will as a result begin to change in ways that are specific to one area. The third process is adaptation to particular climates and habitats, expressed through various pressures, including temperature, humidity, and other living organisms with which the population in question coevolves. Fourth is the effects of gene recombination produced by breeding within or beyond the boundaries of a population's gene pool.

The range of habitat for *Homo sapiens* is very nearly the Earth itself. We are a global species, and we have been one for several tens of millennia. Nevertheless, the human species does not consist of a single interbreeding population.[80] We live in locally interconnected populations (called "demes") that engage in social relationships with neighboring populations, and among these relationships is the exchange of mates. Genes can move from one population to another by two mechanisms: by the exchange of mates (a process known as "gene flow"), or by the expansion of an entire group from its range to that of another group (known as "invasion").

When genes move via gene flow, it is assumed that the territory in question is continuously inhabited, genetic differences are the product of distance only, and diversity is represented by gradual shadings of gradient lines known as "clines." When genes have been moved by invasion, it is assumed that today's populations have been formed by splitting away from a parent population, and the progeny populations diverge from their parents because of their physical isolation. In this case, genetic distance is a function of time; that is, the more similar two populations are genetically, the more recently they shared a common ancestral population—and of course the opposite is true as well. When both gene flow and invasion occur together, that is, when population A enters the territory of population B and the two begin to exchange mates, the process is called "demic diffusion."

The great diversity that is humankind illustrates the effects of several hundred thousand millennia of changes that took place within relatively isolated habitats. Whether these changes occurred because of the pressures of climate, or simply by the arbitrary local definitions of beauty, the fact remains that different forms of a number of important genes are not distributed evenly across the Earth. Some important phenotypical differences are easily apparent (skin pigmentation, facial contours, stature), whereas others are hidden deep within our bodies (blood groups, lactose intolerance, resistance to AIDS or malaria). Of interest to us here are these questions: As human migration expanded, and as more and more people moved farther and farther from their place of birth, what happened to the human gene pool, and what will continue to happen in the future as the human gene pool becomes truly globalized?

"The movement of people from place to place," writes Barry Bogin, "is a major determinant of the biological structure of human populations."[81] This movement of *Homo sapiens* has occurred in phases that correspond roughly to the level of economic and technological development achieved by humans at the time.[82] Within Africa and across Eurasia, the initial wanderings of human groups proceeded by their entry into territory uninhabited and unimpeded by others. The word "migration" hardly captures what was occurring there, since movement was very gradual and only over relatively short distances. By about twenty to forty thousand years ago, most of the far reaches of Eurasia had been settled; from that point on, migrants there and in Africa were likely to encounter other people, even though migration to the Americas and Australia continued for millennia thereafter.

Although the Eurasian distances to be covered were great, populations almost certainly continued to exchange mates and thereby keep the gene flow going.

Jonathan Marks warns against exaggerating the degree of isolation of local populations or gene pools far back in history.[83] One of the stereotypes of world demographic history is that European explorers encountered peoples "frozen in time," people who were genetically isolated from all outside contact until the Europeans arrived. But Marks asserts that there has always been considerable gene flow between gene pools since the beginning of humankind's tenure on Earth. Jonathan Kingdon agrees:

> Genes had a much greater mobility in prehistoric people than has generally been allowed for. Although there is much to support the idea of prolonged genetic isolation in Australia, Hokkaido and a few other enclaves, the major continental populations cannot and should not be conceived as monolithic races. The erection of "racial types" . . . is wrong. They are not only likely to be false as scientific models but also wrong at the popular and moral level in that they create false entities and false identities too.[84]

The arrival of agriculture at the local level introduced a new dynamic into human gene movement. Small population clusters became increasingly sedentary, but there was still movement of individuals, families, and even entire villages to new sites as land was exhausted. However, since surplus production had not yet reached the stage where states and armies could exist and be used as instruments of expansion, it is improbable that entire demes systematically expanded and displaced others via invasion. Rather, the random movement, especially of single individuals, was likely to lead to considerable irregularities in genetic frequency patterns. Genetic clines drawn on maps would look somewhat chaotic, with little order and considerable genetic "patchiness."

Before too long, however, agriculture reached the stage where it both required and supported the systematic expansion of farmers into lands previously occupied by foraging peoples. Chapter 5 examined the spread of agriculture into Europe, in what was probably the first ever instance of large-scale demic diffusion. Here, so many people moved more or less at the same time, with such overpowering technology, and displaced the previous inhabitants so thoroughly, that the map of genetic clines portrays even waves of changes in genetic frequency as one moves from Turkey north and west toward Britain and Scandinavia. Although the evidence is necessarily fragmentary and the proposition is contested, somewhat the same kind of thing seems to have occurred in the Americas *before* agriculture. Here the original inhabitants, the Paleo-Indians, arrived perhaps twenty thousand years ago, and were succeeded and displaced in Alaska and Canada by two populations, the Athapascans and the Eskimo-Aleuts. These waves of migration are still preserved today in the divergent gene pools of these three groups scattered across the Western Hemisphere.

The movement of human genes has clearly accelerated and broadened in the past ten millennia, especially since the Industrial Revolution. What has made this possible has been the creation of large state systems, with armies and

bureaucracies, that can conquer distant lands, move large numbers of new settlers into those lands, administer their new holdings from a distance, and eventually kill, absorb, or drive out most of the natives. In many historical instances,
particularly the movement of Europeans into the Americas, these factors have
been reinforced by the high death rates among natives from alien diseases and the
high population growth rates of the invaders.

Human populations have clearly gone beyond demic diffusion and now moved
themselves by true genetic invasions. The past ten thousand years have seen the
reduction of the barriers to the exchange of life forms and the creation of ever
larger and more nearly homogeneous gene pools, until today many gene pools,
including human, are virtually global in scope. All of these changes are so novel
that we hardly know what to make of them. The contemporary patterns of genetic mixing—that is, large numbers of people moving far beyond the boundaries of their natal gene pool—are no more than a dozen or so generations old,
and demographic experts disagree about the long-term consequences.

For one thing, the globalization of the human gene pool is causing us to re-
consider the meaning of the word "race" as a genetic marker of human identity.
Jonathan Marks asserts that the human use of culture to meet environmental
challenges has had the side effect of making us more biologically homogeneous.[85]
Ironically, he says, the reduction in biological diversity has been matched by a rise
in cultural distinctiveness. A sense of group identification and of group contrast
is a universal property of human societies. Unfortunately, these cultural divisions
are often widely misperceived as having their origin in biology, when in fact human differences such as race are cultural artifacts, categories to which people are
assigned (by themselves or by others) regardless of their biological history and
endowments.

Steve Jones reports that an analysis of 18 variable genes in 180 different populations reveals that about 85 percent of the total diversity for this sample comes
from the differences between two individuals from the same population—such
as two randomly chosen Englishmen or Nigerians.[86] About 5 to 10 percent of the
variation is explained by differences between "national" populations—for example,
the people of England and Spain, or of Nigeria and Kenya. The remaining differences, also between 5 and 10 percent, stem from different "races," such as Africans and Europeans. Thus, Jones asserts, "individuals—not nations and not
races—are the main repository of human variation for functional genes. A race,
as defined by skin color, is no more a biological entity than is a nation, whose
identity depends only on a brief shared history."[87] Since human migration consists of the movement of individuals, this paramount source of diversity is being
spread across greater and greater distances, with greater speed and in greater volume than has ever been the case in the past.

Some observers, such as Jonathan Kingdon, believe that the movement of a large
proportion of the human population from one habitat to another has yielded (and
will continue to yield) greater diversity of the gene pool;[88] but this appears to be

a minority opinion among population biologists. A majority think that this trend is producing greater genetic homogeneity overall, even while it is causing increased diversity at the local level. One of these latter is D. F. Roberts, who propounds that "migration . . . is the vehicle for the mechanism of evolution that today is producing the greatest evolutionary effect, allowing the incorporation of new genes into established gene pools, enhancing intrapopulation and reducing interpopulation variability."[89] Kenneth Weiss goes even further, predicting that "in the long run, . . . if this [pattern of mixing] continues we can expect a worldwide homogenization of the human gene pool."[90] Steve Jones agrees that the speed with which the world's populations are mixing together is increasing.[91] Nevertheless, global genetic homogeneity is still a long way into the future. Jones estimates that it will take as many as 500 years to erase the genetic differences between populations in England and Scotland, so we are witnessing only the early stages of a process that will require millennia to unfold.

These differences of opinion may stem from different definitions of the term "gene pool" as well as from different time perspectives. While it may be true that, as G. W. Lasker and C. G. N. Mascie-Taylor put it, "Human migration is the mechanism that injects DNA from one gene pool into another,"[92] it is apparent that different kinds of migration produce different effects on the gene pools affected: that of the originating population, that of the receiving population, and that of the migrants themselves. Random migration (that in which the migrants are not selected because of some genetically encoded features or traits) supposedly reduces the genetic distance between the originating and the receiving populations and thus promotes genetic homogeneity, whereas selective migration is supposed to produce the opposite. There are different effects if the migrants move as single individuals, families, or large groups; whether they move before or after marriage; how they are received into the new host population; whether the migration is continual and across generations, or occurs only once; whether they move long distances or short; how long it takes the fertility rate of the migrating population to come to resemble that of the receiving population; and so forth. To take one example: even if a particular migrant flow is random, if entire families are moving together, their presence in the migrating gene pool is magnified (what is called the "booster effect") and tends to skew the pool toward a somewhat more nonrandom profile.[93]

We are obviously witnessing a phenomenon of extreme complexity, making long-term predictions especially risky. However, all other things being equal, an increase in the movement of large numbers of people over long distances to reside permanently in a new population should result in these changes: first, an increase in the genetic diversity in the local receiving population and in the migrating population; second, a decrease in the genetic differences between the migrating and receiving populations; third, a decrease in the genetic diversity of the original population from which the migrants came; and fourth, over the very long term, a decrease in the genetic diversity of the entire global population, the human gene pool. In these ways, migration fulfills its role as one of the major mechanisms of evolution, defined as change in gene frequency of the population.[94]

Finally, some geneticists, including Steve Jones, believe that human evolution is winding down, that we have used technology to insulate ourselves so well from the forces of natural selection that we have essentially ceased changing as a species.[95] Moreover, since humans are intermixing more than ever before, and mating with people born in locations farther away, we are erasing the isolation of populations that produces speciation, or the emergence of a new species. If so, then the only way the human species can continue to evolve is through the establishing of colonies on distant worlds, a subject to which we turn in the final chapter.

NOTES

1. Niles Eldredge, *Life in the Balance: Humanity and the Biodiversity Crisis* (Princeton: Princeton University Press, 1998); Richard Leakey and Roger Lewin, *The Sixth Extinction: Patterns of Life and the Future of Humankind* (New York: Doubleday, 1995). For a different perspective, see Vaclav Smil, *Energy, Food, Environment: Realities, Myths, Options* (Oxford: Clarendon Press, 1987), pp. 237–46.

2. Paul Martin and Richard Klein, eds., *Quaternary Extinctions: A Prehistoric Revolution* (Tuscon: University of Arizona Press, 1984), esp. Paul Martin, "Prehistoric Overkill: The Global Model," chapter 17; Leakey and Lewin, *Sixth Extinction*, chapter 10.

3. Colin Tudge, *The Time before History: 5 Million Years of Human Impact* (New York: Simon & Schuster, 1996), chapter 8.

4. William Stevens, "Disease Is New Suspect in Ancient Extinctions," *New York Times*, April 29, 1997.

5. Jared Diamond, "Historic Extinctions: A Rosetta Stone for Understanding Prehistoric Extinctions," in Martin and Klein, *Quaternery Extinctions*, chapter 38, pp. 838–46.

6. Yvonne Baskin, *The Work of Nature: How the Diversity of Life Sustains Us* (Washington, D.C.: Island Press, 1997), pp. 153–54.

7. Paul Ehrlich, *The Machinery of Nature: The Living World around Us—and How It Works* (New York: Simon & Schuster, 1986), p. 75 (emphasis in the original).

8. Tyler Volk, *Gaia's Body: Toward a Physiology of Earth* (New York: Springer-Verlag, 1998), pp. 66–76.

9. Edward Wilson, *The Diversity of Life* (Cambridge: Harvard University Press, 1992), pp. 195–99.

10. Wilson, *Diversity of Life*, p. 199.

11. Ruth Patrick, "Biodiversity: Why Is It Important?" in *Biodiversity II: Understanding and Protecting Our Biological Resources*, ed. Marjorie Reaka-Kudla, Don Wilson, and Edward Wilson (Washington, D.C.: Joseph Henry Press, 1997), p. 17.

12. Leakey and Lewin, *Sixth Extinction*, chapters 9, 12.

13. Edward Wilson, "Introduction," in *Biodiversity II*, ed. Reaka-Kudla, Wilson, and Wilson, p. 1.

14. Thomas Lovejoy, "Biodiversity: What Is It?" and Nigel Stork, "Measuring Global Biodiversity and Its Decline," both in *Biodiversity II*, ed. Raeka-Kudla, Wilson and Wilson;

Edward Wolf, "Avoiding a Mass Extinction of Species," in *State of the World: 1988,* ed. Lester Brown (New York: W. W. Norton, 1988), table 6.3, pp. 104–07.

15. John Thompson, *The Coevolutionary Process* (Chicago: University of Chicago Press, 1994), pp. 9–12.

16. Thompson, *Coevolutionary Process,* p. 8.

17. David Quammen, "Small Things Considered," *The Sciences* (November/December 1997): 28–33.

18. Terry Erwin, "Biodiversity at Its Utmost: Tropical Forest Beetles," in *Biodiversity II,* ed. Reaka-Kudla, Wilson, and Wilson.

19. Stork, "Measuring Global Diversity," pp. 50–55.

20. Diamond, "Historic Extinctions," pp. 825–38; David Quammen, "Life in Equilibrium," *Discover* (March 1996): 66–77.

21. John Fleischman, "Mass Extinctions Come to Ohio," *Discover* (June 1997): 84–90; Karen Schmidt, "Life on the Brink," *Earth* (April 1997): 26–33.

22. "The Foundering Ark," *The Economist* (January 6, 1990): 83–84.

23. Diamond, "Historic Extinctions," pp. 838–46.

24. "The Foundering Ark," p. 83.

25. See Wilson, *The Diversity of Life,* chapter 12, for anecdotal evidence on the loss of biodiversity.

26. Leakey and Lewin, *Sixth Extinctions,* chapter 13.

27. Edward Wilson, "The Current State of Biological Diversity," in *BioDiversity,* ed. Edward Wilson (Washington, D.C.: National Academy Press, 1988), chapter 1, p. 13. See also A. J. McMichael, *Planetary Overload: Global Environmental Change and the Health of the Human Species* (Cambridge: Cambridge University Press, 1993), chapter 9.

28. Wilson, *The Diversity of Life,* p. 276.

29. John Tuxill and Chris Bright, "Losing Strands in the Web of Life," in *State of the World: 1998,* ed. Lester Brown, Christopher Flavin, and Hilary French (New York: Norton, 1998), chapter 3; Les Line, "1,096 Mammal and 1,108 Bird Species Threatened," *New York Times,* October 8, 1996; Rick Weiss, "One-Fourth of Mammal Species Face Extinction," *Washington Post,* October 4, 1996.

30. "Richly Diverse," *Washington Post,* December 27, 1997.

31. William Stevens, "Latest Endangered Species: Natural Habitats of America," *New York Times,* February 14, 1995.

32. William Stevens, "'Hot Spots' for American Endangered Species Cover Surprisingly Little Land," *New York Times,* January 24, 1997; Jon Luoma, "Treasure of Biodiversity Discovered, and It's in Nation's Yard," *New York Times,* September 16, 1997.

33. "Extinct Species in America: An Update," *New York Times,* February 25, 1997.

34. Irwin Forseth, "Plant Response to Multiple Environmental Stresses: Implications for Climatic Change and Biodiversity," in *Biodiversity,* eds., Reaka-Kudla, Wilson, and Wilson, chapter 12, p. 187.

35. Curt Suplee, "1 in 8 Plants in Global Study Threatened," *Washington Post,* April 8, 1998; William Stevens, "One in Every 8 Plant Species Is Imperiled, a Survey Finds," *New York Times,* April 9, 1998.

36. William Dicke, "Numerous U.S. Plant and Freshwater Species Found in Peril," *New York Times,* January 2, 1996.

37. "The Foundering Ark," pp. 83–84; Leakey and Lewin, *Sixth Extinction,* chapter 8.

38. Rick Weiss, "Moonstruck: Cosmic Cuisine," *Washington Post,* April 1, 1998.

39. Cynthia Mills, "Blood Feud," *The Sciences* (March/April 1998): 34–38.

40. Patrick, "Biodiversity."

41. Carol Kaesuk Yoon, "Ecosystem's Productivity Rises with Diversity of Its Species," *New York Times*, March 5, 1996; Joby Warrick, "Diversity Is Not Enough to Ensure Hardy Ecosystems," *Washington Post*, August 29, 1997; Carol Kaesuk Yoon, "New Studies Reassess Importance of Biodiversity," *New York Times*, September 2, 1997.

42. Baskin, *Work of Nature.*

43. Stephen Buchmann and Gary Paul Nabhan, *The Forgotten Pollinators* (Washington, D.C.: Island Press, 1996).

44. Mark Sagoff, "Can We Put a Price on Nature's Services?" *Philosophy and Public Policy* 17, no. 3 (summer 1997): 7–13.

45. William Stevens, "Congress Asks, Is Nature Worth More than a Shopping Mall?" *New York Times*, April 25, 1995.

46. Stephen Budiansky, *The Covenant of the Wild: Why Animals Chose Domestication* (New York: Morrow, 1992), p. 165.

47. Norman Myers, "The Rich Diversity of Biodiversity Issues," in *Biodiversity II,* ed. Reaka-Kudla, Wilson, and Wilson, esp. pp. 127–28; William Booth, "Lake Victoria's Ecosystem, Vital to Millions, May Be Unraveling," *Washington Post*, June 5, 1989; Susan Okie, "Lake's Bounty Becomes Its Bane," *Washington Post*, July 7, 1992.

48. Peter Goodman, "Close Encounters of the Bear Kind," *Washington Post*, March 16, 1998.

49. Eric Lipton, "Hunters, Wolves to Rescue?" *Washington Post*, December 3, 1996.

50. Jane Brody, "Wild Turkeys Return to American Fields," *New York Times*, November 25, 1997.

51. Christopher Wills, *Yellow Fever, Black Goddess: The Coevolution of People and Plagues* (Reading, Mass.: Addison Wesley, 1996), pp. 23–26, chapters 11, 12.

52. Rick Potts, *Humanity's Descent: the Consequences of Ecological Instability* (New York: Morrow, 1996), p. 251.

53. Baskin, *Work of Nature,* chapter 2.

54. Baskin, *Work of Nature*, pp. 153–56.

55. Peter Vitousek, Paul Ehrlich, Anne Ehrlich, and Pamela Matson, "Human Appropriation of the Products of Photosynthesis," *BioScience* 36, no. 6 (June 1986): 368–73.

56. "Dwindling Diversity," *Washington Post*, February 15, 1997.

57. Myers, "Rich Diversity," p. 131.

58. Paul Shepard, *The Others: How Animals Made Us Human* (Washington, D.C.: Island Press, 1996); Keith Thomas, *Man and the Natural World: A History of the Modern Sensibility* (New York: Pantheon, 1983).

59. Vaclav Smil, *Cycles of Life: Civilization and the Biosphere* (New York: Scientific American Library, 1997), p. 129; Charles Heiser, *Seed to Civilization: The Story of Food* (Cambridge: Harvard University Press, 1990), chapter 4.

60. Boyce Rensberger, "A Rescue Mission for Dying Breeds," *Washington Post*, February 3, 1992; Boyce Rensberger, "Nurturing a Cornucopia of Potential," *Washington Post*, October 20, 1993.

61. Budiansky, *Covenant of the Wild,* chapter 6.

62. "Sustainable Arguments," *The Economist* (June 21, 1997): 83; "Taming the Wildlife Trade," *Washington Post*, June 7, 1997; William Branigin, "Mexico's Other Contraband—Wildlife," *Washington Post*, June 24, 1989; Sheryl WuDunn, "South Koreans,

Lusting after Cures, Are Imperiling the Species," *New York Times*, May 7, 1997; "Unrelenting Contraband in Nigeria: Animals," *New York Times*, August 17, 1997.

63. "No Longer Burning Bright," *Washington Post*, January 24, 1998.

64. "Reigning Cats and Dogs," *Washington Post*, May 2, 1998.

65. Budiansky, *Covenant of the Wild*, chapter 6.

66. Paul Ehrlich, "The Loss of Diversity: Causes and Consequences," in Wilson, *BioDiversity*, p. 21.

67. John Curtis, "The Modification of Mid-latitude Grasslands and Forests by Man," in *Man's Role in Changing the Face of the Earth*, ed. William Thomas (Chicago: University of Chicago Press, 1956), pp. 734–35.

68. Leakey and Lewin, *Sixth Extinction*, chapter 13.

69. Richard Norgaard, "The Rise of the Global Exchange Economy and the Loss of Biological Diversity," in Wilson, *BioDiversity*, p. 206.

70. Jonathan Kingdon, *Self-Made Man: Human Evolution from Eden to Extinction?* (New York: Wiley, 1993), p. 87.

71. Kingdon, *Self-Made Man*, p. 87.

72. Tudge, *Time before History*, pp. 299–300.

73. Kent MacDougall, "Worldwide Costs Mount as Trees Fall," *Los Angeles Times*, June 14, 1987.

74. "Shrinking Forests," *Washington Post*, October 11, 1997.

75. William Wood, "Tropical Deforestation: Balancing Regional Development Demands and Global Environmental Concerns," *Global Environmental Change* (December 1990): 23–40.

76. Kent MacDougall, "Need for Wood Forestalled Conservation," *Los Angeles Times*, June 17, 1987.

77. Wilson, *The Diversity of Life*, p. 42.

78. Jonathan Marks, *Human Biodiversity: Genes, Race, and History* (New York: Aldine DeGruyter, 1995), p. 33.

79. Kingdon, *Self-Made Man*, chapter 7.

80. Kenneth Weiss, "In Search of Times Past: Gene Flow and Invasion in the Generation of Human Diversity," in *Biological Aspects of Human Migration*, ed. C. G. N. Mascie-Taylor and G. W. Lasker (Cambridge: Cambridge University Press, 1988), p. 130.

81. Barry Bogin, "Rural-to-Urban Migration," in *Biological Aspects*, ed. Mascie-Taylor; and Lasker, p. 90.

82. Weiss, in *Biological Aspects*, Mascie-Taylor; and Lasker, pp. 135–52.

83. Marks, *Human Biodiversity*, pp. 176–80.

84. Kingdon, *Self-Made Man*, p. 303.

85. Marks, *Human Biodiversity*, pp. 44–46, 199–200.

86. Steve Jones, *The Language of Genes: Solving the Mysteries of Our Genetic Past, Present and Future* (New York: Doubleday, 1995), pp. 205–06.

87. Jones, *Language of Genes*, p. 206.

88. Kingdon, *Self-Made Man*, p. 221.

89. D. F. Roberts, "Migration in the Recent Past," in *Biological Aspects*, Mascie-Taylor; and Lasker, p. 67.

90. Weiss, "In Search of Times Past," p. 149.

91. Jones, *Language of Genes*, p. 247.

92. G. W. Lasker and C. G. N. Mascie-Taylor, "The Framework of Migration Studies," in *Biological Aspects,* Mascie-Taylor; and Lasker, p. 2.

93. Roberts, "Migration in the Recent Past," pp. 59–60.

94. Roberts, "Migration in the Recent Past," pp. 51–52.

95. William Stevens, "Evolution of Humans May at Last Be Faltering," *New York Times,* March 14, 1995.

Chapter Twelve

Where Do We Go from Here?
The Biology of Interplanetary and Interstellar Migration

Whatever else one may think about our species, we cannot deny its extraordinary biological achievements.[1] We are the first terrestrial species to live virtually everywhere, and the first to live at densities far higher (three orders of magnitude higher) than nature provides. As Paul Colinvaux pointed out, we are the first (and only) species to expand its niche without speciating (that is, without giving up its old niche) or without giving up our old breeding strategy, a feat we accomplished by grafting ourselves onto the niche of a handful of other species.[2] We are the first to globalize other species—those plants, animals, and microörganisms with which we coevolved, and which have accompanied us on our global adventure; and we are the first to acquire the capacity to effect changes in the global biosphere. All living organisms have an impact on their immediate surroundings and for a brief moment; we are the first to have an impact on ecosystems halfway around the world, and for decades or centuries into the future. We accomplished these things by coevolving with packages of other species that are our food supply, and by defeating attempts by other species to make us their food supply (although, in the case of microörganisms, these victories have been only partial and temporary, with the exception of smallpox).

While a huge controversy rages today over the nature of the Earth's carrying capacity and the degree to which that capacity limits our further growth, few people doubt that there must be a limit to how many of us can live at any one time on the planet.[3] The only real issues are these: when we will reach that limit; how big our population will be when the limit is reached; how we will respond to these limits—through public policies and private choices that add up to a zero-growth world that preserves some degree of freedom and human dignity, or through violence and destruction; and when we reach the limit, where we will go from there. Answers to the question "How many people will the Earth hold?" vary tremendously, depending on what kind of life people want to experience. But no matter what the answer is, even the highest estimates will be reached in a matter of centuries. At that point, our descendants must either limit their own population voluntarily, experience involuntary limits, go somewhere else to live, or devise some combination of the above. In this concluding chapter, I want to explore these issues, and end by speculating on the biological implications of what appears to some to be the only real solution in the very long term: migrating to another world. We will discover, however, that this "solution" implies a quite unexpected fate for the human species.

HOW MANY PEOPLE WILL THE EARTH HOLD?

In its most basic and general form, the term "carrying capacity" means "the maximum number of animals of a given species that a particular area can support during the harshest part of the year, or the maximum biomass it can sustain indefinitely."[4] There are numerous variations on that basic theme (see table 12.1).[5] In basic ecology (that is, without human behavior, or culture, factored in), the term usually refers to the ability of a given area to support a species population indefinitely. Once human activities are taken into account, this definition is of limited value. The human use of technology and social organization to expand the planet's resources enabled our species to exceed the Earth's biological carrying capacity some ten millennia ago.

It appears that the population will continue to grow at a gradually decreasing rate for about the next two centuries, when it is expected to stabilize at about 10.7 billion. While demographers do not doubt that we will reach stability, and prob-

Table 12.1 Definitions of Carrying Capacity in Basic and Applied Ecology

Basic ecology, used for nonhuman populations

1. The population size at which the birth rate equals the death rate, as determined by population density
2. The average population size at which the population neither grows nor declines
3. The population size set by the least available critical resource, also known as **Liebig's Law of the Minimum**

Applied ecology, assuming human activity

1. The population size at which the standing stock of animals (e.g., a herd of livestock) is maximal
2. The population size at which the steady yield of animals is maximal
3. The animal population size that maintains a maximal plant population (i.e., for grazing purposes)
4. The size of a harvested population belonging to a single owner
5. The population size of an open-access resource (i.e., of a commons accessible to multiple users and owners such that no single owner has an incentive to restrict their exploitation)

Source: Joel Cohen, *How Many People Can the Earth Support?* (New York: Norton, 1995), chapter 12.

ably within 200 years or less, the exact level at which population stabilizes is dependent on many variables, most of which we can only speculate about. In 1990, for example, the U.S. Census Bureau published a series of projections for population until 2080. The Bureau's most commonly used projection, based on a total fertility rate (TFR) of 1.8 children per woman, estimated the country's population would peak in 2038 and be slowly declining by 2080, by which time it would have reached 292 million. In contrast, the Bureau's high fertility scenario, based on a TFR of 2.2, produced a population that would reach 421 million by 2080 and continue growing by 20 million per decade.[6]

This next doubling (or near doubling) of the global population promises to be the last such increase we will ever experience; but it may prove to be the final and decisive assault on the planet's carrying capacity. Whether the planet's resources will permit future generations to attain this population level and to sustain it over the long term remains very much a controversial question. There may be general agreement that carrying capacity places absolute limits on populations of species other than *Homo sapiens*, and there may even be agreement that there are limits to human populations at certain times or in certain places. But there is no consensus about whether there is a general carrying capacity for the Earth as a whole that will some day restrict the number of humans who can live here at any given time. The complex interconnectedness of population, food, energy, land, climate, fossil fuel consumption, and many other variables makes such predictions extremely unreliable.[7]

One important reason why no consensus exists is that any answer to this question requires that we make choices that involve what one might term "the quality of life." Joel Cohen has identified a set of questions that must be addressed before one can estimate what the carrying capacity of the Earth might be.[8] These include the following: at what average level of material well-being do we wish to live; with what pattern of distribution of that material wealth; with what technology; with what domestic and international political, economic, and demographic arrangements; with what tastes and values; in what physical, chemical, and biological environments; with what degree of variability or stability; with what degree of risk or robustness (that is, how close to the edge of catastrophe do we want to get); and for how long.

Table 12.2 summarizes the various opinions one can hold on this issue and the policy implications that flow more or less inescapably from each of these. One can believe, for example, that the limits imposed by the Earth's carrying capacity are very real, and they will be reached soon, perhaps in the lifetime of people alive today, in which case zero-growth policies are called for immediately. Or one may believe that the very concept of a planetwide carrying capacity is fallacious—that technology, capitalism, the profit motive, and entrepreneurial innovation will always provide for those who live here, that a growing population is as much a stimulus for progress as it is a cause for alarm, and that zero-growth policies will never be needed, now or at any time in the future.

Table 12.2 **Policy Implications of Beliefs Regarding Earth's Carrying Capacity**

| | Does the Earth's carrying capacity limit population or economic growth? | |
	Yes	No
Limits are literally and absolutely real*	Policies to produce zero growth immediately	No policy limits on growth, now or ever
Limits are only "virtually" real**	Zero growth policies may be necessary someday in the distant future, but do not seem warranted today. Such policies may be implemented gradually as conditions warrant. However, there is a strong probability that . . .	
	such policies will be needed, so we should start moving in this direction now	technology will solve our problems, so there is no need to limit growth yet

Note: *Limits to growth will be physically reached either soon, or never. **While limits may be reached someday, that day is so far into the future and/or so uncertain that we cannot use this belief as a guide to responsible policy today.

There are those, however, who believe that the idea of carrying capacity exists as a kind of "virtual reality"; that is, there may be some kind of ultimate limit to population, but it is so uncertain or so far off into the future that the concept cannot provide us with a guide for reasonable and responsible policy choices to-day. What can it possibly mean to a policymaker to talk of sustaining population levels "indefinitely": one century, one millennium? If by "indefinite" one really means "forever," then no policy can accommodate that definition. Within these limits, one can argue that the probability is such that zero-growth policies will be needed someday, in which case we would be advised to begin now; or the alternative, that technology will probably solve most of our food, resource, and pollution problems for the medium term (say, 100 to 200 years), so we do not need to begin to restrict growth just yet. Implicit in these beliefs is the opinion that future generations will enjoy enough time to respond to the approach of onrushing limits, so we today do not need to sacrifice unduly in anticipation of a problem that can be solved later. While all sides in this dispute present data to buttress their position, what one believes depends significantly on values and intangibles like one's faith and intuition as much as on the historical and scientific evidence, a lot of which is (unfortunately) contradictory.

Much of the debate around carrying capacity and limits to growth turns on one's view of the time available to adapt. To say that we want a sustainable population "indefinitely" is operationally meaningless. To begin to operationalize such a concept, we might define "indefinitely" as meaning the time needed to secure another habitat—that is, sustaining our population long enough to mount a successful interplanetary or interstellar migration stream. The next sections of this chapter address how long that might be. If, as seems likely, the journey to other planets and eventually to the stars will require a very long time indeed to prepare, then we will need to sustain our population for more than simply a few generations or centuries. If this is the case, we need to take policy steps in the not-too-distant future that will not only reduce growth rates to zero but will actually begin to reduce the population itself.

Let us be clear about one thing: the exploration and colonization of space can never solve the population pressures on Earth. We will never possess the capacity to lift off the surface of our planet more than an extremely tiny fraction of its population at any one time. Virtually all the near-term interplanetary migration scenarios presume crews and passenger populations in the range of 10s to the low 100s, only approaching the range of 1,000 to 10,000 several hundred years into the colonization process. Under the most wildly optimistic scenarios, to transport as many as 1,000 or 10,000 people to another planet over the course of a decade seems to represent the absolute outer limits of our technology. Yet this feat would still transport only between 0.0001 and 0.00001 percent of a population currently growing at the rate of 1.5 to 2.0 percent each year and that is sure to exceed 10 billion before stabilizing. Thus, interplanetary and (especially) interstellar migration should be seen only as a way of preserving our species by colonizing distant worlds where our descendants can continue to live after our time here is over. While such a paradigm may make this topic even more speculative than it is already, by redefining the challenge in this way we free ourselves of more constraining time limits, since it is clear that we are dealing here with a "post-Earth" epoch that stretches tens to hundreds of millennia into the future.

MIGRATION TO THE PLANETS AND BEYOND

It is not difficult to find critics of proposals to colonize other worlds; some of the most passionate are those who believe that simply discussing such a possibility weakens our commitment to protect the Earth today and for the foreseeable future. These critics argue that proposals to go to Mars and beyond not only drain away scarce public resources from more immediate and pressing needs here at home, but also erode our resolve to be more responsible inhabitants of the world as it is today. They assert that if people really thought there was a chance to solve our population and consumption problems by simply going to another world, they would have no incentive to limit our numbers or to protect and clean up this habitat.

There are several responses to these criticisms that reconcile space exploration with population limitations and environmental protection.[9] First, we have to recognize the very real possibility that such an ambitious project as reshaping the surface of Mars or going to a planet circling another star is going to turn out to be simply beyond our technological capabilities, in which case we need to hedge our bets by treating this planet as gently as we can. Even if such projects are successful, we in this generation will never know it, given the enormous time lags between inception and successful completion. Second, even if these projects work, they will require a very long time to prepare, so we need to slow down current consumption rates to give ourselves and future generations the time and resources they need. And finally, what we learn from making the effort will help us greatly in our endeavors to protect and cherish the Earth for as long as we have to live on it. In engineering a new biosphere for Mars, or a new coevolved life system to sustain humankind on a distant world, we will learn more about how species fit together and how ecosystems function; this knowledge should improve our ability to care for the Earth today and for the next several centuries.

How much time it will take to colonize another world depends on which of two options we select. (We may, of course, choose to pursue both, in the belief that what we learn from one will help us achieve the other.) The near-term option (the first steps of which are attainable within a century or so) is to replicate an "Earth-like" environment capable of supporting life on another planet in our solar system. Mars is the obvious choice, and the technology is known as "terraforming." The long-term option (which we can begin within half a millennium or so) is to migrate to another star system with a planet capable of supporting ourselves and our coevolved life systems. To travel these long distances will require either achieving speeds approaching some significant percentage of that of light (probably not feasible for any payload that includes a large human population) or planning for a very long trip that will last many generations and be completed in stages.[10]

Advocates of these journeys assume that no known laws of physics make these voyages inherently impossible; and for us to go much beyond this point to examine in detail the engineering requirements of these options would take us far away from our central theme. To be able to assess the biological dimensions of interplanetary or interstellar colonization, however, we do need to know the distances to be traveled, the time required to do so (dependent on propulsion technologies) and whether the journey is round trip or one way; the cost per unit of weight of the trip; the total cost of a generic trip; the time required to build the technologies to accomplish the trip; the crew and passenger requirements (minima) and allowances (maxima); the degree to which the colonists can be supported from Earth or from some intermediate site (such as asteroid bases); any special hazards, dangers, or barriers that we need to plan for; and the degree of safety we wish to build into the technologies (a dimension not unrelated to the sense of urgency with which we undertake these adventures).

The Near-term Strategy: To Mars

On June 20, 1989, while celebrating the twentieth anniversary of the *Apollo 11* moon landing President George Bush announced a long-term agenda for the U.S.

space program, called the Space Exploration Initiative (SEI), that proposed putting an expedition on Mars sometime in the first decades of the twenty-first century. Later, he set the year 2019 as the target date for the Mars landing.[11]

Ever since the 1890s, when the American astronomer Percival Lowell misinterpreted the lines on the surface of the planet as "canals," Mars has fascinated generations of experts and lay observers. A century later, extensive reconnaissance of the solar system has confirmed that only Mars of all our neighboring planets offers even the remotest prospects for human colonization. But when the National Aeronautics and Space Administration (NASA) reported back to Bush that the trip would cost between $450 and $500 billion, the enormity of the project began to register, enthusiasm waned, and the idea was dropped.

In the late 1990s, however, NASA's interest in Mars was reawakened, partly because the cost estimates for a Mars mission dropped dramatically as researchers and engineers looked for less expensive ways of completing the expedition, especially in the areas of fuel and weight. Analysis of planetary orbits revealed that every twenty-six months between 1996 and 2005 Mars and Earth would be positioned in respect to each other so that reconnaissance trips requiring reasonable expenditures of fuel would be feasible; as a result, NASA planned for a series of flights, beginning in November and December 1996.[12] Russia also planned several flights in 1996 and 2001, and Japan scheduled a flight for 1998. The announcement in August 1996 by scientists at NASA and Stanford University that "unusual characteristics in a meteorite known to have come from Mars could most reasonably be interpreted as the vestiges of ancient Martian bacterial life"[13] excited the public's interest in Mars, as did the pictures relayed back to Earth from the Martian surface by the *Mars Pathfinder* television camera in July 1997. This flurry of excitement encouraged NASA administrators to announce a number of preliminary research projects directed at laying the groundwork for a Mars mission. NASA's goal was to be able to show the President and Congress by 2003 or 2004 how a mission to Mars might be accomplished within eight to ten years of a set starting date, and for a price tag in the range of $50 billion.

Planning for a Mars flight begins with the chief obstacle: distance.[14] Even at its closest approach, on average Mars is about a thousand times farther from Earth than is the moon, so a flight to Mars would last a thousand times longer than to the moon (about ten years, one way) if a spacecraft could achieve no more than the velocity of the Apollo flights. In fact, a Mars-bound ship could use the Earth's own velocity as a springboard, and thus could reduce the elapsed time of a Mars trip to between six months and a year, assuming that the craft traveled at a speed (relative to Earth) only two to three times that of the Apollo missions. Achieving these speed increases, however, is neither easy nor cheap, since each increase in final speed can be achieved only by adding extra fuel, that additional fuel adds weight, that weight requires additional fuel, and so on.

To raise the final speed of the craft to four times the exhaust speed of the propellant requires increasing fuel by a factor of more than thirty. This additional fuel requires a sturdier and heavier craft, and the result is that the weight of the ship and the fuel at launch has to be fifty-five times the weight of the ship without fuel. These restrictions dictate that, for ships powered by chemical propellant, speeds of three to four times the exhaust speed of the propellant define the upper limit.

Added to this dilemma are the interconnected problems of time and weight. Under optimal conditions, a round trip to Mars will last two to three years: six months or so in travel time each way, and approximately 500 days on the Martian surface. This latter parameter is determined not only by our desire to get our money's worth in research from such an expenditure, but also more importantly by the fact that travel between the two planets is feasible only when their solar orbits bring them together at their closest approach, which occurs every twenty-six months. To sustain a crew in the hazardous conditions of space (zero gravity and atmosphere; bombardment of radioactive particles) and the only slightly improved conditions of Mars requires a portable, light, robust habitat capable of providing the living and working quarters for four to six people. To deal with this, in the late 1990s NASA engineers began design of the "TransHab," an inflatable module encased in layers of puncture-resistant fabric similar to that used to make bullet-proof vests.[15] This module would be inflated in space, provide the living quarters for the astronauts both en route and on the Martian surface, and remain behind when the crew leaves, to be part of a series of modules that will eventually be connected to form a Mars colony. Despite major advances in lightweight materials and designs, the TransHab will still weigh five tons empty, and the food, water, and other essentials will add even more to the payload. (Astronauts and space colonists will each require about four kilograms of food and water per day. Much of this can be obtained by recycling; but most will have to be carried as payload.)

The real breakthrough in weight reduction was achieved (at least in theory) by the unveiling in the early 1990s of a radical new strategy for the Mars trip. The designer of this approach, rocket engineer Robert Zubrin, has asserted that "two of the most fundamental axioms of exploration are that it is necessary to have mobility, and that true mobility can only be obtained if the resources required to support it can be obtained from the environment whose exploration is desired."[16] In other words, Zubrin argues, space colonizers, like all colonizers before them, must "live off the land."

Zubrin's plan, known as "Mars Direct," eliminates the need to carry the fuel for the return trip to Earth.[17] Instead, Zubrin proposes using the Martian atmosphere, which is 95 percent carbon dioxide, to manufacture the fuel for the return trip. Several years before the astronauts are scheduled to leave Earth, a ship would be launched carrying the equipment to manufacture the fuel, plus a small quantity of hydrogen to react with the CO_2 to produce methane and water. The oxygen would be separated from the water, refrigerated, and stored; the hydrogen would be recycled; and the methane would be stored. By the time the astronauts arrived on Mars, the system would have produced 107 tons of oxygen-methane, enough fuel for the return trip. To leave Mars, the oxygen and methane would be mixed to yield the rocket's propellant. NASA has not endorsed Zubrin's plan, partly because it does not include any backup in case of system failure; but NASA engineers think enough of the idea that the Mars Surveyor lander scheduled for launch in 2001 will carry equipment to evaluate the Martian atmosphere as a source of rocket fuel. Other schemes for powering future flights are under investigation by NASA and may yield even better solutions for the critical propulsion problem.

The Long-term Strategy: To the Stars

Once we have determined to reach beyond the solar system in our search for new worlds, our tasks become much more daunting, principally because of the enormous distances to be traveled, the high speeds that must be achieved and sustained, the extraordinary spans of time that will be required, the costs of such an adventure, and the uncertainties and hazards surrounding the enterprise. If the Mars Direct plan stretches our imagination and challenges our credulity, talk of going to the stars can be dismissed as science fiction. Let us suspend judgment momentarily, however, to consider what exactly would be involved in such a journey, and how we would meet its biological challenges.

Let's begin with the most obvious: We do not know today where such a journey ought to go, or even whether there is a real destination "out there." That is, we do not have unequivocal evidence that there exists outside our solar system another planet capable of harboring life, or even one that could do so after a moderate degree of terraforming. In the 1970s, the advocates of space exploration and colonization argued that the extremely small probability of there being such a planet, and of our finding it among the literally billions of (quite distant) alternatives, precluded a "planet-focused" strategy. Our goal, they asserted, should be to build artificial worlds, enormous space stations on which millions of people could find a second home. More recently, scholars have returned to the planetary option, partly because they have found the space station option either too expensive or too confining, and partly because we are beginning to acquire information that suggests that other Earth-like planets might not be so rare after all.

Several scholars, including Martyn Fogg and Paul Halpern, have addressed in a theoretical way the question of what the destination of an intersellar colonization voyage should be. Fogg identifies three types of planets that might serve as our destination:

1. habitable planets, with an environment sufficiently similar to Earth to allow human habitation without the need for life-support systems
2. biocompatible planets, possessing the necessary physical properties (such as planetary mass, surface temperature, orbital eccentricities, liquid water, stellar illumination) for life to flourish on its surface even if life is not yet implanted there
3. easily terraformable planets, which might be rendered habitable by modest

planetary engineering techniques within the limited resources of a starship with about the size, resources, and population of a city-state.[18]

This last requirement, by the way, effectively rules out any Mars-like planets we might find around other stars. The terraforming of Mars will stretch to the limit the resources of Earth itself and would be quite beyond the capabilities of a single vessel at the end of an extremely long voyage.

Halpern has identified in somewhat more specific terms what we might look for to identify suitable planets.[19] He begins with the four characteristics that signal the stars most likely to support habitable planets:

1. They should be on what astronomers call the "Main Sequence"—that is, they should be stable in size, and burn hydrogen slowly and for a long span of time.
2. They should be of the right spectral class (type G), which burns steadily and brightly for billions of years.
3. They should be of the right age, about three to five billion years, old enough for the evolution of life on their planets, young enough to offer billions of years more of energy.
4. They should harbor the organic molecules from which living tissue is formed—carbon, nitrogen, oxygen, and iron.

A fifth criterion involves the distance of the planet from the star—that is, it should be within the "ecosphere" of the star, so that its surface temperature would yield liquid water, neither so cold as to freeze, nor so hot as to vaporize.

Halpern next looks at the physical characteristics of the planet itself. The planet's atmospheric conditions need to be taken into account: to what degree greenhouse gases are present, and how well-endowed is the atmosphere with oxygen, ozone, methane, and other gases associated with life-giving processes. Another consideration is the magnitude of their orbital eccentricities. Nearly circular orbits produce more even climatic conditions on the planet; oval orbits produce climates with extreme variations. Usually, planet hunters would avoid multiple stars because of the variations of the planetary orbits around them; but twin stars very close together may still harbor planets with more or less regular orbits. Two other factors astronomers consider are the planet's equatorial inclination (its slant relative to the star) and its rotation rate (spin). Extremely high values in either of these two criteria would likely produce a planetary climate of great extremes, not conducive to the evolution of life. The final physical criterion of the planet involves its mass. Huge planets the size of Jupiter would have a crushing gravity force; tiny planets would have too little gravity for life to take hold.

Once the parameters of the problem have been set forth in this way, our search for a destination can focus on the age of the star and of its planets, and on the distances between them. The age of the bodies is crucial. There was a time when the Earth was not habitable for humans because its atmosphere had too little oxygen and too much carbon dioxide, and there will come a time when it again will not be habitable because of the rising temperature from an aging and expanding Sun. Likewise, there was a time in the distant past when Mars was more easily terraformable than it is today—when the surface temperature was higher, and liquid water more readily available. These parameters—stellar and planetary ages, distances from star to planets—dictate the probability that a given star is circled by a biocompatible or easily terraformable planet.

Fogg applied these criteria by means of a computer program written to identify stars most likely to harbor Earth-like planets. Beginning rather arbitrarily with the one hundred thousand stars closest to Earth, he eliminated those that are multiple-star systems (twins or triplets), because their gravitational perturbances would prevent planets from forming, and very old and very young stars, because their planets would not be within the desired age range. After these deletions, his computer program still found 210 stars that could possess a habitable planet, 2,640 that could have a biocompatible planet, and 2,692 that could have an easily terraformable planet. Fogg then narrowed his scanning range to the 100 stars closest to Earth, the farthest of which is about twenty-two light-years away. Of these 100 stars, his program discovered fourteen that could possess planets suitable for colonization, and twenty-eight if we were to include multiple-star systems. From these data, Fogg concluded that the search for a planet for colonization is not exactly the "needle-in-a-haystack" adventure that earlier paradigms suggested.

In the past, it was not possible to gather and record visual images of extrasolar planets from Earth because the brilliance of the star overwhelms reflected light bouncing off the planet. In 1998, scientists using the Hubble Space Telescope recorded an image of what may be an extrasolar planet circling a star 450 light-years from Earth.[20] This discovery, if confirmed, raises significantly the prospects for finding another Earth-like planet somewhere in the cosmos.

For the most part, however, our search for extrasolar planets has employed techniques that focus on the signals they (or the civilizations they harbor) send out.[21] In 1960, a program known as the Search for Extraterrestrial Intelligence (SETI) began scanning the heavens in search of radio signals sent from distant planets; the hypothesis was that if civilizations exist on other worlds, they probably have invented devices for communicating via radio waves. During the 1960s and 1970s, there were about forty SETI searches in all, all severely limited in funding and in telescopic use time; but the total absence of results weakened public support for SETI. In the early 1980s, a group of well-known scientists led by Carl Sagan sought to promote SETI and lobbied to get Congress to fund additional searches. This increased support culminated in the launching in October 1992 of NASA's High Resolution Microwave Survey (HRMS) project. Within a year, however, Congress cut off all further funding for SETI. Since then, the searches have gone ahead with some modest private financial support, but in more than thirty-five years of systematic scanning, SETI has not detected even a single radio signal that could be identified unambiguously as the product of extraterrestrial intelligence.

There are other ways to pursue the objective, however. For over a decade, other astronomers have been looking for the signature of distant planets—not by finding the planet itself, but by observing its effects on other bodies in space. One of the best known and most productive of these techniques, known as astrometry, relies on the fact that when a star has a planet in orbit around it, the star tends to wobble back and forth. Because of their mutual gravitational pull, the planet attracts the star just as the star pulls on the planet. The result is a minute change in the star's position as the planet moves around it. By recording thousands of observations of the movement of a star over very long spans of time, astronomers can determine whether the star is wobbling, and whether an orbiting planet is the cause. Another technique, known as spectroscopy, concentrates on the observed spectrum of light produced by a star. It is known that that spectrum is affected by the star's motion relative to the observer. If the star is moving away from the viewer, the light is shifted in wavelength toward the red end of the spectrum; if the star is moving closer to the observer, the light is shifted toward the blue and violet end of the spectrum. By recording changes in the wavelength of a star's light, observers can detect stellar motion toward or away from their position.

The first success with astrometry came in early 1992 when Alexander Wolszczan, an astronomer working out of the Arecibo Observatory in Puerto Rico, detected a wobbling star with at least three planets in orbit around it. As the search continued, however, spectroscopy became the preferred technique, and in October 1995, astronomers Michel Mayor and Dider Queloz at the Geneva Observatory in Switzerland announced the first confirmed discovery of a planet orbiting a star like our sun.[22] The star, named 51 Pegasi, is about forty-eight light-years from Earth. Soon there was a succession of confirmations of other extrasolar planets, and by mid-1998 astronomers had confirmed the existence of at least twelve planets orbiting around stars similar to our sun, two of them only 35 light-years away—relatively close by cosmic standards.[23] At least as many more stars were thought to have planets around them, pending confirmation by additional data.

Bear in mind that simply finding an extrasolar planet does not confirm it as a suitable destination for interstellar colonists. To be capable of harboring life, the planet must circle a star similar to our sun and at about the same distance (between 95 and 115 percent) as our Earth is from the Sun. The planet must also resemble Earth in size and mass. Most of the planets so far discovered are far too large and massive; some of them are many times the size of Jupiter. Astronomers believe planets this large must be gaseous rather than solid and thus not biocompatible; but they may have rocky moons around them where a human colony could survive.

Even if we are able to detect extrasolar planets we think capable of supporting human life, the exceedingly difficult challenges lie in the distances to be traveled. The closest star that Fogg identified as a candidate for colonization is the twin star, Alpha Centauri, some 4.38 light-years away. If it turns out that twin stars cannot harbor planets, then the next closest is Epsilon Eridani, 10.69 light-years distant from Earth. So far, the closest confirmed extrasolar planets are thirty-five to forty light-years away. There are, as Gordon Woodcock puts it, only three ways to travel such distances: fly slow (a multigeneration voyage), fly fast (achieve and sustain speeds some appreciable percentage of that of light), or fly tricky (meaning to invoke some scheme currently known only in science fiction, such as spacewarp, using black holes, or travel in other dimensions).[24]

Common sense dictates that we discard the "tricky" options and concentrate on flying "fast" or "slow." Carl Sagan, for one, believed that human civilization may be approaching traveling at the speed of light in the next several centuries.[25] In the twentieth century alone, we have increased the speed of transport by a factor of 3,000, from 10 miles per hour for early automobiles to 30,000 miles per hour for the *Voyager* spacecraft (see figure 12.1, above). Simple extrapolation of any of several recent growth curves suggests that our descendants will approach the speed of light in the next 100 to 600 years (see figure 12.1, below). If we do manage to accomplish such a feat, then travel to the stars within the lifetime of the crew

Figure 12.1 Recent Trends in the Speed of Transportation, Extrapolated into the Future

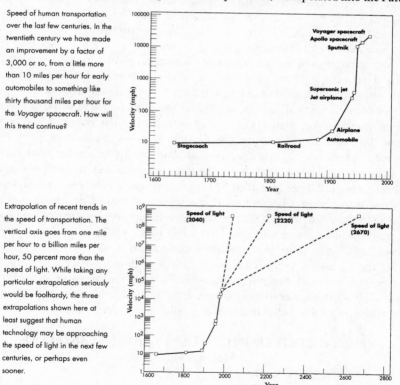

Source: Carl Sagan, *Pale Blue Dot: A Vision of the Human Future in Space* (New York: Random House, 1994), p. 396. © Estate of Carl Sagan. Reprinted by permission.

becomes imaginable. At a speed half that of light, the journey to the closest detected extrasolar planet would require about seventy years, probably within the life expectancy of people born half a millennium into the future. It is obvious, though, that these are one-way trips undertaken solely for colonizing purposes.

To achieve sustainable speeds three or four orders of magnitude greater than the highest achieved to date will require novel propulsion technologies that exist today only in the imagination of space-travel engineers (and science-fiction writers).[26] The chief goal with all these inventions is to employ a fuel much lighter and less massive than the chemical propellants that today's spacecraft use. Nuclear fusion, for example, offers the promise of such a propellant, but a workable fusion reactor is still decades away, and some engineers are skeptical that it can ever be made to work, at least on the scale required for a spacecraft. Another plan is to use antimatter particles to trigger a fusion reaction of deuterium and tritium (heavy forms of hydrogen), but these reactions, equivalent to millions of tons of TNT, cannot yet be contained in a combustion chamber. Other exotic plans include solar sails (huge sheets of aluminum spread out to catch the hydrogen atoms streaming out from the sun in plasma form), laser sails (a similar technology, using huge mirrors to concentrate a laser beam on a sail), or solar-electric engines (using solar cells to convert sunlight to electricity, which is used to ionize and accelerate a nonreactive gas such as xenon).

Some barriers to flying fast cannot be overcome, however, no matter what propulsion technology we devise. Energy requirements are one. Accelerating a spacecraft with astronauts aboard to one-third light speed will require a power output roughly equivalent to all the power generating plants on Earth working together for several years. Any plan to send a ship outside our solar system would require a space infrastructure of power plants, factories, asteroid-mining operations, housing for workers in deep space, and so on. And finally, no matter what sorts of propellants engineers may devise in the distant future, they will still not be able to overcome the barrier identified by Einstein: as velocity increases, so does mass. With each increment of acceleration, the spacecraft and its occupants and payload all become heavier. By the time the craft reaches three-quarters of light speed, its mass will have increased to one and a half times what it was when it started. Increasing the thrust yields virtually no acceleration at all.

For these reasons, flying fast is not a realistic option. If we want to think seriously about interstellar colonization, we will have to face the prospects of flying slow, with a multigenerational voyage. How such an adventure will affect the population of humans that undertakes it will be considered in the next section.

THE BIOLOGY OF INTERPLANETARY/INTERSTELLAR MIGRATION

The colonization of space will present our descendants with many questions: The first concern is population: How many crew and passengers can be transported?

According to what criteria will they be selected? How should they organize a trip that will last much longer than the life span of the original colonists? How will the colonists' population grow and evolve over the long term? What about food: How will food be grown in low-gravity environments where space and weight are severe constraints? What will be the principal food sources for space colonists? What kind of diet will they have? Then there are the biological issues: Which species should they take with them as parts of their coevolved life systems? How do they keep those organisms alive and functioning during the trip and the adjustment time when they reach the new world? How will terrestrial species interact with the indigenous species (if there are any)? Over the very long term, what will be the biological relationships between the colonists and the descendants of the people who remain on Earth? And don't forget the issues related to diseases: How can the colonists be protected from microörganisms on the new world? How can organisms on the new planet be protected from terrestrial microörganisms? What should colonists do to ensure that pathogens do not accompany them? If germs do get aboard, how will colonists deal with epidemics under the stressful conditions of life in space?

While these problems are certainly not easy to solve, those associated with the transport of human populations to Mars, the cultivation of their food crops, and their protection from diseases do not seem insurmountable. Interstellar migration, however, presents much more serious challenges. In either case, terraforming (that is, the deliberate intervention by humans to alter a planet's ecosystem to render it habitable for them) raises many of the issues in the creation and maintenance of life systems that people have confronted throughout the process of globalization.

Population

Early advocates of space colonization took it for granted that travel to other planets and eventually to the stars was possible, and they believed that our civilization would expand so long as there were exploitable resources available that would enable it to do so.[27] Four possible barriers were seen to space colonization:

1. physical limits, such as distance and the time required to travel between planets
2. a loss of motivation, accompanied by a desire to live within a no-growth society here on Earth
3. self-inflicted disasters such as warfare or ecological catastrophes
4. contact with other civilizations, whose members resisted our expansion.[28]

But few forecasters actually believed that these forces were powerful enough to prevent humans permanently from migrating across the reaches of space.

One early proposal for space settlement was that of Gerard O'Neill who, in the early 1970s, foresaw the construction of extremely large habitats in space to accommodate up to twenty million people apiece.[29] Each habitat would be up to four miles in diameter and twenty miles long, and would have a land area of about seven thousand square miles. Each structure would supply its own food, and its people would enjoy a varied environment that featured forests, rivers, lakes, animals, and even its own weather. Indeed, life in such surroundings would be so attractive that within two centuries, O'Neill believed, more people would be living in space than on Earth. Other researchers estimated the carrying capacity of our sun and its planets, asteroids, and other bodies in the solar system as sufficient to support a human population of 10^{21}, or a sextillion.[30] At a historical rate of growth of 0.5 percent a year, this population would be reached in only 5,400 years, a span of time similar to that which separates us today from the Bronze Age. Expansion beyond the limits of our solar system would be accompanied by similar population explosions, spread out over much longer spans of time, of course.

In Robert Zubrin's Mars Direct plan, colonists would begin to travel to Mars on a regular basis about twenty-five years after the initial exploration.[31] Without relying on any exotic or futuristic technologies for propulsion, dwellings, or life support, Zubrin envisions spacecraft that could transport twenty-four people to Mars on a one-way trip, and he believes that four such trips could easily be made each year. With 100 or so colonists making the trip each year, divided evenly between male and female, and all migrants between ages of twenty and forty, a population growth rate of 2 percent annually would not be unrealistic. If the fertility rate of "Martian" women were 3.5, then the population of the colony would pass the 10,000 mark about 40 years after its founding, and the 100,000 mark a little more than a century after original settlement, or only 150 years or so after the first humans walk on the Martian surface. Such a population growth rate compares favorably with the expansion of the colonial population in North America in the seventeenth century.

When it comes to interstellar migration, the challenges and obstacles rise substantially. Recent assessments have scaled down considerably the ability of humans to find other habitats beyond our solar system. As Carl Sagan explains,

> Our universe is *almost* incompatible with life—or at least what we understand as necessary for life: Even if every star in a hundred billion galaxies had an Earthlike planet, without heroic technological measures life could prosper in only about 10^{-37} the volume of the Universe. . . .The rest is cold, radiation-riddled black vacuum.[32]

If the places in the universe that can harbor human life and civilization are so few and far between, and if we can assume that reaching these places by "flying fast" will forever remain technologically infeasible, then "flying slow" in a multigenerational voyage becomes the only feasible strategy.

A voyage that will require centuries to complete can be contemplated only if there are intermediate resources, "rest stops" along the way, where the colonists can pause for a time to refuel before resuming their journey. Indeed, many writers assume that interstellar migration will begin with the exploration of the bodies that Sagan calls "rogue worldlets": the near-Earth asteroids.[33] Using a diameter of one kilometer as the bottom cut-off point, Sagan estimates that there are several million asteroids in interplanetary space, none larger than one thousand kilometers across. Some are rocky, others metallic, still others rich in organic matter. Many contain abundant quantities of ice, from which water can be extracted; others possess methane or ammonium deposits from which nitrogen can be extracted to aid the terraforming of Mars. And many have orbits that colonists can exploit to "hitch a ride" to the deeper recesses of the solar system, thus saving precious fuel.

The migration of large populations across space in journeys that will last for many generations raises the question of how to sustain such populations.[34] We have to assume that such a trip is one way—that the colonists will leave Earth fully aware that they will never return. The enormous distances and times to be spanned by such a voyage under any conceivable circumstances make a return trip out of the question. Even going only one way, the challenges will be difficult enough.

For one-way interstellar travelers, one possible solution lies in time dilation.[35] Einstein showed that time moves more slowly aboard a craft as it nears the speed of light, so colonists traveling through space at high speed would age more slowly than they would on Earth. Colonists en route to the planet around 51 Pegasi, for example, at an average speed about 99 percent that of light would age only about three years even though the trip would last more than forty. Recall, however, the problems raised by traveling near light speed: as speed increases, so does mass. To achieve a reduction in aging, colonists must pay a huge price in the propellant necessary to fuel a craft whose mass is increasing at the same time.

Another possible solution may lie in cryonics: the deep freezing of human bodies with the intention of reviving them as the craft nears its destination. At very cold temperatures, human tissue does not deteriorate, so space colonists might survive the trip by going to sleep for most of the journey, to be awakened near the end by some automatic device or robot. This solution would have the additional benefit of reducing the consumables aboard the craft, such as food, water, and oxygen.

A third solution would be to transport not the actual humans themselves but their embryos, sperm and eggs, or perhaps merely their DNA, to be fertilized and "born" once the destination is within, say, twenty years of arrival time. Such a solution would have to provide for the care of the newborns for the two decades they would have to grow and mature before they could assume responsibility for themselves and their craft, to teach them what they need to know as space colonists, and so forth.[36]

All the foregoing "solutions" are only speculation, because they all require the development of technologies not yet available or even contemplated to be available within the next several centuries.[37] Therefore, a multigenerational voyage to the stars will probably be carried out by the much simpler method of breeding

generation after generation of the population aboard the space ship. But this solution, while technologically simpler, carries its own peculiar kind of social and
ethical problems.

What would be the minimum size of the population that could undertake and
successfully complete such an extraordinary voyage? While such a trip would be
possible only after we have learned much by colonizing much closer worlds, the
survival of the crew and passengers would still rely heavily on their ability to
manage an extremely complex, high-technology society. As Gordon Woodcock
observes, "We must take along enough skills and knowledge to operate, repair,
rebuild, replicate, and improve all of the machinery and equipment we need to
live and prosper, perhaps on a moon-like body."[38] Woodcock estimates that a
minimum of ten thousand people would be needed to sustain such a huge enterprise and be biologically self-sustaining themselves.

The small size of the original population of space colonists, and their permanent separation from any other population, raises issues of genetic inheritance,
selection, and evolution. For example, some observers believe that a major concern early on will be the "founder effect," the skewing of the genetic composition
of a population because its founding members are very few.[39] There is a danger
that the founding members may share deleterious genes that will increase in the
population through interbreeding. Screening of the population to maximize genetic variation has been suggested as one way to ensure the future healthy growth
of the colonist population; others have proposed very strict taboos, legal or merely
cultural, against marriage and breeding between close relatives. At the rate scientists are increasing their knowledge of the human genome, our descendants will
certainly possess the knowledge necessary to sustain the genetic variability and
health of a population of space migrants, but the social and political intrusion
into their personal lives may come to resemble that of a police state. Perhaps space
colonists will come to view genetic engineering as a natural component of their
civilization, but if not, managing the interpersonal tensions that arise from these
restrictions may prove to be one of the chief issues confronting multigenerational
journeys through space.

It may be, however, that these fears are unwarranted, and that the founder effect can be avoided even with an initial population as small as ten persons. An-
thropologist Joseph Birdsell points out that there have been historical cases of
colonization by extremely small founding populations, such as those that settled
isolated islands in the Pacific Ocean, where genetic diversity was maintained even
though the members of the population did not possess much knowledge of genetics.[40] He maintains that in real populations, biological inbreeding (that is, the
mating of close relatives) occurs very infrequently, that very few individuals are
affected, and the impact is negligible. Birdsell does caution, however, that space
colonists will have to be carefully screened to ensure that no harmful recessive
genes are present. Blood types could be screened to select only persons with O
type (so they could be universal donors and recipients) and Rh positive (to avoid

problems during pregnancy and birth experienced by an Rh-negative woman carrying an Rh-positive child).

Finally, the migration of large numbers of people out of our solar system raises the question of speciation, and thus exposes the fundamental irony of interstellar colonization.[41] Ever since Darwin, biologists have known that new species arise when a population is separated in such a way that the two resulting populations may no longer interbreed and thereby mix their genes.[42] As time passes and each population experiences the differing pressures of natural selection, they grow apart biologically, until finally they become so different that they could not interbreed and produce fertile offspring even if they were reunited once again. For many generations there may exist intermediate cases, individuals whose ability to interbreed is ambiguous—that is, they may be able to interbreed but just not want to do so. Over time, these cases will disappear, leaving two groups that are in fact reproductively isolated, two species where only one had been before.

In his 1994 book, *Pale Blue Dot*, Carl Sagan wrote that "every surviving civilization is obliged to become spacefaring—not because of exploratory or romantic zeal, but for the most practical reason imaginable: staying alive."[43] The supreme irony is that *Homo sapiens*, in order to save itself, must go to live on some distant world where, separated from its parent population, its members will inevitably evolve into a species with different characteristics. Thus, to save our species means to redefine its nature in ways impossible to predict, to change it into something that is not *Homo sapiens*. Of course, the same thing will happen to all of our companions in the coevolved life system that has served us so well for ten millennia.

Food

It is interesting to look back at early forecasts of life in space, when such adventures still belonged to the realm of science fiction, and to contrast these descriptions with the challenges faced today by NASA and university researchers and others who are trying to design and build actual systems to support space-faring populations. For example, one forecaster in the mid-1970s thought that growing food in space would be so easy that future Earth populations might be fed with crops and animals raised in outer space.[44] Space-based farms could grow not only cereal grains such as wheat and maize, but also poultry and pork. The raw materials, including water, nitrogen, and oxygen, could be obtained by mining the asteroids; and closed ecosystems could be designed so as to control the length of growing seasons, pests, diseases, drought, and other forces that limit agricultural productivity on Earth. Power would be generated by solar power stations mounted on satellites. The food to support six billion people would require about half a million square kilometers, which would represent about 5×10^{10} tons of asteroidal material. Such an enormous structure (or, more likely, structures) could be built, according to this vision, for not much more than it would cost for irrigation and agricultural development in the Third World between the 1970s and 2000.

We now understand that the task of growing food for space colonists will be neither so easy nor so cheap. Consider, for starters, the availability of water.[45] To sustain human life, at least two quarts of drinking water are required each day, much more if the individual is engaged in heavy work and is sweating profusely. But water is also heavy (two quarts weigh about four pounds) and cumbersome to handle, especially in a weightless environment. Researchers believe that water is abundant on Mars and the asteroids, but it is locked up in places and forms that are inaccessible to us given current or near-term technologies. Fortunately, humans produce considerable water as part of their metabolic processes. NASA engineers have been working on regenerative life-support systems that use microbes to clean waste water before it is filtered through a conventional reverse-osmosis purification system. In December 1997, NASA completed a ninety-one day experiment in which four participants lived in a sealed chamber with only their own recycled waste water to drink. The biological system recovered 99 percent of the waste water. Of the 210 gallons originally loaded, the filter system eventually processed a total of 2,300 gallons.[46]

The production of food in space or on Mars confronts researchers with problems that derive not only from the peculiar conditions under which colonists will have to work but from the special dietary requirements of astronauts as well.[47] For people forced to live in cramped, monotonous quarters for long periods, food takes on a special meaning as one of the few sources of variety in daily life. Astronauts must have a special diet that is low in sodium in order to reduce salt in the urine that is recycled to irrigate food crops, but also because salt accelerates bone loss. Astronauts need more vitamin D than people on Earth, but less iron. Meals must be high in calcium to offset bone loss under conditions of weightlessness; and the food must be especially attractive since space dwellers must eat well to maintain their general overall health. In particular, spices must be increased since one's taste buds tend to become less sensitive in space.

Because of space and weight constraints, Mars colonists must be fed with food made from plants grown in microgravity hydroponic gardens, probably under the light of high-pressure sodium lamps. Animals cannot be a part of a space-based food system, since they compete with humans for oxygen, water, and living space; and the disposal of animal wastes would place extra burden on waste recycling systems. So diets will be not just vegetarian but vegan—that is, eschewing even dairy products. Plants that require insects to pollinate them cannot be used either, since astronauts will not want to share a cramped space station with bees or other pollinating insects. Other plants will have to be genetically engineered to accommodate a space environment: for example, dwarf varieties with shorter growing seasons and shorter stalks to fit into a confined space, plants adaptable to light-dark cycles that differ from Earth's twenty-four-hour period. In addition, many plants we will want to grow in space are gravity dependent—they need to extend their roots "down" and their stalks "up." In a weightless environment, such plants may not adapt well, so they may have to be genetically engineered.

One major problem to be overcome involves the simple food ingredient of sugar. Americans typically consume between 100 and 125 grams of sugar a day; astronauts have been weaned to need only 50 or so grams. But the customary plant sources of sugar, such as cane, are not amenable to hydroponic culture, and honey requires bees; so plans now are for sugar to be part of the spaceship's payload. For a crew of ten on a three-year mission, this adds up to more than half a ton of sugar. Cooking oil has also proven to be a problem, and extracting oil from peanuts grown in hydroponic culture has not been promising. Research into feeding a Mars colony is in its initial stages, but so far the diet appears to be restricted to wheat, potatoes, sweet potatoes, soy, peanuts, common beans (lentils), chard, cabbage, lettuce, tomatoes, carrots, quinoa (the Andean grain), rice, and assorted other vegetables.

NASA has begun several collaborative projects with university researchers to design food production and processing systems for space facilities and colonies on Mars and the moon. In May 1996, NASA established a research center in New Jersey to investigate and solve problems associated with a bioregenerative life-support system (BLSS).[48] This center, staffed by researchers from Rutgers University and Stevens Institute of Technology, is charged with designing a food-producing system that is self-renewing and depends on recycling of oxygen and water; nature itself is the model for such a system. Natural processes using plants and microbes will replace the energy-intensive life-support systems currently used in spacecraft. Plants will replace technology to clean the air, produce food and drinking water, and break down wastes. The center's goal is to build a system that can operate for years without resupply.

Once the food is grown, it must be turned into meals for astronauts and space colonists. Researchers at Cornell University began working in 1997 on a three-year project funded by NASA to devise menus for Mars colonists that use almost no foods imported from Earth, are easy to prepare, and meet taste tests for palatability. NASA guidelines allow utilization of Earth-based food to supply between 10 and 15 percent of caloric requirements, but most of these foods are for "celebration meals" like Thanksgiving turkey. After a year of research, Cornell's nutritionists were able to boast that they had kept the Earth-based food percentage down to only 5 percent of the total in their meals.

Experiments in growing food in space have been taken into a space environment as well. American astronaut Shannon Lucid, during her six-month stay aboard the Russian space station Mir, carried out an experiment in growing wheat in a greenhouse in one of the station's modules.[49] Lucid planted the dwarf variety wheat in a bed of zeolite, an absorbent granular material. Light and moisture were applied under the control of a computer program. The mature plants were harvested, and their seed heads returned for analysis. When researchers at Utah State University opened the heads, however, they found them all empty. They speculated that low levels of ethylene in the atmosphere of the space station may have interfered with the ripening of the wheat seeds.

Disease

Diseases are seldom treated in discussions of life in space;[50] in fact, death in general is a topic almost never raised, a remarkable oversight given its inescapable nature. Such a blind spot in visions of the future reveals a lot about the conception many people have of off-Earth living: clean, hygienic, devoid of the pestilences and misery we have had to endure on our home planet. Whether space colonists can achieve such a degree of collective health remains to be determined.

No doubt extraordinary measures will be taken to ensure that space travelers do not suffer from communicable diseases. As Harry Stine describes it, "Space facilities are the healthiest of all human living situations and must be maintained that way."[51] The isolated and enclosed nature of the migrating space community makes public-health measures not just important but essential to the survival of the entire population. Illnesses, especially of epidemic magnitude, must be prevented at all cost. All space travelers will be assigned critical operational and maintenance responsibilities, and it is unlikely that there will be enough people aboard to have replacements for anyone who falls ill. If an epidemic were to gain a foothold in a small self-contained population like that of a spaceship, it could very easily destroy the colony either outright or by so weakening the population that the travelers would be unable to keep their vessel in working order. The experience of Amerindians when confronted with the pathogens of Europeans demonstrates vividly the fate of such a population.

Candidates for the journeys to Mars or to the stars will be subjected to a rigorous physical screening to ensure they do not carry in their genes some predisposition to maladies such as diabetes or glaucoma. But defense against the introduction of micröorganisms into the colony will require additional procedures. All candidates will have to be placed in long-term quarantine before being allowed on board. Even then, pathogens may still sneak aboard in cargo, hair, clothing, skin, or gut: The human body, awash with bacteria and viruses, is one of the most difficult of all objects to sterilize. And since many bacteria are not only helpful but absolutely essential to human health, we will not want to destroy these. But many micröorganisms can hide deep within organs like the liver or the gut—even in parts of the immune system itself—and escape detection.

Personal and environmental hygiene will have to receive the highest priority, as will the treatment and recycling of human waste. There will be strict limits on the other organisms that can be brought aboard with the colonists, and only those absolutely necessary for survival, such as food crops, will be allowed. (Prevention of the introduction of pathogens is another reason why animals will not be included in the food-production system.) Some accounts stress that space is a good environment for manufacturing pharmaceuticals, so there should be no shortage of medicines and drugs, but there will be no way to prepare for the rapid mutation of a pathogen once it enters the human body. A drug designed to defeat a strain of influenza on Earth in the 1990s will be of little use to an isolated population confronted with a mutated strain in space a century later.

Some critics of space exploration have cautioned against exposing Earth organisms to the micröorganisms of other planets, a threat known as "back contamination." Without any experience with, or resistance to, extraterrestrial micröorganisms, humans will be supremely vulnerable to infections for which there is no cure. Of course, the potential threat runs the opposite direction as well: extraterrestrial beings unfamiliar with micröorganisms we take for granted, like bacteria in our gut, will be at risk from infections from our microparasites.

Robert Zubrin calls the fear of back contamination "not only illusory, but hallucinatory."[52] He reasons that Martian or extrasolar micröorganisms, if they exist, will have evolved in an environment so unlike that of Earth, and in the company of host organisms so unlike the fauna of Earth, that they could not possibly penetrate the immune-system defenses of the human body. "This is why," he writes, "humans do not catch Dutch elm disease, and trees do not catch colds." And the differences between possible extraterrestrial micröorganisms and humans will be much greater than any differences between humans and trees.

Still, prudence and a respect for alien life dictate that space colonists approach the organisms of other worlds with extreme caution, at least until they are sure that Zubrin is right. In 1998, NASA issued a set of guidelines for treating with extreme caution any life forms encountered on probes looking for extraterrestrial life on nearby bodies such as the moons of Jupiter. The report concluded:

> The risks of pathogenicity from putative life forms are extremely low because it is highly unlikely that extraterrestrial organisms could have evolved pathogenic traits in the absence of host organisms. However, because there are examples of opportunistic pathogens from terrestrial and aquatic environments that have not coevolved with their hosts, the risks cannot be described as zero.[53]

Terraforming

Terraforming is the ultimate expression of the construction by human beings of a coevolved life system whose purpose is the sustenance of human life. Martyn Fogg, the author of the standard text on the subject, defines "terraforming" as

> a process of planetary engineering specifically directed at enhancing the capacity of an extraterrestrial planetary environment to support life. The ultimate in terraforming would be to create an unconstrained [i.e., one without artificial enclosures—RPC] planetary biosphere emulating all the functions of the biosphere of the Earth—one that would be fully habitable for human beings.[54]

In the opinion of some, humans have been engaged in a version of terraforming since the Neolithic Revolution some ten thousand years ago, using our own Earth as the object of transformation.[55] But this experience has been much less challenging than what awaits us on Mars or beyond our solar system because our ancestors were given a planet to work with that was already abundantly endowed with life forms, and they had plenty of time in which to experiment with species of plants and animals and their interconnections.

Our first true experiment in terraforming, called Biosphere 2, took place in the Sonora Desert of Arizona, and its results were not encouraging.[56] This eight-story laboratory constructed of glass and steel at a cost of $200 million (funded by Texas oil billionaire Edward Bass) was intended to test the limits of human knowledge about how ecosystems are organized and how they function. The habitat's three acres were divided into several zones for intensive farming, plus other zones given over to desert, grasslands, and rainforest. The rainforest was stocked with more than 300 plant species from the Amazon, and a coral reef was flown in from the Caribbean to equip the miniature ocean. Pieces of the Everglades marsh were brought in trucks for the wetlands, and the desert was stocked with plants from Israel, Namibia, and Chile. Construction began in 1984, and the project's eight scientists entered its sealed environment in September 1991. When they emerged two years later, it was not in triumph but in defeat, for Biosphere 2 had turned into an ecological nightmare.

The goal of Biosphere 2 was to place humans and four thousand other species of plants and animals into a closed life-support system that would receive nothing from the outside world except sunlight. The complexities of biological interaction soon confronted researchers with severe and unexpected problems. While researchers had concentrated on plant assemblages, they had given little thought to gas exchange, and this oversight eventually doomed the project. Oxygen levels fell by one-third, largely because the microbes in the soil were working harder than expected, consuming more oxygen and producing more carbon dioxide. Eventually, pure oxygen had to be pumped into the habitat to keep its occupants alive. Carbon dioxide levels rose much more quickly than expected, and plants intended to soak up the CO_2 grew wildly, eventually overrunning food crops. Morning glory flowers were particularly problematic; since no animals that eat them had been included in the habitat, they quickly took over much of the farm area. For the humans, CO_2 scrubbers had to be installed to keep the air breatheable. Large trees became brittle and prone to collapse. Nineteen of the twenty-five vertebrate species went extinct, as did all the pollinators, which doomed many plants to eventual extinction as well. Most insects died except for those hardy survivors, cockroaches and ants. Air temperatures soared higher than expected, the light filtering through the glass panes was dimmer than expected, and too much rain turned the desert into grasslands. As grasses invaded the desert, its native species were all crowded out. The crop soil become contaminated with a pathogenic nematode, a tiny worm that ate crop roots (since this pest is unknown elsewhere in Arizona, the site was placed under quarantine by the State Department of Agriculture). When the scientists finally emerged from the building in 1993, they had lost on average more than ten kilograms apiece and some of them had become quite ill.

After three years of neglect, Biosphere 2 was taken over by Columbia University to be used for experiments in the ecology of global warming. To restore the facility to usefulness required more than a year of work and $45 million. But the habitat stands today as a monument to our ignorance of many of the complexities of ecosystem operations. As one consultant to the project put it, "Biosphere 2 taught us we're not quite ready to manage the planet."

Clearly, terraforming is substantially beyond the technologies and engineering knowledge that Earth's civilization possesses today, but its proponents believe that many of its fundamental principles are grounded in current scientific understanding. The advocates of terraforming assert that most of the problems associated with it are questions of engineering, not of basic science: We know enough to be able to do most of these things, even if we lack the technological capabilities to achieve them today.

Martyn Fogg identifies several categories of life-support systems, ranging from "open-loop" systems (virtually completely resupplied from external sources) and environmentally closed systems (those in which essentials such as air and water are recycled within the facility), to small and large contained biospheres (facilities with artificial enclosures, large enough to house multiple ecosystems and even to experience their own weather, including cloud formations and rain, among other things), to, finally, uncontained biospheres such as present-day Earth, where everything is recycled (except sunlight), and all components are kept in place by the force of gravity.[57] The goal of terraforming is to enable the colonists of a distant world to make the transition from open and closed life-support systems to uncontained biospheres so that they can live, work, and move about unimpeded. Ideally, the new biosphere should be reliant principally on free energy (from sunlight), self-contained (especially in energy), self-replicating, self-maintaining, self-stabilizing, autonomous, and aesthetically pleasant to live in.

How to transform a lifeless planet like Mars into an uncontained biosphere capable of supporting a large population of human beings presents challenges to engineering far beyond anything yet achieved here on Earth.[58] But the first step toward achieving the goals of terraforming is to free onself from the constraints of a limited imagination, which Fogg's research is intended to do.

The work of terraforming Mars begins with what we know about the planet's atmosphere (thin and mostly carbon dioxide) and temperature (cold).[59] It is believed the planet's climate is unstable, and with a modest push from the outside, some of its latent resources an be freed to begin a self-sustained process of change. The critical "nudge," they believe, is to warm up the southern polar ice cap, which will release CO_2 into the atmosphere, which in turn will initiate a runaway greenhouse effect. Several options have been proposed for achieving this warming, but the least intrusive into the Martian landscape is to place a mirror 125 kilometers in diameter in space about 214,000 kilometers from the planet's surface. Aluminum to produce this gigantic device could be mined from asteroids and then steered into position using solar sailing. Since the foil will be tissue-paper thin, the mirror will weigh only about 200,000 tons—about the same as a supertanker on Earth. In the span of perhaps a few decades, the southern polar cap will have melted, yielding a thicker carbon dioxide atmosphere, which in turn will warm the surface even more. As the permafrost begins to melt, more CO_2 will be released, and the greenhouse effect will be strengthened. If need be, factories can be set up on Mars to manufacture other greenhouse gases, such as chlorofluorocarbons (CFCs). Along with rising temperatures will come a release of liquid waster now locked up in the planet's substantial stores of ice, and little by little Mars will become a wet planet again.

Terraformers now split into two camps. One group would halt human intervention at this point, leaving Mars to regenerate its own biosphere through its own processes. If there were long-dormant Martian organisms in the soil, they would presumably respond to these changes. If not, then organisms not needing oxygen could be introduced from Earth. This level of planetary engineering, known as "ecopoiesis" (the birth of an ecosystem), would still leave Mars far short of supporting human life.

The second group of terraformers advocates the application of much higher levels of technology to accelerate the processes of change on Mars, leading relatively quickly to an atmosphere capable of supporting complex plants, animals, and eventually humans. For this, oxygen levels would have to increase, and essential gases like nitrogen would need to be introduced. These changes would require much higher levels of energy (one estimate of the requirements is about twice the total energy produced on Earth in a year), and the techniques proposed to acquire and direct this energy all represent enormous challenges to engineering. Fogg admits that "the most fundamental assumption" of terraforming involves energy supplies: Can Earth's civilization generate sufficient energy surpluses above what it needs for its own uses to invest in planetary engineering while at the same time acquiring additional energy resources from Mars itself and other sources in the solar system?[60]

To accomplish the tasks of this second stage, Fogg advocates what he calls a "synergic scenario," some combination of mirrors in orbit: a huge lens to focus the sun's rays, production of additional greenhouse gases, and bombardment of Mars with either hydrogen bombs or asteroids, or both.[61] After several centuries of this treatment, the Martian atmosphere could reach the point where it could be seeded with simple plants such as mosses or lichens, which could then begin to produce tiny amounts of oxygen. Complex plants would follow, and then, perhaps a millennium or two later, animals.

Critics and skeptics of terraforming are abundant. Some believe that such ideas are simply science fiction dressed up with the jargon and data of science; others criticize the economic illogic of the scheme (who could possibly want to pay the enormous price of planetary engineering?) or its insensitivity to ethical concerns (what right do we humans have to rearrange Mars or some other world just to suit our purposes?). But the proponents of terraforming shrug off these criticisms as tangential to their main concern: How could our descendants achieve such a huge task, one that will be essential to the survival of our civilization?

As if the terraforming of Mars were not enough, its advocates see our neighboring planet as only the beginning. What engineers learn on Mars would be applied millennia hence on other worlds by interstellar migrants. Indeed, some modest degree of terraforming seems virtually essential to any strategy to carry our civilization away from Earth. If our descendants are restricted to only those very few worlds that already possess an Earth-like biosphere, then the challenges of interstellar migration rise to even more daunting levels. We can only hope that by the time our descendants achieve the technological maturity necessary to reconstruct the ecosystem of a planet in orbit around some distant star, they will have learned to appreciate and care for Earth as well. If not, the biological tragedies that have accompanied the process of globalization will simply be repeated on other worlds for a very long time into the future.

NOTES

1. Deborah Franklin, "The Successful Animal," *Science* 86 (January/February 1986): 55–59.

2. Paul Colinvaux, *Why Big Fierce Animals Are Rare: An Ecologist's Perspective* (Princeton: Princeton University Press, 1978), chapter 18.

3. Bill McKibben, "A Special Moment in History," *Atlantic Monthly* (May 1998); pp. 55–78.

4. Sally Morgan, *Ecology and Environment: The Cycles of Life* (New York: Oxford University Press, 1995), p. 21.

5. Joel Cohen, *How Many People Can the Earth Support?* (New York: Norton, 1995), chapter 12; Joel Cohen, "Maximum Occupancy," *American Demographics* (February 1996): 44–51; Garret Hardin, *Living within Limits: Ecology, Economics, and Population Taboos* (New York: Oxford University Press, 1993), chapter 20; "World Population: Poor in Abundance," *The Economist* (June 13, 1987): 51–54.

6. Carl Haub, "2050: Standing Room Only?" *Washington Post,* July 8, 1990.

7. Charles Mann, "How Many Is Too Many?" *Atlantic Monthly* (February 1993): 47–67; John Bongaarts, "Can the Growing Human Population Feed Itself?" *Scientific American* 270, No. 3 (March 1994): 36–42. It is revealing that so many of the articles discussing this issue carry titles that are questions.

8. Cohen, *How Many People,* chapter 13; Joel Cohen, "How Many People Can the Earth Support?" *The Sciences* (November/December 1995): 18–23.

9. Carl Sagan has argued that space exploration can never be justified in economic terms (job creation, for example) or technological spin-offs (Teflon, Tang) because these objectives can always be achieved more cheaply if they are sought directly rather than as the by-product of the space program. For his discussion of the costs and benefits of space exploration, see Carl Sagan, *Pale Blue Dot: A Vision of the Human Future in Space* (New York: Random House, 1994), chapters 14–16.

10. See Marshall Savage, *The Millennial Project: Colonizing the Galaxy in Eight Easy Steps* (Boston: Little, Brown, 1992) for a description of how space colonization could be accomplished in stages.

11. Warren Leary, "NASA Still Dreams of Mars Outpost," *New York Times*, February 3, 1998.

12. "Blazing a Trail to Mars," *The Economist* (November 9, 1996): 97–99.

13. Everett Gibson, David McKay, Kathie Thomas-Keptra, and Christopher Romanek, "The Case for Relic Life on Mars," *Scientific American*, 277, no. 6 (December 1997): 59.

14. Lawrence Krauss, "It's Only Rocket Science," *Discover* (May 1997): 59–66.

15. Leary, "NASA Still Dreams."

16. Robert Zubrin, "The Magnetic Sail," in *Islands in the Sky: Bold New Ideas for Colonizing Space*, ed. Stanley Schmidt and Robert Zubrin (New York: Wiley, 1996), p. 199.

17. Robert Zubrin, with Richard Wagner, *The Case for Mars: The Plan to Settle the Red Planet and Why We Must* (New York: Free Press, 1996); Robert Zubrin and David Baker, "Mars Direct: A Proposal for the Rapid Exploration and Colonization of the Red Planet," in *Islands in the Sky*, ed. Schmidt and Zubrin, chapter 3.

18. Martyn Fogg, "A Planet Dweller's Dream," in *Islands in the Sky*, ed. Schmidt and Zubrin, chapter 9.

19. Paul Halpern, *The Quest for Alien Planets: Exploring Worlds Outside the Solar System* (New York: Plenum, 1997), chapter 7.

20. Curt Suplee, "Picture This: An Extrasolar Planet," *Washington Post*, May 29, 1998; Malcolm Browne, "Image Is Believed to Be the First of a Planet Beyond Solar System," *New York Times*, May 29, 1998.

21. Halpern, *Quest for Alien Planets*, esp. chapter 8.

22. "All Possible Worlds," *The Economist* (January 25, 1997): 71–73; John Noble Wilford, "Life in Space? 2 New Planets Raise Thoughts," *New York Times*, January 18, 1996; John Noble Wilford, "New Discoveries Turn Astronomers toward Hunt for New Planets," January 23, 1996; Sam Flamsteed, "Impossible Planets," *Discover* (September 1997): 78–83.

23. Halpern, *Quest for Alien Planets*, p. 9, Kathy Sawyer, "Two New Planets Found Outside Solar System," *Washington Post*, September 24, 1998.

24. Gordon Woodcock, "To the Stars!" in *Islands in the Sky*, ed. Schmidt and Zubrin, chapter 11. See also Eric Jones and Ben Finney, "Fastships and Nomads: Two Roads to the Stars," in *Interstellar Migration and the Human Experience*, ed. Ben Finney and Eric Jones, (Berkeley: University of California Press, 1986), chapter 5.

25. Sagan, *Pale Blue Dot*, p. 396.

26. See three articles from *Islands in the Sky*, ed. Schmidt and Zubrin: Zubrin, "The Magnetic Sail," chapter 12; John Cramer, "The Tachyon Drive: Infinite Exhaust Velocity at Zero Energy Cost," chapter 13; and Robert Forward, "The Negative Matter Space Drive," chapter 14. See also Fred Guterl, "A Small Problem of Propulsion, *Discover* (October 1995): 100–08; Freeman Dyson, "21st Century Spacecraft," *Scientific American* (September 1995): 114–116a.

27. William Gale and Gregg Edwards, "Models of Long Range Growth," in *Life in the Universe: The Ultimate Limits to Growth*, ed. William Gale (Boulder, Colo.: Westview, 1979), chapter 4.

28. Michael Michaud, "Improving the Prospects for Life in the Universe," in Gale, *Life in the Universe*, pp. 114–15.

29. Leonard David, "Space Exploration: Prospects and Problems for Today and the Future," in Gale, *Life in the Universe*, pp. 59–60.

30. Gale and Edwards, "Models of Long Range Growth," p. 76.

31. Zubrin and Baker, *Islands in the Sky*, pp. 61–67, esp. figure 3.1, p. 64.

32. Sagan, *Pale Blue Dot*, p. 34 (emphasis in the original).

33. Sagan, *Pale Blue Dot*, chapter 17.

34. Edward Regis, "The Moral Status of Multigenerational Interstellar Exploration," in Finney and Jones, *Interstellar Migration*, chapter 16.

35. Halpern, *Quest for Alien Planets*, pp. 269–70.

36. William Hodges, "The Division of Labor and Interstellar Migration: A Response to Demographic Contours," in Finney and Jones, *Interstellar Migration*, chapter 8.

37. Michael Hart, "Interstellar Migration, the Biological Revolution, and the Future of the Galaxy," in Finney and Jones, *Interstellar Migration*, chapter 18.

38. Woodcock, "To the Stars!" pp. 191–92.

39. Richard Terra, "Islands in the Sky: Human Exploration and Settlement of the Oort Cloud," in Schmidt and Zubrin, *Islands in the Sky*, pp. 107–09.

40. J. B. Birdsell, "Biological Dimensions of Small, Human Founding Populations," in Finney and Jones, *Interstellar Migration*, chapter 6.

41. James Valentine, "The Origins of Evolutionary Novelty and Galactic Colonization," in Finney and Jones, *Interstellar Migration*, chapter 17.

42. Daniel Dennett, *Darwin's Dangerous Idea: Evolution and the Meanings of Life* (New York: Simon & Schuster, 1995), pp. 43–45.

43. Sagan, *Pale Blue Dot*, p. 371.

44. Brian O'Leary, "Limits to Growth Implications of Space Settlements," in Gale, *Life in the Universe*, chapter 2, pp. 35–37.

45. G. Harry Stine, *Living in Space: A Handbook for Work and Exploration beyond the Earth's Atmosphere* (New York: Evans, 1979), chapter 8.

46. Leary, "NASA Still Dreams."

47. Rick Weiss, "Moonstruck: Cosmic Cuisine," *New York Times*, April 1, 1998; Jane Brody, "What to Serve for Dinner, When Dinner Is on Mars," *New York Times*, May 19, 1998; Mark Wheeler, "Figs in Space," *Discover* (September 1998): 38–41.

48. Information on this research center can be obtained from the World Wide Web at this address: <http://www-rci.rutgers.edu/-biorengg/njnscort>.

49. Shannon Lucid, "Six Months on Mir," *Scientific American* 278, no. 5 (May 1998): 46–55.

50. One of the rare exceptions is Alfred Crosby, "Life (With All Its Problems) in Space," in Finney and Jones, *Interstellar Migration*, chapter 13.

51. Stine, *Living in Space*, p. 187.

52. Zubrin, *The Case for Mars*, pp. 132–35.

53. "Biology: A Guide for Handling Extraterrestrial Microbes," *Washington Post*, July 20, 1998.

54. Martyn Fogg, *Terraforming: Engineering Planetary Environments* (Warrendale, Penn.: Society of Automotive Engineers, 1995), p. 9.

55. Fogg, *Terraforming*, chapter 4.

56. Yvonne Baskin, *The Work of Nature: How the Diversity of Life Sustains Us* (Washington, D.C.: Island Press, 1997), pp. 207–09; William Broad, "Paradise Lost: Biosphere Retooled as Atmospheric Nightmare," *New York Times*, November 19, 1996.

57. Fogg, *Terraforming*, chapter 2.

58. For a graphic description of the terraforming of Mars, see Sagan, *Pale Blue Dot*, chapter 19.

59. "The Terraformers' Dream," *The Economist* (December 23, 1995–January 5, 1996): 97–100.

60. Fogg, *Terraforming*, p. 146.

61. Fogg, *Terraforming*, chapter 6.

Index

globalization, 3–26; coevolution and, 15–22; of culture, 50; definition of, 23n4; of diet, 242; and disease, 39, 93, 99, 101–6, 270–71; episodes in, 44; factors affecting, 22; history of, 15–22; of humans, 42–50; and loss of biodiversity, 277–300
global life systems: definition of, 3; and North America, 182–86
global warming: and agriculture, 62; and disease, 254
goats, 58, 120, 128, 140; domestication of, 73–74, 130
Gobi Desert, 143
goldenseal, 291
Gorrie, John, 197
gorse, 211
Gould, Stephen Jay, 85
gourds, 170
Gouveia, Lourdes, 237
Grant, Susan, 65
grapes, 120, 153
grasses: cereal, 72; European, 178; native American, 176–77; in New Zealand, 210–11
grasslands: and agriculture, 201, 204–5; biodiversity of, 287; in New Zealand, 208–9
grazer-host systems, 13–14, 64–65
grazers, 58–59, 147, 204
great pines, 171
Great Plague of London, 160
Great Wall of China, 143, 147
Greece, 118, 197, 234
green-cheeked parrot, 291
Green Revolution, 229–30
Gregg, Charles, 260
Gregg, Susan Alling, 14, 126–27, 129, 131–32, 182–83, 213
Guangzhou, 145

Haber, Fritz, 229
habitable planets, 313
habitat tracking, 42
haddock, 203, 238
Halpern, Paul, 313
Halstead, Paul, 114, 130
Han Dynasty, 146–48, 152

hantavirus, 96, 250, 254
Harappan civilization, 98
Härd, Mikael, 8
Harrison, James, 199
Hawaii, 283
hawksbill turtle, 291
hemoglobin E, 95
hemorrhagic fevers, 250, 253
Hengeveld, Rob, 46
Henle, Jacob, 84
hepatitis, 91, 254
herbivores, evolution of, 56
herd immunity, 88
herding, 59
Hessian flies, 178
hierarchy, development of, 125
High Resolution Microwave Survey (HRMS), 315
hindgut digesters, 58, 154
HIV: evolution of, 265–66. *See also* AIDS
Hobhouse, Henry, 3
homeothermy, 28, 57
hominization, 50
Homo erectus, 3, 28, 30; food choices of, 68; migration of, 43–45
Homo sapiens, 3, 27–34; brain of, 33; digestive system of, 59; range of habitat of, 295–96. *See also* humans
horse cavalry, 147
horses, 58, 121, 128, 130, 151; domestication of, 73–74, 154; in North America, 175, 277; of Silk Road, 154–55; technologies of, 48
Howard, Henry, 197
Hsiung-nu (Huns), 147–48, 155
HTLV viruses, 250
human leukocyte antigen (HLA), 94–95
humans: agriculture and, 132–34; coevolution with diseases, 11, 83, 85, 89–95; diet of, 59; diffusion of, 46–48; energy needs of, 64, 78; evolution of, 300; genetic diversity of, 295–300; globalization of, 42–50. *See also Homo sapiens*
hunter-gatherers: interaction with farmers, 126–27; social organization of, 115–16; survival curve for, 37–38
hypnozoites, 100

About the Author

Robert Clark has been professor of government and politics in the Department of Public and International Affairs at George Mason University since 1977. He is currently coordinator of the disciplinary minor in global systems. Professor Clark received his B.A. degree in political science and Latin American studies in 1962 from Tulane University in New Orleans. He received a master's degree and a Ph.D. in international studies from the Johns Hopkins University, School of Advanced International Studies, Washington, D.C.

Professor Clark conducted field research in Honduras, Venezuela, Spain, and France, and he has taught in Spain and Venezuela. He has authored, coauthored, or edited thirteen books, more than thirty scholarly articles, and more than three dozen professional conference papers and presentations.

Deutsch *aktiv* Neu

Ein Lehrwerk für Erwachsene

Arbeitsbuch 1A

Gerd Neuner, Theo Scherling, Reiner Schmidt und Heinz Wilms

LANGENSCHEIDT

BERLIN · MÜNCHEN · LEIPZIG · WIEN · ZÜRICH · NEW YORK

Zeichnungen und Layout: Theo Scherling
Fotografie: Ulrike Kment (s. a. Quellennachweise, S. 135)
Umschlaggestaltung: Theo Scherling, unter Verwendung eines Fotos
© Presse- und Informationsamt der Bundesregierung, Bonn
Redaktion: Gernot Häublein
Verlagsredaktion: Sabine Wenkums

Deutsch aktiv Neu

Ein Lehrwerk für Erwachsene

Stufe 1A

Lehrbuch 1A	49100
Arbeitsbuch 1A	49101
Lehrerhandreichungen 1A	49102
Glossar Deutsch-Englisch 1A	49103
Glossar Deutsch-Französisch 1A	49104
Glossar Deutsch-Italienisch 1A	49105
Glossar Deutsch-Spanisch 1A	49106
Glossar Deutsch-Türkisch 1A	49107
Glossar Deutsch-Polnisch 1A	49108
Glossar Deutsch-Griechisch 1A	49109
Glossar Deutsch-Russisch 1A	49111
Glossar Deutsch-Rumänisch 1A	49112
Glossar Deutsch-Portugiesisch 1A	49113
Cassette 1A/1 Hörtexte	84550
Cassette 1A/2 Sprechübungen	84551
Begleitheft zu Cassette 1A/2	49110
Folien 1A	84552

Druck:	11.	10.	Letzte Zahlen
Jahr:	95	94	maßgeblich

© 1987 Langenscheidt KG, Berlin und München

Druck: Druckhaus Langenscheidt, Berlin
Printed in Germany · ISBN 3-468-49101-8

Inhaltsverzeichnis

Unterrichten und Lernen mit dem Arbeitsbuch

Informationen für Lernende und Lehrende

Da Ihre Kursteilnehmer gerade beginnen, Deutsch zu lernen, verstehen sie natürlich diese Arbeitshinweise noch nicht. Bitte erklären Sie als Lehrer(in) deshalb die wichtigsten Hinweise in der Muttersprache der Lernenden; oder machen Sie einfach vor, wie eine Aufgabe gelöst werden soll.

1. Das *Arbeitsbuch* bietet zu fast jedem Abschnitt des *Lehrbuchs* eine oder mehrere Übungen. Die Bezeichnun der Abschnitte (z. B. 2A1, 2B1) ist in *Lehrbuch* und *Arbeitsbuch* identisch. Innerhalb der A-Teile und innerhalb der B-Teile sind die einzelnen Übungen durchnumeriert. (Ü1, Ü2, ...).

2. Es gibt zwei Gruppen von Übungen: (a) Übungen, zu denen es in der Regel nur eine richtige Lösung gibt; diese haben das Symbol ⌐••. Die Lösungen finden sich im "Lösungsschlüssel." Sie sind insbesondere für die häusliche (Nach-)Arbeit geeignet, können aber auch zuvor mündlich und/oder schriftlich im Unte richt durchgeführt werden. – (b) Übungen, die zunehmend "freieren" Sprachgebrauch von den Lernenden fo dern; sie reichen von der Rekonstruktion von Dialogen/Gesprächen mit Hilfe von Verlaufsdiagrammen (vgl. 2A1, Ü1) über die gesteuerte Produktion (vgl. 2A1, Ü2) bis zur freien Produktion (vgl. 2A4, Ü9). Die Lösung dieser Aufgaben muß von dem/der Lehrenden auf jeden Fall überprüft und evtl. korrigiert werden.

3. Um mehr Übungen aufnehmen zu können, wurde das *Arbeitsbuch* so angelegt, daß alle Schreibaufgaben, bei denen Schreiben ins Buch nicht unumgänglich ist, von den Lernenden auf einem Extrablatt ausgeführt werden; bei diesen Schreibaufgaben erscheint das Symbol ✐. Die Lernenden sollten alle Arbeits- blätter in einem Schnellhefter sammeln.

4. Zu allen reinen Hörtexten 📷 des *Lehrbuchs* enthält das *Arbeitsbuch* Übungen, vor allem in Form von Lückentexten (z. B. 2A3); dabei entspricht jedem fehlenden einzusetzenden Wort ein Strich _____. Da das Hörverstehen neben dem Sprechen und als Voraussetzung des Sprechens die höchsten Anforderungen an die Lernenden stellt, wird es hier konsequent und extensiv geübt. Dabei kann jede Höraufgabe durch Vor gabe weiterer Wörter (vgl. *Lehrerhandreichungen,* wo alle Hörtexte 📷 abgedruckt sind) weiter verein facht und so dem Leistungsvermögen der Lernenden angepaßt werden. Nach Lösung dieser Aufgaben haben auch die Lernenden den jeweiligen Hörtext in schriflicher Form vorliegen. Bei anders gearteten Hörauf gaben, z. B. Richtig-Falsch-Aufgaben oder Fragen zum Text (vgl. 7A2), kann der/die Lehrende den voll- ständigen Text aus den *Lehrerhandreichungen* zur Verfügung stellen.

5. Bei allen Übungen und Aufgaben werden Vorschläge zu möglichen Arbeitsformen gemacht, die alternativ bzw. nacheinander eingesetzt werden können; die verwendeten Symbole am Seitenrand bedeuten: ▢ = Einzelarbeit, ⬚ = Partnerarbeit, ⬟ = Gruppenarbeit, ⬡ = Arbeit im Plenum.

6. Am Ende der A-Teile jedes Kapitels (wobei die Kapitel 1 und 2 als eine Einheit behandelt werden) finde sich Spiele und Rätsel; sie dienen vor allem der Wiederholung und sind deshalb mit W gekennzeichnet (vgl. 3AW, Ü1-Ü3).

7. Am Ende eines Blocks von jeweils vier Kapiteln finden sich Wiederholungsübungen, gekennzeichnet mit z. B. 1-A4W: Dabei müssen die Lernenden Redemittel zu den wichtigsten Sprechintentionen anwenden und werden gezielt auf den entsprechenden Teil der mündlichen Prüfung des "Zertifikats Deutsch als Fremdsprache" vorbereitet. Ebenfalls zu je 4 Kapiteln gehören Kontrollaufgaben (z. B. 1-4K) zu den Lernzielbereichen A: Wortschat B: Grammatik, C: Orthographie, D: Lesen, E: Sprechen, F: Schreiben. Sie können als informelle Tests in der Klasse oder in häuslicher Einzelarbeit eingesetzt werden.

8. Im Anhang finden sich Lösungsschlüssel, Wörterverzeichnis und Grammatikübersicht (zu jedem Kapitel in der Reihenfolge des Auftretens). Die Grammatikübersicht ist für das "Nachschlagen" gedacht, die Wörter verzeichnisse dafür, daß die Lernenden sich die jeweils neuen Wörter noch einmal vergegenwärtigen können (falls sie über kein *Glossar* zum *Lehrbuch* verfügen).

Viel Spaß bei der Arbeit!

Ü1 Wer sagt was?

3 **Ü 2** **Buchstabieren Sie bitte** 🔑

G	wie Gustav	B	wie Berta	C	wie Cäsar
E	wie Emil	A	wie Anton	O	wie Otto
I	wie Ida	R	wie Richard	N	wie Nord Pol Nordp
G	wie ~~Georg~~ Gustav	B	wie Berta	R	wie Richard
E	wie Emil	I	wie Ida	A	wie Anton
S	wie Samuel	E	wie Emil	D	wie Dora
		R	wie Richard		
		I	wie Ida		

Ü 3 **Sprechen Sie und schreiben Sie die Zahlen** 🔑

1	eins	0	null	9	neun
3	drei	2	zwei (zwo)	8	acht
5	fünf	4	vier	10	zehn
7	sieben	6	sechs	11	elf
12	zwölf	13	dreizehn	14	vierzehn
17	siebzehn	16	sechzehn	15	fünfzehn
18	achtzehn	20	~~zwanzig~~ zwanzig	19	neunzehn

Ü 4 **Nummer ① : Wer ist das?** 🔑

Weltelf

Maier ①

Vogts ② Maradona ④ Beckenbauer ⑤ Smith ③

Rivera ⑥ Pelé ⑩ Platini ⑧

Eusebio ⑦ Krankl ⑨ Garrincha ⑪

Nummer ① : Wer ist das? – Nummer ① ist Maier.
Er kommt aus Deutschland. – Nummer ② ...

Der Deutschkurs

Ü 5 Schreiben Sie bitte

Der Deutschkurs _hat_ zwölf _Teilnehmer_, _fünf_ Frauen und

sieben _Männer_. Der Lehrer heißt _Peter Bauer_. Nummer 11 ist

Michiko _Tanaka_, sie kommt _aus_ _Japan_.

Jim Sampson _ist_ aus _Australien_. Nummer 9 _ist_

aus _Brasilien_. Herr und Frau Scoti _sind_ aus _Italien_.

Frau Scoti _ist_ nicht da, sie _ist krank_. Aber ihr Mann _ist da_.

Maria Barbieri _ist_ auch _da, sie kommt aus Italien._

1 Ü1 Schreiben Sie bitte   Ü2 Schreiben Sie bitte

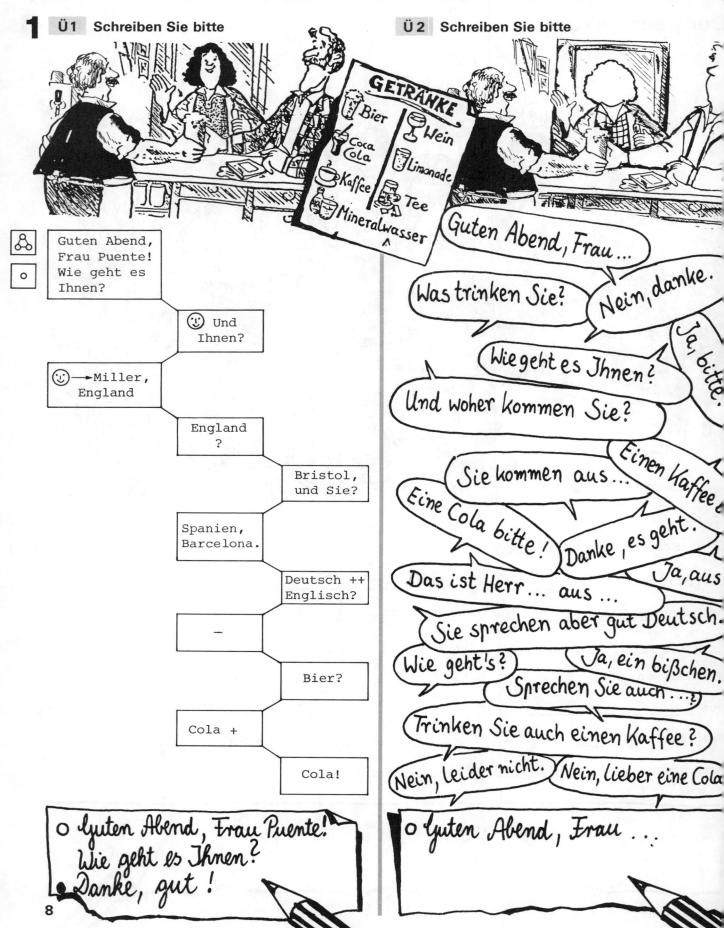

Ü3 Zeichnen Sie bitte

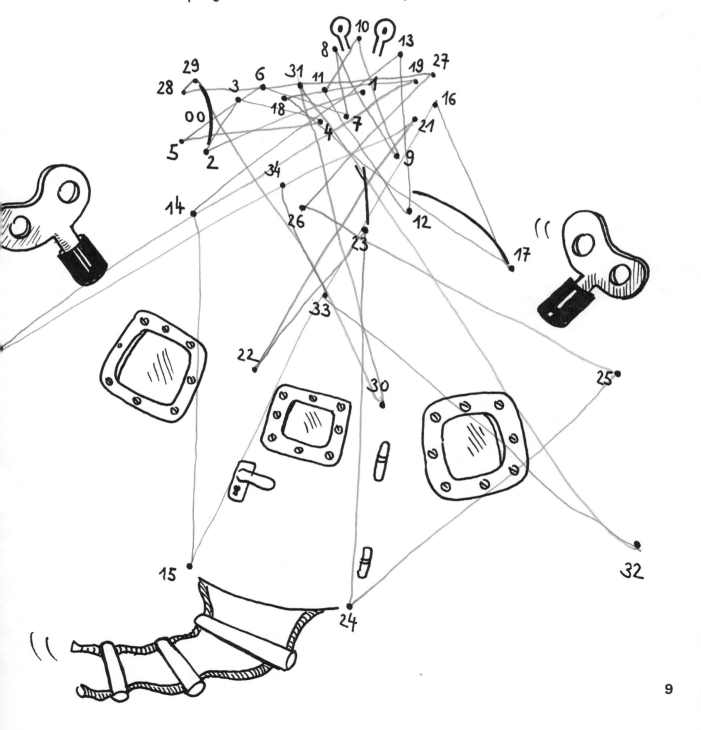

ins → sieben → vier → zwei → fünf → achtundzwanzig → neunundzwanzig → drei →
chs → achtzehn → einunddreißig → elf → acht → zehn → dreizehn → neunzehn → siebenund-
wanzig → sechzehn → einundzwanzig → neun → zwölf → dreiundzwanzig → sechsund-
wanzig → vier → vierunddreißig → vierzehn → ✶✶!! → zwanzig → fünfzehn →
weiundzwanzig → dreißig → vierundzwanzig → zweiunddreißig → fünfundzwanzig →
iebzehn → dreiunddreißig → vierzehn — FERTIG!!

3

Ü 4 **Hören Sie das Gespräch.**
Lesen und ergänzen Sie bitte 🔑

O Auskunft 1O. Grüß Gott!

● Bitte _____ _____ von Willi Decher _____ Kirtorf.

O Wie, wie _____ der Ort?

● Kirtorf. Das wird geschrieben KARL - _____ - RICHARD - THEODOR - _____
_____ - _____ - FRIEDRICH.

O _äh... bla... chr..._

● Kirtorf.

O Wo ist das in der Nähe?

● In Hessen. Ich _____ nochmal: _____ - _____ -
_____ - _____ - _____ - _____
_____ . Kirtorf.

O Wie heißt der Teilnehmer?

● Willi _____ .

O Decher mit _____ am Anfang, ja?

● _____ , genau.

O _____ _____ , Moment mal, null - sechs - _____
- _____ - _____ .

● _____ _____ _____ _____ _____

O Und die Rufnummer: zwo - _____ - _____ .

● _____ - _____ - _____ . Herzlichen Dank. Auf Wiederhören!

O _____ _____ !

10

Ü5 Notieren Sie die Rufnummern bitte

1. siebeneinssechsneun: *7169*
2. zehnachtundvierzigachtundfünfzig: *10 48 58*
3. dreizwoeinsdreisieben: _____ 4. achtdreidreisechsnull: _____
5. sechsfünfnullsechssieben: _____ 6. achtdreieinsneunzwo: _____
7. siebenvierneunsechs: _____ 8. zwölfeinundzwanzigdreiundsechzig: _____
_____ 9. zehnzweiunddreißigvierundachtzig: _____
10. dreiunddreißigsechsundvierzigvierundneunzig: _____
11. siebzehneinundneunzigsiebenundfünfzig: _____ .

Ü6 Schreiben Sie bitte

157 *einhundertsiebenundfünfzig*

① 423 ② 648 ③ 395 ④ 276 ⑤ 567 . . . .

Ü7 Schreiben Sie und sprechen Sie bitte

Widdenhausen (Bü) - Bünde (0 52 23) (En) - Enger (0 52 24x) (He) - Herford (0 52 21)

Flessner A. BünderStr. 335	(He) 5 45 25	
Fliege Karl WaldeckerStr. 7	(Bü) 7 50 50	
Flömer Dietmar AmLienkamp 3	(Bü) 7 43 17	
Focke Horst Betr.Ltr. AmReesberg 12	(Bü) 7 34 27	
Foerdermann Horst Massage Bachstr. 6	(Bü) 7 30 75	
Foerster Josef AlterSchulweg 37	(He) 5 42 29	
Förster M. Wiesenstr. 18	(He) 5 27 48	
Förster Manfred LöhnerStr. 280	(Bü) 7 60 35	
Foerster Willi Schöneberger Str. 24	(He) 5 44 92	
Fordemann	(He) 5 19 69	
Fordemann Barbara FriedrichEbertStr. 4	(He) 5 47 66	
Fordemann Karl jun. Großküchenplanung Gesch.Führer	(Bü) 5 90 10-1 (He) <5 91-0>	
Forth Karl	(Bü) 7 33 60	
Fring Werner AlterSchulweg 41	(He) 5 36 43	
Frischmann Lothar AlterKirchweg 22	(He) 5 17 66	
Fritsche Johannes HansBöcklerStr. 23	(He) 5 10 40	
Fritz Dieter GrünerWeg 48	(Bü) 7 46 05	
Fritz Jürgen Malerstr. 13	(He) 5 29 39	
Froböse Friedrich Bäckerei HerforderStr. 195	(He) 5 53 73	
Frölich Karl-Heinz jun. Dieselstr. 22	(Bü) 7 65 02	
Froese Heinrich Elisabethstr. 12	(He) 5 47 87	
Froesta Lufttech- nische Anlagen u. Gerätebau GmbH DunstabsaugAnl. Dieselstr. 22	(Bü) 7 80 40	
Frölich Karl-Heinz jun. Großplanung Lufttechn.Anl. Dieselstr. 22	(Bü) 7 80 40	
Frowitter Hans Buchenkamp 9	(Bü) 7 39 57	
Gaststätten		
Alter Dorfkrug BünderStr. 221	(He) 5 17 81	
Am Bustedter Holz Industriestr. 52	(Bü) 7 45 86	
Am Felsenkeller BünderStr. 38	(He) 5 22 24	
Böke Edith Holtstr. 82	(He) 5 13 36	
Candle-Light LöhnerStr. 165	(Bü) 7 89 77	
Dorett-Bar Nightclub HerforderStr. 434	(He) 5 33 52	
Generotzky Friedrich-Wilhelm HerforderStr. 217	(He) 5 14 74	
Grünewalds Krug Engerstr. 2	(He) 2 22 55	
Haus Schäfer CharlottenburgerStr. 12	(Bü) 7 22 85	
Kreuzeck ObereWiesenstr. 61	(He) 5 20 06	
Kuhlmann August HerforderStr. 136	(He) 6 13 09	
Meyer	(He) 6 50 79	
Generotzky Wolfgang WurstwarenAgt. HerforderStr. 204	(He) 5 16 51	
Gennrich Elfriede Steinstr. 1	(He) 5 56 88	
Gennrich Erhard Schäfferbrink 11	(He) 5 20 62	
Gennrich Karl- Heinz Flachsweg 7	(He) 5 36 79	
Geppert	(Bü) 7 60 10	
Geppert Wolfgang ImWerregrund 3	(He) 5 43 52	
Gerber Baldur AmReesberg 5	(Bü) 7 43 89	
Gerber Wilhelm TrockeneWiese 3	(Bü) 7 49 05	
Gerbsch Heinz Brunnenstr. 23	(He) 5 27 31	
Gerbsch Herbert Brunnenstr. 23	(He) 5 53 00	
Gerdes Elisabeth Pestalozzistr. 4	(He) 5 51 07	
Gerdes Volker AlterKirchweg 36	(He) 5 55 55	
Gerdt Uwe	(He) 5 24 25	

1. Karl Fliege wohnt in Widdenhausen. Er hat die Telefonnummer 7 50 50, Vorwahl 0 52 23 (Bünde).
2. Barbara Fordemann . . . . .
3. Karl-Heinz Frölich . . . . .
4. Elisabeth Gerdes . . . . .
5. Die Gaststätte "Alter Dorfkrug" hat die Telefonnummer 5 17 81, ...
6. Die Gaststätte "Candle-Light" . . . . .
7. Die "Dorett-Bar" (Nightclub) . . . . .
. . . . .

4 | Ü8 | Spielen Sie das Interview und notieren Sie bitte

Wie heißen Sie?

Woher kommen Sie?

(Stadt?) (Geburtstag?)

Wo wohnen Sie?

Wie ist Ihre Telefonnummer? (Straße?)

(Beruf?)

Name: _____

Vorname: _____

Land: _____

Stadt: _____

Geburtstag: _____

Wohnort: _____

Straße: _____

Telefonnummer: _____

Beruf: _____

Ü9 | Beschreiben Sie die Person aus Ü8

Das ist _____ . Er/Sie kommt _____

_____

_____

_____

_____

Ü 10 Richtig? – Falsch? (→ Lehrbuch, S. 20) 🔑

	richtig	falsch
1. Marlies Demont wohnt in Bern.	X	
2. Sie ist Ärztin.		
3. Sie spricht Deutsch und Italienisch.		
4. Peter Martens wohnt in Leipzig.		
5. Er ist Ingenieur.		
6. Er spricht Deutsch und Russisch.		
7. Fritz Wenzel ist Lehrer.		
8. Er spricht Deutsch und Englisch.		
9. Anni Sinowatz wohnt in Wien.		
10. Sie ist Studentin.		
11. 100 Millionen Menschen lernen Deutsch.		

Ü 11 Ergänzen Sie bitte 🔑

. Marlies Demont w_____ in Bern. Sie spr_____ Deu_____ _____

Franz_____. Sie i_____ Stud_____.

. Fritz Wenzel w_____ in Leipzig. Er i_____ Lehrer und sp_____ Deu_____

und Russ_____.

. Alexandra Karidakis le_____ schon 15 Ja_____ in München. Sie s_____

Griech_____ und Ital_____.

. Miza Lim k_____ aus Korea. Sie stud_____ Deu_____ i____ Bielefeld.

Sie i_____ 24 Jahre alt.

. Mustafa Benhallam i_____ Mar_____, er k_____ aus Fez. Jetzt arb_____

er in Berlin. Mustafa i_____ Arzt.

. Barış Önal a_____ der Tür_____ ist Arb_____ bei Ford. Er w_____

schon sehr lange i_____ Köln. Die Fam_____ ist da_____ in d_____

Türkei.

. 100 Millionen Menschen spr_____ Deu_____. Und 15 Mil_____

Men_____ ler_____ D_____ als Fremdsprache.

13

Ü1 1. Wer ist das? – Raten Sie bitte
2. Beschreiben Sie die Personen
(→ Lehrbuch)

Das ist Frau Abramczyck.
Sie wohnt in Frankfurt,
Bockenheimer Landstraße 4.

Beruf:
Ärztin

Aus Italien;
krank

Adresse:
Frankfurt,
Bockenheimer
Landstraße 4

Aus
Spanien;
spricht gut
Deutsch

Beruf:
Arbeiter

Studiert
in
Bielefeld

Aus
Leipzig

Telefon-
nummer:
089/34 11 84

Arbeitet
bei
Siemens

Beruf:
Ingenieur

Ü2 "So ein Mist!"

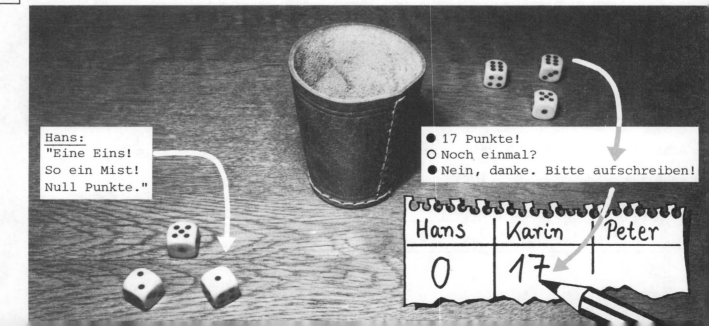

Hans:
"Eine Eins!
So ein Mist!
Null Punkte."

● 17 Punkte!
○ Noch einmal?
● Nein, danke. Bitte aufschreiben!

Hans	Karin	Peter
0	17	

3 **Wie heißen die Wörter?**

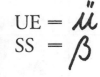

UE = ü
SS = ß

T	E	I	L	N	E	H	M	E	R	A	W	C	F
E	R	T	B	E	W	E	I	N	H	K	O	W	S
E	L	F	O	U	N	I	S	L	M	V	H	E	A
P	R	U	T	N	U	S	T	U	D	I	E	R	T
W	I	E	V	A	U	S	W	B	I	E	R	Z	Z
O	C	N	A	R	B	E	I	T	E	R	B	S	A
D	W	F	N	Z	E	L	T	A	G	H	I	P	K
K	O	M	M	T	M	L	A	N	D	L	D	A	S
R	H	E	I	N	O	E	L	E	R	N	E	N	T
A	N	N	E	P	R	B	I	E	R	T	S	I	E
A	T	C	O	L	A	T	E	K	A	F	F	E	E
K	U	W	Z	A	O	U	N	E	H	M	E	N	X

aus, Arzt, _____

_____

4 **Machen Sie Wörter**

, ärz

i, bier

, den, di, dol

e

f, ken, kran

, leh, li

mat, met, mi, mo

na, ne, nieur

plo

ral, rer, rin

sche, schwe

ser, ster, stu

~~tee~~, ter, tin, tin

was, wein

Beruf	Getränk
Arbeiter	Tee

Ü5 Das Länder-Spiel

1 Wo ist Bonn?

Stadt	Fluß	⊞
Bonn	*Rhein*	A5
Hamburg		
Köln		
München		
Frankfurt		
Dresden		
Mainz		
Dortmund		
Kassel		
Bremen		
Würzburg		
Stuttgart		
Heidelberg		
Magdeburg		
Koblenz		
Ludwigshafen		
Saarbrücken		
Düsseldorf		
Halle		
Karlsruhe		
Duisburg		
Regensburg		

2 Wie heißt der Fluß?

○ Bonn: Wie heißt der Fluß?

● Rhein. Das ist A5.

○ Hamburg: _____

● _____

· · · · ·

3 Wie heißt die Stadt?

○ Wie heißt die Stadt?

● Buchstabe?

○ K.

● Kassel?

○ Nein.

● Fluß?

○ Rhein.

● Köln?

○ Nein.

● Karlsruhe?

○ Ja!

4 Wie heißen die Städte?

A4: Duisburg, Düsseldorf, Köln,

     Bochum

D7: · · · · ·

· · · · ·

1 Ü1 Wort und Satz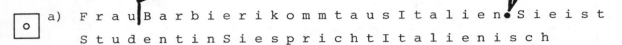

a) F r a u B a r b i e r i k o m m t a u s I t a l i e n. S i e i s t
S t u d e n t i n S i e s p r i c h t I t a l i e n i s c h

b) W i e i s t I h r N a m e P u e n t e W i e s c h r e i b t m a n d a s
B u c h s t a b i e r e n S i e b i t t e W o w o h n e n S i e I n
F r a n k f u r t W i e i s t I h r e T e l e f o n n u m m e r

c) D e r d e u t s c h k u r s h a t 1 2 t e i l n e h m e r f r a u p u e n t e
k o m m t a u s s p a n i e n n u m m e r 2 i s t f r a u b o u c h e r a u s
k a n a d a h e r r d u p o n t i s t a u s f r a n k r e i c h f r a u
s c o t i i s t n i c h t d a s i e i s t k r a n k

a) Frau Barbieri ...
b) Wie ist ...
c) Der Deutschkurs....

2 Ü2 (Verb)

1. Ich (heiße) Anne. Wie heißt du? - Toni.

2. Ich komme aus England. Woher kommst du?

3. Mein Name ist Abramczyk. - Verzeihung, wie ist Ihr Name?

4. Trinken Sie auch ein Bier? - Nein, danke, ich nehme lieber eine Cola

Ü3 Nominativergänzung (Subjekt)

1. Herr Miller kommt aus England. Er spricht Englisch. Er trinkt ein

Bier. Frau Puente kommt aus Spanien. Sie trinkt eine Cola.

Herr und Frau Scoti kommen aus Italien. Sie lernen Deutsch.

Kommen Sie aus England? – Ja, aus Bristol. Und woher kommen Sie? –

Ich komme aus Barcelona. – Sie sprechen aber gut Deutsch! Sprechen

Sie auch Englisch? – Nein, leider nicht. – Trinken Sie auch ein Bier?

4 | Verb |—| Nominativergänzung | **3** ▫

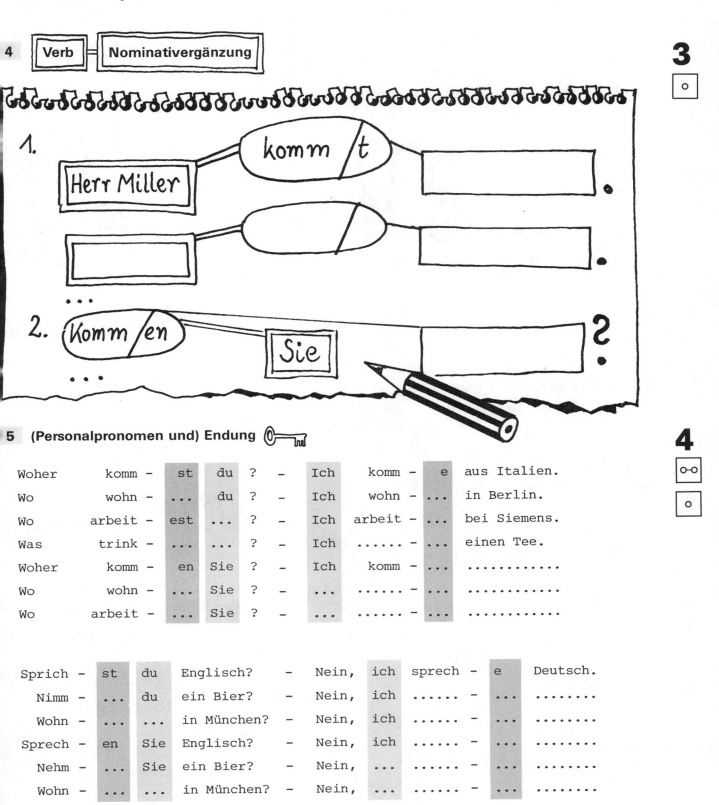

1. Herr Miller — komm/t — ____ .

   ____ — (___) — ____ .

   ...

2. Komm/en — Sie — ____ ?

   ...

5 (Personalpronomen und) Endung 🔑   **4** ⊶ / ▫

Woher	komm –	st	du	?	–	Ich	komm –	e	aus Italien.
Wo	wohn –	...	du	?	–	Ich	wohn –	...	in Berlin.
Wo	arbeit –	est	...	?	–	Ich	arbeit –	...	bei Siemens.
Was	trink –	...	...	?	–	Ich	...... –	...	einen Tee.
Woher	komm –	en	Sie	?	–	Ich	komm –	...	....
Wo	wohn –	...	Sie	?	–	...	...... –	...	....
Wo	arbeit –	...	Sie	?	–	...	...... –	...	....

Sprich –	st	du	Englisch?	–	Nein,	ich	sprech –	e	Deutsch.
Nimm –	...	du	ein Bier?	–	Nein,	ich	...... –	...	....
Wohn –	...	...	in München?	–	Nein,	ich	...... –	...	....
Sprech –	en	Sie	Englisch?	–	Nein,	ich	...... –	...	....
Nehm –	...	Sie	ein Bier?	–	Nein,	...	...... –	...	....
Wohn –	...	...	in München?	–	Nein,	...	...... –	...	....

19

c) Miza Lim:

Sie	komm	–	t	aus Korea.
Sie	studier	–	...	Deutsch.
...	wohn	–	...	in Bielefeld.
Sie		is	t	24 Jahre alt.

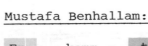

Mustafa Benhallam:

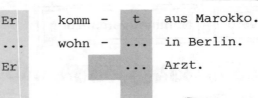

Er	komm	–	t	aus Marokko.
...	wohn	–	...	in Berlin.
Er			...	Arzt.

Alexandra Karidakis:

...	leb	–	...	in München.
...	arbeit	–	...	bei Siemens.
...	komm	–	...	aus Griechenland.

Barış Önal:

...	....	–	...	aus der Türkei.
...	....	–	...	in Köln.
...	....	–	...	bei Ford.
...			...	Arbeiter.

Ü 6 Verb-Stamm und Endung

7 Die Aussage ●

5
○

heiße

Ich   Anne .

Ich (komme) aus England.
2

Ü8 Die Aufforderung !

Hören Sie

das Gespräch !

Notieren Sie die Nummer!
1

9 Die Frage ?

kommt

oher   sie ?

Wo (wohnt) sie ?
2

Sprechen

Sie   Englisch ?

Trinken Sie einen Tee ?
1

10 Die Aussage und die Frage. – Antworten Sie oder fragen Sie

Das ist Herr Dupont. – <u>Wer</u> ist das?

Er kommt <u>aus Frankreich</u>. – ....

Ich heiße <u>Peter Bauer</u>. – ....

Ich wohne <u>in München</u>. – ....

Ich arbeite <u>bei Siemens</u>. – ....

6. <u>Wie</u> heißen Sie? – ....

7. <u>Woher</u> kommen Sie? – ....

8. <u>Wo</u> wohnen Sie? – ....

9. <u>Wo</u> arbeiten Sie? – ....

10. <u>Wie alt</u> sind Sie? – ....

11. Trinken Sie auch ein Bier? – Ja/Nein, ...

12. Sprechen Sie Englisch? – ....

13. Kommen Sie aus Italien? – ....

14. Wohnen Sie auch in Köln? – ....

15. Arbeiten Sie auch bei Ford? – ....

2 Ü1 Was ist Nummer ...? 🗝

Nr. 14, wie heißt das auf deutsch?

"Stuhl"

① _____   ⑥ _____   ⑪ _____

② _____   ⑦ _____   ⑫ _____

③ _____   ⑧ _____   ⑬ _____

④ _____   ⑨ _____   ⑭ *der / ein Stuhl*

⑤ _____   ⑩ _____   ⑮ _____

📼 Ü2 Hören und ergänzen Sie bitte 🗝

o Was _____ das?

o Ein - wie _____ _____?

o Ein _____ .

o Ein _____ .

   Und _____ _____ ,

   ist das eine _____ ?

o Oh, _____ _____ , bitte!

o Ist _____ _____ ?

• _____ Tonbandgerät.

• _____ !

• Ein _____ !!!

• _____ , _____ Tageslichtprojektor.

• _____ .

• Ja, das _____ auf deutsch: Tageslichtprojektor.

Ü 3 Text und Bild 🔑

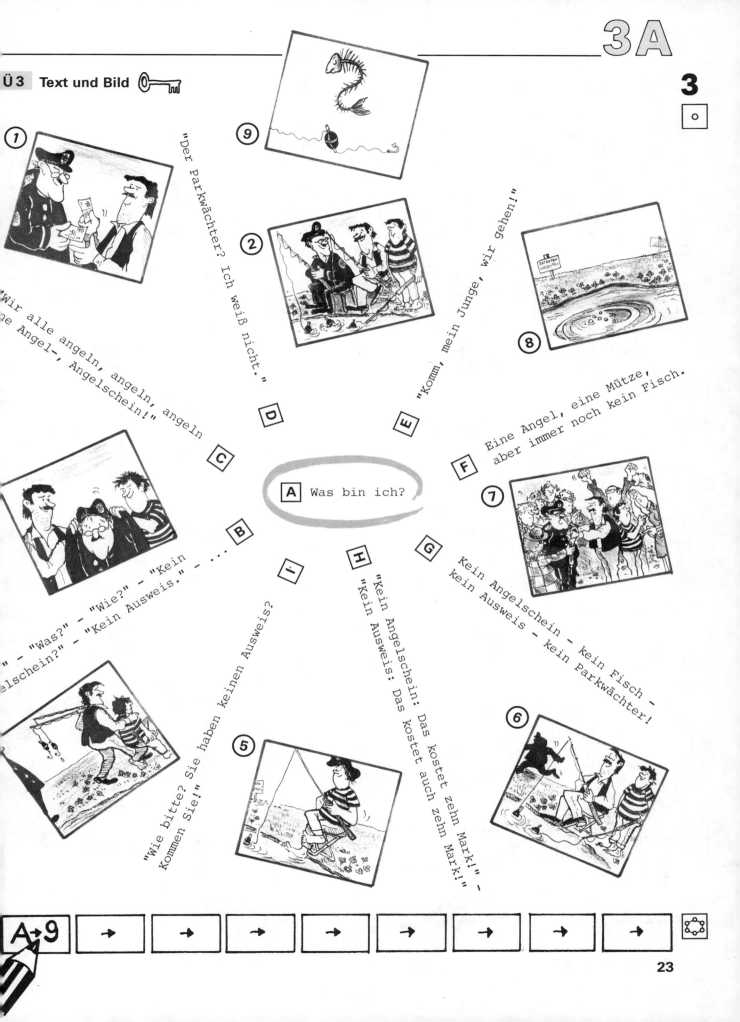

"Der Parkwächter? Ich weiß nicht."

"Wir alle angeln, angeln, angeln / ...e Angel-, Angelschein!"

[C]

[D]

[E] "Komm, mein Junge, wir gehen!"

[F] Eine Angel, eine Mütze, aber immer noch kein Fisch.

[A] Was bin ich?

[B] ...lschein?" – "Was?" – "Wie?" – "Kein / ... – "Kein Ausweis." – ...

[I]

[H]

[G] Kein Angelschein – kein Fisch – kein Ausweis – kein Parkwächter!

"Kein Angelschein: Das kostet zehn Mark!" – "Kein Ausweis: Das kostet auch zehn Mark!"

"Wie bitte? Sie haben keinen Ausweis? / Kommen Sie!"

A→9 → → → → → → → → →

4 Ü4 Schreiben Sie bitte

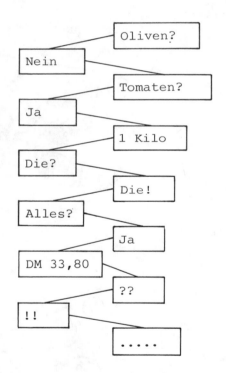

	Oliven?
Nein	
	Tomaten?
Ja	
	1 Kilo
Die?	
	Die!
Alles?	
	Ja
DM 33,80	
	??
!!	
	.....

Haben Sie Oliven?

...

Ü5 Schreiben Sie bitte

Nein, heute leider nicht.
Und Salat?
Haben Sie Orangen? ....
Ja, hier! ......
Was kostet der Fisch? ....
....
Ja, der! Das kostet sechs Mark
Der da?
Eine Cola. 1 Kilo Kartoffeln, bitt
Zwei Joghurt, bitte! Alles
2 Kilo Lammfleisch, bitte!
....
Zehn Eier, bitte! Wie bitte?
...Mark... alles zusammen.

Haben Sie Orangen?
Nein, ...

j 6 Mark und Pfennig: Schreiben Sie bitte

 = DM 18,68

achtzehn Mark achtundsechzig

achtzehn Mark und achtundsechzig Pfennig

    =

5 **Ü7** **Wieviel Geld brauchen *Sie* im Monat?**

Getränke

_____ DM _____ DM _____ DM _____ DM

_____ DM _____ DM _____ DM _____ DM

_____ DM _____ DM _____ DM _____ DM

Ü8 **Schreiben Sie bitte**

Für Essen und Trinken brauche ich /brauchen wir
. . . . . .

Ü9 **Wieviel sind . . . ?**

Eine Mark sind ____ Dollar.
_____ ____ Franc.
_____ ____ Lire.
_____ ____

40 Mark sind ____ Dollar.

	Tageskurse		Verkauf	Kauf
0 1 8 9 5 0	England	1 £	2 9 3	2 7 8
0 1 6 9 5 0	Frankreich	100 FF	3 1 2 4	2 9 5 0
0 7 3 4 0 0	Griechenland	100 Dr.	1 7 0	1 1 0
0 2 3 0 5 0	Italien	1000 Lit.	1 4 9	1 3 9
0 2 0 0 5 0	Jugoslawien	100 Din.	8 5	2 5
0 6 1 9 0 0	Holland	100 hfl.	8 9 2 5	8 7 2 5
0 7 1 9 0 0	Österreich	100 öS	1 4 3 3	1 4 0 9
0 1 5 6 8 0	Schweden	100 skr.	3 0 0 0	2 8 2 5
0 2 9 0 0 0	Schweiz	100 sfrs.	1 2 4 0 0	1 2 1 0 0
0 4 4 7 5 0	Spanien	100 Pts.	1 5 7	1 4 8
0 6 0 8 0 0	USA	1US $	.	.
0 5 4 9 0 0	weitere Kurse am Schalter			

10 Regine Klein: Hören Sie bitte 🔑
Richtig oder falsch?
Machen Sie ein Kreuz! ☒

	r	f
. Regine Klein ist achtundzwanzig Jahre alt.		
. Sie ist Lehrerin.		
. Sie hat ein Haus.		
. Andrea ist 5, Tommy ist 6 Jahre alt.		
. Der Mann verdient 3.200 Mark netto, das ist nicht gut.		
. Die Wohnung ist schön, groß und sehr teuer.		
. Sie brauchen für die Wohnung ungefähr 1.350 Mark im Monat.		
. Für Essen, Trinken, Auto, Reisen, Kleidung brauchen sie etwa 800 Mark.		
. Sie sind immer pleite, aber sie sind gesund und haben viele Freunde.		

11 Was kostet eine Gulaschsuppe? (→ Lehrbuch, S. 34 und 36) 🔑

6/7

DM 1,95   DM 4,—   DM 2,40
   DM 1,60   DM 3,50
DM 3,50   DM 1,90
   DM 4,50 DM 1,80 DM 2,60   DM 1,80
DM 3,50   ~~DM 2,40~~   DM 3,60
   DM 3,70   DM 3,20   DM 3,50
DM 2,20   DM 4,80   DM 2,50
   DM 3,90   DM 2,50   DM 19,80
DM 19,80   DM 2,50

Eine Bratwurst kostet DM 2,40
(zwei Mark und vierzig Pfennig)
.....

Suppen

Bayer. Leberknödelsuppe

Gulaschsuppe nach Wiener Art

Hühnersuppe mit Nudeln

Steaks
vom Rind 180 g Frischgewicht

„Texas"-Steak
mit Kräuterbutter, Pommes frites und Saisonsalat

Zigeuner-Steak
mit einer Sauce aus Paprika, Zwiebeln, dazu Reis und Saisonsalat

Salate & Beilagen

Gemischter Salat
je nach Saison

Kartoffelsalat

Kartoffeln

Eiernudeln

Ü 12   **Machen Sie Dialoge**

Ü 13 Wer ist das? Was ist das?

Ü 14 Antworten Sie und schreiben Sie

1. Was ist heute?
2. Wer macht Picknick?
3. Wie ist der Tag?
4. Was macht Frau Wolter?
5. Was hat sie?
6. Was macht Herr Lang?
7. Wer ist dick und faul?
8. Was macht Stephan?
9. Was macht Susanne?
10. Wer ist krank?
11. Was sagt Frau Wolter?

Heute ist Sonntag . . .

9 **Ü 15** "Rocko – ein U. L."

Richtig oder falsch? – Machen Sie Kreuze

	r	f
1. Ein U.L. hat Durst.	X	
2. Ein U.L. trinkt Bier.		
3. Ein U.L. trinkt keinen Kaffee.		
4. Ein U.L. trinkt Ö.L.		
5. Ein U.L. hat Hunger.		
6. Ein U.L. frißt Wurst.		
7. Ein U.L. frißt Pommes frites.		

Rocko bestellt......

	r	f
8. ..... eine Tasse Kaffee.		
9. ..... ein Glas Tee.		
10. ..... ein Glas Bier.		
11. ..... eine Flasche Wein.		
12. ..... eine Flasche Milch.		
13. ..... eine Dose Cola.		

Ü 16 **Hören Sie und notieren Sie**

1. Was möchte Rocko?

2. Wie heißen der Mann und die Frau (Vornamen)?

3. Woher kommt Rocko?

4. Woher kommen der Mann und die Frau?

5. Was bringt der Ober?

6. Was macht Rocko?

7. Was essen der Mann und die Frau?

8. Was frißt Rocko am liebsten?

Ü 17 **Schreiben Sie bitte**

Rocko möchte ...

1 Raten Sie: Was ist Nummer 13? 🔑

ä = AE

BUNDESREPUBLIK DEUTSCHL...
PERSONALAU...
IDENTITY CARD / ...
123...0016
MUSTERMANN
GEB. GABLER
ERIKA
12.09.45   MÜNCHEN
DEUTSCH / 01.10.91
Erika Mustermann
...MANN<<ERIKA<<<<<<<<<<<<
...0110912<<<<<<6

1
2
3
4
5
6
7
8
9
0
1
2

13

Ü 2   **Raten Sie:**
Was kaufen wir im Supermarkt?

Crossword grid (letters shown):

```
                    M  I
                 F     C  H
      S  C  H  I        B  R
         B     T        R
            W           C  H  E  N
            T  O  M        N
               O     I     E
      B  R  A  T           E
               K           E  E
         K              B  R
      P  O              F  R
         B              R
      S  U  P  E  R  M  A  R  K  T
```

ü = UE

ä = AE

Ü 3   **Machen Sie Wörter**

brat, but	mi, mi, mü
co	ne, ner
dier	pe, pe
ei, er	ra, ral, re
fee, fel	sa, sche, se, se,
gal, ge, geu,	ser, steak, sup
gu, gum	ta, ter, tof
kä, kaf, kar, ky	was, whis, ~~wurst~~
la, lam, lasch, lat	zi

SPEISEN
B ~~Bratwurst~~
G _____
K _____
Z _____

GETRÄNKE
C _____
K _____
M _____
W _____

ESSEN
B _____
E _____
G _____
K _____

SACHEN
L _____
R _____
R _____
T _____

Ü1 "der", "das" oder "die"?

Sortieren Sie. Benutzen Sie das Lexikon 🔑

Ü2 Sortieren Sie auch die Sachen aus 3A2 (→ Lehrbuch, S. 29)

2 Ü3 Schreiben Sie Sätze 🔑

..... schreibt einen Satz.

.... heißt Al Capone.

..... arbeitet bei Siemens.

.... trinkt einen Kaffee.

..... ist 6 Monate alt.

.... kommt aus Japan.

.... spielt.

..... wohnt in München.

..... spricht Englisch, Französisch und Spanisch.

..... hat zwölf Teilnehmer.

Studentin

Arbeiterin

Lehrerin

Dolmetscherin

Nummer ③: Das ist ein Deutschkurs. Der Deutschkurs hat zwölf Teilnehmer.

Nummer ①: ...

4   Sprechen Sie und schreiben Sie

Nummer 1: Das ist ein Telefon. – Was ist das? – Ein Telefon.
Nummer 2: Das ist Peter Bauer. – Wer ist das? – Peter Bauer.
Nummer 3:

4 Ü5 **Machen Sie Sätze**

Ich esse .....

Ich nehme .....

Möchtest Du .....?

Ist das .....?

Möchten Sie .....?

Wer möchte .....?

Das ist .....

Essen wir .....?

Nehmen wir .....?

Trinken Sie .....?

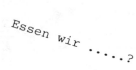

Möchtest du eine Bratwurst?

.....

5 Ü6 **Ergänzen Sie und antworten Sie**

1. Woher komm____ du?   – Ich .....
   komm____ Sie?

2. Sprich____ du
       auch Englisch? – .....
   Sprech____ Sie

3. Wie heiß____ du?   – Ich .....
   heiß____ Sie?

4. Ha_____ du
       auch Hunger? – .....
   Hab____ Sie

5. B____ du
       krank? – .....
   S____ Sie

6. Nehm____ ihr
       auch ein Steak? – .....
   Nehm____ Sie

7. Wohn____ ihr
       auch in Berlin? – .....
   Wohn____ Sie

8. S____ ihr
       auch aus Italien? – .....
   S____ Sie

Ü 7   Ergänzen Sie bitte

a) Familie Lang und Familie Wolter

ma_____ Picknick. Sie s_____

im Park. Sie h_____ Wurst

und Käse, Brot und Bier.

Michael, Stephan und Susanne

s_____ da; aber Gabi i____

nicht da, sie _____ krank.

Frau Wolter r_____: "Das Essen

i____ fertig, wir f_____ an!"

b) Das _____ Rocko. Auch Rocko _____ Hunger und

Durst. Aber Rocko i_____ kein Brot und keine Wurst,

er f_____ Metall und Mineralien (M.M.).

Er _____ auch kein Mineralwasser, er

_____ nur Ö.L.

Er _____ mit Paula und Rainer Schmidt;

er sagt: "Ich _____ Rocko, wer _____ Sie?

Was _____ Sie? Ich _____ nur M.M."

Ü 8   Fragen Sie bitte

Familie Lang und Familie Wolter
machen Picknick.

. Heute ist Sonntag. 2. Frau Wolter
macht das Essen. 3. Sie hat Wurst,
Brot und Bier. 4. Herr Lang arbeitet.
. Er schreibt einen Brief. 6. Gabi
ist nicht da.

Wer macht Picknick?
Was machen sie?
1. ...

1 Ü1 **Wie heißen die Körperteile?**

Krater (Ausschnitt)
Kampf der Kentauren und Lapithen
Drittes Viertel des 5. Jahrhunderts v. Chr.
Florenz, Archäologisches Museum

Schreiben Sie bitte

① *der Kopf* _____

② _____

③ _____

④ _____

⑤ _____

⑥ _____

⑦ _____

⑧ _____

⑨ _____

⑩ _____

⑪ _____

⑫ _____

⑬ _____

⑭ _____

⑮ _____

❓ _____

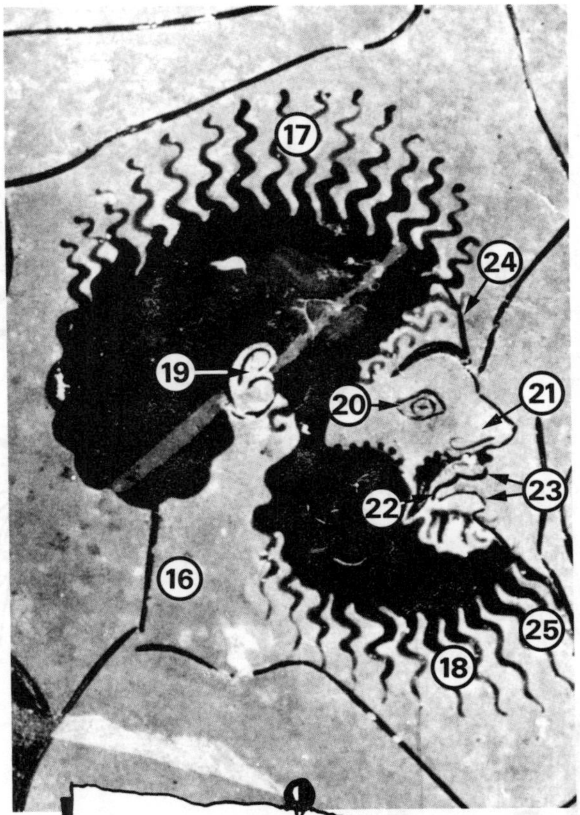

( ) _____

( ) _____

( ) _____

( ) _____

( ) _____

( ) _____

( ) _____

( ) _____

( ) _____

( ) _____

( ) _____

Attische Schale (Ausschnitt): *Kampf*
Zweites Viertel des 5. Jahrhunderts v. Chr.
Florenz, Archäologisches Museum

2

Ü2 Suchen Sie die Organe

die Organe:

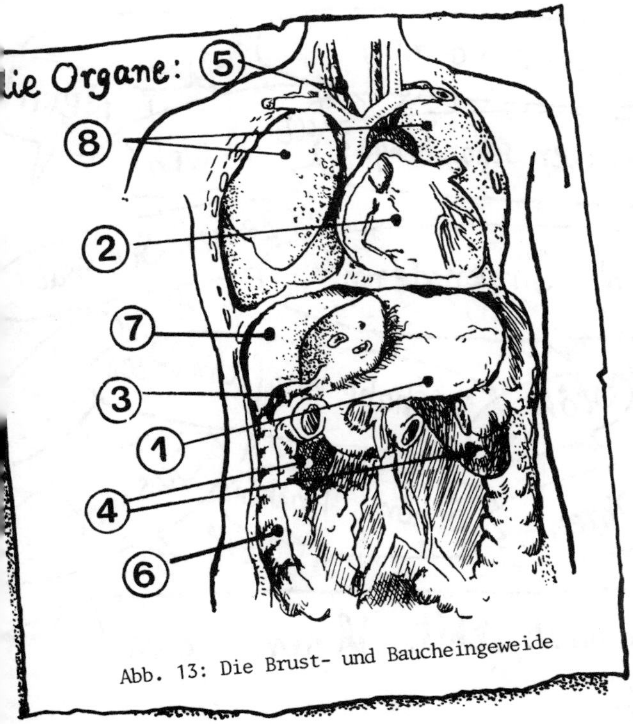

Abb. 13: Die Brust- und Baucheingeweide

○ die Schlagader _____

○ die Lunge _____

○ das Herz _____

○ die Leber _____

③ die Gallenblase _____

○ der Magen _____

○ die Niere _____

○ der Darm _____

Ü3 Wie heißen die Organe in Ihrer Sprache?

39

① Akosan-Saft

Soweit vom Arzt nicht anders verordnet, nehmen Erwachsene und Kinder im akuten Stadium als Anfangsdosis 1mal 1 Eßlöffel Saft und danach stündlich 1 Teelöffel (5 ml) Saft ein: nach Abklingen der Symptome täglich 3mal 1 Teelöffel einnehmen (ca. 2–3 Tage lang).

② Nasovit
Spray gegen Schnupfen

Dosierungsanleitung, Art der Anwendung
Soweit nicht anders verordnet, nach Bedarf, etwa 3–4mal täglich, durch leichten Druck auf die Sprayflasche in die Nase sprühen.

Aurimed Ohrentropfen

weit nicht anders verordnet, gibt man 3–4mal täglich
Tropfen in das schmerzende Ohr. Die Ohrentropfen
ten vor der Anwendung auf Körpertemperatur erwärmt
rden.

④ Tussidural-Tropfen
gegen Husten und Bronchitis

Erwachsene und Jugendliche	3mal täglich 15 bis 20 Tropfen
Kinder	3mal täglich 10 bis 15 Tropfen
Kleinkinder	3mal täglich 7 bis 10 Tropfen
Säuglinge	3mal täglich 1 bis 7 Tropfen
	(1 Tropfen pro Lebensmonat)

⑤ ntihustin
pfen
r Hustenstillung und
chleimverflüssigung

lls vom Arzt nicht anders verordnet, gilt folgende
osierung:
äuglinge (4–12 Monate) nehmen 5 Tropfen, Klein-
inder 5–10 Tropfen, 1–2–3mal täglich; ältere Kinder
0–20 Tropfen, Erwachsene 25–35 Tropfen, bei Bedarf auch mehr, mehrmals täglich ein.

⑥ TRANSPIRIN

Anwendungsgebiete: Fieber und Schmerzen; Erkältungskrankheiten; Schmerzen wie Kopf-, Zahn-, Muskel- oder Glieder-Schmerzen; Entzündungen.

Alter	Einzeldosis
unter 2 Jahre	– nach ärztlicher Verordnung
2–3 Jahre	– 1 Tablette
4–6 Jahre	– 2 Tabletten
7–9 Jahre	– 3 Tabletten

Ossogen Tabletten

altabletten
ei Entzündungen im Mund- und Rachenraum

Soweit nicht anders verordnet, alle 2–3 Stunden eine Tablette; nicht
angsam unter der Zunge oder im Munde zergehen lassen; nicht
schlucken und nicht kauen.

⑦ Immunix forte ⑧

Zur Steigerung der körpereigenen Abwehrkräfte

Soweit nicht anders verordnet, nehmen Erwachsene dreimal täglich 50 Tropfen ein, Kinder und Säuglinge, je nach Alter, dreimal täglich 10–30 Tropfen.

J6 Sammeln Sie Informationen

	Medikament	Form	Indikation	Dosierung
①	Akosan	Saft	Grippe/Fieber	Erwachsene + Kinder: 1 mal 1 Eßlöffel, dann 1 Teelöffel pro Std.
②				

J7 Schreiben Sie Gespräche

Beispiel: o Ich habe Husten.   ● Hier, nimm das, das ist gut gegen Husten.

o Und wie oft?   ● Dreimal täglich eine Tablette.

4

Ü 8 Ordnen Sie zu (benutzen Sie ein Lexikon)

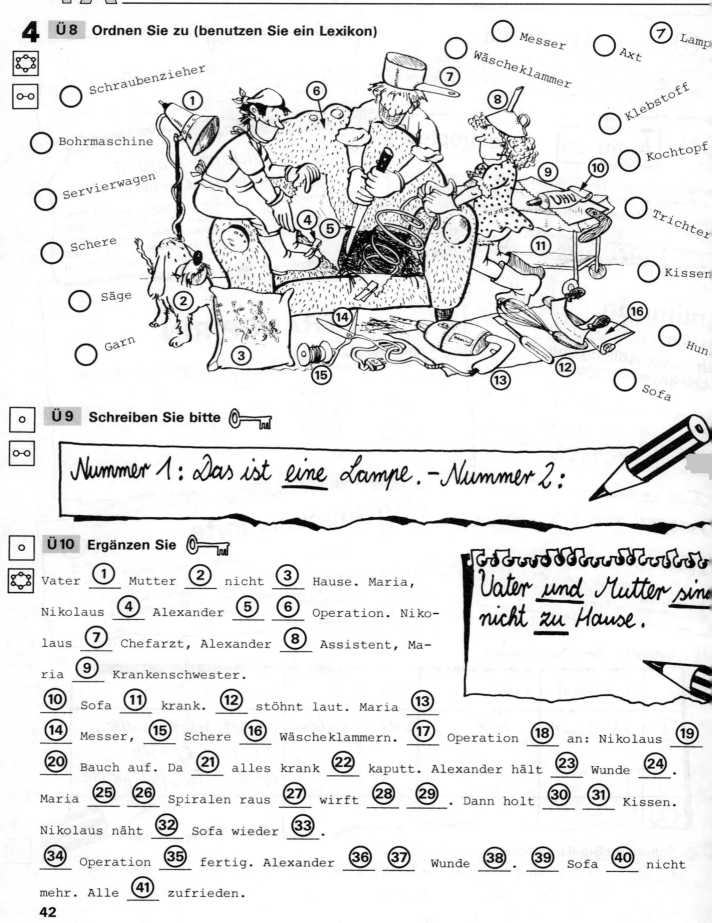

Schraubenzieher

Bohrmaschine

Servierwagen

Schere

Säge

Garn

Messer

Wäscheklammer

Axt

Lamp

Klebstoff

Kochtopf

Trichter

Kissen

Hun

Sofa

Ü 9 Schreiben Sie bitte 🔑

Nummer 1: Das ist <u>eine</u> Lampe. – Nummer 2:

Ü 10 Ergänzen Sie 🔑

Vater ① Mutter ② nicht ③ Hause. Maria, Nikolaus ④ Alexander ⑤ ⑥ Operation. Niko- laus ⑦ Chefarzt, Alexander ⑧ Assistent, Ma- ria ⑨ Krankenschwester.

⑩ Sofa ⑪ krank. ⑫ stöhnt laut. Maria ⑬ ⑭ Messer, ⑮ Schere ⑯ Wäscheklammern. ⑰ Operation ⑱ an: Nikolaus ⑲ ⑳ Bauch auf. Da ㉑ alles krank ㉒ kaputt. Alexander hält ㉓ Wunde ㉔ . Maria ㉕ ㉖ Spiralen raus ㉗ wirft ㉘ ㉙ . Dann holt ㉚ ㉛ Kissen. Nikolaus näht ㉜ Sofa wieder ㉝ .

㉞ Operation ㉟ fertig. Alexander ㊱ ㊲ Wunde ㊳ . ㊴ Sofa ㊵ nicht mehr. Alle ㊶ zufrieden.

Vater <u>und</u> Mutter sin nicht <u>zu</u> Hause.

Ü11 Schreiben Sie Sätze und machen Sie einen Text

Milchgeschäft Wilhelm Etzin, Lausitzer Straße 38, Berlin-Kreuzberg

...ilhelm Etzin		1908
...r		im Keller
...err und Frau Etzin	**war –**	billig
...ie		kühl im Keller/Souterrain
...as Milchgeschäft		der Besitzer
...as Geschäft	**hatt –**	in Berlin-Kreuzberg
...s		eine Frau und zwei Kinder
...ie Miete		noch keinen Kühlschrank
...in Glas Milch		Milch und Sahne, Brot und Butter
...as		damals nicht teuer

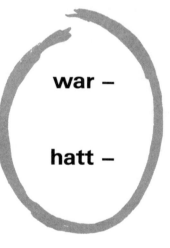

Das Milchgeschäft war in Berlin – Kreuzberg.

6 **Ü12** Hören Sie den Text und ergänzen Sie

1. Früher hatte ich keine _____.

   Ich hatte _____, ein _____, _____ tolles

   _____, ein _____, eine Villa.

   Ich _____ verheiratet, und ich _____

   Kinder, und _____, ja, ich _____

   _____, 'ne Menge _____, hm

   Aber ich hatte _____ Zeit. Nie _____

   _____ Zeit.

2. Ich war _____.

   Ich hatte 'ne Menge _____. Ich war _____

   _____. Und ich hatte viele _____.

   Überall. In _____, _____,

   in _____ und Hollywood.

3. Ja, und dann - dann war ich _____.

   Ha, ja, da hatte ich _____. Ich hatte ein

   dickes _____ und _____ _____

4. Aber dann hatte ich _____!

5. Jetzt, jetzt hab' ich _____ _____

   mehr. Meine _____ ist weg, mein _____

   ist weg, meine _____ ist _____ weg, _____

   ist weg. So ist _____ eben.

   Jetzt hab' ich _____ mehr. Ich bin _____

   Aber ich hab' 'ne _____ _____.

Ü13 Bilder – Wörter: Ordnen Sie zu

Rhein

Industrie

Bayern

SA

Kaiserreich

BMW

München

Berge

Nazis

Folklore

Großstadt

Tierliebe

Polizei

Niederlage

Tennis

Alpen

Mercedes

Sieg

Hitler

2. Weltkrieg

Sport

Automobile

Schäferhund

Preußen

Wirtschaftswunder

Ü1 **Was ist das?**

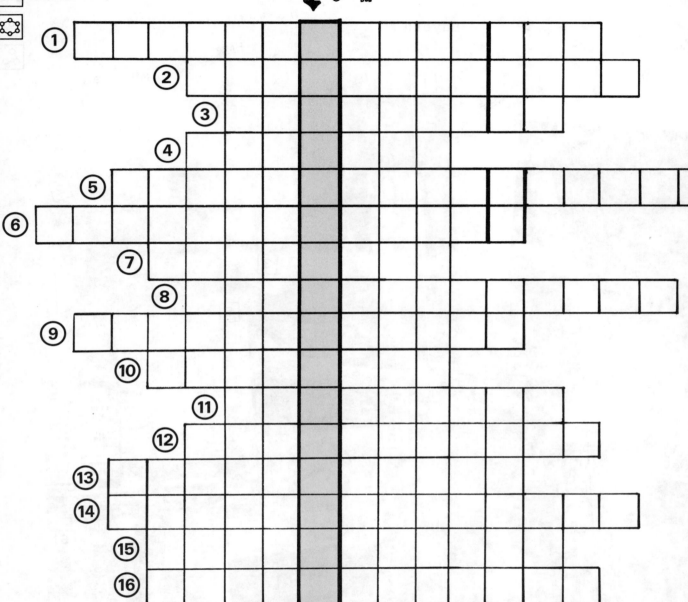

ä = *ae* , ö = *oe* , ü = *ue*

 ①  ③

 ② 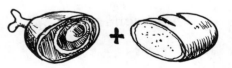  ④

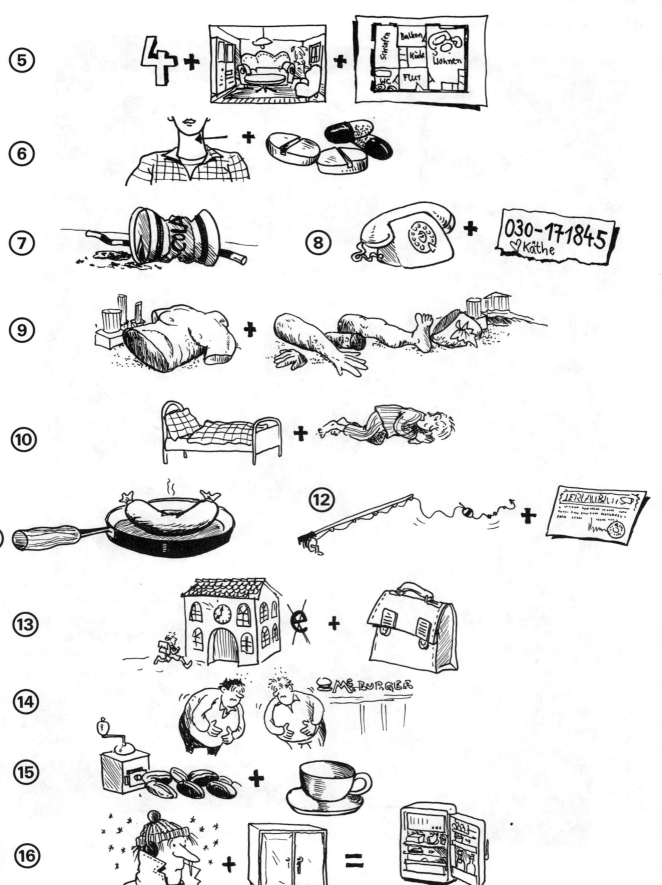

1 Ü1 **Wie viele Körperteile sehen Sie?**

Fernand Léger
Die Tänzerinnen mit den Vögeln, 1953
Öl auf Leinwand, 130 x 89 cm; Oslo, Sammlung Sonja Henie

Ich sehe .... und vier __Köpfe__ ...

....

Ü2 **Wie heißt der Plural?**

maskulinum: der

der Arbeiter, der Arm	der Gast	der Name
der Arzt, der Ausweis	der Hals, der Hamburger	der Paß, der Polizist
der Brief, der Bruder	der Junge	der Radiergummi
der Clown, der Computer	der Kopf, der Kuli	der Schmerz, der Schrank
der Deutschkurs	der Lehrer	der Star, der Stuhl
der Diplomat	der Mann	der Tag, der Teilnehmer
der Finger, der Fisch	der Mensch	der Termin, der Tisch
der Freund, der Füller	der Monat, der Motor	der Vater, der Vorname
der Fuß		

femininum: die

die Adresse	die Konferenz	die Stunde, die Suppe
die Dose	die Lampe, die Lippe	die Tablette, die Tasche
die Fahrkarte	die Mutter	die Tasse
die Flasche	die Nase, die Nummer	die Tomate
die Frau	die Olive	die Uhr
die Hand	die Party	die Wohnung
die Idee	die Schwester	die Zahl, die Zehe
die Information	die Stadt, die Straße	die Zeitung

neutrum: das

das Auge, das Auto	das Glas	das Ohr
das Baby, das Bein	das Haus, das Heft	das Radio
das Bild, das Brot	das Jahr	das Spiel
das Buch	das Kännchen, das Kind	das Steak
das Ei, das Essen	das Land	das Wort
das Foto	das Mädchen	das Zimmer

2 Ü3 **Lesen Sie die Wörter laut und sortieren Sie** 🔑

anfangen einkaufen beschreiben aufhören anrufen verdienen aussehen aufhalten rausziehen weitergehen aufschneiden verstehen ergänzen einladen zunähen mitbringen wegwerfen bezahlen benutzen aufschreiben zukleben

Trennbare Verben:

an|fangen

Nicht trennbare Verben:

beschreiben

Ü4 **Ergänzen Sie bitte Wörter aus Ü3** 🔑

1. Wann _____ der Deutschkurs _____?

2. Was _____ Frau Puente _____?

3. _____ Sie bitte einen Teilnehmer aus dem Deutschkurs!

4. Ich würfle nicht mehr; ich _____ _____.

5. Wieviel _____ Herr Klein im Monat?

6. So _____ ein Gefängnis _____:

7. Sie sind mein Gast, ich _____ Sie zum Essen _____.

8. _____ Sie Deutsch? – Ja, ein bißchen.

9. _____ Sie bitte die Sätze!

10. _____ Sie ein Lexikon!

11. _____ Sie mir bitte Ihre Telefonnummer _____!

    Ich _____ Sie morgen _____.

12. Wer _____ die Rechnung?

J5 Ergänzen Sie bitte

① _warst_ ② _____ ③ _____ ④ _____ ⑤ _____

Herr Schmidt hat drei Freunde. Sie gehen jeden Mittwoch in ein Gasthaus und spielen Karten. Letzten Mittwoch _____ Herr Schmidt nicht da. Er _____ krank,
er _____ Grippe. Aber heute _____ er wieder da. Seine Freunde fragen
ihn, wo er letzten Mittwoch _____.

J6 Gestern. – Fragen Sie bitte

1. _____? – Doch, ich war gestern zu Hause.

2. _____? – Nein, ich hatte keine Zeit.

3. _____? – Ja, ich hatte Husten.

4. _____? – Nein, Susi war nicht da.

5. _____? – Ja, ich war krank.

6. _____? – Nein, ich hatte kein Fieber.

7. _____? – Nein, ich hatte auch keine
     Kopfschmerzen.

8. _____? – Nein, ich war nicht beim Arzt.

Was sagen (fragen) Sie?

1. Sie sagen <u>Ihren</u> Namen, <u>Ihre</u> Adresse und
   <u>Ihre</u> Telefonnummer.

   _____

   _____

2. Ein Mann sagt: "Mein Name ist Abr--." -
   Sie verstehen den Namen nicht.

   _____

   _____

3. Herr Müller fragt Sie: "Trinken Sie
   auch ein Bier?" - Sie möchten lieber
   Mineralwasser.

   _____

   _____

4. Frau Puente fragt Sie:

   a) "Woher kommen Sie?"

   b) "Sprechen Sie auch Englisch?"

   a)_____

   b)_____

5. Goethe-Institut München, Zentrale:
   Telefon: ...../...................?
   Sie rufen die Auskunft an.

   _____

   _____

6. Eine Frau fragt Sie: "Sind Sie Leh-
   rer(in)?" - Sie sind kein(e) Lehrer(in),
   Sie sind .....

   _____

   _____

7. Ihr(e) Freund(in) fragt Sie: "Hast du
   heute Zeit?" - Sie haben keine.

   _____

   _____

8. Tomaten/Oliven DM .....? Fragen Sie!

   _____

9. Zweizimmerwohnung, 56 m²;
   Miete DM .....? Fragen Sie!

   _____

   _____

10. Ihr(e) Freund(in) fragt Sie: "Was essen
    wir heute?"

    _____

    _____

11. Der Arzt fragt Sie: "Was fehlt Ihnen
    denn?" (Fieber, Schmerzen, ...)

    _____

    _____

12. Der Lehrer fragt: "Wo waren Sie
    gestern?" (zu Hause, krank, ...)

    _____

A **Wörter: Machen Sie ein Kreuz**

1. Wie ..... es Ihnen?

a	trinkt
b	ist
c	kommt
d	geht

2. Wo ..... Sie?

a	kommen
b	nehmen
c	wohnen
d	heißen

3. Sie ..... aber gut Deutsch!

a	fragen
b	sprechen
c	hören
d	sagen

4. Wie ..... Sie? – Fischer.

a	sind
b	sprechen
c	heißen
d	fragen

5. Wie ..... man Ihren Namen?

a	ist
b	möchte
c	schreibt
d	heißt

6. ..... Sie eine Tasse Kaffee? – Ja, gerne.

a	Möchten
b	Essen
c	Kommen
d	Heißen

7. Der Deutschkurs ..... 20 Teilnehmer.

a	trifft
b	ist
c	hat
d	schreibt

8. Was ..... das? – Eine Mark achtzig.

a	heißt
b	tut
c	kostet
d	hat

9. Dr. Müller: "Was ..... Ihnen?"

a	geht
b	fehlt
c	tut
d	möchte

10. "..... die Brust auch weh?"

a	Tut
b	Fehlt
c	Hat
d	Ist

11. "Haben Sie die ..... schon lange?" –

a	Husten
b	Hals
c	Schmerzen
d	Ohren

12. "..... ist das?" – "Frau Müller."

a	Was
b	Wo
c	Wie
d	Wer

B Grammatik: Machen Sie ein Kreuz

1. Verzeihung, wie ..... Ihr Name?

a	bist
b	sein
c	ist
d	sind

2. Wie ..... das auf deutsch?

a	heiße
b	heißen
c	heißt
d	heiß

3. ..... du auch Englisch?

a	Spricht
b	Sprichst
c	Sprechen
d	Spreche

4. ..... Sie aus Berlin?

a	Bist
b	Ist
c	Sein
d	Sind

5. Das macht 5,80 DM. ..... du?

a	Bezahlst
b	Bezahlen
c	Bezahlt
d	Kostet

6. Herr Scoti, wo ..... Sie gestern?

a	warst
b	waren
c	war
d	wart

7. ..... du gestern keine Zeit?

a	Haben
b	Hattest
c	Hast
d	Hatte

8. Das ist ..... Füller.

a	eine
b	einer
c	eines
d	ein

9. Suchen Sie ..... Bleistift?

a	ein
b	einen
c	eine
d	eines

10. Ist das ..... Tee oder Kaffee?

a	eins
b	---
c	einer
d	eine

C Orthographie: Schreiben Sie bitte die Wörter

Beispiel: Guten Abe(0)! ➝

0	*Abend*

o Gu(1)en Abend, Herr Santos! Wie g(2)t es Ihnen?

● Gan(3) gu....., danke! Und wie g.....t es Ihnen, Herr Klein?

o Au(4)h gu....., danke. Das is(5) Frau Bührle aus München.

● Fre(6)t mich, Frau B--? Verzeihung, wie schr(7)bt man das?

oo B-ü-h-r-l-e.

● Noch einm(8)l, bitte!

oo B-ü-h-r-l-e. Sind Sie aus Fran(9)reich, Herr Santos?

● Nein, aus Bra(10)ilien. Was (11)rinken Sie?

oo Cola.

o Ich ne(12)me l(13)ber ein Bier.

oo Spre(14)chen Sie auch Franz(15)sisch?

● Nein, l(16)ider nicht. Aber ich spre.....e Englis(17)

oo Woher in Brasilien sin(18) Sie?

● Aus Rio.

1	
2	
3	
4	
5	
6	
7	
8	
9	
10	
11	
12	
13	
14	
15	
16	
17	
18	

D Lesen – Machen Sie ein Kreuz: richtig ☒ oder falsch ☒ ?

Das Picknick

Familie Bauer und Familie Scoti machen Picknick. Die Sonne scheint heute nicht, aber es ist auch nicht kalt. Frau Bauer macht das Essen. Sie hat Wurst und Käse, Eier, Butter, Milch, Cola und Mineralwasser. "Ich möchte ein Bier!" sagt Herr Bauer. Herr Scoti möchte auch ein Bier. "Bier habe ich nicht", antwortet Frau Bauer. "Aber hier ist Cola und Milch." Herr Scoti trinkt ein Glas Cola und ißt fünf Eier. Nach dem Essen gehen Herr Bauer und Herr Scoti angeln. Frau Scoti hört Radio, Frau Bauer schläft.

Herr Scoti kommt zurück. Er hat Bauchweh! "Das waren die fünf Eier und die Cola!" sagt Frau Scoti. "Hier, trink ein Glas Mineralwasser!" – "Nein, nein!" ruft Herr Scoti. Er hat Schmerzen. Er möchte nach Hause.

	richtig	falsch
1. Die Sonne scheint.		
2. Frau Bauer macht das Essen.		
3. Sie essen Hamburger.		
4. Herr Scoti und Herr Bauer trinken Bier.		
5. Herr Scoti ißt ein Ei.		
6. Frau Scoti schläft.		
7. Herr Scoti und Herr Bauer gehen angeln.		
8. Herr Bauer hat Bauchweh.		
9. Herr Scoti trinkt Mineralwasser.		
10. Herr Scoti möchte wieder angeln gehen.		

E Sprechen: Was sagen Sie? – Machen Sie ein Kreuz ☒ ⌐᠊ᠬ

1. Sie verstehen einen Namen nicht:

a	Mein Name ist Braun.
b	Verzeihung, wie ist Ihr Name?
c	Karlsson.
d	Guten Tag, Herr Karlsson.

2. Herr Braun sagt: "Woher kommen Sie?" – Sie antworten:

a	Er ist aus Brasilien.
b	Ich spreche Englisch.
c	Sie kommt aus Schweden.
d	Ich komme aus (Japan, den USA, der Türkei .....).

3. Sie stellen Herrn Conrad vor:

a	Das ist Herr Conrad.
b	Hallo, Herr Conrad!
c	Verzeihung, wie ist Ihr Name?
d	Wie geht es Ihnen, Herr Conrad?

4. "Möchten Sie eine Tasse Tee?"

a	Das geht nicht.
b	Das ist zuviel.
c	Nein, vielen Dank.
d	Nein, das ist zu teuer.

5. Dr. Kroll: "Haben Sie Schmerzen?"

a	Ja, sie ist krank.
b	Ja, mein Hals tut weh.
c	Ja, prima.
d	Ja, das ist eine Entzündung.

F Schreiben: Eine Bildergeschichte. Schreiben Sie zu jedem Bild zwei Sätze

1. _____

_____

2. _____

_____

3. _____

_____

4. _____

_____

5. _____

_____

6. _____

_____

geszeit und Uhrzeit

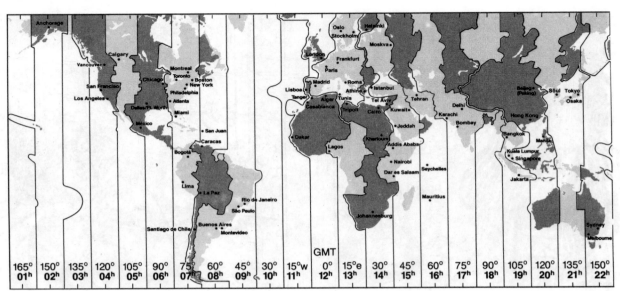

„Morgen"	= ca. 5.00 – 9.00 Uhr	„Nachmittag"	= ca. 14.00 – 18.00 Uhr
„Vormittag"	= ca. 9.00 – 12.00 Uhr	„Abend"	= ca. 18.00 – 22.00 Uhr
„Mittag"	= ca. 12.00 – 14.00 Uhr	„Nacht"	= ca. 22.00 – 5.00 Uhr

Ü1 Lesen Sie bitte

Frankfurt, Paris und Rom ist es jetzt
ttag, 13 Uhr. Aber in Tokyo ist es schon
end, 21 Uhr. In Rio de Janeiro ist es
tzt erst 9 Uhr am Vormittag. In New York
t es gerade Morgen, 7 Uhr. In San Fran-
sco und Los Angeles ist es noch Nacht,
Uhr.

Ü2 Wo ist es jetzt Morgen/Mittag/Abend?

Schreiben Sie die Städte und sprechen Sie
nach folgendem Beispiel:
"In Mexico City ist es jetzt Morgen." -
"Wieviel Uhr?" - "6 Uhr."

Morgen	Mittag	Abend
Mexico City	Madrid	Bangkok
. . . . . .	. . . . .	. . .

Ü3 Sprechen und schreiben Sie

er Zeitunterschied zwischen <u>Tokyo</u> und
rankfurt ist acht Stunden."

eking - Teheran / Lima - Casablanca /
Oslo - Bangkok / Montreal - Istanbul /
. . . . .

Ü4 Sprechen und schreiben Sie

"In <u>Frankfurt</u> ist es Morgen, <u>5 Uhr</u>.
Dann ist es in <u>New York</u> Nacht, 23 Uhr."

Rom - 20 Uhr - Sydney / Stockholm -
15 Uhr - Peking / Paris - 2 Uhr - Buenos
Aires / Montreal - 8 Uhr - Madrid / . . . . .

2 Ü5 Schreiben Sie einen Dialog: Wann treffen wir uns?

J 6 Hören Sie noch einmal die Texte an und ergänzen Sie 🔑

3

) Durchsagen am Flughafen

Ausland International
Abflug / Departures

• _____ British Airways _____ _____,

Flugsteig A _____.

• _____ Condor _____ Palma de

Mallorca und Ibiza, _____ _____.

• Abflug _____ _____ _____ Athen, _____ _____.

• _____ Hopier, Passagier _____ _____, _____ zum Lufthansa-Flug-

scheinschalter _____ _____.

• Letzter _____ Lufthansa _____ _____ _____, _____ _____.

) Durchsagen am Bahnhof

ZEIT	ZUGLAUF		ZIEL	GLEIS	HINWEIS
15 22	FD Rosenh Freilassing		BERCHTESGADEN	15	ca. 30 Min später
15 32	D Holzkirchen		TEGERNSEE/LENGGR	25	ca. 10 Min später
15 52	IC Augsburg Stuttgart	Mannheim Frankfurt	KASSEL	13	
15 55	S		DEISENHOFEN	35	
15 56	E Pfaffenh Wolnzach		INGOLSTADT NORD	33	
15 57	IC Augsburg Würzburg	Frankfurt/← Köln	DORTMUND	22	
16 00	D Tutzing Weilheim	Murnau Garmisch-P	MITTENWALD	29	
16 01	E Buchlon		MEMMINGEN	17	

ZEIT	ZUGLAUF		ZIEL	GLEIS	HINWEIS
16 04	N Pfaffenh Wolnzach		LOURDES	14	
16 05	N Markt Schwaben		INGOLSTADT	32	
16 07	N Freising		MUEHLDORF	9	
16 10	IC Kempten Lindau	Bregenz St Gallen	LANDSHUT/BAY	23	
16 10	E Holzkirchen		ZUERICH	20	
16 15			BAYRISCHZELL	36	

• Am _____ _____ bitte _____, _____ schließen, Vorsicht

bei der _____.

• _____ Gleis _____ _____ _____ der Schnellzug 892 _____ Salzburg zur

Weiterfahrt _____ Karlsruhe. _____ Uhr _____.

• _____, _____ private Durchsage: Werner _____ Dieter Steiner,

_____ und _____ Steiner, möchten _____ zum Kundendienst der

_____ am _____ _____ _____.

• _____ _____ _____ _____ _____ der Intercity _____ "Ernst

Barlach" aus Hamburg-Altona. Ankunft _____ _____ _____.

• _____ _____ _____ _____ in Kürze _____ _____ verspätete Fernexpreß

_____ "Berchtesgadener Land" _____ Dortmund zur _____ _____

Berchtesgaden, mit _____ _____ Salzburg. .....

59

5A

4 Ü7 "Richtig" (r) oder "falsch" (f)?

Lesen Sie noch einmal den Text (→ Lehrbuch, S. 66) und kreuzen Sie an!

	r	f
1. In Frankfurt ist jedes Jahr die Internationale Buchmesse.	X	
2. 10.000 Menschen kommen in die Stadt.		
3. Brigitte Weiß möchte auch zur Buchmesse.		
4. Sie ruft ein Hotel an.		
5. Sie möchte ein Hotelzimmer in Kelkheim.		
6. Sie braucht das Zimmer nur für eine Nacht.		
7. Sie kann nur noch ein Privatzimmer in Kelkheim bekommen.		
8. Von Kelkheim bis nach Frankfurt (City) sind es nur 15 Kilometer.		
9. Sie kann mit dem Bus fahren.		
10. Die Telefonnummer ist: null - sechs - eins - neun - fünf - acht - neun - null - drei.		

Ü8

"Kommt ihr mit nach Frankfurt zur Buchmesse?"

Ergänzen Sie das Gespräch

o .....

o Vielleicht. _____ fahrt_____ denn genau?

o Und _____ _____ ihr zurück?

o Wir _____ nur Zeit bis Donnerstag.

o _____ ihr schon ein _____?

o Gut, danke schön, bis dann!

● Hallo, Sabine, hier _____ Elke. Wir _____ nächste Woche _____ Frankfurt zur Buchmesse. _____ ihr _____

● Am Dienstagvormittag, _____ 8 _____

● Das wissen _____ noch nicht genau; vielleicht am Donnerstag oder ____ Freit

● Gut, dann bleiben wir auch nur bis _____.

● Nein, aber ich _____ gleich die Touristen-Zentrale in _____ _____ Dann rufe _____ dich wieder _____

● Bis dann. Tschüs!

60

9 Schreiben Sie das Datum, bitte. 🔑

ispiel:

.1.1987: (1) Heute ist der erste Januar neunzehnhundertsiebenundachtzig.

(2) Heute haben wir den ersten Januar neunzehnhundertsiebenundachtzig.

11.12.1996; 13.3.1989; 31.8.1988; 20.6.1989; 17.2.1992; 16.9.1987; 3.5.1989;
8.10.1990; 25.4.1993; 7.7.1991; 12.11.1994; 31.12.1999

10 Beantworten Sie bitte die Fragen 🔑

1. In Nordrhein-Westfalen ...

Schulferien	Frühjahr Ostern	Himmelfahrt Pfingsten	Sommer	Herbst	Winter Weihnachten
Baden-Württemberg	13.4. – 25.4.	1.6. – 5.6.	2.7. – 15.8.	26.10. – 30.10.	23.12. – 5.1.
Bayern	13.4. – 25.4.	9.6. – 20.6.	30.7. – 14.9.	—	23.12. – 9.1.
Berlin	4.4. – 25.4.	6.6. – 9.6.	25.6. – 8.8.	2.10. – 10.10.	23.12. – 6.1.
Brandenburg	14.4. – 16.4.	5.6. – 9.6.	29.6. – 7.8.	5.10. – 10.10.	23.12. – 6.1.
Bremen	1.4. – 21.4.	—	25.6. – 8.8.	5.10. – 13.10.	23.12. – 6.1.
Hamburg*	16.4. – 21.4.	29.5.	18.6. – 1.8.	5.10. – 17.10.	21.12. – 2.1.
Hessen	3.4. – 22.4.	—	22.6. – 31.7.	5.10. – 16.10.	23.12. – 8.1.
Mecklenburg-Vorpommern	15.4. – 21.4.	5.6. – 9.6.	13.7. – 21.8.	12.10. – 17.10.	23.12. – 2.1.
Niedersachsen	1.4. – 21.4.	6.6. – 9.6.	25.6. – 5.8.	9.10. – 10.10.	23.12. – 6.1.
Nordrhein-Westfalen	6.4. – 25.4.	9.6.	16.7. – 29.8.	19.10. – 24.10.	23.12. – 6.1.
Rheinland-Pfalz	6.4. – 25.4.	9.6.	23.7. – 2.9.	19.10. – 24.10.	23.12. – 9.1.
Saarland	13.4. – 27.4.		23.7. – 5.9.	26.10. – 31.10.	21.12. – 6.1.
Sachsen	16.4. – 24.4.	4.6. – 9.6.	6.7. – 14.8.	15.10. – 24.10.	23.12. – 6.1.
Sachsen-Anhalt	13.4. – 21.4.	4.6. – 10.6.	20.7. – 28.8.	19.10. – 23.10.	22.12. – 5.1.
Schleswig-Holstein	9.4. – 25.4.		18.6. – 1.8.	5.10. – 17.10.	23.12. – 7.1.
Thüringen	13.4. – 16.4.	5.6. – 9.6.	13.7. – 21.8.	19.10. – 24.10.	23.12. – 2.1.

Jeweils **erster** und **letzter** Ferientag   * Frühjahrsferien: 9.3. – 21.3.   Stand: Februar – ohne Gewähr

. Wann haben die Kinder in Nordrhein-Westfalen Schulferien?

. Wo beginnen die Weihnachtsferien am dreiundzwanzigsten Dezember?

. Wo dauern die Osterferien bis zum einundzwanzigsten April?

. Wie viele Tage Osterferien haben die Kinder a) in Bayern, b) in Berlin,

c) in Hessen, d) in Sachsen, e) in Thüringen?

. Von wann bis wann dauern die Sommerferien a) in Brandenburg, b) in Hamburg,

c) in Niedersachsen, d) im Saarland?

. Wann / Von wann bis wann / Wie lange haben die Kinder in Ihrem Land Ferien?

Ü 11 Wann ist Teddy Panther wo?
Hören Sie noch einmal die Radio-Ansage und ergänzen Sie die Städte und das Datum 🔑 📼

Das ist die Stimme von Teddy Panther. Der Sänger macht im April eine Tournee durch

ie Bundesrepublik. Hier die Stationen: Sein erstes Konzert ist am _____

n _____ in der Ostseehalle. Am _____ tritt er in_____

uf. Und weiter geht's: Am _____ in _____, am _____ und

_____ in _____, am _____ in _____ .

om _____ bis _____ gastiert Teddy Panther in _____. Am _____

n _____, und am _____ und _____ das Finale in _____,

n der Olympiahalle."

6 "Hier Praxis Dr. Huber."

Ü12 Was sagt Herr Pasolini?
Hören und schreiben Sie bitte 🔑

Hier Praxis Dr. Huber, guten Tag!

Guten Tag, mein Name ist Pasolini. Ich habe Zahnschmerzen. Haben Sie einen Termin für mich? Möglichst bald!

Am Dienstag, den dreiundzwanzigsten, um 8 Uhr.

Am Freitag, den zwölften Februar. Um zwölf Uhr fünfzehn ist noch ein Termin frei.

Nein, das geht leider nicht. Freitagnachmittag ist die Praxis geschlossen.

Ja, zwölf Uhr fünfzehn. - Verzeihung, wie ist Ihr Name?

Ü13 Frau Petersen ruft an.
Hören Sie das Gespräch und ergänzen Sie bitte 🔑

o Hier Praxis Dr. Huber, guten Tag!

● Guten Tag, _____ _____ Petersen

  Ich _____ einen _____ für

  _____ nachmittag.

o Ja, _____, _____ Uhr _____

● Ja, richtig. _____ das _____

  leider _____. Meine Tochter ist ...

  _____ Sie _____ nachmittag

  einen _____ _____?

o Morgen ist _____. Da ist

  _____ _____. Aber Donners

  tagvormittag ...

● _____ Vormittag _____ ich leider

  _____. _____ es _____ ____

  _____?

o _____ Uhr?

● Ja, _____ _____ _____

o _____ _____ _____

  _____, 17 _____

● _____ Dank, auf Wiederhören!

o Wiederhören.

14 **Herr Bamberg ruft an.**
Hören Sie das Gespräch und beantworten
Sie die Fragen

Wie heißt Herr Bamberg mit Vornamen?

Warum ruft Herr Bamberg an?

Was möchte Herr Bamberg?

War Herr Bamberg schon einmal bei Dr. Huber?

Warum hat Herr Bamberg keine Zeit?

Wann möchte Herr Bamberg zu Dr. Huber kommen?

Was sagt die Sprechstundenhilfe?

Kommt Herr Bamberg heute zu Dr. Huber, oder kommt er nicht?

15 **Herr Riad hat "Fieber". – Ergänzen Sie bitte**

rr Riad hat am 30. Juli Examen. Heute ist Montag, der 29. Juli. Herr Riad _____

gst. Sein Kopf tut weh. "Ich habe _____!" sagt Herr Riad.

_____ den Arzt an. Er _____ einen Termin. Die

_____ sucht einen Termin. "_____

e das Fieber schon _____?" fragt die Sprechstundenhilfe. "Nein, erst

it _____ früh", antwortet Herr Riad. "Gut, dann _____

e bitte morgen, 10 Uhr!" - "Nein, das _____ nicht! Ich _____ heute

ch kommen!" ruft Herr Riad. "Ich habe sehr _____ Schmerzen!" - Die Sprechstun-

nhilfe sagt: "Moment mal, also dann heute, _____ , 17 Uhr 30."

"Vielen _____", sagt Herr Riad.

16 **Verstehen Sie das? Ganz einfach! – Ergänzen Sie bitte**

				6 Sa
		vor-gestern		7 So
		gestern		8 Mo
		heute	→	9 Di
		morgen		10 Mi
		über-morgen		11 Do
				12 Fr

te ist heute heute.
te ist gestern gestern.
te ist morgen morgen.

rgen ist heute gestern.
rgen ist gestern *vorgestern*
rgen ist morgen _____
rgen ist übermorgen _____

ermorgen ist heute _____
ermorgen ist morgen _____
ermorgen ist übermorgen _____

Am neunten ist der neunte heute.
Am neunten ist der achte gestern.
Am neunten ist der zehnte morgen.

Am zehnten ist der *neunte* gestern.
Am zehnten ist der _____ vorgestern.
Am zehnten ist der _____ heute.
Am zehnten ist der _____ morgen.

Am elften ist der neunte _____
Am elften ist der zehnte _____
Am elften ist der elfte _____

7 Die Autopanne

Ü 17 Was steht im Text (→ Lehrbuch, S. 69)? Korrigieren Sie bitte

Was ist hier anders? Unterstreichen Sie: | **Und was steht im Text? Schreiben Sie bitte**

Herr Gröner hat *ein Auto.*

Er braucht Hilfe. Er ist nicht in Eile:
Um achtzehn Uhr hat er eine Konferenz in
Duisburg. Jetzt ist es kurz nach sechzehn
Uhr. Herr Gröner findet eine Tankstelle,
die ist noch offen. Der Meister sagt, er
hilft sofort; vielleicht ist nur der Ben-
zintank leer - das geht ziemlich schnell.
Der Meister schreibt die Autonummer von
Herrn Gröner auf. Dann ruft er die Polizei. Herr Gröner fährt mit seinem Auto
nach Duisburg.

Herr Gröner hat eine Autopanne.

Ü 18 Lesen Sie den Text. Schreiben Sie dann das Telefongespräch

"Kein Bild, kein Ton, wir kommen schon."

Es ist Samstagnachmittag, 15 Uhr. Frau Weber möchte ein Tennismatch aus Wimbledon sehen. Sie macht den Fernsehapparat an - aber der Apparat ist kaputt. Frau Weber ruft
Fernseh-Service an. Der Mann am Telefon sagt, er kann den Apparat heute nicht mehr r
rieren. Er hat keine Zeit, und seine Kollegin ist krank. Aber er kann Frau Weber ein
neuen Apparat bringen; das dauert höchstens dreißig Minuten. Dann kann Frau Weber da
Tennismatch sehen. .....

Ü1 **Suchen Sie 27 Verben und machen Sie Sätze**

M	B	E	S	U	C	H	E	N	C	J	M	X	E
I	E	B	A	N	F	A	N	G	E	N	S	F	I
T	G	E	B	E	N	B	Y	D	A	U	E	R	N
F	I	N	D	E	N	E	P	H	R	O	G	A	S
A	N	R	U	F	E	N	G	R	B	F	N	G	T
H	N	H	S	C	H	L	A	F	E	N	E	E	E
R	E	G	K	U	M	S	T	E	I	G	E	N	I
E	N	E	O	F	E	K	O	S	T	E	N	B	G
N	E	H	M	E	N	A	V	S	E	H	E	N	E
A	Z	E	M	H	E	L	F	E	N	U	D	T	N
W	D	N	E	E	W	O	H	N	E	N	L	C	K
K	O	E	N	N	E	N	B	L	E	I	B	E	N

Beispiel: "schlafen": *Ich kann nicht schlafen*

Ü2 **Wie heißen die Wörter? (Ergänzen Sie die Sätze)**

① ② ③ ④ ⑤ ⑥ ⑦ ⑧ ⑨

←____?

1. Frau Weiß möchte zur Buchmesse; sie braucht ein ___①___ .

2. Der Motor ist ___②___ .

3. Herr Gröner braucht ___③___ .

4. Die ___④___ dauern vom 26.
Oktober bis zum 2. November.

5. Wir treffen uns um 7 Uhr
am ___⑤___ .

6. ___⑥___ Dupont bitte zum
Flugscheinschalter!

7. Es ist genau fünf ___⑦___
vor acht.

8. Am ___⑧___ drei bitte einsteigen, Türen schließen!

9. Halb acht ist zu spät, wir
haben noch keine ___⑨___ .

5B

1 **Ü1** "Ich möchte…" / "Wann kann ich…?" – Ergänzen Sie bitte. 🔑

o Ich _____ morgen

nach Berlin. Wann

_____ ich fliegen?

o Das ist zu früh.

_____ ich auch am Mittag fliegen?

o Und wann _____ ich übermorgen wieder

zurückfliegen? Ich _____ am Abend

wieder zu Hause sein.

● Sie _____ am Vor-

mittag um 7 Uhr fliegen.

Dann sind Sie um 8 Uhr in

Berlin.

● Ja, da _____ Sie auch fliegen,

um 11 Uhr 15.

● Sie _____ um 18 Uhr 35 fliegen,

dann sind Sie um 19 Uhr 40 in Düsseldo

Ü2 **Ergänzen Sie bitte** 🔑

a) _____

o Wir _____ in den Osterferien

nach Paris fahren, kommt ihr mit?

● Wie lange _____ ihr denn bleiben?

o Vier oder fünf Tage.

● Und wann fahrt ihr los?

o Am Freitag.

● Hm. Ich rufe Gisela an, vielleicht

_____ sie mitfahren; dann _____

_____ wir zusammen mit dem Auto fah-

ren.

b) _____

● Hallo, Gisela! Sabine und Peter _____

_____ am Freitag nach Paris fahren

..... Ja, nach Paris ..... _____

du auch mitfahren? Ich _____

dich einladen ..... Ja, ich habe Zeit

ich _____ mitfahren ..... Du

_____ wirklich nicht? Das ist

aber schade. ..... Natürlich _____

ich das verstehen, ... ach so, du

_____ nach Athen. Wann denn

..... Im Mai? Da _____ ich leider

nicht. ..... Wie bitte? Das macht

nichts? ..... _____

du denn ganz allein fahren, ohne mich

..... Schade, da _____ man nich

machen. Tschüs!

c) _____

● Also, Gisela _____ nicht nach

Paris. Sie _____ im Mai nach

Athen, aber allein.

Jetzt _____ ich erst einmal

einen Kognak.

Ü3 **Schreiben Sie die Sätze zu den richtigen Modellen (auf Seite 67 und 68) und fragen Sie**

<u>Beispiel</u>: Die Sprechstundenhilfe sucht einen Termin: <u>Was</u> sucht die Sprechstunden-
hilfe? - <u>Einen Termin.</u>

1. Herr Pasolini möchte einen Termin. 2. Ein Termin um 14 Uhr ist besser. 3. Wir kommen mit zur Buchmesse. 4. Peter Martens ist Ingenieur. 5. Der Zug fährt um 14 Uhr 30. 6. Sie besuchen ein Fußball-Länderspiel. 7. Eine Fahrkarte nach Amsterdam kostet 143 Mark. 8. Er nimmt eine Schlaftablette. 9. Die Sommerferien sind lang. 10. Sie fahren zum Oktoberfest nach München. 11. Brigitte Weiß ruft die Touristenzentrale an. 12. Sie braucht ein Hotelzimmer. 13. Wir fahren fast sechs Stunden. 14. Wilhelm Etzin war der Besitzer. 15. Alle sind zufrieden. 16. Barış Önal kommt aus der Türkei. 17. Die Sprechstundenhilfe notiert den Termin. 18. Sie weiß den Namen (nicht mehr). 19. Herr Pasolini ist krank. 20. Herr Gröner fährt (mit dem Taxi) nach Düsseldorf. 21. Die Schule beginnt erst am Montag. 22. Der 13. Juni ist der erste Ferientag. 23. Herr Gröner hat eine Autopanne. 24. Er braucht Hilfe. 25. Die Kinder sind (noch) zu klein. 26. Es ist fünf Minuten vor zwölf. 27. Herr Pasolini buchstabiert seinen Namen. 28. Deutsch ist leicht. 29. Das ist eine Entzündung. 30. Der Flug dauert zwei Stunden. 31. Frau Braun geht zu Herrn Spiros.

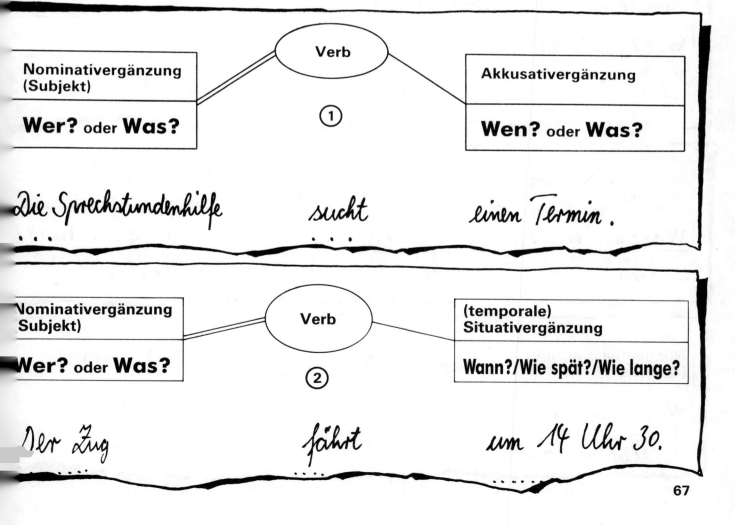

32. Der 4. August ist ein Sonntag.   33. Herr Gröner findet eine Autowerkstatt.
34. Ich war (früher) berühmt.   .35. Ich war Schauspieler.   36. Peter Martens kommt
aus Hamburg.   37. Der Meister schreibt Adresse und Telefonnummer von Herrn Gröner
auf.   38. Dann ruft er ein Taxi.   39. In Nordrhein-Westfalen dauern die Ferien vom
18. Juni bis zum 3. August.   40. Mustafa Benhallam stammt aus Fez.   41. Ich hole den
Wagen (morgen) ab.   42. Maria ist Krankenschwester.   43. Der Tag ist schön und warm.
44. Der Zug kommt um 12 Uhr 15.   45. Maria holt ein Messer.   46. Herr Fischer hat
Fieber und Schmerzen.   47. Ich gehe nach Hause.   48. Die Ferien fangen (aber erst)
am 1. August an; sie dauern bis zum 16. September.   49. Früher hatte ich Geld, ein
Auto, ein Haus.   50. Herr Klein verdient 3.200 Mark netto.   51. Herr Dupont kommt
aus Frankreich.   52. Anni Sinowatz ist Ärztin.   53. Die Miete ist sehr hoch.   54. Ich
möchte eine Bratwurst und eine Flasche Bier.   55. Wir nehmen eine Portion Kaffee.
56. Barış Önal ist Arbeiter.   57. Ich habe eine Idee.   58. Herr Myers kommt aus den
USA.   59. Miza Lim studiert Deutsch.   60. Sie trinkt eine Cola.

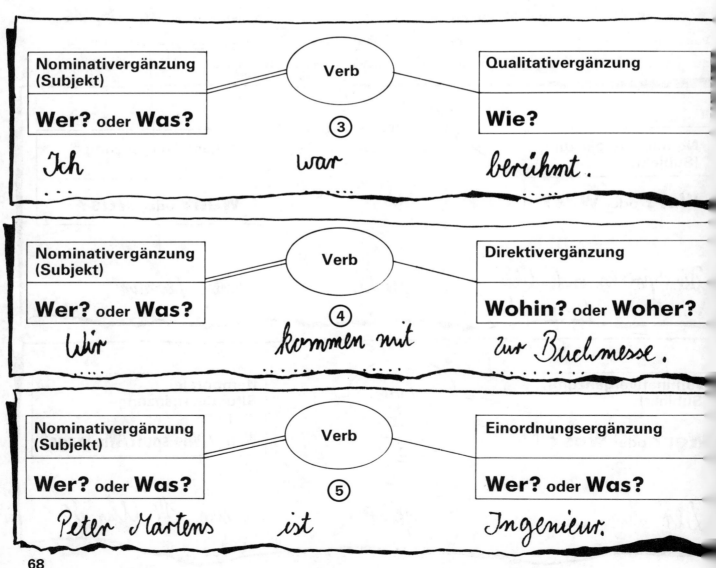

Nominativergänzung (Subjekt)	Verb	Qualitativergänzung
Wer? oder **Was?**	③	**Wie?**
Ich	war	berühmt.

Nominativergänzung (Subjekt)	Verb	Direktivergänzung
Wer? oder **Was?**	④	**Wohin?** oder **Woher?**
Wir	kommen mit	zur Buchmesse.

Nominativergänzung (Subjekt)	Verb	Einordnungsergänzung
Wer? oder **Was?**	⑤	**Wer?** oder **Was?**
Peter Martens	ist	Ingenieur.

Ü1 **Dichtung und Wahrheit – korrigieren Sie Herrn Rasch**

1

Dichtung   und   **Wahrheit**

1. Herr Rasch erzählt: "Um neun Uhr war viel Verkehr. ·····

Um neun Uhr war nicht viel Verkehr. Die Straße war leer. ···· Herr Rasch

2. Ich war erst um zehn Uhr da. ·····

3. Dann habe ich eine Stunde gewartet. Herr Meinke hat gerade Briefe diktiert. ······

4. Ich habe bis halb zwei mit Herrn Meinke geredet. ·····

5. Dann habe ich schnell einen Hamburger geholt."

6A

1 Ü2 **Schreiben Sie Geschichten zu den Bildern**

Am Morgen ist Herr Rasch

Ü3 **Hören Sie den Dialog und ergänzen Sie**

Vater:

● Wo _____ _____ jetzt her?

● Und was _____ du da so lange _____?
  _____ ist es _____ vor _____!

● Hausaufgaben? _____ _____

  Hausaufgaben? Um eins _____ die

  Schule aus!

● Und _____ ist deine _____ _____?

● Pluto?

● Ihr _____ Fußball _____!

Fritz:

o _____ Mario.

o Hausaufgaben.

o Ja, um _____ _____ _____ _____
  bei Mario - dann _____
  und dann _____ wir Hausaufgabe
  _____. Das _____ so _____
  Deutsch, Mathe, Bio ..... Ich _____
  Mario Mathe _____.

o Das _____ Pluto _____

o Der _____ von Mario.

o Nein, wir _____ _____, wir
  _____ _____. Frag Mario

Ü4 **Was hat Mario wirklich gemacht? Schreiben Sie die Geschichte (➜ Lehrbuch, S. 75)**

Ü 5 Was kostet wieviel? Hören Sie noch einmal die "Durchsagen im Supermarkt" **2**

1.29
-.99
1.⁴⁹
0
1.49
1.99

Pepsi-Cola

Italienische **Blutorangen** Kl. II

1 Ltr. **THIELE Tee** Broken Spezial

Holländische Markenbutter

1.⁹⁹

8.⁹⁹
0

12.99

13.98

Norwegischer **Ridderkäse** 60 % Fett i. Tr.

Jacobs Kaffee Edelmocca

Kognak Napoleon 0,7 Ltr.

"Paulaner Hell" Bier 20 Fl. à 0,5 Ltr.

Ital. oder franz. **Blumenkohl** Kl. II

Frischmilch

Ü 6 "Durchsagen im Supermarkt": Ergänzen Sie bitte

1. Verehrte Kunden! Wir _____ Ihnen _____ _____ Sonderangebote

   zu _____ _____ . Zum _____ : 500 _____ Jacobs _____

   "Edelmocca" oder, _____ Teefreunde, Thiele Tee "Broken Special", _____

   500 Gramm – _____ Packung nur _____ Mark _____ .

2. Die _____ des Südens _____ unseren _____ : _____ Blutorangen,

   Handelsklasse 2, 1,5 Kilogramm _____ _____ eine Mark 99! _____Blumenkohl,

   _____ _____ oder _____ - nur _____ Mark _____ pro Stück.

3. Bei uns _____ Sie die _____ Kraft der _____ zu Minipreisen: Frisch-

   milch nur 99 _____ pro _____ ; Holländische Markenbutter, _____

   _____ _____ eine Mark 99! Magerer gesunder Speisequark _____

   _____ uns nur _____ _____ der 250-Gramm-Becher. _____ _____ nor-

   wegische Spezialität: Ridderkäse mit _____ Prozent Fettgehalt gibt's _____

   _____ unglaubliche eins 49 je _____ Gramm.

4. Und abends _____ _____ durstig: _____ , die Literflasche _____

   für _____ _____ , Paulaner Hell, das frische _____ für die _____

   _____ , der Kasten nur _____ _____ _____ . Und _____

   _____ ein besonderes Gläschen _____ : Kognak "Napoleon", die 0,7-Liter-

   Flasche zu _____ _____ _____ . .....

3 **Ü7** "Richtig" (r) oder "falsch" (f)?

Hören und lesen Sie noch einmal die Dialoge (→ Lehrbuch, S. 78 – 79) und kreuzen Sie an:

	r	f
1. Die Chefin hat vor zehn Minuten angerufen.	X	
2. Die Chefin ruft noch einmal an.		
3. Die Chefin hat mit Maria gesprochen.		
4. Was hat die Chefin gesagt? Maria hat es vergessen.		
5. Maria hat vor zehn Minuten gegessen.		
6. Emil ruft die Chefin an.		
7. Emil hat eben angerufen.		
8. Die Chefin glaubt, Maria hat nicht verstanden, was sie gesagt hat.		
9. Die Firma Busch hat das Auto repariert.		
10. Emil hat die Firma Busch angerufen.		
11. Emil hat das Auto repariert, aber es funktioniert nicht.		
12. Die Batterie ist kaputt.		
13. Emil möchte das Auto morgen früh holen.		
14. Emil holt das Auto heute noch.		
15. Die Chefin braucht das Auto heute noch.		

Ü8 **Was sagt Emil? Schreiben Sie bitte**

Es ist 22 Uhr. Emil kommt ins Gasthaus. Er ist sehr müde; er hat bis 21 Uhr gearbeitet. Das Auto von Firma Busch .....

Seine Freunde fragen: "Warum kommst du denn jetzt erst? Wo warst du denn so lange?"

Emil erzählt:

"Also, das war so:...

Ü9 **Aber die Freunde glauben die Geschichte nicht.
Spielen (und schreiben) Sie das Gespräch weiter**

Ü 10 Hören und lesen Sie noch einmal "Verloren!" und "Gefunden!" (→ Lehrbuch, S. 80 – 81) und beantworten Sie die Fragen: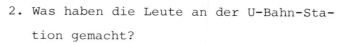

<u>Verloren</u>

1. Was sucht der Mann?

2. Wo sind der Mann und die Frau (über-all) gewesen?

3. Was haben sie am Kiosk gemacht?

4. Wo waren sie dann? / Was haben sie dann gemacht?

5. Und dann?

<u>Gefunden</u>

1. Der Mann hat gesucht. Wo war er zuerst?

2. Was haben die Leute an der U-Bahn-Station gemacht?

3. Was hat der Mann im Kaufhof gemacht?

4. Wie hat er das Geld gefunden? / Wo war das Geld?

Ü 11 **Frau Weiß überlegt...: Schreiben Sie bitte**

Frau Weiß ist heute von Köln nach Frankfurt zur Internationalen Buchmesse gefahren. Jetzt ist sie im Hotel. Aber ihre Tasche ist weg! .....

"Am Kölner Hauptbahnhof habe ich ...

6 **Ü 12** **Was ist hier falsch?**
Vergleichen Sie mit dem Text auf S. 82 (→ Lehrbuch) und korrigieren Sie!

Er ist *nicht schnell* ins
Bad gegangen; er war müde.
...

FR. 13. September

Um 8 Uhr ist Peter aufgestanden und <u>schnell</u> ins Bad gegangen.
Er war nur fünfzehn Minuten im Bad; dann hat er sich angezogen.
Um Viertel vor neun war das Frühstück fertig.
Er hat Tee getrunken, Brot gegessen und die Nachrichten gehört.
Um 10 Uhr ist er mit der U-Bahn in die Stadt gefahren; er ist einmal umgestiegen.
Er hat für Monika Blumen gekauft und eine Stunde lang auf sie gewartet.
Aber Monika ist nicht gekommen; sie hat keine Zeit gehabt.
Um 12 Uhr 40 ist Peter nach Hause gefahren; dabei hat er sein Geld verloren.
Um drei Uhr ist er nach Hause gekommen. Er war sehr traurig.
Er hat einen Brief an Monika geschrieben. Dann hat er Susi angerufen.

Ü 13 **Hören Sie das Telefongespräch zwischen Monika und Susi.**
Notieren Sie Stichwörter zu den folgenden Fragen:

1. <u>Wo</u> ist Monika gewesen?

2. <u>Was</u> hat sie gesucht?

3. <u>Was</u> hat sie gekauft?

4. <u>Wen</u> hat sie <u>wo</u> getroffen?

5. <u>Was</u> erzählt Monika von Peter?

6. <u>Was</u> hat sie vergessen?

1. (In der) Stadt
2. ....
3. ....
4

7. "Und was machen wir jetzt?" <u>Welchen Vorschlag</u> macht <u>Monika</u>, und was sagt Susi dazu?

8. <u>Welchen Vorschlag</u> macht <u>Susi</u>? <u>Warum</u>?

Ü 14 **Schreiben Sie nun den Inhalt des Telefongesprächs**

Susi hat Monika angerufen. Monika ist gerade nach Hause gekommen. Sie ...

r Einbrecher! Frau Gieseke erzählt...

5 Hören Sie den Text und ergänzen Sie

as _____ eine Aufregung! Ich _____ was _____,

o um _____, ein Klirren, einer _____ die

_____ kaputtgemacht.

nd wie! _____ ich habe die _____ leise

_____, und _____ _____ _____!

a, der _____.

a, _____, _____!

ch _____, er hat _____ _____.

r hat _____ aufgemacht und _____.

ch _____ ihn _____: "_____ Sie mal,

_____ machen _____ _____?"

Der sagt: "Entschuldigen Sie, _____ _____

Bahnhofstr. Nr. 9?" - "Ja, _____," sag ich,

Bahnhofstr. 9." _____ _____ sagt er: " Ja,

_____ _____ mich denn _____ _____?"

Und ich sag:"_____, ich _____ _____ nicht,

wer _____ Sie _____?" Und er: "Na, ich _____

doch ein _____ _____ Hermann!"

- Haben Sie_____

_____ _____?

- Wer??

- Ein _____?

- Oh Gott!

- Und _____ haben _____

gemacht?

- Und er?

- So eine Frechheit!

- Von Hermann??

o Ja, Hermann _____ _____ Mann. Also, ich sag zu

ihm: "Nein, _____ Sie sich mal _____. Ich

mach Ihnen erst ne _____ _____, und

_____ _____ ich Hermann _____."

● _____ _____ denn

Ihr Mann?

o Der _____ nicht ___ _____. Also ich _____

_____, und der _____ da und schwitzt.

● Schwitzt??

o Na klar, der hat _____ _____.

● Ich _____, _____

haben _____ geha

o Ja, _____ ich, _____ _____ er. Und _____

habe ich _____. .....

Ü 16 **Und wie geht die Geschichte weiter?**
(Malen und) schreiben Sie bitte:

Das sind ja tolle Geschichten!

Urlaubsgeschichten

Science fiction

Kriminalgeschichten

6B

Ü1 **Regelmäßige Verben: Wie heißen die Partizipien II?** 🗝️

ge /......... /(e)t	.../ge/........ /(e)t	.........../(e)t
ge/ leb /t	ein/ge/ kauf/t	verdien/t
ge/arbeit/et		

leben, arbeiten, einkaufen,   kaufen, fehlen, zeigen,   ergänzen, brauchen, wohnen,
verdienen, (sich) freuen,   besuchen, kosten, stöhnen,   aufmachen, reden, holen,
meinen, antworten, angeln,   erzählen, suchen, dauern,   machen, ausräumen, schicken
zunähen, flirten, zukleben,   stecken, einpacken,   haben, sagen, übernachten,
spielen, hören, nachschauen,   kaputtmachen, warten,   kochen, fragen, schwitzen,

Ü2 **Unregelmäßige Verben: Wie heißen die Partizipien II?** 🗝️

		ge/........./en	.../ge/....../en	........../en
① a)	bleiben	geblieben	/	/
	schreiben			
	beschreiben	/	/	beschrieben
	aufschreiben			
	einsteigen	/	eingestiegen	/
	umsteigen			
b)	schneiden	geschnitten	/	/
	aufschneiden			
	unterstreichen			

	ge/............/en	.../ge/........../en	............/en
a) schließen	geschlossen	/	/
b) verlieren			
a) trinken	getrunken	/	/
finden			
b) beginnen	/	/	begonnen
a) sprechen	gesprochen	/	/
kommen			
werfen			
mitkommen			
zurückkommen			
wegwerfen			
b) essen	gegessen	/	/
vergessen			
a) nehmen	genommen	/	/
mitnehmen			
b) lesen	gelesen	/	/
sehen			
heben	gehoben	/	/
a) schlafen	geschlafen	/	/
anfangen			
aufhalten			
b) fahren	gefahren	/	/
abfahren			
rufen	gerufen	/	/
laufen	gelaufen	/	/
anrufen			

6B

☐ **Ü3** Ausnahmen: Lernen Sie diese Partizipien II

stehen	*gestanden*	wissen	*gewußt*
verstehen	*verstanden*	bringen	*gebracht*
aufstehen	*aufgestanden*	wiedererkennen	*wiedererkannt*
gehen	*gegangen*	tun	*getan*
anziehen	*angezogen*	sein	*gewesen*
rausziehen	*rausgezogen*		

6 **Ü4** Verben auf "-ieren": Wie heißen die Partizipien II? 🗝️

notieren	*notiert*	funktionieren	
buchstabieren		fotografieren	
studieren		passieren	
diktieren		telefonieren	
reparieren			

7 **Ü5** Machen Sie Sätze

verlieren · vergessen · umsteigen · aufmachen · besuchen · anrufen · kaputt machen · aufstehen · ...

Der Einbrecher		sein Geld
Horst	hat	Lebensmittel	ge ...	t / et / er
Der Mann	ist	um 8 Uhr
Frau Gieseke	haben	......
Die Chefin	sind	.....
Sie (Plural)		
...		

1. Horst hat Lebensmittel eingekauft.
2. ....

80

Ü6 Perfekt mit "haben" – Perfekt mit "sein" 🔑

4

Das Verb bezeichnet eine "Ortsveränderung".

Das Verb hat das | "Perfekt mit "sein": |

Beispiel: Horst <u>hat</u> im Supermarkt eingekauft.
Dann <u>ist</u> er nach Hause gefahren.

Aufgabe: Welche Verben bezeichnen eine "Ortsveränderung"? ⟶ ⬭
Bilden Sie von allen Verben Sätze im Perfekt.

einkaufen, (fahren,) verdienen, erzählen, kommen,
beginnen, umsteigen, verlieren, einsteigen,
trinken, mitkommen, essen, abfahren, finden,
zurückkommen, wissen, laufen, gehen, schreiben,
aufstehen, spielen, arbeiten

Achtung! ⚠
Auch "bleiben" und "sein"
haben ein Perfekt mit "sein".

Perfekt mit "haben"	Perfekt mit "sein"
Horst <u>hat</u> im Supermarkt eingekauft.	Dann <u>ist</u> er nach Hause gefahren.
. . . . .	. . . .

Ü7 Ergänzen Sie die Sätze 🔑

7

○

kaputtgemacht   hat   hat   gesagt   gekocht   hat
aufgemacht   gesucht   habe   hat   gefragt   gesucht   habe
gehört   hat   hat

Der Einbrecher   die Scheibe
Er   das Fenster   .
Er   Geld   .
Er   Uhren und Bilder in den Sack
Die Frau   den Einbrecher   .
Sie   die Tür   und   den
Einbrecher   :
"Was machen Sie hier?"
Da   der Einbrecher   :
"Entschuldigen Sie bitte! Ich   hier
früher   . Ich   die alte Uhr
Da   die Frau ihm Kaffee   .

gesteckt   aufgemacht   hat   gewohnt

Hermann Hesse

Im Nebel

Seltsam, im Nebel zu wandern!
Einsam ist jeder Busch und Stein,
Kein Baum sieht den andern,
Jeder ist allein.

Voll von Freunden war mir die Welt,
Als noch mein Leben licht war;
Nun, da der Nebel fällt,
Ist keiner mehr sichtbar.

Wahrlich, keiner ist weise,
Der nicht das Dunkel kennt,
Das unentrinnbar und leise
Von allen ihn trennt.

Seltsam, im Nebel zu wandern!
Leben ist Einsamsein.
Kein Mensch kennt den andern,
Jeder ist allein!

Bertolt Brecht

Der Radwechsel

Ich sitze am Straßenrand.
Der Fahrer wechselt das Rad.
Ich bin nicht gern, wo ich herkomme.
Ich bin nicht gern, wo ich hinfahre.
Warum sehe ich den Radwechsel
Mit Ungeduld?

Johannes R. Becher

Ende

Was kommt am Ende
Dabei heraus,
Wenn Menschen nicht
Mit Menschen sprechen?

Sie schießen
Aufeinander...

Darum:
Deutsche, sprecht
Mit Deutschen!

Ingeborg Bachmann

Schatten Rosen Schatten

Unter einem fremden Himmel
Schatten Rosen
Schatten
auf einer fremden Erde
zwischen Rosen und Schatten
in einem fremden Wasser
mein Schatten

eter Handke

elbstbezichtigung
(Ausschnitte)

Dieses Stück ist ein Sprechstück für einen Sprecher und ne Sprecherin. (. . .)

ch bin auf die Welt gekommen. (. . .)

h habe mich bewegt. Ich habe Teile meines Körpers ewegt. Ich habe meinen Körper bewegt. Ich habe mich uf der Stelle bewegt. Ich habe mich von der Stelle ewegt. Ich habe mich von einem Ort zum andern ewegt. Ich habe mich bewegen müssen. Ich habe mich ewegen können.

h habe meinen Mund bewegt. Ich bin zu Sinnen gekom-en. Ich habe mich bemerkbar gemacht. Ich habe eschrien. Ich habe gesprochen. Ich habe Geräusche hört. Ich habe Geräusche unterschieden. Ich habe eräusche erzeugt. Ich habe Laute erzeugt. Ich habe öne erzeugt. Ich habe Töne, Geräusche und Laute rzeugen können. Ich habe schweigen können.

Ich habe gesehen. Ich habe Gesehenes wiedergesehen. Ich bin zu Bewußtsein gekommen. Ich habe Gesehenes wiedererkannt. Ich habe Wiedergesehenes wieder-erkannt. Ich habe wahrgenommen. Ich habe Wahrge-nommenes wiederwahrgenommen. Ich bin zu Bewußtsein gekommen. Ich habe Wiederwahrgenommenes wieder-erkannt. (. . .)

Ich habe gelernt. Ich habe die Wörter gelernt. Ich habe die Zeitwörter gelernt. Ich habe den Unterschied zwi-schen sein und gewesen gelernt. Ich habe die Hauptwör-ter gelernt. Ich habe den Unterschied zwischen der Ein-zahl und der Mehrzahl gelernt. Ich habe die Umstands-wörter gelernt. Ich habe den Unterschied zwischen hier und dort gelernt. Ich habe die hinweisenden Wörter gelernt. Ich habe den Unterschied zwischen diesem und jenem gelernt. Ich habe die Eigenschaftswörter gelernt. Ich habe den Unterschied zwischen gut und böse gelernt. Ich habe die besitzanzeigenden Wörter gelernt. Ich habe den Unterschied zwischen mein und dein gelernt. Ich habe einen Wortschatz erworben. (. . .)

7A

1 **Ü1** Oben – unten – vorne – hinten – links – rechts: Schreiben Sie bitte 🔑

(oben)

1   2

3   4

5   6

7   8

① ist *links oben hinten*

②

③

Ü2 Was ist wo? Raten und ergänzen Sie bitte 🔑

①

Links ist ein _____

_____ ist ein H

Oben ist ein _____

_____ ist ein S

Das ist ein _____

②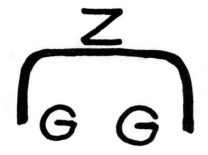

_____ ist ein _____.

_____ ist ein U.

_____ sind zwei _____.

Das ist ein _____!

③

Links und rechts ist ein U.

In der Mitte ist ein _____

und ein _____.

_____ sind zwei _____.

Das ist ein _____!

④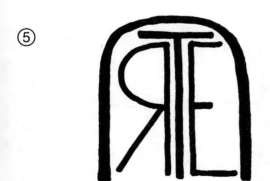

_____ ist das B.

Rechts ist das _____.

_____ ist das T.

Und wo ist das O? ➞ ⬭

Das ist ein _____!

⑤

_____ ist ein R.

Rechts ist auch ein _____!

In der Mitte ist ein _____.

Und wo ist das U? ➞ ∩

Das ist eine _____!

7A

2 **Ü3** **Hören – Sehen – Verstehen – Ergänzen – Notieren** 🔑

① Hören Sie und ergänzen Sie bitte

o Entschuldigen Sie! Wie _____ _____ zum
   Josephsplatz?

● _____ Josephsplatz? _____ _____ geradeaus und _____ an der Kreuzung _____ .
   Dann _____ _____ direkt _____ Josephsplatz.

② Hören Sie und notieren Sie bitte

a) Der Mann möchte zur _____ .
b) Die Frau sagt: Gehen Sie _____ .
c) Wie weit ist das? _____ .

③ Richtig oder falsch? Hören Sie bitte und kreuzen Sie an

	r	f
a) Der Mann möchte zur Georgenstraße.		
b) Das ist nicht weit.		
c) Der Mann hat ein Auto.		
d) Die Frau sagt: "Bis zur zweiten Kreuzung, dann rechts .... ."		
e) Die Georgenstraße ist eine große Querstraße zur Arcisstraße.		
f) Die Georgenstraße ist eine Parallelstraße zur Theresienstraße.		

④ Hören Sie und ergänzen Sie bitte

o _____ suche _____ Polizei.

● Die Landpolizeidirektion?

o Ja, _____ .

● Gehen Sie _____ die Theresienstraße _____ , bis _____ _____ Kreuzung
   dann _____ , und die _____ _____ _____ .

o Bis _____ _____ , dann _____ , und dann die _____
   _____ _____ .

● Genau, und _____ noch zwei- bis dreihundert Meter _____ ,
   und dann auf der _____ Seite das große Gebäude.

o Vielen _____ , das _____ ich bestimmt!

86

Ü 4   Wie komme ich zu …? – Schreiben Sie bitte

Rocko ist auf der Deutzer Brücke.
Sehen Sie ihn? - Ja? - Zeigen Sie ihm den Weg:

(1) Er möchte zum Neumarkt.

(1) _Gehen Sie_ _____

_____

(2) Er möchte zum Hohenzollernring.

(2) _____

_____

(3) Er möchte zur Brückenstraße.

(3) _____

_____

(4) Er möchte in die Breite Straße.

(4) _____

_____

(5) Er möchte zur Komödienstraße.

(5) _____

_____

3 Ü5 Schreiben Sie bitte 🔑

Wie heißt das auf deutsch?

① der Teppich	⑥ _____	⑫ _____
② _____	⑦ der Gummibaum	⑬ die Fotografie
③ _____	⑧ der Zwerg	⑭ das Kissen
④ der Käfig	⑨ der Blumentopf	⑮ _____
⑤ der Vogel	⑩ _____	⑯ der Telefonhörer
	⑪ _____	

Wo steht/sitzt/liegt/hängt.....?

Der Teppich liegt auf dem Boden.
. . . .

Ü6 **Hören Sie bitte und ergänzen Sie: Wo sucht der Vater den Fotoapparat?** 🔑

Der Vater sucht den Fotoapparat zuerst _____ Wohnzimmer, _____ dem Sofa, dann

_____ dem _____; aber da ist er auch nicht.

Dann sucht er den Fotoapparat _____ dem Regal, _____ von der _____.

Schließlich sucht er ihn _____ der _____; _____ Kühlschrank?

Vielleicht _____ dem _____ oder _____ einem _____? Mal sehn!

7 Vergleichen Sie mit dem Text 7A4 (⟶ Lehrbuch S. 98): Was ist falsch?

Unterstreichen Sie bitte

Der Mann hat sein Auto verkauft. 2. Er war die ganze Zeit auf dem Automarkt.

Er war beim TÜV, in der Werkstatt und im Theater. 4. Er ist zu Fuß zum TÜV

aufen. 5. Beim TÜV hat er den Abgastest gemacht. 6. Von der Autowerkstatt

er direkt zum Automarkt gefahren. 7. Dort hat er sein Auto verkauft.

Dann hat er sich einen anderen Wagen gekauft.

Korrigieren Sie bitte: Schreiben Sie jetzt die Sätze richtig

1. Der Mann hat sein Auto nicht verkauft.

2. ...

8 Tagesablauf: Was haben *Sie* gestern, vorgestern ... gemacht?
Zeichnen und schreiben Sie bitte.

Um ... Uhr bin

...

5 Ü9 Was ist was?
Benutzen Sie ein Lexikon und suchen Sie die Sachen ①–㉕ auf dem Bild 🔑

Schuhe ① Sonnenbrille ◯ Schwimmflossen ◯ Rettungsring ◯ Kleiderhaken ◯

Schirm ◯ Zahnbürste ◯ (Spazier-)Stock ◯ Nachttisch ◯ Nachttopf ◯

Bett ◯ Toilettenpapier ◯ Fensterbank ◯ Gardinenstange ◯ Fisch ◯

Sieb ◯ Hemd ◯ Krawatte ◯ Hut ◯ (Sardinen-)Dose ◯ Strumpf ◯

Einmachglas ◯ (Schweizer) Käse ◯ Bettdecke ◯ Blumentopf ◯

Ü10 **Was hat er gemacht? Schreiben Sie bitte**

Er hat die Schuhe an den Kleiderhaken gehängt. Er ...

Verben:
hängen
legen
stellen
stecken
setzen
......

Ü1   Fragen Sie und antworten Sie bitte

1/2

der Fotoapparat	in
die Uhr	an
die Zeitung	auf
der Paß	unter
die Tasche	vor
das Geld	hinter
die Hose	neben
.....	zwischen

..... Bücher
..... Wand
..... Boden
..... Vase
..... Tisch
..... Stuhl
..... Sofa
..... Regal
..... Schrank
..... Tür

? – Vielleicht ...

**? – Nein, ... !
Ja, ...**

1. Wo ist der Fotoapparat? Vielleicht auf dem Tisch?
– Nein, da ist er nicht. – Dann vielleicht im Regal?
– Ja, da ist er!
2. ...

Ü2   Wohin? – Wo? – Woher?

3

a) Wohin gehst du? – Zum Deutschkurs.
b) Wo warst du? – Im Deutschkurs.

| Wo | Wohin? Woher? | ich du Sie wir ..... | geh- fahr- war- komm- ..... | zu nach bei an auf in von aus | Arzt Bahnhof Post Flughafen Autowerkstatt Schule Deutschkurs Italien Spanien "... Hause" Berlin ..... |

c) Woher kommst du? – Vom Deutschkurs.
d) ...

4 Ü3 Wohin hat sie das Essen gestellt?
Wo steht das Essen jetzt?

1. Sie (hat) den Kuchen auf den Boden (gestellt).

_____ _____

_____ _____

2. Der Kuchen (steht) jetzt auf dem Boden.

_____ _____

_____ _____

4 **Ergänzen Sie bitte Präposition (und Artikel)** 🗝

5

◻

1. Wieviel hast du _____ _____ Auto bezahlt?   2. "Sie fahren _____

Fahrausweis! Das kostet 20 Mark."   3. "Gehen Sie bitte _____ _____

nächste Tür rechts!"   4. Wir brauchen 800 Mark _____ _____ Miete.

5. Wer kommt da _____ _____ Ecke?   6. Das Auto ist _____ _____

Baum gefahren.   7. Der Kurs beginnt _____ 19 Uhr und dauert _____

21.30 Uhr.   8. Die Tabletten sind gut _____ Halsschmerzen.

9. Ich bleibe _____ zu_____ 30. Juni in München.   10. Wir sind _____

_____ Pfennig aus dem Urlaub zurückgekommen!   11. Wir waren

_____ _____ Tag nach Weihnachten in Urlaub.   12. _____ _____

Paß kann man nicht nach Amerika fliegen.

W

1 **Science fiction mit Präpositionen** 🗝

◻

①

②

Rocko fliegt _____ _____

UFO _____ Führerschein

_____ _____ Fenster _____

_____ Wohnzimmer; er fliegt ein-

mal _____ _____ Lampe und landet

dann _____ _____ Tisch.

Er klettert _____ _____ UFO,

läuft einmal _____ _____ Blu-

menvase herum; dann springt er

_____ Tisch _____ _____ Stuhl

und schaut sich um. _____ Stuhl

springt er _____ _____ Sofa und

landet _____ _____ Katze Mira.

Die Katze faucht.

③

Rocko hat Angst; er rennt weg;

er rennt _____ _____ Kopf _____

_____ Wand.

④

Er steht wieder auf. Wohin?

Er rennt _____ _____ Kinder-

zimmer _____ Peter und Anneliese.

_____ _____ Ecke findet er eine

Kiste _____ Spielsachen: Autos,

Puppen und ..... . Was ist denn

das? Noch ein UL? .....

⑤

Ein Roboter _____ einem Auge und

_____ vier Armen steigt _____

_____ Kiste. Rocko springt

_____ _____ Kleiderschrank und

versteckt sich _____ _____

Kleidern.

⑥

Am Morgen stehen Peter und

Anneliese auf. Anneliese geht

_____ Kleiderschrank; sie

macht die Tür auf .....

94

3

1 Was sagen die Leute? Schreiben Sie bitte die Gespräche

2 Rekonstruieren Sie bitte den Text

Weihnachten - Fest - Deutschland

25. + 26.12 - Weihnachtsfeiertage

24.12. - der "Heilige Abend"

24.12 - viele Menschen - Kirche -

danach: zu Hause

Wohnung - "Christbaum" (Kerzen, Kugeln,

Figuren - Sterne)

Baum - Geschenke

Weihnachten - "Schenk-Tag"

"Geschäft" - Geschäfte

Weihnachten: Lebkuchen, ..., Plätzchen,

....., Spezialitäten

Weihnachten ist das größte Fest ...

4

5 **Ü3** Was ist was? 🔑

○ der Koffer ○ das Bild ○ die Angel
○ der Revolver ○ das Paar Hosenträger ○ die Babyflasche
○ der Füller ○ das Paar Skier ○ die Armbanduhr
○ der Radiorecorder ○ das Fahrrad ○ die Flasche Kognak
○ der Computer ○ das Paket ○ die Krawatte
○ der Fußball ○ das Dreirad ○ die Puppe
○ der Kerzenleuchter ○ das Radio ○ die Pfeife
○ der Kochtopf ○ das Paar Hausschuhe *Was fehlt?*
○ der Knochen

Ü4 Was ist für wen?
Schreiben Sie bitte

1. Der Koffer ist für die Mutter; er gehört jetzt der Mutter.
2. Der Revolver ....

Ü5 Wer hat wem was geschenkt? Schreiben Sie bitte

Die Oma hat dem Opa die Hosenträger geschenkt.
. . . .

Ü1 Antworten Sie bitte mit "Ja" oder "Nein"

1. a) Ist dieser Brief für Sie?

"Ja, der ist für mich."
"Nein, der ist nicht für m..."

   b) Ist er vielleicht für Herrn Petrovic?

   c) Oder vielleicht für Herrn Henschel?

2. Ist das Paket für mich?

3. Sind die Geschenke für die Kinder?

4. Sind die Bücher für uns?

5. Ist der Kaffee für Sie?

6. Suchst du mich?

7. Habt ihr uns gesucht?

8. Brauchst du mich noch?

9. Besucht ihr uns mal?

10. Kannst du mich mitnehmen?

11. Habt ihr uns nicht gesehen?

12. Rufst du mich mal an?

13. Habt ihr mich verstanden?

14. Erkennst du mich nicht wieder?

Ü2 Beantworten Sie bitte die Fragen 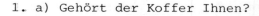 **1**

1. a) Gehört der Koffer Ihnen?

   b) Wem gehört der Koffer denn?

2. a) Gehört die Tasche euch?

   b) Vielleicht der Frau da drüben?

3. Gehört der Computer dir?

4. Gehören die Bücher Herrn und Frau Puente?

5. Gehört das Radio Peter?

6. Zeigst du mir mal die Geschenke?

7. Erzählen Sie mir noch einmal diese Geschichte?

8. Schickt ihr uns mal eine Karte?

9. Kannst du mir Zigaretten mitbringen?

10. Können Sie mir heute noch das Auto reparieren?

11. Gehört der Wagen Ihnen?

12. Können wir euch helfen?

**Ü3 Antworten Sie bitte mit "Ja, ..."
oder "Nein, ..."**

. a) Ist das dein Buch?

   b) Vielleicht das Buch von Frau Scoti?

. a) Ist das ihre Tasche?

   b) Vielleicht die Tasche von Herrn Bauer?

. a) Ist das euer Koffer?

   b) Vielleicht der Koffer von Herrn und Frau Puente?

. Sind das eure Kinder?

. Sind das deine Zigaretten?

. Sind das deine Schlüssel?

. Ist das Ihr Zimmer?

. Ist das Ihr Paß?

**Ü4 Beantworten Sie bitte
die Fragen**  **2/3**

Beispiel: Gehört der Koffer ihm/ihr/ihnen? - Ja/Nein, das ist (nicht) sein/ihr/ihr Koffer.

1. Gehört das Gepäck ihnen?

2. Gehört der Füller ihnen?

3. Gehört der Fotoapparat ihm?

4. Gehört der Paß ihr?

5. Gehört der Platz ihnen?

6. Gehören die Schlüssel ihnen?

7. Gehört das Auto ihr?

8. Gehört der Computer ihm?

9. Gehören die Bücher ihnen?

10. Gehören die Zigaretten ihm?

2/3 **Ü5** **Ergänzen Sie bitte** 🔑

1. Ich lebe mit m_____ Familie in Berlin. 2. Wir freuen uns auf u_____ Urlaub. 3. Herr Bauer spielt mit s_____ Freunden Skat. 4. Zeigst du mir mal d_____ Geschenke? 5. Wir besuchen u_____ Freunde in Italien.

6. Der Vater erzählt s_____ Kindern eine Geschichte. 7. Ich suche m_____ Fotoapparat; hast du ihn nicht gesehen? 8. Hast du auch d_____ Führerschein eingesteckt? 9. Ich habe I_____ Computer nicht kaputtgemacht!

10. Sie wartet schon seit einer Stunde auf i_____ Mann. 11. Wir brauchen e_____ Hilfe. 12. Ein Einbrecher ist gestern in i_____ Wohnung eingestiegen.

13. Peter schenkt s_____ Freundin eine Schallplatte. 14. Komm, wir fragen u_____ Lehrer! 15. Wir können bei u_____ Freunden übernachten.

16. Beschreiben Sie bitte I_____ Nachbarn! 17. Ich habe m_____ Brieftasche verloren! 18. U_____ Kurs beginnt um 19 Uhr. 19. Hast du schon mit d_____ Lehrerin gesprochen? 20. Habt ihr e_____ Karten vergessen?

21. Kannst du m_____ Tasche mitnehmen? 22. Hast du schon d_____ Mutter angerufen? 23. Notieren Sie bitte hier I_____ Adresse! 24. Ich habe gerade mit I_____ Chef telefoniert.

4 **Ü6** **Gebrauchen Sie die Personalpronomen** 🔑

Beispiel:

a) Rocko zeigt <u>seinem Freund</u> <u>die Geschenke</u>.

b) Rocko zeigt *ihm* die Geschenke.

c) Rocko zeigt *sie* *ihm*.

d) Rocko zeigt *sie* seinem Freund.

Aufgaben:

1. Rocko gibt seinem Freund einen Knieschützer.

2. Peter schenkt seiner Freundin ein Buch.

3. Susi leiht ihrer Freundin ein Fahrrad.

4. Susi schickt ihrer Freundin ein Paket.

5. .....

5

7 Ergänzen Sie bitte

Rocko hat schon s_____ ein___ Stunde Bauchschmerzen. 2. Er möchte z__ ein____
zt. 3. N_____ d_____ Frühstück fährt er m____ d____ Bus i____ d____ Stadt.
Er fährt b__ z___ Marktplatz. 5. Dort steigt er a____ d___ Bus aus.
Die Arztpraxis liegt direkt g_____ d___ Rathaus. 7. Rocko fährt
___ d_____ Lift b____ z____ dritten Stock. 8. Aber der Arzt ist nicht da,
e Praxis ist v_____ zehnten August b____ z____ ersten September geschlossen.
Rocko fährt z_____ nächsten Arzt, aber auch der ist nicht da. 10. B_____
itten Arzt hat Rocko drei Stunden lang gewartet. 11. Erst a_____ Abend ist
cko wieder z___ Hause. Er hat immer noch Bauchschmerzen - und Hunger.

6

8 Wer ist wer? – Was ist was? – Erklären Sie bitte

ispiel: Der Hodscha verläßt <u>sein</u> Haus.   <u>sein</u> Haus: das Haus <u>des Hodscha</u>

<u>Seine</u> Frau sieht <u>das</u> und fragt <u>ihn</u>:
"Was suchst <u>du</u>?"
<u>Er</u> antwortet:
"<u>Mein</u> Ring ist weg; <u>ich</u> habe
<u>meinen</u> Ring verloren."
"Ich suche <u>ihn</u> schon seit einer Stun-
de."
<u>Sie</u> fragt weiter:
Wo hast <u>du</u> <u>ihn</u> denn verloren?"

1. <u>Seine Frau</u>: ....

7

9 Sagen Sie das anders

ispiel: Dieser Koffer gehört Peter.   Das ist <u>der Koffer von Peter</u>.
                                              Das ist <u>Peters Koffer</u>.
                                              Das ist <u>sein Koffer</u>.

Diese Bücher gehören Fernando.
Dieses Auto gehört meiner Frau.   6. Diese Knieschützer gehören Rocko.
Dieser Paß gehört Frau Barbieri.   7. Diese Puppe gehört dem Mädchen.
Diese Tasche gehört Maria.   8. Diese Pfeife gehört Opa.
Dieses Gepäck gehört Herrn und   9. Dieser Kochtopf gehört Vater.
Frau Berger.

Was sagen (fragen) Sie?

1. Sie sind im Theater. Sie haben die Platznummer 126; aber da sitzt schon eine Frau.

2. Der Mann am Zoll fragt: "Gehört der Koffer Ihnen?"
   a) Es ist <u>nicht</u> Ihr Koffer.
   b) Es ist Ihr Koffer.

3. Eine Dame fragt Sie: "Welches Datum haben wir heute?"
   a) Sie wissen es auch nicht.
   b) Sie wissen es.

4. Maria möchte ins Kino. Ihr Freund möchte zum Fußball.
   a) Sie sind die Frau.
   b) Sie sind der Freund.

5. Sie sind zu Besuch. Sie möchten eine Zigarette rauchen.

6. Eine Freundin ruft Sie an; sie möchte mit Ihnen ins Kino. Sie aber haben Zahnschmerzen.

7. Ein Mann fragt Sie: "Wie komme ich zum Bahnhof?"
   a) Sie wissen es auch nicht.
   b) Der Bahnhof ist in der zweiten Querstraße links.

8. Peter fragt Sie: "Wo ist mein Fotoapparat?"
   a) Sie wissen es auch nicht.
   b) Er ist in seiner Tasche.
   c) Sie haben den Fotoapparat in den Schrank gelegt.

9. Ihre Freundin fragt Sie: "Was hast du heute gemacht?" Sie erzählen es.

10. Sie können Ihren Paß nicht finden. Sie fragen Ihre Frau / Ihren Mann.

11. "Verzeihung, wie spät ist es?"
    a) Das wissen Sie auch nicht.
    b) Sie sagen es.

12. "Wann und wo treffen wir uns?"
    a) 8 Uhr - Bahnhof
    b) 7 Uhr - Kino

13. Sie möchten mit dem Zug nach Amsterdam. Fragen Sie die Auskunft.

14. Sie möchten eine Fahrkarte nach Paris.

15. Sie brauchen ein Hotelzimmer. Rufen Sie die Touristen-Zentrale an.

16. Sie fahren zur Buchmesse. Vielleicht möchte Ihr(e) Freund(in) auch zur Buchmesse? Rufen Sie sie/ihn an.

17. Sie brauchen einen Termin beim Zahnarzt. Rufen Sie an.

18. Sie haben eine Autopanne. Rufen Sie eine Werkstatt an.

19. Sie kommen am nächsten Tag zur Werkstatt; aber ihr Auto ist immer noch nicht repariert. Sie brauchen das Auto <u>sofort</u>.

20. Sie haben eingekauft. Sie kommen nach Hause und haben kein Geld mehr. Ihr Mann / Ihre Frau fragt Sie: "Was hast du mit dem Geld gemacht?"

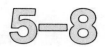

. Sie haben Ihre Brieftasche verloren. Wo kann das passiert sein?
Sie überlegen .....

. Sie haben die Brieftasche wieder-
gefunden. Wo war sie? Erzählen
Sie bitte.

. "Der Einbrecher und Frau Gieseke".
Erzählen Sie Ihrem Freund / Ihrer
Freundin die Geschichte.

. Der Weg zum Bahnhof?

a) Fragen Sie bitte.

b) Beschreiben Sie den Weg (Kreuzung rechts - 2. Querstraße links -
geradeaus - ca. 200 Meter)

. Sie suchen

a) die Post

b) das Einwohnermeldeamt

26. Ihr(e) Freund(in) macht eine
Reise. Wohin? Wie lange?
Fragen Sie sie bitte.

27. Sie möchten Herrn Otramba besuchen. Sie wissen die Adresse
nicht genau. Fragen Sie bitte.

28. Ihr Kugelschreiber ist kaputt.
Vielleicht leiht Ihnen Ihr Nach-
bar einen Kugelschreiber?
Fragen Sie bitte.

29. Der Kugelschreiber Ihres Nachbarn ist kaputt. Sie haben zwei.

30. Jemand fragt: "Ist das die Tasche
von .....?"

a) Sie wissen, wem die Tasche gehört.

b) Es ist _Ihre_ Tasche?

31. Sie haben Ihr Deutschlehrbuch
    verloren:
  a) Sie suchen nicht weiter.
  b) Sie nehmen das von Ihrem Lehrer.
  c) Sie schreiben an den Verlag ...

A **Wörter: Machen Sie ein Kreuz**

X	

1. "Wie ..... ist es bitte?" - "7 Uhr 20."

a	alt
b	spät
c	früh
d	schnell

2. "Wie ..... fahren wir?" - "Ungefähr zwei Stunden."

a	früh
b	spät
c	lange
d	oft

3. Montag - Dienstag - ..... - Donnerstag

a	Freitag
b	Sonntag
c	Samstag
d	Mittwoch

4. "..... sind Sie gestern abend gewesen?" -
   "Ich war im Kino."

a	Wo
b	Warum
c	Wie
d	Wann

5. Der Chef fragt Herrn Rasch: "Haben Sie
   Herrn Meinke .....?" - Herr Rasch: "Ja, um
   10 Uhr war ich da und habe mit ihm geredet."

a	gesucht
b	besucht
c	geholt
d	geschrieben

6. "Emil, du sollst zur Post fahren! Die Chefin
   hat eben ..... ."

a	angerufen
b	geschrieben
c	erzählt
d	gekommen

7. "..... bist du im Urlaub gefahren?" -
   "Nach Spanien."

a	Wozu
b	Wann
c	Wohin
d	Warum

8. "Ich möchte ein Auto anmelden. Wo kann ich
   das machen?" - "....."

a	Auf dem Einwohnermeldeam
b	Bei der Ausländerbehörde
c	Auf der Zulassungsstelle
d	Auf dem Standesamt.

9. "Zum Nachtisch gibt es heute .....!" -"Sehr gut!"

a	Würstchen
b	Bier
c	Schinken
d	Kuchen

10. "Heiliger Abend" - das ist in Deutschland
    der ..... Dezember.

a	24.
b	25.
c	26.
d	31.

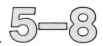
Grammatik: Machen Sie ein Kreuz

X

"Was ..... Sie trinken?" - "Ein Bier, bitte."

a	magst
b	möchten
c	mag
d	mögt

"..... du mir bitte helfen?" - "Ja, gern".

a	Können
b	Kann
c	Kannst
d	Könnt

"Ich kann nicht bezahlen! Ich habe mein Geld .....!"

a	gegessen
b	vergegessen
c	gevergessen
d	vergessen

Herr Baier ist mit dem Zug von München nach Kassel gefahren. Er ist zweimal ..... .

a	umstiegen
b	umsteigen
c	umgestiegen
d	umgesteigt

"Wo ist mein Buch?" - "Dort liegt es doch! Auf ..... Tisch!"

a	das
b	der
c	den
d	dem

"Ich hatte das Buch aber auf ..... Stuhl gelegt!"

a	das
b	den
c	der
d	dem

"Woher kommst du denn jetzt?" - "..... Arzt."

a	Vom
b	Von
c	Von der
d	Von das

"Ist der Kaffee für .....?" - "Ja, natürlich, der ist für Sie."

a	mir
b	mich
c	mein
d	meine

"Ist das ..... Tasche, Herr Baier?" - "Ja, sie gehört mir."

a	seine
b	ihre
c	Ihre
d	deine

"Da liegen ja meine Zigaretten! Kannst du .... bitte herübergeben?"

a	mich sie
b	sie mir
c	sie mich
d	Sie mir

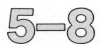

C   Orthographie: Schreiben Sie bitte die Wörter

Beispiel: Guten Ta(**0**)!

An Wei(**1**)nachten feier(**2**) die Deutschen

am l(**3**)bsten zu (**4**)use in der Famil(**5**).

Am Heiligen Abe(**6**) gehen viele Mens(**7**)en

zur Kir(**8**)e. In den meisten W(**9**)nungen

steht ein Chr(**10**)baum, geschmü(**11**)t mit

Ker(**12**)en und Sternen.

Besonder(**13**) sch(**14**)n ist das Fest für

die Kind(**15**). Sie bek(**16**)men viele Ge-

schen(**17**)e. Es gibt viele gute S(**18**)hen,

wie Lebku(**19**)en, zum E(**20**)en.

o	*Tag*
1	
2	
3	
4	
5	
6	
7	
8	
9	
10	
11	
12	
13	
14	
15	
16	
17	
18	
19	
20	

D   Lesen: Machen Sie ein Kreuz

1. Frau Scoti telefoniert mit ihrer Freundin.
   Sie wollen am Sonntag nach Italien fahren.
   Der Zug geht am Morgen, Viertel vor acht, von
   München ab.

   Sie fahren um
a	7 Uhr 45
b	8 Uhr 45
c	7 Uhr 15
d	7 Uhr 04 ab.

2. Frau Scoti wohnt in Aachen. Sie muß schon am
   Samstag nach München fahren. Sie sagt zum
   Beamten am Schalter: "Nach München, bitte,
   einfach."

a	Sie möchte allein fahren.
b	Sie möchte hin und zurück fah[...]
c	Sie möchte 2. Klasse fahren.
d	Sie möchte eine Fahrkarte ein[...]

3. Der Beamte sagt zu Frau Scoti: "Nach
   München gibt es leider keine direkte
   Verbindung."

a	Sie kann nicht fahren.
b	Sie muß 1. Klasse fahren.
c	Sie muß später fahren.
d	Sie muß umsteigen.

4. Herr Baier fragt seinen Kollegen, Herrn
   Steger: "Wann machst du in diesem Jahr
   Urlaub?" - "Im Juli", antwortet Herr Steger..

   Herr Steger macht Urlaub:
a	im Frühling
b	im Sommer
c	im Herbst
d	im Winter

5. Jedes Bundesland hat andere Ferientermine.
   Frau Scoti ruft ihre Freundin in München an
   und fragt: "Wann fangen in Bayern die Ferien
   an?" - "Anfang nächster Woche", sagt die
   Freundin.

   Das ist
a	am Montag
b	im Juni
c	am Morgen
d	im Sommer

6. Im Frühling machen die deutschen Hausfrauen ihre Wohnungen ganz gründlich sauber. "Eine Stunde habe ich heute den Boden geputzt", erzählt Frau Baier ihrer Mutter. Mit welchem Gerät hat sie den Boden geputzt?

a	Mit einem Bügeleisen.
b	Mit einem Schrubber.
c	Mit dem Werkzeugkasten.
d	Mit der Wäscheleine.

7. Eva Harre, 67, ist ziemlich allein. Sie hat eine kleine Wohnung. Ihre Kinder sind verheiratet und wohnen in einer anderen Stadt.

a	Bei Frau Harre wohnt ihre Tochter.
b	Ihre Kinder sind weit weg.
c	Ihre Wohnung hat fünf Zimmer.
d	Sie arbeitet als Sekretärin.

8. Herr Müller will am Abend ins Kino gehen. Die Eintrittskarte hat er schon am Nachmittag gekauft. Er kommt etwas zu spät. Im Kino sind alle Plätze besetzt! Auch auf seinem Platz sitzt ein Mann.

a	Er bekommt keine Karte mehr.
b	Alle Plätze sind schon reserviert!
c	Sein Platz ist noch frei.
d	Ein Mann ist zuviel im Kino!

9. Der Fuchs trifft den Raben. Der Rabe hat ein Stück Käse im Schnabel. Er sagt zu ihm: "Wie schön du bist! Wie berühmt du bist! Kannst du auch schön singen?!"

a	Der Rabe gefällt dem Fuchs.
b	Der Fuchs möchte den Raben besuchen.
c	Der Fuchs möchte den Käse haben.
d	Der Fuchs möchte mit dem Raben singen.

0. Der Hodscha sucht seinen Ring: im Haus und vor dem Haus. "Wo ist bloß mein Ring!", ruft er, "vor einer halben Stunde hatte ich ihn noch!"

a	Er hat seinen Ring verloren.
b	Er hat seinen Ring verkauft.
c	Er hat seinen Ring verschenkt.
d	Er hat seinen Ring versteckt.

E Sprechen – Was sagen Sie? ⊙━🔑

1. Sie rufen am Bahnhof an. Sie wollen <u>am Abend</u> mit dem Zug fahren. Der Auskunftsbeamte sagt zu Ihnen: "Es gibt einen Zug um 15.45 Uhr." Sie sagen:

a	Der ist mir zu teuer.
b	Ich möchte nach 18 Uhr fahren.
c	Den nehme ich.
d	Muß ich da umsteigen?

2. Sie waren letzte Woche nicht im Deutschkurs. Ein Freund fragt: "Wo bist du gewesen?" Sie antworten:

a	Ich hatte eine Erkältung.
b	Ich hatte Durst.
c	Es tut mir leid.
d	Ich <u>war</u> im Deutschkurs!

3. Sie essen mit einer Freundin im Restaurant. Das Essen ist sehr gut. Sie fragen:

a	Na, wie schmeckt´s dir?
b	Was kostet das Bier?
c	Wie geht es dir?
d	Hast du ein Menü?

. Ihr Freund hat ein Auto gekauft. Es ist fast ganz neu. Sie möchten das Auto sehen. Sie sagen:

a	Ich habe ein schönes Auto.
b	Wie gefällt dir mein Auto?
c	Zeigst du mir dein Auto?
d	Willst du ein Auto?

. Sie wollen sich eine Hose kaufen. Sie haben nur 60 Mark. Der Verkäufer im Geschäft sagt: Hier, diese Hose ist besonders billig. Sie kostet nur 85 Mark!"

a	Nein, leider nicht.
b	Die gefällt mir.
c	Das ist mir zu teuer.
d	Die habe ich gekauft.

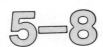
6. Herr Kiener hat am Nachmittag auf der Autobahn in der Nähe von Frankfurt eine Panne. "Die Reparatur dauert zwei Tage," sagt der Mechaniker. Herr Kiener muß aber um 19 Uhr bei seiner Familie in Frankfurt sein. Er bittet den Mechaniker:

a	Können Sie mir ein Taxi rufen?
b	Können Sie das Auto noch heute reparieren?
c	Kann ich den Wagen morgen holen?
d	Kann ich hier übernachten?

7. Der Chef hat Herrn Schnell zur Post geschickt. Nach drei Stunden kommt er endlich wieder. "Da sind Sie ja endlich!" ruft der Chef. "Wo sind Sie denn so lange gewesen?!" Herr Schnell antwortet:

a	Ich war am Montag krank.
b	Ich habe Urlaub gemacht.
c	Ich mußte zwei Stunden warten.
d	Ich war doch immer hier!

8. Frau Müller hat ein Kleid gekauft. Es hat ihr gleich sehr gut gefallen. Sie hat viel Geld ausgegeben. Zu Hause zeigt sie es ihrem Mann. Aber der ist sehr böse und schreit:

a	Wie lange warst du weg?!
b	Wann ziehst du es an?
c	Das ist ja viel zu teuer!
d	Das ist wirklich sehr schön!

9. Ein Bekannter fragt Sie: "Günther Grass hat einen neuen Roman geschrieben. Hast du ihn schon gelesen?
Sie haben den Roman noch <u>nicht</u> gelesen, aber Sie wollen es nicht sagen. Was antworten Sie?

a	Was hat Grass gelesen?
b	Wie findest du denn das Buch?
c	<u>Wie</u> heißt der Mann?
d	Wer ist Grass?

10. Sie sitzen im Cafe und lesen Zeitung. Neben Ihnen sitzt ein Mann. Er nimmt Ihre Tasse und trinkt Ihren Kaffee! Was sagen Sie?

Entschuldigen Sie,
a	wie ist Ihr Name?
b	das ist mein Kaffee.
c	wo wohnen Sie?
d	haben sie eine Zeitung?

F **Schreiben: Hier sind einige Stichwörter. Schreiben Sie einen Brief an ...**

Sie waren auf der Buchmesse in Frankfurt:

- kein Hotelzimmer in Frankfurt -

- Privatzimmer -

- 20 Kilometer von Frankfurt -

- Taxi: 30 Mark, einfach -

- sehr viele Leute -

- Schriftsteller, sehr berühmt -

- Freunde aus München -

- Abendessen -

- sehr müde -

- Auf Wiedersehen -

Liebe/r ...

2 Gustav-Emil-Ida-Gustav-Emil-Samuel;
Berta-Anton-Richard-Berta-Ida-Emil-Richard-Ida;
Cäsar-Otto-Nordpol-Richard-Anton-Dora.

3 eins, drei, fünf, sieben, zwölf, siebzehn, achtzehn;
null, zwei, vier, sechs, dreizehn, sechzehn, zwanzig;
neun, acht, zehn, elf, vierzehn, fünfzehn, neunzehn.

4 Nummer ② ist Vogts. Er kommt auch aus Deutschland. - Nummer ③ ist Smith. Er kommt aus England. - Nummer ④ ist Maradona. Er kommt aus Argentinien. - Nummer ⑤ ist Becken-bauer. Er kommt aus Deutschland. - Nummer ⑥ ist Rivera. Er kommt aus Italien. - Nummer ⑦ ist Eusebio. Er kommt aus Portugal. - Nummer ⑧ ist Platini. Er kommt aus Frankreich. - Nummer ⑨ ist Krankl. Er kommt aus Öster-reich. - Nummer ⑩ ist Pelé. Er kommt aus Brasilien. - Nummer ⑪ ist Garrincha. Er kommt auch aus Brasilien.

5 hat - Teilnehmer - fünf - Männer.
Peter Bauer.
Michiko Tanaka - aus Japan.
kommt - Australien.
kommt - Brasilien.
kommen - Italien.
ist - ist krank.
ist da.
kommt - aus Italien.

4 die Nummer - aus. heißt. Ida - Otto - Richard.
buchstabiere - Karl - Ida - Richard - Theodor - Otto - Richard - Friedrich. Decher. Dora. Dora. Die Vorwahl - sechs - drei - fünf. null - sechs - sechs - drei - fünf. null - vier. zwo - null - vier. Auf Wiederhören.

5 1. 71 69; 2. 10 48 58; 3. 3 21 37; 4. 8 33 60; 5. 6 50 67; 6. 8 31 92; 7. 74 96; 8. 12 21 63; 9. 10 32 84; 10. 33 46 94; 11. 17 91 57.

6 ① vierhundertdreiundzwanzig;
② sechshundertachtundvierzig;
③ dreihundertfünfundneunzig;
④ zweihundertsechsundsiebzig;
⑤ fünfhundertsiebenundsechzig.

7 2. Barbara Fordemann wohnt in Herford. Sie hat die Telefonnummer 5 47 66, Vorwahl 0 52 21 (Her-ford). 3. Karl-Heinz Frölich wohnt in Bünde. Er hat die Telefonnummer 7 65 02, Vorwahl 0 52 23 (Bünde). 4. Elisabeth Gerdes wohnt in Herford. Sie hat die Telefonnummer 5 51 07, Vorwahl 0 52 21 (Herford). 5. Die Gaststätte "Alter Dorfkrug" hat die Telefonnummer 5 17 81, Vor-wahl 0 52 21 (Herford). 6. Die Gaststätte "Candle-Light" hat die Telefonnummer 7 89 77, Vorwahl 0 52 23 (Bünde). 7. Die "Dorett-Bar" (Nightclub) hat die Telefonnummer 5 33 52, Vor-wahl 0 52 21 (Herford).

10 1. richtig; 2. falsch; 3. falsch; 4. falsch; 5. richtig; 6. falsch; 7. richtig; 8. falsch; 9. richtig; 10. falsch; 11. falsch.

11 1. wohnt - spricht - Deutsch und Französisch - ist - Studentin.
2. wohnt - ist - spricht - Deutsch - Russisch.
3. lebt - Jahre - spricht - Griechisch - Italienisch.

4. kommt - studiert - Deutsch - in - ist.
5. ist - Marokkaner - kommt - arbeitet - ist.
6. aus - Türkei - Arbeiter - wohnt - in - Fa-milie - daheim - der.
7. sprechen - Deutsch - Millionen - Menschen - lernen - Deutsch.

1A-2AW **Ü3** aus, Arzt, kommt, Italien, (Rhein), lernen, Bier, sie, Kaffee, nehmen, Land, Arbeiter, Teilnehmer, neun, woher, wer, Satz, Tag, die, vier, das, Tee, Cola, fünf, elf, wie, wohnt, lebt, Spanien.

Ü4 Berufe: Krankenschwester, Studentin, Lehrer, Ingenieur, Ärztin, Diplomat, Dolmetscherin:
Getränke: Bier, Cola, Kaffee, Wein, Mineral-wasser, Limonade.

2B1 **Ü1** a) Frau Barbieri kommt aus Italien. Sie ist Studentin. Sie spricht Italienisch.
b) Wie ist Ihr Name? Puente. Wie schreibt man das? Buchstabieren Sie bitte! Wo wohnen Sie? In Frankfurt. Wie ist Ihre Telefonnummer?
c) Der Deutschkurs hat 12 Teilnehmer. Frau Puente kommt aus Spanien. Nummer 2 ist Frau Boucher aus Kanada. Herr Dupont ist aus Frankreich. Frau Scoti ist nicht da. Sie ist krank.

2B2 **Ü2** 1. heiße, heißt; 2. komme, kommst; 3. ist, ist; 4. trinken, nehme.

Ü3 1. Herr Miller, Er, Er, Frau Puente, Sie, Herr und Frau Scoti, Sie.
2. Sie, Sie, Ich, Sie, Sie, Sie.

2B4 **Ü5** a) Woher kommst du? - Ich komme... .
Wo wohnst du? - Ich wohne ... .
Wo arbeitest du? - Ich arbeite ... .
Was trinkst du? - Ich trinke ... .
Woher kommen Sie? - Ich komme ... .
Wo wohnen Sie? - Ich wohne ... .
Wo arbeiten Sie? - Ich arbeite ... .

b) Sprichst du ...? - Nein, ich spreche ... .
Nimmst du ...? - Nein, ich nehme ... .
Wohnst du ...? - Nein, ich wohne in ... .
Sprechen Sie ...? - Nein, ich spreche ... .
Nehmen Sie ...? - Nein, ich nehme ... .
Wohnen Sie ...? - Nein, ich wohne ... .

c) Miza Lim: Sie kommt / studiert / wohnt / ist ... .

Mustafa Benhallam: Er kommt / wohnt / ist ... .

Alexandra Karidakis: Sie lebt / arbeitet / kommt ... .

Barış Önal: Er kommt / lebt, wohnt / ar-beitet / ist ... .

Ü6 komm/e, komm/en; sprech/e, sprich/st; sprech/en, sprich/t; heiß/e, heiß/en; nimm/st, nimm/t, nehm/en, nehm/e; lern/en; arbeit/en, ar-beit/et, arbeit/est; wohn/e, wohn/st; studier/en, studier/st, studier/t; versteh/t; notier/en; schreib/en, schreib/t; buchstabier/en; trink/en; leb/t.

Ü10 2. Woher kommt er? 3. Wie heißen Sie? 4. Wo wohnen Sie? 5. Wo arbeiten Sie? 6. Ich heiße... .
7. Ich komme aus ... . 8. Ich wohne in ... .
9. Ich arbeite bei ... . 10. Ich bin ... (Jahre alt). 11. Ja, ich trinke auch ... / Nein, ich

trinke kein ... . 12. Ja/Nein, ich spreche ... . 13. Ja/Nein, ich komme aus ... . 14. Ja/Nein, ich wohne in ... . 15. Ja/Nein, ich arbeite bei ... .

3A2 Ü1 1: der Radiergummi, 2: die Tasche, 3: das Heft, 4: die Lampe, 5: der Füller, 6: das Regal, 7: das Bild, 8: die Landkarte, 9: der Tisch, 10: das Buch, 11: ???, 12: die Kreide, 13: das Tonbandgerät, 14: der Stuhl, 15: der Tageslichtprojektor.

Ü2 ist - ein - heißt das - Tonbandgerät - Tonband - Tonbandgerät - Tonbandgerät - Nummer 15 - Lampe - Nein, ein - noch einmal - Tageslichtprojektor - das - deutsch - heißt.

3A3 Ü3 A9, B7, C2, D6, E4, F5, G8, H1, I3.

3A4/5 Ü6 2. sechsundsiebzig Mark fünfzehn, sechsundsiebzig Mark und fünfzehn Pfennig; 3. sechshundertzwei Mark dreiundfünfzig, sechshundertzwei Mark und dreiundfünfzig Pfennig; 4. tausendfünfhunderteinunddreißig Mark, eintausendfünfhunderteinunddreißig Mark; 5. hundertsechzig Mark sechsundsechzig, einhundertsechzig Mark und sechsundsechzig Pfennig; 6. vierzehn Mark vierzehn, vierzehn Mark und vierzehn Pfennig; 7. zehn Mark vierundzwanzig, zehn Mark und vierundzwanzig Pfennig.

3A5 Ü7 Miete ... - Möbel/Hausrat - Körperpflege - Essen - Gesundheit - Fernsehen/Zeitung - Auto/Fahrtkosten - Telefon - Kleidung - Restaurant - Sonstiges.

Ü10 1. richtig; 2. richtig; 3. falsch; 4. falsch; 5. falsch; 6. richtig; 7. richtig; 8. falsch; 9. richtig.

Ü11 Eine Gulaschsuppe kostet DM 3,50 (drei Mark und fünfzig Pfennig); ein Paar Würstchen kostet DM 3,60 (drei Mark und sechzig Pfennig); eine Bratwurst kostet DM 2,40 (zwei Mark und vierzig Pfennig); ein Schinkenbrot kostet DM 3,70 (drei Mark und siebzig Pfennig); ein Käsebrot kostet DM 3,20 (drei Mark und zwanzig Pfennig); ein Hamburger kostet DM 3,50 (drei Mark und fünfzig Pfennig); eine Portion Pommes frites kostet DM 1,80 (eine Mark und achtzig Pfennig); ein Glas Tee kostet DM 1,95 (eine Mark und fünfundneunzig Pfennig); eine Tasse Kaffee kostet DM 2,40 (zwei Mark und vierzig Pfennig); ein Kännchen Kaffee kostet DM 4,- (vier Mark); ein Glas Milch kostet DM 1,60 (eine Mark und sechzig Pfennig); eine Dose Cola kostet DM 1,90 (eine Mark und neunzig Pfennig), ein Viertel Wein kostet DM 4,50 (vier Mark und fünfzig Pfennig); eine Flasche Bier kostet DM 2,60 (zwei Mark und sechzig Pfennig).
Die Leberknödelsuppe kostet DM 3,50 (drei Mark und fünfzig Pfennig); die Gulaschsuppe kostet DM 4,80 (vier Mark und achtzig Pfennig); die Hühnersuppe kostet DM 2,20 (zwei Mark und zwanzig Pfennig); das "Texas"-Steak kostet DM 19,80 (neunzehn Mark und achtzig Pfennig); das Zigeunersteak kostet DM 19,80 (neunzehn Mark und achtzig Pfennig); der gemischte Salat kostet DM 3,90 (drei Mark und neunzig Pfennig); der Kartoffelsalat kostet DM 2,50 (zwei Mark und fünfzig Pfennig); die Kartoffeln kosten DM 2,50 (zwei Mark und fünfzig Pfennig); die Eiernudeln kosten DM 2,50 (zwei Mark und fünfzig Pfennig).

3A9 Ü15 1. richtig; 2. falsch; 3. richtig; 4. richtig; 5. richtig; 6. falsch; 7. falsch; 8. richtig; 9. richtig; 10. falsch; 11. richtig; 12. falsch; 13. richtig.

3AW Ü1 1. Picknick; 2. Auto; 3. Radio; 4. Käse; 5. Wein; 6. Ausweis; 7. Essen; 8. Cola; 9. Hamburger; 10. Telefon; 11. Eier; 12. Regal; 13. PARKWAECHTER

Ü2 Milch - Fisch - Schinkenbrot - Butter - Wuerstchen - Tomaten - Oliven - Bratwurst - Kaffee - Kaesebrot - Pommes frites - Bier - MINERALWASS

Ü3 Speisen: Bratwurst - Gulaschsuppe - Kartoffelsalat - Zigeunersteak
Getränke: Cola - Kaffee - Mineralwasser - Whisky
Essen: Butter - Eier - Gemüse - Käse
Sachen: Lampe - Radiergummi - Regal - Tasche

3B1 Ü1 der Paß - der Star - der Salat - der Gangster - der Clown - der Computer - der Hamburger - die City - die Garage - die Cassette - die Hostess - die Nummer/die Zahl - das Auto - das Baby - das Glas - das Radio - das Telefon

3B2 Ü3 1. Die Studentin kommt aus Japan. 2. Das Baby ist 6 Monate alt. 3. Der Deutschkurs hat 12 Teilnehmer. 4. Die Arbeiterin arbeitet bei Siemens. 5. Bjarne wohnt in München. 6. Der Gangster heißt Al Capone. 7. Die Dolmetscherin spricht Englisch, Französisch und Spanisch. 8. Das Radio spielt. 9. Die Lehrerin schreibt einen Satz. 10. Die Frau trinkt einen Kaffee.

3B3 Ü4 3: Das ist ein Radio. - Was ist das? 4: Das ist ein Computer. - Was ist das? 5: Das ist Anni Sinowatz. - Wer ist das? 6: Das ist eine Cassette. - Was ist das? 7: Das ist ein Hamburger. - Was ist das? 8: Das ist eine Garage. - Was ist das? 9: Das ist Rocko. - Wer ist das? 10: Das ist ein Tonbandgerät. - Was ist das? 11: Das ist ein Tageslichtprojektor. - Was ist das? 12: Das ist ein Gangster. - Wer ist das? 13: Das ist ein Buch. - Was ist das? 14: Das ist eine Tasche. - Was ist das? 15: Das ist Marlies Demont. - Wer ist das? 16: Das ist ein Bild. - Was ist das? 17: Das ist Herr Müller. - Wer ist das? 18: Das ist Herr Miller. - Wer ist das?

3B5 Ü6. 1. Woher kommst du / kommen Sie? 2. Sprichst du / Sprechen Sie auch Englisch? 3. Wie heißt du / heißen Sie? 4. Hast du / Haben Sie auch Hunger? 5. Bist du / Sind Sie krank? 6. Nehmt ihr / Nehmen Sie auch ein Steak? 7. Wohnt ihr / Wohnen Sie auch in Berlin? 8. Seid ihr / Sind Sie auch aus Italien?

Ü7 a) machen - sind - haben - sind - ist - ist - ruft - ist - fangen;
b) ist - hat - ißt - frißt - trinkt - trinkt - spricht - bin - sind - essen - (fr)esse.

Ü8 1. Was ist heute? 2. Wer macht das Essen? Was macht Frau Wolter? 3. Wer hat Wurst, Brot und Bier? Was hat sie? 4. Wer arbeitet? 5. Wer schreibt einen Brief? Was schreibt er? 6. Wer ist nicht da?

4A1 Ü1 2: der Oberarm; 3. die Schulter; 4. die Brust; 5. der Bauch; 6. der Rücken; 7. der Unterarm; 8: die Hand; 9: der Oberschenkel; 10: der Unterschenkel; 11: das Knie; 12: der Fuß; 13: der Knöchel; 14: die Zehe; 15: der Finger; 16: der Hals; 17: die Haare; 18: der Bart; 19: das Ohr; 20: das Auge; 21: die Nase; 22: der Mund; 23: die Lippen; 24: die Stirn; 25: das Kinn.

4A2 Ü2 5, 8, 2, 7, 3, 1, 4, 6.

Ü9 Nummer 2: Das ist ein Hund; Nummer 3: Das ist
ein Kissen; Nummer 4: Das ist eine Wäscheklammer; Nummer 5: Das ist ein Messer; Nummer 6:
Das ist ein Sofa; Nummer 7: Das ist ein Kochtopf; Nummer 8: Das ist ein Trichter; Nummer
9: Das ist eine Säge; Nummer 10: Das ist Klebstoff; Nummer 11: Das ist ein Servierwagen;
Nummer 12: Das ist ein Schraubenzieher; Nummer
13: Das ist eine Bohrmaschine; Nummer 14: Das
ist eine Schere; Nummer 15: Das ist ein Garn;
Nummer 16: Das ist eine Axt.

Ü10 (1) und (2) sind (3) zu;
(4) und (5) machen (6) eine;
(7) ist (8) ist (9) ist;
(10) Das (11) ist;
(12) Es;
(13) holt (14) das (15) die (16) und;
(17) Die (18) fängt;
(19) schneidet (20) den;
(21) ist (22) und;
(23) die (24) auf;
(25) zieht (26) die (27) und (28) sie (29) weg;
(30) sie (31) das;
(32) das (33) zu;
(34) Die (35) ist;
(36) klebt (37) die (38) zu;
(39) Das (40) stöhnt;
(41) sind.

Ü11 Das Milchgeschäft war in Berlin-Kreuzberg.
Wilhelm Etzin war der Besitzer. Er hatte eine
Frau und zwei Kinder. Herr und Frau Etzin hatten noch keinen Kühlschrank. Sie hatten Milch
und Sahne, Brot und Butter. Das Geschäft war
im Keller. Es war kühl im Keller/Souterrain.
Die Miete war billig. Ein Glas Milch war damals nicht teuer. Das war 1908.

Ü12 1. Zeit - Geld - Auto - ein - Auto - Haus -
war - hatte - Freunde - hatte - Freunde -
Freunde - keine - hatte - ich.
2. Schauspieler - Erfolg - berühmt - Termine -
Rom - Paris - London.
3. Politiker - Macht - Flugzeug - viele -
Telefone .
4. Pech.
5. keine - Freunde - Villa - Geld - Frau -
auch - alles - das - nichts - allein - Menge -
Zeit.

Ü1 1: Milchgeschäft; 2: Schinkenbrot; 3: Landkarte; 4: Tonband; 5: Vierzimmerwohnung;
6: Halstabletten; 7: Coladose; 8: Telefonnummer; 9: Koerperteile; 10: Bettruhe;
11: Bratwurst; 12: Angelschein; 13: Schultasche; 14: Bauchschmerzen; 15: Kaffeetasse;
16: Kuehlschrank
EIN BILDERRAETSEL

Ü3 *Trennbare Verben:*
anfangen, einkaufen, aufhören, aussehen,
aufhalten, rausziehen, weitergehen, aufschneiden, zukleben, einladen, zunähen, mitbringen, wegwerfen, anrufen, aufschreiben.
Nicht trennbare Verben:
beschreiben, verdienen, verstehen, ergänzen,
benutzen, bezahlen.

Ü4 1. fängt ... an; 2. kauft ... ein; 3. Beschreiben; 4. höre auf; 5. verdient;
6. sieht ... aus; 7. lade ... ein; 8. Verstehen; 9. Ergänzen; 10. Benutzen;
11. Schreiben ... auf; rufe ... an; 12. bezahlt.

4B3 Ü5 a) 2: hattest; 3: waren; 4: war; 5: hatte;
b) war; war; hatte; ist; war.

Ü6 (Lösungsbeispiele)
1. Warst du gestern nicht zu Hause?
2. Hattest du keine Zeit?
3. Warst du krank? / Hattest du Husten?
4. War Susi (nicht) da?
5. Warst du krank?
6. Hattest du Fieber?
7. Hattest du Kopfschmerzen?
8. Warst du (nicht) beim Arzt?

1-4W (Lösungsbeispiele)
1. Ich heiße Barbara Fordemann; ich wohne in
Herford, Blumenstraße 13; meine Telefonnummer
ist 54 766.
2. Verzeihung, wie ist Ihr Name? (Verzeihung,
wie heißen Sie?)
3. (Nein, danke), (ich möchte/trinke) lieber
ein Mineralwasser.
4. a) (Ich komme) aus ...
   b) (Ja), (ein bißchen). / (Nein), (leider
      nicht).
5. Bitte, die Nummer von: Goethe-Institut,
Zentrale, in München.
6. Nein, ich bin kein(e) Lehrer(in), ich bin ...
7. Nein, ich habe heute (leider) keine Zeit.
8. Was kosten die Tomaten? Und die Oliven?
9. Wie hoch ist die Miete für die (Zwei-
zimmer)-Wohnung?
10. "Eine Bratwurst und eine Portion Pommes
frites."
11. Ich habe Kopfschmerzen und Fieber.
12. Ich war zu Hause; ich war krank.
12. Ich war zu Hause; ich war krank.

1-4K **Kontrollaufgaben**

A Wörter
1d; 2c; 3b; 4c; 5c; 6a; 7c; 8c; 9b; 10a;
11c; 12d.

B Grammatik
1c; 2c; 3b; 4d; 5a; 6b; 7b; 8d; 9b; 10b.

C Orthographie
1: Guten; 2: geht; 3: Ganz; 4: Auch; 5: ist;
6: Freut; 7: schreibt; 8: einmal; 9: Frankreich; 10: Brasilien; 11: trinken; 12: nehme;
13: lieber; 14: Sprechen; 15: Französisch;
16: leider; 17: Englisch; 18: sind.

D Lesen
1: falsch; 2: richtig; 3: falsch; 4: falsch;
5: falsch; 6: falsch; 7: richtig; 8: falsch;
9: falsch; 10: falsch.

E Sprechen
1b; 2d; 3a; 4c; 5b.

5A1 Ü3 ... zwischen Peking und Teheran ist vier Stunden; ... zwischen Lima und Casablanca ist
fünf Stunden; ... zwischen Oslo und Bangkok
ist sechs Stunden; ... zwischen Montreal und
Istanbul ist acht Stunden ...

Ü4 In Rom ist es Abend, 20 Uhr. Dann ist es in
Sydney Morgen, 5 Uhr.
In Stockholm ist es Nachmittag, 15 Uhr. Dann
ist es in Peking Abend, 22 Uhr.
In Paris ist es Nacht, 2 Uhr. Dann ist es in
Buenos Aires Abend, 22 Uhr.

In Montreal ist es Morgen, 8 Uhr. Dann ist es in Madrid Nachmittag, 14 Uhr ...

5A3 Ü6 a) *Durchsagen am Flughafen*
1. Abflug British Airways 959 nach Manchester, Flugsteig A6.
2. Abflug Condor 2212 nach Palma de Mallorca und Ibiza, Flugsteig A4.
3. Abflug Lufthansa 306 nach Athen, Flugsteig A18.
4. Herr Hopier, Passagier nach Kairo, bitte zum Lufthansa-Flugscheinschalter Nummer 9.
5. Letzter Aufruf Lufthansa 796 nach Hamburg, Flugsteig B12.

b) *Durchsagen am Bahnhof*
1. Am Gleis 19 bitte einsteigen, Türen schließen, Vorsicht bei der Abfahrt.
2. Auf Gleis 19 fährt ein der Schnellzug 892 aus Salzburg zur Weiterfahrt nach Karlsruhe. Ankunft 15 Uhr 47.
3. Achtung, eine private Durchsage: Werner und Dieter Steiner, Werner und Dieter Steiner möchten bitte zum Kundendienst der Bundesbahn am Gleis 26 kommen. ...
4. Auf Gleis 22 fährt ein der Intercity 683 "Ernst Barlach" aus Hamburg-Altona. Ankunft 16 Uhr 24.
5. Auf Gleis 19 fährt in Kürze ein der verspätete Fernexpreß 728 "Berchtesgadener Land" aus Dortmund zur Weiterfahrt nach Berchtesgaden, mit Kurswagen nach Salzburg. Planmäßige Ankunft 15 Uhr 10.

5A4 Ü7 1: richtig; 2: falsch; 3: richtig; 4: falsch; 5: falsch; 6: richtig; 7: richtig; 8: falsch; 9: richtig; 10: falsch

Ü8 (Lösungsbeispiel)
● Hallo, Sabine, hier ist Elke. Wir fahren nächste Woche nach Frankfurt zur Buchmesse. Kommt ihr mit?

o Vielleicht. Wann fahrt ihr denn genau?

● Am Dienstagvormittag, um 8 Uhr.

o Und wann kommt ihr zurück?

● Das wissen wir noch nicht genau; vielleicht am Donnerstag oder am Freitag.

o Wir haben nur Zeit bis Donnerstag.

● Gut, dann bleiben wir auch nur bis Donnerstag.

o Habt ihr schon ein Zimmer?

● Nein, aber ich rufe gleich die Touristen-Zentrale in Frankfurt an. Dann rufe ich dich wieder an. ...

Ü9 Heute ist der elfte Dezember neunzehnhundertsechsundneunzig / Heute haben wir den elften Dezember ... ;
... der dreizehnte März neunzehnhundertneunundachtzig / ... den dreizehnten März ... ;
... der einunddreißigste August neunzehnhundertachtundachtzig / ... den einunddreißigsten August ... ;
... der zwanzigste Juni neunzehnhundertneunundachtzig / ... den zwanzigsten Juni ... ;
... der siebzehnte Februar neunzehnhundertzweiundneunzig / ... den siebzehnten Februar ... ;
der sechzehnte September neunzehnhundertsiebenundachtzig / ... den sechzehnten September ... ;
... der dritte Mai neunzehnhundertneunundachtzig / ... dritten Mai ... ;

... achte Oktober neunzehnhundert(und)neunzig / ... den achten Oktober ... ;
... der fünfundzwanzigste April neunzehnhundertdreiundneunzig / ... den fünfundzwanzigsten April ... ;
... siebte Juli neunzehnhunderteinundneunzig / ... den siebten Juli ... ;
... der zwölfte November neunzehnhundertvierundneunzig / ... den zwölften November ... ;
der einunddreißigste Dezember neunzehnhundertneunundneunzig / ... den einunddreißigsten Dezember ... .

5A5 Ü10 (Lösungsbeispiele)

1. In Nordrhein-Westfalen haben die Kinder vom sechsten April bis zum fünfundzwanzigsten April, vom sechzehnten Juli bis zum neunundzwanzigsten August, vom neunzehnten Oktober bis zum vierundzwanzigsten Oktober und vom dreiundzwanzigsten Dezember bis zum sechsten Januar Schulferien.

2. Am dreiundzwanzigsten Dezember beginnen die Weihnachtsferien in allen Bundesländern bis auf Hamburg, Saarland und Sachsen-Anhalt.

3. Bis zum einundzwanzigsten April dauern die Osterferien in Bremen, Hamburg, Mecklenburg-Vorpommern, Niedersachsen und Sachsen-Anhalt.

4. a) Bayern: 13 Tage; b) Berlin: 22 Tage; c) Hessen: 20 Tage; d) Sachsen: 9 Tage; e) Thüringen: 17 Tage.

5. a) In Brandenburg dauern die Sommerferien vom neunundzwanzigsten Juni bis zum siebten August.
b) In Hamburg dauern die Sommerferien vom achtzehnten Juni bis zum ersten August.
c) In Niedersachsen dauern die Sommerferien vom fünfundzwanzigsten Juni bis zum fünften August.
d) Im Saarland dauern die Sommerferien vom dreiundzwanzigsten Juli bis zum fünften September.

Ü11 "Das ist die Stimme von Teddy Panther. Der Sänger macht im April eine Tournee durch die Bundesrepublik. Hier die Stationen: Sein erstes Konzert ist am 3. April in Kiel in der Ostseehalle. Am 6.4. tritt er in Hamburg auf. Und weiter geht's: am 9.4. in Bremen, 13. und 14. in Hannover, am 16. April in Köln. Vom 18. bis 20.4. gastiert Teddy Panther in Frankfurt. Am 23.4. in Stuttgart, und am 26. und 27. April das Finale in München, in der Olympiahalle.

5A6 Ü12 ... Am dreiundzwanzigsten, das ist zu spät! Ich habe Schmerzen!
... Oh, das ist zu früh! Ich arbeite bis halb drei; um drei Uhr, paßt das? Geht das?
... Gut, dann frage ich meinen Chef. Also: Freitag 12 Uhr 15.
... Pasolini, Pa - so - li - ni.

Ü13 o Hier Praxis Dr. Huber, guten Tag!

● Guten Tag, hier ist Petersen. Ich habe einen Termin für heute nachmittag.

o Ja, heute, 15 Uhr 30.

● Ja, richtig. Aber das geht leider nicht. Meine Tochter ist ... Haben Sie morgen nachmittag einen Termin frei?

o Morgen ist schlecht. Da ist nichts frei. Aber Donnerstagvormittag ...

● Am Vormittag kann ich leider nicht. Geht es auch am Nachmittag?

○ 17 Uhr?

● Ja, das ist gut.

○ Also, am 15., Donnerstag, 17 Uhr.

● Vielen Dank, auf Wiederhören!

○ Wiederhören.

(Lösungsbeispiele)
1. (Herr Bamberg heißt mit Vornamen) Günter.
2. Herr Bamberg hat große Zahnschmerzen.
3. Herr Bamberg möchte Tabletten.
4. (Nein,) Herr Bamberg war noch nicht bei Dr. Huber.
5. Herr Bamberg macht morgen Examen.
6. Er möchte überhaupt nicht kommen.
7. Die Sprechstundenhilfe sagt: "Kommen Sie gleich, es geht ganz schnell."
8. (Ja,) Er kommt, in zehn Minuten.

(Lösungsbeispiel)
Herr Riad hat am 30. Juli Examen. Heute ist Montag, der 29. Juli. Herr Riad hat Angst. Sein Kopf tut weh. "Ich habe Kopfschmerzen!" sagt Herr Riad. Er ruft den Arzt an. Er möchte einen Termin. Die Sprechstundenhilfe sucht einen Termin. "Haben Sie das Fieber schon lange?" fragt die Sprechstundenhilfe. "Nein, erst seit heute früh", antwortet Herr Riad. "Gut, dann kommen Sie bitte morgen, zehn Uhr!" - "Nein, das geht nicht! Ich möchte heute noch kommen!" ruft Herr Riad. "Ich habe sehr große Schmerzen!" - Die Sprechstundenhilfe sagt: "Moment mal, also dann heute, nachmittag, 17 Uhr 30." - "Vielen Dank", sagt Herr Riad.

(Lösungsbeispiel)
Er ist sehr in Eile. Um 19 Uhr hat er eine Konferenz in Düsseldorf. Jetzt ist es kurz nach siebzehn Uhr. Herr Gröner findet eine Autowerkstatt, aber die ist schon zu. Der Meister sagt, er hilft am nächsten Morgen. Vielleicht ist der Motor kaputt - das geht nicht so schnell. Der Meister schreibt die Adresse und die Telefonnummer von Herrn Gröner auf. Dann ruft er ein Taxi. Herr Gröner fährt mit dem Taxi nach Düsseldorf.

(Lösungsbeispiel)
○ Ich möchte morgen nach Berlin. Wann kann ich fliegen?

● Sie können am Vormittag ...

○ Das ist zu früh. Kann ich ...?

● Ja, da können Sie ...

○ Und wann kann ich übermorgen ...? Ich möchte am Abend ...

● Sie können um 18 Uhr 35 fliegen, ...

a) ○ Wir möchten in den Osterferien ...

● Wie lange möchtet ihr denn bleiben?

○ ...

● Hm. Ich rufe Gisela an, vielleicht möchte sie mitfahren; dann können wir zusammen mit dem Auto fahren.

b) ● Hallo, Gisela, Sabine und Peter möchten am Freitag nach Paris fahren ... Möchtest du auch mitfahren? Ich möchte dich einladen ... ich kann mitfahren ... Du kannst wirklich nicht? ... Natürlich kann ich das verstehen, ... du möchtest nach Athen. ... Da kann ich leider nicht ... Möchtest du

denn ganz allein fahren? ... Schade, da kann man nichts machen. Tschüs!

c) ● Also, Gisela möchte nicht nach Paris. Sie möchte im Mai nach Athen, ... Jetzt möchte/ brauche ich erst einmal einen Kognak.

5AW **Ü1** *Waagerecht:*
besuchen, suchen, anfangen, dauern, finden, anrufen, schlafen, umsteigen, kosten, nehmen, sehen, helfen, wohnen, können, bleiben.
Senkrecht:
mitfahren, fahren, beginnen, gehen, kommen, nehmen, haben, essen, arbeiten, fragen, einsteigen.

Ü2 1. Hotelzimmer; 2. kaputt; 3. Hilfe;
4. Herbstferien; 5. Bahnhof; 6. Passagier;
7. Minuten; 8. Gleis; 9. Fahrkarte
? = LUFTHANSA

6A1 **Ü3** ● Wo kommst du jetzt her?
○ Von Mario.
● Und was hast du so lange gemacht? Jetzt ist es 20/zwanzig vor acht!
○ ...
● Hausaufgaben? Sieben Stunden Hausaufgaben? Um eins war die Schule aus!
○ Ja, um halb zwei waren wir bei Mario - dann haben wir Hausaufgaben gemacht. Das war so viel: ... Ich habe Mario Mathe erklärt.
● Und warum ist deine Hose kaputt?
○ Das hat Pluto gemacht.
● ...
○ Der Hund von Mario.
● Ihr habt Fußball gespielt!
○ Nein, wir haben gearbeitet, wir haben gelernt. Frag Mario!

6A2 **Ü6** "Durchsagen im Supermarkt":
1. Verehrte Kunden! Wir bieten Ihnen heute wieder Sonderangebote zu kleinen Preisen. Zum Beispiel: 500 Gramm Jacobs-Kaffee "Edelmocca" oder, für Teefreunde, Thiele Tee "Broken Special", auch 500 Gramm, jede Packung nur 8/acht Mark 99! ...
2. Die Sonne des Südens auf unseren Tisch: Italienische Blutorangen, Handelsklasse 2, 1,5 Kilogramm für nur eine Mark 99! Oder Blumenkohl, aus Italien oder Frankreich - nur 1/eine Mark 49 pro Stück. ...
3. Bei uns bekommen Sie die ganze Kraft der Milch zu Minipreisen: Frischmilch nur 99 Pfennig pro Liter; Holländische Markenbutter, 250 Gramm für 1/eine Mark 99! Magerer gesunder Speisequark kostet bei uns nur 39 Pfennig der 250-Gramm Becher. Und eine norwegische Spezialität: Ridderkäse mit 60 Prozent Fettgehalt gibt's heute für unglaubliche eins 49 je 100/hundert Gramm. ...
4. Und abends sind alle durstig: Cola, die Literflasche schon für eins 29; Paulaner Hell, das frische Bier für die ganze Familie, der Kasten nur 12/zwölf Mark 99. Und Vater hat ein besonderes Gläschen verdient: Kognak "Napoleon", die 0,7-Liter Flasche zu 13/dreizehn Mark 98. ...

6A3 **Ü7** 1: richtig; 2: falsch; 3: richtig; 4: richtig;
5: falsch; 6: richtig; 7: falsch; 8: richtig;
9: falsch; 10: falsch; 11: richtig; 12: falsch;
13: richtig; 14: richtig; 15: falsch

6A4/5 **Ü10** (Lösungsbeispiele)
Verloren
1. Der Mann sucht sein Geld. 2. Sie sind am Kiosk und im Kaufhaus gewesen, und sie sind mit der U-Bahn gefahren. 3. Am Kiosk haben sie

die Zeitung gekauft (mitgenommen). 4. Dann haben sie die Hose gekauft. 5. Dann sind sie mit der U-Bahn gefahren.

Gefunden
1. Er war zuerst am Kiosk. 2. Die Leute an der U-Bahn-Station haben das Fundbüro angerufen. 3. Im Kaufhof hat der Mann die Verkäuferin gesucht. 4. In der alten Hose. Die Verkäuferin hat die alte Hose eingepackt; das Geld war noch in der alten Hose.

6A6 Ü13 (Lösungsbeispiele)
1. (in der) Stadt; 2. (ein) Geschenk (für Vater); 3. (eine) Hose (für sich); 4. Peter, (in einem) Restaurant; 5. komischer Typ, Blumen mitgebracht (für Monika); 6. (die) Blumen; 7. Monika: ins Kino (gehen)? Susi: Film schon gesehen; 8. Susi: Komm zu mir! Besuch; Peter, Blumen.

6A7 Ü15 o Das war eine Aufregung! Ich hab was gehört, so um 11/elf ein Klirren, einer hat die Scheibe kaputtgemacht.
● Haben Sie keine Angst gehabt?
o Und wie! Aber ich habe die Tür leise aufgemacht, und da war er!
● Wer??
o Na, der Einbrecher.
● Ein Mann?
o Ja, groß, stark!
● O Gott!
o Ich glaube, er hat Geld gesucht. Er hat alles aufgemacht und ausgeräumt.
● Und was haben Sie gemacht?
o Ich habe ihn gefragt: "Sagen Sie mal, was machen Sie hier?"
● Und er?
o Der sagt: " Entschuldigen Sie, ist hier Bahnhofstr. Nr. 9?" - "Ja, natürlich," sag ich, "Bahnhofstr. 9." Und dann sagt er: "Ja, kennen Sie mich denn nicht mehr?"
● So eine Frechheit!
o Und ich sag: "Nein, ich kenne Sie nicht, wer sind Sie denn?" Und er: "Na, ich bin doch ein Kollege von Hermann!"
● Von Hermann??
o Ja, Hermann ist mein Mann. Also, ich sag zu ihm: "Nein, setzen Sie sich mal hin. Ich mach ihnen erst ne Tasse Kaffee, und dann rufe ich Hermann an.
● Wo war denn ihr Mann?
o Der war nicht zu Hause. Also, ich mach Kaffee, und der sitzt da und schwitzt.
● Schwitzt?
o Na klar, der hat Angst gehabt.
● Ich denke, Sie haben Angst gehabt!
o Ja, zuerst ich, aber dann er. Und dann habe ich telefoniert. ...

6B2/5 Ü1 gelebt - gearbeitet - eingekauft - verdient - (sich) gefreut - gemeint - geantwortet - geangelt - zugenäht - geflirtet - zugeklebt - gespielt - gehört - nachgeschaut - gekauft - gefehlt - gezeigt - besucht - gekostet - gestöhnt - erzählt - gesucht - gedauert - gesteckt - eingepackt - kaputtgemacht - gewartet - ergänzt - gebraucht - gewohnt - aufgemacht - geredet - geholt - gemacht - ausgeräumt - geschickt - gehabt - gesagt - übernachtet - gekocht - gefragt - geschwitzt.

6B3/5 Ü2 1. geblieben - geschrieben - beschrieben - aufgeschrieben - eingestiegen - umgestiegen - geschnitten - aufgeschnitten - unterstrichen
2. geschlossen - verloren
3. getrunken - gefunden - begonnen
4. gesprochen - gekommen - geworfen - mitgekommen - zurückgekommen - weggeworfen - gegessen - vergessen

5. genommen - mitgenommen - gelesen - gesehen
6. gehoben
7. geschlafen - angefangen - aufgehalten - gefahren - abgefahren
8. gerufen - gelaufen - angerufen

6B6 Ü4 notiert - buchstabiert - studiert - diktiert - repariert - funktioniert - fotografiert - passiert - telefoniert

6B7 Ü5 (Lösungsbeispiele)
Der Einbrecher hat die Scheibe kaputtgemacht.
Er hat das Fenster aufgemacht.
Er hat Geld gesucht.
Er hat Uhren und Bilder in den Sack gesteckt.
Die Frau hat den Einbrecher gehört. Sie hat d[ie] Tür aufgemacht und hat den Einbrecher gefragt "Was machen Sie hier?"
Da hat der Einbrecher gesagt:
"Entschuldigen Sie bitte! Ich habe hier früh[er] gewohnt. Ich habe die alte Uhr gesucht."
Da hat die Frau ihm Kaffee gekocht.

6B4 Ü6 Ich bin ... gefahren. Ich bin ... gekommen. Ich bin ... umgestiegen. Ich bin ... eingestiegen. Ich bin ... mitgekommen. Ich bin ... abgefahren. Ich bin ... zurückgekommen. Ich bin ... gelaufen. Ich bin ... gegangen. Ich bin ... aufgestanden.
Ich bin ... geblieben.
Ich bin ... gewesen.

7A1 Ü1 ① ist links oben hinten / oben links hinte[n] oben hinten links / links hinten oben / hint[en] oben links (diese Varianten sind auch bei ⑧ möglich)
② ist hinten rechts oben; ③ ist vorne li[nks] oben; ④ ist vorne rechts oben; ⑤ ist hint[en] links unten; ⑥ ist hinten rechts unten; ⑦ vorne links unten; ⑧ ist vorne rechts unten[.]

Ü2 ① Links ist ein A, rechts ist ein H, oben ist [ein] U, unten ist ein S; Das ist ein HAUS!
② Oben ist ein Z, in der Mitte ist ein U, unt[en] sind zwei G. das ist ein ZUG!
③ Links und rechts ist ein U. In der Mitte is[t] ein A und ein T. Unten sind zwei O. Das ist [ein] AUTO!
④ Links ist das B, rechts ist das R, unten ist das T, und wo ist das O? Das ist ein BR[OT]
⑤ Links ist ein R, rechts ist ein E, in der Mitte ist ein T; und wo ist das U? Das ist [eine] TUER!

7A2 Ü3 ① o Entschuldigen Sie, wie komme ich zum Jos[ephs]platz?
● Zum Josephsplatz? Gehen Sie geradeaus un[d] dann an der Kreuzung links. Dann kommen [Sie] direkt zum Josephsplatz.

② a) Der Mann möchte zur Technischen Hochsch[ule.]
b) Gehen Sie immer geradeaus, diese Straße geradeaus, ... und am Ende ist die Tech[ni]sche Hochschule.
c) Vielleicht ein Kilometer, zehn Minuten [zu] Fuß.

③ a) richtig; b) falsch; c) falsch; d) falsc[h] e) richtig; f) richtig

④ o Ich suche die Polizei.
● Die Landpolizeidirektion?
o Ja, richtig.
● Gehen Sie hier die Theresienstraße entla[ng] bis zur zweiten Kreuzung, dann rechts, [die] zweite Straße links.

112

o Bis zur Kreuzung, dann rechts, und dann die zweite Straße links.
● Genau, und dann noch zwei- bis dreihundert Meter geradeaus und dann auf der rechten Seite das große Gebäude.
o Vielen Dank, das finde ich bestimmt.

5 1: der Teppich; 2: das Sofa; 3: das Bild; 6: die Hose; 10: der Plattenspieler; 11: der Schrank; (das Regal); 12: die Vase; 15: die Bücher.

6 Der Vater sucht den Fotoapparat zuerst im Wohnzimmer, auf dem Sofa, dann unter dem Sofa; aber da ist er auch nicht. Dann sucht er den Fotoapparat auf dem Regal, links von der Vase. Schließlich sucht er ihn in der Küche; im Kühlschrank? Aber vielleicht auf dem Tisch oder auf einem Stuhl. Mal sehn!

7 a) Falsch ist :
1. hat verkauft; 2. die ganze Zeit (auf dem Automarkt); 3. im Theater; 4. ist zu Fuß zum TÜV gelaufen; 5. beim TÜV; 6. direkt zum Automarkt; 7. verkauft; 8. hat er sich einen anderen Wagen gekauft.

9 Schuhe ①; Sonnenbrille ㉔; Schwimmflossen ㉒; Rettungsring ㉓; Kleiderhaken ②; Schirm ③; Zahnbürste ⑤; (Spazier-)Stock ④; Nachttisch ⑰; Nachttopf ⑭; Bett ⑬; Toilettenpapier ⑮; Fensterbank ⑲; Gardinenstange ㉑; Fisch ⑩; Sieb ⑨; Hemd ⑫; Krawatte ⑧; Hut ⑦; (Sardinen-)Dose ⑪; Strumpf ⑥; Einmachglas ⑯; (Schweizer) Käse ⑳; Bettdecke ⑱; Blumentopf ㉕ .

13 1. Sie hat den Kuchen auf den Boden gestellt.
Sie hat den Fisch hinter das Bild gesteckt.
Sie hat den Schinken neben das Sofa gelegt.
Sie hat das Huhn in die Schublade gelegt (gesteckt).
Sie hat das Bier zwischen die Bücher gestellt.
Sie hat das Dessert unter den Tisch gestellt.
Sie hat die Würste an die Wand gehängt.
Sie hat die Suppe auf das Sofa gestellt.

2. Der Kuchen steht jetzt auf dem Boden.
Der Fisch steckt jetzt hinter dem Bild.
Der Schinken liegt jetzt neben dem Sofa.
Das Huhn liegt jetzt in der Schublade.
Das Bier steht jetzt zwischen den Büchern.
Das Dessert steht jetzt unter dem Tisch.
Die Würste hängen jetzt an der Wand.
Die Suppe steht jetzt auf dem Sofa.

14 1. für das; 2. ohne; 3. durch die; 4. für die; 5. um die; 6. gegen den/einen; 7. um ... bis; 8. gegen; 9. bis zum; 10. ohne einen; 11. bis einen; 12. Ohne einen.

1 ① Rocko fliegt in/mit einem UFO ohne Führerschein durch das/ein Fenster in das/ein Wohnzimmer; er fliegt einmal um die Lampe und landet dann auf dem Tisch.

② Er klettert aus dem UFO, läuft einmal um die Blumenvase herum; dann springt er vom Tisch auf den Stuhl und schaut sich um. Vom Stuhl springt er auf das Sofa und landet auf der Katze Mira. Die Katze faucht.

③ Rocko hat Angst; er rennt weg; er rennt mit dem Kopf gegen/an die Wand.

④ Er steht wieder auf. Wohin? Er rennt in das Kinderzimmer von Peter und Anneliese. In der Ecke findet er eine Kiste mit Spielsachen: Autos, Puppen und ...

⑤ Ein Roboter mit einem Auge und mit vier Armen steigt aus der Kiste. Rocko springt

in den Kleiderschrank und versteckt sich zwischen den Kleidern.

⑥ Am Morgen stehen Peter und Anneliese auf. Anneliese geht zum Kleiderschrank; ...

8A5 Ü3 ① der Koffer; ② der Revolver; ④ der Füller; ⑥ der Radiorecorder; ③ der Computer; ⑩ der Fußball; ⑪ der Kerzenleuchter; ⑬ der Kochtopf; ㉓ der Knochen; ⑨ das Bild; ⑲ das Paar/die Hosenträger; ⑳ das Paar/die Skier; ㉑ das Fahrrad; ㉒ das Paket; ㉔ das Dreirad; ㉕ das Radio; ⑮ das Paar/die Hausschuhe; ⑦ die Angel; ⑧ die Babyflasche; ⑤ die Armbanduhr; ⑫ die Flasche Kognak/der Kognak; ⑱ die Krawatte; ⑯ die Puppe; ⑰ die Pfeife. Es fehlt: ⑭ die Bücher.

8B1 Ü1 (Lösungsbeispiele)
1. a) Nein, der ist nicht für mich.
   b) Nein, für ihn ist der Brief auch nicht.
   c) Ja, (vielleicht ist er) für ihn.
2. Ja, (das Paket ist) für mich.
3. Ja, (die Geschenke sind) für sie.
4. Ja, (die Bücher sind) für euch/uns.
5. Nein, (der Kaffee ist) nicht für mich.
6. Ja, dich. / Nein, dich nicht.
7. Ja, (wir haben) euch (gesucht).
8. Nein, ich brauche dich nicht mehr.
9. Ja, wir besuchen euch mal.
10. Ja, ich kann dich mitnehmen.
11. Nein, wir haben euch nicht gesehen.
12. Ja, ich ruf' dich mal an.
13. Ja, wir haben dich verstanden.
14. Nein, ich erkenne dich/Sie nicht wieder.

Ü2 (Lösungsbeispiele)
1. a) Nein, mir (gehört der Koffer) nicht.
   b) Vielleicht ihr/ihm?
2. a) Nein, uns (gehört die Tasche) nicht.
   b) Ja, vielleicht ihr.
3. Ja, (der Computer gehört) mir.
4. Ja, (die Bücher gehören) ihnen.
5. Ja, (das Radio gehört) ihm.
6. Ja, ich zeig' sie dir mal.
7. Gut, ich erzähle sie Ihnen noch einmal.
8. Ja, wir schicken euch mal eine (Karte).
9. Ja, ich kann dir Zigaretten mitbringen.
10. Nein, ich kann es Ihnen heute leider nicht mehr reparieren.
11. Nein, mir (gehört der Wagen) nicht.
12. Nein, ihr könnt uns leider nicht helfen.

8B2/3 Ü3 (Lösungsbeispiele)
1. a) Nein, das ist nicht mein Buch.
   b) Ja, (das ist) vielleicht ihr Buch.
2. a) Nein, das ist nicht meine Tasche.
   b) Ja, vielleicht seine (Tasche).
3. a) Nein, das ist nicht unser Koffer.
   b) Ja, (das ist) vielleicht ihr Koffer.
4. Ja, (das sind) uns(e)re (Kinder).
5. Nein, das sind nicht meine (Zigaretten).
6. Nein, das sind nicht meine (Schlüssel).
7. Ja, das ist mein Zimmer.
8. Ja, das ist mein Paß.

Ü4 (Lösungsbeispiele)
1. Ja, das ist ihr Gepäck.
2. Ja, das ist ihr Füller.
3. Nein, das ist nicht sein Fotoapparat.
4. Ja, das ist ihr Paß.
5. Nein, das ist nicht ihr Platz.
6. Ja, das sind ihre Schlüssel.
7. Ja, das ist ihr Auto.
8. Nein, das ist nicht sein Computer.
9. Nein, das sind nicht ihre Bücher.
10. Ja, das sind seine Zigaretten.

Ü5 1. mit meiner Familie; 2. auf unseren Urlaub;
3. mit seinen Freunden; 4. deine Geschenke;
5. unsere Freunde; 6. seinen Kindern; 7. meinen Fotoapparat; 8. deinen Führerschein;
9. Ihren Computer; 10. auf ihren Mann; 11. eure Hilfe; 12. in die Wohnung; 13. seiner Freundin; 14. unseren Lehrer; 15. bei unseren Freunden; 16. Ihren Nachbarn; 17. meine Brieftasche;
18. Unser Kurs; 19. mit deiner Lehrerin;
20. eure Karten; 21. meine Tasche; 22. deine
Mutter; 23. Ihre Adresse; 24. mit ihrem Chef.

8B4 Ü6 1. Rocko gibt ihn ihm.
2. Peter schenkt es ihr.
3. Susi leiht es ihr.
4. Susi schickt es ihr.

8B5 Ü7 1. seit einer Stunde; 2. zu einem Arzt;
3. Nach dem Frühstück ... mit dem Bus in die
Stadt. 4. bis zum Marktplatz; 5. aus dem Bus;
6. gegenüber dem Rathaus; 7. mit dem Lift bis
zum dritten Stock; 8. vom 10. August bis zum
1. September; 9. zum nächsten Arzt; 10. Beim
dritten Arzt; 11. am Abend ... zu Hause.

8B6 Ü8 1. Seine Frau: Die Frau des Hodscha;
das: Der Hodscha verläßt sein Haus;
ihn: den Hodscha.
2. du: der Hodscha.
3. Er: der Hodscha.
4. Mein Ring: der Ring des Hodscha;
ich: der Hodscha;
meinen Ring: den Ring des Hodscha.
5. Ich: der Hodscha.
ihn: den Ring;
6. Sie: die Frau des Hodscha.
7. du: der Hodscha;
ihn: den Ring.

8B7 Ü9 1. Das sind die Bücher von Fernando.
Das sind Fernandos Bücher. Das sind seine
Bücher.
2. Das ist das Auto von meiner Frau. Das
ist ihr Auto.
3. Das ist der Paß von Frau Barbieri. Das
ist Frau Barbieris Paß. Das ist ihr Paß.
4. Das ist die Tasche von Maria. Das ist
Marias Tasche. Das ist ihre Tasche.
5. Das ist das Gepäck von Herrn und Frau
Berger. Das ist Herrn und Frau Bergers Gepäck. Das ist ihr Gepäck.
6. Das sind die Knieschützer von Rocko. Das
sind Rockos Knieschützer. Das sind seine
Knieschützer.
7. Das ist die Puppe von dem Mädchen. Das
ist die Puppe des Mädchens. Das ist seine
Puppe.
8. Das ist die Pfeife von Opa. Das ist Opas
Pfeife. Das ist seine Pfeife.
9. Das ist der Kochtopf von Vater. Das ist
Vaters Kochtopf. Das ist sein Kochtopf.

5-8W (Lösungsbeispiele)
1. Entschuldigen Sie, haben Sie auch Platznummer 126? (Sie sitzen auf meinem Platz. /
Das ist mein Platz!)
2. a) Nein, das ist nicht mein Koffer.
b) Ja, der gehört mir.
3. a) Tut mir leid, das weiß ich nicht.
b) Heute ist der (12. Juli).
4. a) Ich möchte aber ins Kino; immer Fußball,
das ist langweilig!
b) Komm doch mit zum Fußball; die Weltelf
spielt!
5. Entschuldigen Sie, kann ich eine Zigarette
rauchen?
6. Tut mir leid, ich kann nicht (mitkommen),
ich habe Zahnschmerzen.
7. a) Tut mir leid, das weiß ich (auch) nicht.

b) Gehen Sie bis zur zweiten Querstraße,
dann links; der Bahnhof ist auf der linken/rechten Seite.
8. a) Das weiß ich doch nicht!
b) In deiner Tasche.
c) Im Schrank. / Ich habe ihn in den Schrank
gelegt.
9. Zuerst habe ich ..., dann bin ich ...
10. Ich kann meinen Paß nicht finden. Hast du
(nicht) meinen Paß gesehen?
11. Tut mir leid, das weiß ich nicht (; ich
habe auch keine Uhr).
12. a) Um 8 Uhr am Bahnhof.
b) Um 7 Uhr am Kino/vor dem Kino.
13. Ich möchte (morgen früh) nach Amsterdam.
Wann kann ich fahren? Wann ist der Zug in
Amsterdam?
14. Nach Paris und zurück, 2. Klasse bitte.
15. Ich brauche nächste Woche (vom 5. bis zum
7. November) ein Hotelzimmer (in Berlin).
16. Hallo, Peter/Petra, ich fahre am Montag zur
Buchmesse nach Frankfurt. Kommst du mit?/
Möchtest du (nicht) mitkommen?
17. Guten Tag, ich habe Zahnschmerzen, ich brauche einen Termin / kann ich sofort kommen?
18. Guten Tag, mein Auto ist kaputt. Können Sie
es heute noch reparieren?
19. Sie haben gesagt, ich kann das Auto heute abholen; und jetzt ist es immer noch nicht fertig! Ich brauche das Auto sofort!
20. Das siehst du doch, ich habe eingekauft! Die
Sachen waren sehr teuer!
21.-22. Im Geschäft habe ich sie noch gehabt, da habe
ich die Sachen bezahlt; danach waren wir noch
im Restaurant, da habe ich sie auch noch gehabt; und dann sind wir mit der U-Bahn gefahren ...
24. a) Entschuldigen Sie bitte, wie komme ich
(von hier aus) zum Bahnhof?
b) Gehen Sie an der Ampel rechts, dann geradeaus bis zur zweiten Querstraße, dann
links und dann immer geradeaus, noch ungefähr 200 Meter.
25. a) Entschuldigen Sie bitte, ich suche die
Post. / Wie komme ich zur Post?
b) Wo ist bitte das Einwohnermeldeamt?
26. Wohin fährst du? Und wie lange bleibst du?
27. Entschuldigen Sie bitte, wohnt hier Herr
Otramba?
28. Entschuldigen Sie, mein Kugelschreiber ist
kaputt; können Sie mir einen Kugelschreiber
(oder einen Bleistift) leihen?
29. Ich kann Ihnen meinen leihen, ich habe zwei.
30. a) Ja, das ist (Petras) Tasche.
b) Nein, das ist meine Tasche/die Tasche gehört mir!

5-8K Kontrollaufgaben

A Wörter
1b; 2c; 3d; 4a; 5b; 6a; 7c; 8c; 9d; 10a.

B Grammatik
1b; 2c; 3d; 4c; 5d; 6b; 7a; 8b; 9c; 10b.

C Orthographie
1: Weihnachten; 2: feiern; 3: liebsten; 4: Haus;
5: Familie; 6: Abend; 7: Menschen; 8: Kirche;
9: Wohnungen; 10: Christbaum; 11: geschmückt;
12: Kerzen; 13: Besonders; 14: schön; 15: Kinder;
16: bekommen; 17: Geschenke; 18: Sachen; 19: Kuchen; 20: Essen.

D Lesen
1a; 2d; 3d; 4b; 5a; 6b; 7b; 8d; 9c; 10a.

E Sprechen
1b; 2a; 3a; 4c; 5c; 6a; 7c; 8c; 9b; 10b.

Wörterverzeichnis

pitel 1

1

r
t (sein)
s
me, der
rname, der
ourtstag, der
ourtsort, der
öße, die
rbe, die
ge, das
ün
lefon, das

2
t
g, der
h
ißen
llo!
rzeihung, die
e
r-
edersehen, das
f Wiedersehen!
au, die
rr, der
d

her
mmen (aus)

ssen
cht
auben
s
euen
ch
in

formation, die
utschkurs, der

3
hreiben
n
chstabieren
e
tte
hl, die

Buchstabiertafel,
 die
noch
einmal
langsam
also
danke
Adresse, die
Landstraße, die
wo
wohnen (in)
Sie
in
Fräulein, das
Intonation, die

1.4

Frankreich, -
Spanien, -
Kanada, -
Indien, -
USA, die
Italien, -
Brasilien, -
Australien, -
Japan, -
Lehrer, der
haben
Teilnehmer, der
Mann, der
Nummer, die
dann
dasein
krank
aber
England, -
Bundesrepublik
 Deutschland, die
Griechenland, -
Telefonnummer, die
Kurs, der
Liste, die
Kursliste, die
Schweiz, die
Uruguay, -
Israel, -
Österreich, -
Belgien, -
Partner, der
Interview, das
Partner-Interview,
 das

---

beschreiben
Partnerin, die

Kapitel 2

2A1

gehen (es geht)
sprechen
Englisch, -
was
trinken
Cafeteria, die
Bier, das
Cola, die
Kaffee, der
Wein, der
Limonade, die
Tee, der
Mineralwasser, das
ein-
ah!
Abend, der
es
ganz
Deutsch, -
auch
nein
leider
lieber
ein bißchen
Schottland, -
gern(e)
Mars, der

2A2

die
von

2A3

Auskunft, die
oder
Vorwahl, die
hören
Gespräch, das
notieren
spielen
Lotto, das
machen
Kreuz, das
Gewinnzahl, die
Spiel, das

2A4

Arbeiter, der
Ausländer, der
Berlin
Korea, -
studieren
Pädagogik, die
Jahr, das
alt
meinen
schön
Heimweh, das
Diplomat, der
leben
schon
lange
hier
daheim
sagen
Marokkaner, der
stammen (aus)
jetzt
arbeiten
Arzt, der
bei
noch
gehen
nach
Haus, das
nach Hause
Familie, die
Dolmetscherin, die
Freund, der
Deutscher, -
bleiben
sehr
allein
Major, der
British Army, die
erst
Monat, der
schwer
Vietnam, -
Krankenschwester,
 die
kalt
Mensch, der
freundlich
viel
Finnland, -
Marokko, -
Griechenland, -

Türkei, die
Koreaner, der
Koreanerin, die
Finne, der
Finnin, die
Marokkanerin, die
Grieche, der
Griechin, die
Franzose, der
Französin, die
Türke, der
Türkin, die
Engländer, der
Engländerin, die
Vietnamese, der
Vietnamesin, die
Koreanisch, -
Finnisch, -
Arabisch, -
Griechisch, -
Französisch, -
Türkisch, -
Vietnamesisch, -
korrigieren

2A5

als
Muttersprache, die
Fremdsprache, die
Studentin, die
Ingenieur, der
verstehen
Dänisch, -
Schwedisch, -
für
Russisch, -
Ärztin, die
Italienisch, -
Spanisch, -
antworten
lernen
Gemeinschaft Unab-
  hängiger Staaten,
  die
Südkorea, -
Holland, -
Niederlande, die
Jugoslawien, -
Polen, -
Indonesien, -
andere -
Land, das

2B1

Satz, der
Satzteile, die

2B2

Verb, das
Nominativergänzung,
  die
Subjekt, das

2B3

Personalpronomen,
  das
Verbstamm, der
Endung, die

2B4

Konjugation, die
Präsens, das
Infinitiv, der
Singular, der
Person, die
Plural, der

2B5

Satzart, die
Aussage, die
Frage, die
Wortfrage, die
Fragewort, das
Satzfrage, die
Aufforderung, die
Imperativ, der
lesen
ergänzen
fragen
Beispiel, das
Aufgabe, die
Aufforderungssatz,
  der

Kapitel 3

3A1

Hauptbahnhof, der
City, die
Messegelände, das
Telefon, das
Clown, der
Spray, das
Steak, das
Park, der
Auto, das
Gangster, der
Star, der
Hamburger, der
Cassette, die
Hostess, die
Baby, das

Paß, der
Garage, die
Radio, das
Zigarette, die
Computer, der

3A2

Radiergummi, der
Schultasche, die
Heft, das
Lampe, die
Regal, das
Tageslichtprojek-
tor, der
Tonbandgerät, das
Bild, das
Stuhl, der
Landkarte, die
Buch, das
kein-
Ahnung, die
vielleicht
Kuli, der
Füller, der
Tisch, der

3A3

Angelschein, der
wir
Fisch, der
Ausweis, der
Sonntagnachmittag,
  der
Langeweile, die
sein-
Vater, der
heute
Zeit, die
ja
Idee, die
angeln
prima!
kosten
Mark, die
warum
egal
mehr
nicht mehr
zu
spät
zu spät
Polizist, der
Parkwächter, der
bezahlen
weitergehen
Geschichte, die

3A4

Olive, die
Pfennig, der
Pfennigstück, das
Markstück, das
einkaufen
im (in dem)
Supermarkt, der
Spezialität, die
Milch, die
Butter, die
Margarine, die
Joghurt, das/der
frisch
Ei, das
Stück, das
Sonderangebot, das
Lammfleisch, das
Schweinefleisch,
  das
Rindfleisch, das
Tomate, die
Schokolade, die
Tafel, die
Cornflakes, die
Öl, das
Apfel, der
Birne, die
Salat, der
Obst, das
Gemüse, das
Kartoffel, die
Kilo, das
gr. (= Gramm, das)
alles
zusammen

3A5

Miete, die
hoch
Kind, das
Mädchen, das
Junge, der
Vierzimmerwohnung,
  die
m² (= Quadratmeter,
  der)
Heizung, die
extra
verdienen
netto
Lehrerin, die
klein
Schulden, die
Lebenshaltungs-
kosten, die

essen, das
rinken, das
rom, der
sser, das
hrtkosten, die
bel, das
bel, die
usrat, der
eidung, die
itung, die
no, das
rnsehen, das
ise, die
isen, das
sundheit, die
rperpflege, die
nstiges, –
chtig
lsch
hein, der

_A6_

asche, die
eise, die
laschsuppe, die
ar, das
rstchen, das
n Paar Würstchen
t
ot, das
atwurst, die
hinkenbrot, das
isebrot, das
rtion, die
mmes frites, die
las, das
sse, die
nnchen, das
se, die
iertel, das
nger, der
ssen
r
uviel
urst, der
öchte-

_A7_

ast, der
exas-Steak, das
alat, der
h!
euer
uerst
uppe, die
ank, der

---

bayerisch
Leberknödelsuppe,
  die
nach
Art, die
nach Wiener Art
Hühnersuppe, die
Nudel, die
Kräuterbutter, die
Saisonsalat, der
Zigeuner-Steak, das
Sauce, die
Paprika, der
Zwiebel, die
dazu
Reis, der
Matjesfilet, das
Rahmsoße, die
Salzkartoffeln, die
Forelle, die
blau
Forelle blau
Petersilienkartof-
  feln, die
Seezunge, die
braten
je
Saison, die
je nach Saison
Beilage, die
gemischt
Kartoffelsalat, der
Eiernudeln, die

_3A8_

Picknick, das
kommen
Essen, das
fertig
Sonntag, der
warm
Sonne, die
scheinen
Wurst, die
Käse, der
Brief, der
schlafen
dick
faul
Fußball, der
Schwester, die
Radio, das
zu Hause
Kopf, der
weh tun
anfangen

_3A9_

unbekannt
Lebewesen, das
Sprudel, der
fressen
Metall, das
Mineralien, die
Teeglas, das
Kaffeetasse, die
Coladose, die
Weinflasche, die

_3B1_

Genus, das
maskulinum
neutrum
femininum

_3B2_

unbestimmt
Artikel, der
bestimmt

_3B3_

Sache, die

_3B4_

Deklination, die
Nominativ, der
Akkusativ, der
Dativ, der
Genitiv, der

_3B5_

genauso
benutzen
Lexikon, das

Singen und Spielen

Singen, das
Spielen, das
Hahn, der
tot
können
Meister, der
Glocke, die
viel
Glück, das
Buchstabe, der
raten
Gefängnis, das
aussehen
so
Strich, der
Kreis, der
Wort, das
kennen

---

welche-
Zentimeter, der
groß
lustig
blau
blond
Haar, das
Würfelspiel, das
Pech, das
Würfel, der
würfeln
Punkt, der

Kapitel 4

_4A1_

Ohr, das
Fuß, der
Hand, die
Arm, der
Bauch, der
Brust, die
Popo, der
Bein, das
Vorsicht, die
Busen, der
Lippe, die
Knie, das
Nase, die
Mund, der
Hals, der
Finger, der
Zehe, die
deutsch
Volk, das

_4A2_

fehlen
denn
Schlagader, die
Lunge, die
Herz, das
Leber, die
Gallenblase, die
Magen, der
Niere, die
Darm, der
Eingeweide, das,
  die
Fieber, das
Schmerz, der
Schmerzen, die
aha!
zeigen
mal (_einmal_)
vorn(e)

Husten, der
etwas (*ein bißchen*)
Angina lacunaris,
  die
Entzündung, die
links
täglich
Tablette, die
Kamille, die
inhalieren
Bettruhe, die
Woche, die
schlecht

4A3

mehrmals
Halstablette, die
Anwendungsgebiet,
  das
Mundschleimhaut-
  entzündung, die
Rachenentzündung,
  die
Schluckbeschwer-
  sen, die
Kehlkopfentzün-
  dung, die
Zahnfleischentzün-
  dung, die
Dosierungsanlei-
  tung, die
Art, die
Dauer, die
Anwendung, die
falls
Arzt, der
verordnen
zergehen
lassen
Behandlung, die
sollen
nach
Abklingen, das
Beschwerden, die
fortsetzen
Arzneimittel, das
für
unzugänglich
aufbewahren
gegen
Halsschmerz, der
Halsschmerzen, die
Grippe, die
Angina, die
suchen
weitersuchen

4A4

Operation, die
Mutter, die
Chefarzt, der
Assistent, der
Sofa, das
stöhnen
laut
Messer, das
Schere, die
Wäscheklammer, die
aufschneiden
kaputt
Wunde, die
aufhalten
rausziehen
Spirale, die
wegwerfen
Kissen, das
holen
wieder
zunähen
zukleben
zufrieden
klingeln

4A5

war (sein)
Sahne, die
selbstgebacken
Kuchen, der
Milchgeschäft, das
Besitzer, der
Sohn, der
Geschäft, das
Souterrain, das
Keller, der
billig
kühl
hatte- (haben)
Kühlschrank, der
damals
früher

4A6

Lebensgeschichte,
  die
Geld, das
verheiratet
nie
Schauspieler, der
Erfolg, der
berühmt
Termin, der
Politiker, der
Macht, die
Flugzeug, das

weg
sammeln

4A7

Empfindungswort, das
aha!
Deutschen, die (*Pl.*)
ei!
hurra!
pfui!
ach!
nanu!
oho!
hm
jaja!

4B1

Substantiv, das
Plural-Computer,
  der
Silbe, die
Typ, der
Konsonant, der
Endbuchstabe, der

4B2

trennbar

4B3

Präteritum, das
Präteritumsignal,
  das

Kapitel 5

5A1

wieviel
Uhr, die
Uhrzeit, die
halb
vor
Minute, die

5A2

spät
wann
treffen
uns
fahren
fast
Stunde, die
um
am (an dem)
Bahnhof, der
Zug, der
früh
genug

Fahrkarte, die
pünktlich
Wecker, der
anrufen
Schlaftablette, die
bis
morgen
Abflug, der
Inland, das
dauern
Flug, der
etwa
Maschine, die
so
ab
direkt
umsteigen
einfach
hin
zurück
Klasse, die

5A3

Durchsage, die
Flughafen, der
Flugsteig, der
Passagier, der
Flugscheinschal-
  ter, der
Aufruf, der
letzte-
Schalter, der
Abfahrt, die
Ziel, das
Gleis, das
bei
einsteigen
Tür, die
schließen
auf
einfahren
Schnellzug, der
zur (zu der)
Weiterfahrt, die
Achtung, die
Ankunft, die
privat
Kundendienst, der
Bundesbahn, die
Intercity, der
unterwegs
Kürze, die
verspätet
Fernexpreß, der
Kurswagen, der
planmäßig

5A4

Bus, der
jede-
international
Buchmesse, die
Stadt, die
überfüllt
Journalistin, die
Touristenzentrale,
 die
brauchen
Hotelzimmer, das
Hotel, das
besetzt
nur
für
Nacht, die
Privatadresse, die
Kilometer, der
bis
Messe, die
mit
Platz, der
übernachten
Rückfahrt, die
Fahrt, die
per
Anhalter, der
per Anhalter
besuchen
Fußball-Länder-
 spiel, das
Oktoberfest, das

5A5

Ferien, die
Ordinalzahl, die
Ordinalzahlen
 1-100.
Schulferien, die
Ostern, -
Pfingsten, -
Sommer, der
Herbst, der
Weihnachten,-
Januar, der
Februar, der
März, der
April, der
Mai, der
Juni, der
Juli, der
August, der
September, der
Oktober, der
November, der

Dezember, der
Ferientag, der
Frühjahrsferien, die
Sommerferien, die
Sonntag, der
deshalb
Montag, der
beginnen
Schule, die
lang
Osterferien, die
gleich
Weihnachtsferien,
 die
Pfingstferien,die
Herbstferien, die

5A6

vorgestern
gestern
übermorgen
Dienstag, der
Mittwoch, der
Donnerstag, der
Freitag, der
Zahnschmerzen, die
Zahnarzt, der
möglichst
bald
Sprechstundenhil-
 fe, die
frei
besser
Freitagnachmittag,
 der
Praxis, die
geschlossen
Chef, der
unterstreichen
Text, der
wichtig
Telefonat, das

5A7

brauchen
sofort
Hilfe, die
Autopanne,die
Eile, die
Konferenz, die
kurz
Autowerkstatt, die
helfen
nächste-
Motor, der
schnell
Taxi, das

abend
leid tun
eilig
bis
Wagen, der
nachschauen
aus
Sprechblase, die
Dialog, der

5A8

raus
rein
selber
lehrreich
Reich, das
reichen
Markierung, die
Wende, die
Krieg, der

5B1

Modalverb, das
Konjunktiv, der

5B2

Akkusativergän-
 zung, die
Qualitativergän-
 zung, die
Direktivergänzung,
 die
.Einordnungsergän-
 zung, die
temporal
Situativergänzung,
 die

Kapitel 6

6A1

ganz-
Vormittag, der
beim (bei dem)
endlich
Co. (= Compagnie)
schicken
Verkehr, der
warten
gerade
diktieren
reden
wirklich
Freundin, die
Sekretärin, die
kochen

erzählen
flirten
Spaziergang, der
fotografieren
Pause, die
Zeitung, die
Bank, die
müde
Nachmittag, der
Bildgeschichte, die

6A2

Zucker, der
Honig, der
Orange, die
böse
Brathering, der
Vollkornbrot, das
Markenbutter, die
Sorte, die
Becher, der
jede-
Auswahl, die
Gulasch, das
Rind, das
Schwein, das
Blumenkohl, der
Blutorange, die
Bienenhonig, der
Speisequark, der
mager
Rahmspinat, der
gefroren
Musik-Kassette,
 die
Frischmilch, die
Kognak, der
Knacker, die

6A3

Moment, der
verdammt!
genau
los sein
möglich
Firma, die
reparieren
funktionieren
Batterie, die
Paket, das
Mittagessen, das
Post, die
Abendessen, das

6A4

Mist, der
Mist!

verlieren
vergessen
mitnehmen
danach
Hose, die
stimmen
U-Bahn, die

6A5

zuerst
sehen
U-Bahn-Station,
 die
Fundbüro, das
Kaufhof, der (Ei-
 genname)
Verkäuferin, die
gleich
wiedererkennen
neu
anziehen
einpacken
laufen
geben = (existie-
 ren)
Manteltasche, die

6A6

aufstehen
ziemlich
Bad, das
Frühstück, das
schneiden
dünn
Brötchen, das
hart
Nachricht, die
Blume, die
wenig
Brieftasche, die
traurig
Pizza, die
Jeans, die
Restaurant, das
früher-

6A7

Einbrecher, der
Fenster, das
Fensterscheibe, die
Zimmertür, die
Wohnzimmerschrank,
 der
kaputtmachen
aufmachen
steigen
Schublade, die

ausräumen
Sack, der
stecken
Angst, die
Mütze, die
schwitzen
Mitternacht, die

6A8

viele -
manche -
einige -
ein paar -
wenige -
keine -

6B1

Perfekt, das

6B2

Aktiv, das
regelmäßig

6B3

unregelmäßig
Ablaut, der

6B5

Präfix, das
Partizip, das
vorige-
Kuchen, der

Deutschsprachige Literatur im 20. Jahrhundert

deutschsprachig
Literatur, die
Jahrhundert, das
Roman, der
Kaufmannsfamilie,
 die
Nobelpreis, der
emigrieren
sterben
Schwarzwald, der
Steppenwolf, der
 (Eigenname)
seit
Staatsbürger, der
Literaturnobel-
 preis, der
Kulturminister,
 der
Gedicht, das
bekannt
Romanschrift-
 stellerin, die

Heimatstadt, die
Architektur, die
Drama, das
Tagebuch, das
Lyrikerin, die
Hörspiel, das
veröffentlichen
sozialkritisch
Figur, die
Theaterautor, der
Filmautor, der
Blechtrommel, die
 (Eigenname)
besonders
durch
satirisch
Erzählung, die
ausfüllen
Biographie, die

Kapitel 7

7A1

rechts
Stock, der
Etage, die
Erdgeschoß, das
Parterre, das
oben
Leben, das
bunt
unten
arm
Hund, der
Mitte, die
Bayer, der
vorn(e)
Zoo, der
hinten
Klo, das
Postkarte, die
Schloß, das
Brücke, die
Luftaufnahme, die
Partie, die
Neckar, der (Ei-
 genname)
Partie am Neckar,
 die
Schloßhof, der
Faß, das
Kornmarkt, der
 (Eigenname)
Heiliggeistkirche,
 die (Eigenname)

diese -
Raum, der
zeichnen
Zimmer, das

7A2

Rathaus, das
müssen
entlanggehen
Hauptstraße, die
ungefähr
Seite, die
Park, der
Markt, der
Kirche, die
Einwohnermeldeamt,
 das
geradeaus
Ausländeramt, das
Treppe, die
höher
Reisepaß, der
bekommen
anmelden
Zulassungsstelle,
 die
heiraten
Standesamt, das
Zollamt, das
Entschuldigung,
 die
Querstraße, die
entschuldigen
Kreuzung, die
Fotoapparat, der

7A3

auf
unter
hinter
neben
in
zwischen
vor
Blumentopf, der
Vase, die

7A4

Automarkt, der
TÜV, der
Theater, das
ablaufen
Riesenschlange,
 die
Abgastest, der
Papier, das
Ordnung, die

errückt
rnen, das
ausaufgabe, die
ernsehen, das
ltern, die
sko, die
ußballmannschaft, die

5
nntagmittag, der
ttagstisch, der
tzen
echen
nderbar
hinken, der
hn, das
m (zu dem)
chtisch, der

tt, der
lle, der
Gottes willen!
nladen
en, der
geleisen, das
sen, der
aubtuch, das
tztuch, das
ndbesen, der
hrschaufel, die
rste, die
inigungsmittel, as
hrubber, der
scheleine, die
mer, der
aubsauger, der
rkzeugkasten, er
gelbrett, das

6
hweizer, der
s (in das)
sland, das
lt, die

---

aufpassen
stehlen
Koffer, der
geben
Beutel, der
Hemd, das
eingenäht
Unterwäsche, die
Klang, der
Elend, das

7A7
Kollege, der
Bewegung, die
Schreibtisch, der
immer
dasselbe
Schlimmste, das
Bude, die
Luft, die
fest

7B3
wohin
an

7B4
Wechselpräposition, die
stehen
stellen

7B5
durch
um

Kapitel 8

8A1
doch
bloß
hergeben
nett

8A2
Taxifahrer, der
Tennislehrer, der

Katze, die
Hausfrau, die
Automechaniker, der
Postangestellte, die
pensioniert
Besuch, der
Briefträger, der

8A3a
gehören

8A3b
voll
Karte, die
Reihe, die
Platznummer, die
Tasche, die

8A4
Fest, das
Weihnachtsfeiertag, der
heilig
feiern
Christbaum, der
schmücken
Kerze, die
Kugel, die
Stern, der
Geschenk, das
schenken
Lebkuchen, der
Spekulatius, der
Plätzchen, das
Stollen, der

8A5
Wahnsinn, der
Knieschützer, der
passen
irre
leihen
beide-
Oma, die
Opa, der

8A6
Rabe, der
Schnabel, der
Fuchs, der
denken
herrlich
Fell, das
hübsch
König, der
Wald, der
natürlich
stolz
Ring, der

8A7
verlassen
drinnen
draußen
dunkel
hell
Possessivpronomen, das

8A8
Haut, die
Gewehr, das
Krieg, der
Schuld, die
Mauer, die

8B2
vergleichen

8B5
Präposition, die

8B6
Referenzmittel, das
Zugehörigkeit, die
Besitz, der

Wiederholungsspiel
Spielregel, die
zählen
Szene, die
uff!
geschafft!

Grammatikübersicht

Die Satzarten

→ Lehrbuch, S. 23–24

1 Die Aussage

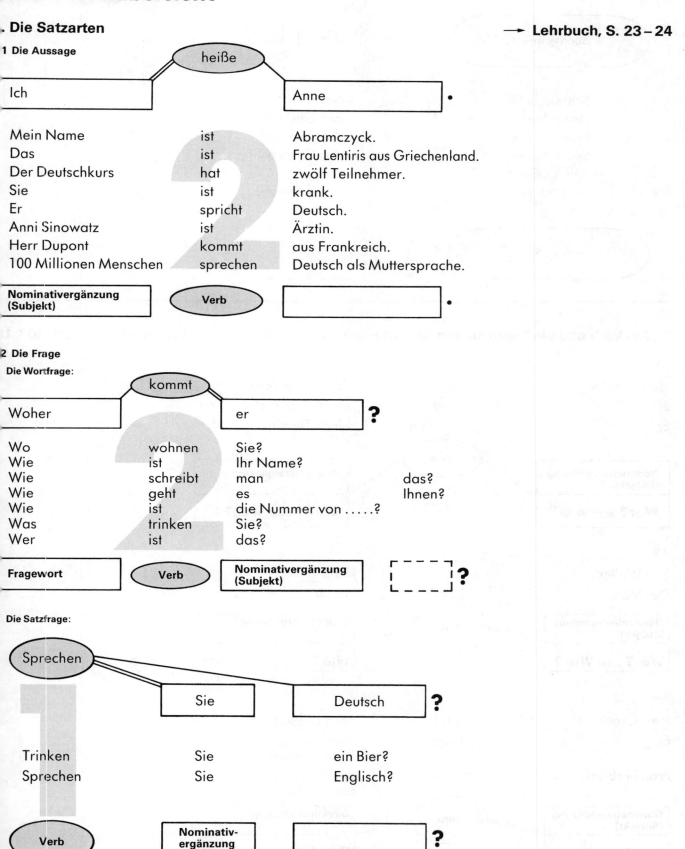

Ich	heiße	Anne	

Mein Name	ist	Abramczyck.
Das	ist	Frau Lentiris aus Griechenland.
Der Deutschkurs	hat	zwölf Teilnehmer.
Sie	ist	krank.
Er	spricht	Deutsch.
Anni Sinowatz	ist	Ärztin.
Herr Dupont	kommt	aus Frankreich.
100 Millionen Menschen	sprechen	Deutsch als Muttersprache.

Nominativergänzung (Subjekt) — **Verb** — ☐ .

2 Die Frage

Die Wortfrage:

Woher	kommt	er	?

Wo	wohnen	Sie?	
Wie	ist	Ihr Name?	
Wie	schreibt	man	das?
Wie	geht	es	Ihnen?
Wie	ist	die Nummer von ..... ?	
Was	trinken	Sie?	
Wer	ist	das?	

Fragewort — **Verb** — **Nominativergänzung (Subjekt)** — ☐ ?

Die Satzfrage:

Sprechen	Sie	Deutsch	?

Trinken	Sie	ein Bier?
Sprechen	Sie	Englisch?

Verb — **Nominativergänzung (Subjekt)** — ☐ ?

1.3 Die Aufforderung: Imperativ (1)

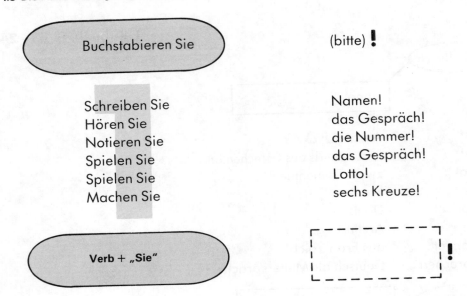

Buchstabieren Sie	(bitte) !
Schreiben Sie	Namen!
Hören Sie	das Gespräch!
Notieren Sie	die Nummer!
Spielen Sie	das Gespräch!
Spielen Sie	Lotto!
Machen Sie	sechs Kreuze!

Verb + „Sie"

---

2. Das Verb und die Ergänzungen (Satzglieder)

→ Lehrbuch, S. 71 – 72, 103, 118

2.1

Herr Pasolini	hat	Zahnschmerzen.	
Er	ruft	einen Zahnarzt	an.
Er	möchte	einen Termin.	

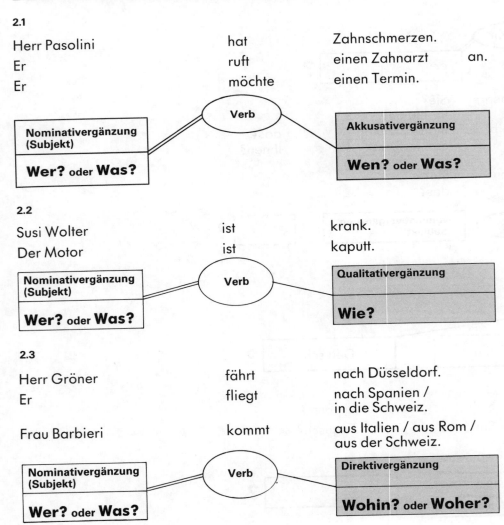

Nominativergänzung (Subjekt)	Verb	Akkusativergänzung
Wer? oder **Was?**		**Wen?** oder **Was?**

2.2

Susi Wolter	ist	krank.
Der Motor	ist	kaputt.

Nominativergänzung (Subjekt)	Verb	Qualitativergänzung
Wer? oder **Was?**		**Wie?**

2.3

Herr Gröner	fährt	nach Düsseldorf.
Er	fliegt	nach Spanien / in die Schweiz.
Frau Barbieri	kommt	aus Italien / aus Rom / aus der Schweiz.

Nominativergänzung (Subjekt)	Verb	Direktivergänzung
Wer? oder **Was?**		**Wohin?** oder **Woher?**

.4

| Das | ist | ein Tageslichtprojektor. |
| Marlies Demont | ist | Studentin. |

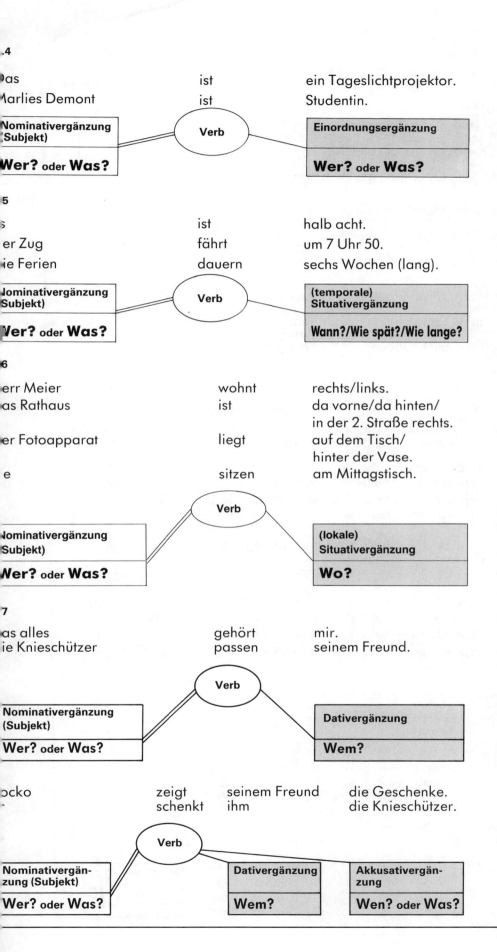

Nominativergänzung (Subjekt) — **Wer? oder Was?** — Verb — **Einordnungsergänzung** / **Wer? oder Was?**

5

s	ist	halb acht.
er Zug	fährt	um 7 Uhr 50.
ie Ferien	dauern	sechs Wochen (lang).

Nominativergänzung (Subjekt) — **Wer? oder Was?** — Verb — **(temporale) Situativergänzung** / **Wann?/Wie spät?/Wie lange?**

6

err Meier	wohnt	rechts/links.
as Rathaus	ist	da vorne/da hinten/ in der 2. Straße rechts.
er Fotoapparat	liegt	auf dem Tisch/ hinter der Vase.
e	sitzen	am Mittagstisch.

Nominativergänzung (Subjekt) — **Wer? oder Was?** — Verb — **(lokale) Situativergänzung** / **Wo?**

7

| as alles | gehört | mir. |
| ie Knieschützer | passen | seinem Freund. |

Nominativergänzung (Subjekt) — **Wer? oder Was?** — Verb — **Dativergänzung** / **Wem?**

| ocko | zeigt | seinem Freund | die Geschenke. |
| - | schenkt | ihm | die Knieschützer. |

Nominativergänzung (Subjekt) — **Wer? oder Was?** — Verb — **Dativergänzung** / **Wem?** — **Akkusativergänzung** / **Wen? oder Was?**

3. Das Verb

3.1 Trennbare Verben

→ Lehrbuch, S. 59

án/fangen

Wann **fängt** die Operation **an** ?

Die Operation **fängt** gleich **an** .

Fängt die Operation gleich **an** ?

zú/kleben

Alexander **klebt** die Wunde **zu** .

Klebt Alexander die Wunde **zu** ?

Wie **klebt** er die Wunde **zu** ?

eín/kaufen

Was **kauft** Frau Braun **ein** ?

Sie **kauft** Tomaten **ein** .

Kauft sie auch Oliven **ein** ?

3.2 Die Konjugation: Präsens

→ Lehrbuch, S. 41, 71

Infinitiv		kommen	sprechen	heißen	antworten	
Singular			⚠	⚠		
1. Person	ich	komm- e	sprech- e	heiß- e	antwort- e	-e
2. Person	du	komm- st	sprich- st	heiß- t	antwort- est	-(e)st
	Sie	komm- en	sprech- en	heiß- en	antwort- en	-en
3. Person	er sie es	komm- t	sprich- t	heiß- t	antwort- et	-(e)t
Plural						
1. Person	wir	komm- en	sprech- en	heiß- en	antwort- en	-en
2. Person	ihr	komm- t	sprech- t	heiß- t	antwort- et	-(e)t
	Sie	komm- en	sprech- en	heiß- en	antwort- en	-en
3. Person	sie	komm- en	sprech- en	heiß- en	antwort- en	-en

Hilfsverben

	sein	haben
	⚠	⚠
	bin	habe
	bist	hast
	sind	haben
	ist	hat
	sind	haben
	seid	habt
	sind	haben
	sind	haben

Modalverben

Infinitiv		können	mögen	⚠	Konjunktiv II von „mögen"	
Singular						
1. Person	ich	kann- —	mag- —	- —	ich	mö**ch** -t-e
2. Person	du	kann- st	mag- st	-st	du	mö**ch** -t-est
	Sie	könn- en	mög- en	-en	Sie	mö**ch** -t-en
3. Person	er sie es	kann- —	mag- —	- —	er sie es	mö**ch** -t-e
Plural						
1. Person	wir	könn- en	mög- en	-en	wir	mö**ch** -t-en
2. Person	ihr	könn- t	mög- t	-t	ihr	mö**ch** -t-et
	Sie	könn- en	mög- en	-en	Sie	mö**ch** -t-en
3. Person	sie	könn- en	mög- en	-en	sie	mö**ch** -t-en

a) Regelmäßige Verben: Partizip II

Was	hat	Herr Rasch	ge-	mach	-t ?
Er	hat	die Sekretärin		**be**such	-t .
Er	hat	ihr etwas		**er**zähl	-t .
Sie	hat	Kaffee	ge-	koch	-t .
Er	hat	mit der Sekretärin	ge-	flir**t**	-et .
Sie	haben	einen Spaziergang	ge-	mach	-t .
Er	hat	sie		fotograf**ier**	-t .
Er	hat	auf Herrn Meinke	ge-	war**t**	-et .
Er	hat	mit Herrn Meinke	ge-	re**d**	-et .
Er	hat	einen Hamburger	ge-	hol	-t .

„hab-en" → **Perfekt (Aktiv)** ← ge- **Stamm** -(e)t

d) Verben auf „-ieren": Partizip II

Infinitiv	Partizip II
dikt**ier**en	dikt**ier** - t
fotograf**ier**en	fotograf**ier** - t
telefon**ier**en	telefon**ier** - t
	ier - t

b) Unregelmäßige Verben: Partizip II

Sie	hat		an-	ge-	ruf	-en .
Das	habe	ich			**ver**gess	-en .
Ich	habe	mein Geld			**ver**lor	-en !
Wo	hast	du es		ge-	fund	-en ?
Sie	haben	nichts		ge-	seh	-en .

„hab-en" → **Perfekt (Aktiv)** ← ge- **Perfekt-Stamm** -en

HUGH! Ich habe gesprochen.

Trennbare Verben – nicht trennbare Verben: Partizip II

Infinitiv	Partizip II	Infinitiv	Partizip II
ein/kaufen	**ein** - ge - kauf - t	**be**suchen	**be**such - t
an/rufen	**an** - ge - ruf - en	er**zähl**en	er**zähl** - t
mit/nehmen	**mit** - ge - nomm - en	**ver**gessen	**ver**gess - en
auf/stehen	**auf** - ge - stand - en	**ver**lieren	**ver**lor - en
um/steigen	**um** - ge - stieg - en		
kaputt/machen	**kaputt** - ge - mach - t		
aus/räumen	**aus** - ge - räum - t		

PRÄFIX - ge - STAMM - { t / en }   STAMM - { t / en }

e) Das Perfekt mit „haben" – **das Perfekt mit „sein"**

	„haben"		Partizip II		„sein"		Partizip II
Er	hat	sich	geschnitten .	Er	ist	um acht Uhr aufgestanden .
Er	hat	Kaffee	getrunken .	Er	ist	ins Bad	gegangen .
Er	hat	Brötchen	gegessen .	Er	ist	in die Stadt	gefahren .
Er	hat	die Zeitung	gelesen .	Er	ist	einmal	umgestiegen .
Er	hat	den Bus	genommen .	Sie	ist	schließlich	gekommen .
Er	hat	einen Brief	geschrieben .				
Sie	hat	keine Zeit	gehabt .	Er	ist	müde	gewesen .

f) Die Konjugation: Perfekt

		Perfekt mit „haben"		Perfekt mit „sein"	
Singular					
1. Person	ich	habe	gesprochen	bin	gegangen
2. Person	du	hast	gesprochen	bist	gegangen
	Sie	haben	gesprochen	sind	gegangen
3. Person	er				
	sie }	hat	gesprochen	ist	gegangen
	es				
Plural					
1. Person	wir	haben	gesprochen	sind	gegangen
2. Person	ihr	habt	gesprochen	seid	gegangen
	Sie	haben	gesprochen	sind	gegangen
3. Person	sie	haben	gesprochen	sind	gegangen
		PRÄSENS von „haben"	+ PARTIZIP II	PRÄSENS von „sein"	+ PARTIZIP II

3.4 Die Konjugation: Präteritum von „sein" und „haben"

Infinitiv		**haben**		**sein**	
Singular					
1. Person	ich	ha-**tt**-e	-e	**war**-—	-—
2. Person	du	ha-**tt**-est	-est	**war**- st	- st
	Sie	ha-**tt**-en	-en	**war**- en	- en
3. Person	er				
	sie }	ha-**tt**-e	-e	**war**-—	-—
	es				
Plural					
1. Person	wir	ha-**tt**-en	-en	**war**- en	- en
2. Person	ihr	ha-**tt**-et	-et	**war**- t	- t
	Sie	ha-**tt**-en	-en	**war**- en	- en
3. Person	sie	ha-**tt**-en	-en	**war**- en	- en

-tt- ←→ Präteritum-signal ←→ war

128

4. Das Substantiv

4.1 Das Genus
→ Lehrbuch, S. 39

m = maskulinum	n = neutrum	f = femininum
der Clown	das Auto	die Cassette
der Computer	das Baby	die City
der Paß	das Glas	die Cola
der Hamburger	das Radio	die Garage
der Salat	das Steak	die Party
der Star	das Telefon	die Hostess
. . .	. . . .	die

4.2 Der unbestimmte Artikel – der bestimmte Artikel

Das ist **ein** Clown.

Der Clown heißt Pippo.

Das ist **ein** Baby.

Das Baby ist drei Monate alt.

Das ist **eine** Hostess.

Die Hostess spricht Deutsch, Englisch und Französisch.

4.3 „ein-" – „kein-"

→ Lehrbuch, S. 42

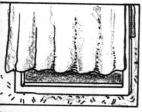

„Was ist das? Ist das **ein** Bild ?" –

„ Nein , das ist **kein** Bild ,

das ist **eine** Landkarte !"

129

Typ 1:

Singular	maskulinum **der** Arm	neutrum **das** Bein	maskulinum **der** Stuhl	femininum **die** Hand
Plural	die Arm-**e** die -**e**	die Bein-**e** die -**e**	die Stühl-**e** die -**e**	die Händ-**e** die -**e**

Typ 3:

Singular	maskulinum **der** Finger	neutrum **das** Essen -er, -el, -en	(maskulinum) **der** Vat⌊er⌋	(femininum) **die** Mutt⌊er⌋ ⚠
Plural	die Finger-— die -—	die Essen-— die -—	die Väter-— die ¨ -—	die Mütter-— die

Typ 2a:

Singular	femininum **die** Lipp-e -e	(maskulinum) **der** Nam-e ⚠	(neutrum) **das** Aug-e ⚠
Plural	die Lippe-**n** die -**n**	die Name-**n** die -**n**	die Auge-**n** die -**n**

Typ 4:

Singular	← neutrum → **das** Bild	**das** Glas 1silbig	(maskulinum) **der** Mann ⚠
Plural	die Bild-**er** die -**er**	die Gläs-**er** die ¨ -**er**	die Männ-**er** die ¨ -**er**

Typ 2b:

Singular	femininum **die** Wohnung Konsonant	(maskulinum) **der** Schmerz ⚠	(neutrum) **das** Ohr ⚠
Plural	die Wohnung-**en** die -**en**	die Schmerz-**en** die -**en**	die Ohr-**en** die -**en**

Typ 5:

Singular	maskulinum **der** Clown	neutrum **das** Steak Fremdwort	femininum **die** Party
Plural	die Clown-**s**	die Steak-**s** die -**s**	die Party-**s**

4.5 Die Deklination:

→ Lehrbuch, S. 10

	maskulinum	neutrum	femininum
Singular			
Nominativ	der /ein-— Tisch	das /ein-— Buch	die /ein-e Vase
Akkusativ	den /ein-en Tisch	das /ein-— Buch	die /ein-e Vase
Dativ	dem /ein-em Tisch	dem /ein-em Buch	der /ein-er Vase
Genitiv	des /ein-es Tisches	des /ein-es Buches	der /ein-er Vase
Plural			
Nominativ	die /— Tische	die /— Bücher	die /— Vasen
Akkusativ	die /— Tische	die /— Bücher	die /— Vasen
Dativ	den /— Tischen	den /— Büchern	den /— Vasen
Genitiv	der /— Tische	der /— Bücher	der /— Vasen

Genauso wie   ein Tisch: **k**ein Tisch,   ein Buch: **k**ein Buch,   eine Vase: **k**eine Vase

Das Personalpronomen

→ Lehrbuch, S. 116

	Nominativ	Akkusativ	Dativ
Singular			
1. Person	ich	mich	mir
2. Person	du	dich	dir
	Sie	Sie	Ihnen
3. Person	er	ihn	ihm
	sie	sie	ihr
	es	es	ihm
Plural			
1. Person	wir	uns	uns
2. Person	ihr	euch	euch
	Sie	Sie	Ihnen
3. Person	sie	sie	ihnen
	Wer?	**Wen?**	**Wem?**

Das Possessivpronomen

→ Lehrbuch, S. 117, 118

.1 Possessivpronomen + Substantiv: alle Personen

Personal-pronomen	Possessivpronomen + Substantiv		
	maskulinum	neutrum	femininum
ich	mein - — Koffer	mein - — Buch	mein - e Tasche
du	dein - — Koffer	dein - — Buch	dein - e Tasche
Sie	Ihr - — Koffer	Ihr - — Buch	Ihr - e Tasche
er	sein - — Koffer	sein - — Buch	sein - e Tasche
sie	ihr - — Koffer	ihr - — Buch	ihr - e Tasche
es	sein - — Koffer	sein - — Buch	sein - e Tasche
wir	unser - — Koffer	unser - — Buch	uns(e)r - e Tasche
ihr	euer - — Koffer	euer - — Buch	eu(e)r - e Tasche
Sie	Ihr - — Koffer	Ihr - — Buch	Ihr - e Tasche
sie	ihr - — Koffer	ihr - — Buch	ihr - e Tasche
Vergleichen Sie:	ein - — Koffer	ein - — Buch	ein - e Tasche

6.2 Die Deklination: Possessivpronomen + Substantiv

Singular								
Nominativ	mein - ——	Koffer	mein - ——	Buch	mein - e	Tasche		
Akkusativ	mein - en	Koffer	mein - ——	Buch	mein - e	Tasche		
Dativ	mein - em	Koffer	mein - em	Buch	mein - er	Tasche		
Genitiv	mein - es	Koffers	mein - es	Buches	mein - er	Tasche		
Plural								
Nominativ	mein - e	Koffer	mein - e	Bücher	mein - e	Taschen		
Akkusativ	mein - e	Koffer	mein - e	Bücher	mein - e	Taschen		
Dativ	mein - en	Koffern	mein - en	Büchern	mein - en	Taschen		
Genitiv	mein - er	Koffer	mein - er	Bücher	mein - er	Taschen		

Vergleichen Sie:

der
ein - —— } Koffer

das
ein - —— } Buch

die
ein - e } Tasche

---

7. Die Präpositionen

7.1 Die Präpositionen mit Akkusativ

⟶ Lehrbuch, S. 1(

Wir sind **bis** einen Tag nach Weihnachten in Berlin.

Der Einbrecher ist **durch** das Fenster in die Wohnung gestiegen.

Wir brauchen 800 Mark **für** die Miete.

Ohne einen Angelschein ist Angeln verboten.

Das Auto fährt **gegen** die Wand.

Wer schaut da **um** die Ecke?

bis durch für
ohne gegen um

AKKUSATIV

→ Lehrbuch, S. 119

	Mustafa kommt aus **der** Türkei.
	Er war bei**m** (= bei dem) Arzt.
	Der Supermarkt liegt gegenüber **dem** Rathaus.
	Fährst du mit **uns** nach Italien? Wir fahren mit **dem** Auto.
	Der Tannenbaum ist mit Kerzen geschmückt.
	Er ist nach **dem** Frühstück in die Stadt gefahren.
	Er sucht seinen Ring schon seit **einer** Stunde.
	Er kommt vo**m** (= von dem) Arzt.
	Die Ferien dauern vo**m** achtzehnten Juni .... bis zu**m** dritten August.
	Der Fuchs läuft zu**m** (= zu dem) Raben.

DATIV

aus bei gegenüber mit nach seit von zu

133

Wohin tut/stellt sie das Essen? –   **Wo** ist/steht das Essen?

Sie tut/stellt das Essen . . . . .   Das Essen ist/steht . . . . .

     . . . . . in **den** Topf.   . . . . . **im** (= in **dem**) Topf.

     . . . . . an **die** Wand.   . . . . . an **der** Wand.

     . . . . . auf **den** Tisch.   . . . . . auf **dem** Tisch.

     . . . . . unter **die** Bank.   . . . . . unter **der** Bank.

     . . . . . vor **den** Mann.   . . . . . vor **dem** Mann.

     . . . . . hinter **die** Tür.   . . . . . hinter **der** Tür.

     . . . . . neben **das** Bett.   . . . . . neben **dem** Bett.

     . . . . . zwischen **die** Bücher.   . . . . . zwischen **den** Büchern.

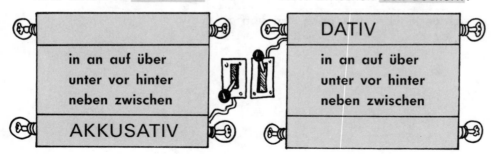

	DATIV
in an auf über unter vor hinter neben zwischen	in an auf über unter vor hinter neben zwischen
AKKUSATIV	

Quellennachweis für Texte und Abbildungen

S. 14 Foto: Barbara A. Stenzel, München
S. 16 Karte: Polyglott Verlag, München
S. 26 Foto: Sabine Wenkums, München
S. 31 Foto Personalausweis: Barbara A. Stenzel, München
S. 33 Foto Reisepaß: Barbara A. Stenzel, München
S. 34 Fotos: Arbeiterin: Herrad Meese, München;
       Paßfoto: Bjarne Geiges, München;
       Studentin und Lehrerin: Sabine Wenkums, München
S. 38 Foto: aus: Tony Spiteris, Griechische und etruskische Malerei, Band 3 der Weltgeschichte der Malerei, Hg. Claude Schaffner, Editions Rencontre, Lausanne/Paris 1966, S.70
S. 39 Foto: (wie S. 38) S. 73
S. 43 Foto: aus: Alte Berliner Läden, © 1982 Nicolaische Verlagsbuchhandlung, Berlin
S. 45 Fotos: ③ Bjarne Geiges, München; ④, ⑥, ⑦, ⑨ Süddeutscher Verlag, München
S. 48 Foto: aus: Georges Charensol, Die großen Meister der modernen Malerei, Band 22 der Weltgeschichte der Malerei, s.o., Lausanne/Paris 1967, S. 52
S. 57 Weltzeitkarte aus: Lufthansa Bordbuch © Deutsche Lufthansa AG
S. 82 Fotos: Süddeutscher Verlag, München
    Johannes R. Becher, Ende, aus: Gedichte 1949-1958, S. 195 © Aufbauverlag Berlin und Weimar 1973;
    Hermann Hesse, Im Nebel, aus: Stücke I. © Suhrkamp Verlag Frankfurt am Main 1977;
    Bertolt Brecht, Der Radwechsel; aus: Gesammelte Werke IV. © Suhrkamp Verlag Frankfurt am Main 1967;
    Ingeborg Bachmann, Schatten Rosen Schatten, aus: Werke Band I, S. 133 R. Piper & Co. Verlag, München 1978
S. 83 Foto: Joachim Thode, Mönkeberg, von einer Aufführung des Stücks "Selbstbezichtigung" von Peter Handke durch die Bühnen der Stadt Kiel Peter Handke, Selbstbezichtigung, aus: Stücke I., © Suhrkamp Verlag Frankfurt am Main 1972, S. 69-70
S. 86 Stadtplanausschnitt: Heinz Fleischmann Gmbh & Co., München
S. 87 Stadtplan: Verkehrsamt der Stadt Köln
S. 95 Foto u.: Bavaria Verlag, Gauting; Foto o.: Bjarne Geiges, München

Alle anderen Photos: Ulrike Kment, München